Praise for *Philip Larkin: Life, Art and —*

'Booth's supplement to Andrew Motion's biography – the light to his shadow – should render further attention by biographers superfluous for several years' Blake Morrison, *Guardian*

'Booth is absolutely excellent on the work . . . To read this book through, turning back to the poems in sequence, is to appreciate Larkin's development more intimately than has been possible before' *Evening Standard*

'A very good biography, both judicious and generous' *Scotsman*

'Booth's poem-by-poem account of Larkin's evolution as a poet is compelling and makes clear how unmistakeably Larkin belongs among the greats' *Spectator*

'His examination of the poems is exemplary, always intelligent and free of jargon, and the manner in which he relates them to Larkin's life will enhance many readers' appreciation of the poetry and deepen their enjoyment' *Scotsman*

'The narrative is peppered with close analysis of many of the poems which doesn't detract from the life story, so much as enhance it' *Yorkshire Post*

'Impressive . . . If Booth finally succeeds in correcting the view of Larkin and reminding us of the glories of the poetry, he will have done us all a service' *Herald*

'By dwelling on the poems as well as the life Booth will awaken readers to the complexity and weight of Larkin's accomplishment' *London Review of Books*

A NOTE ON THE AUTHOR

JAMES BOOTH edited Philip Larkin's early girls'-school stories and poems as *Trouble at Willow Gables and Other Fictions* (2002) and has published two critical studies of the poet's work: *Philip Larkin: Writer* (1991) and *Philip Larkin: The Poet's Plight* (2005). He is Literary Adviser to the Philip Larkin Society and Co-Editor of its journal, *About Larkin*. Professor Booth recently retired from the Department of English at the University of Hull, where he had been a colleague of Larkin for seventeen years.

PHILIP LARKIN

Life, Art and Love

James Booth

BLOOMSBURY
LONDON • NEW DELHI • NEW YORK • SYDNEY

For the friends and lovers of Larkin who
contributed to the writing of this book

Bloomsbury Paperbacks
An imprint of Bloomsbury Publishing Plc

50 Bedford Square
London
WC1B 3DP
UK

1385 Broadway
New York
NY 10018
USA

www.bloomsbury.com

BLOOMSBURY and the Diana logo are trademarks of Bloomsbury Publishing Plc

First published in Great Britain 2014
This paperback edition first published in 2015

© James Booth, 2014

James Booth has asserted his right under the Copyright, Designs and Patents Act,
1988, to be identified as Author of this work.

British Library Cataloguing-in-Publication Data
A catalogue record for this book is available from the British Library.

ISBN: HB: 978-1-4088-5166-1
PB: 978-1-4088-5169-2
ePub: 978-1-4088-5167-8

2 4 6 8 10 9 7 5 3

Typeset by Hewer Text UK Ltd, Edinburgh
Printed and bound in Great Britain by CPI Group (UK) Ltd, Croydon CR0 4YY

MIX
Paper from
responsible sources
FSC® C020471

To find out more about our authors and books visit www.bloomsbury.com.
Here you will find extracts, author interviews, details of forthcoming events
and the option to sign up for our newsletters.

The ultimate joy is to be alive in the flesh.

(Larkin to James Sutton, 23 June 1941)

Contents

Author's Note

Quotations are from *The Complete Poems* (2012). The *Collected Poems* (1988), though less comprehensive, has the great advantage, for those wishing to follow Larkin's biography, of printing the poems in the order in which they were written. Since individual works are easily located in these volumes I have omitted page references.

Introduction

Larkin is, by common consent, the best-loved British poet of the last century. Phrases and lines from his poems are more frequently quoted than those of any other poet of his time: 'What are days for?'; 'Sexual intercourse began / In nineteen sixty-three'; 'What will survive of us is love'; 'Never such innocence again'. Already during his lifetime the publication of a Larkin work was an event. Within days of the appearance of a new poem in the *New Statesman*, the *Listener* or the *Times Literary Supplement*, 'people would have it by heart and be quoting it over the dinner table'.[1] A recent blogger speaks for many when he recalls reading his slim volumes 'to tatters'.[2] Since his death Larkin's poetic reputation has become even more secure. A 2003 poll of several thousand readers by the Poetry Book Society and the Poetry Library voted his heart-warming celebration of marriage, 'The Whitsun Weddings', the most popular poem of the previous half-century.[3] His harrowing self-elegy 'Aubade' was seventh on the list. The witty, humorous poems are equally popular. As he himself wryly reflected: '"They fuck you up" will clearly be my Lake Isle of Innisfree.'[4] His poetic range seems all-encompassing.

He remains, however, a controversial figure, both as a poet and as a man. Even the apparently neutral question of which of his poems deserve to be printed under his name raises fierce passions. During Larkin's lifetime the mature collections, *The Less Deceived* (1955), *The*

Whitsun Weddings (1964) and *High Windows* (1974), established an oeuvre which gave all the appearance of perfection. The modulated sequences in these books seem to carry the same authority as the text of one of his poems. So when, following his friend's death, Anthony Thwaite was called upon to edit the *Collected Poems*, his task seemed simple. Editorial tradition required him to reproduce these volumes in their original form, adding poems published in magazines or newspapers in a separate section. Important unpublished works might perhaps be printed in an appendix; unfinished poems must be excluded. However, Thwaite faced a dilemma. There existed a hitherto hidden version of Larkin's life's work, more comprehensive than that of the existing publications, and carrying equal if not greater authority. Larkin had constructed his oeuvre with rare deliberation. For three and a half decades, from October 1944 to November 1981, he had written virtually all his poetic drafts in pencil in a series of eight manuscript workbooks, entering dates, usually to indicate a 'final' version, and sometimes inserting typescripts with last-minute changes. These workbooks contain his most intimate poetic autobiography.

Archie Burnett notes that Coleridge advocates 'a thoroughgoing chronological arrangement' for a poet's work, since this enables the reader readily to follow a development from early to late.[5] Confronted with the workbooks, Thwaite made the bold decision to adopt this policy in the *Collected Poems* of 1988. Moreover a number of workbook poems which had remained unpublished, including 'An April Sunday brings the snow', 'The View' and 'Love Again', were clearly of comparable quality to poems already published. Thwaite therefore inserted into the sequence sixty-one 'new' poems, including the key incomplete work, 'The Dance'. The result was revelatory. In an early letter to his friend James Sutton, Larkin referred to his writing as a record of his 'soul-history'.[6] In Thwaite's edition, this soul-history was laid bare in a new and unexpected way. It was revealed, for instance, that Larkin had been unable to complete a poem for eleven months following the death of his father in 1948. In the abandoned draft of 'The Dance' (1963–4) readers were able to follow his never-resolved mid-life crisis. The final poems in the eighth workbook showed his inspiration guttering in the mid-1970s.

The Whitsun Weddings volume of 1964 conducts the reader, with artful contrasts of comic and tragic, reflective and dramatic, from the opening chords of 'Here', through the gloomy meditation of 'Dockery and Son' to the yearning finale of 'An Arundel Tomb'. Thwaite's sequence reveals, instead, the poet's emotional journey. 'An Arundel Tomb', reflecting his commitment to Monica Jones, was completed in 1956. The serene 'Here' came five years later in October 1961, when he was still safely in his thirties, his professional career was at its most satisfying and his relationship with his Hull muse, Maeve Brennan, was at its happiest. By the time of 'Dockery and Son', eighteen months later, he had passed the threshold of forty and was descending into crisis. Those who wish to follow the narrative of Larkin's life as a man and an artist will find Thwaite's 1988 *Collected Poems* a surer guide than the lifetime volumes.

Thwaite's reconfiguration of Larkin's life's work caused a furore. He was accused of disregarding the poet's 'intentions' by destroying the harmony of the lifetime volumes and of releasing 'second-rate material' which Larkin had not seen fit to print.[7] His critics forgot that publication had not always been simply a matter of Larkin's intention. One of the reasons he was so hesitant to publish even some of his best work was the trauma of 1948 when his volume *In the Grip of Light* was rejected by six publishers. Fourteen of the poems in this collection remained unknown until 1988 simply because no publisher had seen fit to print it.

In the 2003 edition of *Collected Poems* editorial orthodoxy was reasserted. The sixty-one additional poems were omitted altogether and the order of the lifetime volumes was restored. In 2005 A. T. Tolley complicated the picture by publishing, in *Early Poems and Juvenilia*, a large number of works written when Larkin was in his teens. Then, in 2012, a certain closure was achieved in Archie Burnett's *The Complete Poems*, which aimed to print 'all of Larkin's poems whose texts are accessible'.[8] Despite his respect for Coleridge's chronological principle, Burnett reproduced the order of the lifetime volumes; but added, in a separate section, the 'new' 1988 works, the juvenilia and also some hitherto unknown fugitive squibs from letters. The very completeness of Burnett's project offended some. He was accused of 'diluting a major oeuvre and distracting from the real source of its power',[9] and of publishing 'every napkin- or matchbook-jotting'.[10]

The possessive passion which so many readers felt towards the established lifetime canon offers a pointer to the unique nature of Larkin's poetic achievement. Readers deplored the insertion of works which seemed to lack the authority, the *necessary* quality of his familiar masterpieces, and they resented seeing his poems placed in the contingent context in which they had been written. These readers need not have worried. As the dust settles it is clear that there has been an expansion rather than a 'dilution'. Disregarding most (not all) of the juvenilia and the doggerel squibs, the larger Larkin oeuvre revealed in the *Collected Poems* and *The Complete Poems* has a rigour and economy equal to and more organic than that of the volumes published in Larkin's lifetime. Larkin's complete works contain only a tiny proportion of dross compared with those of, say, Wordsworth or Auden.

At the age of thirty in 1953 Larkin set out his aim in a tone of jokey presumptuousness: 'I should like to write about 75–100 new poems, all rather better than anything I've ever done before, and dealing with such subjects as Life, Death, Time, Love, and Scenery in such a manner as would render further attention to them by other poets superfluous.'[11] He largely succeeded in his aim. Among literary forms the lyric is at the extreme of verbal economy and concentration; a great lyric poem strikes the reader as the distilled 'last word' on a universal theme. Larkin's mature oeuvre has been said to contain 'a remarkable percentage of the definitive poems of his time'.[12] For the moment he seems to have had the last poetic word, on love, on death, on the Great War, on parents, on ageing, on hedgehogs. Poets writing on these subjects today struggle to escape his 'definitive' voice and find their own.

He achieved this definitiveness by the extreme economy of his genres, forms, types of rhyme, even individual words. Larkin's oeuvre does not comprise, as do those of, say, Yeats, Housman or Hopkins, numerous poems on similar themes and with repeated or overlapping forms. Those who have taught his poetry will be familiar with the frustration of attempting to move on with their students to another Larkin poem similar to 'An Arundel Tomb' or 'This Be the Verse' or 'Sunny Prestatyn', only to be compelled to start again from scratch, since there are no other poems 'like' these. Each of his works is 'its own sole freshly created universe',[13] comprehensively differentiated from the others in terms of form, style and voice. As he put it in an arresting metaphor, 'Poetry is not like surgery, a technique that can be copied: every operation the poet performs is unique, and need never be done again.'[14]

Larkin's mature body of poetry contains a single mourning elegy ('An April Sunday brings the snow'), a single prayer ('Solar'), a single graveyard meditation ('Church Going'), a single extended narrative poem ('The Dance'), and so on. Every poem has its own rhyme-colour and its own idiomatic register. Often enough, also, it has its unforgettable key-word or words. Larkin remarked of his abandoned novels of the late 1940s: 'they were over-sized poems. They were certainly written with intense care for detail. If one word was used on page 15 I didn't re-use it on page 115.'[15] Indeed, a startlingly large number of the words in the mature post-1945 section of the 1988 *Collected Poems* occur in a single poem only.[16] Larkin, it seems, waits for the best time to employ each word, gives it the most memorable context he can contrive and then never uses it again. This is not only the case with distinctive, intrinsically memorable words: 'unmolesting', 'Blindingly', 'fishy-smelling', 'Immensements'. Larkin also asserts his copyright over more commonplace words, which become unforgettable in the poems in which they make their unique appearances: 'unsatisfactory', 'wonderful', 'welcome', 'useful', 'afresh', 'singular'. His instinct for verbal refinement ensures that the briefest snatch brings to mind a whole poem: 'Such attics!', 'awkward reverence', 'the exchange of love', 'we shall find out', 'sure extinction'. This is the source of what Martin Amis terms the 'frictionless memorability' of Larkin's poetry.[17] Could this uncanny control be connected perhaps with the 'deep-seated abnormality in the left cerebral hemisphere' which revealed itself when he was X-rayed in 1961?[18]

Larkin's reputation as a poet is secure. His reputation as a man is, however, in a less healthy state. The frequently retold story of his fall from grace following the publication of Anthony Thwaite's edition of the *Selected Letters* in 1992 and Andrew Motion's official biography, *A Writer's Life*, in 1993 has taken on the quality of a modern morality tale. The *Independent* set the tone when it headlined an interview with Motion: 'Mr Nice tackles Mr Nasty'.[19] Ideological commentators such as Terry Eagleton, Lisa Jardine and Tom Paulin uncovered 'the sewer under the national monument'.[20] Many readers today believe that Larkin was 'a Tory snob with sexist and racist tendencies', and 'a singularly unattractive man'.[21] One reviewer declared of Burnett's Commentary in *The Complete Poems*: 'The only thing we're reminded of is what a shit Larkin was in real life.'[22] Even those who admire the poetry feel it acceptable to refer to 'the vile mess that was Larkin',[23] and accuse him of living a sterile life. Martin Amis believes that the success of his poetry was earned at the expense of 'failure' in his personal life.[24] Larkin, he writes, 'siphoned all his energy, and all his love, out of the life and into the work'. He had 'no close friends', and his life story was one of 'gauntness', 'with no emotions, no vital essences, worth looking back on'.[25]

There is, of course, no requirement that poets should be likeable or virtuous. But we might ask whether art and life can have been so deeply at odds with each other that the poet who composed the heart-rending 'Love Songs in Age', the euphoric 'For Sidney Bechet' and the effervescent 'Annus Mirabilis' had no emotions, or was a shit in real life. Larkin's negative public image is built neither on his poetry nor on the evidence of those who knew him well. Those who shared this life simply do not recognize the Mr Nasty version. Dismay and puzzlement at Larkin's poor image is universal among those I interviewed in writing this book: the women with whom he was romantically involved, Ruth Siverns (Bowman), Monica Jones, Winifred Dawson (Arnott), Maeve Brennan and Betty Mackereth, his friends Anthony and Ann Thwaite, Judy Egerton and Jean Hartley, and his University colleagues, Eddie Dawes, John White, Brenda Moon and Father Anthony Storey. All those who were close to him remember him with affection and feel privileged to have known him. Typically, they found him 'witty', 'entertaining', 'considerate' and 'kind'.

Jean Hartley, who knew him for thirty years, recalls his spontaneous empathy: 'he gave his full attention to everyone he had dealings with. I myself never had the feeling that he was waiting for a gap in the conversation in order to inject his own views. He seemed invariably to follow one's train of thought rather than his own.'[26] His generous inclination to identify himself with the widest range of his fellow beings is central to the appeal of his poetry. He enters into the feelings of young mothers at a playground, a rabbit dying of myxomatosis, his own harassed American biographer. Such wide sympathies, however, bring problems in 'real life'. Listening to the speakers at the memorial for Larkin in Hull in 1986, Jean Hartley was surprised to discover 'Philip's chameleon-like nature'. His interests and sympathies were clearly much wider than she had thought.[27] Those who imagined that they knew Larkin tended to see only those aspects which suited their own conceptions. This is one reason why Larkin's reputation was damaged in some quarters on the publication of the *Selected Letters*.

In what seems a deliberate strategy, he maintained long-term correspondences with the widest spectrum of people: the earnest would-be artist Jim Sutton, the irrepressible philistine novelist Kingsley Amis, the flamboyant University lecturer Monica Jones, the liberal-voting art historian Judy Egerton, the right-wing historian of Soviet atrocities Robert Conquest, the left-wing Anglican Anthony Thwaite, the conservative novelist Barbara Pym, the ingenuous Catholic Maeve Brennan, and his lonely widowed mother, to whom he wrote at least twice a week for a quarter of a century. A key motive seems to have been the compulsion to express himself in the widest possible range of literary registers, from civilized formality to intimate gossip. There are 'almost as many different voices' in the *Selected Letters* 'as there are correspondents'.[28] (Unfortunately one voice is missing, since none of the letters to his mother were included.) As long as these letters remained private, their contradictory Larkins could cause no offence. On the publication of the *Letters*, however, he was accused of duplicity. He said one thing to one correspondent and something different to another. He compartmentalized his life. Maeve Brennan was dismayed by the language of his letters to Amis and Conquest; Amis was baffled by the softer sentimental side of his character. Readers were offended by his inability to be polite about the faults of his poetic contemporaries.

Dryden was suspicious of the Earl of Shaftesbury because of the breadth and intensity of his interests: 'A man so various, that he seemed to be / Not one, but all Mankind's Epitome'.[29] To some, omnivorousness of spirit will always seem a sign of deviousness and insincerity. But self-contradiction is part of the human condition; and Larkin's contradictions are central to his greatness. He was a man of many parts and many roles, ironic and unironic. Larkin the poet, for instance ('Why should I let the toad *work* / Squat on my life?'), coexisted over the decades with Larkin the hard-working librarian, who oversaw the building of the first new post-war British university library at the same time as managing an inexorable expansion of staff and service provision. An academic from another university, enthusiastically joining in when he overheard Larkin praised at a conference, was puzzled to find that the topic was poetry. He had no idea that the pioneering librarian was also a poet.[30] Larkin's secretary, Betty Mackereth, recalls him pointing to the shelf of bound Library Committee minutes and remarking with glum satisfaction, that this also was part of his oeuvre.[31] After his death the Library Association published a volume in his honour.[32] Some of Larkin's fellow writers feel that his 'day-job' casts a shadow across the poetry. Seamus Heaney imitates the poet's self-deprecating tone, ventriloquizing a Larkin who describes himself defeatedly as 'a nine-to-five-man who has seen poetry'.[33] Martin Amis implicitly compares his own father's genuinely 'bohemian' life with Larkin's provincial life as a 'nine-to-five librarian, who lived for thirty years in a northern city that smelled of fish'.[34]

The mercurial shifts of persona in Larkin's interviews, essays and letters have been the cause of many misreadings. Larkin claimed in his celebrated *Observer* interview that he did not want 'to go around pretending to be me'. However, he conceded elsewhere that 'one has to dramatize oneself a little'.[35] As Jonathan Raban remarked, Larkin spoke to interviewers in the voice of 'a well-scripted character whose tone was pitched midway between the reactionary acerbities of W. C. Fields and the self-deprecating complaints of Eeyore the donkey'.[36]

Some readers fail to register the performative playfulness of Larkin's self-caricatures: 'Deprivation is for me what daffodils were for Wordsworth'; 'there's not much to *say* about my work'; 'I don't want to sound falsely naive, but I often wonder why people get married'; 'Children are very horrible, aren't they?' These are not the words of a gaunt, emotionless failure, but of an ebullient provocateur with an instinct to entertain. He began his interview with the *Observer* in 1979: 'I like to think of myself as quite funny.'[37] It is easy to see why those who knew him enjoyed his company so much.

The various ideological Larkins who raise the passions of some critics, are provisional personae. The fervent nationalist Larkin, for instance, is the product of performance as much as of ideology. Tom Paulin speaks of Larkin's 'rock-solid sense of national glory'.[38] His elegy for the wasted lives of the Great War, 'MCMXIV', tells a different story. The famous photograph of the poet sitting inscrutably on the boundary-sign 'England' tells us more about his relationship with the woman who took it, Monica Jones, than about its subject, for whom 'elsewhere' was always more comfortable than 'home'.[39] Larkin expressed his instinctive view in a letter to Monica: 'my God, surely nationalism is the surest mark of mediocrity!'[40] Similarly, the ardent Tory Larkin proclaims 'I adore Mrs Thatcher.'[41] But when they met and she misquoted a line from his poem 'Deceptions', 'Your mind lay open like a drawer of knives,' as 'Her mind was full of knives,' he remarked slyly, 'she might think a mind full of knives rather along her own lines', hastening to correct himself: 'not that I don't kiss the ground she treads'.[42]

Larkin the racist is a similar fiction. It is frequently remarked that his handful of racist comments, some of them indeed very unpleasant, are confined to private letters written to prejudiced correspondents. But his self-irony escapes the notice of critics, as it no doubt escaped the notice of the original correspondents. In a letter to Monica Jones, he depicts himself settling down for a lazy evening after a dinner of haggis, neeps and claret: '& by God wasn't the toast "Mr Enoch Powell"! Then jazz records *to my taste*, especially Armstrong.'[43] Approval for the politician who prophesied rivers of blood if 'the black man' gained the whip hand in Britain is followed by a grateful surrender to black music. It is to be regretted that, on rare occasions, Larkin used the words 'nigger', 'wog' and 'yid' in writing to particular correspondents. However at a time when most British middle-class households would have possessed a tin of 'nigger brown' Cherry Blossom shoe polish, and have had in their kitchens jars of Robertson's marmalade with a golliwog on the label (a feature withdrawn only in 2001), such language was not always the sure sign of poisonous prejudice it has since become. Whatever language Larkin might use, he would never have theorized about racial inferiority or degeneracy, as did some writers of the century. During his early years in Hull Larkin recommended E. R. Braithwaite's anti-racist novel *To Sir, With Love* to his staff, and for a time they addressed him, half-ironically, as 'Sir'.[44] In 1946 he dreamt he was a black man walking through race-course crowds with Amis's future wife, Hilly Bardwell, sobbing with fear that he might be lynched.[45] His subconscious was not racist.

It is a similar story with Larkin the misogynist. Motion detected in the poet's youthful high-camp pastiches of girls'-school stories 'the wish to dominate' women.[46] Another commentator refers to Larkin's 'creepy interest in sadistic pornography'.[47] In fact domination and sadism were alien to his temperament, and his 'Brunette Coleman' writings express, first and foremost, his imaginative desire to be a girl. In our internet era the surviving remnants of his pornography retain little power to shock. There are a few distinctly half-hearted 'bondage' photographs, but the majority of the images show a spectrum from stocking-and-suspender titillation to idealized haughty nudity: on the one hand the smiling invitation of the girl next door, on the other a Platonic or Keatsian aestheticism.[48] It is these erotic proclivities which underlay his fear of domestic entanglement with Ruth Bowman or Monica Jones, and his muse-adoration of Winifred Arnott and Maeve Brennan. However, in a variant on the usual literary pattern, even his unattainable muses are also, in his own memorable formulation, real girls in real places. His empathy with women was strong, and this made him, as Nuala O'Faolain records, 'a most attractive man'.[49]

His comments on children show a particularly revealing clash between self-dramatization and reality. In his *Observer* interview he calls them 'Selfish, noisy, cruel, vulgar little brutes'.[50] Exasperated by his duties in Wellington Library, he told his parents: 'Children I would willingly bayonet by the score.'[51] On the other hand, he also told them that a 'pleasant old lady' had complimented him on how good he was with the children. (He added, self-critically, 'I don't feel I'm good with anybody.')[52] He went to the trouble, one Christmas, of buying dolls for the daughters of his publishers, the Hartleys, and gave Alison Hartley a piggy-back ride during a walk along the Humber estuary.[53] Bridget, Judy Egerton's elder daughter, recalls: 'Philip was the friend of my parents I liked the best. He never talked down to me.'[54] In a letter decorated with comic sketches of a rabbit and himself in a bow-tie he makes his handwriting round and distinct for her youthful eye.[55] He drew sketches in the autograph books of Anthony and Ann Thwaite's four daughters, patiently admired their card tricks and helped them search for lost balls.[56] In a letter to his mother he expressed concern about the 'squashed & timorous' demeanour of the Amises' infant sons in their chaotic domestic environment: 'Even their crying seems subdued.'[57] In his poem 'Coming', he compares an intimation of spring to the uncomprehending happiness of a child caught up in a scene of adult reconciling. And in 'To the Sea' he observes 'the uncertain children' on the beach, 'grasping at enormous air'. As Colm Tóibín observes, he was 'a great big sour softie'.[58]

Larkin was puzzled when he was accused of lacking feeling. He was aware, on the contrary, of having to strive to avoid emotional excess: 'I always think that the poems I write are very much more naïve – very much more emotional – almost embarrassingly so – than a lot of other people's. When I was tagged as unemotional, it used to mystify me; I used to find it quite shaming to read some of the things I'd written.'[59] The key to Larkin, the poet and the man, is an ingenuous openness to life's simplest pleasures and pains. He wrote to his mother from Belfast in 1954: 'the trees round Queen's are well-budded and stand in a circle of daffodils. Spring never fails us, does it? How beautiful it is, even though it isn't spring for *us!*'[60] Shortly after moving to Hull in 1955 he set out energetically on foot from his digs in Cottingham: 'People had told me to "walk to the Wolds" or the Dales or something':

Near home I stopped and watched half a dozen Jersey cows. How lovely
they are! like Siamese cats, almost: the patches of white round the eyes
and the soft way the coffee-colour melts into the white underbody. They
were licking each other affectionately in pairs, on the chest and along
the neck. When one stopped the other would begin licking back! The
Peaceable Kingdom! In the end I found I'd walked about II miles [. . .][61]

No poet was less likely to contemplate suicide. To a writer like Graham
Greene life is intrinsically empty. It requires Russian roulette, a dangerous career in espionage or a fear of Hell to give it relish. Larkin possessed
the opposite temperament: 'Everyday things are lovely to me.'[62] The
sight of a lamb in snow, the sound of a sustained note on a saxophone,
a glimpse of newly-weds from a train, flood his life with meaning and
pleasure. By the same token, the suffering of a diseased rabbit, the
thought of lonely widowhood, or of his own death, drain his life of joy.
No poet shows a more poignant apprehension than Larkin of the
'million-petalled flower / Of being here'.

His life was a success. On the public level he took satisfaction from
his achievements at the Library in Hull and in his Fellowships of the
Royal Society of Literature and the Library Association. He was proud
to receive the Queen's Gold Medal for poetry, a CBE and innumerable
honorary degrees, and, in his final days, to be made a Companion of
Honour. On the personal level he knew that he had the love and respect
of those around him. His day-to-day life was packed with affections
and epiphanies. And he gained the profoundest satisfaction from
writing his poetry. He was, nevertheless, haunted by failure. In some
moods his refusal of the social normality of marriage and procreation
appeared to him not as the inevitable consequence of his artistic
commitment, but as the selfishness of a flawed character. Towards the
end, after his poetic inspiration had died, his despairing moods became
more frequent. He told Andrew Motion: 'I used to believe that I should
perfect the work and life could fuck itself. Now I'm not doing anything,
all I've got is a fucked up life.'[63]

But the failure which haunted him most deeply and persistently was
simpler and more universal than this. From the beginning he was

horrified that our precious existence, here, now, must inevitably falter and be extinguished in death. Larkin's biological clock ticked more loudly than those of other people. Unalloyed happiness was, he felt, unattainable, if only 'because you know that you are going to die, and the people you love are going to die'.[64] His poems feature the most uncompromising reflections on death outside the soliloquies of Shakespeare:

> The sure extinction that we travel to
> And shall be lost in always. Not to be here,
> Not to be anywhere,
> And soon; nothing more terrible, nothing more true.

Lunching with a young colleague in the staff canteen of Hull University a few months before he died, he asked her how old she was. She told him she was thirty-one. Looking down at his failing body he declared passionately: 'It's not fair!'[65]

I

Dear Fambly
1922–40

In 1953, on holiday in Weymouth, Philip Larkin was moved to hear his widowed mother Eva quoting snatches of poems by Thomas Hardy which she had learnt by heart 'simply to please my father'. He was prompted to reflect on his parents' first meeting, half a century earlier in 1906:

> O frigid inarticulate man! He met my mother on the beach at Rhyl. He was there for 3 days only, on a cycling tour, but before leaving he had a picture of them taken together & exchanged addresses [. . .] & despite a separation of several years his intentions didn't alter. I find all that very strange & romantic, partly because unlike the father I knew. He must have been as intensely idealistic as a young man as he was nihilistically disillusioned in middle age.[1]

Sydney Larkin had been impressed that Eva, a teacher, had continued to read her book while they sheltered from the rain together. But this had been the result of shyness rather than strength of mind, and she became a timid, nervous wife. Beneath his confident exterior Sydney also was painfully inhibited. When his young son claimed shyness he responded crushingly: 'You don't know what shyness is.'[2] Taking stock of his parents in a letter to his friend James Sutton in 1943 at the age of twenty Larkin wrote: 'I realized that I contain both of them [. . .] It intrigues me to know that a thirty-years struggle is being continued in me, and in my sister too. In her it has reached a sort of conclusion – my father winning. Pray the Lord my mother is superior in me.'[3]

After his father's death Larkin analysed the marriage with brutal objectivity: 'I think the situation was technically his fault. His personality had imposed this taut ungenerous defeated pattern of life on the family, and it was only to be expected that it would make them miserable and that their misery would react on him. And despite the fact that my mother grew to be such an obsessive snivelling pest I think if my father had handled her properly she would have done much better.'[4] It was his parents' example that taught him his passionate misogamy. The 'monotonous whining monologues' that his mother inflicted on the family, 'resentful, self-pitying, full of funk and suspicion', remained in his mind 'as something I mustn't, *under any circumstances*, risk encountering again'. The marriage 'left me with two convictions: that human beings should not live together, and that children should be taken from their parents at an early age'.[5] On the other hand, in his interview with the *Observer* in 1979, he expressed relief that his line 'They fuck you up, your mum and dad' had not been included in the current *Oxford Dictionary of Quotations*: 'I wouldn't want it thought that I didn't like my parents. I did like them. But at the same time they were rather awkward people and not very good at being happy.'[6]

Sydney planned his family, delaying the birth of the second child until he achieved advancement in his career. Philip was born on 9 August 1922, the year his father was promoted from Deputy Treasurer of Coventry to Treasurer. He was ten years younger than his sister Kitty. His father was thirty-eight at the time of his birth, and his mother thirty-six. Kitty remarked: 'Really, Philip could do no wrong in his father's eyes. Or his mother's. They worshipped him.'[7] This emotional closeness made Sydney's influence on Philip intense and lasting. The father's brusque precision of expression and emotional idealism are echoed in his son. Sydney gives a glimpse of his personality in a brief account of his early days published in the journal of the Local Government Financial Officers Association a few weeks before he died. He opens with Housman's famous stanza, 'That is the land of lost content', and then, with whimsical self-deprecation, likens borough treasurers to the damned souls of Bunyan's *Grace Abounding*. His focus then shifts to Bunyan's 'very clear English'. Bunyan does not use 'any such muddle-headed expression as "and/or" in his works. I do not remember that he uses "implement" as a verb or that he misuses "will" and "would" for "shall" and "should".' Sydney's reticence trembles when he reminisces about his sixteen-year-old first love, now lost in the past: 'I would not have missed the episode for anything.'[8] Philip's deep intimacy with this passionate, thwarted man, who had such high expectations of him, may have been partly responsible for the stammer from which the poet suffered throughout his youth. He himself always dismissed the idea that it had anything to do with early 'trauma', and recorded that it finally faded away in his mid-thirties.[9]

Like his librarian son after him, Sydney Larkin rose to the top of his profession. In 1926, four years after taking over the finances of Coventry he established a stabilized, level rate, which, as an anonymous obituary recalls, ushered in a period of prosperity and growth in the city. He also 'introduced mechanical book-keeping in trading accounts and gained for the position of City Treasurer an international reputation', travelling 'many times' to the continent.[10] He attended international conferences on accountancy in Berlin in July 1933, 1936, 1938 and 1939,[11] and his reputation brought him briefly to the notice of Hjalmar Schacht, Minister for Economics in the Third Reich from 1934 to 1937, the man whose cautious fiscal policies were widely credited with bringing German inflation under control.[12] In 1936 Sydney received the ultimate recognition of election to the Presidency of the Institute of Municipal Treasurers and Accountants.[13]

An insight into Larkin's earliest years is provided by the diaries which Sydney kept of the family's holidays between 1927 and 1933. He shows an acute self-consciousness. In Lyme Regis in 1927 he carries his bathing costume and towel everywhere, so as not to betray that he is a new arrival, and goes through embarrassing contortions while changing on the beach: 'I have never seen a rabbit skin itself but the operation must be similar to me trying to get the upper part of a two-piece bathing costume off my wet body.' In a pattern repeated on later holidays, he sets out to make the family distinctive by buying himself some shorts and 'Mamma' a 'jazz kerchief': 'sufficient to lend that amount of distinction to us that I like in a holiday place. Henceforth, we shall not be ciphers in Lyme Regis. We shall be known.'[14] One constant theme is the attractive women around him ('five very fine girls'; 'beautiful girls'; 'a vision in turquoise blue'). Philip, as the child of the family, was 'spoilt', and was allowed his independence. In 1929 in Ventnor: 'Philip did not bathe but reported that he had had three fights with different people.'[15] Several times his son's holiday illnesses elicited fatherly concern. In Newquay in 1930: 'Philip would not eat his lunch and so he went to sleep in the afternoon, on the bed, and I sat with him.'[16] In Falmouth in 1931 the nine-year-old Philip dominated one outing with his moody sentimentalism: 'After lunch we hiked to Maenporth, Philip being in a vile mood. Half way there we palled up with a black dog [. . .] As time went on Philip became a picture of misery owing to his anxiety over the welfare of the dog – whether he was happy, tired &c and whether he would get home.'[17]

Sydney admitted that, as time went on, these holidays shared by four very disparate people became strained. As he wrote before their trip to Bigbury on Sea in 1932: 'This holiday is even more doomed to failure than the last one (which in spite of the cold was not too bad.) The whole family agree that it is impossible to have an enjoyable holiday with four people all afraid to do what they would really like for fear of upsetting the others.'[18] In 1933, they took their last holiday together as a complete family. As an experiment and an economy, Sydney booked them into the new-fangled 'holiday camp' opened by the National Association of Local Government Officers near Scarborough. Philip had just turned eleven and his sister was approaching twenty-one. Sydney anticipated the trip with wry pessimism: 'This year we are taking the biggest gamble ever by going to the Nalgo holiday camp at Cayton Bay [. . .] it will probably be cold and wet. No one has, so far, had a bright word to say about the holiday. We are the funniest family on earth.'

On the first evening in the camp at an 'initiation ceremony', 'we were christened Oxo, Pussy, Snooker and Godiva – which Kitty and

Philip voted to be a bit "balmy"'. Sydney encouraged his family to enter into the spirit of things: 'We all filed down to the beach hut where we had community singing to the light of the numerous fairy lamps and Chinese lanterns. Philip got to bed very late.' With something of the diffident self-ridicule characteristic of his son, Sydney joked that he had come close to winning the booby prize in a whist competition. On the other hand he boasted that he and Kitty had walked to Scarborough and back in one and a half hours, 'a thing no camper has done before'. His verdict on the holiday was mixed: 'Mamma was not at all well during the whole period and could not enjoy it properly. Kitty is not cut out for camp life – not speaking to any other person unless spoken to. Philip enjoyed the table tennis and bathed occasionally but caught cold.' Nevertheless, Sydney calculated, the holiday had cost only 'about one half the usual and was therefore much better value for money. Philip ought to take his spectacle case.'[19]

Sydney was delighted when his son passed the entrance examination for the respected King Henry VIII School in Coventry. But the surviving drafts of his school reports show that Philip made a hesitant start. In 1934 the Headmaster, A. A. C. Burton, wrote: 'Inclined to take things too easily, perhaps.' In 1935 at the age of twelve he was ranked about the middle of his year-group, and since he was more than a year younger than his classmates it was decided that he should repeat the year. This easing of pressure had its effect and in April 1936 he was rated 'Very Good' in some areas, but: 'Would be better still if he would bring more enthusiasm to his work.' From July 1936 onwards he regularly came first in English, but showed no enthusiasm for other subjects. By Christmas 1937, at the age of fifteen, his future was in the balance. Burton commented: 'unlikely to pass the School Certificate unless he devotes himself to the task'. In 1938 his report reads: '*Conduct*: Moderate. Tendency to foolishness must be checked; *Progress*: Much too one-sided. His considerable ability in English is more than off-set by weaknesses in languages and science. This must be corrected if he is to pass S.C.' He was now placed twentieth out of twenty-eight boys. Then in the summer of 1938 he joined the Arts Sixth and no longer needed to apply himself to mathematics or sciences. The result was a dramatic improvement. He came second in a class of eight, his friend Noel Hughes being placed first. In his final report, on 26 July 1940, Larkin was placed first in English and History, and third in French, German and Latin. He left King Henry VIII School a lanky youth, already six feet tall, but weighing only ten stone seven pounds.[20]

At school Larkin developed two contrasted relationships: a pattern which was to be repeated in different forms throughout his life. He shared his deepest feelings with a paying pupil, James Sutton, an aspiring painter and son of a local builder. But he was also inseparable from the cocky defier of authority, Colin Gunner, who would throw paper darts around the Assembly Hall and then deflect collective punishment by gamely owning up to his crime.[21] Larkin later described Gunner as 'a small, agile, tough boy, with a face like a nut', and remembered sharing fantasies out of the boys' weekly magazine, the *Magnet*, *Tom Brown's Schooldays*, *Dracula* and 'the more colourful aspects of the Hitler regime' with him. When pupils were each presented with a George VI coronation mug, he recalled his friend 'shying his own into the squalid sewer the River Sowe (I have mine still)'.[22] The young Larkin took care himself that his 'tendency to foolishness' did not land him in serious trouble and, in a school regime in which corporal punishment played a prominent role, it seems that he avoided ever being beaten. His father, it seems, would not have permitted it. Though the obscure reference to 'violence a long way back' in Larkin's late poem 'Love Again' (altered in drafting from 'difference a long way back') has led some to speculate that Sydney might have been prone to domestic violence, the evidence is quite to the contrary. Larkin's father was sensitive to any hint of physical duress. He recollected in his autobiographical essay that he had himself been beaten, as a boy, by a sadistic woman teacher: 'I always thought she herself seemed to get a thrill out of it too.'[23]

For two years there were no family holidays. In 1934 and 1935 Sydney and Eva holidayed on their own in Germany and then Switzerland. Then in 1936 they took Philip with them to Germany, and again around the time of his fifteenth birthday in 1937. As Sydney's holiday diaries show, he now felt at home in Germany. He paid his dutiful respects to

German culture: 'Beethoven was a remarkable man. We saw his piano [. . .] He was a most wonderful genius and his life is worth studying.'[24] But his main pleasures were of a simpler kind: lake bathing, beer drinking and fleeting encounters with young women, though he always refers to 'Mamma' with proper respect. Glued into the diaries of 1934 and 1935 are photographs of 'Kath', 'les girls' and 'Backs of girls'. In Königswinter in 1936, he writes: 'we left the awful dullness of the Mattern Hotel' after dinner, and 'went to the Bier Klause, where the fun was fast and furious. Tired at last we went to bed.'[25] He does not mention whether Philip accompanied them on this occasion, but a repeated theme of the diaries of 1936 and 1937 is his determination to find a good place for 'bier', in order to initiate his son into this adult masculine pleasure.

But though the poet was indeed to become a confirmed beer-drinker, he did not share his father's enthusiasm for Germany. 'My father liked the jolly singing in beer-cellars, three-four time to accordions [. . .] think of that for someone who was just buying the first Count Basie records!'[26] His recollections of these two holidays were of embarrassment: 'I found it petrifying, not being able to speak to anyone or read anything, frightening notices that you felt you should understand and couldn't.'[27] His most excruciating German experience, he later told Kingsley Amis, arose from a failure of language. On one trip, given pride of place at the front of a bus, he assumed that the driver had asked 'Have you been to Germany before?' and replied 'No.' He was puzzled when the driver took offence and avoided him for the remainder of the excursion. Later he was mortified to learn that his words had actually been 'Do you like Germany?'[28] These early expeditions, he later wrote, 'sowed the seed of my hatred of abroad'.[29] Possibly because of Philip's resistance to a third German trip, in 1938 the family spent their holiday in Sidmouth, and in 1939 in Jersey.[30] Then, the day after returning from Jersey, on 16 August 1939, father and son set out on a tour of Somerset, taking the train to Bath and spending a week cycling together between Radstock, Glastonbury and Ilminster. Reading between the lines of Sydney's sparse diary, this outing seems to have been an idyll. At the end he proudly recorded: 'Philip's cyclometer indicated that we had ridden 162 miles.'[31] Much of Philip's leisure time in Belfast and during his early years in Hull was to be spent in the countryside on a bicycle.

Larkin claimed that when he later tried to 'tune into' his childhood in 1 Manor Road, Coventry, the emotions he picked up were 'over-whelmingly, fear and boredom'. It seems, however, that with two doting parents in a 'dull, pot-bound, and slightly mad' home his childhood was happier than most.[32] 'It was all very normal: I had friends whom I played football and cricket with and Hornby trains and so forth.'[33] His short essay 'Not the Place's Fault', written in 1959, breathes a warm nostalgia. He attributes 'the slight scholarly stoop in my bearing today' to his habit of looking for cigarette cards of 'Famous Cricketers' in Coventry gutters.[34] His schoolfriend Noel Hughes later recalled the 'intimidating tidiness' of his house, 'its highly waxed furniture and the practice of hushed conversation', though Mrs Larkin always welcomed him with 'unfailing graciousness'.[35] The young Philip would escape for long hours to the more relaxed atmosphere of James Sutton's home: 'One of my strongest memories of their house is of its long attic, that ran the whole length of the house, and which contained among many other things the debris of a hat-shop the family had once owned.'[36] He would give Sutton novels by Lawrence, and Sutton gave him books on Cézanne. The description in 'Coming' of the poet's childhood as 'a forgotten boredom' rings true in its poetic context. But Larkin's child-hood was, in fact, a vividly remembered scene of pleasurable activity.

His warmest recollections were of jazz. 'I became a jazz addict at the age of 12 or 13, listened avidly to all the dance bands of the day and tried to learn to play the drums.'[37] At first he felt some highbrow reserva-tions. In a letter written on 9 August 1939, his seventeenth birthday, and signed 'Snooker', he told Sutton: 'you simply can't think of Jazz after Beethoven. It's a physical impossibility [. . .] it's just "big", that's all. Jazz isn't big . . . but I refuse to start theorizing again on Jazz and its ethics, morals, foundations etc. etc.'[38] It was not long before jazz over-whelmed him: 'On Saturday afternoons we sat, frowning intently, in the glass cubicles at Hanson's, trying to decide whether both sides of the latest Parlophone Rhythm-Style Series or Vocalion Swing Series were sufficiently good to justify expenditure of the record's stiffish price of three shillings.'[39] Looking back from 1968, in the Introduction to *All What Jazz*, he rises to lyrical eloquence:

> Sitting with a friend in his bedroom that overlooked the family tennis-court, I watched leaves drift down through long Sunday afternoons as we took it in turn to wind the portable HMV, and those white and coloured Americans, Bubber Miley, Frank Teschmacher, J. C. Higginbotham, spoke immediately to our understanding. Their rips, slurs and distortions were something we understood perfectly. This was something we had found for ourselves, that wasn't taught at school (what a prerequisite that is of nearly everything worthwhile!), and having found it, we made it bear all the enthusiasm usually directed at more established arts.[40]

In a letter to Jim Sutton at the time, he declared, 'I'd back coloured against white most times, and as Count Basie is top of the coloured outfits I think I'm right in saying that he is the tops.'[41] Sydney Larkin raised no objection to his son's passion for what a German Fascist would have seen as degenerate negro music. Indeed Sydney went to the expense of a subscription to the Chicago-based magazine *Down Beat*, and also a drum kit on which his son could express his passion for 'hot' music: 'I battered away contentedly, spending less time on the rudiments than in improvising an accompaniment to records.'[42]

On the day war was declared, 3 September 1939, full of anger and frustration at the untold death and destruction which he foresaw would befall Britain and Germany, Sydney began a new, more formal diary in a large hard-bound volume. It was to run to twenty volumes, and continued into 1946.[43] His political instincts were coarse, and he shared the anti-Semitism of many of his class and generation. During the thirties he had brightened up his office in Coventry with Nazi paraphernalia brought back from conferences and Nuremberg rallies. Motion reports that John Kenyon, Professor of History at Hull University, related that Philip told him that his father 'had a statue of Hitler on the mantel-piece [at home] which at the touch of a button leapt into a Nazi salute'.[44] Richard Bradford elaborated Motion's description, referring to 'a 12-inch statue'.[45] However, when this object came to light in 2002, it turned out, in fact, to be a tiny hand-painted figurine, barely three inches high, with brown shirt and piercing blue eyes – the kind of souvenir which many tourists to Germany in the 1930s would have brought home. There is no button; the arm simply props up on a catch.[46] Philip later denied Noel Hughes's claim that his father's commitment to Nazism had extended to membership of the fascistic Anglo-German friendship organization, the Link.[47] Indeed it seems likely that such membership would have been ruled out by his public office.[48] As Philip records, Sydney called himself 'a conservative anarchist',[49] placing himself in an English, rather than a German, intellectual tradition. His personal views did not alter his devotion to his work nor affect his service on the wartime National Savings Committee, for which he was awarded the OBE.

Rejecting his beloved father's simplifications, and also as his mother's son, Philip was beginning to develop the empathy and self-doubt which were to mark his mature writing. His response to the declaration of war is a subtle and complex cartoon, 'Portrait of the Author and Family', drawn in a letter to Sutton of 6 September 1939. His father, 'Pop', appears as an endearing eccentric, leaning back in his chair, his balding head seen from behind, one hand gesticulating, the other holding a newspaper with the headline 'WAR'. In a speech balloon he defends Hitler, 'The british govt. have started this war . . . Hitler has done all he could for peace,' and launches into a farrago worthy of Lawrence's *Fantasia of the Unconscious*: 'This is the end of civilisation . . . after all, man has to be superseded, sooner or later . . . we're only a stage in the earth's development . . . a very unimportant stage, too.' 'Mop' mildly replies: 'Oh, do you think so? I wonder what we ought to have for lunch tomorrow . . . don't scrape the floor like that, Philip [. . .] I hope Hitler falls on a banana skin.' Meanwhile 'Sister' is preoccupied by what Joyce told her about her missed date with a storm trooper she had met on a recent trip to Munich. The poet himself, in a bow-tie, sits at the far left, pencil in hand, looking out of the picture, his face coloured with embarrassment and a huge exclamation mark above his head.[50] The assured blend of affection and detached irony in this cartoon is astonishing in a young man of seventeen.

Philip soon developed his own attitude to the war. He wrote to Sutton in 1942, 'the German system is, from all accounts, much more evil than last time',[51] and recast his father's apocalyptic despair into a disengaged quietism of his own: 'I believe we must "win the war". I dislike Germans and I dislike Nazis, at least what I've heard of them. But I don't think it will do any good. And I have no driving power to bring it about [. . .] I can't believe that anything I can do as an Englishman would be of the slightest use, nor do I see any "hope" in the future.'[52] In one of his earliest letters to Sutton, written probably when he was seventeen, he had ventriloquized his father's anti-Semitism: 'As for photos in "Down Beat" . . . our worst fears. All oily Jews.'[53] But three years later he wrote to his family from Oxford: 'My bookplate has aroused dislike as it is in the shape of a Star of David. On the wave of anti-semitism that is almost bound to come after the war I may be hung up on the nearest lamp post.'[54] His early exposure to Sydney's controversial views had the lifelong effect of neutralizing Larkin's political instincts. It is a key feature of his sensibility that he disclaims any coherent political ideology. There are virtually no expressions of political belief in Larkin's letters of the later 1940s and 1950s and those which are detectable show him leaning towards the left. By the time he met Monica Jones in 1947 it seems that his left-wing views were pitted against her unreflecting conservatism.

He remained in crucial respects, however, his father's son. Philip learnt his religious scepticism from Sydney, who told him never to believe in God. Sydney also imparted to his son his own adventurous appetite for literature. Larkin later recalled with gratitude that though 'most boys of my class were brought up to read Galsworthy and Chesterton as the apex of modern literature, and to think Somerset Maugham "a bit hot"', his father had filled the house with works by Hardy, Shaw, Samuel Butler, Wilde, D. H. Lawrence, Huxley and Katherine Mansfield. From an early age, also, Philip made full use of the local lending library: 'I suppose I must have read a book a day.' He also took early to writing, pouring out prose and verse in abundance, resting his pages on a record of Beethoven's opus 132 quartet, the only classical disc he owned.[55] Like his father he used for preference a 2B

Royal Sovereign pencil, and his handwriting, fluent and regular, is uncannily similar to his father's.[56] His earliest datable writing was printed in the school magazine, the *Coventrian*, in 1933, when he was eleven. It is a prose description entitled 'Getting Up in the Morning', already assured in its focus, with no evidence of stumbling over phrasing or idiom. He regarded reading and writing as his own province, without reference to school: 'I did not much like the senior English master, and I do not think he much liked me.'[57] He neatly transcribed or typed his earliest poems and sewed them into dainty booklets.

By the time he was in his final years at school he had developed a writer's sense of different audiences. He earned the approval of teachers by such contributions to the school magazine as his first 'published' poem, 'Winter Nocturne', which appeared in the *Coventrian* in December 1938 when he was sixteen. It is a fluent Shakespearean sonnet:

> Mantled in grey, the dusk steals slowly in,
> Crossing the dead, dull fields with footsteps cold [. . .]
>
> As quiet as death. The sky is silent too,
> Hard as granite and as fixed as fate.

He ends with an echo of Gray's *Elegy*: 'Dark night creeps in, and leaves the world alone.' It is notable that 'Going', the first-written poem in his first mature volume, *The Less Deceived*, is essentially this same poem in a more accomplished form.

He was also producing less public writing for the entertainment of his friends and schoolmates. 'Coventria' is a scurrilous parody of the school song, making fun of the teachers:

> We are the school at the top of the hill,
>   That Henry the King did will,
> If he came back and saw it now
>   The sight would make him ill!
> The Head's a lout – Hardy's a weed
>   With his lop-eared, pop-eyed gaze [. . .][58]

'Phippy's Schooldays' is a spoof biography of the English teacher, in dramatic prose, its farcical mayhem owing something to the Billy Bunter stories:

> Bates hurled himself across the study, and crashed Philipson to the floor. The Hon. Percy was not far behind. There was a rending sound as a cheap waistcoat and jacket split up the back, and a squeal of anguish.
>
> 'OOOHH . . . Bates, I shall report you to the Head Prefect . . . Oh! . . . ow . . . my jacket . . . my waistcoat . . .'
>
> The remains of the punch were swamped over Phippy's meagre features, and his steel-rimmed spectacles were cracked into a thousand pieces. A pair of poor-fund boots were dragged off and thrown into the fire.[59]

There were also comical accounts of 'the combat between Gunner and myself and the sponges' (conformist pupils), and a 'Tour of K.H.S.', in which the Headmaster A. A. C. Burton shows a visitor around, enthusiastically thrashing the wretches under his charge as he goes.[60]

Very different are three poems concerned with Philip's schoolfriend Earnest Stanley Sanders, which show the influence of Auden:[61]

> Disparaging my taste in ties
>   Relaxèd warmly on my lap,
> I gazed into his lovely eyes
>   And saw the snow beyond the gap [. . .]
>
> For life is not a storm of love,
>   Nor a tragedy of sex;
> It only is a question of
>   Deriving joy from shapely necks.
>
>   ('À un ami qui aime')

The confident form and tone of these poems is as remarkable as their lack of inhibition, at a time when homosexuality was a taboo topic: 'I, fascinated, watch your tongue / Curl pink beyond your little ivory teeth' ('Stanley et la Glace'). It seems certain however that Larkin was not yet sexually active.

It was decided that, like John Kemp, the protagonist of his later novel, *Jill*, he should take the Oxford scholarship examination a year early, since in five years' time Oxford and Cambridge might well 'be nothing but ruins'.[62] King Henry VIII School had two 'closed scholarships' at St John's College, so it was there that he went for the examinations in March 1940. He was awarded a scholarship in English, while Noel Hughes gained the other place to study Modern Languages. A few months earlier the seventeen-year-old Larkin had reviewed his writings up to that point, burning much and preserving an anthology of the best: fragments of novels, poems, satirical playlets and essays. With the instinct for balance and symmetry which shows itself throughout his life, he took care to devote exactly equal numbers of pages to prose and to poetry.[63] He had ambitions to be a novelist, but poetry always came more easily to him than prose, and it was in poetry that he made his first real start. Before going up to Oxford he sent five poems to the *Listener*, one of which, 'Ultimatum', was accepted for publication, and appeared in the issue of 28 November 1940. It is an Audenesque sonnet with self-consciously obscure imagery: 'For on our island is no railway station, / There are no tickets for the Vale of Peace, / No docks where trading ships and seagulls pass.'

As an undergraduate Larkin wrote a steady stream of informative and entertaining letters and cards to his parents, 'Pop' and 'Mop', or 'Dear Fambly', sometimes separately, sometimes jointly. On his first arrival he wrote to tell his father that he had seen an original letter of D. H. Lawrence in Blackwell's, priced at fifteen shillings. He had also attended his 'first and (I trust) last chapel':

On Monday I attended my first lecture – Edmund Blunden talking about biography. Very strange. B. was a nervous man with a shock of hair, a nose like a wedge, and a twitching mouth. He delivered his lecture in staccato phrases, semi-ironically, only half concealing his genuine enthusiasm for his subject. After that I heard Nichol-Smith talking about Dryden, and yesterday Prof. Wyld on the History of English. The latter was very interesting but hard to follow.[64]

The description of the matriculation ceremony is clearly intended for his proud mother's eyes:

> This entailed dressing up in all the full apparel – I didn't look half bad at all – and shambling down to Divinity Schools to receive the Statutes of the University and being blessed in Latin by the Vice Chancellor. This was only a very hasty affair – cut down to a mere nothing – and conducted to the accompaniment of bombers overhead. God, there are *hundreds*! My Latin name, by the way, is Philippus Arturus Larkin.[65]

The city was under-populated and the atmosphere muted. The age and specifications for call-up into the army were constantly being revised and undergraduates knew that their studies might be interrupted at any time. The traditional routines and rituals were reduced. Rooms were shared, students were rationed to one bottle of wine a term from the buttery, and meals could no longer be taken in one's rooms. As Larkin wrote later in his Introduction to *Jill*: 'This was not the Oxford of Michael Fane and his fine bindings, or Charles Ryder and his plovers' eggs.'[66] Bombers took off continually from the nearby aerodrome: 'I heard that old Brett-Smith, lecturing on mediaeval romance, paused in his discourse, peered over his spectacles, and inquired "Do I hear an unacademic sound? . . ." Everyone roared with laughter and the lecture continued.'[67] At first Larkin associated only with his tutorial mate Norman Iles and friends from his school, particularly Noel Hughes with whom he shared his room at St John's, and Jim Sutton who was at the Slade School of Art, which had been relocated to the Ashmolean Museum.

Then on 14 November 1940, only weeks after he had left Coventry, the first major blitz of the war was visited on his home city, killing 554 people and injuring 1,000. Sydney Larkin stayed all night at his post in the Council House, which was hit by two bombs and several incendiaries. Two days later he sent a telegram to his son, consisting with characteristic thrift of the minimum number of letters: 'Am quite safe. Daddy.'[68] Sydney decided to shut up the house in Manor Road and took Eva to stay with relatives in Lichfield. On 17 November, before receiving this telegram, Larkin hitch-hiked home with Noel Hughes to see the damage. His desperate anxiety is recalled in his novel *Jill*, written three years later. The protagonist John Kemp 'gasped aloud that he would do anything, promise anything, if only it would be all right. Any attempts at a personal life he had made seemed merely a tangle of a hypocritical selfishness: really he was theirs, dependent on them for ever.'[69] Larkin's parents may have fucked him up but he loved them deeply.

In sharp contrast, in the letter to 'Dear Fambly' which he wrote on 18 November, after receiving Sydney's telegram, he strikes an insouciant tone. Larkin recounts his and Hughes's hitch-hiking strategies and relates that they had not been able to approach the city centre because it was being dynamited. But the main account of what they have seen comes in a retrospective which he depicts himself delivering with mock-heroic self-importance to his undergraduate friends over dinner:

> I was able to hold forth to an astonished commoners' table – 'By God . . . Just back from Coventry . . . What a sight . . . pass the peas . . . any factories hit? . . . Ha, ha! . . . all be out of production for a month . . . blowing up the city . . . streets full of broken glass . . . pass the pota-toes . . . no gas . . . all candles . . . no electricity – can't hear the news on the wireless – absolutely no communications . . . bread please . . . getting water from shellholes . . . danger of typhoid . . .'

At the end of the letter, in '*Remarks to Mop*', he puts the bombing at an even further distance, addressing his mother in a tone of soothing trivi-ality: 'I broke the handle from a tea-cup the other day, unfortunately. This is the first breakage of any sort we have had. We *lost* the strainer the other day, but on questioning the Scout found it had only been mislaid. It is still the best thing we have.'[70] By this sophisticated literary strategy he quite defuses the impact of his disturbing subject matter.

In his later undergraduate memoir 'Biographical Details', Larkin relates that he could not write poetry while actually in Oxford: 'in fact, all my best poems have always been written at home. Oxford lacks silence.'[71] One of the best of his juvenile works, 'Out in the lane I pause', dates from his first vacation, Christmas 1940, spent in Lichfield, where his family had taken refuge with relatives. The poet stands alone under a starless sky beside the railway bridge, contemplating the futures of the 'Girls and their soldiers from the town' whose steps he can hear on the steep road towards the shops.[72] From his invisible vantage point he contemplates the disappointments to come: 'Each in their double Eden closed / They fail to see the gardener there / Has planted Error.' There is a touch of Donne about the biblical rhetoric and also the poem's complicated rhymed stanzas. The poet imagines the lovers going their separate ways from each other, and turning back in the future 'with puzzled tears':

> So through the dark I walk, and feel
> The ending year about me lapse,
> Dying, into its formal shapes
>   Of field and tree;
> And think I hear its faint appeal
> Addressed to all who seek for joy,
>   But mainly me.

It is a studied, self-conscious exercise, but the assured authority of the poem's lonely detached voice is impressive from a writer of just eighteen.

In tracing Larkin's literary development we are naturally mainly concerned with close and explicit influences: Auden, Yeats, Hardy, Laforgue. But of crucial importance also are the attitudes which he absorbed from his official undergraduate studies. Larkin was very much the product of the Oxford English Faculty of his day. English had been established as a respectable academic 'discipline' only two decades earlier as a result of the pioneering work of I. A. Richards in 'Practical Criticism' in Cambridge. From the beginning Oxford took a more historically based, less ideological approach. As an undergraduate Larkin attended lectures by J. R. R. Tolkien on Anglo-Saxon, Nevill Coghill on Chaucer and Shakespeare, C. S. Lewis on medieval and Renaissance literature, Charles Williams on Milton, Edmund Blunden on the Lake Poets and Lord David Cecil on the Romantics.[73] He recollected that his first college tutor, Gavin Bone, an Anglo-Saxon specialist, 'was mildly condescending', and 'very kind' to him and Norman Iles, appearing 'to regard us both as village idiots. I don't really blame him, considering the work and remarks we used to produce.'[74] Amis later made much of Larkin's contempt for Anglo-Saxon: 'I can just about stand learning the filthy lingo it's written in. What gets me down is being expected to *admire* the bloody stuff.'[75] But in fact Larkin never shared Amis's philistinism. He admired, absorbed, parodied and derided writing of all periods, learning lessons for his own work.[76]

Larkin's fundamental attitudes towards art are rooted in the principles he imbibed at Oxford. His insistence that poetry is 'not an act of the will'[77] owes much to that favourite discussion topic in the Romantic section of the syllabus of his day: Coleridge's distinction between Imagination and Fancy in *Biographia Literaria*. When Larkin later insists that writing is an involuntary attempt to satisfy 'that mysterious something that has to be pleased',[78] he is echoing Coleridge's idea of 'secondary imagination' which 'dissolves, diffuses, dissipates, in order to recreate', or at all events 'struggles to idealize and to unify'. In contrast, Larkin's 'required' writings, the reviews and the commissioned poems, are the product of Coleridge's 'fancy', a 'mode of memory' manipulated by 'the will' and dealing only with 'fixities and definites'.[79]

Most influentially, T. S. Eliot's 1919 essay 'Tradition and the Individual Talent' had set the prevailing theoretical context of literary studies. Eliot argued that the work of a great poet distils all previous poetry while also being quite new. The poet, he argued, must 'write not merely with his own generation in his bones, but with a feeling that the whole of the literature of Europe from Homer and within it the whole of the literature of his own country has a simultaneous existence and composes a simultaneous order'.[80] Eliot's language is elitist and nationalistic. Larkin is less ideologically strained. In his 'Conversation with Ian Hamilton' in 1964, he mocks the self-consciousness of Eliot and Pound. They were 'keen on culture, *laughably* keen': 'every poem must include all previous poems, in the same way that a Ford Zephyr has somewhere in it a Ford T Model – which means that to be any good you've got to have read all previous poems. I can't take this evolutionary view of poetry. One never thinks about other poems except to make sure that one isn't doing something that has been done before.'[81] Larkin chooses his words carefully. He rejects not tradition but the reification of tradition. The Oxford syllabus of his day was aimed at making him thoroughly familiar with what 'has been done before', while Oxford's relaxed cultural omnivorousness exposed him to many other influences outside the syllabus.

Larkin's reading was as wide and deep as Eliot's; but it was not driven by a self-conscious idea of culture. Consequently he achieves a wider range of spontaneous poetic effects than Eliot. The reader need not be aware of it, but a subtext of tradition serves to give depth and resonance to his poems. After the apprenticeship of his Oxford years, he could wait 'for it to come to me, in whatever shape it chose',[82] safe in the knowledge that the shapes it chose would carry within them the accumulated force of centuries of poetic precedent: Donne, Marvell, Gray, Pope, Keats, Gautier, Baudelaire, Tennyson, Laforgue, Yeats, Hardy and Auden. When he finally graduated from Oxford, he gained not merely the qualification which secured him a job in librarianship; he graduated as a poet.

2

Exemption
1941–3

Jim Sutton was called up into the 14th Field Ambulance Corps in April 1941, after only two terms in Oxford. In early June Larkin wrote another Audenesque sonnet, 'Conscript', which he later dedicated to his friend when it became Poem V in *The North Ship*. A young man's land is 'violated' by a 'bunch of horsemen' whose leader asks for his help in a war for which, obscurely, 'he was to blame'. The young man scorns evasion or 'replacement', and resigns himself fatalistically to 'follow further / The details of his own defeat and murder'. The poem was published later in the year in the fugitive magazine *Phoenix* (October–November 1941). Another Audenesque sonnet, 'A Writer', had been published in *Cherwell* in May. However Larkin's hopes of a smooth rise to literary prominence were disappointed when he was excluded from *Eight Oxford Poets*, edited in 1941 by Michael Meyer and Sidney Keyes. Kingsley Amis records that Keyes may have intended a deliberate slight, being aware 'that Philip considered him a third-rate personage'.[1] Larkin never forgave this rejection, expressing his contempt for Keyes even after his death in action at the age of twenty in 1943.

Over the next decade Larkin was to reveal his most intimate thoughts in letters to Sutton. Shortly after his friend's departure he described to him a series of lectures on psychology delivered in Oxford by the Jungian anthropologist John Layard. Layard, who had featured as 'Barnard' in Christopher Isherwood's *Lions and Shadows* and had

had an affair with Auden (who called him 'loony Layard'), made a great impression on Larkin. On 15 May, after one of the lectures, he devoted much of a six-page letter to his sister Catherine[2] to Layard's ideas on the common symbolism of ancient Egypt and modern Yugoslavian peasants, and to diagrams of the 'hypothetical line of perfection' between 'God' and 'animal' in the human psyche. It was, he told her, 'like an evening spent with truth'.[3] He explained to Sutton later in June: 'The solution as he saw it was that women should be the priestesses of the unconscious and help men to regain all the vision they have lost.' Since women are 'rubbing shoulders with all these archetypes and symbols that man so needs', they need to 'bring them up and give them to man. How this is to be done, he didn't really know.'[4] Earnest though he is he ends characteristically with a shrug of scepticism.

Larkin found an alternative, less problematic access to his unconscious in jazz. While still at school he had theorized pretentiously about the centrality of jazz to the modern predicament: 'Jazz is the new art of the unconscious [. . .] the unconscious is in a new state, and has a new need, and has produced a new art to satisfy that need [. . .]'[5] As he recorded in an account of his Oxford years, typed in September 1942 and October 1943 under the title 'Biographical Details: OXFORD', the first friendships he made in Oxford outside his own school and college circle came 'via hot jazz'. These evenings of beer and records were 'the most exciting thing about Oxford I had yet encountered'.[6] He wrote to Sutton: 'I rushed out on Monday & bought "Nobody Knows The Way I Feel Dis Morning". Fucking, conting, bloddy good! (sic) Bechet is the great artist. As soon as he starts playing you automatically stop thinking about anything else and listen. Power and glory.'[7]

On 5 May 1941, within days of Sutton's departure, Larkin encountered Kingsley Amis, in many ways Sutton's opposite. Amis was to take the subversive role in Larkin's life which had been filled by Colin Gunner at school. Larkin's later account of their first meeting is carefully nuanced. He was walking across the quadrangle with Norman Iles:

a fair-haired young man came down staircase three and paused on the bottom step. Norman instantly pointed his right hand at him in the semblance of a pistol and uttered a short coughing bark to signify a shot – a shot not as in reality, but as it would sound from a worn sound-track on Saturday afternoon in the ninepennies.

The young man's reaction was immediate. Clutching his chest in a rictus of agony, he threw one arm up against the archway and began slowly crumpling downwards, fingers scoring the stonework. Just as he was about to collapse on the piled-up laundry [. . .] he righted himself and trotted over to us. 'I've been working on this,' he said, as soon as introductions were completed. 'Listen. This is when you're firing in a ravine.'

We listened.

'And this is when you're firing in a ravine and the bullet ricochets off a rock.'

We listened again. Norman's appreciative laugher skirled freely: I stood silent. For the first time I felt myself in the presence of a talent greater than my own.[8]

There is a twinkle in that last sentence: the 'talent' in question is, after all, merely the ability to mimic the conventions of 'western' films.

This hint of dubiety underpins the lifelong relationship between the two men. They at once developed an intimate masculine bond. But theirs was always a very unequal relationship. Motion writes that Amis's was a 'sensibility very like Larkin's', one which 'checked lyricism with mockery, and spurned any sign of pretension'.[9] But though this is an accurate description of Amis, it covers only one small part of Larkin. Amis later recalled that Larkin's was 'the stronger personality [. . .] I was always full of ridiculous, foolish, very young man's ideas. But he seemed to have grown up.'[10] Richard Bradford observes that Larkin 'corresponded with virtually every one of his acquaintances, from Sutton and Gunner through his Oxford friends to his mother and father', while 'Amis wrote almost exclusively to Larkin.'[11] Amis demanded that his friend be 'an exact replica of himself'. 'I enjoy talking to you more than to anybody else [. . .] because you are savagely

uninterested in all the things I am uninterested in.'[12] Larkin obliged by
adopting Amis's tone of beer-drinking, jazz-loving ribaldry, and even
outdid his friend in contempt for the Oxford Literature syllabus:
Anglo-Saxon was 'ape's bumfodder'; *The Faerie Queene* and *Paradise
Lost* vie with each other for the title of 'the most *boring* poem in
English'.[13] It was in Amis's copy of Keats's *Eve of St Agnes* that Larkin
wrote against the lines: 'like a throbbing star / Into her dream he
melted' – 'YOU MEAN HE FUCKED HER.'[14]

Larkin soon introduced his new friend to his record collection:
'Kingsley's enthusiasm flared up immediately. I suppose we devoted to
some hundred records that early anatomizing passion normally reserved
for the more established arts.' The clarinettist Pee Wee Russell 'was,
mutatis mutandis, our Swinburne and our Byron. We bought every record
he played on that we could find.'[15] Amis was also an ally in Larkin's quest
for poetic recognition. As Larkin wrote in 'Biographical Details', 'Keyes
was rapidly forging ahead, and winning a reputation for himself that
extended far beyond the limits of Oxford.'[16] Amis became editor of the
Labour Club Bulletin, and published Larkin's poems 'Observation' and
'Disintegration' in the issues of November 1941 and February 1942:

> Time that scatters hair upon a head
> Spreads the ice sheet on the shaven lawn;
> Signing an annual permit for the frost
> Ploughs the stubble in the land at last [. . .]
>
> ('Disintegration')

The young poet was still convinced that his best route to success lay
through ventriloquizing Auden. He was also aware that he was beginning to lose his head of fine fair hair.

In his early months in Oxford Larkin made his first serious attempts
at narrative prose. Four stories from 1941–2, three in typescript and one
a substantial handwritten fragment, give thinly fictionalized accounts
of conversations and drunken outings with his Oxford friends, who for
a brief period named themselves 'The Seven'. Larkin explained in
'Biographical Details':

This arose from an idea that we should form some definite group with definite ideas, set against the college authorities and all the intellectuals and scholars we disliked. As a matter of fact, after one meeting the ideas and ideals degenerated into one big supper-party per week, supplied by two people. These suppers were perhaps the most thrilling and amusing things in the whole year. They may have been only projections of 'dorm feeds' onto a college scale, but they were never so enjoyable when only a few of us were there. It is quite impossible to recall just what went on.[17]

Norman Iles remembered the group, in a more serious tone, as a hand with seven digits: 'We made a fist against the Dons [. . .] I see myself as the thumb. Next to me is Philip Brown. In the middle come Nick Russel, Hilary Morris, and David Williams. Kingsley Amis is the third finger. The little finger, the opposite to me, is Philip Larkin.'[18]

The atmosphere of Larkin's stories echoes the schoolboy context of Christopher Isherwood's *Lions and Shadows*. The first typescript is dated 'January–July 1941', and the title added in pen, 'Story 1', indicates that Larkin regarded it at the time as a significant start in his writing. In a plain, dogged third person it follows the students from lecture to pub to party, achieving vividness only towards the end when one of them realizes that homosexual desire has overcome him at a college 'drunk'. He staggers spectacleless and blinded by cigarette smoke back to his room, which has, in the meantime, been wrecked by his fellow students. His sexual hysteria develops into a long unparagraphed purple patch of melodrama. He feels 'absolute shame' as he recalls 'the loathsome rapid servility of his hands to execute the vapid mirages of mind. Hands swam before his eyes, grasping, touching, manipulating, cleverly overcoming obstacles so that the mind could gratify its absurd beliefs, half-desires, and hallucinations, conspiring like vicious and unimaginative courtiers to burden further the patient and ox-like peasantry of the body.' The imagery becomes picturesquely phallic: 'That which, left alone, would like a lupin point for the sky in admirable symmetry he had, and not in the few previous hours only, warped and torn like an imbecile gardener [. . .] He was foul. Foul. Foul.'[19] Was

Larkin himself perhaps drunk when he wrote this comic sub-Lawrentian farrago?

The holograph prose fragment 'Peter', written a short time later, reveals the passive, relaxed mood of his early months in Oxford: 'Peter felt his university life to be happily and even creatively aimless. The beauty and luxury of the colleges pleased him; he did not feel his work either difficult or unpleasant [. . .]'[20] The choice of name for the protagonist alludes archly to a record by the high-voiced, gender-ambiguous jazz-singer Billy Banks ('Oh Peter, you're so nice. It's Paradise. When you're by my side, that's when I'm satisfied. Come on and kiss me do, and hug me tight.')[21] Larkin's narrative, however, has no such sophistication, amounting to little more than a desultory diary, the awkward third-person narrator clearly being 'Peter' himself. Norman Iles appears as 'Edwin':

> Each despised academic work, social polish, and intellectual discussion: each unspokenly believed that personal relationships were the only things worth caring for. Each was restless, sexually unsatisfied and nervous, yet capable of great personal loyalty, if not wholehearted passion.
>
> On the other hand, there were too many differences between them for them to be inseparable. Edwin was impetuous, honest, unthinking, child-like; any emotion or thought he experienced he immediately expressed. It rarely occurred to him that he could be in the wrong, and in consequence he had no sympathy with people who differed from him.[22]

The friends visit a medical student, 'Philip' (Philip Brown with whom Larkin was later to share a room), who shows them slides on his microscope, including human semen. Edwin comments: 'I never knew it looked so beautiful.' Peter refuses to look. They sit by the fire and Edwin aims an imaginary revolver into the centre of the flames. The narrator reflects that Peter and Edwin are 'day boys' and 'completely virgin', in contrast to their more sexually experienced boarding school contemporaries.[23] 'Geoffrey' who appears at dinner, is clearly Amis. 'Peter despised Geoffrey ultimately, but had a liking for him because he flattered him and could make him laugh. He had a gift for mimicry of a very high order: any peculiarity he could caricature and use as a nucleus for a fantastic monologue, that always the same, passed into the repertory of the group's humour'. While admiring 'his talent' Peter finds Geoffrey 'impossible to take seriously'.[24] The fragment ends as Peter visits Edwin next morning, to find him still in bed. They talk uneasily about 'this buggery business'.[25]

In June 1941 Sydney Larkin moved the family home from 1 Manor Road, Coventry to a new house at 73 Coten End, Warwick. Here the young Larkin found himself, during vacations, in the first of the high, secluded rooms in which he was to live most of his creative life. He described the house to Sutton: 'It is long and tall. I sleep in one of the attics and write this in the other. Everywhere junk is piled.'[26] On his return to Oxford in October 1941, the pattern repeated itself: 'My room, due to a misunderstanding with the Senior Tutor, was an attic in the president's lodgings.' Again he found himself in a solitary retreat up flights of stairs: 'I preferred it to college. The room had a small but vehement electric fire, and this I kept on all day and most of the night – frequently all night. This was before the days of fuel-rationing and so on. Consequently the room grew like a tiny oven, and earned the scorn of my friends. But I liked it.'[27]

In 'Biographical Details' his imagination is fired by the topic of living rooms. He is entranced by the stylish decadence of a new fresh-man, Hilary, who had 'a childish mane of fairish flopping hair, and pouting lips'. Hilary's room boasts 'two silky cushions – if not more – of green and orange, peculiar pictures (one seemed like a Japanese print), and a white, voluptuous lambskin on the floor':

I might digress on the subject of rooms. Norman's was redolent of a smashed culture [. . .] Kingsley's was also squalid and untidy, but without the debauched culture [. . .] His room, which grew to be our centre, was gradually made chaotic: records, papers, teacups and plates, books borrowed and not returned – all were thrown about the room in astonishing confusion. Nor would his fire ever burn. Nor would his cupboard shut. The scouts had a horror of our rooms. I don't wonder. Philip's, on the same staircase as Hilary's, betrayed no character. It had a picture or two, a few books and a microscope, and mice: it could be very draughty in the winter [. . .] My own room was a mixture of natural chaos and neurotic tidiness – it *looked* untidy, but everything was actually in its place.[28]

Then he makes an unexpected poetic leap:

I learnt something about untidiness when visiting an empty set of rooms in New [College] for some money. Needless to say, the owner was out, but the room was *expensively* untidy, with dozens of delicious books jumbled everywhere, mixed with letters, bottles, invitations, rackets, records, more books, and to top it all a chessboard with men neatly arranged to suggest a game or problem still in progress, ledged on the corner of a trunk.[29]

He is entranced by a glimpse of the deserted room of someone he will never meet. The inscrutable chessboard on the trunk has the air of a poetic symbol.

His determination to be in the literary swim was intense. He told his sister in a letter of 24 January 1941 that he was about to pay 2s 6d to join the Ark, a Christian association, 'just to hear and see' T. S. Eliot. 'I want to confirm my opinion that he really is an unpleasant guy.'[30] He became Treasurer of the University English Club, and over the next two years was involved in entertaining a wide variety of speakers, including Stephen Spender, R. H. Wilenski and Lord Berners. On 3 March 1943 he wrote to his parents: 'Met George Orwell, who is very nice, though not quite Pop's political line.' The visit which made the greatest impact was that of Dylan Thomas in the winter of 1941. Larkin was eager to put the image in Augustus John's celebrated portrait to the test: 'To my mind, his face was smaller and more triangular than John made it, and his hair (composed of beautiful curls seeming to range in colour from lemon to prussian blue) more luxuriant. His lips were more loose, and were perpetually holding an out-thrust cigarette.'[31] Larkin records every gesture and mannerism, noting that he 'did not drink as much sherry as I expected'. They talked about the documentary films Thomas had made for the Ministry of Information. 'I told him I sincerely admired "Balloon Site", which he seemed to find incredible [. . .] He smoked perpetually, lighting fresh cigarettes from the stubs of old ones.'[32] As they waited 'in some girl's room' in St Hilda's College, the ambitious young undergraduate attempted to make an impact on his distinguished guest: 'I said I had been reading "Contemporary Poetry and Prose", a little surrealist magazine in which D.T. had published stories and poems. He gave a brief biography of Roger Roughton the editor, commenting on his suicide "Bloody little fool".'[33]

During the reading Thomas, still in his coat, sat near the fire, hunched over 'a great wad of typescript, dogeared and scribbled'. After 'a little pyrotechnic introduction, full of bad puns and spoonerisms ("pillars of the Swiss")' and 'a topical poem of which all I can remember is "As I tossed off on Pembroke Bridge"', Thomas read two passages from a draft novel and 'about four poems: "Paper and sticks and shovel and match", A Centenarian Killed in an Air Raid, and two others I don't recall. These too seemed wonderful to me. He read very slowly, lingering on the vowels.' Larkin's past tense is deliberately chosen. By the time he records his enthusiasm for this 'wonderful' reading it has already faded. In a letter to Sutton, written the week following the visit, he had given a brisker, upbeat account, mentioning that Thomas ('Hell of a fine man: little, snubby, hopelessly pissed bloke') had read 'a parody of Spender entitled "The Parachutist" which had people rolling on the floor'.[34]

In view of Thomas's extravagant bardic image it is notable that what particularly impressed Larkin was his refusal of pretension: 'One girl questioned the phrase "innocent as strawberries"; DT admitted he had no sinful desires about strawberries [. . .] a long discussion of his Poem in October ensued, DT saying that he'd merely gone for a walk along a seashore in October and felt a bit queer, and wanted to make the reader feel queer also.'[35] Larkin carefully assesses his own shifting reactions. His final, dismissive judgement comes as a slight surprise: 'On the whole, he was rather a pathetic figure. It was difficult to connect the man and his poetry. I felt impatient because of his social manner, which I thought assumed. He seemed to use it as an artful protection.'[36]

On 16 November Larkin attended a very different performance. He wrote to Sutton that 'McCready and I shagged up to London to attend a Jam session at HMV Studios in S. John's Wood.' He was filled with excitement at being present at an historic occasion, the first jam session, indeed, to be recorded in England. He conceded that the quality of the music was not high, but criticism was disarmed:

> the audience was in front, behind, underneath, hanging from the lights, and so on. There was a beautifully informal atmosphere as they shat about at first, all dropping one by one into 'My Blue Heaven' as practice. Then the engineer asked them to play something to test the recording apparatus. 'Honeysuckle Rose' was then bashed out for 10 minutes [. . .] we left at 5.30 and just caught our 'bus. The outstanding player on the session was Carl Barriteau, a negro clarinet player who sounded wonderful in the flesh. Played hellish loud, as Bechet would.[37]

The experience made him aware that 'an *American* session would be colossal'. 'Barriteau was amazingly good: every one of his sides ended with a terrific cheer from the audience, which I hope goes on the record. It deserves it.' The listener today can hear Barriteau playing in 'Tea for Two' at this very recording session on the CD set of *Larkin's Jazz*.[38]

The young poet was enjoying his new experiences. He was popular and happy. He wrote to Sutton with shocking candour: 'Perhaps you think I am being a bit selfish but I just don't want to go into the Army. I want to pretend it isn't there; that there's no war on.'[39] But the shadows were gathering, and on 16 December he was called for his medical examination. He was told that if his eyesight was graded at 4 or below he would be exempt. As term came to an end he sold all his books and burnt his lecture notes. He would, it seemed, be in uniform within a matter of weeks. 'So it all came to an end,' he wrote portentously in 'Biographical Details':

> Everybody – that is, Norman, Philip, Nick, and Kingsley – gave me a Bessie Smith record each, which touched me more deeply than I showed. I was staying on till Christmas, firewatching, and I saw Philip and

Norman off [. . .] The parting was one of the most harrowing things I had to go through, and I returned blindly to college in the December gloom, to play a record or two before dinner.[40]

This valedictory diminuendo is followed by a dramatic reversal: 'On New Year's Day I received my hideous letter marked O.H.M.S. in bed. It informed me that my medical category was IV. Never have I, except at the news of the Munich agreement, felt so relieved.'[41] The equation of his personal exemption with the national relief of 1939 is rich with comic euphoria. The Munich agreement had of course turned out to be a temporary delusion.

For the time being his dearest wish was fulfilled. He was exempt and could pretend there was no war on. At the beginning of 1942 he returned to his beloved Oxford free of the shadow which had haunted him. He moved with Philip Brown, who as a medical student was in an exempt category, into 125 Walton Street, not quite an attic, but a large, first-floor room with a piano,[42] and they became a homosocial couple, 'the two Philips' or 'big Philip and little Philip'. Brown gave Larkin a copy of Housman's *A Shropshire Lad*. He recalled in 1991: 'Philip may have been in love with me [. . .] there were a few messy encounters between us, yes. Nothing much. Philip's sexuality was so obscured by his manner of approach and his general diffidence that frankly I would be surprised to hear that he ever had sex with anyone.'[43] Larkin's 'crush' on him, he recalled, did not lead to 'any serious action. Besides, I was extremely interested in girls. And so was he.'[44] Larkin wrote in 'Biographical Details': 'We were all still very childish about sex.' But though Larkin lacked experience he adopted an assured attitude towards sexual matters in his writing. In a letter of 16 May 1942 he wrote to his mother: 'Tell Pop that a friend has found an unexpurgated version of "Lady Chatterley's Lover" behind the bookcases in his digs. I am impatiently waiting for him (and his wife) to finish it.' It is difficult to imagine many other nineteen-year-olds making such a joke to their parents at this period.

Around this time both Larkin and Amis were paying court to a Czech student. Kingsley, Philip wrote, was attempting 'to ensnare

Chitra by a reformed-pervert appeal'. He goes on to describe her: 'striking, with a comical head of black hair and scarlet lips. One couldn't call
her beautiful – anyway she would probably regard beauty as being
slightly bourgeois – but she had a good figure and was decidedly attractive. She was, however, a full time party-line girl. She was known to
interrupt kisses to say: Remember, the party comes first.'45 While Amis
invented strategies to cajole Chitra into bed, Larkin explored his feelings for her: 'In a drunken fit of bravado I asked her to tea, and she
came. We ate toast and marmalade and she told me I was decadent.
Nothing else happened. My ventures with women had up to this time
been continually depressing, but I liked her and I still do – not that I
ever did anything about it. She did not ask me back.'46 Without 'doing
anything about it' he finds that he 'likes' her, and attributes her lack of
response to his own inadequacies rather than to any failure on her part.

Towards the end of the following term Larkin found himself further
isolated in his exemption when Amis followed Sutton into the army,
being commissioned into the Signals. Larkin's mood during the summer
vacation in 1942 is vividly evoked in parallel letters to Sutton and Amis
written from his new Warwick family home shortly after his twentieth
birthday. He begins his letter to Sutton on 17 August in a mood of pure
jouissance: 'I have gone for a walk in the Park. I have seen a man & six
white puppies. The paddling-pool is full of children [. . .] There is a
light, withy, breeze.' His ebullience overflows into surreal inner music:
'I am hearing an audible voice singing "Arseholes cheap today, cheaper
than yesterday." etc.'47 Since their letters have been crossing in the
wartime post, he decides that 'general meandering is the best way to
write at present'. 'I enjoyed your letter by the way – pissed myself over
Ross & a few other bits.'48 He briefly mentions the 'buggering silly' war
work in which he is engaged in the Warwick Fuel Office, sorting letters
and forms, and then turns to his writing: 'I am still undecided as to
whether I am a poyte or a writah. At present I am writing a story about
a mad woman in an air-raid, much influenced by Dylan Thomas,
whom I very much admire [. . .] The novel has expired – bricks without
straw. You remember Auden in "Letters from Iceland" said that novels
were much harder than poetry. I agree!'49

Later he resumes the letter with a different topic: 'My favourite jazz record at present is Condon's "Friar's Point Shuffle" in the 1940 Chic. Album. It is sodding fine [. . .] Bessie is still huge and monumental.' He then shifts time and scene again. He is back in the park:

> This evening is purely beautiful – a whitish sky near the sun, sweeping over to deep blue in the east. The stone wall is yellow. Shadows of poplars are very translucent at the tips. Dogs run through the stream. People wheel bicycles between the flowerbeds. The river runs between green, rounded banks and is lined with trees. A woman wheeling a pram, and a soldier, have come up to this seat. The soldier has his thumbs in his pockets and is quite at his ease. Planes crawl like lice over the sky. I'm afraid I'm not much good at description.
>
> The park is full of soldiers. The baby is crying uneasily, waving tiny paws over the wool coverlet.[50]

As dusk descends Philip wishes Jim many happy returns on his twenty-first birthday and reflects seriously on their future: 'At no point can one say "Now I am this, or that". One discovers it slowly [. . .] The sun has sunk and shows a great, cloud-paced sky, etched and whorl[ed]. It is a bit colder. Yesterday I rode 30 miles and feel fine. If we had peace and a bit of money we could live damned well. Also read "The Rainbow" again.'[51]

Next day he picks up his account as he listens to jazz. He compliments Jim on his letters ('They express something firm and unshaken'), and tells him that the previous evening he wrote a poem: 'My poytry is all to buggery at present. The pure wine of Auden has been shamefully adulterated by Spender's still lemonade and Dylan's Welsh whiskey.' He suddenly dramatizes his immediate writing process: 'I rather like this paper I am writing on. Large and opulent [. . .] Fuck this bastiobating pen.'[52] He brings the letter to an end with a reflection that all his friends, with the exception of Philip Brown, are in the army or navy. He, in contrast, is on the edge of events, lonely but safe. He signs off with verve: 'Well, I'll cock off. Whenever you read this, in darkness or sea-dingle, I hope you'll be well & happy. I will write again shortly. Yours ever, *Philip*.' The enclosed poem shifts borrowed tones between the yearning Yeats ('I stand at the kerb, and hear / The day of shops break over my feet'), the 'modern' Auden ('the crowd / Wave in the cinema like weed'), and the 'metaphysical' Dylan Thomas ('the navigating worm'). Nevertheless it conveys real emotion:

> I hear you are at sea, and at once
> In my head the anonymous ship
>   Swings like a lamp;
> I think of equipment and meals, and the long
> Sane hours of a funnel
> Against the birdless, interleaving plain.[53]

The letter to Amis, written two days later on 20 August 1942, is more edgy and argumentative. After complimenting his friend on his latest letter ('I read it on the way to the office, cackling liberally'), he resumes an ongoing disagreement with a show of finger-wagging pomposity: 'Might I remind you that the greatest artists and philosophers did not enjoy the benefits of heterosexuality. If I were not too lazy, I would get up a few references for you.' Then, apprehending that his tone might antagonize his friend, he humours Kingsley's homophobic prejudices: '(NB This is *not* serious – do you catch the note of hysteria.) I put my mental age as fifteen; and likely to remain so many moons, I should imagine.'[54] Amis has sent him a blues lyric which he found 'highly entertaining', and he promises to enclose his own 'Fuel Form Blues composed & illuminated at the office'. He has just been listening on the radio to 'the History of Jazz, Ch 16': 'Very good – after each programme I make frenzied notes of records to buy when I go back to Oxf., if I do [. . .] I have a great admiration for Armstrong – "he hath outsoared the shadow of our night" etc.'[55]

With calculated abruptness he shifts to more personal matters: '2.3 was the reading on my flogging chart. I'm not quite sure what it *signifies*: it's either times per day, or days per time. The former, I rather fancy. Present reading is 2.2.' After this masturbatory calculation he abruptly turns to a set-piece description of his fellow workers at the Fuel Office, displaying his skill in characterization for his aspiring novelist friend. Mr Turner, 'an enormous comic ex-policeman', 'thrusts a pile of papers on my desk & says "You might just check that, Mistah – er –" I remain Mister Er, although he knows my name *perfectly* well [. . .] His favourite phrase is "I think we've done enough, for today" said in monumental simplicity & sincerity.'[56] Larkin has, it seems, developed a more interesting relationship with his closest office colleague:

> After cautious fencing, Mrs Glencross & I have begun to swear. I say sod, bugger, bloody, and balls. She says bugger, bloody, and bum. The latter amuses me intensely. I have an awful moral compulsion to say fuck & shit as well, but haven't dared to yet. It might horrify you that such things become important. They do. This morning, after she had been scoffing[57] abt Prince George,[58] I made a flippant remark like 'One less to shoot when the Revolution comes' which, before I knew where I was, had developed into the kind of conversation 'Well, I always say to people who run England down, if you know a better, *go* to it!' However, we compromised by agreeing that Hitler could have made Germany 'the finest country in the world'.[59]

To preserve masculine solidarity with Amis, Larkin presents this verbal brinkmanship as a skirmish in the battle of the sexes, omitting the facts which he records in a separate biographical fragment, that Mrs Glencross's husband was a prisoner of war and she had recently given birth.[60] By referring to her always as 'Mrs Glencross' he also obscures the fact that she was only twenty-seven. There is more friendship and fellow feeling in this relationship than he reveals to Amis.

Richard Bradford attributes the difference between the levels of Larkin's and Amis's sexual activity at this period to Larkin's lack of attractiveness: 'he did not have Amis's enviable combination of charm, wit and looks'.[61] However, Amis was certainly no more charming and witty than Larkin, and Larkin's empathy with and respect for women made him less aggressive than Amis in the pursuit of sexual conquest.[62] Philip Brown remembered that Larkin was popular with the women in the Oxford English Club: 'most of the officers of the Club were girls, and they used to lionize Philip a bit, asking him to tea and so on [. . .] he was charismatic, you see. Girls wanted to find out about him.'[63] At this time Larkin still had the silky fair hair seen in early photographs; though not for much longer. Nuala O'Faolain was later to comment on Larkin's subtle sexual magnetism. She found him 'a most attractive man, sending out both a nonthreatening message and a message about being more threatening than his nonthreatening image made him appear'.[64]

Larkin's letter to Amis comes to an abrupt close on the pretext that 'there's no more of this paper left'. He ends with a suggestive compliment on his correspondent's sexual adventures:

> . . . God I want to piss. How's Lizzie?
>   Busy?   (don't misinterpret.)
> Wishes –

Here, in embryo, is the caricature relationship between the two men seen later in 'Letter to a Friend about Girls': Larkin the timid, unadventurous wimp, Amis the rampant sexual adventurer. The promised lyric, 'Fuel Form Blues', is enclosed as a separate typescript.

> Oh see that Fuel Form comin' through the post
> Oh *see* that Fuel Form comin' through the post
> It's five weeks late and worse filled up than most.
> [. . .]

> I'd rather be a commando, or drive a railway train,
> I'd rather be a commando, Lord! drive a railway train,
> Than sort dem Fuel Forms into streets again.
> [. . .]

> Fuckin' Fuel Forms, gonna carry me to my grave, carry me to my grave.

He adds a vigorous pen sketch of a seven-piece band: piano, double bass, saxophone, guitar, drummer, trumpeter and clarinettist, all jamming away in angular enthusiasm. Motion's description of

Larkin's mood at this period seems unduly negative: 'Reading the letters he wrote at the time, it is impossible not to be impressed by the ferocity of his misery. It is also hard not to suspect [. . .] a degree of complacency.'[65]

These letters to Sutton and Amis show Larkin's already highly developed literary sense. Texture and tone are calculated to suit the correspondent. To have written to Amis with the earnest sincerity of his letters to Sutton would have incurred sceptical derision; while Sutton would not have appreciated the crude sexual references and sharp caricatures of the letters to Amis. Significantly Larkin scarcely mentions Sutton in his letters to Amis, or Amis in his letters to Sutton; they feed quite different, contradictory aspects of his sensibility. What both letters have in common, however, is their omnivorous, magnanimous appetite for experience of all kinds. It is easy to see why Larkin's friends so looked forward to receiving his letters, with their vivid interest in the correspondent, evocative epiphanies, quirky self-ironic euphoria and manifest enjoyment of the process of writing itself.

At the end of the first section of the 'Biographical Details' typescript, completed on 9 September 1942, Larkin added a brief list of omissions in pen. Then, in different handwriting and at a slant he inserted the name 'Penelope'. The second section, describing his final year, begins with his fire-watching duties and reading of Dryden and Pope. He then continues: 'I soon found out that Penelope Scott-Stokes, a girl resembling an Eton boy and whom I had been gently attracted to the term previously had left Somerville and been married. So a sonnet, So through that unripe day . . ., was proved correct.'[66] These enigmatic references hint at a private subtext. Penelope, already lost when he first mentions her, was his first muse, and her ambiguous image haunts his work for the next two years. In the winter term of 1941 Larkin had attended a performance of *Twelfth Night* in Somerville College, where he was struck by the first-year student playing Viola. Penelope Scott Stokes's father 'had wanted her to be a boy and thus had her hair cut short and dressed her in boy's clothes'.[67] Decades later she herself recalled their failed encounter: 'He invited me to tea, but I evaded that, making some paltry excuse. We're talking about *1941* when probably tea was just that. No bed glimpsed through carefully half-opened door. Just a bright fire, toast and cakes fetched from Oliver & Gurden [. . .] One way and another, perhaps at 18 I was wise! The girl-boy in me (Viola well chosen) he found provocative.'[68] Penelope appealed to the young poet's intense literary eroticism. He found himself 'gently' attracted by her slight figure, 'gently' meaning 'overwhelmingly'.

It seems a plausible speculation that there was also some more substantial incident which they both later suppressed. In a letter to Amis written on his birthday three years later, in 1945, Larkin recalls: 'the only advance I ever made to a woman was productive of such scorching embarrassment that the wound is still rawly open. (In response to your unspoken question it wasn't anyone you knew.) That was over two years ago and if I forget it in ten I shall be agreeably surprised.'[69] Robin's abrupt embrace of Katherine on the punt in his 1947 novel *A Girl in Winter* may perhaps be a version of this incident.[70] It is not impossible that he is referring to a different woman, but it seems likely that he made a clumsy physical advance to Penelope, eliciting a vulnerable response which filled him with shame.

'Sonnet: Penelope, August, 1942',[71] to which he refers, became Poem XXX in *The North Ship*. It begins with an Audenesque evocation of an ungendered victim enduring the bitterness of 'that unripe day', cruelly tested before his/her time by some undefined ordeal. It then shifts abruptly to the poet's perspective:

> Instead,
> It was your severed image that grew sweeter,
> That floated, wing-stiff, focused in the sun
> Along uncertainty and gales of shame
> Blown out before I slept.

Despite his obscure uncertainty and 'shame', the poet cherishes his beautiful recollection, which floats in his imagination like a stiff-winged butterfly. She is now 'Long since embedded in the static past':

> Summer broke and drained. Now we are safe.
> The days lose confidence, and can be faced
> Indoors. This is your last, meticulous hour,
> Cut, gummed; pastime of a provincial winter.

The delicate promise of summer has sunk into the safe Eliotic sterility of winter. As he had predicted in the poem, Penelope was unable to take the strain, and left Oxford to be married. In accordance with tradition the muse is distant, unattainable. Significantly, however, in the poem the speaker also sympathizes with the real suffering girl. Watching Penelope's performance as Viola, he had intuited her nervous, vulnerable temperament, and felt protective towards her.

The very different 'Poem for Penelope abt. the Mechanical Turd', written in anticipation of his return to Oxford in autumn 1942, seems to dramatize an intimate birthday stocktaking.[72] It survives only in holograph on a single sheet torn from a manuscript book, and shows a number of draft changes. Archie Burnett considers it merely three separate fragments. However, the text arises from a single mood and a continuous, finished text can be inferred. Larkin has drawn a large cross over the second and third sections, but he did not destroy the page. This is a more private poem than 'So through that unripe day', with a mix of elements unprecedented in Larkin's previous poetry. The title parodies a poem by Sidney Keyes, addressed to his girlfriend, 'Poem for Milein about the Mechanical Bird', which had been published in Keyes's first collection *The Iron Laurel*, in 1942.[73] The opening line, however, echoes Keyes's 'Elegy' on his grandfather, which includes the lines: 'It is a year again since they poured / The dumb ground into your mouth.' These eloquent lines, it seems, roused Larkin's competitive envy. His pastiche insults Keyes (presumably the 'mechanical turd'), with gratuitous obscenity: 'August again, and it is a year again / Since I poured the hot toss into your arse' ('arse' replaces the earlier drafted 'mouth'). The image of buggery or oral sex may perhaps express self-disgust at his clumsy advance to Penelope a year earlier.

After an asterisk the poem continues its retrospective on the past

year, but in a different register, focusing, with a further echo of
Keyes, on the poet's current claustrophobia at home with his parents:

> Choking, I pull open a door. It is evening out there.
> But the house is building still behind my back
> Room over room, cells of a great mad brain,
> And all are threaded on my parents' voices
> Crossing like scissors in the stale air.
>
> The bright road crawls with placid faces.
> And I leave tomorrow eager to have done
> With the sandwiches they are cutting for me to take
> – For they love me – but I turn again in despair.

The reference to his parents' home as the 'cells of a great mad brain'
elaborates the surrealist imagery of Keyes's 'Elegy': 'Your brain / Lives
in the bank-book, and your eyes look up / Laughing from the carpet
on the floor.'[74] The speaker acknowledges his parents' affection without irony; but, as the long vacation comes to an end, he is eager 'to
have done' with their love and sandwiches. Larkin anticipated his
final year at Oxford with contradictory feelings. 'One by one my
friends left: Nick, Jimmy, and David and David West to the Navy,
Norman, Mervyn Brown, Kingsley, to the Army: Hilary was due for
the R.A.C. [Royal Armoured Corps] [. . .] Now there would be one
more posthumous year.'[75] It was to be one of the most momentous
years in his life.

In October 1942 John Layard returned to Oxford to deliver a
lecture about the symbolism of dreams. Shortly afterwards, a friend
of Brown's, Karl Lehmann, a keen Jungian, came and stayed in Walton
Street. Larkin recalls: 'We each began a recording of our dreams, and
up to the present ['Dec 19th 1942' penned in the margin] I have
amassed nearly seventy. Karl gave us indications as to how to interpret them, and we began searching for "problems". I don't believe
Philip had one. I had.'[76] Between 26 October 1942 and 4 January
1943, Larkin typed out ninety-five numbered dreams, painstakingly

illustrated with diagrams showing the relations between 'myself' or 'my path' and people, animals, buildings and streets. In one simple realistic dream he pulls Philip Brown out of the path of an unlighted car as they 'whizz' on their bicycles out of Hertford Street into Greyfriars Lane in Coventry. Less realistically, in another dream he is singing a hymn, resigned to marrying 'a girl called "Helen Rose" whom I disliked'. He consoles himself that 'anyway I can get divorced immediately afterwards, and then I shall be even more sophisticated'. Another dream resembles a thriller film. He is 'a member of a secret service in some eastern town' where, ambushed in a conference room, he kills two hostile agents by firing his revolver repeatedly at their advancing bodies. Another dream is a brief moral fable: 'Someone was playing with a cat that obviously wanted to escape. When it at last did so, it had shat all over his hands. I regarded this as just.'

Other dreams are surreal. In one, headed 'A visit to the home of Christopher Isherwood', he sneaks away from Isherwood and his mother to try out a piano in a 'wonderful room' with bookshelves ascending out of sight under an 'immensely high ceiling'. But he becomes lost in the dark and, hearing two women laughing in the next room, runs away. In another he has volunteered to commit suicide by putting his name on a list posted up in the gym, and is annoyed to find that the shoes he is to wear when he jumps off the roof have not been laid out ready for him. Other dreams are purely absurd, such as one concerning 'an extremely savage rabbit that I made kill someone'. In a dream recorded on Christmas Day he is driving a car that grows smaller and smaller until he can push it along with his foot.[77]

Some of the dreams have obvious 'Freudian' interpretations: 'someone took the lid off a hamper, which was filled with a huge snake. It began uncoiling and I fled in horror.' In a dream of sexual self-doubt he finds himself 'in the custody of four girls', including Margaret Flannery, an Oxford acquaintance:

> It seemed that I was going to bed with her. We two went back to the first room and she lay on the floor. She was wearing a flame coloured skirt and brilliant yellow knickers. I began fucking her and she talked

dreamily about copulation. After a while I stopped fucking, not feeling I was getting anywhere, and we both stood up. She maintained her dreamy indifference.[78]

In another he is kissing a male friend on a sofa near Carfax in the centre of Oxford. 'I disliked this intensely but remained polite.'

Other dreams feature encounters with 'negroes'. In one he strangles and drowns a 'great tiger' which threatens to stop him reaching Lil Armstrong (Louis's second wife) and a 'negro band' performing on the far bank of a river. In a more delicate psychological wish-fulfilment dream he meets 'a most beautiful negress' as he walks through a symbol-ist landscape 'along a path between several rivers and canals'. 'We remained together for some time, and I was going to ask to meet her again. Someone called her "a new Billie Holiday".' In another dream comedy takes charge: 'I was making a violent speech against Louis Armstrong, the President of the United States. I said "The only merit of this buffoon is that he has not had the effrontery to submit any laws to Congress." Voices called out from other bedrooms, telling me to shut up, because it was assumed I was talking in my sleep. One voice was my Father's.'[79]

Though his imagination throws up some colourful psychological and subliterary material, Larkin's dream diary failed in its primary psychoanalytical purpose of defining his 'problem'. He wrote wryly to Sutton on 7 January: 'I have dropped my dream-business, (where? into the Thames?): presumably I am the individuated man.'[80] A more focused stimulus to his literary development was provided the follow-ing month, February 1943, when the poet Vernon Watkins spoke at the Oxford English Club about W. B. Yeats. Larkin's early poems already show Yeatsian influence, but now Watkins's crusading enthusiasm for Yeats's elliptical symbolism overwhelmed his sceptical defences. As he later recorded, 'I spent the next three years trying to write like Yeats, not because I liked his personality or understood his ideas but out of infatuation with his music (to use the word I think Vernon used).'[81] Larkin abruptly ditched his knowing Audenesque detachment in favour of loud Yeatsian self-dramatization. Watkins's own impact on Larkin was ambiguous. Though he inspired his enthusiasm for Yeats's music, in himself he presented a poetic example quite different from either Yeats or Thomas. In peacetime he had been a bank clerk. He did not adopt a poetic pose 'as an artful protection'. He seemed to Larkin 'a genuinely modest, genuinely dedicated person, who had chosen, in Yeats's phraseology, perfection of the work rather than of the life. To anyone who, like myself, was on the edge of the world of employment his example was significant. Indeed, it was almost encouraging.'[82] Watkins 'made it clear how one could, in fact, "live by poetry"; it was a vocation, at once difficult as sainthood and easy as breathing'.[83]

Three poems which Larkin wrote at this time show the impact of the various new influences on him. 'I dreamed of an out-thrust arm of land' ends with a glamorous Yeatsian dramatization of the poet as rejected lover:

> Till your voice forsook my ear
> Till your two hands withdrew
> And I was empty of tears,
> On the edge of a bricked and streeted sea
> And a cold hill of stars.

In contrast, 'Mythological Introduction' is an entry from his dream diary turned into poetry. A 'white girl' sings in Blakean mode, 'I am your senses' crossroads, / Where the four seasons lie', but then:

> She rose up in the middle of the lawn
> And spread her arms wide;
> And the webbed earth where she had lain
> Had eaten away her side.

Eros and Thanatos are juxtaposed in a visually exact image ('webbed earth') reminiscent of paintings by Salvador Dalí. These two poems were published in *Arabesque* (Hilary Term 1943). The third poem, 'A Stone Church Damaged by a Bomb', shows the influence of the Thomas of 'A Centenarian Killed in an Air Raid'. The Dylanesque contortion of thought sits uneasily with the poem's simple religious scepticism. With 'metaphysical' wit the poet finds 'magnificence' in the bomb's destructive work in contrast with the Church's feeble spell against death. When Ian Davie accepted all three poems to appear alongside works by Drummond Allison, Sidney Keyes, Michael Meyer, Michael Hamburger and John Heath-Stubbs in the volume *Oxford Poetry 1942–3*, Larkin could feel that he was beginning to make some progress as a poet. The volume appeared in June 1943, by which time he had already embarked on a quite different literary adventure, as a 'lesbian' writer of girls'-school stories.

3

Brunette Coleman
1943

In the spring of 1943 Larkin adopted a new and radical literary strategy. He began to experiment with female styles and genres. At the same time he adopted a tone of frivolous comedy, at an opposite extreme from Yeats's high seriousness. During summer and autumn 1943 he devoted much energy to writing girls'-school fiction under a female pseudonym. This seems a strange development for a twenty-year-old male undergraduate in the middle of a war. One motive was simple escapism. He wanted to pretend there was no war on. The abrasive masculine Amis had left, and with so many male academics and students away in the army Larkin found himself in an Oxford which was overwhelmingly female. He described the candidates for the Final Examination in a letter to his parents in June 1943 as 'a sea of women, a little thin file of men [. . .] 6 of us in all out of 70 or 80'.[1] In his experiments with women's writing he embraces his exempt situation, *hors de combat*.

But there were also deeper and more personal motives. In a dialectic characteristic of his sensibility, a restless literary instinct impelled him to contradict the serious tones of his earlier attempts at fiction, and the earnest pretension of his Audenesque and Yeatsian poems. Male critics have made heavy weather of Larkin's 'lesbian' phase, interpreting it as distasteful heterosexual pornography or trivial flippancy. But, immature as he was, Larkin had the sure instinct of an original writer. It is a mistake to raise our eyebrows in prurient embarrassment at these works. Apart from their considerable success as high-camp comedy, they add a key new element to his developing literary repertoire. A keen sensitivity to different genres, and particularly to the idioms and motifs of popular culture, figures largely in the mature poems.

Two new friends, both of whom lived a stone's throw from St John's, played their part in Larkin's literary modulation from earnest, idealistic young man to witty, subversive woman. Bruce Montgomery was a year older than Larkin, though since his Modern Languages course took four years rather than three they were to take their Final Examinations at the same time:

> Bruce lived in Wellington Square, and could make a very strong impression on the unwary, being a good pianist, a fluent composer, and author of several unpublished books. He also seemed very rich. Under his immediate influence, I suddenly revolted against all the things I had previously worshipped – poetry, Lawrence, psychoanalysis, seriousness, the creative life, and so forth. It was like being back in the fourth form again. Bruce's irresponsibility and self-confidence were exactly what I needed at the time and our friendship flared up like a flame in oxygen. In return I lent him jazz records.[2]

Montgomery 'professed to do very little work, and usually hung round the Playhouse and the Randolph [the most prestigious hotel in Oxford]. The only books he read were detective stories.'[3] During the Easter vacation of 1943 he completed a detective novel, *The Case of the Gilded Fly*, which he was seeking to publish under the pseudonym 'Edmund Crispin'. Larkin's relationship with Montgomery had none of the edgy rivalry of that with Amis. In his 1964 Introduction to *Jill* Larkin wrote: 'For the next three years we were in fairly constant contact, and I wrote continuously as never before or since.' He continued: 'Possibly his brisk intellectual epicureanism was just the catalyst I needed.'[4] Out of deference to Amis, Larkin retrospectively underplayed Montgomery's influence. But Montgomery radically altered the direction of his writing. He also confirmed Larkin's lifelong fascination with French literature.

The second new influence, Diana Gollancz, Larkin's first female friend of any importance, was a student at the Slade School of Art. She remains elusive, and it is difficult to gauge how seriously he took her. A daughter of the left-wing Jewish publisher Victor Gollancz, she adopted the image of a socialite and projected her rooms in Beaumont Buildings, off St John Street, as a salon for talented and fashionable undergraduates.[5] Larkin's attitude towards her was, however, familiar and affectionate: 'Diana Gollancz, the only publisher's daughter I have yet encountered, was a pale, excitable girl of boundless cheerfulness and good nature. She painted. We spent a great many evenings drinking together, either at The Gloucester Arms or more often the Lord Napier in Observatory Street.'[6] He told Sutton, a touch unconvincingly, that he was physically attracted to her: 'I like publishers' daughters. Oh, I *do* like publishers' daughters! The more we mix together, etc. I'd like to brush some of the dust off her myself. She is quite a good painter and dislikes the Slade intensely.'[7] Though he affected a lordly disdain for Oxford women, he made an exception for Diana, 'who is really lesbian and therefore probably a better artist'.[8]

Larkin's new literary voice is heard first in 'An Incident in the English Camp', written in the month following Vernon Watkins's appearance at the Poetry Club. The story, celebrating the life of a wartime female undergraduate in the style of a woman's magazine, is dated 'March 15th 1943', and appears to have been composed compulsively during the course of one day as a deliberate exercise, as if the author were setting himself a challenge. Larkin even calculated, as he went, exactly how many pencilled words would be needed to fill all the pages of the small lined notebook in which it is written. He missed one page in the middle, to which he returned for the final words of the story.[9] The subtitle, 'A Thoroughly Unhealthy Story, by P. A. Larkin', suggests that the author is aiming at a transgression beyond the lukewarm homoeroticism of the earlier stories. It even seems possible that 'P. A. Larkin' is female. What is remarkable about the story, in contrast with his earlier fiction, is its assured narrative voice and accomplished tone. The author is no longer the ingenuous autobiographer of 'Story 1' and 'Peter', but a master of the professional skills of romantic-magazine writing.

At the outset the reader is immersed in a closed world of female domesticity. Pamela Fenton fetches her milk-ration from the College kitchen, in 'a small Poole jug', amid the smell of fishcakes, the 'ripple of high voices' and the sounds of freshers 'doing each others' hair' in one of the bathrooms. The anticipated boring afternoon of reading and fire practice is suddenly dispelled when the portress tells her that a 'gentleman visitor' has called. She rushes up to her room:

> the sun poured in from windows in two walls on her hearth rug, her books, the pussy willow catkins in her Poole vase, and her camouflaged divan-bed. And as she opened the heavy door, with her name slipped crookedly in the socket outside, the room burst upon her like a bomb of sunshine, streaming from the mirror and the backs of the hairbrush and handmirror on the dressing table, and winking from Robbie's gold buttons and 'pips' as he stood, magnificently astride, his cap, gloves, and cane thrown carelessly across her bed, in the very centre of her room.
>
> 'Hallo, Pam!'
>
> 'Hallo, Robbie!'
>
> To conceal her emotion she put the milk jug down on a copy of *The Complete Poems of John Donne*, saying:
>
> '*What* brings you here? Surely you aren't on another leave, are you?'
>
> 'I've got four days. As a matter of fact –' his voice grew selfconscious, proud and sad – 'it's embarkation leave.'[10]

Unlike the edgily masculine rooms described in 'Biographical Details', this feminine room is orderly, domestic, charming. Arch allusions to the war, the 'camouflaged' divan-bed and the bursting 'bomb' of sunshine serve merely to emphasize the innocuousness of the scene. We may be reminded of Larkin's letter to his family following his visit to the blitzed Coventry, foregrounding a broken tea-cup handle and a mislaid strainer.[11]

Robbie's conventional masculine good looks and military bearing are seen through Pamela's admiring, but also gently mocking, eyes. He has a 'tiny tidy little moustache the same colour as his fair hair that waved like a toy sea from left to right of his small peashaped head'.[12] 'Pamela parted her lips in a half smile: "You have got the officer and gentleman badly, Robbie.'" The narrator reveals that Pamela's books disturb him with their cosmopolitanism: 'He noticed with some alarm a few new additions since he last inspected the shelf: *Fleurs du Mal*, by Charles Baudelaire. French, eh? He frowned.' (Enid Starkie's edition of *Les Fleurs du Mal*, published in November 1942, was the focus of some scandal at this time.)

This archetypical English couple go on to spend an afternoon of wartime solidarity together. She challenges him to a game of squash: 'Pamela, her hair tossing lightly on her neck, fought bitterly for every point, each muscle in her body tigerishly taut.' To the gratification of both, he finally overcomes her 'brave defence', in his borrowed 'togs'. They go on to Elliston's tea-house where they consume 'cress and paste sandwiches, sponge cake and china tea', and afterwards they attend a morale-boosting variety performance at the theatre. Robbie, who, we are told, runs a discussion group on the British Empire back in his camp, enthuses about his desire to 'go abroad somewhere and help keep the English tradition of fair ruling going'. The show ends with community singing: 'There'll Always Be an England' and 'God Save the King'.[13]

The ending of the story at dusk on the platform of Oxford Station is a scene to be played by Trevor Howard and Celia Johnson (Noël Coward's film *Brief Encounter* was released two years later in 1945):

> The signals dropped: a bell rang. Far away in the mouth of darkness a red light appeared, and in a moment the train drew up steaming to the platform. Silently soldiers and civilians got out and in. Robbie was leaning from a window, his peaked cap casting a shadow over his face. 'Goodbye, darling,' he whispered, and she put her face up to his. For a minute they clung until the whistle sounded and the dark train drew slowly out.[14]

Then, in the final paragraphs, the knowing narrator makes fun of Pamela's exalted emotions, revealing the narcissism beneath:

> Pamela watched it go, without regret, almost with exaltation, for now she could face life alone again. She almost wished Robbie could be

struck dead, his words would have been so beautiful, and then she could cherish his memory and live as he would have wished. She walked in exaltation through the black streets, her heart glowing like a coal with deep love.[15]

With its playful enjoyment of the stereotypes and idioms of romantic-magazine writing, and its blend of comic satire and warm sympathy, this is an extraordinary piece of writing from the pencil of a twenty-year-old.

During his final term in summer 1943, 'on the whole one of the most purely enjoyable I have spent',[16] Larkin fell into a mood of pleasantly fatalistic euphoria. In a letter to Sutton in May he depicts himself in the role of an effete dandy: 'You ask me what I am doing – I am preparing to take Finals, and the prospect is an expanding shite. I am also dressed in red trousers, shirt, & white pullover, and look very beautiful [. . .] In fact I am happy.'[17] In a letter to his parents written the following day he elevates a shopping trip into a mock-heroic adventure of whimsical sentimentalism: 'after standing in the Cadena queue yesterday for half an hour I staggered out with blood-shot eyes clutching two "trifles" and a couple of currant buns. I then bought a very sad looking lettuce. "It's got a good heart," said the shopkeeper, pinching it cruelly, like a warder speaking of a prisoner's conduct. I bought it out of pity.'[18]

With Bruce and Diana as his audience, Philip found himself plunging deeper into irresponsible literary transgression. Montgomery had written a detective story under a male pseudonym. Larkin decided he would go one better and write a girls'-school story under a female pseudonym. So the gender-ambiguous 'P. A. Larkin' became the female 'Brunette Coleman', her name suggested by Blanche Coleman, whose All-Girl Band was popular at the time.[19] He wrote to Amis later: 'Blanche Coleman is Brunette's sister, a natural ashblonde.'[20] Looking back in 1964 in the Introduction to *Jill* Larkin seems still a little taken aback by the unaccountable originality of this move: 'Even in that last term, with Finals a matter of weeks away, I began an unclassifiable story called *Trouble at Willow Gables*, which Bruce and Diana Gollancz would come back to read after an evening at the Lord Napier.'[21]

The impetus continued through his final examinations. Glumly he prepared his parents for that 'hallmark of imbecility', a third-class degree.[22] But he was more successful than he expected, underlining 'FIRST' thirteen times in a letter to Sutton of 18 July.[23] Following the award ceremony on 24 July he celebrated with lunch at the George Hotel together with his family, Bruce and Diana. Then he returned to Warwick, and, in an extended limbo briefly broken by attempts to secure a job, he completed the 'Brunette Coleman' canon: *Trouble at Willow Gables*, its Oxford sequel *Michaelmas Term at St Bride's*, the essay 'What Are We Writing For?' and his most impressive writing so far, the verse-sequence *Sugar and Spice*. He later recalled: 'leaving Oxford was like taking a cork out of a bottle. Writing flooded out of me.'[24] It was the adoption of a female persona that uncorked the bottle.

He devoted great care to *Trouble at Willow Gables*, typing it out neatly on 143 pages of poor war-quality paper. It is comic parody, but the parody of affectionate homage rather than satire. Larkin treated this disregarded genre with all the respect due to D. H. Lawrence or Dylan Thomas. He read numerous examples, absorbing their conventions and idioms. In her essay 'What Are We Writing For?' Brunette cites seven works, most of them recently published. In chronological order of publication they are: Dorita Fairlie Bruce, *Dimsie Moves Up Again* (1922), Elsie J. Oxenham, *The Abbey Girls Win Through* (1928), Dorothy Vicary, *Niece of the Headmistress* (1939), Phyllis Matthewman, *The Queerness of Rusty: A Daneswood Book* (1941), Joy Francis, *The Girls of the Rose Dormitory* (1942), Judith Grey, *Christmas Term at Chillinghurst* (1942) and Nancy Breary, *Two Thrilling Terms* (1943). There are also unspecific references to Elinor Brent-Dyer's *Chalet School* stories and the Farm School stories by Josephine Elder. Two of his particular favourites, he told Amis, 'charming in their way', were Vicary's *Niece of the Headmistress*, and Breary's *Two Thrilling Terms*.[25]

Though the plot and language of *Trouble at Willow Gables* are more complex than those of actual girls'-school stories, Larkin/Brunette still submits to the key imperatives of the genre. The characters, for instance, show the proper age hierarchy. The junior fourth-formers, Marie and Myfanwy, have an innocent pre-adolescent narcissism. The protagonist, Marie, is based on Dorita Fairlie Bruce's heroine in the popular Dimsie series of the 1930s, sharing Dimsie's ingenuous, impulsive nature and appetite for second (and third) helpings at dinner. The sixth-formers Hilary, Ursula and Pamela are more adult, affecting the dignity of seniors. When *Trouble at Willow Gables* was published in 2002 Sue Sims, editor of *Folly*, the magazine for devotees of the girls'-school story, found it a charming if unorthodox example of her beloved genre. Some passages, she wrote, 'could have come straight out of Dorita Fairlie Bruce or Elsie J. Oxenham'.[26]

The story is intricately plotted. It centres on a £5 note sent to Marie by her aunt Rosamond, who seems to be Rosamond Lehmann, author of the novel of lesbian love *Dusty Answer*:

> 'Now isn't that jolly decent of her?' Marie cried joyously, her amber hair shaking. Across her mind danced a preposterous procession of what £5 could buy: tennis racquets, evening frocks, wristlet-watches, slave-bangles, bicycles, underwear of finest silk, puppies, mountains of soap and cosmetics, rivulets of expensive Paris perfume, or even the collected morocco-bound works of Sir Hugh Walpole.[27]

Her joy is cut short, however, when the note is spitefully confiscated by the prefect Hilary, since girls are not permitted to possess more than two pounds pocket-money during term-time. When the headstrong Marie is discovered to have stolen the note back from the Headmistress's study, the Headmistress forces her, under moral blackmail, to donate it publicly to the school's Gymnasium Fund. The note is then stolen again, this time not by Marie, though the Headmistress mercilessly beats her for the crime and locks her in the punishment room, where she is consoled clandestinely by her friend Myfanwy:

> Her golden hair fell rhapsodically over the remains of her cup of tea.
> 'Marie!' Myfanwy called softly, and her friend looked swiftly round.
> 'Myfanwy!'
> She ran lightly down the dormitory, and knelt by Marie's bed, her eyes filling with tears. Marie hastily shoved the teatray out of the way.

'Oh, Marie!—'

For a second they clung together, Myfanwy's lips pressed against her chum's hair. Then Marie gave an uneasy wriggle, and slid down onto her side. Myfanwy, guessing the cause, gazed with an infinity of pity at the small girl lying in her arms.

'Oh, Marie, how awful!—'

'Oh, it's all right,' said Marie gallantly. 'It doesn't hurt, much.'

'The old beast!' Myfanwy hissed with all the anger of which she was capable.[28]

Larkin/Brunette relishes this fourth-former 'chumminess', one of the staple elements of the genre, evoking its ingenuous charm with an affectionate detachment which would be lacking in any actual girls'-school story.

The characterization of the senior Hilary, with her wilfulness and taste for violence, owes something to Una Vickers in Dorothy Vicary's *Niece of the Headmistress*. Larkin, however, pushes the genre beyond its conventional limits by making Hilary's lesbianism explicit. In Vicary's *Niece of the Headmistress*, and in Elsie J. Oxenham's novels, lesbianism is merely a suppressed, if sometimes clamorous, subtext. In a delicious variation on the stereotypical sixth-former, Hilary is depicted as a sophisticated decadent who smokes and plays cards with the other prefects in her study. The 'crush' of the conventional girls'-school genre becomes, in Hilary's case, an aestheticist obsession with the 'young lioness', Mary Beech, a hockey-playing junior to whom she is giving secret midnight coaching in French and Latin.

Hilary's most prized possession, Brunette tells us, is a calf-bound copy of Théophile Gautier's scandalous novel *Mademoiselle de Maupin* (1835), in which the hapless idealist d'Albert searches for the perfect woman: 'someone whom I have never seen, who must exist somewhere, and whom, if it please God, I shall find. I know just what she is like and, when we meet, I shall recognize her.'[29] D'Albert believes he has achieved his goal when he makes the delectably feminine Rosette his mistress, only to be left comically bereft when Rosette rejects her subject role and elopes with Mademoiselle de Maupin, a bisexual member of the 'third sex', whose members lack both the 'imbecile submissiveness' of women and the 'disgusting crapulence and bestial propensities' of men.[30] Gautier's imagery frequently alludes to the Greek myth of Pygmalion, the sculptor whose statue of the sea-nymph Galatea was of such beauty that he fell in love with it. In Ovid's version the gods took pity and rewarded the artist by breathing life into his creation. But, as in other post-Romantic variations on the myth, such as Wilde's *Picture of Dorian Gray* and Hardy's *The Well-Beloved*, in Gautier's and Larkin's versions the coming to life of the statue brings only disillusion.

Larkin/Brunette takes delight in reformulating decadent French aesthetic doctrine in terms appropriate to an English sixth-former with a crush on a fourth-former. Like d'Albert, Hilary builds an impossible dream in her imagination. She yearns to possess Mary's unselfconscious pre-adolescent innocence: 'the early flowering into a quiet beauty of soft, silken skin, ribboned hair, print dresses, socks and sensible shoes, and a serious outlook on a world limited by puppies, horses, a few simple ideas, and changing Mummy's book at Boots". Hilary has nothing but contempt for the version of six years later: 'a painted savage dressed in bangles and skins, chock-full of feminine wiles, dodges, and other dishonesties directed to the same degrading sexual end'.[31]

Fatally, when Mary drowses off during one of their secret French lessons, Hilary, deluded by the passivity of the thinly clad form, mistakes dream for reality and makes a clumsy advance. At this point Mary wakes up and, deeply shocked, rushes back to her dorm. The prefect chases after her, only to come upon Margaret Tattenham, the girl who has actually stolen the confiscated £5 note, in the act of returning it to the Headmistress's study (she had needed it to bet on a cert in the Oaks). Hilary wrestles with Margaret in the dark and, having been baulked of Mary, blackmails the sporty girl into bed with her.

> With a smile she stroked Margaret's cheek where her blows had landed, and felt under her hand a solid body. Mary Beech was, alas, not for her, but here in her possession was the slender, horse-riding body of Margaret Tattenham, who, Hilary reflected, brutally, would do. Moth-wings of passion ran all over her body, and she released Margaret's wrists.[32]

The scene owes something to the passage in Dorothy Vicary's *Niece of the Headmistress* in which Una, who has been reading *Torture through the Ages*, inflicts a chinese burn on the defenceless Dora: 'Her strong, hard little hands dealt mercilessly with Dora's slender white wrist. Dora flushed and grew pale, and struggled to free herself, but, failing, put her head back against the wall and took her lip between her teeth. "You – you utter bully," she stammered.'[33] It is notable that Vicary's depiction of sado-masochistic violence has a direct vividness which makes Brunette's version sound studied and literary in comparison.

The story ends, as the typical girls'-school story so often does, with a dangerous excursion beyond the safe school bounds. Marie, having escaped from the punishment room and blundered about the country-side all night, treading in cowpats and tearing her trousers on barbed wire, is tracked down by Hilary and the other prefects, who have been dispatched by the Headmistress to bring her back, her innocence having been established by Margaret's confession. Margaret has also escaped from the punishment room, by means of a rope made from her underclothes, and ridden off across the fields on Toby, the school pony:

> they started to gallop across the next field, the wind blowing her short tunic precisely against her body, and her flying hair making her look like some exquisite nymph riding the horse of the dawn over the Pan-guarded slopes of Arcady. Mentally, with pardonable epicureanism, she noted for future reference that bare-backed riding without knickers was a pleasurable occupation. The sun shone warmly on her bare arms and legs.[34]

Finally the plot, with elegant complication worthy of Beaumarchais, brings all the characters together in a country lane at exactly the moment when Marie's chum Myfanwy, the school's water-polo captain, out for morning swimming practice, floats past in the river about to drown through cramp. Margaret redeems herself by leaping in and saving Myfanwy's life. They then all return to the school to receive inevitable justice at the Headmistress's hands. The lesbian Hilary is expelled, Margaret is forgiven because of her heroism, and the story ends with Marie visiting Myfanwy in the sanatorium: '"Everything's settled . . .

Everyone's happy. Nobody's been punished. And ... Myfanwy!" She leant closer. "They've started a Swimming-Bath Fund!"'[35]

Trouble at Willow Gables is not pornography. The narrator is empathetic rather than lubricious. Motion cites 'the wish to dominate' as one of Larkin's motives in writing the story.[36] But Larkin/Brunette has no more wish to dominate women than do Dorita Fairlie Bruce or Nancy Breary, and arguably less than Dorothy Vicary. He was, however, content to allow Amis to interpret his motives in terms of his own predatory sexuality. He told his friend gleefully that the lesbian seduction scene 'gave Diana Gollancz quite a "crisis des nerfs" or whatever the French is'.[37] And he complained that there was not enough lesbianism in the stories written by women: 'It's nice when the girls kiss each other and get into each others' beds and quarrel and twist each others' wrists, but in between there is an awful lot of waffle, and the authoresses are very stupid women, without a grain of humour in their tiny little minds.'[38] Significantly, he represents his disappointment as literary as much as sexual. And he seems to attribute a private, specifically literary meaning to the word 'lesbianism'. On 7 September 1943 he wrote to Amis: 'homosexuality has been completely replaced by lesbianism in my character at the moment – I don't know why'.[39] He chooses his words carefully. His early stories had taken their tone, uneasily, from Christopher Isherwood's celebration of homosocial boyhood in *Lions and Shadows*, and the near-explicit homosexuality of Julian Hall's Eton novel, *The Senior Commoner* (1934).[40] He had now achieved a more objective artistic outlet for this same fictional impulse by transposing it into the female mode.

Recently the feminist critic Terry Castle has perceived tragic implications in Larkin's impersonation of Brunette: 'Pretending to be a middle-aged invert named Brunette was a bookish young man's way of neutering himself at the starting gate – of announcing second-tier status and yielding in advance to the competition.'[41] But Castle underestimates Larkin's imaginative control of this literary exercise. Outside his writing he did not neuter himself; nor, despite the show of wimpishness with which he flattered Amis's ego, did he yield to 'the competition' in his dealings with women. His transgendering was not a symptom of sexual timidity.

Larkin was severely selective in what he disclosed about his 'lesbian' story to his correspondents, and we would understand his motives better were the letters to Montgomery available; but they are embargoed in the Bodleian until 2035.[42] Larkin did not mention Willow Gables to Sutton, and it seems that he shared his interest in Gautier with Montgomery alone. He does not mention *Mademoiselle de Maupin* in his letters to Sutton or Amis, who would have had no sympathy with such foreign sophistication. Larkin made a show of furtiveness, begging Amis: 'Please don't ask me to send it, because I simply daren't let it out of my sight, it's too valuable and incriminating.'[43] Startlingly, however, the typescript gives evidence that he made an attempt to have the work published. At some point after its completion he went through the text with a pen, altering the names of his real Oxford contemporaries to fictional ones. Marie Woolf becomes Marie Moore; Margaret Flannery Margaret Tattenham; Mary Burch Mary Beech; Hilary Allen Hilary Russell, and so on. He also included in the stapling an unnumbered typed sheet listing the 'Correct Nomenclature'. The only conceivable reason for these indications is to guide a typesetter. The tattered wallet-file which contains the typescript bears two ink-stamps of 'Rochefort Productions (Literary Property) Ltd', a literary and film agency with which Victor Gollancz, Diana's father, was briefly associated.[44] Larkin, it seems, attempted to see the work into print in 1943, trusting that, 'unclassifiable' though it was, it would find some kind of readership.

Both Montgomery and Amis also tried their hand at writing in a female voice. But their attempts are in different styles, and on a different scale from Larkin's. Among Montgomery's papers there is a very brief, 126-word fragment in which a woman nostalgically reminisces about having been stripped and spanked, as a naughty fifteen-year-old, by her handsome thirty-year-old stepfather.[45] It is closer to the male pornography of *Fanny Hill* than to Brunette's writings. Amis took the literary challenge more seriously, developing his own lesbian alter ego, 'Anna Lucasta', in parallel with Brunette. In their letters the two men tell each other about Brunette's and Anna's projects, including a novel concerned with lesbian art-students in Oxford, referred to as 'Iwdafy' ('I Would Do Anything for You'), whose title comes from a song by

Billy Banks.[46] A surviving fragment, included in a letter to Larkin of early 1945, gives an idea of the camp luridness of Anna's style:

> 'all I want is to be close to you, but somehow we never seem to be close enough to one another.' For answer, Jennifer pulled her on to her lap and held her mouth in a long, shuddering kiss. Marsha flexed her slim body and pressed herself to her. And then there was nothing but their closeness as the shadows lengthened and the sunlight paled and dusk swam into the still, silent room.[47]

This soft-core sentimental pornography is very different from Larkin's complex genre-gender adventure.

Isolated in Warwick during the autumn of 1943 the precocious young writer pursued his Brunette impulse further into other 'unclassifiable' forms. Most remarkable perhaps is the essay 'What Are We Writing For?', neatly typed and stapled in October 1943. It begins with a camp self-portrait of the chain-smoking professional writer, Brunette, breakfasting with her assistant Jacinth, who has 'great intelligent topaz eyes'. Jacinth has been reading George Orwell's famous essay published in *Horizon* in 1940, 'Boys' Weeklies',[48] and suggests that Brunette might write an answering piece on the girls' version of the genre. Brunette is taken with the idea and, putting aside her routine labours on *Wenda's Worst Term*, she settles down to write a defence of her profession. Orwell's pioneering essay was one of the first which subjected popular subliterature to serious analysis. It is a classic of ideological demystification, decoding the apparent trivialities of the boys'-school story in terms of British imperialist ideology. For Orwell, 'All art is to some extent propaganda.'[49] Britain's imperialist wars, he asserts, were won on the playing-fields of Eton by people like Tom Brown in Thomas Hughes's novel, or Frank Nugent and Bob Cherry in the Billy Bunter books by Frank Richards. With the casual sexism of his day Orwell makes only perfunctory reference to the girls'-school story, implying half-heartedly that a similar analysis would be possible. But Brunette will have none of this. In her view Orwell's analysis is irrelevant to her genre. It is possible to read feminist motives into Brunette's response. She can be seen as anticipating the work of recent

feminists such as Alice Walker, who champion disregarded female cultural
pursuits like quilt-making or gardening. In her 1992 study of the genre
Rosemary Auchmuty includes the girls'-school story in this ideological
programme, asserting that it 'offered me as a young woman a temporary
escape and refuge from the pressures of that profoundly heterosexual
society I lived in'.[50] More philosophically, in French feminist jargon, the
girls'-school story could be seen as *écriture féminine*, outside the 'symbolic
order' of patriarchy.

In evading his masculine destiny as a war-combatant Larkin could
also be seen as escaping heterosexual patriarchy. But he is neither a
political demystifier like Orwell nor an ideological feminist like
Auchmuty. Brunette rejects altogether what we would now call 'histori-
cist' interpretations. Instead she proclaims in tones of magisterial
authority the doctrine that art transcends politics and ideology.

> I am too familiar with Mr Orwell, and others of his kidney, to pay any
> attention to their ephemeral chatter; it seems to me to be a self-evident
> fact that Art cannot be explained away – or even explained – by foreign
> policy or trade cycles or youthful traumas, and that these disappointed
> artists whose soured creative instinct finds an outlet in insisting that it
> can are better ignored until Time has smoothed away all that they have
> scribbled on the sand.[51]

Even the personal psychology of the author ('youthful traumas') is
irrelevant to the impersonal world of art. There is a delicious impu-
dence in this arrogant attack by a twenty-one-year-old on a distinguished
older contemporary, presented in the voice of a hard-bitten lesbian
hack-writer. Larkin is, however, quite serious. William Empson's brilliant genre study, *Some Versions of Pastoral* (1935), had familiarized
Larkin's generation with the idea that ancient literary tropes and
patterns persist in transmuted modern forms. Larkin/Brunette detects
in the conventions of the girls'-school story a version of timeless pastoral. This 'closed, single-sexed world' contained within the walls of the
school is life simplified into a concentrated metaphor.[52] It affords the
writer a stock of simple images no less powerful than the groves of

Theocritus' Sicily, the 'Pan-guarded slopes of Arcady' of Ovid and Virgil, or the ploughland and blue vistas of Housman's shires. The stereotypes of popular culture may be as universal as the archetypes of high culture. In the previous year, 1942, the naturalized American T. S. Eliot had constructed in 'Little Gidding' a timeless England of Anglican tradition and prayer. Brunette, like Eliot, believes, as she declares in the preface to *Sugar and Spice*, that in this time of war 'more than ever a firm grasp on the essentials of life is needed'. However, she finds these essentials not in theology but in the secular clichés of girls'-school fiction. Behind Brunette we glimpse the mature Larkin of 'Lines on a Young Lady's Photograph Album', 'Essential Beauty' and 'Sunny Prestatyn', who found tears in things as trivial and familiar as advertisement hoardings, sentimental piano pieces and holiday snapshots.

It is the seven poems of *Sugar and Spice* that most convincingly make Brunette's aesthetic case: 'The False Friend', 'Bliss', 'Femmes Damnées', 'Ballade des Dames du Temps Jadis', 'Holidays', 'The School in August' and 'Fourth Former Loquitur'. They are extraordinarily accomplished for a writer at such an early stage of development. Larkin showed the value he placed on the sequence by typing out the first six poems with three carbon copies, and stitching them, with an elaborate title-page in two colours, into booklets with covers of black art-paper, thereby creating the most limited of editions.[53] In Brunette Coleman's poems we hear for the first time the inflections of the mature Larkinesque poetic style. 'The False Friend' adopts a confident demotic register far from the Yeatsian languour of the poems written in his own name at this time: 'Joan always said, she wondered how I stuck you, / And now I see that she was jolly right.' 'The School in August', like a number of his mature poems, depicts an empty room:

> The cloakroom pegs are empty now,
> And locked the classroom door,
> The hollow desks are dim with dust,
> And slow across the floor
> A sunbeam creeps between the chairs
> Till the sun shines no more.

> Who did their hair before this glass?
> Who scratched 'Elaine loves Jill'
> One drowsy summer sewing-class
> With scissors on the sill?

The questions are rhetorical in the purest sense. Elaine and Jill are the author, or the readers themselves. What matters is not who they were, but that they are lost in time:

> Ah, notices are taken down,
> And scorebooks stowed away,
> And seniors grow tomorrow
> From the juniors today,
> And even swimming groups can fade,
> Games mistresses turn grey.

The rituals and recurrences of school life, its seniors, juniors and score-books, become a metonym of all existence. Transience is the more poignant when it afflicts a timeless symbol; games mistresses are by definition forever young.

The last and most ambitious poem in the series, 'Fourth Former Loquitur' ('Fourth Former Speaks') was finished after he had bound up the booklet, and survives only in pencil script on an inserted sheet in Larkin's own copy. Its tone owes something to Fairlie Bruce's moving poem 'To the Old Girls of Clarence House, Roehampton', from which Brunette quotes in her essay.[54] It begins in the leisurely manner of his mature reflective elegies, by evoking a lazy afternoon on the cricket pitch. The shadows have lengthened, the deckchairs have been abandoned and the final score has been hung up: 'To show for once the Old Girls had been licked'. Only a single fourth-former remains 'now they are gone':

> Here they lay,
> Wenda and Brenda, Kathleen, and Elaine,
> And Jill, shock-headed and the pockets of

> Her blazer full of crumbs, while over all
> The sunlight lay like amber wine, matured
> By every minute.

The phrasing is touchingly clumsy: 'Jill, shock-headed and the pockets of / Her blazer full of crumbs'. Transcending her persona to become, for a moment, a prophetic seer, the fourth-former reassures her classmates that they are still at the mid-point of their idyll. Three years of school are behind them, but they still have three more to come. As the poem approaches its end, however, this secure perspective becomes blurred:

> Wenda, Brenda, Kathleen and Elaine
> Have flattened down the long grass where they've lain,
> And brownlegged Jill has left her hat,
> For they have gone to laugh and talk with those
> Who've played the Old Girls' match out to its close.

From her vantage point alone on the outfield the timeless fourth-former delicately hints at an elision of the generations: girls and old girls. With elegiac gravity, she observes the passing of the day, and also the passing of life. The grass, vivid to the eye in the present, has been flattened, in a sudden foreshortening of time, by girls who have returned to the pavilion to join those who have played the match of life out to its close. Larkin's mature poetic voice it seems owes as much to Dorita Fairlie Bruce as to Yeats, Hardy or Auden. Larkin was not to write anything as assured and moving as this again until 'At Grass' seven years later.

Brunette's plentiful quotations from *Mademoiselle de Maupin* in *Trouble at Willow Gables* show that Larkin read the novel in French, and in a development which resonates throughout his mature work, two of Brunette's poems imitate French originals. Though he never mastered the language with fluency, Larkin was fascinated by French poetry and culture. A poem written at school in 1939 had initially been entitled 'Homage to Daddy Lamartine',[55] and some of his juvenile lyrics have French titles. During his second year at Oxford he had briefly associated with a group of students from Exeter College, who, unlike the blokish 'Seven', 'read modern languages, and quoted La Rochefoucauld with relish'.[56] Now his friendship with Montgomery inspired a fresh enthusiasm for French literature. He later recalled that when, in the 1940s, Charles Madge put before him some prose by Mallarmé, his 'plume-de-ma-tante French wasn't up to it'.[57] On the other hand in a letter of 21 June 1953 he told his mother that he was reading Flaubert's letters in French. Larkin saw French literature, with its formal exactitude, its lack of inhibition on sexual issues and its symbolist sublimities, as offering an intimate Other to his own Englishness. His use of French literary inflections was to become a way of refining and testing his English voice or, more radically, of evading his Englishness.

Brunette impudently states that though 'suggested' by their namesakes in French her 'paraphrases' of Villon and Baudelaire 'are not, of course, "renderings" in any sense. In my opinion they are improvements.'[58] Larkin told Amis that Brunette considered 'Ballade des Dames du Temps Jadis' 'the best thing she has done',[59] and it remains one of his most moving poems. Without satire or subversion Larkin/Brunette transposes François Villon's fifteenth-century elegy for the fatal women of history into the mode of Willow Gables. Villon contemplates the fates of classical and historical women: Thais the mistress of Alexander the Great, Eloise the lover of Abelard, Blanche of Castile, and Joan of Arc. Brunette mock-heroically elegizes typical twentieth-century schoolgirls: Valerie, the tomboy with golden-red hair, Julia improvising on the Londonderry Air, brown-legged Jill, Patricia, who played Rosalind:

> Tell me, into what far lands
> They are all gone, whom once I knew
> With tennis-racquets in their hands,
> And gym-shoes, dabbled with the dew?

Brunette's Jacqueline and June with their blazers and badges are as much the stuff of legend as Villon's 'Flora la belle Romaine' or 'la très sage Heloïs'.

> Now the ponies all are dead,
> The summer frocks have been outgrown,
> The books are changed, beside the bed,
> And all the stitches that were sewn
> Have been unpicked. [. . .][60]

Brunette touchingly domesticates Villon's celebrated refrain 'Mais où sont les neiges d'antan?' ('Where are the snows of yesteryear?') in terms of the school calendar: 'So many summer terms away'. The English girls' school is a version of pastoral as poignant as Villon's historical vista.

The other French paraphrase has a more vexed relationship with its original model. 'Femmes Damnées' ('Lesbians') brilliantly subverts the murky French melodrama of Baudelaire's original poem, subtitled 'Delphine et Hippolyte' ('À la pâle clarté des lampes languissantes').[61] Baudelaire expands on these 'damned women', through twenty-six stanzas of prurient fascination and horror, concluding with magisterial condemnation:

> – Descendez, descendez, lamentables victimes,
> Descendez le chemin de l'enfer éternel!
> Plongez au plus profond du gouffre, où tous les crimes,
> Flagellés par un vent qui ne vient pas du ciel,
>
> Bouillonnent pêle-mêle avec un bruit d'orage.

('Descend, descend, lamentable victims, descend the path to eternal hell! Plunge to the deepest abyss where all crimes, whipped by an infernal wind, boil pell-mell with the noise of a tempest.') Brunette distils the initial seduction into six mock-heroic quatrains, and transfers the scene into an English suburban context:

> the living-room is ruby: there upon
> Cushions from Harrods, strewn in tumbled heaps
> Around the floor, smelling of smoke and wine,
> Rosemary sits. Her hands are clasped. She weeps.

Brunette has a good case for arguing that her version is an 'improve-ment'. Where the poem comes closest to actual translation her version is indeed more sharp and vivid than the original:

> Étendue à ses pieds, calme et pleine de joie,
> Delphine la couvait avec des yeux ardents,
> Comme un animal fort qui surveille une proie,
> Après l'avoir d'abord marquée avec les dents.

Brunette renders this:

> Stretched out before her, Rachel curls and curves,
> Eyelids and lips apart, her glances filled
> With satisfied ferocity; she smiles,
> As beasts smile on the prey they have just killed.

Baudelaire's hectic moralism is replaced by a tone of 'brisk intellectual epicureanism'.

Brunette's poem focuses on a detailed empirical description of a room: the milk on the step, *The Guardian* neglected in the letterbox since dawn, beds unslept in upstairs. From the upper windows can be seen labourers on the way to work, a Green Line bus and plots of cabbages. This ordinary world, the reader gathers with a frisson, has been subverted by exotic 'vice'. The innocent world of Rosemary's books and pictures ('Dance'; 'The Rhythmic Life'; 'Miss Rachel Wilson in a cap and gown') has been destroyed by the damned lesbian animal stretched out before her, presumably this same 'Miss Rachel Wilson'. But how seriously is the reader meant to take this seduction? 'The only sound heard is the sound of tears.' The disembodied ominousness of tone oddly forecasts the enigmatic serio-comic confrontations of Harold Pinter's plays a generation later.[62]

As the end of Larkin's long exemption approached, his imagination multiplied ideas with ever greater inventiveness. He seems to have been writing at a frenetic rate, as if determined to make the very most of his precious Oxford inspiration before turning to the real world. The sequel to *Trouble at Willow Gables*, *Michaelmas Term at St Bride's*, takes all the original characters, improbably, to Oxford. The sexual frisson of the girls'-school milieu disappears, and the tone is reminiscent of Max Beerbohm's *Zuleika Dobson* or early Evelyn Waugh. Unlike Willow Gables, Oxford rewards rather than condemns Hilary's lesbian aestheticism. Arriving in college, Mary Burch is horrified to discover that she is sharing a room with Hilary.[63] For a time she succeeds in preserving the proper distance, but then, disappointed at failing a trial for the University hockey team, she succumbs to the sympathetic Hilary's brandy and black Russian cigarettes.[64] No disaster ensues, and these cheerful English 'damned women' become companionable lovers, setting out, like Gautier's Mademoiselle, to wreak havoc in the world of heterosexual masculinity. Hilary tumbles accidentally-on-purpose into the Cherwell from the bridge in the University Parks, so that Pilot-Officer Clive Russell Vick can gallantly rescue her, glimpsing stocking tops and wet clinging fabric as he does so. Besotted, he showers invitations upon her and sends bunches of flowers which Hilary tells Mary to stuff down the toilet.

Montgomery had set Larkin in revolt against 'Lawrence, psychoanalysis, seriousness',[65] and in this spirit of self-contradiction *Michaelmas Term* satirizes his own recent preoccupations. The undergraduate Marie, still the same impetuous innocent as in *Trouble at Willow Gables*, is deeply impressed by the lectures of 'John Barnyard': 'She bought a large metal-edged book, costing nearly a pound, which she soon filled with accounts of dreams, in her sprawling childish handwriting.'[66] Then Marie discovers that her elder sister Philippa is a belt fetishist:

Coiled neatly, sometimes three within each other, they lay, in all shapes and sizes. There were very thin leather thongs, with single businesslike buckles; there were summery ones of canvas, in gay green and yellow [. . .] Finally, at the back of the drawer, were a selection of Philippa's favourite kind: ponderous thick leather ones, three inches or more broad, heavily inlaid with ornamental metal figures, strong enough to stand any imaginable strain.

'Thirty-seven!' repeated Marie, awestruck. 'It's fantastic.' She uncoiled one, as if expecting it to give a sudden wriggle in her hands.

'That's made of rhinoceros-hide,' said Philippa casually, smoothing her dress down. 'The buckle is solid horn. Hand it over, will you? I think I'll wear it.'[67]

Marie is horrified to see how tightly her sister pulls the belt, securing it by the last hole, which, she notices 'was rather ragged round the edges and was obviously home-bored'.[68] There is serious insight into the anorexic temperament here. However, broad farce takes over when Marie determines to shock her sister out of her belt-fixation by planting earthworms about her rooms, since, as Barnyard has revealed, belts are really symbols of worms. Philippa's friend Penelope Scott Stokes, reduced here to a comic stereotype, becomes the accidental victim of this stratagem when she discovers three worms in a teacup: 'Penelope clutched both hands to her unemphatic bosom: worms always had a curious effect on her.'[69]

Finally Marie persuades Philippa to join her in a symbolic pub crawl into her Unconscious: 'If you got drunk it would be a kind of descent into Hell to rescue your soul. Orpheus-Eurydice legend, you see.'[70] In one of the pubs the barmaids reveal themselves to be Eileen and Pat, former servants at Willow Gables. Pat explains that she is no longer at the school because 'That story's over now, Miss Marie [. . .] Willow Gables doesn't exist any more.' Marie is disconcerted to be told that she is only a fictional character, and asks where she can find real life. Pat points out the Smoke Room door, which opens on to a busy scene of dart-playing and jazz, in the midst of which Diana Gollancz and Bruce Montgomery are discussing the title of Bruce's novel. Unimpressed by reality Marie decides she would rather stay within the fictional story, and closes the door. Like her creator, she fears the onset of hard reality. The manuscript breaks off as she sets out into the darkness of a blacked-out Oxford, in pursuit of Philippa's distant torch, dimmed with green tissue-paper.[71] Larkin's notes indicate detailed plans for the work's completion, and he had already begun to type up the final copy when, overtaken by events, he was forced to abandon it. At this point he glued the typed pages over the initial pages of the holograph and added it to his archive for the attention of posterity. He was already working on *Jill*, which was, after all, a better prospect for publication than any of his Brunette works.

The charmed world he had inhabited over the last few months was fading about him. The period of freedom which began with his exemption from military service on New Year's Day 1942 finally drew to an end. On his birthday, 9 August, Larkin had submitted himself, miserably, to be interviewed for a job in the Civil Service. His application was rejected. In September he was considered for a Foreign Office post doing secret work at Bletchley Park, and was again rejected. Ashamed of his failure, he fumed to Amis: 'I detest being inspected and weighed up and classed as unfit for this imbecile job or fit for that imbecile job or suitable for such and such lunatic task. I boil and spit with fury.'[72] He returned to his attic in Warwick, to Brunette and to the beginnings of his first novel. Finally, early in November his future was decided: 'I was sitting at home quietly writing *Jill* when the Ministry of Labour wrote to me asking, very courteously, what I was doing exactly. This scared me and I picked up the *Birmingham Post* and saw that an urban district council in Shropshire wanted a librarian, so I applied and got it.'[73] As he had anticipated, he was to follow the example of the bank clerk Vernon Watkins, making his living in an ordinary job and applying himself to 'perfection of the work'. The comic impulse central to the Brunette works withered for the time being, not to return until he found his mature poetic voice in the early 1950s.

4

Nothing So Glad
1943–5

Larkin arrived in Wellington on 1 December 1943, an inexperienced, unworldly young man of twenty-one. It was, on the face of it, an unpromising place to start a literary career. 'Too large to have the community spirit of a village and too small to engender the cultural activities of a larger town, it was an unremarkable little place with a built-in resistance to new ideas and even perhaps to newcomers.'[1] On his arrival he simply stayed in lodgings for a while: 'The idea of getting a flat for myself was, you know, beyond my imagination.' Once he had found more permanent digs in a 1930s detached house, 'Glentworth', his social life settled into a bachelor pattern.[2] He played snooker at the local YMCA; he visited Sidoli's and Brittain's cafés and the town's three cinemas with local girls, including Jane Exall, the 'bosomy English rose' of 'Wild Oats'. Writing to Sutton in mid-December, he made a show of disdain for the duties of his new position: 'I am entirely unassisted in my labours, and spend most of my time handing out tripey novels to morons. I feel it is not at all a suitable occupation for a man of acute sensibility and genius.'[3] By March 1944 he was seeing some advantages to his situation: 'I intend to devote myself to writing and doing my boring job without enthusiasm or slackness. I only took it on account of being able to write in the intervals: it's not so easy, I must say, but it's possible.'[4] Indeed, from a literary point of view, wartime Wellington did offer what he needed. He occupied a respected position in the local community, and was largely his own master.

In his brief memoir 'Single-handed and Untrained', written in 1977, Larkin recalled his days in Wellington with affection.[5] He began each morning by stoking the boiler, and later in the day it was his task to light the gas-mantles with long, dripping tapers. He set about modernizing the Library's antiquated systems and procedures, arguing with the Urban District Council about the need for improvements, and renewing the interior decoration. He enrolled on a correspondence course leading to membership of the Library Association and secured the appointment of an assistant librarian. When he arrived the Library's stock consisted of only 4,000 books, and his purchases of works by Lawrence, Forster, Joyce and Isherwood gained him a reputation for 'filling the Library with dirty books'.[6] In a letter to Sutton of March 1944 he expressed a somewhat baffled respect for the 'quiet men in cloth caps who take out books of a rather serious kind with a serious expression on their faces, as if they are seriously trying to get a grip on things'. The reading choices of the female library-users disappointed him: 'It's the women that are the stupid sods. I hate women when it comes to choosing books.'[7] But he expressed such views only to distant correspondents, and rose to the social demands of his position, involving himself in the needs and ambitions of the local library-users. With a dynamism inherited from his father he persuaded the Urban District Council to raise the municipal rate by a penny in the pound to support the purchase of new books.[8] He took pride in the increase in inter-library loans, 'chiefly to sixth-formers, and those readers with precise interests and courses of study'.[9] To older readers 'he was unfailingly courteous, and his diffidence and nervous stammer, together with his patient willingness to find them books they would enjoy, won them over completely'.[10]

One library-user on whom he made a particularly deep impression was Ruth Bowman, in 1943–4 a sixteen-year-old schoolgirl:

The arrival of Philip made life suddenly brighter. Here was someone, a mere handful of years older than myself, glamorized by an Oxford degree – not all that common in Wellington at that time – mature, learned and successful, who was yet willing to discuss with me books I had read, advising me on what I should read and actually interested in my reactions. I was dazzled. Annoyingly, some of my contemporaries developed a sudden and unlikely interest in English literature and hung around the library shelves in what I felt was a distinctly predatory manner, but Philip, whose maturity I had over-estimated, regarded these giggling sixth-formers with some complacency.[11]

Philip and Ruth's feelings for each other developed in a decorous, hesitant way. By early 1944 there was amused gossip in the town about the awkward couple they made. At school she was warned to 'stop bothering the new librarian'. An acquaintance at the time often saw them together 'reciting poetry to each other [. . .] She looked at him with such adoring eyes.'[12] They would walk on Sundays on the wooded slopes of the Ercall, above Wellington (joined on one uneasy occasion by Kingsley Amis).[13] In 1991 Ruth recalled that she had been shocked by 'the robustness' of Philip's language and his outrageous sentiments, 'but if I found any part of his conversation distasteful and said so he might grumble at my prudishness but he would carefully avoid such expressions again. Oddly enough he had a Puritan streak which made him outraged if I attempted to reply in kind.'[14] He attempted to shake her religious beliefs, but gave up when she remained steadfast. And he joined her in her passion for cats. Their liaison was symbolically cemented when she stole a copy of Yeats's poems from her school for him. Over the previous two years Larkin had run the gamut of attitudes towards sexuality and gender, from Théophile Gautier to D. H. Lawrence; from W. H. Auden to Dorothy Vicary. Now, still a virgin, he had to cope with a vulnerable, serious-minded schoolgirl, with no conception of his inner life, eager for a relationship with him, and also hoping for the only end of such a relationship. Over the next six years his entanglement with Ruth became an increasingly insistent element in his poetry and fiction.

During his time in Wellington writing still continued to pour from the bottle uncorked by W. B. Yeats and Dorita Fairlie Bruce. Bruce

Montgomery was now teaching at Shrewsbury School, and regularly on Tuesday, his evening off at the Library, Larkin would visit him in his 'sumptuous' house, a sharp contrast to his own makeshift 'digs'. In turn Montgomery would visit Larkin in Wellington where they would sit for hours in the Raven or the more upmarket Charlton Arms, drinking and discussing literature.[15] When 'Edmund Crispin's' *The Case of the Gilded Fly* was published in February 1944, Larkin redoubled work on his own novel, *Jill*, first mentioned in letters to Sutton in August of the previous year. Urged on by Montgomery he completed the manuscript on Sunday 14 March 1944. Montgomery suggested changes to the final chapter and then sent the typescript to Charles Williams, a founding member of the Inklings and a director of Oxford University Press, in the hope that he might pass it on to Faber and Faber. Larkin was filled with excitement and a sense of unreality. T. S. Eliot worked at Faber and might see his book.[16] But Williams wrote saying that he was unable to help. Montgomery immediately sent the typescript to Gollancz. Months went by, and Larkin began to feel that he had been left behind by his more successful friend.

In contrast, opportunities to publish his poems came readily, confirming his conviction that the novel was the more difficult, serious form. R. A. Caton, owner of the Fortune Press, wrote asking him to contribute to a volume, *Poetry from Oxford in Wartime*, edited by William Bell of Merton College. Larkin sent him 'So through that unripe day' and nine recently written poems in Yeatsian style. These were immediately accepted and the volume was published in November 1944. In the meantime Caton had written to a number of Oxford poets, including Larkin, asking if they had enough work for a volume. The Fortune Press's fiction list included, as Larkin joked, many 'master-pieces' for 'students of intersex': *Boys in their Ruin*, *A Brute of a Boy*, *Bachelor's Hall*. Caton had been prosecuted in 1934 for 'obscene libel'.[17] But the Press's poetry list was, in contrast, impressive, including Dylan Thomas, Gavin Ewart, Roy Fuller, Tambimuttu, Drummond Allison and Vernon Scannell. Surprisingly Larkin did not respond immediately to Caton's approach. He was by this time engaged on his second novel, then entitled *The Kingdom of Winter*, which probably seemed a more important priority. But he may also have felt that his poetic voice was not yet secure enough to justify a volume. Montgomery, his stalwart ally when it came to fiction, was derisive of his enthusiasm for Yeats: 'I remember Bruce Montgomery snapping, as I droned for the third or fourth time that evening *When such as I cast off remorse, So great a sweetness flows into the breast. . .*, "It's not his job to cast off remorse, but to earn forgiveness."'[18]

Nevertheless, when Caton repeated his inquiry in October Larkin cast doubt aside and assembled a collection of thirty-one pieces, *The North Ship*. The fact that he headed each poem with a roman numeral, only eight of the poems being given titles, imitates Part One of Auden's *Another Time*, which also runs from I to XXXI, but it may also betray a certain haste. He included the ten poems from *Poetry from Oxford in Wartime*, but most of the volume was made up of Yeatsian works written in the early months of 1944. Caton was notorious for not paying royalties to his authors, and when Larkin wrote asking about terms, Caton assured him 'that no agreement was necessary'.[19] A publication date of February 1945 was mentioned, and when proofs did not arrive until March Larkin was consumed with impatience. Nevertheless, their final arrival prompted him to send Caton the typescript of *Jill*, despairing of finding a more respectable publisher. The novel was, after all, in its way, a work of 'intersex'. Caton accepted it at once, though again no financial terms were mentioned.

Larkin's first published volume, *The North Ship*, finally appeared on 31 July 1945, six months later than had originally been promised. The evocative, symbolist manner of *The North Ship* is at an opposite extreme from the witty demotic of Brunette ('I'm very cross: I think you've been a beast'):

> I put my mouth
> Close to running water:
> Flow north, flow south,
> It will not matter,
> It is not love you will find.

Here, as in the later mature poem 'Solar', the elements of nature are dispassionate, immutable, clear of the human element. The running water and the wind are beyond love, beyond death:

> You have no limbs
> Crying for stillness, you have no mind
> Trembling with seraphims,
> You have no death to come. (XIII)

The phrasing shows a refined ear for the music of vowels and consonants: 'Trembling with seraphims'.[20] Even more exquisite is the jewel-like miniature, 'This is the first thing' (XXVI):

> This is the first thing
> I have understood:
> Time is the echo of an axe
> Within a wood.

This lyric, in plain indicative mood, elusive in literal meaning but immediately emotionally comprehensible, would be perfectly in place in one of Ezra Pound's anthologies of imagist poetry.

One major strand of the volume is an aestheticist celebration of beauty for its own sake in a tone of secular worship or awe. In 'Like the train's beat' (XII), the poet glimpses transcendent beauty in the eyelashes and 'sharp vivacity of bone' of a Polish airgirl in a corner seat, lit through the window of the swaying train by the 'swinging and narrowing sun':

> all humanity of interest
> Before her angled beauty falls [. . .]

Her beauty has an abstract precision, as loveless and deathless as the running water and wind in 'I put my mouth'. Her fluttering foreign words are as 'meaningless' as the 'whorling' notes issuing from a bird's throat. A similar pure lyric impulse informs 'Is it for now or for always'

(XXVIII), a *carpe diem* poem, playing with words to conjure exalted euphoria from an assertion of transience:

> Shine out, my sudden angel,
> Break fear with breast and brow,
> I take you now and for always,
> For always is always now.

The ecstatic rhetoric cannot conceal the irony familiar from ancient and Renaissance examples of the genre. The only permanence the poet can offer his beloved is the livelong minute: we are always here; always is always now. Life is never more than a moment long.

To achieve a unifying tone of pure lyricism, Larkin entirely excluded the humour and irony of his Brunette persona from the volume. He also banished the postures of his earlier Audenesques in favour of a more direct address to the reader. Larkin dedicated the first poem in the volume 'To Bruce Montgomery', but though his friend was generous about it ('I *like* the North Ship'), he still preferred the Brunette works: 'I adore WGO [*Willow Gables at Oxford*]. There's a sort of brisk heartlessness about it, and it is extraordinarily funny.'[21] Partly perhaps because of Montgomery's lack of enthusiasm, but also because of the long delay before publication, Larkin always felt disappointed with *The North Ship*. His dissatisfaction resurfaced when the collection was reprinted in 1966 in the wake of the success of *The Whitsun Weddings*. In the Introduction to the reissue he derided his youthful pretension: 'Then, as now, I could never contemplate it without a twinge, faint or powerful, of shame compounded with disappointment. Some of this was caused by the contents but not all: I felt in some ways cheated. I can't exactly say how. It was a pity they had ever mentioned February.'[22]

In 1966 Larkin reflected that the volume contained 'not one abandoned self but several', and added self-deprecatingly that 'The search for a style was merely one aspect of a general immaturity.'[23] An alert reader will catch the widest range of verbal echoes: Keats, Tennyson, Matthew Arnold, Ernest Dowson, A. E. Housman, Gerard Manley Hopkins, the French symbolists, T. E. Hulme, W. H. Auden and Dylan

Thomas. But, though some of the poems in the volume are second-hand and weakly characterized, it does not deserve his later scorn. It is remarkable how often a poem in *The North Ship* appears upon examination to be an early, less forceful version of a later mature poem. The symbolist 'One man walking a deserted platform' (XXII) was later recast in his later 'Movement' demotic style, as 'Poetry of Departures'; 'Morning has spread again' (XXV) anticipates 'No Road'. 'Like the train's beat' (XII), with its image of the 'meaningless' beauty of the Polish airgirl, looks forward to the poet's 'useless' encounter with beauty in 'Latest Face'.

In 1966 Larkin was apologetic about his 'infatuation' with the particularly potent music of Yeats, 'pervasive as garlic', pleading in excuse that it has 'ruined many a better talent'.[24] Later in life he became fixed in condemnation, referring to 'that shit Yeats, farting out his histrionic rubbish'.[25] There may be a personal, biographical explanation for this puzzlingly disproportionate antipathy. The most headily Yeatsian works in *The North Ship* are Larkin's first real love poems. 'Morning has spread again' (XXV) could easily be read, for instance, as an immature attempt to dictate the script of his relationship with Ruth Bowman. The poet dreams that the love affair has run its course to the end; the lovers have 'worn down love good-humouredly', and are left:

> Talking in fits and starts
> As friends, as they will be
> Who have let passion die within their hearts.

The couple in Yeats's 'Ephemera' sighed similarly that 'Passion has often worn our wandering hearts.'[26] This is very satisfying and poetic. But, following this valediction, the speaker expresses puzzlement that 'love can have already set / In dreams, when we've not met / More times than I can number on one hand.' The cosy ventriloquism of Yeats is broken by the poet's dismay that he is rehearsing the end of the relationship when he should by rights be rejoicing at its beginning.

Similarly it is easy to read 'Love, we must part now' (XXIV) as a Yeatsian spell, designed to avert the threat of Ruth's growing emotional dependence by anticipating the end of the relationship in *fin de siècle* world-weariness:

> Love, we must part now: do not let it be
> Calamitous and bitter. In the past
> There has been too much moonlight and self-pity [. . .]

There is a whiff of the nineties decadents Dowson and Symons here. And the young poet was only too aware that such gorgeous rhetorical gestures were irrelevant to his real situation. His and Ruth's parting, nearly six years later, was indeed to be 'calamitous and bitter'. But he could not realistically expect her to share his enjoyment of his gaudy rhetoric of tall ships 'wet with light', 'waving apart' as the sun boldly paces the sky. The poem's tone, indeed, is so high-falutin that one might suspect the young poet of mocking himself, in Montgomery mode, inserting invisible inverted commas of irony: 'There is regret. Always, there is regret. / But it is better that our lives unloose [. . .]' It seems that following the bitter reproaches and self-reproaches of his long engagement to Ruth he felt painfully embarrassed by the manipulative bad faith of these poems. The quarrel was perhaps less with Yeats's rhetoric itself than with his own use of it in the emotional mistreatment of Ruth.

Implicit in the imagery of *The North Ship* is an ominous gender theme. At times we see a Larkin concerned to empathize with women in a straightforward human way. The speaker of 'Ugly Sister' (XIX), disregarded, climbs the thirty steps to her high room.

> Since I was not bewitched in adolescence
> And brought to love,
> I will attend to the trees and their gracious silence,
> To winds that move.

This lonely, ugly girl offers a protest against simplificatory gender archetypes which do not allow ugly sisters to be objects of empathy. But she is not quite a real girl in a real place. The theme is expressed in the terms of the 'myth-kitty'; she finds her consolation in a symbolic attic, communing with the elements. Overwhelmingly in the volume, women remain archetypal and idealized. They are muses, 'sudden angels', sweet severed images, floating wing-stiff in the sun; or, like the Polish airgirl, they are embodiments of Beauty. They may even be, as in 'The North Ship', *femmes fatales*.

In the most complex poem in the volume, 'I see a girl dragged by the wrists' (XX), the girl is on the one hand the male poet's unattainable muse; on the other she shows, in Brunette vein, his intense desire to 'be that girl!' The mixing of the two motives makes for a powerful but muddled effect. The poem opens with a stark antithesis between the girl rejoicing in the flux of life and the male poet alienated and self-doubting. With affected world-weariness he regrets his inability to identify himself with this girl as she is dragged laughing across the snow in courtship horseplay:

> Nothing so wild, nothing so glad as she
> Rears up in me,
> And would not, though I watched an hour yet.

He will never, as he had once hoped, 'be / As she is'. Remarkably, the man who is dragging the girl by the wrists is of no concern to the poet. He feels no rivalry, no envy of this man's masterful control over the girl. Instead he strains to identify himself with *her* delighted passivity. His vain hope had been to achieve her breathless submission to life. On this level the poem propounds, if with an unusual gender twist, the familiar *fin de siècle* theme of the alienated poet's exclusion from the everyday world which his poetry serves and celebrates.

However, his resignation to his lot has, it seems, caused the 'first brick' of a new imaginative building to be laid, and he finds himself suddenly excited 'to fever-pitch again' by the sight of 'two old ragged men' clearing the drifts 'with shovels and a spade':

> The beauty dries my throat.
> Now they express

> All that's content to wear a worn-out coat,
> All actions done in patient hopelessness [. . .]

The beauty he had seen in the young girl reappears in the epiphany of these two shabby old men. They 'sweep the girl clean from my heart'. Here it seems is a different version of the muse, realer and less conventionally beautiful than the girl. The structure of the poem imitates that of Yeats's early Platonic meditation 'To the Rose upon the Rood of Time'. Yeats sought 'Eternal beauty wandering on her way' in the symbolic rose itself, but then found that he must come down to earth and turn his attention also to the 'rose-breath': to the reflection of eternal beauty in the mortal world of 'common things that crave'.[27] Larkin retreads Yeats's tortuous poetic steps, turning from the transcendent beauty of the girl to the less obvious beauty of the commonplace old men. The speaker claims, 'I'm content to see / What poor mortar and bricks / I have to build with.'

But at this point the young poet begins to slip and slide between alternative inspirations and the momentum falters. He abruptly reverts to his hopeless desire to be the girl, and the old men change from alternative muses into metaphorical artists:

> Damn all explanatory rhymes!
> To be that girl! – but that's impossible;
> For me the task's to learn the many times
> When I must stoop, and throw a shovelful [. . .]

The poem ends by leaping to a quite different evocation of the beauty he seeks, in the form neither of the girl nor of the two old men, but of a preposterous Yeatsian 'snow-white unicorn', which in reward for his service may 'Descend at last to me, / And put into my hand its golden horn.' Are there invisible inverted commas of irony here? Unicorns traditionally entrust themselves to virgins; is he perhaps making derisive reference to his own virginal state? The word 'horn', which in letters to male friends Larkin uses frequently in its vulgar meaning, also hints at an obscene joke. The poet conjures an image of a girlish muse while holding a horn in his hand as he stoops to throw a shovelful.

On its publication in the summer of 1945 *The North Ship* received only a single brief notice, in the *Coventry Evening Telegraph* (26 October 1945), which gives every sign of having been written by Larkin himself: 'He has an inner vision that must be sought for with care. His recondite imagery is couched in phrases that make up in a kind of wistful, hinted beauty what they lack in lucidity.'[28] Nevertheless his literary career was at last on track, however modestly. In May, shortly after Victory in Europe Day, he completed work on his second novel, *The Kingdom of Winter*, in 'Proustian' mood, and Montgomery's agent Peter Watt agreed to seek a publisher for it. By now Montgomery had completed his own second novel, *The Moving Toyshop*, intensifying Larkin's feeling of impatience at not yet being a published novelist. He remained passive, however. Kingsley Amis, demobbed in September 1945, was horrified to find that the finished manuscript of *The Kingdom of Winter* was still untyped. Larkin wrote to his parents asking for help and they paid the £5 typist's fee. He sent the book to Watt in October 1945. Months were to pass before, in June 1946, he heard that no less a publisher than Faber had accepted it, offering an advance of £30. At last, it seemed, he was breaking into the larger literary world. Then in October 1946 the Fortune Press published *Jill*. He sent a copy to his father who, characteristically, responded with a cheque in payment.[29] Faber followed, in February 1947, with *The Kingdom of Winter*, the title having been changed after discussion to the more saleable *A Girl in Winter*, though Larkin had earlier rejected this as 'Mills & Boony'.[30] With a volume of poems and two novels in print, Larkin now had some reason to feel that he had arrived as a writer.

5

The Novels
1943–5

The momentum created in his final months at Oxford had driven Larkin forward, and he had completed two novels in less than two years, between August 1943 and May 1945. They are highly precocious works for a writer in his early twenties. But they led him into an artistic and personal dead end. He was not fully to regain creative self-possession until he moved to Belfast in 1950 and abandoned his ambitions as a novelist. The narratives of both works drive inexorably towards negative conclusions. Self-depreciation was, as John Banville has said, 'not second but first nature' to Larkin,[1] and a strong subtext of both novels is a scathing critique of his own masculine selfishness and immaturity. As a *Bildungsroman*, or coming-of-age novel, *Jill* is very sour. Unlike Lawrence's Paul Morel or Joyce's Stephen Daedalus, Larkin's Kemp has no promising future. Similarly *A Girl in Winter*, contradicting its final published title, is the bitterest of anti-romances. He later said 'I always think of [it] as The Kingdom of Winter', and it seems appropriate to employ the original title here rather than the misleadingly sentimental version forced on him by Faber.[2]

Jill, like *Michaelmas Term at St Bride's*, which he was writing when he first conceived it, transfers Willow Gables to Oxford. The protagonist, Kemp, is a Pygmalion aesthete enchanted, as was Hilary, by a dream of innocence. But grim heterosexual reality replaces comic lesbian fantasy. Hilary's dream of Mary ultimately became flesh; Kemp's dream of Jill is from the start unattainable. The delightful pastoral of Willow Gables is reduced to the obsessive delusion of 'a very poor young man who goes to Oxford who is exceptionally nervous and rather feminine', and whose 'complicated sexless daydream' is broken by the appearance of a real-life Jill. As Larkin put it, with brisk relish, in a letter to Sutton, written shortly after he first conceived the novel: 'the rest of the story, in action and in a long dream, serves to disillusion him completely'.[3]

In a later interview he dismissed the idea that *Jill* had the 'political overtones' of later works by Sillitoe, Wain, Waterhouse and Amis. His ineffectual, moody protagonist is no class champion or victim, but a displaced version of himself: 'John's being working-class was a kind of equivalent of my stammer, a built-in handicap to put him one down.'[4] At first sight Kemp might seem a similar self-projection to Jim Dixon in Amis's *Lucky Jim*, 'unlucky John' perhaps. Larkin's and Amis's protagonists are both versions of the blundering 'northern scholar', invented by Larkin and his undergraduate friends.[5] Both descend into a spiral of disaster, ending in drunkenness and physical mayhem. But the tones of the novels are quite different. *Lucky Jim* takes sides with its protagonist. The reader is encouraged to identify him or herself with the young man's pursuit of the girl and the money. The desires of Larkin's 'exceptionally nervous' protagonist are altogether more elusive.

Kemp's is a fundamentally poetic sensibility. As early as 1940 Larkin had declared to Sutton that 'A novel should be a diffused poem,'[6] and in August and September 1943 his letters were full of admiring references to George Moore's 'real prose poem', *Esther Waters*, the elusive novels of Henry Green and, most enthusiastically, the poetic prose of Katherine Mansfield. Kemp's consciousness is rendered with something of Mansfield's cool descriptive precision:

> From the stone façades pigeons fluttered down on to the pavements and waddled uneasily about, casting a wary eye at him, but he paid no attention to them. The wind blew and a whole wall of ivy danced in the sun, the leaves blowing back to show their white undersides. So in him a thousand restlessnesses yearned and shook.[7]

On one level Larkin was trying again to 'be that girl' by writing, as he announced to Sutton, with 'double-distilled purity of essence-of-Mansfield'.[8] But, characteristically, even as he was embarking on the novel he was doubting this strategy, ridiculing his poetic prose in the Lawrentian dialect of a Mr Morel: 'It's got no guts, no earth. Wheer keeps tha ba's, lad?'[9] *Jill* was, he told Sutton, 'very tiny and thin' compared with *Sons and Lovers*, which he could feel mocking him from the bookcase, '*breathing*, very slightly'.[10]

On the realistic level, Kemp's fantasy is a barely plausible attempt to impress his public-school room-mate, Warner, who regrets not being closer to his own sister. But the novel insists on a more aesthetic version. The fantasy takes on an imaginative life of its own. Kemp is an artist offering selfless devotion to a muse. An emotional climax is reached when he starts writing letters to the imagined Jill, and posting them: 'He was trembling when he dropped [the letter] into a pillar-box, and leant against the wall a moment, filled with exultation at the idea of thus speaking with nothingness. He envisaged the envelope wandering around England, collecting pencilled scribbles of suggestions on the front and back until, perhaps a year or more hence, it came to rest in some dusty corner of a dead-letter office.'[11] In Gautier's theory 'there is something grand and beautiful about loving a statue; the love is perfectly disinterested, there is no fear of satiety nor conqueror's disgust, and you cannot reasonably hope for the miracle that happened to Pygmalion'.[12] Kemp is such a selfless aesthete, absorbed in his own creation, speaking excitedly with nothingness.

Like his creator before him Kemp seeks to bring his vision closer by literary transgendering. He pursues the Pygmalion miracle by writing Jill's diary, in a pale version of the Willow Gables mode:

All my kirbi-grips had vanished for a start this morning (yes, and WHO took them?), so what with searching for them and trying to find a slide, I hadn't time to get my hymn-book before prayers – and of course the Badger had to choose today to inspect them, as she said she'd seen too many girls sharing recently. I suppose she thinks I *like* sharing with Molly.[13]

But, like the blessing of the gods which breathes life into the statue, or the visitation of the poet's muse, the epiphany cannot be forced or willed. When it does come, it is quite unexpected, and catches him unawares:

> The final possession came one day at lunch, when he was quietly eating bread and cheese and listening to casual talk [. . .] The sensation he had was of looking intently into the centre of a pure white light: he seemed to see the essence of Jill, around which all the secondary material things formed and reformed as he wrote them down. He thought he saw exactly what she was and how he should express it: the word was *innocent*, one he had used dozens of times in his own mind, and yet until that moment had never understood.[14]

In a version of the hyacinth-girl episode in *The Waste Land*, Kemp looks 'into the heart of light, the silence'.

By the time Larkin came to write the later part of the novel reality had caught up with his artificial fiction. Just as Kemp comes upon the very Jill of his imagination in an Oxford bookshop, with her blue woollen gloves, her belted fawn coat with flaps over the pockets and her Wellingtons, so the young Larkin had met the all-too-real schoolgirl Ruth Bowman. In the novel Gillian insists on being a real girl in a real place. She is, indeed, the cousin of Elizabeth, the sexually aware girl-friend of Kemp's room-mate, the odious public-school 'hearty', Warner. Warner's friends, Patrick and Eddy, crudely mock Kemp's obsession: 'This man's got a letch on your kid cousin.' He can only protest feebly, 'I'm not a damn baby snatcher',[15] and cling stubbornly to his dream: 'The door to the different world had been left half ajar and swiftly, lightly, coolly, calmly, he must slip through it and be for ever safe.'[16] However, his preparations to entertain Jill to tea take on a hopeless fatalism as he makes his room tidy and neat, sets out large quantities of cakes and lettuce, and then rushes out distractedly to buy a too-large packet of salt. Dream cannot possibly become reality. And, indeed, instead of Gillian it is Elizabeth who arrives. Gillian, she quite properly insists, is too young and fragile for his attentions.

Until this point the war has scarcely registered with the reader. None of the characters has shown any interest in the progress of the conflict, and casual references to the black-out, fire-watching and changes in the age of the army call-up have served merely to reinforce the atmosphere of insecurity. Now, it seems, the bombing of his home town is to bring about Kemp's awakening to reality. As he sets out on the train to discover his parents' fate, he 'seemed to be leaving a region of unreality and insubstantial pain for the real world where he could really be hurt'.[17] Ominously, however, he remains a self-obsessed neurotic, imagining that his parents must have been killed to punish him personally for his neglect: 'he deserved to be punished in this way [. . .] he was tormented with thinking the worst had happened, they had been killed because he treated them lightly'.[18] He views the ruins of the city with refined objective detachment: familiar streets uncannily deserted; 'broken bricks, lurching floors and laths sticking out like delicate broken bones'.[19] On his visit to Coventry Larkin had been accompanied by Noel Hughes. In the novel, however, John roams the ruins of Huddlesford poignantly alone. Personal tragedy and loss are omitted. John's own area of the city is untouched and he discovers that his family is safe in Preston. The most vivid image is the Larkinesque deserted living room of his family home:

> Bending close to the window-pane, he looked into the front room: it was tidy as usual, there were ornaments on the mantelpiece and the clocks showed the right time. There was a pile of newspapers on the table and behind a glass vase he could see the half-dozen letters he had written home all put neatly together. It was strange, like looking into a doll's house, and putting his hands against the window frames he felt as protective as a child does feel towards a doll's house and its tiny rooms.[20]

A numb, traumatized quality infuses the narrative. The pub-goers seem embarrassed rather than sympathetic as they listen to the commercial traveller whose wife has been killed in a direct hit on their hotel: '"I reckon they'll do this to everywhere," said the young man, looking up again. "Everywhere. There won't be a town left standing." His voice had a half-hysterical eager note as if he desired this more than anything.'[21]

As Kemp boards his train and leaves behind him the brightly moonlit 'blank walls and piles of masonry that undulated like a frozen sea', he, like the commercial traveller, internalizes the destruction he has seen.[22] The blitz becomes an agent of his unconscious Jungian will:

> he thought it represented the end of his use for the place. It meant no more to him now, and so it was destroyed: it seemed symbolic, a kind of annulling of his childhood. The thought excited him. It was as if he had been told: all the past is cancelled: all the suffering connected with that town, all your childhood, is wiped out.[23]

The final sequences of the novel powerfully dramatize Kemp's nervous breakdown. Suddenly, for no apparent reason, he finds himself wrecking the 'garret-like' room[24] of an impoverished fellow student, Whitbread: shoving pats of butter into his slippers, filling the pockets of his jackets with sugar and tea, pouring his milk into the coal scuttle and stealing a pound note. Whitbread is a working-class boy from the North like himself, and his act of destruction is less of Whitbread's room than of the structure of his own life. In contrast to the farcical class-based embarrassment of parallel scenes in *Lucky Jim*, this destruction has a systematic, abstract quality to it. Kemp is confirming his own alienation. 'A great cheerfulness came over him now and he sauntered out through the cloisters into the dark. There was a letter from his parents in the Lodge, but he did not even trouble to pick it up.'[25] There is keen insight into the psychology of the self-harmer here.

At the close of the novel Kemp compulsively places himself beyond the pale, refusing the challenge to engage with reality. After a solitary pub-crawl, he gate-crashes a party and kisses Gillian, reducing the vulnerable, fifteen-year-old schoolgirl to tears. Warner and his friends throw him into a fountain and the novel comes to an inconclusive close with the protagonist in a hectic fever, tended by his devoted parents. As Larkin promised, Kemp has been completely disillusioned. Though the fictional Kemp is not the real Larkin, the novel offers no alternative to

Kemp's viewpoint, and the author inevitably seems an active partici-
pant in Kemp's self-destruction. On one level the novel is displaced
autobiography, a chapter of Larkin's own 'soul-history', and its verdict
on himself, as both man and artist, seems bleak indeed.

Like Kemp, Katherine Lind, the protagonist of *The Kingdom of
Winter*, experiences complete disillusion. But she embodies a more
subtle and artistic sublimation of the author's autobiography. Katherine
is a woman, and also, with metaphorical, poetic resonance, a 'displaced
person'. Larkin's plan for the novel, written in June 1944 in a small
black notebook, sketches a ruthless nihilistic diagram:

> Katherine Lind, a refugee to England, works in a branch library in a
> fairly large provincial city.[26]
>
>   The story describes about the whole of a day in her life.
>
>   It demonstrates through various selected incidents how she awakes
> from the loneliness beyond which nothing seemed to exist or matter, to
> a state where loneliness as being alone is a positive quality.[27]

Katherine's fate is to be more positive than Kemp's, but only because
she embraces her disillusion, and finds strength in 'loneliness as being
alone'. Larkin's mood as he settled into the writing of the novel is
revealed in a letter to Sutton of 10 December 1944: 'The weather is very
cold today, snow blowing in the rain and wind and not settling [. . .] do
you feel that winter is more true than summer? It is nearer death and I
am vaguely concerned about death these days, which shows probably a
lack of spiritual understanding &c.'[28]

The protagonist shares Mansfield's name, and in his letters Larkin
cited another female influence: 'If I write like anybody, it is like Virginia
Woolf – but much better, or it will be.'[29] In December 1944 he reread
Woolf's most poetic work, *The Waves*, and declared 'it knocked me for
six'.[30] The ternary, ABA structure of *The Kingdom of Winter* may owe
something to Woolf's *To the Lighthouse*, two sections in a wintry present
framing a contrasted section in a past summer. There is a laconic poetry
in the description of Katherine's journey through a snowbound town-
scape with her pathetic, toothache-stricken colleague, referred to always,

impersonally, as 'Miss Green'. 'The Library was an ugly old building built up on a bank, where laurel bushes grew: the bank was now covered with snow and littered with bus-tickets. A newspaper had been carefully folded and thrust into a drift, where it was frosted stiff.'[31] In the scene at the dentist's surgery Larkin keeps a relentless focus on the precisely observed symptoms of physical pain: 'The drilling started again, and the little quavering moans. This time there was a definite crackling sound, quite audible. One of Miss Green's feet lifted a second from the iron foot-rest, then was jammed back again as quickly.'[32] Katherine cannot believe that the anaesthetic has dispelled the girl's pain:

> she felt an upswerve of terror lest the girl should still be half-conscious but unable to move or speak. Her head stirred as he first pulled, and he put his free hand on her forehead, rumpling her hair, before giving another dragging wrench in the other direction. Katherine could almost feel the pain exploding beneath the anaesthetic and nerved herself against a shriek. It seemed impossible for the girl to feel nothing.[33]

The fact that she has nothing in common with Miss Green, and does not like her, makes Katherine's empathy with her all the more primitive and intense.

From the start the reader has doubts about Katherine's wan romantic excitement at the coming visit of her English friend Robin Fennel. Ominously she re-established contact with him after noticing in the newspaper that his sister's infant daughter had died. In the middle, summer section of the novel, Larkin develops a female variant on the Pygmalion myth. Robin, an ordinary conventional Englishman, not dissimilar to Warner, becomes the desired statue. During her three weeks with the family before the war, the schoolgirl Katherine builds an imaginary romance around her 'harmless but dull' English host.[34] She imagines that love prompts him to take her on a bus visit to Oxford, and is touched by his apparent foresight, when he gives her a mackintosh from his haversack to keep off the rain. Then she finds his sister's name tag on the gloves in its pockets, and realizes that he is simply doing his sister's bidding, and the whole trip was her idea:

she had been constructing an elaborate pagoda out of nothing, and
the shame she now felt was a punishment for this. In fact she could
not have made a bigger fool of herself if she had tried carefully. At that
moment she hated England and everybody in it – this would never
have happened if she could have understood all the foreign inflexions
and shades of meaning.[35]

The biographical implications seem cruelly explicit. Like Ruth Bowman,
this sixteen-year-old schoolgirl has built her unreal hopes on a man
from a world she does not understand, and who is in reality unworthy
of her love.

What gives the novel a touch of real distinction, is its all-pervasive
metaphor of foreignness. Katherine's nationality and personal history
are deliberately withheld. As Larkin wrote in his preparatory notebook: 'What city, what Katherine's original name and nationality
were, etc all left unstated.' (In an early draft she answers a query about
her name: 'Katherine Lind is near enough [. . .] It's not exactly the
name on my passport, but it will do.')[36] He manages the evasion with
considerable skill. First-time readers of the novel not infrequently
assume that they have simply missed this detail, and they must have
been told somewhere that Katherine is Belgian or Scandinavian. If one
were forced to assign Katherine a nationality she would surely be
German, if only because Larkin's own first-hand experience of Europe
had been largely limited to Germany. His preparatory note indicating
that Katherine's nationality should be left 'unstated' is written on the
inside cover of the notebook under the heading 'Notes Germane to
the Opposite'.[37] The pun seems deliberate. He was aware that, whether
he intended it or not, Katherine would be bound to be more German
than anything else. Miriam Plaut, the 'displaced' German Jew in
Oxford to whom Larkin gave one of the typescripts of *Sugar and Spice*,
claimed that she was the 'original' of Katherine. Larkin remarked,
with teasing equivocation, that this was 'not very true'.[38] But though
Miriam Plaut or Germany may have been in his mind, it is clear that
his theme is not the social and political situation of enemy aliens in
Britain in 1944; it is foreignness as a metaphor of the human

condition. Larkin ensures that Katherine neither says nor does anything specifically German.[39]

This is a novel written in English and set in England, in which England is foreign territory. Larkin subtly translates his own childhood difficulties as a foreigner in Germany into Katherine's confusions as a foreigner in England. Like him she is baffled by the unfamiliar language. Mrs Fennel comments that the proximity of their house to the river '"makes the place rather damp, do you know? And it's mournful in winter." This last remark, spoken as it was in a foreign language, came to Katherine with something of the impact of a line of poetry.'[40] Robin's Englishness gives him glamour in Katherine's eyes. She comments on a local gymkhana that 'It was very English and interesting.' Robin's sister Jane counters: 'I am English, more's the pity. And I know a lot of those people, rot them, and they aren't at all interesting.'[41] The fact that her brother is 'the perfect Englishman' seems to Jane a great defect.[42]

Just as Larkin had tried to write like a woman in the Brunette works, here he tries to write like a foreigner. The language of the novel sometimes takes on an oddly bilingual quality. Before she comes to England her schoolfriends nickname Katherine's pen friend 'the bicyclist', rather than the more normal English 'cyclist', and the phrases through which they project her future relationship with him have a slightly stilted simplicity which marks them as clearly not English.[43] Jack Stormalong, with his ridiculous name, his 'dark crimson sports car', his protruding front teeth, his habit of calling Mr Fennel 'Sir' and his tall tales about tiger-shooting in India, seems a cartoon Englishman from Hergé's *Tintin* rather than a novelistic caricature conceived by an English author.[44]

More intriguing still, the literary texture of the novel at times aligns it, uniquely among Larkin's works, with contemporary continental fiction. *The Kingdom of Winter* sounds faintly like a translation. In conversation with Montgomery he referred to it as *Winterreich*, perhaps remembering Königswinter, where the Larkin family had holidayed in 1936. In a letter to Amis he calls it *Le Royaume d'Hiver*.[45] In his *débat* 'Round the Point' written six years later, the failed novelist Geraint rejects modish continental avant-gardism: 'I don't lie awake sweating about my vocation as a European, I don't read Gide or Hölderlin or

Rilke or Kafka or Sartre, I don't go to the Academy cinema [. . .]'[46]
However, in the mid-1940s Larkin had been less hostile to continental
influence. Bruce Montgomery will surely have introduced him to
Camus' recently published *L'Étranger* (*The Foreigner*, or *The Outsider*,
1942), and Sartre's *L'Être et le Néant* (*Being and Nothingness*, 1943). Like
Kafka's K, Katherine moves through half-understood situations, never
sure of her ground. Like Roquentin in Sartre's *La Nausée* (*Nausea*,
1938), she has to create her own meaning from a series of meaningless
epiphanies. However, Larkin never uses continental philosophical
vocabulary. He writes about 'loneliness' rather than 'alienation', and the
final epiphany is less a matter of Katherine's rejection of 'false consciousness' or Sartrean *mauvaise foi* (bad faith), than of Hardyesque pessimism:
'if way to the Better there be, it exacts a full look at the Worst'.[47]
Nevertheless, despite himself, Larkin has to some extent been caught
up in the European current of Existentialism which was flowing so
strongly at this moment.

The novel ends on the brink of the post-humanist void. Like Kemp,
Katherine burns all her boats in a humiliating confrontation with her
boss, Mr Anstey, over a telegram which Robin has sent to her at the
Library. (Larkin's self-depreciation perhaps shows itself in the depiction
of the librarian as a self-important bully.)[48] She confirms her outsider
status by addressing Anstey 'with an exaggerated foreign accent she had
learned annoyed people'.[49] More practically she compounds her difficulties as a refugee by giving up her job. But Larkin makes nothing of
her practical financial plight. Instead we follow her back to her attic,
where her tenuous English dream of summer collides with wintry
reality in the form of the real Robin, a provincial auctioneer, now a
soldier, 'rather drunk' and importunate for sex. Wearily she succumbs,
naming 'a condition that he accepted', presumably a contraceptive
strategy such as avoidance of full penetration.[50] United in their alienation the foreign woman and the Englishman drift together into sleep:

> There was the snow, and her watch ticking. So many snowflakes, so
> many seconds. As time passed they seemed to mingle in their minds,
> heaping up into a vast shape that might be a burial mound, or the cliff

of an iceberg whose summit is out of sight. Into its shadow dreams crowded, full of conceptions and stirrings of cold, as if icefloes were moving down a lightless channel of water [. . .] Unsatisfied dreams rose and fell about them, crying out against their implacability, but in the end glad that such order, such destiny, existed. Against this knowledge, the heart, the will, and all that made for protest, could at last sleep.[51]

The writing is tenuous and insubstantial, imitating the drift into sleep. But it is also a touch forced and artificial.

Though Larkin later expressed a certain affection for *Jill*, recollecting his Oxford undergraduate days with nostalgia, he developed an active distaste for *A Girl in Winter*. He wrote to Barbara Pym in 1961: 'I can't *bear* to look at *A G. in W.*: it seems so knowing and smart.'[52] There seems something painfully personal behind his feeling. Perhaps its association with his own early experiences in Germany, or with his failed relationship with Ruth, or with the miserable winter of 1944 in provincial Wellington, unduly coloured his judgement of this minor masterpiece of poetic prose. Or perhaps his dislike was simply a result of bitter disappointment that, despite all his efforts, he never succeeded in following it with a third novel.

6

The Grip of Light
1945–8

On his twenty-third birthday, 9 August 1945, Larkin gave Amis a gloomy account of his relationship with Ruth, 'the school captain', or 'Misruth' as they called her: 'As long as she keeps on talking about me I am flattered. When she criticizes me, or speaks of herself, I am bored.' He attempted to titillate his friend: 'she has begun to write a novel about her school days, with a lot of lesbianism in it'.[1] But in reality Ruth had no interest in his literary 'lesbianism'. She expected straight-forward commitment, and her ingenuous devotion put him off the idea of sex: 'I really do not think it likely I shall ever get into the same bed as anyone again because it is so much trouble, almost as much trouble as standing for Parliament. I have formed a very low opinion of women [. . .]' His phrasing is evasive. He was at this time effectively still a virgin. Amis was puzzled that his friend failed to follow through his pursuit of sexual satisfaction. But Larkin feared for his freedom. Earlier in this letter he mentioned a 'brawny young man' he knew in Wellington 'who has just married and fucked his wife without a french letter so that she is now going to have a baby'.[2]

Ruth was five years younger than Larkin, and suffered from an inher-ited condition which made her slightly lame. She shared with Penelope Scott Stokes a vein of victimhood, confiding to Philip: 'When I was small if anything I ate had a peculiar flavour I immediately suspected that my mother had grown tired of me and was trying to poison me.'[3]

Larkin felt protective towards her and wished to give her the affection for which she longed. He related a dream to Sutton in which, 'at some richly-coloured wedding celebrations I met – or, as it almost seemed, remet – a beautiful lame girl, whom I gladly felt was mine for keeps. This cheered me up for a bit.'[4]

In September 1945, now eighteen, Ruth was accepted to read English at King's College London. Her imminent departure prompted their first sexual encounter. Shortly afterwards she wrote humbly from London: 'The fact that you like me and have made love to me is the greatest source of pride and happiness in my life.'[5] There is something ominous in her past perfect tense – 'and have made love to me' – as though she were steeling herself for the end of the relationship. But Philip remained loyal. He travelled to London at weekends and some-times met Ruth secretly in Wellington after the Library closed. They went on trips together to D. H. Lawrence's Eastwood and Hardy's Dorchester. The emotional quality of the relationship would be easier to imagine if we could read any of the 'over four hundred letters' which, as he recalls in his later poem, 'Wild Oats', he sent to her over seven years. But when the relationship ended her grandfather persuaded her to destroy them.[6] Today we see the relationship only as refracted through the scathing self-criticism of Larkin's letters to Sutton and the ribaldry of his letters to Amis. September 1945 was also the month Amis was demobbed. But Philip at first avoided bringing Kingsley and Ruth together. They met for the first time only in January 1946. Ruth recalled that Kingsley 'wanted to make Philip a "love 'em and lose 'em" type. He was possessive of Philip and tried to keep me separate from him.'[7]

Shortly before he sent the typescript of *The North Ship* to Reginald Caton in October 1944, Larkin had begun to write the drafts of his poems in a substantial limp-bound manuscript workbook.[8] Of little apparent significance at the time, the move seems in retrospect momen-tous. This was the first of eight books in which Larkin would compose virtually all his mature poetry. By the time he moved on to the second workbook in 1950 he had become a great poet. As time went on, his drafting became increasingly consistent. He wrote in pencil, generally working on one stanza at a time and often inserting dates when he considered a work complete. From April 1959 onward he generally started a fresh page whenever he began a new session of drafting. In many cases he produced a separate typescript including final corrections. He thus made it possible, to a degree unknown in other poets, to follow the sequence of his poems, to see the relative ease or difficulty with which he brought, or failed to bring them to completion, and to relate them to the events of his life. His sense of the importance of this record of the creative process was shown by his donation, in 1964, of his first workbook, covering 1944–50, to the British Library. At that time he tore out several pages containing material too personal to be made public. Significantly, however, he did not destroy them, but kept them to await ultimate restoration after his death.[9] His sense of the integrity of his oeuvre is strong.

At first, however, his poetry showed little change. There is an eloquent epigrammatic bleakness in the five lines of 'To S.L.' in which the poet craves the 'gift' of his father's 'courage and indifference' in the face of a hostile world.[10] However, the other poems completed during 1945 do not reach this level. 'Coming at last to night's most thankful springs' is irritatingly obscure; 'Plymouth', a portrait of an aged seafarer, is clumsily phrased; 'Lift through the breaking day', 'Portrait' and 'Past days of gales' are elusively symbolist.[11] However, 'Who whistled for the wind', written in December, has hidden surprises:

> Who whistled for the wind, that it should break
> Gently, on this air?
> On what ground was it gathered, where
> For the carrying, for its own sake,
> Is night so gifted?

Montgomery no doubt easily found the answer to the poem's riddle. This gently breaking, whistled-for wind, gathering and then 'gifting' the night, is a fart, a poetically appropriate, if unconventional reminder of the process of corruption and decay: 'Mind never met / Image of death like this [. . .]' Perhaps the poem is a disrespectful end-of-year farewell to the Yeatsian mode.[12]

The following month, January 1946, Larkin moved into new lodgings at 7 Ladycroft, Wellington, the windows of which faced east.[13] As the days lengthened he was woken earlier and earlier in the morning by the sun. The impact of this insistent dawn light was powerful, long lasting and ambiguous. In numerous later poems light figures as a source of exaltation ('Wedding-Wind', 'Here', 'Livings II'), or alternatively as the threatening agent of exposure ('Deceptions', 'Aubade'). His light-enforced wakefulness coincided with a new literary influence: 'It seemed too early to get up, so I used to read, and it happened that I had Hardy's own selection of his poems, and I began to read them and was immediately struck by them. I was struck by their tunefulness and their feeling, and the sense that here was somebody writing about things I was beginning to feel myself.'[14] Here, it seemed, was a poet who had more direct relevance to Larkin's life in Wellington than his previous models: 'I was beginning to find out what life was about, and that's precisely what I found in Hardy [. . .] He's not a transcendental writer, he's not a Yeats, he's not an Eliot; his subjects are men, the life of men, time and the passing of time, love and the fading of love.'[15] Read in the hard light of dawn, Hardy offered Larkin a corrective to the metaphysics of Dylan Thomas and the twilight of Yeats. 'When I came to Hardy it was with the sense of relief that I didn't have to try and jack myself up to a concept of poetry that lay outside my own life – this is perhaps what I felt Yeats was trying to make me do. One could simply relapse back into one's own life and write from it.'[16]

The influence of Hardy on Larkin was all-pervasive. Some of his later writing echoes the earlier poet. The conclusion of 'An Arundel Tomb' has the same rhetorical turn as that of 'The Darkling Thrush', building poignant hope on transparently flimsy foundations. The jam in Larkin's 'An April Sunday brings the snow' metonymically recalls his father's life in the same way as the burning logs recall Hardy's sister in 'Logs on the Hearth'. 'No Road' is Larkin's version of 'Neutral Tones'. 'Skin' and 'Send No Money' may be compared with 'I Look into My Glass'. 'Nothing To Be Said' seems to owe something to 'The Dead Man Walking'. Less specifically there is something Hardyesque about such subjects as old-fashioned sheet music in a piano stool ('Love Songs in

Age'), an evangelical preacher ('Faith Healing'), an empty church viewed with a sceptical eye ('Church Going'), the picturesque muddle of provincial weddings ('The Whitsun Weddings'). More generally, he shares Hardy's empathy with marginalized or victimized women.

As Larkin's sensibility matured, his poetry underwent an unobtrusive transformation. The fourteen poems completed in 1946 are all more clearly focused and assured than the 1945 works. Anthony Thwaite's decision, in the 1988 *Collected Poems*, to separate the 'early poems' from the mature poetry at the beginning of 1946 seems all but inevitable. 'Going', completed on 23 February 1946, and at first untitled, stands at the beginning of his mature phase. Like 'Who whistled for the wind' it is a primitive riddle, the answer being 'Death'. Indeed it would not seem out of place in a collection of Anglo-Saxon riddles. But it is also a latter-day imagist poem. Its rhymelessness, its symbolist imagery, the abrupt sentences and final rhetorical question align it with such poems as 'The Pool' and 'Sea Rose', by HD. And the way the initial regular iambs disintegrate into unmetrical free verse imitates the darkening of dusk/death in the way recommended by Ezra Pound in his descriptions of the *'image'*. The result is a memorable jewel of a poem. In 1947 in the typescript of *In the Grip of Light* he titled it 'Dying Day', eliding the dying of the light at sunset with the day of the speaker's death. He also included it, untitled, in *XX Poems* (1951) and it became, with its final title, the earliest written of the works included in his first mature collection, *The Less Deceived*, in 1955.

As the quality of his poetry improved, Larkin's poetic output slowed. The collected *Early Poems and Juvenilia* (2005), containing work written over eight years (1938–46), comprises 255 poems and takes up 344 pages.[17] In contrast the (slightly overlapping) first section of the 1988 *Collected Poems*, containing poetry written over three and a half decades (1946–82), comprises 176 poems and takes up 219 pages.[18] From 1946 onwards he scrupulously rations his forms, rhetorical devices and, most remarkably, individual words in order to make each poem tell with the greatest possible force. In hindsight it seems that in the late 1940s Larkin set about consciously constructing an oeuvre, his life's work, a task which he was to pursue single-mindedly for the next three decades.

Antagonistic though they were towards each other, Ruth and Kingsley shared the view that Philip's difficulties would be dispelled by a full sex life. But he was hesitant. In 'Deep Analysis' he adopts the voice of a woman reproaching her lover for his unresponsiveness:

> I am a woman lying on a leaf;
>   Leaf is silver, my flesh is golden,
> Comely at all points [. . .]
>
> Why would you never relax, except for sleep,
>   Face turned at the wall [. . .]
>
> Your body sharpened against me, vigilant,
>   Watchful, when all I meant
> Was to make it bright, that it might stand
>   Burnished before my tent?[19]

Echoes of the biblical Song of Songs ('comely', 'burnished', 'assuaged'), of D. H. Lawrence ('your straight sides') and of Yeats ('only your grief under my mouth') dramatize female abjection with an embarrassing intensity. Larkin is determined to make Ruth's case for her as eloquently as he can.

In April 1946 Amis grew impatient: 'When these things have reached a certain stage they must be completed. Why don't you have it all out with her (that's right)?'[20] The contrast of sexual register between the poem and Amis's letter is stark. It was to the more understanding Sutton that Larkin gave the explanation of his difficulty:

in my character there is an antipathy between 'art' and 'life'. I find that once I 'give in' to another person, as I have given in not altogether voluntarily, but almost completely, to Ruth, there is a slackening and dulling of the peculiar artistic fibres that makes it impossible to achieve that mental 'clenching' that crystallizes a pattern and keeps it still while you draw it [. . .] this letting-in of a second person spells death to perception and the desire to express, as well as the ability. Time & time again I feel that before I write anything else at all I must drag myself out of the water, shake myself dry and sit down on a lonely rock to contemplate glittering loneliness. Marriage, of course (since you mentioned marriage), is impossible if one wants to do this.[21]

Images of dawn and light haunt the poetry of 1946. 'Come then to prayers', completed in May, shows the incongruous influence of T. S. Eliot's religious writing. In an echo of *Murder in the Cathedral*, we are required 'to give up pride', including the 'pride in being humble', and our reward will be the freedom to greet the dawn with gladness: 'the dawn / Hunts light into nobility, arouse us noble'. There is something strained about Larkin's attempt to dispel his domestic difficulties with Eliotic light.

This was an unsettling time. In June Kingsley Amis introduced him to his new girlfriend, Hilary Bardwell, then not yet eighteen years old, among whose attractions was an enthusiasm for jazz. Amis encouraged Philip's relationship with her. On 24 June 1946 he wrote insinuatingly: 'Hilary liked you very much which is nice isn't it?' He relates her impressions of Philip: 'charming stammer', 'amuses me a lot', 'the nicest of all your friends'. On 15 July Kingsley tells Philip: 'Hilary is very nice, as you will agree (she dreamed you were kissing her the other night).'[22]

Larkin was becoming restless in Wellington, which did not offer him the professional challenges he needed. A letter to Sutton, written in July, reflects his desultory, dissatisfied mood:

some silly sod in South Africa sent us a book the other day for the library: it was privately printed and was on very good paper. Inside were about two hundred aphorisms, with a little row of asterisks between each one. They were of the 'As the Daisy opens to the Sun, so the force of Personality opens to the force of Love' variety. When I had read perhaps ten, I opened a razor blade and slit the linen at the back so that the boards could be easily ripped off. Then I cut the sewing and taking each set of pages tore them neatly into four. After that I felt a lot better. Lot of bloody rubbish. For Christ's sake![23]

Wellington, he told Sutton, was a 'hole of toad's turds', and he needed to escape.[24] Since 1944 he had applied unsuccessfully for posts with Chambers Encyclopaedia in London, and in the university colleges of Liverpool[25] and Southampton.[26] In June 1945 his father had even ghost-written his application for a post at University College London. Philip had written gratefully: 'things reach a pretty pass when I don't even write out my own applications, but I really am grateful to you when you do it for me. I shrink from it – I hate laying myself open – I hate being prodded and turned over and pinched like fish on a slab.'[27] Now he applied for the post of Deputy Librarian at University College, Leicester. He was interviewed at the end of June, and this time he was successful. He was to take up his new position in September.

Once his escape was certain he began to feel a sentimental affection for Wellington. The reaction of users of the Library was 'embarrassingly regretful. I am beginning to long for someone to come up & say, "You're goin', eh? Good riddance to rotten bad rubbish!"'[28] He could not, however, resist the witticism: 'I'd have missed it for anything.'[29] Around the time of the move to Leicester his poems show a rise in emotional temperature. In mid-September he completed a beautiful, moody reflection on death: 'And the wave sings because it is moving'.

> Death is a cloud alone in the sky with the sun.
> Our hearts, turning like fish in the green wave,
> Grow quiet in its shadow. For in the word death
> There is nothing to grasp; nothing to catch or claim;
> Nothing to adapt the skill of the heart to [. . .]

There is little evidence here of echo or influence.

The second of the 'Two Guitar Pieces', completed a few days later, is the first of Larkin's poems to deal explicitly with the poet's vocation. He casts the tension between art and life in terms of an elaborate room allegory. The speaker shares a cigarette with his lover as he looks out through a window at a 'platz' where a man is walking among wreckage. We are, it seems, in the continental world of Auden and Isherwood. Behind the pair their friend is collecting up the cards, though the pack is short, 'And dealing from now till morning would not bring / The highest hands.' When this friend turns to playing a guitar the speaker finds himself unbearably moved. The music 'builds within this room a second room; / And the accustomed harnessing of grief / Tightens [. . .]' However this room of art is not, in reality, a room, 'nor a world; but only / A figure spun on stirring of the air'. At the end of the poem the speaker remains hopelessly caught between the claims of human intimacy and the airy unreal figures of music, which 'spread' him (in a Prufrockian phrase) 'over the evening'.

Ruth was apprehensive that Philip's exposure to new stimuli in Leicester would draw him away from her, and he felt under pressure to reassure her. Towards the end of September this tension prompted another poem in the voice of a woman, 'Wedding-Wind'. By dramatizing the ecstatic joy of a farmer's wife on her wedding morning in terms reminiscent of *The Rainbow* he might perhaps persuade himself into action.[30] In the poem a woman has lain overwhelmed by happiness through her wind-blown wedding night while her husband, an archetypal 'He', attended to the frightened horses. Now he has left her to look at the floods, and she feeds the chickens from a chipped pail, her apron 'thrashed' by the wind:

> Can it be borne, this bodying-forth by wind
> Of joy my actions turn on, like a thread
> Carrying beads? Shall I be let to sleep
> Now this perpetual morning shares my bed?

Completed on 26 September 1946, the poem seems to mark a year to the day since he and Ruth had first slept together. This became a key poem in the construction of his mature oeuvre. It is the only one of the group of his early poems in a woman's voice to be included in his first mature collection, *The Less Deceived*.[31] Also, appropriately enough in view of the importance which the genres were to develop for him, it is both an epithalamium, celebrating a wedding, and an aubade, a poem dramatizing a parting of lovers at dawn.

In a calculated contrast, in 'Träumerei', completed the following day, dawn brings not ecstatic love but the fear of death. The poet describes a surreal dream, in which he walks in a silent crowd under a wall. Another wall closes in, shutting them in 'Like pigs down a concrete passage'. The poet notices a 'giant D' whitewashed high above; he knows already that E will come next. Like water in a sewer the crowd passes beneath a 'striding A' and the 'decapitated cross' of a T. Then:

> The walls of my room rise, it is still night,
> I have woken again before the word was spelt.

With weird superstition he implies that had he slept through until dawn the word would have been completed and he would be dead.

As a work of art 'Wedding-Wind' is eloquent and beautiful, but its intended therapy misfired. Ruth wrote that she might be pregnant.[32] Confronted with the possibility of fatherhood, Larkin wrote, eight days after 'Wedding-Wind' on 4 October 1946, a very different anti-aubade. In 'At the chiming of light upon sleep' a male speaker cowers in his bed in fear of the 'Morning, and more / Than morning' flooding into his room. He had been dreaming of a clenched, evergreen world of frost and 'Unchanging holly'. Now the dawn provokes procreative desire, and pitches him into the cycle of nature. He is compelled to fulfil his biological destiny and expend himself. From blossom comes fruit, and with fruit comes decay. Love, which is death's harbinger, 'Hangs everywhere its light'. With a wild pun on his failure to use a condom, he sees himself repeating the Original Sin of Adam:

> Unsheath
> The life you carry and die, cries the cock
> On the crest of the sun: unlock
> The words and seeds that drove
> Adam out of his undeciduous grove.

He has spent his seed, and his wages are death. This strange masculinist poem owes something to the seventeenth-century misogyny of Marvell's 'The Garden': 'Such was that happy Garden-state, / While man there walk'd without a Mate [. . .] Two Paradises 'twere in one / To live in Paradise alone.'[33]

The poetic ferment of 1946 culminated, less than a fortnight later, in another light-focused poem, reprising the same theme in a more objective philosophical tone. 'Many famous feet have trod', completed on 15 October, depicts each new morning as a miraculous rebirth into light. The rhetoric is reminiscent of Fitzgerald's *Rubaiyat of Omar Khayyam*, his father's favourite poem:[34]

> We are born each morning, shelled upon
> A sheet of light that paves
> The palaces of sight, and brings again
> The river shining through the field of graves.

The tone is sacramental, but Eliotic religiosity has been replaced by secular materialism. Each evening and morning we kneel before the gate of light and dark, of waking and sleep. All we ever achieve is a trembling moment of inconclusive incipience: 'Nothing's to reach, but something's to become.'

At first sight there seems little sign in these 1946 poems of any influence from Hardy. Indeed there is much apocalyptic allegory and surrealism. However in one specific verbal nuance Hardy's influence is clearly audible. Larkin commented in a later review on the 'quaint' element in Hardy's style: 'often in Hardy I feel that the quaintness, if it is quaintness, is a kind of striving to be accurate'.[35] There is a memorable awkwardness of diction at points of high emotion in Hardy's work: 'richened', 'misrepresenter', 'the unseen water's ejaculations', 'wistlessness'. Larkin's use of 'Undeciduous' in 'At the chiming of light upon sleep' has this clumsy Hardyesque memorableness, while the phrase 'the irrecoverable keys' in 'The wave sings because it is moving' stumbles with Hardyesque emotionality. It is difficult to imagine that, without the example of Hardy, Larkin would have arrived at such awkward felicities in his mature poems as 'all but the unmolesting meadows' in 'At Grass', or 'to prove / Our almost-instinct almost true' in 'An Arundel Tomb'.

The alarm following 'Wedding-Wind' passed, but the episode left Larkin tangled in self-criticism and sexual inhibition. His mood can be gauged from the dreams he recorded in the days following Christmas 1946. He had abandoned his dream diary of 1942–3 with the comment that the exercise 'no longer interests me'.[36] Now, once again in quest of his 'problem', he wrote down his dreams. The mixture of tones is much as before. In one he tries to direct a friend on a bicycle to a village whose name he does not know, while a hen walks past carrying a rolled magazine. In another his father cruelly ridicules his sister.[37] The next dream, however, develops a disturbing complexity:

> I am a negro, by definition rather than observation. I go to an American racecourse, where I go in the negroes' entrance & use the negroes' very rickety lavatory. I then meet Hilly, and we walk arm in arm through a very gay scantily dressed beach crowd. I say, with a self-pitying sob, that it is terrible to think I cd be killed (*i.e.* lynched) for walking with her (I may have said sleeping with her). She agrees, and says something about Russia – a similar atrocity.[38]

Larkin's empathy causes him to identify himself with the most oppressed of racial groups. But his habitual self-criticism leads him at once to accuse himself of self-pity. Similarly, the erotic fantasy of the 'scantily dressed beach crowd' is spoiled by a deep anxiety over the dangers of sex.

Two other dreams have a more immediate erotic focus on Gillian Evans, a friend in Wellington to whom he was briefly attracted. Ruth, he told Amis, had been considering abandoning him for a 'young homo', and he had been reviewing alternative possibilities. But his loyalty to Ruth immediately reasserted itself: 'after all we got on much better than I should ever get on with Miss G. C. Evans, or Miss Jane Exall, or anybody else'.[39] The two dreams show a characteristic pattern. In the first an authority figure, in the form of the Chief Clerk of Wellington District Council, puts Gillian through her paces: 'In a gymnastics class presided over by Astley-Jones, Gillian Evans was called upon to do a difficult exercise in a skimpy sort of playsuit. As far as I remember she didn't succeed.'[40] There is sexual excitement here; but it seems that Larkin also feels empathy with her failure. In the second dream the poet attempts his own difficult exercise: 'Deliberately & in my capacity as an integrated adult man kiss Gillian Evans. She then says something like "That was entirely undistinguished & meant nothing to me at all!" & changes into Philip Brown. I slap his face viciously & in real anger.' In this dream Gillian becomes the accusing authority figure, and his response to her humiliating criticism is violent anger. But by the time it is expressed Gillian has become the male Philip.

Amis was baffled by his friend's reluctance either to enjoy sex with Ruth or to move on to someone else. Earlier in December 1946, in the comically misspelled idiom of their correspondence, he had offered to buy contraceptives for him, 'if that's what's worring you'.[41] Three months later he exhorted his friend to conquer his distrust of 'Durex porducts' which are '100 PURSE SENT SAFE',[42] and reassured him that, if the worse came to the worst, 'I can get you abortioning Engines if you find you need them.'[43] Throughout 1946 and 1947 he encouraged Philip to follow his own example of shameless promiscuity. Why did he not make Ruth jealous by paying court to Jane Exall? Or, alternatively, why did he not simply transfer his attentions to Jane? But Larkin feared the emotional and social consequences: 'It seems to me that while pocking Miss Jane Exall is infinitely desirable, preparing Miss Jane Exall to be pocked and dealing with Miss Jane Exall after pocking is not at all desirable – and that pocks do not exist in the void.'[44] It may be about this time that Larkin first conceived a sour quatrain which he seems never to have committed to holograph or typescript:

> To shoot your spunk into a girl
> Is life's unquestioned crown.
> But leading up to it is not;
> And nor is leading down.[45]

The lines are insidiously mnemonic, and Anthony Thwaite could not but remember them when Larkin recited them to him years later.

One simple expedient by which Larkin protected his eroticism from shame and guilt was to keep the unicorn's virginal horn safe in his own hands. As he wrote with excruciating wit in a pocket diary in 1950, sexual intercourse is 'like asking someone else to blow your own nose for you'.[46] He retreated into vicarious sex, sending 'facetia' (pornographic pictures) to Amis with each of his letters. In a contrast of psychologies, Amis was more inhibited about these photographs than about condoms: 'I don't know how you can bear to part with them. I wish I had your courage and could become a subscriber myself.'[47]

Ruth's apprehensions were justified. Shortly after his arrival in Leicester Philip met Monica Jones, an Assistant Lecturer who had joined the English Department a few months before. They had been exact contemporaries at Oxford, he in St John's and she in St Hugh's, though since she had stuck obediently to her studies and avoided the literary scene they had never met. Both had achieved first-class degrees. For the first three or four years their relationship was to remain a respectful friendship. But, within weeks of their meeting he had lent her the proofs of *A Girl in Winter* and a copy of *Jill*, with the self-deprecating comment: 'They are both very much first shots: *Jill* perhaps a bit "firster" than the other. Do not say anything of them if no particular verdict occurs to you: and if you think *Jill* an adolescent bit of rubbish and *Winter* a pompous lifeless platitude don't hesitate to say so.'[48] He was not bored with Monica's opinions as he was with Ruth's. But he hesitated to make a new emotional tie. Indeed, he was eager to move on from Leicester as quickly as possible. Motion mentions applications for posts in the British Museum Library in February 1947, and in the Bodleian in May.[49] In February 1948 he applied for a job at Nottingham University College.[50]

Puzzlingly, following the leap forward of 1946, Larkin completed no further poems for nearly a year. It seems probable that his energies were focused on his novel-writing. When it did come, in December 1947, his next poem, 'Waiting for breakfast while she brushed her hair', resumed the life-and-art debate of 'Guitar Piece II', but with a speaker now cast unambiguously as an artist. He stands at a window, gazing at the hotel courtyard, which seems at first colourless and dull. But then the morning mist wandering 'absolvingly' past the pinpoints of light in the windows transforms the scene:

> The colourless vial of day painlessly spilled
> My world back after a year, my lost lost world
> Like a cropping deer strayed near my path again [. . .]

He is visited by the muse, drained of female attributes and with the aspect of a shamanic animal familiar. Euphoric and confused, he turns and kisses the woman who is combing her hair in the hotel room behind him, only to realize immediately that there can be no reconciliation. If he is to follow the muse's 'tender visiting, / Fallow as a deer or an unforced field', then he must send her 'terribly away'. Significantly, however, the poem ends with a satirical image of himself as 'Part invalid, part baby, and part saint'. This is the first poem in which Larkin explicitly dramatizes the rivalry between the muse of the imagination and the real girl of social commitment. He signalled its importance to his development by adding it to the reissue of *The North Ship* of 1966, even though it postdates all the other poems in that volume by more than three years.

In January 1948 he assembled a collection of twenty-four poems and sent it to his agents A. P. Watt, writing also to Alan Pringle at Faber to tell him that it would soon reach him.[51] He chose the arresting title *In the Grip of Light*, appropriately ambiguous between exaltation and threat. The phrase, he told Sutton grandly, 'occurred to me & seems to sum up the state of being alive'.[52] The contents of the volume have a hidden symmetry. He included six poems carried forward from *The North Ship*, clearly not regarding the Fortune Press book as publication proper. To these he added six poems from 1945. The remaining half of the volume consists of twelve poems from his latest burst of productivity in 1946.[53] Puzzlingly he did not include 'Waiting for breakfast'. The collection is varied in quality, but contains one or two masterpieces. After his previous experience of poetry publishing he could have had no apprehension of the difficulties which lay ahead.

7

Just Too Hard for Me
1945–50

The dated drafts in the first workbook make it easy to track the development of Larkin's poetry in the late 1940s. This is not the case with his fiction, which survives only in discontinuous, usually undated drafts, sometimes written much later than the original inspiration. To compound the difficulty, the accounts which Larkin gives of his fiction in letters to Sutton become increasingly vague and unspecific, while those to Amis show deliberate evasiveness. Moreover Larkin's later verdicts on his fiction show ambiguities. He usually blamed his failure to complete a third novel on his over-poetic conception of the form. 'I wanted to be a novelist. I thought novels were a richer form of literature than poetry; I suppose I was influenced by the kind of critical attitude that you used to get in *Scrutiny* – the novel as dramatic poem. I certainly saw novels as rather poetic things, perhaps too poetic.'[1] But he seems uncertain that this is the real explanation, and remains puzzled as to why fiction had not worked for him: 'When I stopped writing novels it was a great disappointment to me; I went on trying in the 1945–50 period. Why I stopped I don't really know, it was a great grief to me.'[2] To many readers Larkin's lyric poetry will seem a rarer achievement than that of any novelist. But to him poetry, coming so much more easily, always seemed less impressive than the novels he had failed to write: 'novels are much more interesting than poems – a novel is so spreading, it can be so fascinating and so difficult. I think they were just too hard for me.'[3]

In the months following the completion of *The Kingdom of Winter* he put on a brave show of moving forward with Lawrentian purpose. In September 1945 he wrote to Sutton that *The Kingdom of Winter* was 'a deathly book' on the theme of 'the relinquishing of live response to life':

> Now I am thinking of a third book in which the central character will pick up where Katherine left off and develop *logically* back to life again. In other words, the north ship will come back instead of being bogged up there in a glacier. Then I shall have finished this particular branch of soul-history (my own, of course) and what will happen then I don't know.[4]

The future perfect tense in which he looks forward to having 'finished' this branch of his 'soul-history' betrays little relish for the process, and the final sentence has a dispirited, helpless tone. To achieve this re-engagement with life Larkin would surely need, like Lawrence, to commit himself to a Jessie Chambers or elope with a Frieda Weekley. He would have to make a developing relationship with Ruth or Monica the creative centre of his fictional 'soul-history', and wander the world in search of new experience. Intriguingly, the two novels with which he wrestled over the next five or more years do show him, in a muted way, attempting something like this. Both protagonists were, it seems, to find new opportunities for themselves in America. But, crucially, Larkin himself never crossed the Atlantic, and the novels were never finished.

But Larkin is not consistent, and on occasion could give a very different analysis of his fictional ambitions. In an early letter to Sutton of 5 March 1942, he accurately predicted the future shape of his career. He would, he forecast, fail the difficult challenge of fiction 'before I finally sprout wings and turn into a poet dashing forward like a Hussar'.[5] He alludes to Auden's celebrated sonnet 'The Novelist', which contrasts the dashing Hussar poet with the novelist, whose task is to learn 'How to be plain and awkward, how to be / One after whom none think it worth to turn'. The novelist must 'Become the whole of boredom, subject to / Vulgar complaints like love, among the Just // Be just, among the Filthy filthy too'.[6] This notion of the novelist as a passive recorder of life on all its levels offers an alternative to the more elevated, egotistical notion of the novel as diffused poem or Lawrentian soul adventure. Vernon Watkins had offered Larkin a similar example in poetry of self-effacing devotion to 'the work'.

In this version the novelist's task is one of radical empathy. As Larkin later said: 'novels are about other people and poetry is about yourself'.[7] In his unfinished novels of the late 1940s he was attempting to write not poetically about himself, but prosaically about others. He was no longer the inspired or cursed poet, but an ordinary man. In poetry he rejected the examples of Yeats and Thomas, who had encouraged him to jack himself up to 'a concept of poetry that lay outside my own life'.[8] Similarly, in his fiction he would now learn to be plain and awkward, even perhaps 'Become the whole of boredom'. While he was working on *Jill* he boasted to Amis, 'There is not a single intelligent character in the book,' and resolved in future drafts to repress Kemp's growing signs of cleverness.[9]

It is tempting to relate this development to Larkin's association with Kingsley Amis. Between 1947 and 1951 Amis was wrestling with his own ultimately unpublished first novel, *The Legacy*, and constantly demanding his friend's advice.[10] Amis certainly presented Larkin with the example of fiction lacking the poetic refinement of his own published novels. But Larkin's determination to empathize with other people is alien to Amis, and it seems that, while offering Amis plentiful advice, Larkin evaded any interaction between his own fiction and that of his friend. Nevertheless Larkin and Amis found themselves moving with the literary current of the time in broadly the same direction. Fiction had moved beyond the modernism of Joyce and Woolf and was beginning to generate from the social realism of George Orwell's and Graham Greene's novels of the 1930s to the raw post-war 'angry young man' idiom of Braine and Sillitoe. Amis's *Lucky Jim* was to be a key early work in this literary movement.

Two substantial groups of drafts survive among Larkin's papers. Both novels have their biographical origins in the period 1946–8, and he seems to have worked on them in parallel or alternately. One of them, titled in some drafts *No For An Answer*, focuses on Sam Wagstaff, a young 'son of the firm', about to inherit a motor-manufacturing business in Birmingham from his father. The narrative follows Sam's relationship with his girlfriend Sheila Piggott (in some drafts Stella), a reductive caricature of Ruth Bowman as a cultureless provincial girl. They attend a rugby-club dance, encounter Sam's lonely, ill father and visit a pub at Christmas. The prevailing tone of meticulous realism is set in the opening scene. Sheila is opening Christmas cards while her mother reads a novel on the sofa: '"Look at the price of that," she said, tossing one over to Mrs Piggott. "Looks like one-and-six, doesn't it? It's tenpence really. You can see where they've altered it."' ('10d' has been changed to '1/6d'.) Her mother compliments her, '"You're a sharp one,"' bending her library book back 'as if to keep it submissive'.

> Her heavy face had stern good-humoured lines, her grey hair was permanently-waved. She wore horn-rimmed spectacles to read and play bridge. With each breath she blew out a faint blue plume from the cigarette she smoked, using a holder. 'They've no money these days.'
>
> Sheila went on studying [the cards], her small forehead wrinkled as if she were short-sighted. 'This of Jack Ryman's, now that only cost a bob but it looks more, doesn't it? . . . Oh, for heaven's sake.' She extinguished the wireless. 'Where's Sam got to, I'd like to know.' She stretched, shivered. 'It doesn't take all night to drive from Brum.'[11]

It is a perfectly visualized scene and the dialogue is exactly caught. But something is lacking. Does the narrator perhaps not like the Piggotts and Wagstaffs of this world enough to make the writing quite come alive? Or is it that the colourless, omniscient third-person narration precludes the humour, irony and playfulness which give vitality to the Willow Gables works and the later mature poems? Was Larkin repeating the same mistake he had made in *The North Ship*, rejecting mixed tones in favour of a consistent seriousness?

Four main drafts and four subsidiary drafts survive (with overlaps), and the page numbering shows that extensive further drafting was destroyed. Larkin devoted many months to the novel during 1947–9.[12]

The process of composition was clearly strenuous. He repeatedly recast the text, making slight changes of action and wording without changing the basic conception. The high quality of much of the writing makes this puzzling. A less self-critical writer would certainly have pressed on to a finish. Moreover he sets himself new challenges of subject matter and tone. The scene in which Sam and Sheila eat Christmas lunch together, for instance, is peculiarly unsettling:

> For a time they did nothing but eat. As he lifted the first forkful Sam felt water spring in his mouth, and he put in as much at once as he could. The flavour of the turkey, of cloves in the bread sauce, and sage in the stuffing, ran together and ascended his palate in a delicious fume. Every now and then he cleared his taste with bread, or washed the cold metallic claret over his tongue before starting again. They grinned at each other, mouths stuffed full: neither stopped chewing for an instant, but if they had they would have heard the sound of the other's jaws. They did not want to talk. Their knives and forks worked steadily as spades clearing away snow, until the food was reduced to small heaps, then to nothing. Stella finished first by about a couple of mouthfuls.[13]

The detailed description of these two healthy members of the lumpen-bourgeoisie gorging themselves makes for a subtly gross, disgusting effect. The author may not 'want to be' these unpoetic characters in the way that he earlier wanted 'to be that girl', but he certainly takes us uncomfortably into their skins. As Richard Bradford comments, 'Had the novel been completed and found a publisher [. . .] it might have subtly altered the course of post-war literary history,' by anticipating by a decade the work of Braine, Barstow, Sillitoe, Storey, Amis and Wain, whose works showed that 'good writing could coexist with states of mind that had little time for high culture'.[14] The originality and adventurousness of such writing would have transformed the context for later novelists.

The scene which, in his notes to the novel, Larkin calls the 'seduction fiasco' explores, with an insight ahead of its time, the social phenomenon later called 'heavy petting'. The new post-war freedom of the young, no longer respectful of earlier conventions of courtship, was to become a major theme of novels in the 1950s. The encounter, which Larkin rewrote five times with slight variations, also looks further forward to what would now be called 'date rape'. After dinner, Sam and Sheila/Stella engage in horseplay which gets out of hand:

> The sensation was like getting drunk extremely quickly: he forgot every-thing except that he was making love to Stella and that he must go on doing so at all costs. He got his hand under the edge of her long skirt and slid it up her nyloned right leg till she was holding it tightly between her two bare thighs. His cuff caught against the edge of her girdle and again he was impatient to get undressed. He felt desperate to have her, far too desperate to conduct successfully the polite moves necessary to get her, too desperate not to try. A dozen things about her were throb-bing in him all at the same time, smells, sights, tastes, touches, all bucking like a jawful of aching teeth. But try as he might his hand could get no further.[15]

Larkin catches with embarrassing directness the interplay of raw sex and social convention: Sam's blundering impatience; Sheila's clenched thighs and strict sense of propriety. In one of the drafts Sheila slaps Sam's face and exclaims: 'All right, I've had about enough [. . .] No one's going to, to treat me like that. You've had it. Absolutely had it.'[16] It is not surprising that Larkin kept the novel secret from Ruth Bowman. When she first read it fifty years later in 1999, she was understandably offended at this depiction of a crude, inarticulate relationship, so differ-ent from their real-life mutual respect and shared artistic enthusiasms: 'if Sam and Sheila are any metamorphosis of Philip and me it must be left to literary critics to make the connection. They say nothing to me.'[17]

The narrative was to explore a familiar triangle. Sam's affections are divided between the coarse-grained Sheila and the pathetic victim, Grace, a working-class girl whom he knocks over in his car and then visits in hospital. Larkin's plot-outline suggests that Sam was ultimately to be condemned for failing to respond to Grace's love. However, in a contradictory subtext, the novel was, it seems, to celebrate Sam's escape from his tangled guilts and responsibilities. At the end he was to leave both Sheila and Grace behind and take ship for a business trip to the USA. Also on board were to be members of the Washington Band whose 'hot' music was to represent, Larkin's notes indicate with ironic inverted commas, 'the "falsity" of the American brand of spontaneity'.[18] It seems that the attempt to realize a world of ordinary Midland provincial life was to be short-circuited by an escapist wish-fulfilment fantasy not dissimilar to the ending of *Lucky Jim*, though in Larkin's version Sam is not accompanied by a glamorous Christine.

The other explanation which Larkin gave for his inability to complete a third novel, apart from his over-poetic notion of the form, was his deficiency in empathy. 'I think that was the trouble, really. I didn't know enough about other people, I didn't like them enough.'[19] He was morally scathing about his failure: 'I suppose I must have lost interest in other people, or perhaps I was only pretending to be interested in them.'[20] This explanation does not ring true. Larkin was, in fact, capable of the keenest psychological insights. From the comedy of Marie's Jungian experiments and Philippa's belt fetishism in *Michaelmas Term at St Bride's* to the tragedy of Kemp's self-destructive breakdown at the end of *Jill* and Katherine's alienation in a foreign England in *The Kingdom of Winter*, he shows a generous instinct to venture beyond his own immediate subjectivity and a fascination with different worlds of experience.

The four surviving fragments of the second unfinished novel, whose intended title when Larkin abandoned it was *A New World Symphony*, indeed show Larkin attempting a particularly direct and intimate empathy. As in his published novels he turns from a male protagonist, Sam Wagstaff, to a female centre of consciousness, Augusta Bax, a character transparently based on Monica Jones. The first letters of their names perhaps suggest that Augusta and Wagstaff represent alpha and omega in an alphabet of gender. When Larkin began the novel he and Monica were merely colleagues, not committed to a long-term relationship. His attitude to the fictionalized character seems dispassionately exploratory as much as sympathetic. Reality is transposed into fiction with literal directness. Augusta Bax has Monica Jones's bad teeth, migraines and pulsing vein in her temple, as well as her right-wing prejudices. Pamela Hanley, a Library Assistant in Leicester in 1948, observed: 'Augusta has all Monica Jones's physical and personal characteristics, apart from her hair being dyed blonde, not red. Her distinctive flamboyant style of dressing in brightly coloured clothes is exactly described.'[21] Monica's mother frequently visited Leicester at this time, and the opening scene submerges the reader in the intimately feminine relationship between mother and daughter as they scour the shops determined to find a dress of exactly the right colour at a bargain price.

Augusta's name, 'empress' in Latin, suggests a prickly, ironized dignity. She is restless and uneasy in her shared flat, with its jealously guarded spaces of privacy:

> In the larder the seven or eight women who lived in the house each had her small store of food collected inviolably together, surrounded on the slab by a space. 'And this is the dining-room [she tells her mother] – we all take our little messes in, at least, they take their big messes, whenever we feel like – it's just a room to eat in, when you want to eat.' Augusta stared a moment round the characterless furnishings, then led the way back to her room, lightly tucking wisps of hair into place with the tips of her fingers.[22]

There is an ambiguity in the narrator's attitude. Augusta's censoriousness inhibits the emotional identification which the reader felt with Katherine in *The Kingdom of Winter*. The bane of Augusta's life is a Jewish refugee, Mrs Klein,[23] a specialist in Child Psychology ('"Strewth", Mrs Bax commented deliberately'), who insists on calling her 'Bax', despite her own insistence on the formal 'Mrs Klein':

> 'Mrs Klein makes the biggest messes – huge goulaschy messes she sits gorging surrounded by saucepans – on newspapers if she remembers.'
>
> 'This lady sounds as if she needs an agitation working up against her,' said Mrs Bax as if she had seen a non-member crossing a green in high heels.
>
> 'Yes, and don't I wish you were here to do it. And she isn't a lady. I

know that's an old-fashioned thing to say but I shall go on saying it as long as there are people like Mrs K. about. I do really think that the point about the Kleins is that they go about being so terrible and odious until people are forced to band together in sheer self-defence, and then they set up a howl about persecution and move on to deceive a fresh lot of kind souls into helping them.'[24]

Augusta mentions casually that Mrs Klein's husband was murdered during the war: 'Well, I gather the Nazis decided they could get along without him. If he was anything like her I appreciate their point of view for once.'[25] The mean-spiritedness of mother and daughter spoils the comedy.

However, the opening chapters of the novel give only a limited idea of Larkin's intentions. The plot outlines, on which he continued to work in the early 1950s, promise dramatic future developments. Augusta was to quarrel with her mother and Mrs Klein was to develop beyond the anti-Semitic caricature of the initial description. Broader horizons were to open out, breaking down Augusta's defensive small-mindedness. Mrs Klein's American relatives, a family of 'Wonderful loving Yanks',[26] were to offer her a lifeline after she had been sacked from her post. At the end of the novel Augusta was to leave for the USA as companion to the Yanks' delinquent daughter, and the novel was to close with a 'hymn to America': 'a real new world symphony. I mean she feels she's in a new world.'[27] Here Larkin does appear to be making a (much displaced) attempt to develop 'back to life again', bringing the north ship back from the glacier. However, either these later scenes were never written or the drafts were destroyed.

In real life Larkin was developing a protective loyalty towards Monica, intensified by the unremitting hostility of Amis, who was jealous of this new rival. Amis had visited Larkin shortly after he had taken up his post in Leicester and, inspired by a glimpse of the common room, had begun drafting the novel which eventually became *Lucky Jim*, in which Monica Jones features as the neurotic, manipulative Margaret Peel. Amis took every opportunity to ridicule his rival for Larkin's affections. In a letter of 1948 he derided Monica's research on the 'Augustan' poet Crabbe: 'It doesn't surprise me in the *least* that Monica is studding Crab [*sic*]; he's *exactly* the sort of *priggish, boring, featureless* [. . .] *long-winded, inessential* man she'd go for.'[28] Larkin's portrayal of Augusta suggests that he shared some of the criticisms of his friend. But he was attracted by this witty, beautiful, if also difficult and vulnerable woman, to whom he was to become attached for the rest of his life. Larkin kept the content of his novel entirely secret from both of them. Neither Kingsley nor Monica learnt of the novel's existence until half a century later, after Larkin's death.

A New World Symphony foundered on Larkin's risky strategy of making fiction directly out of his own immediate experience. Monica's future was to be nothing like that of Augusta, and as she became a familiar part of his life the novel's imaginative conviction seems to have faded. He could scarcely think of publishing the novel after his relationship with her had deepened in 1950 and become physical. The sensitivities of real-life relationships conflicted with impersonal art. This is not a problem that would have concerned Amis, who took satisfaction in expressing his real-life animosities in fiction, taking 'revenge' on those he disliked. Monica Jones becomes, without a qualm, Margaret Peel, and Amis anticipated with relish putting his father-in-law into a book '*recognisably*, so that he will feel *hurt* and *bewildered* at being so *hated*'.[29]

But Larkin's direct transposition of real-life events also created simpler, more practical difficulties. According to his notes the plot was to reproduce in detail the situation in the Leicester English Department in 1946–7. The character of Butterfield (Praed in some fragments)[30] is based on the popular Head of English, Arthur Collins, who, when professorships were created in the course of college restructuring, was compelled to apply for his own post. He was unsuccessful and suffered a demotion. In the most vividly realized of the fragments the wretched Butterfield spends a Sunday afternoon in comic despair, filling out the professorial application form in the fading light as he drinks sherry direct from the bottle.[31] In Larkin's outlines Butterfield/Praed commits suicide. In real life Arthur Collins continued to work in the Leicester department for many years. Had it been published the novel would have caused the widest offence: to Arthur Collins, to Arthur Humphreys, the new Head of English, and to the then Principal of Leicester University College, Frederick Attenborough (father of Richard and David). It might even have laid Larkin open to litigation. The novel indeed was unpublishable for these reasons alone.

But also perhaps, like *No For An Answer*, it lacked the spark of true inspiration. After reading the drafts in 1999 Monica Jones concluded: 'it wasn't going as he liked. I think that he was realizing that he was drawing on real things and constantly checking with reality – and imagination doesn't come then.'[32] It seems that Larkin did not finally abandon his ambition to be a novelist until the acceptance of *Lucky Jim* by Gollancz in 1953. But by the end of the decade it was already only too apparent that he would never publish a third novel. After all, he found poetry less laborious than fiction: 'When I lapsed back into poetry, it was so much easier, so much quicker.'[33]

8

Crisis and Escape
1947–50

At the end of 1947 Larkin found himself suddenly beset by personal and literary crises. In December, as if to confirm all his inhibitions about sex, Hilary Bardwell became pregnant. Amis reported that attempts to induce a miscarriage with 'a lot of chemicals' had been unsuccessful,[1] and his ignorant confidence in 'abortioning Engines' was shaken when a doctor friend warned him of the dangers of the 100-guinea back-street termination which he had arranged. Larkin looked on as his friend resigned himself with as good a grace as possible to the role of dutiful husband and father. The marriage took place on 21 January 1948,[2] and the Amises' first son, born later in the year, was named Philip after the poet.

Sydney Larkin had realized his ambition to retire early, in June 1944 (his present had been the sixteen-volume complete works of Edmund Burke), and during the following years 73 Coten End had offered the young poet a secure refuge from his troubles. Earlier in 1947 he had been feeling particularly affectionate towards his parents. In May he complimented them on how young they still seemed: 'young in keen response to things [. . .] It makes home a very nice place to come to.'[3] Now this home was broken. At Christmas Sydney Larkin became ill. An operation for gallstones early in the New Year failed to dispel the problem. On 28 January 1948 Philip wrote to Sutton: 'he is still in hospital & I fancy total recovery is by no means inevitable'.[4]

'Really, Philip could do no wrong in his father's eyes. Or his mother's. They worshipped him,' Larkin's elder sister Kitty recalled.

On holiday in Germany, aged fourteen, in 1936: 'frightening notices that you felt you should understand and couldn't.'

Rhöndorf bathing beach, 1934. Eva and Sydney Larkin flanked by a German mother and daughter. Presumably the photograph was taken by the father.

At 73 Coten End, Warwick in the early 1940s. The jam which his father made from plums from this garden features in Larkin's elegy 'An April Sunday brings the snow' (1948).

Larkin's closest school friend, the aspiring painter, James Sutton. They shared a Lawrentian idealism and a passion for jazz.

Sketch in a letter to Kingsley Amis, 1942.

Larkin and Kingsley Amis were inseparable from May 1941 until Amis was called up just over a year later. Amis insisted that his friend be 'savagely uninterested' in all the things he was 'savagely uninterested in'.

In his final year at Oxford (1942–3) Larkin became friends with Bruce Montgomery, who wrote crime fiction under the pseudonym 'Edmund Crispin'. 'Bruce's irresponsibility and self-confidence were exactly what I needed at the time,' Larkin later recalled.

Penelope Scott Stokes (*centre*). Larkin's sonnet 'So through that unripe day' was inspired by this 'girl resembling an Eton boy'.

'Dora is bullied' and 'At the top of her form': illustrations from *Niece of the Headmistress* by Dorothy Vicary (1939), one of the girls'-school stories to which Larkin paid homage in his 'Brunette Coleman' writings.

Philip proposed to Ruth Bowman in 1948. 'The engagement, to me anyway, is to give myself a sincere chance of "opening out" towards someone I do love a lot in a rather strangled way, and to help her take her Finals.' The engagement ended when Larkin left for Belfast in 1950.

'Pop' and 'Mop'. Sydney Larkin O.B.E. and Eva Larkin, newly widowed, in 1949. In May 1947 Philip wrote: 'How young you both are […] young in keen response to things […] It makes home a very nice place to come to.'

'Beautiful handsome girl!' Monica Jones was a Lecturer at Leicester University College when Larkin arrived in 1946. He took this photograph in the early 1950s in his top-floor flat in Elmwood Avenue, Belfast.

Kingsley and Hilly Amis in 1948, the year of their marriage. Kingsley encouraged the flirtation between Hilly and Philip.

Larkin was responsible for the Library Issue Desk at Queen's University, Belfast (1950–55).

Dearest Flopsical - Rabbit,

That's how we are at present!

Are you?

Why did I say it? well, dear,
because, even if we neither ~~at bottom~~
care, the fact ~~does~~ remain that you
explode to the right & I explode to the
left, & that if we are called on to defend
our explosions, you make a better job
of it (in my eyes) than I do (again in my
eyes). That's all!

Larkin's more intimate letters are interspersed with doodles and
sketches in which he depicts himself as a seal (from a childhood pun
on 'sealing' a letter). His most elaborate drawings come in the early
letters to Monica Jones, nicknamed 'Rabbit' or 'Bun'.

Winifred Arnott in Belfast in the early 1950s. Philip's unconsummated courtship with Winifred inspired 'Latest Face' and 'Lines on a Young Lady's Photograph Album'.

Patsy Strang, 1953. Their affair, evoked in the poem 'Whatever Happened?', lasted from spring 1952 to summer 1953. Patsy had lived in Paris and was eager to fall in love with a poet.

She would ~~notice~~ first the varying creep of light,
Fish-brown, puddle-~~grey~~ grey, a string of infected circles
Curdling to mustard and a ~~touch~~ touch of slate

Light that gathers up to the ~~size~~ size of a glove,
Then sickens inclusively outwards. *She ~~would~~ would* also remark
The unwholesome floor, as it might be the skin of a grave,

Everywhere
And ~~the~~ the adhesive sense of betrayal
~~In Flat ~~spheroid~~ Conical and pyramid-shaped~~
~~Makes the whole world seem moulded of ~~ denial~~

on all sides
And ~~everywhere~~ the adhesive sense of betrayal
In planes, spheres, cones and pyramidal shapes
~~Shouldering~~ . But most of all

would
Her pretty head ~~spin~~ at truth's quaint language,
~~Whose words each have~~ contradictory
And wedge ~~the tongue~~ half-chewed bandage,

Showing the world to be a giant neuter
~~be token that the world is great neuter~~
make
Whose forces ~~generate~~ their opposites.
To ~~them~~ useless, now and in the future.

A draft page of 'If, My Darling', May 1950 (Workbook 2). Larkin's feelings for Monica Jones make this one of his most dynamically reworked drafts.

He felt that his creative energy had stalled. He was, he told Sutton, 'fuddling' his head with books on psychology and now imagined himself as 'every kind of neurotic to be found in the early poems of Auden':

> my predominant sensation these days is one of blockage – I feel somewhere I am not functioning – I long for some metaphysical big bad wolf to come & huff & puff & blow the obstruction away as one blows a foul clot out of a pipe stem. [. . .] I'm glad you liked the poems. They are just starting out on their round of publishers. I can't really imagine them being published, but one never knows. The great obstacle lies in the fact that I am 'optioned' – only Fabers can take them with an option on my next [. . .]
>
> Outside it's pissing with rain & I sit in my enormous duffel coat before my lukewarm fire, hands like two chilly frogs.[5]

The 'great obstacle' took an altogether more substantial form when early in February Faber rejected *In the Grip of Light*. Over the following months the volume was turned down by five other publishers: John Lane, J. M. Dent, Macmillan, Methuen and John Lehmann. This failure increased Larkin's self-doubt and he became even more scathing about his own writing. Also in February, Eva fell and broke her wrist. Philip loyally offered to move back into the family home to look after her, but she declined the offer.

On 24 February he wrote to Sutton that it was 'all up' with his father: 'matter of weeks. Please don't tell anyone as *he* doesn't know & we don't want it to become known in Coventry [. . .] I feel that I have got to make a big mental jump – to stop being a child & become an adult – but it isn't easy for me, though I keep trying.'[6] Sydney Larkin died of cancer of the liver on Good Friday, 26 March. Just over a week later on 4 April Larkin wrote to Monica Jones, thoughtfully hoping that she had 'managed to recuperate' from the strain of teaching before going on to relate his own news:

> My holiday was rather as I expected – my poor father grew steadily worse & died on Good Friday. Since then mother & I have been rather

> hopelessly looking at the stock in the house – this morning I shifted 100
> lbs of jam – 1945, 1946, & 1947 years – and about 25 Kilner jars of
> bottled fruit [. . .] I don't know what will happen to it all – I don't like
> sweet things, you remember.[7]

The only poem Larkin had completed during the last sixteen months
was 'Waiting for breakfast', the previous December. Now he composed
what was to remain his only mourning elegy, 'An April Sunday brings
the snow'. In his letter he told Monica: 'It is snowing here at the
moment: this accords very well with mood and circumstance, both of
which are Hardyish.' In the poem mourner and mourned are reduced
to a generic level of basic humanity. The speaker is uncharacterized and
ungendered and the jam-maker could be a mother, a lover or a friend.
The poet's immediate consciousness, however, is intimately evoked as
he moves from cupboard to cupboard storing the jam made by the lost
loved one. Every object mentioned is metonymic of transience. The
wintry snow will be gone in an 'hour or two'; the blossom of spring will
last a little longer. The autumn fruit from these same trees, temporarily
preserved in jars, 'Behind the glass, under the cellophane', will be
consumed at next summer's teas. But the jam-maker will not be there
to enjoy it.[8] With poignant simplicity the jam contains:

> your final summer – sweet,
> And meaningless, and not to come again.

Reticence makes grief the more eloquent. Larkin was aware that this
was one of his finest poems. This may be the poem which he had in
mind when he said in an interview in 1973, 'I wrote my first good poem
when I was 26,' though he did not reach this age until August 1948.[9] It
is an indication of the intensity of its personal grief that he did not
publish it during his lifetime.

It seems that 'An April Sunday brings the snow' was drafted largely
outside the workbook, since, unusually, the version in the book is a
fair copy, occupying a single page, without corrections and more
neatly written than surrounding drafts.[10] Larkin followed this poem

with another poem addressed to his father, 'And yet – but after death there's no "and yet"'. The speaker recalls the dead one's casual words one day on the lawn: 'Death doesn't do you harm.' All the poet can do, now we have 'seen you die; and had you burned', is to hope 'that you were right'. Further lines at the end have been erased with an india-rubber, leaving the piece an incomplete sonnet with eleven lines. Nevertheless there is an eloquence in the broken-off sestet of three unrhymed lines and the work feels, and possibly is, complete.[11] Around this time Larkin was also occupied with *No For An Answer*, one draft of which describes a visit by Sam Wagstaff to his dying father in hospital.

Then, six weeks after Sydney's death, Philip attempted to choose prose over poetry in a literal way, by 'becoming an adult' and proposing to Ruth. She had just turned twenty-one. He wrote to Sutton:

> To tell you the truth I have done something rather odd myself – got engaged to Ruth on Monday. You know I have known her since 1943 or 4; well, we have gone on seeing each other until the point seemed to arrive when we either had to start taking it seriously or else drop it. I can't say I welcome the thought of marriage, as it appears to me from the safe side of it, but nor do I want to desert the only girl I have met who doesn't instantly frighten me away [. . .] I suspect all my isolationist feelings as possibly harmful and certainly rather despicable. 'Are you a bloody valuable vase, man, to be kept so carefully?'

He describes his engagement unpromisingly as 'a sincere chance of "opening out" towards someone I do love a lot in a rather strangled way'.[12] Responsibilities were multiplying. Eva Larkin was disorientated by widowhood and finding it difficult to cope, so Philip submitted to the ordeal of buying a house in Leicester where they could live together. They moved into 12 Dixon Drive in August 1948. He told Sutton dispiritedly, 'It has all been a bother, though I suppose it will be all right in time.'[13] However, it was not all right, and the two years which followed were among the most miserable of his life.

He later tore out a total of twenty-two pages from the workbook following 'An April Sunday brings the snow' (two batches of eight and fourteen pages), probably when he gave the book to the British Library in 1964. The rough violence with which they have been removed, leaving ragged edges and even clipping some words, suggests that he was still haunted by the trauma of these months.[14] But since he preserved these pages, the sequence is not difficult to reconstruct.[15] Following his father's death his poetry failed to come right for nearly a year. After 'And yet – but after death there's no "and yet"' he worked briefly on another poem addressed to his father and then on a seven-part work in free verse, 'Now, without defences', concerned with his inability to write (dated 26 January 1949). Then, in spring 1949, he broke the block with a distinctive group of poems with a traumatized, dispirited tone, ranging between cynicism and quiet humility. 'I am washed upon a rock' (18 March 1949) depicts life, in muted apocalyptic mode, as a moment of transient insecurity:

> My heart is ticking like the sun:
> A lonely cloud drifts in the sky.
> I dread its indecision.
> If once it block the light, I die.[16]

'To Patients', completed shortly afterwards, and renamed 'Neurotics' in the final typescript, is a grim self-admonitory reflection on mental illness.[17] The minds of the neurotics are 'rusted, stiff [. . .] / Like slot-machines only bent pennies fit'.

The next poem, 'Sinking like sediment through the day', is a surreal-ist evocation of blockage and frustration, while 'On Being Twenty-six' is a self-pitying lament over lost promise whose glumness is barely leav-ened by a wan, self-mocking rhyme:

> What caught alight
>
> Quickly consumed in me,
>   As I foresaw.
> Talent, felicity –

> These things withdraw,
> And are succeeded by a dingier crop
>   That come to stop [. . .]

In the middle of work on this poem, Larkin broke off to draft a moving declaration of poetic vocation, 'Once I believed in you', dated 1 May 1949, and titled in the undated typescript 'The Spirit Wooed'.[18] The poet humbly addresses his elusive muse:

> Once I believed in you,
> And then you came,
> Unquestionably new [. . .]
>
> You launched no argument,
> Yet I obeyed [. . .]

The spirit has withdrawn, it seems, because he was overeager, and he resigns himself with the humility of a courtly lover, to a 'pause', 'Longer than life, if you decide it so'. 'Modesties', the only poem of this group that he himself saw into print (in his self-published volume *XX Poems*, 1951), is similarly muted in tone, taking the form of a concise manifesto for a poetry of reticence and sincerity: 'Words as plain as hen-birds' wings / Do not lie, / Do not over-broider things – / Are too shy.'

In sharp contrast, a few days later, on 18 May, he composed 'To Failure', which has something of the wry ironic gusto associated with his later 'Movement' persona. The imagery boldly confuses motifs from different kinds of B movie. Failure, we are told, does not arrive

>   with dragons
> That rear up with my life between their paws
> And dash me butchered down beside the wagons,
>   The horses panicking [. . .]

Reality is less colourful than fantasies of monsters and the Wild West. As he looks out of the window at the chestnut trees 'caked with silence', the poet notices that Failure, personified in didactic eighteenth-century mode, has installed himself unobtrusively at his elbow, 'like a bore'. The poem ends with a lugubrious parenthesis: '(You have been here some time.)'[19] Despite its theme the poem's sulkiness is enjoyable and funny. As he wrote later: 'A good poem about failure is a success.'[20] It is surprising that he never published this work. After this burst of poetic activity between March and May 1949, Larkin completed no other poem for the remainder of the year. He was also making little progress with his fiction. On 24 March 1949 he wrote to Sutton: 'I have given up my novel & Ruth has given up me, not seeing, as you might say, any future in it. Nor do I!'[21]

He turned from the complications of the real schoolgirl to unreal but readily available auto-eroticism. Encouraged by her husband, Hilly even agreed to feature in Philip's pornographic fantasies. Kingsley wrote on 9 May: 'I have asked Hilly about your dirty-picture proposal, and obtained a modified assent. She is prepared to do corset-and-black-stocking or holding-up-a-towel stuff, and bare-bosom stuff ('[. . .] they'll be bigger when I'm feeding the new baby'), but is a bit hesitant about being quite undraped, "though I'll proba-bly get bolder when I start." Does this give you the hron? It does me, slightly, oddly. Do you want "some of us together"? ("Why you narcis-sistic —").'[22] Meanwhile the relationship with Ruth stumbled on, neither Philip nor she having the will or ability to put an end to it. In July Larkin wrote with grim drollery to Sutton: 'Ruth returned and demanded that we continue being friends, so that is what we are continuing being.'[23]

But, around this time, for no obvious reason, Larkin started to recover his self-possession. His spirits began to rise. His letters become more vigorous and a distinctive Larkinesque tone of contrarian *jouis-sance* emerges: 'life seems to have pushed a steamroller up against the door & nailed the windows & stuffed something down the chimney. It is now dancing up & down outside the glass shouting: "Live danger-ously!" I turn round and show it my bum.'[24] It is from this point that we can date the masculine, bloody-minded assertiveness which is to figure centrally in Larkin's 'vernacular' voice. In a letter to Sutton written on 30 October 1949 he tells himself to take control of his own life:

> Most people, I'm convinced, don't think about life at all. They grab what they think they want and the subsequent consequences keep them busy in an endless chain till they're carried out feet first [. . .] *Take what you want – and pay for it [. . .] or you'll get what you don't want, & pay for that too.* My advice to anybody is: *Find out what you want. Then get it.*[25]

He was more certain than ever that what he, Philip Larkin, wanted was not marriage: 'women don't just sit still & back you up. They want children: they like scenes: they want a chance of parading all the emotional haberdashery they are stocked with. Above all they like feeling they "own" you – or that you "own" them – a thing I hate.'[26] In March 1950 he visited the Amises in Swansea, where Kingsley was now a lecturer at the University College, and found this glimpse of married life decidedly uninviting. He began to lay practical plans to escape from his mother and from Ruth: 'My chief handicap at present is this bloody set up here, Christ knows how it will all end. But it can only be broken up by a good excuse like a new job, you see [. . .] I do realize that my mother must live with someone – only I'd rather prefer it not to be me.'[27]

His new self-confidence shows itself in the final pages of the first workbook. The poems he completed in early 1950 breathe a new vigour and assurance. In a deliberate strategy of sharp emotional contrast the calm elegiac 'At Grass' is followed by the tangled anguish of 'Deceptions'. The delicate epiphany of 'Coming' is followed (on the same day) by the acerbic 'Fiction and the Reading Public'. The argumentative 'If, My Darling' is answered a week later by the yearning for oblivion of 'Wants'. The poems shift vertiginously between brutal realism and soft, ingenuous emotion. With the turn of the year and the decade, it seems, Larkin took the signal to make the poetic breakthrough towards which he had been building. Consequently by the time he did escape his personal impasse in October, he had written half a dozen great poems whose tone and emotional texture mapped out the parameters of his first

mature volume, *The Less Deceived*. This year, 1950, was the most productive of his literary life, and saw him achieve full poetic maturity.

The sequence begins with 'At Grass', completed on 3 January. In
retrospect this takes its place as the first in the series of ten great
extended elegies which give structure to his oeuvre over the next
quarter-century: 'At Grass', 'Church Going', 'An Arundel Tomb',
'The Whitsun Weddings', 'Here', 'Dockery and Son', 'The Building',
'The Old Fools', 'Show Saturday', 'Aubade' (some readers might add
'To the Sea'). As frequently in Larkin's work, the poem was prompted
by a casual stimulus. An avid cinema-goer, he was unusually affected
by a short supporting film concerned with Brown Jack, a famous
racehorse of the 1930s, now out to stud. The horses in his poem fall
back into animal anonymity, leaving behind the human world of
which they had no comprehension. Just as his eye can hardly pick
them out, his mind cannot comprehend their world. There is an
elegiac hint in the phrase 'cold shade'; the horses are fading into the
shades, or in the classical terminology are themselves already 'shades'.
Their world is not his, whether because of their animal otherness or
because they are nearing death. The poet is not even confident enough
to attribute motives to them. 'Then one crops grass, and moves about
/ – The other seeming to look on –'. The horse 'seems' to look on. It
is no spectator in the human sense.

The poet now steps back to contemplate a larger distance of time.
Fifteen years earlier these animals were the stuff of human legend,
fabled by their performance over 'Two dozen distances'. The technical
racing term 'distance' subtly intimates the underlying theme of the
poem, which could be fittingly subtitled 'Ode to Distance'. The archaic
pre-war racing scene is evoked in exquisite intricate phrases. The horses'
names 'were artificed / To inlay faded, classic Junes –'. The transferred
epithets make sense only by a complex manipulation of association and
meaning. The strange and dignified verb 'artificed' signifies that their
names were posted up against the dates of their victories in ornamental
lettering (the inlay now faded) in the grandstand roll of fame.
Grammatically the names are 'artificed' to insubstantial time ('classic
Junes'). For all its rituals of 'classics' and almanacks, the world of horse

racing is a matter merely of times, distances and the fleeting victory of
the last race. The flashback of stanzas two and three concludes with a
diminuendo as the cheering of the crowd subsides into the newspaper
report of the race:

> the long cry
> Hanging unhushed till it subside
> To stop-press columns on the street.

Nothing is more poignantly evocative of the transience of life than the
urgent news of the stop-press column once it is no longer new.

The final two stanzas return to the present. The poet toys with the
idea that the horses have memories, plaguing their ears 'like flies'. But
he is not deceived. The simile is illusory: it is real flies that cause the
horses to shake their heads. Similarly their names never had any
meaning for the horses themselves. In retirement they have slipped
both reins and names:

> Almanacked, their names live; they
>
> Have slipped their names, and stand at ease,
> Or gallop for what must be joy,
> And not a fieldglass sees them home,
> Or curious stop-watch prophesies [. . .]

Mortality is hinted at in the suppressed continuation of the sentence:
'their names live; they // [Die]'. The names have 'immortal' life in the
annals of the turf; the animals themselves do not. With an anacrusis
which is to become one of the features of Larkin's greatest mature
poems, the penultimate stanza ends with an anticipatory intake of
breath ('their names live; they // Have slipped their names'). The elaborate diction of the racing world ('handicaps, almanacks, the curious
stop-watch') is suddenly reduced to the formal but simple vocabulary
of 'groom, groom's boy, bridles' and the final verb 'come', with its sense
of consummation. No longer does the 'curious stop-watch' prophesy

the horses' galloping. Indeed the verb 'prophesies' has become unexpectedly intransitive, trailing away to a sudden halt, leaving the final two lines isolated in a hushed pianissimo:

> Only the groom, and the groom's boy,
> With bridles in the evening come.

The men's titles with their long 'o' sounds bring to mind their soothing voices as they lead the horses off into the darkness. Such sounds the animals can understand.[28]

'At Grass' is an elegiac masterpiece of poised detachment and modulation. In contrast 'Deceptions', completed six weeks later on 20 February, vividly dramatizes unresolved emotion.[29] The speaker, doubting his own good faith, strives to sublimate personal motives into detached reflection. The poem's subject is Hardyesque: a ruined Victorian maid. But its treatment is quite unlike Hardy in its complicated 'literary' intertextuality. In a more awkward and dubious 'Ode to Distance', the poet attempts to keep his subject at arm's length by insisting on its mediation through earlier texts. The poem's original title 'The Less Deceived', later transferred to the volume in which the poem ultimately appeared, is an allusion to a scene in *Hamlet*. The prince cruelly tells Ophelia 'I loved you not', and she replies with quiet pathos, 'I was the more deceived.'[30] The biographical parallel with Philip's relationship with Ruth is clear. Both Hamlet and Larkin have lost their fathers and both are tormenting their beloveds with antisocial moodiness. A second, very different intertext is established by the prefatory quotation from *London Labour and the London Poor*, Part IV, by Henry Mayhew. The poet is unable to offer consolation across the years to this long-dead Victorian woman betrayed into prostitution. Worse, he is painfully aware that his masculinity implicates him in the guilt of the man who has raped her.

The subtitle of Mayhew's fourth volume is 'Those That Will Not Work', and in Mayhew's account the woman, already over forty, is 'one of that lowest class of women who prostitute themselves for a shilling or less'. Her own crude verdict on her abandonment is: 'There is always as good fish in the sea as ever came out of it.' Larkin omits this moral and social contextualizing, choosing to focus closely on the original moment of violence, when the innocent sixteen-year-old country girl was drugged and raped. 'I was horrified to discover that I had been ruined, and for some days I was inconsolable, and cried like a child to be killed or sent back to my aunt.'[31] Mayhew, superior and judgemental, gives his verdict on the woman; Larkin in contrast submits himself humbly to her judgement. Clumsily, and uselessly, he intrudes on her grief at the moment of most intimate violation, as she lies 'out on that bed' in a room flooded with 'unanswerable' light. His impulse to share her suffering ('I can taste the grief') appears to him shamefully, uncomfortably egotistical: 'I would not dare / Console you if I could.'

Nevertheless he cannot stop himself putting himself in the rapist's place. She was, he insists, less deceived than he, 'stumbling up the breathless stair / To burst into fulfilment's desolate attic'. Larkin has chosen an extreme metaphor for his mistreatment of Ruth. Is he any better than this Victorian voluptuary abusing his sixteen-year-old victim in his quest for ultimate fulfilment? In an indirect apology, the poet implicitly casts his choice of art over marriage as a rape. And his new-found frank masculinity leads him into what some have read as an apology for rape itself.[32] But the poet makes no claim that the deceived rapist suffers in any way comparable to the less deceived victim. In this traumatic negative aubade the rapist is simply more 'deceived' than she is. The poet is all too aware how lame an excuse this sounds.

Characteristically Larkin followed this stressful self-examination, five days later (25 February), with one of his most serenely beautiful poems, 'Coming' (originally titled 'February'). In something close to free verse, the poet describes a subtle epiphany of existential joy in unobtrusively indicative dimeters and trimeters, unrhymed except for the repeated 'soon' at the centre of the poem ('It will be spring soon') which acts as its emotional fulcrum.

His emotional life was now firmly set on an opposite course from that of the now married but still sexually predatory Amis. As Richard Bradford comments, Larkin must have found Amis's callous assumption that his new wife was in 'contented ignorance' of his infidelities both 'farcical and odious'.[33] Hilly wrote to Philip on 3 March 1950, saying that she was 'simply wild' with jealousy about Philip's involvement 'with this school girl or who ever she is'. Kingsley, she writes, is chasing after other girls, 'Barbara and Terry', while their friend James Michie has a Jamaican girlfriend. She, in contrast, lacks romantic adventures. Kingsley has just departed for the weekend. 'They are having a party on Sat. Night & I'm sure K will "do" all the pretty women there, & here am I stuck at Sketty, Swansea where *all* the men are dull, stupid & too short.' She continues: 'I've got a weekend off in April when I shall be going to London, I dream that I'm meeting you there, & that we'll have loads to drink & then go to bed together, but alas, only a dream.' She ends, 'Lots of love sweet meat – remember no more women – unless it's Hilly x x x x'.[34] Whether or not she was serious, she knew well that Philip would never take the risk of becoming involved with a friend's wife who, moreover, had recently become a mother.

Larkin initiated his second workbook later that month, gluing a photograph of Thomas Hardy on the inside cover above the axiom 'The ultimate aim of a poet should be to touch our hearts by showing his own.'[35] Not surprisingly, given his situation at the time, the first two poems in the new book, revised later in *XX Poems* under the heading 'Two Portraits of Sex', express disillusion. Their contrasted styles wittily imitate the techniques of the visual artist. 'Oils', based on the template of George Herbert's poem 'Prayer', has the wet, rich colour of oil painting; 'Etching' has the dry, acid-traced black on white lines of that very different technique. Nevertheless the theme is the same: sex as the awesome wellspring of existence driving its victims to expend themselves in desire and procreation. In 'Oils', Larkin employs the gaudy imagery of his 'Apocalyptic' manner and a bardic gravity of tone borrowed from Dylan Thomas. A Layardian shaman shakes his magic weed as he dances, while the second stanza takes us into the womb ('Working-place to which the small seed is guided'). At this point the poet's gravity falters. The indelicate line 'Inlet unvisited by marine biologist' is surely a joke. However, he recovers his aplomb, and there is real archetypal force in the strange slow-motion spondaic beat of 'New voice saying new words at a new speed'. The third stanza obscurely laments the iron grip of sex on life, its control even extending to 'the dead' whom death grips and 'begin[s] to use'. Presumably this is a strained way of saying that the organic matter of life is constantly recycled between the living and the dead.

Though the manner of 'Etching' is reductive and ironic, paradoxically it conveys a more intense mood of mythic seriousness than 'Oils'. The crude punning title ('Etching' / 'itching') relieves the poet of the burden of high seriousness, which means that he can get away with extravagant rhetoric in his evocation of the diffused poignancy of orgasm ('The wet spark comes, the bright blown walls collapse, // But what sad scapes we cannot turn from then'). The pretentiousness of 'Oils' is humanized and imbued with pathos. The final lines give an archetypal vision of an impossible imagined 'padlocked cube of light' where sex obtains no right of entry. Marvell's masculinist vision of an Eden where man 'walked without a mate', before the cycle of procreation had begun, is reimagined in terms of modern psychology. Larkin later detached 'Etching' from its less rhetorically secure companion-piece and in *The Less Deceived* it appears under the sexually suggestive title 'Dry-Point' with a sly implied reference to the drinking toast: 'here's lead in your pencil'.

In a pattern repeated several times in his later work, Larkin followed this complex exertion with a very different poem drafted to completion on a single page, 'The Literary World'. This dry indictment of the selfish sexual politics of the male writer, his only free-verse poem, shows virtually no corrections and is dated decisively at the bottom of the page '20/3/50'. He left it unpublished. After this he spent seven pages drafting a poem with a purely descriptive theme, 'Consider the race of birds'.[36] Despite some fine lines it remained uncompleted: 'A nesting thrush pecks up stray fibrous strands / And dashes off. A blackbird faces evening, / Shuddering with vehemence.'

The more personal mood-piece, 'Saturday' or 'Spring and bachelors', retitled 'Spring' in *The Less Deceived*, was completed on 19 May, its drafts overlapping with the bird-meditation. This, the first of the four published mature sonnets, is a complex work, and took more than nine pages of drafting. The first line seems a description of an impressionist painting – 'Green-shadowed people sit, or walk in rings' – and if it were not for the deadpan tone, the visual details would evoke a joyful spring awakening: the calm cloud, the singing bird, the sun 'flashing like a dangled looking-glass', the 'branch-arrested mist of leaf'. There is a contradictory youthful élan about the poet's self-disgust at the end of the octave: 'and me, / Threading my pursed-up way across the park, / An indigestible sterility'. The five accents of the pentameter line are compacted into just two polysyllabic Latinate words, to give an effect of verbal constipation. The reader is forced to stretch out the recitation and dwell on the mean rhyme ('me / sterility'), making the tone snide and aggressive. This perverse effect is highly enjoyable, and it is easy to see that, despite its youthful moodiness, this is after all still a *prima vera* celebration, a traditional lyrical welcome to the most 'gratuitous' of seasons, with its 'fold of untaught flower' and 'race of water'. Paradoxically the less deceived sourness of the poet's tone serves only to intensify the sense of the sweetness of the season, evoked with Keatsian richness and gorgeous sound-writing reminiscent of Hopkins. This ironic contrast between the poet's alienated despair and the freshness of spring is familiar from Shakespeare, Gray and T. S. Eliot. April, with its challenge to our deepest vitality, is indeed the cruellest month.

'If, My Darling', completed four days later on 23 May 1950, is, like 'Deceptions', a dramatic monologue addressed to an innocent woman by a self-critical man. But here the tone is comic rather than tragic. The poem shows the crucial role played by Larkin's relationship with Monica Jones in the development of his new demotic register. The endearment 'my darling' is companionable and intimate. The darling wears a 'float-ing skirt' like Alice in Lewis Carroll. Photographs of Monica at the time show her in a bell skirt.[37] In the title, the heavily stressed 'If' is followed by a deliberate comma, suggesting a provocative question, even a threat. Well, the poet seems to be saying, if you are prepared to take me on, you had better understand what you are letting yourself in for. This humorous combativeness is new to Larkin's poetry. The darling's cosy inner room of imagination has a prissy feel recalling the pathetic insecurity of Margaret Peel in Amis's *Lucky Jim*. The real

Monica, however, will have relished the witty caricature of Victorianism in the mahogany claw-footed sideboards, the 'small-printed books for the Sabbath', the bibulous butler and lazy housemaids which the poet preposterously suggests furnish the inner room of her mind. There may be Amisian hostility in the poem's gauche surliness, but this is subverted by Larkinesque empathy.

The poet's own inner room is a mélange of mediated stereotypes. The higher call of art is imaged crudely as a Grecian statue 'kicked in the privates' and his 'finer feelings' are nothing more than swill fit for a pig. Mixed metaphor swamps the poem and the poet stumbles into incoherence in his eagerness to make as sordid an impact as possible. Judging by the vigorous crossings-out and scribblings in the workbook draft, Larkin spent much energy on perfecting the unhinged metaphorical register of geometry and disease found nowhere else in his poetry. Lit by monkey-brown light, a 'string of infected circles' loiter like bullies, and then 'coagulate'.[38] The geometrical abstractions of his mental processes are soiled and dirtied by his despicable desires. He concludes that if she were aware of his guilty inner secrets she would be knocked 'off her unpriceable pivot'.[39] Deep in the subtext there is an intimate challenge, and in some sense, one must conclude, this is a seduction poem. Philip had, it seems, gauged Monica's temperament well. She was, like him, a complex person, chary of the ingenuous commitments of conventional morality. In an interview at the very end of her life she commented:

> I was really surprised when I learned about it [Larkin's engagement].
> *Did you resent the fact that he didn't tell you about Ruth?*
> No. Not at all! I didn't think he was straightforward.
> *What if he had been? Could you have liked him?*
> I don't think so.[40]

But for the moment Larkin's first priority was not this new relationship. He was intent on securing an escape from his entanglements. An extravagant weariness haunts 'Wants' (2 June 1950). The poet is oppressed by the invitation-cards, 'the printed directions of sex', the family photograph, the life insurance: 'Beneath it all, desire of oblivion runs.' His application for a post in London was rejected, so he applied in late May 1950 for a sub-librarianship at Queen's University Belfast. In early June he crossed by ferry for the interview and, somewhat to his surprise, was appointed. He was to take up his new position in September. He had no connection with the city or the Province, so would be making a bold new start. But though he had taken the decisive step, he still havered. On 17 June, imagining confusedly that 'Ruth and I could start life afresh in a far countrie,' he made 'a garbled proposal of marriage'. But he knew that he could not take Ruth with him, writing the following day to Sutton: 'Now today I cannot think what maggot was in my brain to produce such a monstrous egg.'[41] Only three days after he made his proposal he withdrew it: 'I grabbed back as many of my words as I could and ate them hurriedly, encountering a good deal of scorn and anger in the process, which was understandable enough.'[42] Nevertheless on 3 July he was still contemplating a Lawrentian plunge into commitment: 'Christ knows what I'm going to do. I feel D.H.L. wd sum it all up in a few words. ". . . meanwhile Philip gnawed his fingers, being a Willy Wetleg, and tried to decide whether A Woman was worth more to him than His Art. His most fundamental feeling was one of surprise that any woman should be prepared to marry him at all."'[43]

By the end of July, however, he had finally disentangled himself: 'Despite my fine feelings, when it really comes down to terms of furniture & loans from the bank something unmeltable & immoveable rises up in me – something infantile, cowardly, regressive. But *it won't be conquered*. I'm a romantic bastard. Remote things seem desirable. Bring them close, & I start shitting myself.'[44] Only now, following the break with Ruth, did he begin a physical relationship with Monica Jones. He felt he could take the risk, since he would be in Belfast and Monica in Leicester, so their relationship would necessarily assume what was for him the ideal form: a written correspondence. He would be in control of the time and occasion of any communication, and the relationship could develop without the pressures of physical proximity.

The task of disentangling himself from his mother was also stressful.

His sister Kitty and he made arrangements for the furniture in 12 Dixon Drive to be put in store in anticipation of its sale. On 4 September Eva moved in with her daughter at 53 York Road, Loughborough, though, in her own mind at least, this was only until she could join her son in Belfast. Indeed it was not until more than a year after her move, that she abandoned this hope when a house was bought for her a few doors away from Kitty at 21 York Road. She moved in in December 1951, and was to stay there for the next two decades until she was admitted to Berrystead Nursing Home in 1972.

Larkin was determinedly freeing himself of his responsibilities and their associated guilts. In June 1950 he wrote a self-consciously literary poem, 'Under a splendid chestnut tree', in which three vaguely stereotypical characters, a rector, a schoolboy and a spinster, each suffer from grotesque irrational guilts which spoil their lives. The sour 'Who called love conquering', completed a few weeks later, obscurely laments the vulnerability of love to selfishness. But Larkin was beginning to fight free. On 30 July 1950 he wrote to Sutton that, having listened on the radio to that 'gloomy convincing piece of bullshit', Kafka's *The Trial*, he was determined that his life must change. He was even beginning to question his allegiance to D. H. Lawrence: 'The other night, like a curate in the depths of misery blaspheming against the Almighty, I wrote a short hostile article about D.H.L.'s "freedom".' Why is it, Larkin asked himself, that Lawrence '*never*, seriously or in jest, suggests that he may become a father'?[45] Did he perhaps know that fatherhood was biologically impossible for him? That might explain his strangely uncomplicated attitude towards marriage. Larkin had earlier commented that, though Lawrence declared 'Thank God I'm not free, any more than a rooted tree is free,' it is 'hard to see how he could have been less encumbered in the affairs of life'.[46]

Larkin's impending escape from his own encumbrances also led him to confront his failure to become a novelist. In his letters to Sutton and to Amis of 1948–9 his tone in referring to 'my novel' had become more and more despairing. On 7 March 1950, Amis consoled his friend for his failure to make progress:

Yes, I am sorry about your lack of novel. Sam Wagstaff has finally gone
for a Burton, has he? I'm sorry to hear it, because I thought you were on
to rather a good thing there. I must say that in your shoes I shd. very
likely be so overjoyed at the prospect of being published that I would
(?shd.) be willing to write any old nonsense and send it in.[47]

Now, as he prepared to leave for Belfast, Larkin made a complicated
attempt to theorize his failure in the strange form of a dialectical
playlet, or as he called it a 'débat inédit', 'Round the Point'. Geraint
and Miller, representing different aspects of his own personality,
wrangle over Geraint's failure to write his second novel. Coming
upon his friend tearing up his latest draft, Miller tries to persuade
him to abandon his literary ambitions in favour of a life of ordinary
satisfactions: 'a good easy lucrative job, three bouncing mistresses in
quick succession and then a wife uniting all their good qualities along
with a few of her own, and a house by the sea'.[48] But the idealistic
Geraint desires only to write, though to his dismay he is unable to do
so. With Shavian incisiveness Miller tells him that this is because he
lacks the necessary qualities: massive self-approval, a thick skin and
the conviction of the importance of 'some urgent conception of the
universe and the state of man', which, though inevitably 'arrant tosh',
is necessary to give the writer the stubborn impetus to continue.[49]
Geraint counters with a vision of the artist as 'feminine' and 'passive',
recording experience like the wax of a record or litmus-paper.[50] Miller
concludes, 'your place is in the old ivory tower really', as he kicks the
wastepaper-basket into the auditorium and the curtain falls on the
resulting snowstorm of novel scraps.[51]

The protagonists of the unfinished novels, Sam Wagstaff and Augusta
Bax, were both to have escaped to the new world of the USA. The
actual new world in which Larkin embarked on his self-renewal was
not so far off, nor so exotic. It was none the less a dramatic move for the
young poet. A self-pitying poem of pessimistic anticipation, 'Twenty-
eight, I have walked the length of my mind', petered out after nine
pages of drafting. He was ready for a new start. On Saturday 30
September he embarked at Liverpool for his new life. In 'Single to

Belfast', a poem whose fourteen pages of drafts never reached completion, he put the past behind him:

> the present is really stiffening to past
> Right under my eyes,
>
> And my life committing itself to the long bend
> That swings me, this Saturday night, away from my midland
> Emollient valley, away from the lack of questions,
> Away from endearments [. . .][52]

He could neither marry nor become a novelist. He pushed to the back
of his life his mother's demands, his Lawrentian guilts and his desire to
'be that girl'. Whether he was yet prepared to admit it to himself or not,
his novelistic ambitions were over. In the freer environment of Belfast
he was, as a poet, to dash forward like Auden's hussar. Ireland helped to
renew his sense of himself, and the next few years were to be among the
happiest in his life.

9

The Best Writing Conditions
1950–2

In a long chatty letter to Monica Jones of 1 October 1950 Larkin relished his 'first day in Ireland'. He described his drab lodging in Queen's Chambers, close by the University, grumbled amiably that the green of his candles would clash with the newly painted walls, noted that the roast beef at lunch 'was as pedestrian as a centipede' and lamented that no food was available after seven o'clock. But his complaints barely conceal his exhilaration at starting life afresh in this room of his own:

> No, heark 'ee, cully, this room is grossly underfurnished, the lampshade is made of brown paper, the bulbs are too weak, the noise from the trams tiresome, the sixpenny meter for heat will prove expensive, the students ubiquitous, the servants iniquitous (where's the strap from my suitcase?). Michael Innes[1] speaks somewhere of the combination of refined luxury and barbarous discomfort that is the Oxford don's life: it is the Belfast don's life, too, except for the refined luxury.[2]

There is a sense in this first Belfast letter that he is setting the tone for a substantial future correspondence. Monica is to provide the sounding-board for his responses to his new environment. He ends on an intimate but respectful note:

I hope too your room doesn't look sad & lonely now my lethargic cadging figure isn't in it. Truly I shall always remember the fireplace & the cricket-bin & all the battery of things on the mantelpiece, Fifi & blue Neddy & the flowered lamp. Your life there has come into extremely sharp focus for me now: heating milk, singing in the kitchen, drying stockings, etc.

A burst of nostalgia follows: 'I loved every time I visited you, & do want to thank you again & again for being so kind, so gracious & so generous.'[3] As letters like this arrived regularly over the following months and years it is not surprising that Monica allowed their unresolved long-distance relationship to become a permanent feature of her life.

A serial letter of 28–30 November 1950[4] runs to fourteen sides, complete with a sketch of his room, and a cartoon of a shop-girl refusing to allow him to look through a newly arrived pile of Jazz Collector and Tempo records: 'May I look through these'; 'Oi'd rather you didn't.' He rages: 'cow of Hell! I have never seen any before, & Belfast is the last place I expected to find them.'[5] In the drawing he has accidentally given himself a round-shouldered stoop and huge nose, and writes in the margin: 'This looks like an anti-semitic cartoon in *Die Stürmer*.'[6] The letter ends with a spirited sketch of Monica, seen from behind and above, in her academic gown, flourishing a cigarette. His letters to Monica focus on descriptions of his latest or next anticipated meal, gossip about colleagues, sympathy over her work, fears that guilt will force him to allow his mother to join him in Belfast, and comments on cricket and boxing, Monica's favourite sports. On 7 June 1951 he begins with a delightful sketch of Monica as a rabbit in an apron cooking over a brazier in her burrow, and follows with a vivid sketch of himself exploding across the page at all angles with a sneeze of hay-fever.[7] Monica's letters were often longer than his. In May 1951 he comments that her last letter is 'one of the longest I've ever received, about 7000 words, the length of a couple of short stories or half a dozen *Times* leaders'.[8]

Literature is the predominant theme. In an idiom laced with phrases in French and references to Verlaine, Mallarmé, Flaubert and Montherlant, he discusses the latest book he has read, moving smoothly from Llewellyn Powys to Mrs Gaskell to Oscar Wilde to George Bernard Shaw to D. H. Lawrence to Cyril Connolly to Frances Hodgson Burnett and Beatrix Potter. He exclaims that he longs to know what she thinks of Katherine Mansfield's letters.[9] This is not, however, a correspondence of literary or intellectual equals. Though she shared Philip's love of the English poetic canon, Monica's perspectives were narrower than his. When asked late in life about Théophile Gautier's *Mademoiselle de Maupin*, she recollected:

> I know that I borrowed it from Philip, early on, but I'm not sure I read it. Later I should have had more confidence in my own judgement and therefore wouldn't have read it.
> *How do you mean?*
> Well. I wouldn't be reading a foreign book.[10]

He invited Monica's comments on his poems. She particularly liked 'Spring' and 'Wedding-Wind': 'it's a lovely title, breathing Hardy and Housman'.[11] However she rarely offered advice, and when she did, he did not take it. In June 1951 she warned him against an 'easy lazy flatness you must watch' and hesitantly detected a 'tiny threat' of this in the third stanza of 'At Grass'. He responded vigorously, allowing that there will be a 'prosaic quality' in some of his poetry, 'though I don't find it in the spot you indicate in *At grass* –'.[12]

Larkin rose to the professional challenges of his new post in what he called 'the book barn'. He was put in charge of the Queen's Library issue desk and 'Readers' Services'. A strong mutual respect developed between him and the Librarian, Jacob ('Jack') Graneek, the son of émigrés who had fled a pogrom in Russia. Outsiders from England and elsewhere formed, with Jewish intellectuals like Graneek, a cultural island in the College amid the surrounding sectarianism.[13] Larkin's social life in Queen's was pleasant and stimulating. He learnt bridge from Ansell Egerton of the Economics Department and Alec Dalgarno of Mathematics. In the evenings he would join a group of male colleagues in the Senior Common Room bar, among them Alan Grahame from History, Evan John from Music and Arthur Terry from Spanish. He and Terry widened their horizons by borrowing books from the Library to read overnight and then exchange with each other next day. It was in the course of this reading spree, as Terry later told Motion, that Larkin declared Laforgue's 'Winter Coming On' to be 'the poem I've been trying to write all my life'.[14] It was a stimulating environment for a young poet. Larkin later recalled: 'The best writing conditions I ever had were in Belfast, when I was working at the University there. Another top-floor flat, by the way. I wrote between eight and ten in the evenings, then went to the University bar till eleven, then played cards or talked with friends till one or two.'[15]

In the month following his arrival, determined to rescue his poetic career from the disaster of *In the Grip of Light*, he put together a new collection of poems. Fearing further rejection he determined on self-publication. Housman had, after all, published *A Shropshire Lad* at his own expense. He approached Carswells, a jobbing printer in Belfast, who undertook to produce a booklet for him. On 16 January 1951 he discussed the title in a letter to Monica:

> originally I'd thought of *20 poems for nothing*, but Kingsley shuddered at it: said it was like Roy Campbell. Now I can't think of another: do you think that is so bad? Apart from all the impossible kinds of title, I don't like the drab kind (*Poems*), or the self-denigrating kind (*Stammerings*), or the implied-conceit kind (*Moments of Vision*), or the clever kind (*Stasis*) [. . .] I want something unaffected & unpretentious – for Lord knows there are few to pretend anything about.[16]

He rejected *Speaking from Experience* as sounding like 'broadcast talks by the Radio Padre', and concluded briskly: 'I don't *ask* for advice because in such matters I should be extremely unlikely to take it.'[17] Ultimately he chose the austere *XX Poems*, telling Monica that the title was 'as free from offence as I can manage, & with a slight undercurrent of Guinness double X and Ezra Pound's *Cantos*'.[18] He dedicated it to

Amis. On 27 April 1951, he took delivery of 100 copies, joking that it was printed 'on what I privately called grocer's wrapping paper'.[19]

It is a sign of how rapidly Larkin's poetic self-image was developing at this time that only three pieces were carried forward from *In the Grip of Light*: 'There is an evening coming in' ('Going'), 'The Dedicated' and 'Wedding-Wind'. The new works were: 'Waiting for breakfast', 'Modesties', 'At Grass', 'Even so distant' ('Deceptions'), 'Coming', 'Two Portraits of Sex', 'Spring', 'If, My Darling', 'Wants', 'Who called love conquering' and six poems written since his move to Belfast: 'Since we agreed' (later titled 'No Road'), 'The widest prairies' ('Wires'), 'Since the majority of me', 'Arrival', 'Always too eager for the future' ('Next Please') and 'Latest Face'. In retrospect *XX Poems* seems a trial run for *The Less Deceived*, thirteen of the poems ultimately being carried forward to the later volume.[20] Larkin sent copies to a number of established literary figures who he hoped might review it, including Cyril Connolly and John Lehmann. Later he joked ruefully that the postal rate had just changed and he had put the wrong stamps on the envelopes.[21] His worst apprehensions were realized. Charles Madge was the only recipient to make any response. He passed his copy on to D. J. Enright, who reviewed it in the Catholic journal the *Month*, the only notice it received.[22] Seldom has great poetry been so ignored on its first appearance.

Several of the more recently written poems, dating from the end of 1950 and the beginning of 1951, show what Larkin called his new 'more vernacular' style, basing themselves on proverbs or everyday verbal tags.[23] The metaphor in 'No Road' is, for example, so natural and obvious as scarcely to seem a metaphor at all. The road is 'so little overgrown, / Walking that way tonight would not seem strange, / And still would be allowed'. The tone is conversational, but the syntax becomes tangled as the poet's guilt and embarrassment intensify. In a strained infinitive construction he tells his former lover that it is his 'liberty' to watch 'a world where no such road will run / From you to me' as it rises 'like a cold sun'. The final lopsided couplet stammers with Hardyesque awkwardness:

> Not to prevent it is my will's fulfilment.
> Willing it, my ailment.

With a listless wordplay ('will's / Willing'), pentameter runs into abrupt trimeter, and the poem ends on the wearily offhand misrhyme 'fulfilment / ailment'. The ten high short 'i' or 'e' syllables, and seven 't' sounds in these two lines force the poet's self-distaste aggressively on the reader.

'Wires', based on the familiar saying 'the grass is always greener on the other side of the fence', was drafted to completion on a single page of the workbook, on 4 November 1950. Clearly pleased with the feat, he told Monica that it was written 'straight off before breakfast, in pyjamas'.[24] On the surface it shows little sign of rhetorical ambition. But it is in fact a verbal device of polished artifice. It has the wittily patterned form of a seventeenth-century 'emblem', like the poems by George Herbert in the shape of wings or an altar. Larkin's pattern is more discreet. In the first quatrain the cattle approach the electrified wire apparently without the constraint of rhyme (abcd). They then rebound in the second quatrain, which recoils from the middle repeated word 'wires' (representing a two-strand fence?) as a hidden rhyme scheme makes itself heard (dcba), reversing the first quatrain. The young steers end where they started, except that their encounter with the wires has now made them into old cattle. The fences are now incorporated into their senses.

Larkin commented on 'Wires' to Monica, 'well, just a little verse: no wings'.[25] 'Absences', in contrast, all but completed at the end of the same month, is one of his most sublime works. The first page of drafting beautifully evokes a deserted seascape in delicate phrases which were to undergo much rewriting before the final version:

> Rain patters on the sea, water to waters,
> A small sound in a giant afternoon,
> A sighing floor provoked to tiny craters
>
> And rough winds rub the gloss off water-dunes
> Running like walls, floundering into hollows [. . .][26]

But he hesitated to take poetic wing. Compelled to answer every mood and gesture with its extreme opposite he devoted the following page, headed at the top left *Verlaine*, to a translation of that author's 'À Mademoiselle ***' (*Parallèlement*, 1889):

> Country beauty
> That one has in corners,
> You relish the harvests,
> Flesh and the summer [. . .]
>
> Your swaggering calves,
> Your tempting shoulders –
> And, high-spirited, cheeky,
> Your firm fat bum,
>
> They set in our blood
> A soft stupid fire
> That drives us crazy
> Arse, balls and belly [. . .][27]

The seven dimeter quatrains of Verlaine's original are translated virtually word for word, reproducing faithfully the studied French 'vernacular' of the original.[28] Larkin's new demotic register, it seems, has French as well as English origins. The work occupies a single page (the final stanza being in a second column), suggesting that it may have been dashed off in one sitting. Though there is no attempt to reproduce Verlaine's abba rhyme-scheme, the translation is all but complete; only one word in the penultimate stanza defeated him.[29]

Having, as it were, given himself licence for sublimity by this straight talking, he resumed work on the poem which was to become 'Absences'.[30] It seems that it could have taken a very different direction from the final version. In the workbook the description of the sea, 'tirelessly at play / Where there are no ships and no shallows', is conceived as a consoling daydream of escape from a Kafkaesque courtroom of humiliation. This reassertion of anxious reality was still part of his conception when he briefly revisited the drafting in early 1951. What was to become the resounding final line features as the first line of a *terza rima* stanza:

> Such attics cleared of me! Such absences!
> Such courtroom consolations in a case
> Made up of stale inaudibilities
>
> With somewhere guilt. The thought of any place
> Uncheapened by this vague drawn out disgrace[31]

Ultimately, however, Larkin's symbolist instincts won the day and the courtroom context and the sonnet form were dropped. Three sumptuously pararhymed *terza rima* stanzas and a final isolated line make up a miniature, ten-line sublime ode in the tradition of Coleridge's 'Hymn before Sunrise, in the Vale of Chamouni' or Shelley's 'Mont Blanc'. The poet is rapt out of himself by the idea of a place beyond human observation. As Larkin commented, 'I am always thrilled by the thought of what places look like when I am not there.'[32] Graham Chesters has speculated that the final exclamation may have been suggested by Gautier's 'Sublime aveuglement! magnifique défaut!' in his poem 'Terza Rima',[33] a more elevated example of Gallic lyricism than Verlaine's 'À Mademoiselle ***'. Baudelaire's celebrated 'L'Homme et la Mer' has a similar rhetorical climax: 'Ô lutteurs éternels, ô frères implacables!' Larkin later joked that his poem 'sounds like a slightly unconvincing translation from a French symbolist', adding, 'I wish I could write like this more often.'[34]

Though in other poems of the period he jealously guards his selfhood, here he contemplates a selfless nirvana. The accusing, 'unanswerable' light of 'Deceptions' loses its human, moral quality to become an impersonal 'shoreless day'. And instead of bursting into a sordid attic of fulfilment we are left contemplating sublime attics of emptiness. The violated 'attic' of 'Deceptions' was squalid and humiliating; the uninhabited 'attics' of 'Absences' are exhilarating. The two appearances of the word mark the furthest extremes of emotion which the concept evoked in Larkin, and it was a sure instinct that told him not to use 'attic' again in any subsequent published poem.[35] It seems that he felt doubtful at first about the poem's unabashed transcendence. He omitted 'Absences' from *XX Poems*, though he did include the sulkily argumentative 'Since the majority of me', on which he worked immediately afterwards. 'Absences' certainly did not show the gloomy pessimism which had become a private joke in his letters to Monica: 'we are all on a one way trip to the grave, etc. etc. etc. My usual style.'[36] Monica was the touchstone of his deepest gloom: 'I was struck again by the genuine quality of your pessimism: I play at pessimism but you really are a pessimist.'[37]

In 'Next, Please', on which he worked in January and early February 1951, Larkin plays the pessimist with some gusto.[38] Life, the poet tells us with mock-heroic didacticism, is like queuing:

> Always too eager for the future, we
> Pick up bad habits of expectancy.

The singsong chiming of 'we / expectancy' has a facile self-mockery about it. Cinema clichés embody the ersatz inauthenticity of our dreams. We imagine that a 'Sparkling armada of promises' is headed our way. One day our ship will surely come in, its figurehead gleaming 'with golden tits', as in a Hollywood romance starring Errol Flynn. But in a witty contrast of mediated images, archetype trumps stereotype, and we are sought out by an altogether more sombre metaphorical ship: 'a black- / Sailed unfamiliar', towing behind it a 'huge and birdless silence'. It is a most original and enjoyable exercise on a familiar theme.

A similar proverbial tag underlies 'To My Wife', completed on 19 March 1951. The husband has preferred the fulfilment of a bird in the hand to contemplation of the numerous tease-birds flapping in the bushes. He has given up the Yeatsian 'mask-and-magic-man's regalia' of poetry in return for the wife, who has become, in an excruciatingly sardonic rhyme, 'my boredom and my failure'. The poet feels grim empathy with the woman who shares the disappointment of marriage with him: 'No future now. I and you now, alone.' Larkin did not include this poem in *XX Poems*, perhaps considering it a touch contrived.

'Latest Face', drafted in February 1951, adopts a more elevated tone. Shortly after his arrival in Belfast, Larkin's eye was caught by Winifred Arnott, a twenty-one-year-old Library Assistant who had arrived a month before him. Their relationship was never to develop beyond a romantic friendship, but for this very reason this is one of the most poetically productive of all his liaisons. Winifred indeed became the second of Larkin's muses. 'Latest Face' gives a classic exposition of aestheticist philosophy:

> Admirer and admired embrace
> On a useless level, where
> I contain your current grace,
> You my judgement [. . .]

Like the 'angled beauty' of the Polish airgirl in 'Like the train's beat' this depersonalized, ungendered face dispels 'all humanity of interest'. It does not belong to a 'wife', nor to a 'darling'. It is a Platonic Form, or more romantically a 'precious vagrant': 'useless'. It imposes no demands or obligations. The poet has no desire to possess this bird in the bush. Indeed, he fears what might ensue should 'The statue of your beauty walk', not wishing to wade behind the woman into the 'real untidy air' of 'Bargains, suffering, and love'. There is an ambiguity, however. Winifred's name appears over and over again on the last page of the draft, and though the poet wishes to avoid bargains and suffering there is a hint of warm mutuality in the poem's tone.

In the 'real' world outside the muse-relationship of the poems, this was a friendship bordering on courtship. In retrospect, Winifred played down the suggestion of a romantic attachment: 'He was a working colleague, seven years older than me, already balding. I was 21. I didn't think of him like that.'[39] They would meet over coffee, gossip about mutual friends, and at the weekends she would join him on long bicycle rides in the countryside. 'I think he liked me because I was cheerful.'[40] 'I don't remember him *ever* being sad,' she commented, and added, 'when he expressed melancholy I think everyone took it to be a pose'.[41] The decisive factor for her was his negative attitude towards marriage: 'I never did regard him as a candidate for my husband and the father of my children. I felt our relationship was of a different sort. We never went to bed together though I cheered him up, I think. I was very fond of him.'[42] On the other hand she remembers several conversations in spring 1951 beginning 'If you were married to me . . .'[43] The development of their relationship was, however, suspended when Winifred left for London in August 1951 to take a year's postgraduate diploma course in Librarianship at University College. Philip immediately initiated a correspondence with her, and they met twice during his visits to London.

Within the closed academic world of the University, Larkin was becoming comfortably settled. In a letter to Monica of 13 June 1951 he accepted her envious perception of his 'effortless popularity', and listed his cynical strategies for being liked: 'Never contradict. Be pliable [. . .] Be funny.'[44] By all accounts he was a witty and entertaining companion, imitating the Belfast accent perfectly and always ready with amusing anecdotes. Though he remained essentially an outsider, the Protestant culture of the Province provided him with new experiences and images. In 'March Past', he appropriated the Ulster marching tradition to his own poetic purposes, excluding any mention of politics.[45] Indeed the benign, mock-heroic tone suggests that he might be recalling a Salvation Army march in Coventry. The march is presented in innocent, festive terms, as in an operetta:

> out of the street-shadow into the sun

>> Discipline strode, music bullying aside
>> The credulous, prettily-coloured crowd,
>> Evoking an over-confident, over-loud

>> Holiday where the flags lisped and beckoned [. . .]

Like the later 'To the Sea', the poem celebrates a public ritual of touching human solidarity. But the real theme of the poem seems to be more personal. The full-dress pomp of the march reproaches the poet with a glimpse of a world of glamorous perfection: 'Pure meetings, pure separations, / Honeycombs of heroic apparitions'.[46] This flimsy suggestion of a nobler life overwhelms him with

blind

> Astonishing remorse for things now ended
> That of themselves were also rich and splendid
> But, unsupported, broke, and were not mended –

Reading biographically it seems that Larkin blames himself for breaking off the 'rich and splendid' relationship with Ruth Bowman. He never attempted to publish this poem; possibly he felt that it relied too heavily on unexplained personal feeling. It is difficult to detect the 'rock-solid sense of national glory' which Tom Paulin finds in it,[47] or the 'burgeoning Orange sympathies' to which Andrew Motion refers.[48]

Less than two months after being charmed by this march Larkin was confronted by impure marchings which struck him as anything but poetic. In a letter to Monica of 12 July 1951, he gives a set-piece description of the annual Belfast Orange Day March, very much in the manner of one of D. H. Lawrence's travel essays. Cycling out to the 'nasty little suburb' of Finaghy he watches the Loyal Orange Lodges march by, with their huge silk banners. He is at first amused by the picturesque or absurd images: King William landing at Carrickfergus, the Battle of Aughrim, Protestants drowned in the River Bann ('this was a rather fetching one of plump naked ladies up to their waists in water being gesticulated at by Puritanical-looking fellows in green'). But as the ritual unfolds he is repelled and offended by its self-righteous moral fervour and bad taste. He notes on the banners 'strange symbolic scenes of young women on rocks, clutching at a huge cross ("Our Sole Hope & Refuge"), all done in this pink-yellow-and-purply High Church postcard style'. And he records how the bands of fifes, drums, brass, 'and even accordion', each kept a strong beat, all slightly out of time with each other:

The dominant impression from this endless tramping file of faces was of really-depressing ugliness. Slack, sloppy, sly, drivelling, daft, narrow, knobby, vacant, vicious, vulpine, vulturous – every kind of ugliness was represented not once but tenfold – for you've no idea how *long* it was. They started coming by at 12 noon: at 12.45 I was expecting the end, but no! we left for lunch at 1.15 & the parade didn't finish going by till 2. About 20,000 men in all shambled by, or 280 Lodges. It was a parade of staggering dullness (every face wore the same 'taking-himself-seriously' expression) & stupefying hypocrisy ('Civil & religious liberty' was a catchphrase much repeated, like Ridley & Latimer). Having seen it, I shall *not* see it again. But the drums go beating about the town all day.[49]

In a letter to his mother he drily spelled out the politics behind 'civil and religious liberty': '(i.e. denying civil & religious liberty to Catholics & Nationalists, & damn the Pope, etc.).'[50]

Larkin's new social life was beginning to develop complexities, and around this time he composed a prose interrogation of his misogamist self-possession in the form of 'Round Another Point', a companion *débat* to the playlet concerned with novel-writing of the previous year. Geraint declares that he has 'finished with sex', or rather with the painful rituals involved in its fruitless pursuit: Gillian's 'photograph album of all those filthy foreign towns she's been to, coffee made "a new way", and endless records of that neat little twerp Mozart'.[51] Miller suggests that his friend resorts to a brothel, but Geraint is too sensitive for this recourse. He fantasizes 'sex clubs, rather like tennis clubs, where men and girls could meet each other [. . .] Contraceptives would be on sale and beds available.'[52] Miller counters with an awesome vision of sex as an impersonal imperative in humanity's struggle against death:

On the cloud of innumerable centuries [Life] maintains a thin bright edge of sixty or seventy years. Death enlarges ceaselessly, hoping to obliterate it. But life equally expands, just managing to keep in the lead, and its golden mainspring is sex. Does that convey to you anything of its intense, its exciting all-importance?[53]

Geraint responds by rejecting both Nature, which after all sanctions 'bubonic plague and syphilis', and Society, which produces 'war and lynching-parties'. 'Nature baits the trap of marriage with the cheese of sex. Man wants to eat the cheese without getting nabbed.'[54] Miller appeals to sentiment. The 'ordinary fellow', he argues, actually enjoys having children, 'guiding their first tottering steps, and buying cricket-bats and fishingrods and partyfrocks'. He spells out Geraint's life choice: 'the intricacy, the delicacy, the variety of emotion on the one hand simply towers over the alternative sordid discharge of seed'. Geraint, he alleges, is stuck at an immature stage where 'the hootings of some deplorable "jam session" outshine the Jupiter' (Mozart's last symphony).[55] The phone rings and Miller tells the caller that Geraint would welcome a visitor. Realizing that Gillian is about to arrive Geraint gives a howl, swings about on the chandelier till it breaks, and as the curtain descends falls on top of his friend.

Philip's relationship with Monica was becoming more intimate and familiar. He occasionally felt Lawrentian impulses towards whole-hearted commitment. In a letter of 19 September 1951 he told her, 'I long to abandon myself entirely to someone else,' feeling asphyxiated by his 'monstrous infantile shell of egotism'.[56] However, his tone remains detached and analytical, and in other letters he stresses his need for solitude. From May 1951 onwards, imagery of rabbits becomes a recurrent feature of their correspondence. Letters begin 'Forepaws', 'Ears' or 'Bun' (Bunny-rabbit) in reference to their shared delight in the stories of Beatrix Potter. He adorns his letters with charming sketches of a rabbit in a skirt: watching cricket under a parasol, searching her room for lost scissors, playing croquet, sleeping under a huge mush-room in the rain (complete with slugs and dangling spiders), writing with a quill pen by candlelight. He depicts himself as a rather shapeless seal, in a schoolboy pun on 'sealed with wax' or 'sealed with affection' which goes back to his earliest family letters. His engaging self-drama-tizations and generous concern for Monica's well-being create a secure shared world. In September 1951 he was sent on a tour of universities in the North of England (Leeds, Hull and Durham) to study issue-desk layouts. He regretted being unable to make arrangements for them to meet during his tour, but gave her detailed accounts in his letters: 'there was a cinema in Hull called "The Monica"!'[57]

Back in Belfast his domestic situation improved when, on 13 October 1951, he moved to rooms at the top of 30 Elmwood Avenue. Here he had his own kitchen and could lock his room from the inside, a degree of privacy impossible in his previous accommodation in Queen's Chambers, where the warden enforced strict rules. He described his new arrangements in a letter to Winifred Arnott in London, as 'romantic attics – and delightful they are'. Here, he told her, he would be able to write his poems and play his records of jazz and Monteverdi.[58] His contentment with his new situation put him increasingly out of sympathy with his long-term correspondent James Sutton. Larkin was never to lose his respect for D. H. Lawrence, but he had moved beyond his friend's earnest Lawrentianism. He wrote to his mother that Jim was 'fuller and fuller of windy philosophical tosh about mankind'. Characteristically he added: 'However it shows a nicer, more unselfish nature than mine.'[59]

In a letter ('Sunday') loosely inserted at the end of the second workbook Jim recommends that his friend make a different choice of life:

> For instance physical work, perhaps farming, would surely tend to put to sleep your self conscious mind? Or you could see the world as a tramp – there are casual wards for tramps where they give you a huge sandwich at night & a huge sandwich in the morning, make you have a bath & ask no questions. At least I'm told these places still exist today. I'd be most willing to join you in either of these ventures.[60]

But farming or vagabondage held little attraction for Philip, engrossed as he was in poetry and social activities. He was content with simple, existential pleasures. In October he wrote to Jim: 'By the Gor the weather is fine these days – life turns and beckons to me like an underwater swimmer in a soundless tank, beguiling, impossible.'[61] It would be difficult to imagine a more poignant expression of happiness than this tiny prose poem. At the end of the year Jim paid a visit to Belfast, but Philip was too preoccupied with his own affairs to pay his old schoolfriend much attention. The following month their twelve-year correspondence came to an abrupt end. In his final letter of 21 January 1952 Larkin half apologized for having been 'unjustly neglectful of you during your stay', and reverting, perfunctorily, to their register of high seriousness, wished his friend good luck with his painting: 'if you go grinding away at yourself you will in the end attain an irreducible defiant value'. But this was no longer his idiom. Earlier in the letter he had given an insight into his relaxed, hedonistic mood: 'Every Sunday I wallow in the luxury of freedom, lying on my bed in sheer exultant laziness: to do that every day – Golly! One would feel like a great steaming manure heap in the sun, lazy, pregnant, valuable.'[62]

10

Single in Belfast
1952–3

In 1952 Larkin's self-possession came under threat from a new relationship. Patsy Strang was unlike any other woman in his life, with a sexually adventurous lifestyle and literary ambitions of her own. She was married to a lecturer in Philosophy at Queen's University, Colin Strang, whom Larkin had known briefly in Oxford. The Strangs had helped Larkin move to Elmwood Avenue in October 1951.[1] Patsy, twenty-two years old at this time, was a wealthy South African, the daughter of a diamond-mining magnate. She had read Medicine at Oxford and, inspired by the French tutor at Somerville, Enid Starkie, former lover of André Gide, she was determined to be a writer.[2] She had lived for a time in Paris. Philip gave nothing away in his description of Patsy to Monica in November 1951: 'She is (have you met her?) a large, pale, weak stomached girl, very nice, very charming, but a bit dependent on being with amusing people or in London, which means she spends a lot of time knitting and eating sweets which isn't good for her. She's a doctor.'[3] Winifred Arnott gives a rather different perspective: 'I was frightened of her. She would have quite despised me as a middle-class virginal wimp. She was experienced and sophisticated and rich.'[4]

Patsy's deepest wish was to devote her life to the service of a poet. Philip had told Winifred decisively, 'As far as I'm concerned, other men's wives are completely banned', and it is clear from the diary which

Patsy began on 9 May 1952, inspired by Philip's example, that she took the initiative. He was not, however, totally candid about his own commitments, presenting himself as less experienced than he was and playing down his relationship with Monica: 'You're only my second young lady, and look like being my last.'[5] Patsy's sophisticated cosmopolitanism appealed to the author of 'Femmes Damnées' and *The Kingdom of Winter*. It seems possible that the relationship was precipitated by Patsy's reading his diary when left alone in his room, a transgression which deeply upset him. She was, however, unfazed by its masculine revelations. Among Patsy's papers, now in the McFarlin Library Special Collections, University of Tulsa, is a photograph of the poet leering at a girlie magazine, presumably taken by her.[6]

It was to Colin and Patsy together that Philip wrote to share his enthusiasm for Paris, when he and Bruce Montgomery made a brief trip there in May 1952: 'The street is so noisy & the bed so warm I don't seem to sleep till about 4 a.m. or *want to*. My heart beats in a new, queer way & I daren't lie on my left side for fear of stopping it.' His senses were overwhelmed:

> On Friday night we drank till late, on Saturday we saw the Monet, drank what can only have been a bottle of champagne each in the Ritz bar & saw Benjamin Britten (this, to Bruce, was like being vouchsafed a vision of Martin Luther after years of devout Roman Catholicism), went up the Eiffel tower (never again for me!), & at night after a luxurious meal went to a night club where Bechet was reputed to be appearing. This proved fallacious in fact, but we did hear Claude Luter's band, which I knew from records & was pretty exciting at times. To balance this we intend hearing *Salome* on Monday (*Mayol* tonight . . .) always assuming we have enough money.[7]

When the Strangs returned to England for several months in the early summer of 1952, joint communication was replaced by more intimate letters addressed to Patsy alone. Ruth had been a cat; Monica was a rabbit; he addresses Patsy as 'Dearest Honeybear' or 'Dear Honeyguzzler' in reference to her sweet tooth.

Motion sees this as 'the most happily erotic of all his affairs'.[8] But happy eroticism had no place in Larkin's emotional repertoire. Nor was Patsy a happy person. Winifred relates that one of her standard topics of discussion with Philip was 'why Patsy was so miserable'.[9] In July 1952 Patsy arranged to return secretly to Belfast so that they could spend a weekend together. The visit coincided with the Orange parades, and her diary records that he was alarmed at every sound in the street, in case they might be discovered. Afterwards he wrote to apologize for his 'gibbering funk' that had 'come near to spoiling such a happy weekend, such as I've never had before'.[10] At the end of the month she wrote that she was pregnant by him. But before he could reply to her letter, she suffered a miscarriage. He had already begun an answer ('After feeling sorry & alarmed & guilty, I find it rather thrilling') when he received her second letter, and he continued in a somewhat brutal tone: 'I fancy you should be thankful [. . .] you wd have got pretty tired of "a lifetime of deceit", which really is what it would've turned out to be.'[11] He assumes without question that neither of them would have revealed the child's true paternity. He illustrates his letter with drawings of a seal smiling down on a baby seal, followed by a drawing of the seal waving goodbye to the baby. Perhaps his heartlessness was part of a strategy. By August he was already attempting to disentangle himself. Patsy proposed meeting when he returned to England to visit his mother. But he prevaricated.[12]

Whatever the complexities of their relationship, Patsy made Monica seem insular by comparison. The 'yearly frame' of Philip's and Monica's future relationship was beginning to establish itself: he saw her regularly in Leicester whenever he visited his mother in nearby Loughborough, and they took regular holidays together, though never beyond the British Isles, nor in company with anybody else. But it was by no means inevitable that this would become the permanent pattern of his life. Edgy, defensive, loud and with little interest in other people, Monica was not an easy companion. Anthony Thwaite remembers being baffled, when he first met her a few years later, that the urbane Philip should have paired himself with so socially inept and ungracious a partner. After a holiday in the Lake District in 1952, during which they visited Beatrix Potter's house at Sawrey, Philip allowed himself to express something of the exasperation she caused him. To soften the blow he told her to think of the advice as coming from the wise mother cat in Potter's *The Pie and the Patty-Pan*:

> in my view you would do much better to revise, drastically, the amount you say and the intensity with which you say it. You are vaguely aware of this already, aren't you? You say you 'chatter like a jay' – do you remember saying that, standing on a corner of Clarendon Park Road, after closing time, before catching your bus? – and that you talk 'tediously & unnecessarily': I don't say that exactly: what I do feel is that you've no idea of the *exhausting* quality of yourself in full voice. Perhaps I am unduly (morbidly?) sensitive, but it does affect me just in that way – I feel quite unable to answer, just that I want to go and be quiet somewhere. No doubt you can recall times when I seemed a bit grumpy at Grasmere![13]

He ventures so far as 'to make 3 rules', advising her to restrict herself to two or at the most three sentences at a time, to 'abandon *altogether* your harsh didactic voice, & use *only* the soft musical one (except in special cases)'; and not to 'do more than *glance* at your interlocutor (wrong word?) once or twice while speaking. You're getting a habit of *boring* your face up or round into the features of your listener – *don't* do it! It's most trying.' He realizes he has gone too far and tells her, 'Please don't *mind* what I say.'[14] But it is clear that he does hope she will mind what he says.

Despite the dissatisfactions, Philip remained loyal, and as time passed his developing routines with Monica assumed the aspect of a marriage in every sense except day-to-day cohabitation. In late October 1952, following a visit to Leicester, Monica suspected she might be pregnant. Having recently experienced the threat of Patsy's pregnancy and confident of his own precautions, his response was relaxed: '*really*, I must say I think the chances are *extremely* slender & remote of there being anything in the air. To my certain knowledge I was never within a mile of endangering you.' The alarm was soon over. A letter of the following day, 24 October, begins lightly: 'Dearest Bun, I'm so glad you're out of your worry! So now you can go about your lavender-drying with a cheerful heart.'[15]

The contrast between Monica's and Patsy's personalities focused itself in terms of their attitudes towards animals. A year earlier, in November 1951 Larkin had been startled by a mouse creeping out from behind the fireplace while he was writing to Monica: 'not very nice! First time I've seen him. He *scuttled* back on realizing he wasn't alone.' It is characteristic that he sees the situation from the animal's point of view. But the experience made him sad: 'This depresses me rather – Beatrix Potter's all very well in print but . . .'[16] Now, on 29 November 1952, he wrote to Monica that Patsy had denounced his sentimentalism, condemning Beatrix Potter as 'anthropomorphist', and accusing him 'of not liking animals at all, only Potter ones & ones on my mantelpiece'. Patsy's attack disconcerted him, but he followed his instinct and refused to be consistent: 'I was somewhat at a loss. I do sometimes feel ashamed of liking these sweet little bunnies, but the emotion is there & she [Potter] touches it [. . .] Of course I'm not going to *stop* reading Potter, because I can't defend myself, & I don't take my inability to do so very seriously anyway.'[17] It is notable that his serious animal poems avoid anthropomorphism in favour of detached empathy.

Philip's friendship with Winifred Arnott had been resumed follow-ing her return from London in September 1952. She lived some of the time with her uncle and aunt in Lisburn, eight miles from Belfast, and he would visit her there and play with her two young cousins.[18] He was eager that she should share his literary world, and when she suffered a short illness he lent her a thoughtful selection of five books: *Les Jeunes Filles* by Montherlant, *At Swim-Two-Birds* by Flann O'Brien (both of which she found too masculine for her taste), *Antigua Penny Puce* by Robert Graves, *Dusty Answer* by Rosamond Lehmann and *The Real Charlotte* by Somerville and Ross.[19] Then at the beginning of 1953 she returned from the vacation with the news that she was engaged to be married. In a letter to his mother, he depicts his feelings, with some sincerity perhaps, as those of a disappointed suitor: 'I am feeling a bit balked concerning her – my paw was raised to be brought down on her – and now she scuttles away into the shadow of a rock! Bah!'[20]

Winifred commented that at this point Philip 'became a whole lot more affectionate'.[21] In 'When she came on, you couldn't keep your seat', titled in the workbook 'He Hears that his Beloved has become Engaged', completed in February 1953, the poet reproaches his rival for appropriating his beloved's perfection. He himself has refrained from spoiling her untouched beauty by forcing himself upon her. The successful suitor, in contrast, has blundered straight in and joined the woman in the dance: '*fancying you improve her*'. To the poet such 'love' is only 'interference'. He complains in sulky italics, 'You'll only *change* her.' Like 'Latest Face', this is a very literary poem: a playful exposition of purist aestheticism. And the poet acknowledges, with a bad grace, that he is out of step with society: 'Still, I'm sure you're right.' The suitor is, after all, simply following the instincts of 'the ordinary fellow'. And Winifred herself was only too eager to be changed by marriage. The muse did not share her poet's aesthetic vision. He did not show this poem to her.

Meanwhile Patsy was vigorously acting out her own very different poetic myth, as the helpless victim of a doomed passion. On 16 December 1952 as she prepared to return to England at the end of term she wrote in her diary: 'no post, no job, no child, no home – nothing to look forward to but a few doubtful hours of anxious, taut "pleasure". Weeks of fretful, furtive planning for what, a long day's waiting – and a short night's panting and sobbing. Yet I shall do it all again – if possible.'[22] She was painfully aware that she was more committed than he, and was hurt by his failure to pay any attention to her own writing, beyond polite praise. He flattered her by implying that she, as an experienced self-confident cosmopolitan, was testing his timid limits, but he was not prepared to play the role dictated by her emotional needs. Later Monica Jones told Andrew Motion that Patsy had offered to leave her husband and 'look after Philip and do all the earning so that he could just write'.[23] This was not an arrangement that a man of Larkin's temperament could possibly have borne. His domestic bachelor routines were established, and in the letters to Monica he describes the prospect of tidying his own room with some relish.[24]

In a diary entry of 13 January 1953 Patsy anticipated her return to Belfast with melodramatic rhetoric: 'Desire is a deadly disease. I want I want – the demands vary but have we no other cry? [. . .] Oh Belfast – City of Dreadful Night.'[25] On 9 February she was driven to anguish by Larkin's cold artistic detachment: 'Man and Superman – the artist and the woman. Oh God – must it be as he says. Every natural impulse, then, must be twisted, concealed, mocked. Why? Why?'[26] It is difficult not to contrast this with Geraint's plea in 'Round Another Point': 'I'm not going to bed with [. . .] somebody's daughter who'll tell me she's "two people really" and demand a row and a reconciliation every week-end. I want to screw decent ordinary girls of my own sort without being made to feel a criminal about it.'[27] Tension was high when in April 1953 Philip, Winifred and Patsy all made part of a group which Alec Dalgarno drove to Dublin in his car to hear, appropriately enough perhaps, Wagner's *Tristan and Isolde*.[28] At Easter 1953 Larkin returned to the mainland for a month to visit his mother and Monica, but did not even telephone Patsy in Oxford. Then, when he brought Winifred to her birthday celebration in Belfast in late May, she felt hurt and jealous. The chemistry between Philip and Winifred was clearly apparent:

> Winifred came to dinner last night. She brought cheese biscuits and a box of chocolates [. . .] Did she hope to impress Philip with her generosity, or perhaps she realized she had not been invited because we wanted to see her. So she nearly bought a Bikini printed with cuttings from the News of the World – did she!entos[29]

In a droll clash of perspectives, Winifred remembers that Patsy's exotic food intimidated her and that Philip bent over and whispered subversively: 'Shall I ask for just an egg for you dear?' She has no recollection of the bikini.[30] Patsy attempted to rise above the situation, presenting her jealousy as superior detached philosophy: 'I was not aware of this power of our sex – it seems a cheap weapon, and not, I believe, a very durable one.'[31]

Preparing to leave Belfast at the end of May 1953 to spend the summer in Oxford, Patsy consoled herself with world-weary reflections on the failure of her grand passion: 'No two people travel the same route – they may go a few miles together now and then but it would be very foolish to assume that they will walk together for long [. . .] Still – a little company now and then is very welcome.'[32] She perhaps took heart from Philip's discontent with Monica, with whom he was to go to Skye in July: 'I must say I don't look forward to this bloody holiday', he told her; 'if I feel in as ugly a humour as at present it may be the last we take together. There seems no point in carrying on, if it's out of pure coward-ice as it mainly is. Well! This may be taking an unduly black view. We'll see.'[33] In fact it was the relationship with Patsy rather than that with Monica which was about to end. In August 1953 she wrote that her husband had been appointed to a post in Newcastle, and she was to remain in Oxford.[34] Once the pressure was released, Philip composed, on 6 August, a letter of generous valediction: 'So much of my content in the last two years was due to you [. . .] But oh dear, oh dear! You were so wonderful!'[35] The 'oh dears' hint at his dismay at the impropri-ety of the relationship, and the past tense ('you were') is decisive.

The day before this, 5 August, he had sent Monica a near-final version of 'Days', 'hardly a poem at all [. . .] a change from the old style'. It had been largely drafted early in 1951, and he had now completed it on a single page of the workbook. He was elaborately diffident about it: 'I shouldn't think there's much danger of yr taking it seriously, having just re-read it, but I can't rub it out.'[36] However, he was aware that he had written a timeless masterpiece: the imagist 'Going' reformulated in lighter vein. The *faux naïf* poet asks, 'What are days for?' and answers himself disarmingly, eliding time with place, 'Days are where we live.' That is, of course, until priest and doctor, vividly pictured without explanation 'Running over the fields', usher us away. The poem could be twee; but it isn't. Rarely have ten lines of informal, unrhymed trim-eters and dimeters carried such a pure poetic charge.

Larkin's relationship with Monica weathered the many pressures upon it. Though he was the least political of men, her rigid right-wing opinions occasionally caused friction. He criticized 'the wood of [her] conservatism', and she replied sarcastically that she 'thought you didn't care either way'. 'I certainly *never* knew you fancied yrself a Socialist, &

I must say you've kept it pretty dark.' On 5 August 1953 he attempted to defuse the quarrel:

> the idea of my brooding and fretting over your *political opinions* is enough to make a Staffordshire cat laugh. You know I don't care at all for politics, intelligently. I found that at school when we argued all we did was repeat the stuff we had, respectively, learnt from the *Worker*, the *Herald*, *Peace News*, the *Right Book Club* (that was me, incidentally: *I knew these dictators*, *Marching Spain*, I can remember them now) and as they all contradicted each other all we did was get annoyed. I came to the conclusion that an enormous amount of research was needed to form an opinion on anything, & therefore I abandoned politics altogether as a topic of conversation. It's true that the writers I grew up to admire were either non-political or left-wing, & that I couldn't find any right-wing writer worthy of respect, but of course most of the ones I admired were awful fools or somewhat fakey, so I don't know if my prejudice for the left takes its origin there or not.[37]

Two days later he wrote: 'well dear [. . .] even if we neither at bottom care, the fact does remain that you explode to the right & I explode to the left', conceding that she made 'a better job' of defending her opinions than he of defending his. He drew a caricature rabbit-Monica on a soapbox above a poster reading 'SPEED UP THE BURROWING PROGRAMME', facing a seal-Philip also on a soapbox above a poster reading 'NO CREATURE COMFORT WITHOUT WORK'.[38] A quarter of a century later in the *Observer* interview of 1979 Larkin asserted: 'I've always been right-wing.'[39] In fact his deepest instinct was to avoid politics, while his shallower instincts, contrary to popular opinion, gave him, at least in his earlier years, a 'prejudice for the left'.

During August and September 1953 he devoted thirteen pages of the workbook to drafts of a thirty-first-birthday poem, 'At thirty-one, when some are rich', an engaging meditation on his relationships with women. He wrote 'unfinished' on the typescript,[40] though this seems an expression of personal dissatisfaction rather than an indication of formal incompleteness. The poem is in fact beautifully finished. As summer turns to autumn below his window, in 'deep gardenfuls of air', the poet settles down to write yet another of the letters which have become the measure of his life: less love letters than letters of kindness, or (more cynically) egotistical letters addressed to 'people wise enough to see my worth'. His situation seems pleasant enough, but he is dissatisfied: 'I'm kind, but not kinetic.' These letters 'plot no change'. As he addresses the envelope 'a bitter smoke / Of self-contempt, of boredom too, ascends'.

In 'Mother, Summer, I', written at the same time, and also unpublished during his lifetime, he turns back to the first woman in his life. Taking his cue again from the weather, he notes that his mother hates thunderstorms, and loses her 'worried summer look' only when the rain and frost return. He, her son, 'though summer-born / And summer-loving', also relaxes 'when the leaves are gone'. The 'Emblems of perfect happiness' of summer days offer a challenge to which he cannot rise. Like his mother he awaits:

> A time less bold, less rich, less clear:
> An autumn more appropriate.

The poem has an Eeyorish glumness about it, hinting perhaps at self-parody.

In a letter to Eva he gave a more upbeat version of his mood:

Can you feel the autumn where you are? It seems to hang in the air here, and sharpen my senses, & again I feel a sense of a great waste in my life. We must go again up that road to the wood, where we found the scarlet toadstool, & listen to the wind in the trees [. . .] Here the moon is large and lemon-yellow, & drifts up into the sky at night like a hollow phosphorescent fungoid growth.[41]

After his departure from Leicester in 1950, Philip developed the habit of corresponding with his mother at least twice a week. He addressed her as 'Dearest Mop', 'Dearest Old Creature' or 'My very dear old creature'. She called him 'My dear creature' or 'My very dear creature'. On Sundays he made sure to fill at least four pages with trivial comments, advice and delicate caricatures of mother or son going about their domestic business. She responded in kind. They expected and relied upon next-day postal delivery (including Sundays), and when either of them missed a letter an apology would follow. In October 1953, he wrote that he had not received her usual letter, and she hastened to reassure him by telegram: 'HOPE YOU HAVE LETTER NOW. AM QUITE WELL. MUCH LOVE MOTHER'.[42] This is by far his most consistent and extensive correspondence, running to about 4,000 letters and cards by the time of Eva's death in 1977.

As the time for Winifred's departure from Belfast approached, Philip was moved to write 'Lines on a Young Lady's Photograph Album'. This poem, drafted between August and December 1953, shows the richest combination of genres he had yet attempted. It champions the social realism of photography. But beneath the surface it is both an address to the unattainable muse and also a seduction poem in the witty seventeenth-century cavalier tradition. The woman is a modern muse of real life, a 'real girl in a real place', beautiful, as Jill had been, because of her perfect ordinariness. Photography performs a self-contradictory function. 'Faithful and disappointing' it preserves reality with objective accuracy, recording 'Dull days as dull, and hold-it smiles as frauds'. But it also transfigures the ordinariness of what it records: 'what grace / Your candour thus confers upon her face!' As the spiritual word 'grace' implies, the young lady, though 'empirically true', and blemished, is as transcendentally beautiful as the traditional ideal muse. 'Candour' implies both blunt, ingenuous truthfulness and (from its root in the Latin 'candor') 'brilliant whiteness'. Perhaps Larkin has in mind the hyperreal whiteness of skin in black and white photographs taken outdoors.

But the girl with the album, though a symbol of perfection, has more emotional complexity and humanity than the airgirl in 'Like the train's beat' or the vagrant face in 'Latest Face'. What brings her to life is the poem's chivalrous rhetoric of seduction. Seventeenth-century lovers addressed poems to their 'Lady'. In the subtly different idiom of the 1950s, this poet woos a 'young lady'. Like Marvell or Suckling he appeals to her to take pity on him. Such loudly innocent pleas for mercy conventionally cloak sexual intentions. Here, though sexual innuendo is leeringly signalled ('My swivel eye hungers from pose to pose'), the poet's ultimate aim is quite decorous. He seduces the young lady into surrendering not her body, but her photograph album: 'At last you yielded up the album, which, / Once open, sent me distracted.' The lover's parodic, mock-heroic desire is satiated by images rather than by the woman herself. The nearest we approach to seduction is the poet's brief temptation to steal 'this one of you bathing'. He desires to possess not the flesh-and-blood 'real girl', but her image. He will penetrate no further. Indeed, he is more concerned to arouse the woman's narcissistic appreciation of her younger self in the photographs than to inveigle her into bed.

It is here that Larkin's genre-blending produces its subtlest and most moving effect. This is a muse poem in which the perfect object of desire has descended from her pedestal to become charmingly real and vulnerable. It is also a love poem in which the poet is less concerned with seduction than with the woman's lost youth. The key to the central metaphor is that the 'real girl' in the photographs is the victim of time. She no longer exists:

> Those flowers, that gate,
> These misty parks and motors, lacerate
> Simply by being over; you
> Contract my heart by looking out of date.

Beneath the muse poem and the love poem lies the most universal of all genres: elegy. The photographs, like Plato's unchanging Forms, preserve a reality which we, whose element is time, cannot possess. The photographs are 'Smaller and clearer as the years go by', literally because, photographic materials being hugely expensive at this time, Winifred's snaps are tiny. But they also belong to a distant time made vivid by nostalgia. The poet contemplates 'without a chance of consequence' the growing gulf between the woman's mortal body and her pristine image, now for ever 'out of date'. He joins her on the 'useless' level of her past, that no one now can share, no matter whose her future.

Winifred left Belfast on 27 September 1953. The day before this, by a strange accident, she met Monica for the first and only time, with Philip in the square at Lisburn. It was an awkward, tongue-tied encounter. Winifred immediately wrote to Philip, reproaching him for not properly introducing them, hoping that Monica had not registered the *Numéro Douze* scent, which Philip had given her, and reassuring him that Monica would certainly have noticed her engagement ring. She concluded: 'It's no use my saying how much I shall miss you, and the Library, and Ulster – I wish you could say them for me in a poem. Thank you for all you have been to me this year, when you have had so little in return.' He replied at once, amused at the 'comic encounter', and apologizing for not making the introductions: 'I felt a little like an early Xtian, who feels it hardly necessary to introduce a pair of lions that have met over his recumbent body.' He slyly sympathized with Winifred's nostalgia for their relationship: '*I'm* sorry I had so little in return, too ("he made his Havelock Ellis face"),[43] but, well, as I said, you could have treated me much, much worse, and I have dozens of happy memories which, like pressed flowers, I can spend all winter arranging.'[44]

His poetic version of his affair with Patsy, 'Whatever Happened?', makes a stark contrast with the poems addressed to Winifred. The title has an elusive abstraction about it. Though the question becomes an indicative in the poem's first line, no clear answer emerges. Patsy's cosmopolitanism is reflected in the poem's exotic setting and knowing tone ('Such coastal bedding always means mishap'), reminiscent of a story by Somerset Maugham or Graham Greene. It is implied that some sordid brawl has occurred during a shore visit from a cruise ship, leaving the travellers, a vague collective 'we', with 'trousers ripped, light wallets, and lips bleeding'. Relieved to have escaped, they snap photographs of the port as it recedes 'kodak-distant' into the past, eventually becoming a mere 'latitude' on the map. The impact of Patsy's emotional manipulativeness is reflected in the ripped trousers and bleeding lips. The phrase 'What can't be printed can be thrown away' hints, brutally, at her miscarriage. Obscurity and indirection were essential since

Larkin intended the poem for publication and needed to ensure that its real-life occasion was not recognized by Colin Strang, Winifred or Monica.[45] The form, unique in his work, is a sonnet of four *terza rima* stanzas followed by a concluding couplet (aba, bcb, cdc, ded, ff), the original intended form for 'Absences'. It is formally taut, as if the poet is straining to keep control. Nevertheless repressed emotion finally erupts in short interrogative phrases:

> Curses? The dark? Struggling? Where's the source
> Of these yarns now (except in nightmares, of course)?

Despite its very intimate biographical origin the poem is a brilliant universalized evocation of emotional violation.

On 1 November 1953 Philip sent Patsy a draft of this poem under the title 'The story of an occurrence and a disoccurrence'. In order to deflect her attention from its hostile implications he dates the letter gloomily '*All Hallows*', and speculates on whether he has lung cancer. In deference to her own poetic aspirations he discusses its theme: 'In case it isn't clear, it treats of the way in which the mind gets to work on any violent involuntary experience & transforms it out of all knowledge [. . .] I have tried to keep the wording ambiguous, so that "whatever happened" could be sexual as well as violent.'[46] He implies that Patsy herself, as much as he, is a robbed and victimized traveller. However, he discourages any idea of reviving the affair: 'if a "wrong" thing becomes harder to do, it seems wronger in consequence and – well, we have our obligations. I wish I could write this without sounding priggish & unfriendly.'[47] The following month, on 10 December, he sent Patsy another sonnet, with a more conventional rhyme scheme, 'Autobiography at an Air-Station':

> Delay, well, travellers must expect
> Delay. For how long? No one seems to know.
> With all the luggage weighed, the tickets checked,
> It can't be *long* [. . .]

The poet describes travellers wondering whether to make friends with each other as they await the call to departure. They decide against it in case it spoils their chances in the race for seats: 'You're best alone. Friendship is not worth while.' He made no attempt to publish this poem.

The relationship with Patsy had left him feeling violated. His response was the shameless assertion of bachelor privacy of 'Best Society', drafted in October 1953.[48] This is another of those poems on the typescript of which he wrote 'unfinished', though any other poet would have been satisfied with its refined artistry:

> Our virtues are all social [. . .]
>
> Viciously, then, I lock my door.
> The gas-fire breathes. The wind outside
> Ushers in evening rain. Once more
> Uncontradicting solitude
> Supports me on its giant palm;
> And like a sea-anemone
> Or simple snail, there cautiously
> Unfolds, emerges, what I am.

Never before had he written with such chromatic musicality. In an ababcddc stanza unique in his work, b and d are half-rhymes with subtly shifting vowels ('wrong / thing; get / what; expressed / just; if / chafe; outside / solitude'). These slippages, like accidental sharps and flats in music, perfectly express a wilful, satisfying withdrawal into the self. The open vowel and soft consonant cluster of 'palm' gently but decisively descends to the harder 'am', asserting self-possession in one of the resonant 'what' noun phrases, which were to become a feature of his later poems: 'what I am'. He was determined to resist the intimidation of his socially responsible superego, and to live life rather than allowing life to live him. Larkin never published this intensely personal poem. Perhaps he felt it was too easy to decode the 'vice' of auto-eroticism in the image of the emerging 'simple snail'. Perhaps 'unfinished' was code for 'not for publication'.

After he had finished this poem, he turned, in a characteristic shift of form and mood, to the elegant 'emblem' 'Tops' (originally 'You're the tops'), which he completed in two pages of concentrated drafting (22 and 24 October). The spinning tops become a metonym of life, squirming at first round the floor, then drawing gravely up in a motion so smooth as to seem quite still, 'Until, with a falter, / A flicker – soon gone – / Their pace starts to alter', and they collapse in wobbling, clattering pathos. The metaphor is made explicit with a deft darkening of diction, held back until the last word. The appalling 'first tiny shiver' tells us that the tops are 'starting to die'.

Philip and Patsy continued to correspond occasionally and she depicted Larkin as Rollo Jute in her novel *Playing the Harlot: or Mostly Coffee*.[49] In December 1954 she wrote to say that she was to marry another poet, Richard Murphy. Larkin replied on 7 December, drawing a final line under the affair: 'I reckon, on balance, you treated me better than I treated you. The only thing I hold seriously against you is reading my diary – really. You must not *tell* people if you read their diaries! remember! –'[50] After her marriage in 1955 he sometimes wrote to the Murphys as a couple.

It was during his time in Belfast that Larkin finally abandoned any residual ambition to be a novelist. In his letters to Monica Jones he occasionally implied that he was working on a novel,[51] and as late as April 1952 Amis wrote to him that he was 'interested to hear about your new novel'.[52] It may be that some of the surviving drafts of *No For An Answer* and *A New World Symphony* date from the Belfast years, though the situations they fictionalize belong in 1946–8. A key factor here is Amis's progress on the novel inspired by his glimpse of Larkin in Leicester. Larkin suggested the title *The Man of Feeling* to replace the working title *Dixon and Christine*, but this would have been too literary.[53] In the early stages, the protagonist was closely modelled on Larkin, but in the published novel Jim is an independent comic creation.[54] While keeping his own Leicester novel secret from his friend, Larkin had been reading drafts of Amis's novel since its inception, and when Michael Joseph rejected the typescript of *Dixon and Christine* in June 1952, Larkin helped Amis with the redrafting. 'We should be able to fudge up something good between us', Amis wrote anxiously.[55] 'Would it be asking too much to ask you to skim quickly through the type-script, making marginal indications of anything that displeases you? ("Bad style", "damp squib", bad bit of dialogue & so on, to prevent me using them again).'[56] Larkin wrote amusedly to Monica about his friend's imperious demands, and his intense desire for publication: 'He is prepared to go to endless trouble, & I think if he could get it accepted he'd die happy, but he has no idea how people talk.' Larkin was never-theless aware that Amis's book was 'full of "laughs", and would amuse many people'.[57]

The Harry Ransom Center in Texas holds an incomplete early type-script of *Lucky Jim* bearing Larkin's marginal notes.[58] Its protagonist, Julian Dixon, is more self-confident than the Jim of the final version, and the Bertrand character is quite sympathetically portrayed. It begins with Julian visiting Veronica, the character who was to become Margaret Peel, following her attempt at suicide. He is intent on discovering whether she will now, at long last, begin sleeping with him. Larkin's annotations are not extensive but they show an authoritative involve-ment in the process: 'Forget how we left this, but the device shouldn't be used *twice*'; 'do people talk like this? I never hear them'; 'Absolutely weak kneed. *Please* cut.'[59] Larkin is particularly concerned that Amis's women characters are insufficiently modest and decorous to be plaus-ible: 'Ladies don't talk about sex', 'People don't talk like this, esp. ladies', 'Ladies don't use words like this', 'Ladies etc.' He objects to Christine's response to being kissed: 'A bit *forward*! [. . .] This is going much too fast.' Larkin is confident enough of his friend's receptivity to be frank and trenchant: 'This speech might come from a stage play too BAD to be produced.' 'This speech makes me *twist about* with boredom.'[60] He writes against one passage, 'Horrible smell of arse', and later against another: 'H S of A'. Similarly 'GRUESOME AROMA OF BUM' is repeated as 'G A of B'.[61] In their correspondence the word 'bum' had become a frequent debunking epithet and it remained part of their familiar private language for the rest of their lives.

Though his own unfinished novels are not essentially comic, Larkin's advice tends to transform Amis's original serious realism into broad comedy. He comments that 'Bill Atkinson is bloody funny', and in the final version this character's role is greatly expanded. He deflates Amis's more pretentious dialogue. In the draft, Dixon says to Christine, 'Apart from your obvious physical attractions, what I like best about you is your honesty.' Larkin responds: *'Fearfully* pompous'. At one point Dixon indignantly rejects Veronica's attempt to win him back from Christine by seduction: 'I don't want it [sex] on a plate, thanks, and I won't have it used as a trap.' Larkin is derisively unpersuaded: 'oh yes you do my dear fellow that's just what you do want on a plate'.[62] One cause of tension between them was Larkin's concern over the impact of the novel on Monica Jones. On his insistence Amis agreed to change the name 'Veronica Beale' to 'Margaret Peel',[63] though since Monica's full name was Margaret Monica Beale Jones this scarcely disguised the origin of the character. Amis seems largely to have taken Larkin's advice. Richard Bradford argues that the success of the dialogue in *Lucky Jim* owes much to the texture of Larkin's correspondence with Amis at this time.[64]

When Monica first met Kingsley she was struck by the difference between the two friends. Larkin remained in control of his performances, making a 'Havelock Ellis' face, or acting out an elaborate mime of shoe-fetishism. Amis, she concluded, 'wasn't just making faces all the time, he was actually trying them on. He didn't know who he was.'[65] In *Lucky Jim* Amis turned this insecurity to fictional advantage. The face-pulling antics and insecure fantasies of the fictional Jim Dixon endeared the character to readers, and gave original spice to the novel's humour.

After so many disappointments both Amis and Larkin were caught by surprise when *Lucky Jim* was accepted by Gollancz in 1953, and it was soon apparent that it would be a great success. Larkin's importunate friend had suddenly overtaken him. Richard Bradford concludes: 'Larkin would remain embittered for the rest of his life by what he saw as Amis's act of plagiarism.'[66] But, despite an occasional snide comment, Larkin was not embittered. Nor did he consider *Lucky Jim* 'plagiarized', though he was well aware that Amis could not have written it without his help and support. He wrote to Monica on 14 September 1953 with characteristic generosity: 'I don't think anything can stop it being a howling success: it seems to me so entirely original that my own suggestions really pass unnoticed [. . .] even if he never writes anything else it will remain as a landmark.'⁶⁷

While the typescript of *Lucky Jim* was still being considered by Gollancz, Larkin reviewed his own novelistic efforts in a letter to Patsy Strang: 'I've just dug out 2 unfinished novels of mine & am reading one to see what kind of a thing it was – 233 pages abandoned in Dec. 1949. To me it reads extremely cleverly but without the least flavour of merit.'⁶⁸ Three months later he finally admitted what had been obvious for several years. He wrote to Patsy on 6 July 1953: 'I *can't* write this book: if it is to be written at all it should be largely an attack on Monica, & I *can't* do that, not while we are still on friendly terms, and I'm not sure it even interests me sufficiently to go on. It was planned a long time ago, of course.'⁶⁹ The last dated outline, 'Sundry resurveyings', is headed 'November 1953' and when Charles Monteith, who had taken over from Alan Pringle at Faber, asked to see drafts of the third novel, Larkin told him that it was 'at a halt'.⁷⁰

In a letter to Patsy written on 25 January 1954, two days before the publication of Amis's novel, Larkin balanced admiration against objective critical judgement: 'Of course *Lucky Jim* sends me into prolonged fits of howling laughter [. . .] I do think that it is miraculously and intensely funny, with a kind of spontaneity that doesn't tire the reader at all. *Apart* from being funny, I think it somewhat over-simple.'⁷¹ He was aware that his own novel would have been deeper and more ambitious than Amis's. Augusta Bax is potentially a far more interesting character than Margaret Peel. But once Amis's novel had been published, to the acclaim which Larkin so confidently forecast, he could not think of continuing with his own fiction. At least *Lucky Jim* was dedicated to him.

II

Various Poems
1953–6

At the very end of 1953, Larkin completed a poem of vocation, 'Reasons for Attendance', in which he translated the romantic fervour of 'The Spirit Wooed' and 'Waiting for breakfast' into his new 'vernacular' manner. Though the tone is different, the pattern remains the same. Drawn to the lighted glass by the sound of a trumpet, the poet watches the dancers, face to flushed face, eager for commitment and marriage. He attends instead to art: not now in the form of 'pristine absolutes' or 'tender visitings', but of a demanding 'rough tongued bell / (Art, if you like)'. The casual aside ridicules artistic pretension. Nevertheless, he still obeys the call unquestioningly: 'It speaks; I hear.' He remains the *poète maudit*, and the reader is expected to register the French nuance of 'attend': *attendre à* – to listen to. There is, it seems, as much doubt over 'Life, if you like' as over 'Art, if you like'. However the poet no longer feels on safe enough ground to condemn the ingenuous involvement of the dancers. He justifies his position not by grand Yeatsian gestures, but with a stubborn, sulky shrug. He can't help it; this is just the way he is made. He concludes inconclusively that both the lonely artist outside and the dancers within 'are satisfied': 'If no one has misjudged himself. Or lied.' The poet is less deceived about life than the courting couples, but also less deceived about art than a Yeatsian romantic.

During his years in Belfast Larkin had established an unobtrusive reputation by publication in literary magazines. In 1953–5 a number of his poems (including 'Wires', 'Latest Face' and 'Arrivals, Departures') appeared in the *Spectator*. In 1953 John Wain, his friend from Oxford, became the producer of *First Reading* on the Third Programme, and Larkin's poems began to be heard on the radio. One of the journals in which his work appeared was *Listen*, a small magazine founded in Hull by a twenty-one-year-old former art student, George Hartley, and his wife Jean. Larkin noticed the first number in 1953, and sent the Hartleys 'Spring', 'Dry-Point' and 'Toads', all of which they eagerly accepted for the second issue the following year. 'Poetry of Departures' appeared later in 1954 in *Listen* 3. The Hartleys immediately fell in love with his work. Jean Hartley recalls their excitement at the poems' 'accessibility, wide range of mood and rare combination of wit, lyricism and disenchantment'.[1] In February 1954 Donald Davie invited Larkin to give a talk at Trinity College, Dublin, where he was teaching. Larkin agreed, telling Patsy Strang: 'the sweat runs down my back'.[2]

Through 1954 and into 1955 poems in his new robust manner alternate in the workbooks with poems of elevated emotion. Even in the most 'vernacular' poems a romantic counter-impulse is audible. 'I Remember, I Remember' (8 January 1954) blasphemes against his former Lawrentian faith, debunking the depiction of childhood in novels like *Sons and Lovers*. When the poet's train stops at Coventry, where he was born, the poet is at a loss. The childhood the books tell him he should remember never occurred. He experienced no 'Blinding theologies of flowers and fruits', he did not escape to a neighbouring 'splendid family' and become 'Really myself', nor did his first erotic experience come among the bracken, when 'all became a burning mist'. Coventry, he concludes, is not where he has 'his roots', only where his childhood was 'unspent'. His passionate denials become comic and his companion protests, 'You look as if you wished the place in Hell.' But beneath the plain speaking there are complications. Though the poem is divided into stanzas of five lines, the rhyme-scheme implies a nine-line unit. Larkin claimed, preposterously, that this playful subversion was 'quite accidental really'.[3] The final hanging line required to complete the scheme resonates perplexingly in the mind: 'Nothing, like something, happens anywhere.' At first the words seem merely a glum verdict on the poet's childhood. But they transcend their context, and haunt the reader like a Wittgensteinian puzzle. The impact of this apparently prosaic work is intensely poetic.

In 'For Sidney Bechet', Larkin focused on a very different imagined place: the New Orleans evoked by the narrowing and rising note of Sidney Bechet's saxophone or clarinet. For some, the poet writes, such music builds 'a legendary Quarter / Of balconies, flower-baskets and quadrilles, / Everyone making love and going shares –'. This world of uninhibited freedom is, like the clichés of 'I Remember, I Remember', an 'appropriate falsehood'. However, in this case he has no wish to debunk or deride. Rather he spins his own joyful euphoria from the music: 'On *me* your voice falls as they say love should / Like an enormous yes.' As he wrote in a different context: 'everyone has his own dream of America'.[4] To experience the real New Orleans would be to court disappointment. Later in life Robert Conquest offered to meet Larkin's plane in New Orleans, 'see him to a hotel and so on, so that he could make a local pilgrimage to the blues' historical milieu'. Conquest explains: 'This probably shaky enough project failed when he heard that Congo Square had been subsumed into a *Cultural Center*.'[5]

In contrast 'Born Yesterday', celebrating the birth of Kingsley Amis's daughter Sally on 17 January 1954, presents itself as a plain man's rewriting of Yeats's ceremonious 'A Prayer for my Daughter'. The poet wishes for this baby not beauty, nor innocence and love, but ordinariness, and 'An average of talents'. He hopes that she will be 'Not ugly, not goodlooking', without anything 'uncustomary' to pull her off her balance. It is an assured exercise, but there is something ventriloquial about it. Larkin has ironed out his contradictions in a polite pretence of being Amis or the early Davie. This world of stolid security is as flimsy a dream as any imagined 'Crescent City', but far less exciting. Its tone approaches the 'unassuming commonsense' which Donald Davie saw in his poetry.[6] 'Poetry of Departures', completed only days later, was possibly written in reaction against such dull contentedness. The poet derides the idea of 'home sweet home': 'We all hate home / And having to be there: / I detest my room.' He assumes that 'we' all admire the man who 'just cleared off'. But like 'Reasons for Attendance' the poem ends ambiguously. In Larkin's restless dialectic the Rimbaldian rejection of domesticity seems on reflection a 'step backwards / To create an object'. The stereotypical Hollywood rebel, swaggering the nut-strewn roads, or crouching in the fo'c'sle, 'Stubbly with goodness', is as self-deceived in his 'perfect', 'artificial' life as the conformist with his orderly books and china. Edgy pararhymes prevail, only the d rhyme of the octaves being perfect. The subtle dissonances create an effect of anarchic wilfulness ('epitaph / cleared off; think / junk; home / room; fo'c'sle / artificial; if / life').

This dialectic between realism and fantasy culminated in 'Toads', completed in March 1954. Larkin is virtually alone among twentieth-century poets in writing in a natural, first-hand way about work in the sense of paid employment. No other significant poet, except Wallace Stevens, held down a nine-to-five job with no expectation of becoming a 'full-time' professional writer. Larkin's attitude is profoundly ambiguous. In this poem his 'vernacular' bluster and garish misrhymes build to a pitch of rowdy anarchy; 'lanes' rhymes with 'sardines', 'bucket' with 'like it', 'toad-like' with 'hard luck' and 'blarney' with 'money':

> Ah, were I courageous enough
>   To shout *Stuff your pension!*
> But I know, all too well, that's the stuff
>   That dreams are made on:
>
> For something sufficiently toad-like
>   Squats in me, too;
> Its hunkers are heavy as hard luck,
>   And cold as snow [. . .]

'Made on' rhymes with 'pension', giving Prospero's beautiful phrase from *The Tempest* an unforgettable new context. The poem features in a collage pasted on the surviving inside cover of Larkin's diary for 1954–7. A black and white photograph shows an imposing, large-breasted nude looking out, arms akimbo, with abstracted upward gaze. A smaller photograph of a thin-faced Larkin occupies the space under her armpit, staring at the viewer through large spectacles, tie slightly awry. The woman's right hand presses down on the printed text of 'Toads', which covers the lower part of her body. In the corner is a fragment of a French lesbian romance: 'Sa beauté n'était pas moins insolente que celle de sa soeur' ('Her beauty was no less insolent than that of her sister').[7] The collage presents an engagingly self-deprecating image of the poet's inner landscape.

On 5 and 6 April 1954 Larkin completed two contrasted poems of meditation. 'Skin' is an elegant 'emblem'. The poet sadly sympathizes with his 'Obedient daily dress', which is compelled, in a wan bad joke, to 'learn its lines', parching and sagging under the wind of time. In a charming twist he apologizes that he has not been able to reward its patient loyalty by wearing it to a 'brash festivity [. . .] such as / Clothes are entitled to / Till the fashion changes'. In his new anti-rhetorical manner, death becomes merely a change of 'fashion'. The following day he completed 'Water', equally undeceived, but elevated in tone. It begins in light whimsy as he imagines himself being 'called in' to construct a religion, but modulates into an exalted evocation of the element of water. Borrowing Christian imagery he invents a ritual of drenching and fording to dry clothes, and presents an image of a glass of water in which the 'any-angled' light of dawn 'Would congregate endlessly'. The poem consists only of twelve short lines, and maintains a playful tone throughout. Nevertheless it achieves an impressive pagan gravity.

He later regretted taking Monica's advice to change the original wording of this poem. In a letter of 18 April 1971 he wrote: 'Oh, in the paperb. *TWW* "litany" has been replaced by "liturgy." I rather wish I hadn't listened to you on this: it seems to wreck the whole verse, it's so heavy, as opposed to the dancingness of *litany – liturgy* anticipates *images* in the next line, too, the g sound. I don't think the meaning is sufficient gain, as no one knows what either word means anyway.'[8]

On the day that he composed 'Water' he told Winifred: 'Bruce wrote today to borrow £100! Sent him £50. Why he applies to me & not to Kingsley, God only knows.'[9] Despite his success as novelist and composer, Montgomery was experiencing financial difficulties because of his extravagant lifestyle. Larkin was notoriously penny-pinching in everyday life. Like his father he wrote up monthly accounts of his outgoings, and in matters of trivial expenditure, for instance in paying for rounds of drinks or for haircuts, he was loudly stingy and ungenerous.[10] But when it really mattered he could be open-handed, and even sought out occasions for generosity, as when he later offered to subsidize the publication of Barbara Pym's *Quartet in Autumn*. Over the years, it seems, Montgomery called upon him for frequent financial assistance.

Early in 1954 George MacBeth and Oscar Mellor, editors of the Fantasy Press, which had already published pamphlets of poems by Elizabeth Jennings and Geoffrey Hill, asked Larkin for a selection of his work, and in March five poems appeared in *Fantasy Press Poets, Philip Larkin*, No. 21: 'Lines on a Young Lady's Photograph Album', 'Whatever Happened', 'If, My Darling', 'Arrivals, Departures' and 'At Grass'. At the same time 'Lines on a Young Lady's Photograph Album' and 'Latest Face' appeared in the *Spectator*. He sent the printed versions to Winifred, but she was too preoccupied with her wedding preparations to pay much attention. On April Fool's Day 1954 she sent him a cool letter insisting that her life was not over as his poems implied. On 7 April he replied, saying that he was 'glad, at long last, the two poems eventually got published and you saw them'. He continued: 'frightful as marriage is, it's worse if you don't embrace it whole-heartedly. I shall put away my inconvenient emotions and wish you nothing but good.'[11] Half a century later the muse was still arguing with the dead poet. After two marriages, with three children, three stepchildren and seventeen grandchildren, Winifred was, if anything, even more indignant about Philip's misogamy. She gave a late retort in 2002, in 'Photograph Albums Revisited':

Husbands, children, stepchildren, grandchildren, friends,
Cousins, cats, cars, canals: a cornucopia of pleasures,
The brilliance of the world revealed in a dozen larger, newer albums.[12]

For Winifred life had become clearer and larger with the passage of the years.

In one poem addressed to Winifred, 'Long roots moor summer to our side of earth', Larkin adopted a positive view of marriage. In this, his most deeply felt and personal epithalamium, dated the day of Winifred's wedding, 12 June 1954, though drafted over a longer period, Larkin abjectly concedes his own sterility, renouncing wit and aestheticism to address her as a woman rather than as a muse. The imagery recalls the Lawrentian organicism of 'Wedding-Wind', and like that poem it is also an aubade. The poet awakes to find summer already taller than 'the green / River-fresh castles of unresting leaf'. Procreative nature burgeons around him:

> It unfolds upward a long breadth, a shine
>
> Wherein all seeds and clouds and winged things
> Employ the many-levelled acreage.

He turns away in despair from this epiphany of fertility, feeling 'outdistanced, out-invented'. He is unable to make the only adequate response:

> what
> Reply can the vast flowering strike from us,
> Unless it be the one
> You make today in London: to be married?

A conviction of his failure to rise to the challenge of life is a persistent, tragic element in his sensibility. He left this painfully personal poem unpublished.

On 28 July, after a discontinuous drafting process of three months, Larkin completed what was to become a key work for his early reputation. He had already, in 'At Grass', set the pattern for the long stanzaic Horatian odes or reflective elegies which are a central feature of his middle and late periods. 'Church Going' has a more public theme than 'At Grass', and takes its place in the sequence which was to develop further with 'An Arundel Tomb' (1956), 'The Whitsun Weddings' (1958), 'Here' (1961) and 'Dockery and Son' (1963). Like Keats's odes, each of these poems has a precisely conceptualized abstract theme, though this remains unstated. 'Church Going' is an 'Ode on Faith'. At the time he did not foresee its later popularity, and was diffident about its value. He was dismayed and irritated when he realized it was destined to become a defining work in his public 'Movement' image.

He was aware, as he composed it, that its complex mixture of tones is not wholly coherent. It is easy to read the work as a less deceived retort to T. S. Eliot's 'Little Gidding', published thirteen years earlier in 1942. Like 'A Stone Church Damaged by a Bomb', 'Church Going' subverts Eliot's patriotic belief in the 'significant soil' of English Anglicanism ('You are here to kneel / Where prayer has been valid').[13] The poet's 'awkward reverence' as he removes his bicycle clips is half ironic. He disrespectfully apes the vicar at the lectern ('Here endeth'), and is dismissive about ruin-bibbers who know what rood-lofts are. He donates an Irish sixpence, as he explained to Monica, 'a comic compromise between giving NOTHING and giving REAL MONEY'.[14] The Church represents a moribund authority to which the poet sulkily refuses to defer. However, in writing to Monica, with her more conventional religious attitudes,[15] he stressed his distance as poet from the speaker: 'do remember [. . .] that I write it partly to exhibit an attitude as well as to try to arouse an emotion – the attitude of the "young heathen" of whom there are plenty about these days – the first line, for instance, is designed both as sincere statement of fact & also as heavy irony.'[16]

Thus his ironic disrespect in the phrase 'ghostly silt' mocks Eliot's nostalgia for traditional faith. But it is tempered by more positive feelings. Towards the end the speaker himself adopts the tones of Anglican piety:

> A serious house on serious earth it is,
> In whose blent air all our compulsions meet,
> Are recognised, and robed as destinies.
> And that much never can be obsolete [. . .]

Is this, perhaps, the blather of some Reverend Flannel intoning with poetical inversion 'A serious house on serious earth it is', and speaking vacuously of 'blent air' and 'robed destinies'? No. Dubious though the tone is, there is genuine emotion here. Writing to Monica, Larkin implied that 'blent' is intended as a genuinely moving poeticism.[17] His tone thus allows his pious readers to imagine that the poet himself shares their superstitious self-deception. Christian readers have from the beginning claimed that the poet is expressing here the sincere pensiveness of a fundamentally religious man: 'under the pose he is *homo religiosus*, with an awareness of sacred time and sacred place'.[18]

But it is not religion that prompts the poet's churchgoing. Eliot may deceive himself; Larkin does not. Cultural Anglicanism exerted a powerful hold over him. Echoing A. E. Housman's self-description as 'a High-Church atheist',[19] he termed himself an 'anglican agnostic', and later in 'Aubade' expressed a poignant affection for the 'vast moth-eaten musical brocade' of Christianity. But his atheism is never in doubt. He was disconcerted by religious misreadings of the poem. When Brenda Moon, Assistant Librarian in Hull, called it 'wonderful', Larkin 'looked surprised and said: "If I'd known how popular it would be, I would have taken more trouble over it."'[20] He never quarrelled with sincere religious readers since the poem is not intended as a polemic. However, he objected to those who ingeniously perverted it into an assertion of faith. 'I was a bit irritated by an American who insisted to me it was a religious poem. It isn't religious at all. Religion surely means that the affairs of this world are under divine superveillance, and so on, and I go to some pains to point out that I don't bother about that kind of thing, that I'm deliberately ignorant of it – "Up at the holy end", for instance.' He was even driven to sarcasm: 'Ah no, it's a great religious poem; he knows better than me – trust the tale and not the teller, and all that stuff.'[21] In fact there is no doubt that the House of God in the poem is empty. God is mentioned only in the calculatedly offhand, secular phrase 'God knows'. And the reason the poet gravitates towards the churchyard is secular and conditional: 'If only that so many dead lie round.'

During his final year or so in Belfast Larkin established a

relationship with Judy Egerton, who was to become one of his most significant correspondents. He was detailed to show Judy, a teaching assistant in History and wife of the Economics lecturer, Ansell, round the library. As they went they worked on a *Times* crossword together and became immediate friends. Later she told him how much he had impressed her.[22] The Egertons made a dashing, faintly glamorous addition to the cosmopolitan mix of Queen's. They included him on a trip to Dublin where he visited Donald Davie. He wrote to Patsy on 9 October 1954: 'I went & returned with some married Australians called Egerton, whose big Rover rushed from Davy Byrnes to 30 Elmwood Avenue, through patches of autumnal mist and sending nocturnal rats scuttling to the hedgerows, in two and a half hours flat.'[23] Shortly afterwards he gave more detail:

> They are a rich young Australian couple who've run out of things to say to each other, and are now sucking fresh life from Alec & myself. We play bridge there far too often, & eat good food, & drink good drink. Now they have started buying LP Bechets & giving me recipés, and muttering archly 'I don't know why you call yourself an indigestible sterility . . .' out of the blue. In answer to your unspoken question, no, she isn't attractive: just 'well groomed'. He is about 6'6" and terrifically strong. Plays cricket, of course.[24]

Later Ansell secured him tickets for Test matches at Lords, and his friendship with the Egertons became a permanent strand in his life. He would visit them in London, and he and Judy were to exchange letters regularly for the rest of his life.

Larkin was beginning to feel that his sojourn in Ireland had run its course, particularly after his different adventures with Patsy Strang and Winifred Arnott had come to their ends. Central though it was to his poetic development, Belfast was essentially a diversion. In his next completed poem, 'Places, Loved Ones' (10 October 1954), the speaker meditates on rootlessness, expressing surprise at the way things have turned out: 'No, I have never found / The place where I could say / *This is my proper ground, / Here I shall stay.*' Nor has he found 'that special one' with whom he might share his name. There is no assertion here of artistic vocation. This speaker has happened to miss out on these things for no apparent reason. Larkin was once again beginning to question whether his rejection of the call to join the dance of life was the product of anything more than immaturity. As the second exemption of Belfast drew to an end, his choice of life opened up again. Once he returned to England these issues would confront him with new force.

His thoughts had been concentrated a few weeks earlier when Jack Graneek, the Librarian at Queen's, feeling his abilities needed a new challenge, had encouraged him to apply for a post at Hull, whose Librarian, Agnes Cuming, was about to retire. In September 1954, Hull gained full University status, having until then been a university college awarding external London degrees. This was an opportunity which Larkin felt he could not pass up, though he was diffident of success, since he was still only thirty-two. 'Of course it will be all up if any of the committee has read *Toads – Listen* is printed practically IN *Hull*.'[25] He travelled across for the interview and on 23 November wrote to Monica to say that he had been offered the post. He was to start in March 1955. A few days later, on a chilly 28 November, he reviewed his situation. He was now definitely committed to a career in librarianship, which he depicted as his 'mask', the oppositional alter ego of Yeats's poetic theory. Otherwise he was simply resuming his life where he had left it five years earlier: 'What a hopeless character mine is. In 1950 I ran away from England & the problems it held, but really they're still there unchanged & now I'm *going back* to them . . . Five years older, five years poorer, five years colder, five years . . . can't think of a rhyme. Surer? Surer of what? Brrr.'[26] Graneek commented that he had 'never seen anyone so depressed by promotion'.[27]

Top of the list of the issues to be resolved was whether he would marry Monica. On 15 December, he responded to her hints: 'You seem to suggest that I've yet to throw off my mother & grab myself primary emotional interest in a woman my own age. This may well be true – it sounds true – but it's not a thing one can do by will power.'[28] The relationship had gathered emotional momentum during five years of regular correspondence, visits and holidays. But it had its tensions. In the same letter in which he told Monica about the Hull vacancy in September, he was prompted to take issue with her conservatism. A 'foul article' by Ronald Duncan in the satirical magazine *Punch* had celebrated the advent of myxomatosis in the writer's village: 'when the first bulging-eyed creature was discovered . . . it was drinks all round at the pub that night'. Continuing what was clearly an ongoing debate between them he condemned the magazine: 'it is this sort of thing that makes me look down on *Punch* (you remember you once scolded me for it). It may be the backbone of England, but the *New St.* wd never offend in that way, and I judge them accordingly.'[29] In view of his reputation as a right-wing poet, it is remarkable how many of his occasionally published poems appeared in the *New Statesman* and other left-leaning journals.

The fact that Monica was, in the sentimental language of their letters, 'Ears', 'Paws' or 'Bun', gave the onset of myxomatosis a painful personal significance, and though he finished his poem on the subject on 28 September, he delayed sending it to her until 14 November. He explained awkwardly: 'I'm not keeping "the rabbit one" from you: it's only that in it I kill the rabbit, which makes it totally out of character & rather like a piece of journalism.'[30] There is no hint of anthropomorphism in the poem; the title, 'Myxomatosis', is chillingly clinical. Assuming no more than shared animal sentience, he guesses at what is going on in the animal's consciousness:

> You may have thought things would come right again
> If you could only keep quite still and wait.

'It's not much of a poem,' he wrote to Monica. 'But of course I *felt* strongly enough about it. I hardly dare ask what you think of it. I strove (queer word) to give the essential pathos of the situation without getting involved in argument.' He is anxious about the morality of treating this highly emotive topic at all: 'Oh dear. Is this "using" the rabbits?'[31] The contrast with Ted Hughes is intriguing. Larkin respects the non-human otherness of animals while Hughes endows his birds and rodents with human pride, guilt and deviousness. The world of 'Crow' is far closer to Beatrix Potter than are the horses and rabbit of Larkin's poems.[32] Outside the poem, however, Larkin reverts to the consoling artifice of anthropomorphism. Later in this same letter to Monica he inserts a drawing of a rabbit, her skirt flying in a sprightly dance, accompanied on a rustic shawm by a seal beneath a tree. There is moving pathos in the juxtaposition of the rigorous realism of the poem with the sophisticated sentimentalism of their playful animal personae.

Larkin was aware of the quality of his poetic achievement, and becoming impatient for recognition. In September he sent 'Church Going' and 'Myxomatosis' to the *Spectator*, where they were mislaid, though he did not discover this until a year later. He felt disappointed, writing on 2 October 1954 to Monica, 'No word from the *Spr* about my deathless verse.'[33] Then on 10 October, after the trip to Dublin with the Egertons, he told her that, though Donald Davie had been in favour of the Dolmen Press publishing twelve of his recent poems, Davie's two young Irish co-editors, Thomas Kinsella and Liam Miller, had outvoted him. They thought the poems '"too self-pitying" (I offered Davie this phrase & he gladly accepted it) and "too sexy" (his own words). He was very apologetic, but I think the collection hadn't pleased him as much as he had expected.' Davie had found 'Wires' 'very feeble', though he liked 'Latest Face' enough to set it as an analytical exercise for his classes in Trinity College. Larkin affected indifference: 'So there you are. I was disappointed at the time, but not now.'[34] Despite his show of unconcern, there can be little doubt that he was angered by these blundering criticisms.

'Maiden Name' (January 1955), the last poem Larkin completed in Belfast, returns for the final time to Winifred Arnott and the muse theme. The five light sounds of the maiden name preserve, like the photographs, an innocent perfection now for ever lost. The 'disused' name no longer 'means' her face nor her 'variants of grace'. By marriage she has fallen from grace. There is an ominous undertone in the poet's congratulation to her on being 'thankfully confused / By law with someone else'. The name now survives only in old lists and letters tied with tartan ribbon. Then with a sudden intimate address the poet speaks directly to her: 'Try whispering it slowly. / No, it means you.' But he immediately draws back. This is too intimate a tone to adopt to a married woman. So he re-presents his feeling in the form of a politely circumlocuitous 'what' noun phrase: 'Or, since you're past and gone, // It means what we feel now about you then.' The poem becomes an elegy, mourning her youth:

> How beautiful you were, and near, and young,
> So vivid, you might still be there among
> Those first few days, unfingermarked again [. . .]

Her perfection is spoiled by fingering. There is an unsettling emotional complexity in the story which Amis related years later: 'He had a picture of her in his room. He came back one night full of beer and wrote to say he'd noticed more than usual how it brought out her resemblance to Stan Laurel. "In a hearty way," he said, "I let a bit of beer fall on it and now I can't get it off. I can't get the shine back."'[35] It is likely that Amis's summary lacks nuances present in Larkin's original version. However, the pattern is true to his dialectical sensibility. Whenever he felt a powerful emotion he was impelled to answer it with scepticism or desecration; and vice versa.

On 20 December 1954 George Hartley wrote from Hull that, following the success of the first three issues of *Listen*, he and his wife Jean had decided to venture on a book. Their imprint was to be called the Marvell Press, after Hull's great seventeenth-century poet, with the implication also that it would be a bloody marvel if the plan was a success.[36] They asked him to be their first author. He hesitated, still feeling that it was his destiny to be published by Faber. 'If only he lived in any other city!' he wrote to Monica.[37] But inertia prevailed, and rather than risk a repeat of the traumatic rejection of seven years earlier, he agreed. Nervous about what his new employer and colleagues might think of 'Toads' and 'If, My Darling', he asked the Hartleys not to advertise or distribute the volume around Hull. He was somewhat reassured to learn that neither of the Hartleys had any connection with the University. Remembering his experience with *XX Poems*, he secured assurances that he would not have to pay for anything himself, and that the volume would be printed on good paper.

He made a list of twenty-three possible inclusions, writing to Monica on 8 January 1955: 'I can't decide about *Churchgoing* – it's one of the 23, but I'm not sure. What do you think? [. . .] I should like it for its length!' The title for the volume caused him difficulty: 'I'd *like* to call it *Such Absences*, to draw attention to my favourite poem! Only it doesn't make sense, since my poems aren't *really* "attics cleared of me".'[38] As we have seen, he had omitted 'Absences' from *XX Poems*. Perhaps its sublime theme seemed inappropriate in a collection dedicated to Amis. But his feelings about his friend were now less warm; Amis did not reply to letters nor remember birthdays, and their correspondence was becoming irregular. He was, Larkin told Monica, like a 'fourth form friend' he had outgrown: 'The idea of Kingsley *loving* a book – or a book "feeding" him, as K.M. wd say – is quite absurd. He doesn't *like* books. He doesn't like *reading*. And I wouldn't take his opinion on *anything*, books, people, places, anything. Probably he has been mistaken, to himself, about me.'[39] Other titles Larkin toyed with were: *23 Poems*, *Poems 1946–1955*, *In the same breath* and *True to life*. In the end he sent the typescript to the Hartleys with the title *Various Poems*.[40]

Monica, meanwhile, was doing her best to persuade him to marry her, by the well-calculated strategy of sympathizing with his misogamy. On 22 January 1955 she conceded: 'Well, for one thing, a first thing, you can't marry just because you think it's a sort of moral duty & a nasty one, a punishment that you ought to take.' On the other hand she suggested reasonably: 'One thing that does make me feel we are "suited" is that you can discuss such an idea with me, & that I can hear it without the least offence, & even with understanding – I do see what you mean. But being "suited" & actually wanting to marry is another thing again, too.'[41] It is painful to read her careful angling. He responded, after a week, tantalizing her with arguments in favour of commitment: 'It seemed to me that if we were going to get married this would be a good point to do so. I have a living wage, you want to pack up your job, we both want – or think we want – the same kind of life, we know each other well enough, etc. And we are ageing!' But he continued with a cruel candour which must have put Monica through the emotional mangle: 'The sort of thing that gives me pause (paws) is wondering whether I do more than just like you very, very much and find it flattering and easy to stay with you.'[42] Two weeks later (10 February) he assumed that it was agreed between them that marriage was impossible: 'Really you couldn't say anything more to my way of feeling than that you don't like the idea of *getting* married. I dare say I could go through with it, but [. . .]' He concluded with a crushing Larkinesque aphorism: 'what frightens me most about marriage is the passing-a-law-never-to-be-alone-again side of it'.[43] Monica could be in no doubt where she stood.

Various Poems was a thoughtful choice of title. The volume's range of styles, forms and emotions is more diverse than that of any other poet of the century. The title also has the advantage of avoiding any hint of an ideological programme. The blurb which Larkin wrote at George Hartley's request, but which was never used, is disarming: 'the poems of Philip Larkin have been increasingly well-known for their unusual combination of deep personal feeling and exact, almost sophisticated choice of words'. While 'no less witty and intelligent than his contemporaries', he 'deals with emotion more simply and intensely than is common today'.[44] But, accurate though it was, the title lacked distinctiveness and, following discussion with Hartley, Larkin transferred the intended title of the poem 'The Less Deceived' to the volume, and renamed that poem 'Deceptions'. After a ceremonious request the collection was dedicated to Monica.

It is intriguing to speculate how different the whole period might seem had Larkin's first mature volume been called *Such Absences*. But the abstract noun phrase 'the less deceived' has an authentic Larkinesque quality, and in retrospect the title seems inevitable. With its comparative grammar it stresses the dynamic relativities which Larkin had been exploring in his recent work. The raped girl in 'Deceptions' is less deceived than her rapist. The visitor in 'Church Going' is less deceived than the religious believer. The aestheticist speaker of 'Latest Face' is less deceived than *l'homme moyen sensuel* wading after the statue in untidy air. The speaker of 'If, My Darling' is less deceived than the woman he addresses; or at least so he claims, though with his internal attic full of selfish clutter he is perhaps more deceived than the poet of 'Absences' whose attics are sublimely empty. To be less deceived means to transcend sex or self as often as it means to be disillusioned in the usual sense. Rather than dictating a consistent downbeat tone the title opens up conditional or comparative calculations: 'Whatever happened?'; 'If no one has misjudged himself'; 'Nothing [. . .] happens anywhere'; 'Such attics cleared of me!'; 'what since is found / Only in separation'.

When the volume was published in November 1955 (the title page has 'October'), nine months after Larkin's arrival in Hull, it consisted of twenty-nine poems: thirteen from *XX Poems*,[45] the five poems from the Fantasy Press volume and eleven other recent works: 'Absences', 'Reasons for Attendance', 'I Remember, I Remember', 'Poetry of Departures', 'Toads', 'Skin', 'Age', 'Church Going', 'Places, Loved Ones', 'Myxomatosis' and 'Maiden Name'. Since the Hartleys could not afford to cover the initial production costs, it had been decided to revive the archaic practice of advance subscription. One hundred and twenty subscribers were recruited from the literary world and from among Larkin's and the Hartleys' acquaintances. Larkin called it the 'sucker list'.[46] Anxious about the exact terms of the contract Larkin stipulated a time limit on the option clause for his next volume (this ran out well before the completion of *The Whitsun Weddings*). He agreed that Hartley should have anthology rights following publication, and that, instead of a 10 per cent royalty for the author, the proceeds should be divided according to a 'profit-sharing' arrangement. He commented to Monica, 'this *should* mean 50% of the profits: hope it does'.[47] (A year later he calculated that the result had been similar to that of a 12½ per cent royalty.)[48] Seven hundred copies were printed, but to avoid unnecessary expense if the volume failed to sell, only 400 of these were bound up.

By coincidence, at this point the *Spectator* relocated the typescript of 'Church Going' and published it on 18 November, only days before *The Less Deceived* was published. On seeing the poem Charles Monteith of Faber immediately wrote to Larkin inquiring whether he had enough poems for a volume. Larkin had to reply that he was too late. Already finding his dealings with George Hartley difficult, he commented ruefully in a letter to Monica of 24 November: 'Just suppose *The Spr.* had published it *when they had it* . . . Hartley need never have entered my life [. . .]'⁴⁹

The book was an immediate success and Larkin's reputation was made. On 22 December *The Times* named *The Less Deceived* one of their books of the year. There were favourable reviews in the *Times Literary Supplement*, the *New Statesman* and the *London Magazine*. The 700 copies were sold rapidly and the types were reset for a new impression. Larkin was benefiting from one of those chance intersections between the career of an individual artist and the current of popular culture which make a particular book seem an expression of the *Zeitgeist*. As Britain emerged from the war a new cultural consensus had been building which was at this very moment taking a local poetic habitation and a name in the form of the 'Movement'. In 1954 Anthony Hartley, responding to works by Amis, Gunn and Davie, had written an editorial in the *Spectator* defining a new literary spirit: 'bored by the despair of the Forties, not much interested in suffering, and extremely impatient of poetic sensibility, especially poetic sensibility about "the writer and society" [. . .] The Movement, as well as being anti-phoney, is anti-wet; sceptical, robust, ironic'.⁵⁰ Despite Anthony Thwaite's satirical objection that its supposed members all denied knowledge of it, the term rapidly gained currency.⁵¹ *The Less Deceived* was hailed as a foundational text of the 'Movement', and 'I Remember, I Remember', 'Toads' and 'Church Going' came to be regarded as key 'Movement' works. The labelling was confirmed when in 1956 Larkin's poems appeared in three anthologies alongside those of the other 'Movement' poets: D. J. Enright's *Poets of the 1950s*, Robert Conquest's *New Lines* and G. S. Fraser's *Poetry Today*.

In the 'Statement' written for *Poets of the 1950s* Larkin gave an account of his poetic practice which united no-nonsense 'Movement' plain speaking with intense Romantic idealism. He insisted: 'I make a point of not knowing what poetry is or how to read a page or about the function of myth.' This may seem an odd assertion, given his fascination with the

Pygmalion story. He is, however, thinking not of organic mythic patterns but of the fashionable dropping of classical or biblical names. He continues with Hardyesque clumsiness: 'I write poems to preserve things I have seen/thought/felt (if I may so indicate a composite and complex experience) both for myself and for others, though I feel that my prime responsibility is to the experience itself, which I am trying to keep from oblivion for its own sake.'[52] Beneath the affectation of plain language, this is Walter Pater: 'Not the fruit of experience, but experience itself, is the end [. . .] To burn always with this hard, gem-like flame, to maintain this ecstasy, is success in life.'[53] But Larkin covers his tracks with an offhand, 'conservative' disclaimer: 'Why I should do this I have no idea, but I think the impulse to preserve lies at the bottom of all art.' By a deft sleight he proclaims the unfathomable mystery of inspiration in the tones of a regular unpoetic bloke. However, the effort is a strain, and his Platonic idealism will not be baulked: 'As a guiding principle I believe that every poem must be its own sole freshly created universe.'[54]

Robert Conquest, editor of *New Lines*, was to become one of Larkin's regular correspondents. The two men met for the first time in September 1955 when Philip and Monica stopped off in London on their way to a holiday on Sark. Five years older than Larkin, Conquest had been educated at Winchester, Grenoble and Oxford, and after serving seven years in the army, was now working in the Foreign Office.[55] Surprisingly the two men became fast friends, their relationship cemented by their shared taste for pornography. *New Lines* included poems by Larkin, Amis, Davie, Enright, Thom Gunn, John Holloway, Elizabeth Jennings, John Wain and Conquest himself (the same list as in Enright's volume with the addition of Thom Gunn). Larkin is the dominating presence, represented by eight poems.[56] He was, however, uncomfortable with the polemical tone of Conquest's Introduction, which claimed that the poetry of the fifties 'submits to no great systems of theoretical constructs nor agglomerations of unconscious commands. It is free from both mystical and logical compulsions and – like modern philosophy – is empirical in its attitude to all that comes.'[57] Before the anthology appeared Larkin wrote uneasily: 'no doubt I shall come in for a good deal of anti-Movement sniping'.[58]

By all definitions the 'Movement' foregrounds plain indicatives: empiricism, realism, scepticism and clearly legible irony. It would be difficult to find a less apt description of Larkin's work. It is, in retrospect, astonishing that so many early commentators should have read the label rather than the poems, and accused Larkin of offering 'intense parochialism' and a 'stepped-down version of human possibilities'.[59] By the early 1960s the label had become firmly fixed. Al Alvarez's Introduction to the Penguin volume *The New Poetry*, entitled 'Beyond the Gentility Principle' (1962) cites the 'common sense' and 'gentility' of Larkin's 'Church Going' in an attack on the 'Movement'. Larkin's speaker, Alvarez alleges, offers in 'concentrated form [. . .] the image of the post-war Welfare State Englishman: shabby and not concerned with his appearance; poor – he has a bike not a car; gauche but full of agnostic piety; underfed, underpaid, overtaxed, hopeless, bored, wry.'[60] Alvarez's caricature is utterly inaccurate as a description of Larkin's speaker, who shows not the slightest sign of being shabby, underfed, poor, overtaxed or bored. Larkin is not concerned to speak for a sociologically defined generation, and the poetry is diminished by assuming that he does. It is scarcely surprising that the poet adopts such an acerbic tone in referring to Alvarez in later letters. Alvarez's crude misreading, repeatedly cited, continues to dog his reputation to this day.

But, as Larkin realized, whatever the drawbacks of the 'Movement' label, it gave his work a 'brand' image, and in the literary world, as elsewhere, this is a great aid to publicity. For better or worse, his simplified 'Movement' persona took its place in the nation's cultural consciousness, and over subsequent decades he could not resist pretending to be this persona: 'there's not much to *say* about my work. When you've read a poem, that's it, it's all quite clear what it means.'[61] Already in 1956 the 'Movement' was familiar and established enough to generate self-parody. Amis collected together a sequence for publication, '*All Aboard the Gravy Train: Or, Movements among the Younger Poets*, by Ron Cain'.[62] Larkin produced for the occasion a droll Larkinesque piece, 'The local snivels through the fields'.[63] The poet is discovered, among mums in felt hats, on the final stretch of his train journey back from holiday, comfortably enjoying his disappointment at the end of the spree which the labels on his luggage 'shout' about. In a comic zeugma the mothers are laden with: 'Baby-sized parcels, bags of plums / And bones of gossip'. And the poem ends in a virtuoso anti-climax as the journey 'runs out' in a lopsided 'feminine' misrhyme:

> Death will be such another thing,
> All we have done not mattering.

This may be self-parody, but there is tragic conviction in the gloss he gave to Monica: '*Nothing* will be good enough to look back on. I know that for certain: there will be nothing but remorse & regret for opportunities missed not only for getting on the gravy train but for treating people decently.'[64]

For better or worse the 'Movement' remains a relevant category to Larkin's work, though exactly what it implies is disputed. David Lodge later gave 'Movement' poetics a moral and academic rationale. The 'Movement' poets, he wrote, 'aimed to communicate clearly and honestly their perceptions of the world as it was. They were empiricists, influenced by logical positivism and "ordinary language" philosophy.'[65] But Larkin was as much a Jungian as a logical positivist in the mould of Gilbert Ryle or A. J. Ayer; and in any case, his poetry evokes moods and attitudes rather than proselytizing on behalf of a world view. Blake Morrison has identified the 'Movement' with an anti-Romantic return to tradition,[66] with 'caution and consolidation [. . .] orderliness and rationalism [. . .] neutrality and loss of nerve'.[67] Conquest, on the other hand, writing in 2009, is surprised at the reductive literalism with which his Introduction to *New Lines* was interpreted. Far from being 'anti-Modernist', he took it as read, at the time, that 'We had, indeed, all been brought up on, and had digested, "Modernism" of every type.'[68] Larkin certainly had.

In serious contexts Larkin consistently rejected the label of 'Movement' poet, asserting that he had no common programme with the other writers. He had some acquaintance with Donald Davie, and with John Wain, who had been a freshman in St John's when Larkin

was in his third year. But his only close associate in the group was
Kingsley Amis, with whom he was increasingly out of sympathy: 'we
have inevitably had less time for each other during the last five years or
so'.[69] In later years he mentions the label with irritation: 'Bob Conquest's
New Lines in 1956 put us all between the same covers. But it certainly
never occurred to me that I had anything in common with Thom
Gunn, or Donald Davie, for instance.'[70] Ironically, it was because
Larkin's voice was so independent and unprogrammatic compared with
those of the other poets of the 'Movement' that he became its pre-
eminent representative in the public mind.

12

Hull
1955–7

Arriving in Hull in March 1955 Larkin stayed briefly in University-owned accommodation while he looked for somewhere more permanent to live. In late March he moved into a room in 11 Outlands Road, a modern semi-detached house just off the main road between the University and Cottingham. Here he was badgered by the noise from the landlady downstairs; 'her filthy radio *floods the whole house.*'[1] This uncomfortable episode is reflected in 'Mr Bleaney', completed on 19 May.[2] No other poem by Larkin has such plain, colourless rhymes: abab ('stayed / till / frayed / sill // land / took / hand / hook'). The poet declares that how we live 'measures our own nature', so the lonely working-class caricature Bleaney who formerly occupied his room is probably a fair image of what his own life is worth. The language is truculently unpoetic ('My bit of garden', 'stub my fags', 'Stuffing my ears'), and elegy enters the poem through a bad pun. While living here Mr Bleaney worked at a factory making car-bodies.[3] As the landlady explains, 'He stayed / The whole time he was at the Bodies, till / They moved him,' reminding us that we all stay in our bodies until 'They' move us. Mr Bleaney's room is the most prosaic and literal of spaces; but it is also intensely metaphorical: a figure for failure. 'I'll take it,' the poet says, fatalistically stepping into the shoes of a sad man who keeps the garden properly in order, does the football pools to a system and spends 'Christmas at his sister's house in Stoke'.[4] In letters to Monica over the next few years Larkin looked back to these early days in Hull when he was 'living the life of Bleaney', and would speak of 'Bleaney' as his fate or nemesis.

However, the poem is ambiguous. There is a certain exoneration in having only what one warrants in life, rather than being challenged by something 'better'. The delight in privacy which Larkin expressed in 'Best Society' has faded, but this 'hired box' is still a refuge of self-possession. It presents no threat of 'furniture and loans from the bank', and cannot possibly be shared. On one level this sterile version of 'home', a room without even 'room' for books, suits the poet perfectly. Crucially, its window offers a brief, beautiful epiphany: 'building land, / Tussocky, littered', and 'the frigid wind / Tousling the clouds'. The hidden dialectic here is that dramatized in 'Success Story', written a year earlier in March 1954.[5] The speaker's life is a failure by the usual standards, but 'a curious counter-whispering' late at night tells him that actually he has scored a great success: 'you've dodged the dirty feeding'. He has rejected the 'pretence' that 'the other thing' really matters. His superego tells him he should be disappointed in himself for descending to Bleaney's level, but his vagrant poetic ego whispers that no material success could give him anything more valuable than this glimpse of wind-blown clouds. Bleaney's room reveals itself to be a 'less deceived' version of Yeats's glamorous 'foul rag-and-bone shop of the heart', 'where all the ladders start'.[6]

Larkin's correspondence gives no detailed account of his first impressions of his publishers, the Hartleys. We can only guess, from Jean's vivid account, at the degree of his culture shock. She describes their rented house at 253 Hull Road, Hessle: 'It was a tiny two-up-and-two-down, hundred-and-fifty-year-old, jerry-built workman's cottage, on the main road from Hull, with an outside lavatory, no bathroom, a cold-water tap in the kitchen, a shallow yellow stone sink and indoor slugs.'[7] The Hartleys were at first overawed:

> I was greatly alarmed when I saw a dignified gent, slim, with dark hair (receding), very formally-suited, serious and quite unsmiling. His frequent 'White Rabbit' glances at his pocket-watch did nothing to put

us at our ease [. . .] With his chin well tucked in he paced up and down
our small living-room, his tall body bowed to avoid head-on collision
with the light bulb.[8]

But despite their different backgrounds Philip soon came to rely heavily on the Hartleys for support and companionship. In May he moved
from Outlands Road into rather more comfortable lodgings at 200
Hallgate, Cottingham, a leafy village-suburb, two miles from the
University. His Saturdays soon fell into a routine. He would cycle the
four miles from Cottingham into Hull, buy his groceries in the food
hall of Hammonds, an upmarket department store, and then, with his
purchases in a haversack on his back, cycle the four miles to the Hartleys'
home. Jean Hartley recalls him 'bowling along on his enormous bike
[. . .] the biggest I have ever seen, looking more than life-size as he
pedalled down Hull Road, Hessle'.[9] As in Belfast, though now without
the company of a Winifred, he would explore the local villages, taking
photographs of churches and landscapes. Over the years he was to
develop his talent for photography to a high level.

On 13 June, less than a month after 'Mr Bleaney', he completed 'The
Importance of Elsewhere', a different meditation on how our nature is
measured. In Ireland the prevailing context of strangeness made sense
of the poet's difference. He had been 'separate', exempt from the
reproaches of his peers and of his own conscience. In a characteristic
double negative he was 'not unworkable', his existence 'underwritten'
by elsewhere. Now he has returned home he no longer has this 'excuse'.
In the context of his own 'customs and establishments' the pressure to
conform reasserts itself: 'It would be much more serious to refuse.' But,
in the event, neither the grim image of 'Mr Bleaney' nor the pressure of
his own establishments was powerful enough to make Larkin do what
was expected of him. Neither of the two futures prepared for his return
materialized. On the one hand his mother had the idea that he should
'buy a house, here, & that I should live in half of it, & she, with a
companion-help paid out of my rent, in the other'.[10] On the other
hand, Monica, oppressed by her lecturing duties, wanted marriage. He
acknowledged that he was letting her down: 'I haven't done for you

what I could – take you away from all these trying people & the hard-ship of having a job.'[11] There is perhaps some irony in that last phrase.

On Saturday 23 July 1955, he wrote to Monica:

> 9.50 p.m. I went a long bike ride in boiling weather, enjoying it in snatches [. . .] I went to Beverley in a roundabout way, had tea at the Beverley Arms, then went west in a long arc round the villages and wolds to Kirk Ella & Hessle, for the sake of calling on Jean Hartley to see what the position was now. But she was out & the filthy sluttish mother-in-law merely shouted at me through the window – why is my life in the hands of the workingclass? By the time I got back I must have done nearly 20 miles & felt tired.[12]

Philip was in fact on quite good terms with George's mother, but her manner was loud and grating. When the Hartleys' literary friends visited, she would shout out: 'Them poetry blokes is here.'[13] As an anti-dote to her shouting Larkin evoked in his letter the quiet of St Mary's church, where he had seen the celebrated carving which inspired the White Rabbit in Lewis Carroll's *Alice in Wonderland*:

> In Beverley I went into St Mary's and found the rabbit (see enclosed leaflet). I like this church: I hope one day you'll see it. The rabbit is not a very attractive one: I should say it is sneering rather, and some of it has broken away. Then again it might be a hare, I suppose. But it is certainly wearing a satchel [. . .] a lone invader of a hated eccle-siastical stronghold. I expect the satchel contains carrots. Looking into a small papershop for cricket scores I found a pile of Beatrix Potters, & read Apply Dapply's Nursery Rhymes [. . .] It made me wish you were with me –[14]

A short time earlier, on 26 July 1955, casting about, in a letter to Judy and Ansell Egerton in Belfast, for one 'nice' thing to write about Hull, he had concluded: 'oh yes, well, *it's very nice & flat for cycling*: that's about the best I can say. I usually pedal miles & miles at the week-end, always winding up in the Beverley Arms for tea, not because it's good tea but because I never know where else to go.'[15] From early 1955 on an essential insight into Larkin's moods and activities is given by his letters to Judy Egerton. The chemistry between them was strong, but there was never any question of a sexual relationship, though Ansell was aware that his wife became 'devoted to Philip'. The first half-dozen letters were addressed to both of them. Later Larkin addressed letters to her alone (she would toss them across to her husband but 'he was always more interested in the stock market').[16] Philip would tell her to 'give my regards to Ansell – hope the markets are steady'.[17] Over time they developed routines. He would make sure to write to her on or around Trafalgar Day (21 October), and every year she would send him an illustrated London diary. Philip's tone in writing to this sensitive, Liberal-voting woman, who was later to make an independent career in London as an art historian, lacks the performative hijinks and strategic evasions of his letters to his more intimate correspondents. Over the decades his letters to her become one of the most reliable registers of the course of his life.

He settled into bachelor, or spinsterish, routines. Later he told Jean Hartley that he took 'a lot of pleasure' in washing out his own socks and underclothes: 'Very satisfying dabbling and wringing and then seeing them hang out to dry.'[18] On 3 August he dyed three pairs of white socks mauve: 'They came out blindingly bright.'[19] His mother's loneliness was on his conscience, but his reluctance to bring her to Hull was intensified by a visit to Loughborough shortly before his thirty-third birthday on 9 August. In 'Reference Back', completed later in the month, he dramatized the relationship with touching empathy. The mother calls upstairs from the hall to her son playing jazz records alone in his room: '*That was a pretty one.*' Her touching attempt to make contact across the generations precipitates bitter self-reproach on the son's part for selfishly wasting this time at home 'that you / Looked so much forward to'. In the future, every time he hears Oliver's *Riverside Blues*, the recorded notes played by 'those antique negroes' the year after he was born will remind him how the music 'made this sudden bridge / From your unsatisfactory age / To my unsatisfactory prime'. Having repeated the word 'unsatisfactory' four times in this poem, he made sure never to use it again in his poetry.[20] It would be a mistake to interpret the poem as expressing irritation with his mother. He wrote to Eva a few months later to tell her that 'The one about you saying "that was a pretty one" is being broadcast early in February – you never thought, when you said it, that you'd be repeated over the BBC, did you?'[21]

At the conclusion of the poem the lines lengthen, tetrameters and trimeters becoming spacious pentameters to make one of Larkin's most beautiful, sustained rhetorical climaxes:

> Truly, though our element is time,
> We are not suited to the long perspectives
> Open at each instant of our lives.
> They link us to our losses: worse,
> They show us what we have as it once was,
> Blindingly undiminished, just as though
> By acting differently we could have kept it so.

Such writing has the 'frictionless memorability' which Martin Amis identifies as Larkin's characteristic strength.[22] Every word seems inevitable.

His salary was now twice as large as that he had received in Belfast, but his new post imposed far more responsibility and stress upon him. In letters to his mother he frequently expresses his diffidence: 'God knows how I shall ever get through the next few years, building this new library. A sad life for an unambitious creature!'[23] He had two senior male colleagues, the remaining nine staff being women library assistants. Much of his time was taken up with a busy round of meetings. Having received its University charter only six months before his arrival the University was embarking on a programme of expansion. Plans for an enlarged library had already been agreed under the previous Librarian, Agnes Cuming. But their inadequacy was already apparent. As he wrote to the Egertons: 'The Library they are planning looks at present like a rejected design for a cinema: if it is put up, it will be the laughing stock of the British Isles.'[24] Worse, student access would be inadequate. He involved himself with the Estates Office and architects in the revision of the plan, familiarizing himself with technicalities of design and construction. Early in 1956 the project gathered new impetus when Brynmor Jones, Head of Chemistry at Hull since the 1930s, was appointed internally as the new Vice-Chancellor.

Despite all the professional and domestic pressures, Larkin's spirits were rising. The Hartleys had warned him that 'Hull was the armpit of the East Riding' and had expressed surprise that he should want to come and work in the place from which they had failed to escape.[25] But, though Hull might be 'a frightful dump' and the room in which he was living hideous,[26] he was beginning to feel at home here. On 26 September, returning from a visit to Monica, he wrote:

Dearest,

> Back to this dreary dump,
> East Riding's dirty rump,
> Enough to make one jump
>   Into the Humber –
> God! What a place to be:
> How it depresses me;
> Must I stay on, and see
>   Years without number?

– This verse sprang almost unthought-of from my head as the train ran into Hull just before midday. I'm sure no subsequent verse could keep up the high standard. *Pigs* & *digs* rhyme, of course, likewise *work* & *shirk*, & *Hull* & *dull*, but triple rhymes are difficult. Anyway, it gives an indication of how I'm feeling.[27]

How he was feeling was pretty cheerful. Just as a good poem about failure is a success, so a good piece of doggerel about misery is a tonic. He already has in mind a 'subsequent' version of this poem, and six years later, in a typical Larkinesque dialectic, this glum celebration of Hull was to be recast as the gorgeous, serene 'Here'. He was, as he foresaw, to spend the remaining three decades of his life in the city, and never seriously regretted it.

On 18 August 1955 shortly before the publication of *The Less Deceived* Monica expressed her admiration for his writing: 'I like your poetry better than any that I ever see – oh, I am sure that you are the one of this generation! I am sure you will make yr name! Yr mark, do I mean – really be a real poet, I feel more sure of it than ever before, it is *you* who are the one, I do think so.'[28] Philip's letters to Monica frequently include finished poems or drafts, and occasional requests for advice. However, there was never any significant poetic collaboration between them. The few suggestions she made were not always well judged. She decided, for instance, that the phrase 'that much never can be obsolete' in 'Church Going' is ungrammatical, and that Larkin should have written 'so much'. On the appearance of *The Less Deceived* in November 1955 she wrote: 'I wish you could have altered "that much" – it is a blemish on a lovely stanza of a lovely poem – a bit of grit that scrapes every time.'[29] No other reader would see this problem, and it seems surprising that five months later in March 1956 he should still be 'brooding' over it. He conceded that the phrase is 'grammatically wrong', but insisted that 'so much' would imply, misleadingly, 'that what will never be obsolete is really quite a lot'. In a pattern which was to be repeated, he ostensibly deferred to Monica while rejecting her advice: 'I know you are *right* & I am *wrong*, but there it is.'[30]

His mother now added to his anxieties. She was suffering from depression and the letters show that in early December 1955 she was admitted to Carlton Hayes Hospital, Narborough, for patients with mental problems. On 4 December, the day after his first visit, in a letter headed 'Don't answer if you feel you can't!' Philip wrote that he was sorry she was finding the hospital 'so bewildering and un-private'. 'No doubt the idea is that the company of others (however quaint the others are) is meant to draw you out of the prison of misery you find yourself in [. . .]' She wrote to him on 7 December: 'My very dear Creature, This morning I had my first electrical treatment, but beyond feeling a bit shaky and sick afterwards I felt nothing of it.' On Sunday 11 December, he wrote reminding her that he was to visit her the next Saturday: 'keep your tail up. With very special love, Philip.' A card followed on Wednesday, promising to see her 'as often as possible' over Christmas. On Friday 16 December he wrote in advance of his visit the next day, to tell her that her medical superintendent had given her '"leave of absence for Christmas" from 10 a.m. Dec 24th to 6 p.m. Dec 28th'. He decided to book them both into the Angel Hotel in Grantham, with an excursion on Christmas Day to a hotel in Melton Mowbray where his sister Kitty had booked a family Christmas dinner. Throughout this grim, depressing period his letters maintain a steady flow of calming reassurance. He tells Eva not to worry, to eat well and to recover from her cold. On 20 December he wrote: 'I am looking forward to our time together at Grantham. You will enjoy a trip into the outside world, and I shall be all the happier to be with you at this time of year.'[31]

A constant theme in these weeks was the bitter cold: 'Nowhere is really warm in weather like this.' His sense of exposure, physical and also emotional, found expression on 27 December in 'Pigeons', originally 'Pigeons in Winter', prompted, as he told his mother, by watching the birds from their hotel room in Grantham while she slept through the short afternoons.[32] It is a poem of austere, detached description, evoking the pigeons' restiveness as they shift together on the shallow slates of a roof: 'Backing against the thin rain from the west / Blown across each sunk head and settled feather'. As in 'At Grass' and 'Myxomatosis' there is no anthropomorphism. The distance between human and animal worlds is respectfully observed as the birds become lost to the eye in the dusk:

> Soon,
> Light from a small intense lopsided moon
> Shows them, black as their shadows, sleeping so.

The effect is intimate but impersonal, like a black and white woodcut by Gwen Raverat or Eric Ravilious. The poem was read on the radio in September 1956, and published in the Oxford student magazine *Departure* IV in 1957.

On 1 January 1956 he wrote to Eva from the Royal Hotel, Winchester where he and Monica were staying. He mentions visiting Winchester Cathedral, 'where Jane Austen is buried', and attending evensong at Salisbury Cathedral. By this time Eva was on the road to recovery. By 8 January he was writing to her at The Woodlands, Forest Road, Narborough, 'a nicer place for you to be in than the hospital'. His sister Kitty had told him that 'the agreement is for you to "come out" on January 21st'. At this point he draws a tiny sketch of the seal-like 'old creature' in a mob-cap, peeping timidly out from behind a door.[33] The anxiety of the situation resulted in a brief health scare of his own. He was sent for X-rays, but was able to reassure his mother that there was 'nothing seriously wrong': 'Apparently the pain or discomfort is caused, as I felt, by nervous spasms that contract the oesophagus when I eat & prevent my food getting into the stomach at all. The only sure cure is to stop worrying! So I'm to try to relax before meals, & go on taking belladonna medicine, & hope for the best.'[34]

At this point, as the crisis over his mother subsided and the pressure for him to make immediate decisions about his domestic situation diminished, he wrote one of his greatest poems. During their New Year holiday he and Monica had visited Chichester Cathedral, and on 20 February he completed 'An Arundel Tomb',[35] which, though it takes the form of a detached meditative elegy or ode, is on one level a love poem to the less deceived Monica. It begins simply, gathering rhetorical complexity by degrees. The pre-baroque plainness of the monument 'Hardly involves the eye' until it 'meets' the clasped hands with a 'sharp tender shock'. The aspirated 'h' alliteration takes the reader's breath away: 'His hand withdrawn, holding her hand'.[36] The centuries through which the statues have persisted are unobtrusively telescoped into a medley of kaleidoscopic images:

> Snow fell, undated. Light
> Each summer thronged the glass. A bright
> Litter of birdcalls strewed the same
> Bone-riddled ground. And up the paths
> The endless altered people came [. . .]

The seasons flicker 'undated' over the graveyard, as in a speeded-up film: the snow of winter, the light of summer. Time passes in a sensuous blur of synaesthesia: light thronging the glass, a 'bright / Litter of bird-calls' strewing the ground. Meanwhile, isolated from this lively bustle, the effigies retain their archaic posture: 'Rigidly they // Persisted'. There is even a hint of irritation in the tone. The poet is no 'ruin-bibber' with a sentimental investment in the 'olden days'.

Indeed, in order to ensure the most intense rhetorical effect the poet carries his cynicism beyond what is strictly warranted. There seems no reason why he should assume that the couple 'hardly meant' the affection implied by the 'sweet commissioned grace' of the clasped hands, or that it was less important to them than the 'Latin names around the base'.[37] The gesture is rare in medieval monuments and brasses, and it seems not unreasonable to assume that the couple invested emotional as well as dynastic feelings in the monument which they left for posterity.[38] But, though the poet's cynicism might be felt to make the poem a touch less magnanimous and universal, adding a gratuitous drop of acid to the mix, this scepticism makes the rhetorical coup of the final stanza the more stark and dramatic. The couple lie in stone, and this stone may lie:

> Time has transfigured them into
> Untruth. The stone fidelity
> They hardly meant has come to be
> Their final blazon, and to prove
> Our almost-instinct almost true:
> What will survive of us is love.

A resounding cymbal-clash descends to a poignant diminuendo. The first line lurches with a reversed foot into an abrupt denial of consolation, 'Untruth', with its wrenched accent, coming at the culmination of a three-fold sequence of 'un-' words each of which occurs only here in his work: 'undated', 'unarmorial', 'Untruth'. But, like Keats's Grecian urn, the cold pastoral of the monument teases us out of thought. Logic tells us that love cannot defeat death, but the words stumble with a contradictory Hardyesque awkwardness, and the contorted syntax, by making 'love' the poem's final ringing word, strives to assert permanence. The poet knows that the concluding affirmation is mere rhetoric; but its ineffectuality is precisely what makes it so moving.

Larkin consulted Monica Jones during the drafting of 'An Arundel Tomb' more than in the case of any other poem. Its mix of stark pessimism and yearning despair seems to owe much to her histrionic personality. He claimed that he merely 'played at' pessimism, while Monica was the genuine pessimist,[39] and the flat comment on one page of the workbook draft, 'Love isn't stronger than death just because two statues hold hands for six hundred years', bears the stamp of her acerbic intelligence.[40] He also consulted her over fine points of wording, asking her to adjudicate between 'That what survives of us is love' and 'All that survives of us is love'.[41] She later told Andrew Motion that it was she who had suggested the felicitous medievalism 'blazon', meaning a public, armorial proclamation.[42] It is perhaps Monica's intimate association with the poem which explains his subsequent criticism of it to her. It was published in the May 1956 issue of the *London Magazine* and its classic status was recognized at once. But he was uneasy. In a letter to Monica in December he accused it of being over-clever:

> I don't, myself, like it very much: it belongs to that period after publication when one tries to write *ideas* of poems instead of real poems. In fact I think it's embarrassingly bad! and I fancy you will too when you see it again. Real poems have more bite to them. *Mr Bleaney* is more real. 'Lambs' is not bad: better than *Tomb*.[43]

It is tempting to suspect a personal subtext here. The scepticism of the poem could be read as simply misogamist. Is he trying to reassure Monica about his fundamental loyalty by condemning this poem's artifice, and asserting that he prefers the wry shrug of 'Mr Bleaney', and the ingenuous sentiment of 'First Sight', written immediately after 'An Arundel Tomb'?

Larkin spent Easter 1956 with his mother, now quite recovered. The ten-page letter he wrote to Monica from Loughborough on 31 March is crammed with moment-by-moment experiences. He nearly fell downstairs on Sheffield station, knocking a woman with his case. He has mown his mother's lawn and installed roof-felt on the lean-to over the mower. He is surprised to be enjoying a recently bought record of 'progressive' jazz by Dave Brubeck. He has come upon some early letters that Monica wrote to him 'in 1947 or so'. 'They made very strange reading. You were still a lady.' There was also a letter from Colin Gunner, 'about *Winter*', written when he had been 'mining near Bulawayo', advising that he give the heroine of his next novel 'a love affair with an oran outang [. . .] that'll send up your S. African circula-tion'. The letter continues the following day, evoking the 'maelstrom of boredom, irritation, pathos, anger, fear, remorse, nostalgia, & all the rest' aroused in him by his mother and sister. He has told Eva about Monica's latest fashion accessory, pop beads, and Eva 'thinks she'll buy a lemon twin set for the summer'. He listens to *Macbeth* on the radio and describes a toad he has disturbed in the garden: 'not a very good-looking fellow'. The letter concludes with a Larkinesque aphorism: 'I can't imagine anyone is really happy unless they're old enough to have utterly escaped from home, & young enough not to be thinking about death.'[44] As often in Larkin's correspondence, a bitter conclusion contradicts, or is contradicted by, omnivorous involve-ment with his surroundings.

Back in Cottingham towards the end of April, he rejoices that he will soon be leaving 200 Hallgate, escaping the 'elderly nephew' of the household, who sings Italian opera as he flushes the outside lavatory. He had intended to take a trip across the estuary that afternoon on the New Holland Ferry. But he arrived too late at Victoria Pier and, after a visit to the public lavatory there ('fantastically clean, like the inside of a ship: I complimented the attendant – probably an old sailor'),[45] he ate a lunch of beer and biscuits in the Minerva Hotel. 'After that I cycled round the dock area a good bit, then eventually got out on the west side of Hull, and tried to find Tranby Croft, to photograph it for you.[46] But I got lost, & tried to photograph lambs instead: but as soon as I approached two a sheep lifted its head and said something, & they ran away to her.'[47] On his return he fell asleep in his chair while listening to the radio. 'It's delightful to doze when the wireless is on, it becomes a sort of hallucination, part of one's dreams.' Under the heading 'Nearly bed time' he turns to 'visions of you [. . .] that had better remain untranscribed. Not for the sake of decency so much as because such things always look so silly written down! Or would you like eulogies of your breasts and hips, and the tiny creases your pink shoes make by squeezing your toes together?' He becomes lascivious: 'you've been cavorting round my mind dressed in pink shoes & pink pop-beads and nothing else [. . .] All much to the detriment of my typing.' The next day finds him reading *Dylan Thomas in America*,[48] appalled by the Welsh poet's squandering of his talent, and feeling a '*hatred* of Caitlin – "Is there no man in America worthy of me?" – My God. Had a letter from Kingsley today – repeating that his prof is trying to hold him at the [promotion] bar.'[49] Amis was to remain a lecturer at Swansea until 1961.

Between April and October 1956 Larkin lived at 192a Hallgate, Cottingham, a short distance from his previous lodging. In September he took the opportunity of a conference on librarianship in Liverpool to make a detour to Wellington, where he stayed overnight at the Charlton Arms and saw Ruth. His account of the visit in a letter to his mother is retrospective and mellow. Ruth, he wrote cryptically, was 'much the same as usual. I haven't seen anyone else I know, thank God. It's a curious little town, ugly & graceful all mixed up together. The Library was shut when I arrived, but I could see they have altered it a good deal.'[50] But he was more preoccupied with the new accommodation in Hull into which he was shortly to move. He noted that the cooker and gas fire were the same as those he had had in Belfast: 'the whole thing will be like a superior Belfast – I hope!'[51] On 27 October he moved into a high-windowed, top-floor flat at 32 Pearson Park, a Victorian house belonging to the University overlooking a picturesque but at that time somewhat run-down park, between the University and the city.

As a colleague who lived temporarily in the same building in 1963 recollected, these flats were reserved as transitory lodgings for new

University staff while they searched for something better. But Larkin was unwilling to make another move and 'somehow negotiated continued residence there long after he had ceased to be in any sense a new member of staff'.[52] As he settled in he grumbled amiably to Monica about the cold and the noise: 'The fire has been on full since about 5, but sitting by it I can still feel *a cold breath from the door* [. . .] Funnily enough a Yank mag with Mr Bleaney in it came today. I hope he has receded for a bit.'[53] He names the draught 'Daisy Mae', as if it were an American hurricane, and gives comic descriptions of his attempts to keep it out with newspaper and draft excluders. He complains also about the noise from the flat below, but concedes that he is as noisy as his neighbours, and hopes they are not getting into a competition to drown each other out.[54] In this 'temporary' lodging he was to spend some of the happiest and most creative years of his life. He had found his 'proper ground'. Here he would stay.

Hull, an economically depressed, unpretentious city, with a hinterland of empty vistas and vast skies, had turned out to be more welcoming to him than he cared to acknowledge to his correspondents. One of his early letters to Judy Egerton, of 28 May 1957, suddenly modulates into a self-conscious paean to Hull's seclusion:

> this institution totters along, a cloister of mediocrities isolated by the bleak reaches of the East Riding, doomed to remain a small cottage-university of arts-and-science while the rest of the world zooms into the Age of Technology. The corn waves, the sun shines on faded dusty streets, the level-crossings clank, bills are made out for 1957 under bill-heads designed in 1926, and the adjacent water shifts and glitters, hinting at Scandinavia . . . That's a nice piece of evocation for you.[55]

He had happened upon the ideal solution for a man like him. He needed to submit himself again to his own 'customs and establishments'. But rather than resume where he had left off, in Leicester, Oxford or London, he had stranded himself in an English elsewhere, not dissimilar to the Irish elsewhere of Belfast. Like Belfast, Hull made him feel welcome by insisting on difference. The 'salt rebuff' of the

Northern Irish accent was replicated by the local Hull dialect which makes 'phone' into 'fern' and 'road' into 'rerd'.[56] Belfast had been a ferry journey away, but Hull was almost equally secluded, at the end of the railway line with the North Sea beyond. The language he uses about the two port cities is similar: in Belfast 'the faint / Archaic smell of dockland, like a stable, / The herring-hawker's cry, dwindling'; in Hull 'spires and cranes [. . .] / Beside grain-scattered streets, barge-crowded water'. As he put it in 1979: 'As for Hull, I like it because it's so far away from everywhere else. On the way to nowhere, as somebody put it [. . .] Makes it harder for people to get at you. I think it's very sensible not to let people know what you're like. And Hull is an unpretentious place. There's not so much crap around as there would be in London, at least as I imagine it, or in some other university cities.'[57]

Almost all his remaining poetry was to be written in his rented attic on the edge of things. His public literary and professional career developed in visits to London or Oxford. Otherwise he became 'the hermit of Hull'. In the early days glimpses of Kingsley Amis's literary success gave him a shallow discontent with his lot. After a visit to Amis in January 1956 he wrote to Monica: 'It's not his *success* I mind so much as his immunity from worry and hard work, though I mind the success as well.'[58] But his friendship with Amis was now less cordial. After a meeting in August he wrote to Monica: 'he is really not interested in much more than showing off, and [. . .] once he's shown off sufficiently to oneself he's ready to discard one in favour of the most dreary second-raters'.[59] To increase his jealousy, a film of *Lucky Jim* starring Ian Carmichael was released in 1957. However, as Larkin's own reputation grew, this envy subsided. It is significant that, during his thirty years in Hull, he only once invited Kingsley Amis to visit him. Amis was forced to call off the trip at the last minute, and in the event never visited Hull, coming for Larkin's funeral only as far as the church and cemetery at Cottingham.[60]

13

Poet-Librarian
1956–60

Larkin was increasingly comfortable in his professional role. He appointed Betty Mackereth to the post of his secretary in 1957, commenting to his mother that she seemed 'all right in a way: no doubt she will learn. She'll probably stay all her life [. . .] now.'[1] Betty comments: 'He was a very good boss. He took an interest in people; he spoke to people.'[2] He impressed Library Assistant Maeve Brennan by his combination of shyness and bohemian style: 'At 32 Larkin was tall and slim, with a diffident manner and an embarrassing stammer. By contrast, his dress was unconventional by the standards of the day: sports jacket, corduroy trousers, socks in vivid plain colours, and often a pink shirt, which we considered very daring.' Like his father he wore silk bow-ties, and his clothes marked him off from the only other two men on the Library staff, both of whom wore 'the customary dark, pin-striped suits'.[3] Maeve remembers that the nine women library assistants 'invariably wore regulation pale-blue serge fitted overalls which showed off good figures to advantage!'[4] For a time he was called 'Sir', but with joking ironic reference to the novel *To Sir, With Love* (1959), by the Guyanese writer E. R. Braithwaite, which he recommended to them.[5] He was in his element.

The campus was in post-war disarray, with makeshift huts dotted between the 1920s redbrick buildings of the original University College. The Library was inconveniently housed on the ground and second (top) floor of one of the main 1920s blocks fronting the Cottingham Road. As Betty Mackereth remembers, 'Some of the shelving stacks were fifteen feet high, and required skilful ladder climbing. (No talk then about "Health and Safety at Work".)' At first she was shocked at the contrast with her previous job in the Hull Transport Department, where she had had schedules to prepare and many letters to type:

> In the University it was all hanging around chatting: chat-chat-chat; chat-chat-chat. I found myself asking 'what am I to do now?' And Philip would be evasive. In the early months he found a book in the Institute of Education that was not in the Library. So he borrowed it and told me: 'Copy this book and I'll have it bound.' So I typed it. But doubt whether he really did ever have it bound. It was just something to keep me occupied.[6]

The Librarian's office was on the ground floor overlooking a huge sunken lawn known as the 'soup-plate'. Betty recalls that in the summer Larkin would hold a lens in each hand and adjust them at different distances from his eye to view the women students lying around in the sun. Playing astutely on his youth he allowed his own romantic affections to become the subject of collective interest among his staff, and dramatized his lusts for particular students. One such student, Maeve remembers, 'was of Amazonian build – Philip entertained a fantasy about well-proportioned women – and he named a tiny room in the new Library after her, where, the idea was, he would be able to seduce her'. For a time this was known as 'Miss Porter's room'.[7]

He inherited from Agnes Cuming, his predecessor, a Deputy Librarian, Arthur Wood, who, Betty recollects, was an amiable character not highly regarded by his colleagues. In his letters to Monica Larkin elaborated a running gag of merciless antipathy towards this rotund, cheerful 'pop-eyed little deputy'. 'I should like to feed him into a haychopper', 'little jumped-up sawn-off sod!' 'I saw a van in Newland Avenue called Mobile Butchery Service today: felt like giving them a ring to come and deal with Wood.'[8] But within the Library he was careful to maintain the proprieties.

During his first years in Hull the Library staff had something of the aspect of a family, and his youth gave piquancy to his role of pater-familias. When he moved into the Pearson Park flat he asked his female colleagues for their help. As Maeve Brennan recollects:

> He discussed his furnishing plans with us, asked our advice on the best shops for his needs, and regaled us with his purchases in the weeks before he moved: a rose-pink carpet for the sitting-room, offset by bottle-green chintz arm chairs and settee, book cases, storage units for records and, last but not least, a primrose-patterned tea-service which received much use in the coming months. Once everything was in place, he invited us in twos for tea on Sunday afternoons – a series of mini-house-warmings. We admired in particular the spacious attic sitting-room, with its arched high windows at tree-top level, overlooking the park below.[9]

He could scarcely fail to make an impression: unmarried in his thirties, considerate to the point of ceremoniousness, but refreshingly informal at a time when pre-war deferences and decorums were breaking down.

Following the success of his first mature volume he was now confident of his ultimate poetic destiny. When the Queen paid a brief visit to the University in May 1957 and he was not presented to her, he commented to his mother: 'Ah well, one day I shall meet her as Philip Larkin, not the paltry librarian of a piffling university.'[10] His fame was spreading. It was enthusiasm for *The Less Deceived* which impelled one of his library assistants, Mary Wrench, to apply for her post in 1956. She had been working for some years in the London Institute of Education, and decided to apply for the position in Hull to see what the poet was like, rather than with a serious intention of taking the job. She was, however, charmed at the interview. 'Philip was so nice to me and insisted on seeing me off on the coach, saying "I do hope you'll come".' On her move up to Hull Mary found Maeve Brennan particularly kind and welcoming, and the pleasant informality of the Library made a sharp contrast to the stifling atmosphere at the London Institute: 'He was so friendly with all the staff, using our Christian names and wanting to be called Philip. Everyone liked him. He was very likeable.'[11]

He made a tradition of the staff Christmas parties at which he supplied the drinks while the 'girls' provided the food. Maeve Brennan recollects: 'He joined in the long, extended congas through the book stacks with sheepish enthusiasm [. . .] going out of his way to put everyone, even the youngest junior, at ease.'[12] He followed the love lives of his colleagues, congratulating them on their engagements, and sympathizing with them during their 'disengagements'. Maeve comments: 'I myself experienced both states twice in his first three years!' Her ingenuous exclamation mark catches something of the innocence of the time.[13] Mary Wrench detected a strategic element in the young librarian's attentiveness: 'He was quite wily with it. He would make comments which you would think were only meant for you. But then you realized that he was doing this with everyone.'[14] It was at some point in the mid- or late 1950s that he pasted thirty-five numbered renderings of his own name ('Philip Larkin', 'Philip Larkin Esq') into his diary, cut from envelopes, each written by a different correspondent, from his mother and Ruth Bowman to John Betjeman and C.P. Snow.[15] Perhaps he was meditating on his various identities.

In the period following 'An Arundel Tomb' Larkin's relationship with Monica coarsened. The difference in their characters played its part. Philip was deriving increasing satisfaction from managing the Library, and enjoyed his new status. At the same time he was writing reviews, maintaining several diverse correspondences, and creating the poems which were his main purpose in life. For all its frustrations his life was full and creative. In contrast Monica found her lecturing job a 'hardship', and fretted at its relatively modest demands. Writing from 192a Hallgate on 28 July 1956, Philip erupts at her attitude towards 'holidays':

> You sounded as if I'd irritated you in some way over holidays! Just think
> how lucky you are to be at home all July, *all* August, ALL September
> [. . .] AT HOME, *free*, among your belongings & making your own
> days, never doing any filthy work & money coming into the bank just

the same – twelve *consecutive* weeks . . . I honestly don't think a week at Stratford with my mother & a week at Swansea with Kingsley is in the same street, as How to Live [. . .] you're immeasurably better off. I don't suppose I've had more than 3 weeks consecutive holiday since I left Oxford –[16]

A number of her students recall Monica as a lively, inspirational tutor and lecturer.[17] But she had a perfectionist reluctance, not uncommon among Oxford-educated academics of her generation, to bring her work to publication. Consequently, since research was a requirement of her contract, Leicester University held her at the 'promotion bar' in 1957,[18] and she never moved beyond the lecturer grade. She worked on a study of George Crabbe but nothing ever emerged. It is easy to sympathize with Philip's puzzlement in a letter of 3 November 1958: 'I wonder why you're finding your work hard.'[19]

There was also a lack of accord on literary principles. Not infrequently Philip seems to be deferring to Monica's judgement simply in order to avoid a quarrel. His favourite poem in *The Less Deceived* had been 'Absences'. Monica now wrung from him an assurance that he rejected symbolism in favour of common sense:

Of course I agree with all you say about symbolism! How could I not? My mind is stodgy as usual tonight, but I know I'm with you there, like a rabbit huddled against a warm pipe outside the greenhouse on a frosty night. As soon as you start meaning one thing by saying another you open up a gap & the thing sounds hollow. Rabbits wouldn't understand symbolism.[20]

It is dispiriting to see him deferring to her cosy 'rabbit' philistinism. However, in his poems he remains true to himself. Some of his greatest works rely on the metaphorical gap between saying and meaning.

By the end of 1956 their physical relationship had become the focus of earnest discussion between them. He was baffled by her passivity, and welcomed her explanation of her feelings:

you rarely *seem* to like anything more than anything else. I think, if you analysed it stroke by stroke, my – or anyone's – way of making love is directed as much towards pleasing you as pleasing myself, and probably it grows by learning what you like – so if you don't give any definite signs in this direction, it makes it a little – a little what? Less straightforward? Less confident? Anyway, if you like most things, there's nothing to worry about, is there. I don't reckon I 'understand' you at all, even if I do sometimes![21]

Some months later, in July 1957, a mismatch between their levels of libido caused a problem. Monica complained that his lovemaking was 'impersonal' and not 'tender' enough, whereas he found her lacking in 'lustfulness': 'If you don't feel non-personally lustful too, then clearly a large gap remains to be bridged [. . .]'[22] On 7 August he sent her a two-page letter apologizing for not having organized their annual holiday: 'when it [. . .] came to the point, this year I kept putting off the task of deciding what to do or discussing where to go, partly out of lack of initiative & partly because I doubted if we were likely to make a better success of it than last year, until the time came when it seemed too late. I can quite see how nasty & inconsiderate this has been.' He ended the letter abjectly: 'More later – it's taken nearly an hour to write this.' The following day (the day before his birthday) he seemed inclined to call a halt to their yearly routine: 'I certainly thought at the time *Well, you don't have to go on these holidays if you don't want to*, and while this wasn't a resolve not to, I felt I'd better be sure any further holiday was more likely to succeed.'[23]

Larkin's feelings for Mary Wrench no doubt added to his dissatisfaction with Monica. In a letter written jointly to Maeve Brennan and Betty Mackereth in 1986 following Larkin's death, Mary recollected: 'I used to see quite a bit of him outside the university until my marriage, though I didn't think this was a very wise thing to let the staff generally know [. . .] I think Betty knew all this at the time but I don't know that Maeve did [. . .] Anyway, I was in a long line of female friends and why not?' Their relationship was fresh and innocent. He told Mary never to put jam in an omelette, as Winifred had done in Belfast. Mary recalls, 'he always did the cooking'.

one of my funniest memories [. . .] was that on one of these evenings he drew my attention to something in the corner of the room so that I had my back to him. Then he called me and miaowed and when I turned round he had put on a cat mask. He had made this himself. I think, still, that this revealed a very innocent natural sense of fun which few people who didn't know him, except through the writings, would ever guess that he possessed.[24]

When the University acquired the books from Busby Hall, near Helmsley in North Yorkshire, Betty, the only driver on the Library staff, took Philip, Mary Wrench and another Library Assistant, Wendy Mann, in a hired car to the Moors. (The books travelled separately in the University van.) They stopped for a picnic on the way. In 1986 Mary wrote that her memory of the occasion 'still makes me giggle': 'my trousers began to drop down and very simply and naturally he got on his knees, in the middle of all that rural expanse of moor and wrestled with a safety pin to secure my nether garments. I met Betty's grinning face and we all three girls had difficulty in not exploding with laughter.'[25] At times like this the young Librarian must have felt that the world of Willow Gables had become real and he had been given privileged access to it.

In October 1957 the question of marriage arose again when Monica's Head of Department suggested she might take up a visiting lecturership in New York. Philip responded with exasperating indecision: 'if I'm prepared to marry you it shouldn't need an American invitation to precipitate the proposal [. . .] I am simply terrified at the prospect of us going on year after year & not getting married [. . .] You'll say Mum is at the bottom of all this. Well, if she is, I don't know what to do about it. [. . .] Do you think it wd part us if you went?'[26] In the event she did not take the risk and turned down the offer. In January 1958 Philip suggested bizarrely that theirs was 'a kind of homosexual relation, disguised'. Did she not agree that there was 'something fishy about it'? He continued, 'It seems to me I am spoiling yr life in a hideously ingenious way.'[27] On another interpretation, these subtle wrangles show that they were perfectly matched. Both had sex in the head, and they were involved in an absorbing erotic *agon* which neither would have wished to end.

Larkin's relationship with his mother also remained unresolved. He wrote to Eva as frequently as to Monica, with a continuous stream of reassurance and news. However, it was now apparent that he would not bring her to live with him. On 6 May 1956 he wrote immediately after his return from a visit to express penitence at a rare lapse of patience with her: 'Home safely – am about to go to bed, but I must say how bitterly I regret my inexplicable irritability. *Please* forgive me. You do everything to make my visits enjoyable & then I have to go & upset everything. I have *no* self control, it's awful. I love you very dearly & you mustn't worry about me. I'm sure I'll get better eventually.'[28] On 13 November 1956 he confided to Monica his retrospective sympathy for his father, locked into marriage with this difficult woman:

([. . .] I think he was a terrific romantic; & my mother was the equivalent of Emma Lavinia Gifford [Thomas Hardy's first wife]. Poor father!
My heart bleeds for him. What a terrible fate!) I think there's something quite frightening about all the widows, living effortlessly on,
with their NH specs & teeth & wigs, cackling chara-loads of them,
while in the dingy cemeteries their shadowy men lie utterly effaced – I
want to write a poem on this called *To my mother & the memory of my
father*, but can't/daren't.[29]

It is characteristic of Larkin's genius that the poem he actually completed on this theme, two months later, 'Love Songs in Age', replaces the bitterness of the letter with empathy and compassion.

The first ideas for the poem go back to 1953, the final version being reached after much workbook drafting in January 1957.[30] In contrast to 'Mother, Summer, I' and 'Reference Back', the speaker is uncharacter-ized: a detached, genderless, ageless voice. This ensures that the widow's consciousness dominates the poem. The opening is casual and demotic: 'She kept her songs, they took so little space, / The covers pleased her [. . .]' The songs have waited, disregarded, while her life passed by: one bleached by the sun, one marked by a vase, another mended in 'a tidy fit' when she was young, then 'coloured, by her daughter' when she was old. An anticipatory metrical anacrusis imitates the woman's sudden intake of breath as she is overwhelmed by a rush of recollection:

> and stood
>
> Relearning how each frank submissive chord [. . .]

The songs once again perform their function, and 'the unfailing sense of being young' spreads out 'like a spring-woken tree', singing of freshness and 'That certainty of time laid up in store'. But her store of time has been spent. The promise of the songs to 'solve, and satisfy, / And set unchangeably in order' has been tested and, inevitably, has failed, if only because her husband is now dead. Further anacruses across the ends of the lines imitate the aftershocks which follow her initial discovery:

> ushered in
> Word after sprawling hyphenated word [. . .]

Each syncopated enjambment opens out another long perspective:

> But, even more,
>
> The glare of that much-mentioned brilliance, love [. . .]

The shock slowly subsides and the final anacrusis is merely a quiet monosyllabic sigh:

> So
>   To pile them back, to cry
> Was hard, without lamely admitting how
> It had not done so then, and could not now.

This is a masterpiece in the new poetic manner which was to dominate *The Whitsun Weddings*. The poet's own personality is excluded, the eloquent phrases build to a generous emotional climax, and the rhetorical form is bold and uniquely memorable.

The greatest masterpiece of his new style is the fourth of his great Odes, 'The Whitsun Weddings', which he began later in 1957 and completed on 18 October 1958 after sustained drafting from March onwards. The idea had come to him during the summer bank holiday in 1955 (1 August), when he had travelled to his mother's house in Loughborough, changing from the London train at Grantham. He wrote to Monica on 3 August 1955: 'I went home on Saturday afternoon, 1.30 to Grantham – a lovely run, the scorched land misty with heat, like a kind of *bloom* of heat – and at every station, Goole, Doncaster, Retford, Newark, importunate wedding parties, gawky & vociferous, seeing off couples to London.'[31] He alters the time of the poem to hint at the Christian festival of Pentecost, celebrating the descent of the Holy Ghost on the disciples. Secular though it is, the poem concerns a sacrament. Larkin described the experience in an interview in 1981, adding the final stage into London to his original journey. He was struck, he said, by the 'sense of gathering emotional momentum. Every time you stopped fresh emotion climbed aboard. And finally between Peterborough and London when you hurtle on, you felt the whole thing was being aimed like a bullet – at the heart of things, you know. All this fresh, open life. Incredible experience. I've never forgotten it.'[32] He was fond of claiming that 'Happiness writes white.'[33] In this case happiness wrote in full colour. 'The Whitsun Weddings' introduces a sequence of poems in which Larkin adopts the voice of a celebrant of social rituals, an affectionate observer of contemporary life, rather than an alienated, less deceived artist. As he passionately insisted: 'I don't want to transcend the commonplace, I love the commonplace, I lead a very commonplace life. Everyday things are lovely to me.'[34] For many readers these poems constitute his greatest achievement.

Unlike 'Maiden Name' and 'Long roots moor summer to our side of earth', this wedding poem offers no personal challenge to the speaker, who remains an observer. As in 'Church Going' and 'An Arundel Tomb' the poet settles gradually into his narrative. He catches the exact 'feel' of settling down, exempt from obligation, in the secure travelling room of a train compartment: 'All windows down, all cushions hot, all sense / Of being in a hurry gone'. The feeling of enclosure, the heat of the seats and the smell of 'buttoned carriage-cloth' will be unknown to the younger reader of today. But the feeling of release and escape at the beginning of the journey remains the same, as does the blurred rising and sinking of the passing embankments and hedges, precisely imitated in the poem by enjambment:

> A hothouse flashed uniquely: hedges dipped
> And rose [. . .]

The weddings are described in terms of recognizable stereotypes, affectionately rendered. In instructions for a reading on radio, Larkin commented, 'It is of course humorous, here and there, but any supercilious note should be rigorously excluded.'[35] The girls become metonymic 'heels and veils', 'unreally' separated from the other celebrants by their 'lemons, mauves, and olive-ochres'. The children frown, the fathers have 'never known // Success so huge and wholly farcical'; the women share the secret 'like a happy funeral'. The girls, anticipating the 'religious wounding' of consummation, stand 'posed irresolutely', watching the train depart:

> As if out on the end of an event
>   Waving goodbye
> To something that survived it.

Abstract noun phrases ('the end of an event', 'something that survived it'), transform the prose of the social stereotypes into something more evanescent and elusive: a 'frail / Travelling coincidence':

> – An Odeon went past, a cooling tower,
> And someone running up to bowl –

Everyone who has travelled on a train in England in summer has seen this bowler, snatched from sight before his run-up is complete. But only the poet understands that such glimpses distil the livelong minute of life. The couples are too involved in the event itself:

> – and none
> Thought of the others they would never meet
> Or how their lives would all contain this hour.

As in Hardy's 'The Self Unseeing', they are 'looking away'.[36]

The poem becomes an Ode to Incipience. What the poet or the wedding couples do when they reach their destination, what their different fates will be, are irrelevant questions. The poem is concerned only with the moment, the shared 'hour', in and for itself. In a bold metaphor, London yields a fertile human harvest: 'spread out in the sun, / Its postal districts packed like squares of wheat'.[37] The poet drowses as the train approaches the capital and in a complex image combining kinetic sensation with inner emotion he hears the rushing sound of the brakes as the falling of an arrow shower. There is a specific recollection of the memorable scene in Laurence Olivier's film of Shakespeare's *Henry V*.[38] However, this projectile is fruitful rather than threatening. He vaguely apprehends that the arrows sent 'out of sight' are 'somewhere becoming rain'. There is an unmistakable sexual implication in the imagery here: 'there swelled / A sense of falling'. The journey is consummated and the city is fertilized as the train decelerates in a kind of detumescence.

In an influential essay 'Philip Larkin: The Metonymic Muse', David Lodge placed this poem at the centre of his argument that Larkin is fundamentally unmetaphorical, with limited transcendences. The details of the weddings, he wrote, 'are observed with the eye of a novelist or documentary writer and allowed to stand, untransformed by metaphor'.[39] Metonym is, for Lodge, descriptive and half-hearted in contrast with the explicit rhetorical trope of metaphor or simile. Only at the end of the poem, Lodge asserts, does Larkin surprise us with a simile proper ('like squares of wheat'), 'with its mythical, magical and archaic resonances [. . .] so different from anything else in the poem'.[40] But metaphors are not, as Lodge imagines, cherries studding the plain cake of the literal. Metaphor is the poetic element itself. Lodge fails to mention that a journey is the most ancient metaphor for life itself. T. S. Eliot comments: 'you can hardly say where the metaphorical and the literal meet'.[41] Many of Larkin's poems, Lodge claims, 'have no metaphors at all'.[42] He cites 'Afternoons', 'Myxomatosis', 'Poetry of Departures', 'Days' and 'As Bad as a Mile'. Does he imagine that Larkin 'literally' discussed mortality with rabbits, believed days to be geographically located or worried about his aim with an apple core? Moreover, metonym, in which figurative implications arise organically from the 'literal', is the most profound of metaphorical tropes: 'That vase', 'The apple unbitten in the palm', 'someone running up to bowl'. Larkin is a great master of metaphor.

It is a sign of the constant volatility of Larkin's mood that Motion finds it possible to summarize this period in the poet's life, when he was writing his most exhilarating poetry, as 'a low-key, low-spirited time – burrowing into his flat, digging into his job, feeling alternately bothered and lonely, actively frustrated, dozily feeble. More often than before, he turned to Judy Egerton for the comfort of complaining.'[43]

After 'The Whitsun Weddings', Larkin felt the need to administer an antidote. In a characteristic dialectical reversal, 'Self's the Man', dated in the workbook 5 November 1958, three weeks later than 'The Whitsun Weddings', reverts to his 'vernacular', misogamist register. Here the poet once again characterizes himself as a less deceived bachelor. He may, he readily concedes, be more 'selfish' than his colleague Arnold, a kind of married version of Mr Bleaney. But, after all, he contends, Arnold was 'out for his own ends' just as much as he. He 'married a woman to stop her getting away' and his reward (in a vicious rhyme) is that 'Now she's there all day'. On this, now familiar, poetic ground, Larkin has great fun in elaborating a caricature of henpecked working-class domesticity, reminiscent of the radio monologues of the Northern comedian Al Read, a favourite of Philip and Monica: 'With the nippers to wheel round the houses / And the hall to paint in his old trousers / And that letter to her mother / Saying *Won't you come for the summer.*' The original name in the typescript was 'Arthur', and Larkin admitted that a model for Arnold was the

Deputy Librarian, Arthur Wood, 'horrible cadging little varmint'.[44]
He concludes the poem by admitting that he and Arnold are the
same; the only difference is that the poet knows better 'what I can
stand / Without them sending a van –'. Then with a familiar turn of
self-doubt he adds: 'Or I suppose I can.' Perhaps, after all, it is he who
has made the mistake, not Arnold. The poem is characteristically
confident and at the same time radically self-doubting.

Larkin had by now achieved a significant public reputation. Late in
1957 he accepted an invitation from the PEN Committee to co-edit
with Bonamy Dobree and Louis MacNeice the seventh annual anthology of PEN *New Poems*, a task which occupied him during 1958. In
February 1958 he read a selection of his poems on the Third Programme.
Then a few months later Anthony Thwaite invited him on behalf of the
BBC to contribute to a programme for the European Service entitled
Younger British Poets of Today.[45] He read 'Skin', 'An Arundel Tomb' and
'Church Going'. He met Thwaite for the first time on 2 July 1958 and
they immediately became friends. Thwaite remembers Larkin testing
out the parameters of their relationship on their first meeting. In a taxi
between the BBC and a pub where they were to join Kingsley Amis,
Philip took the opportunity to open the mail he had brought with him
from Hull. One large envelope yielded a 'girlie magazine'. 'This is the
sort of thing that Bob [Conquest] sends me,' he remarked with an
interrogative hint. Thwaite gave a decidedly neutral response, and the
relationship developed along more literary lines.[46]

Thwaite had left Oxford in 1955 and taught in Japan for two years
before joining the BBC as a trainee radio producer. His first volume,
Home Truths, had been published by the Marvell Press a year earlier,
in 1957, and his early poetry, with its 'Movement' imagery and quiet
gravity, appealed to Larkin. Thwaite's Bleaneyesque poem 'Mr
Cooper' became a reference point in their correspondence. The fact
that Thwaite is a sincere, reticent Anglican, with political views very
much to the left, never hindered the relationship; indeed it seems to
have cemented it. Larkin's letters to the younger poet often give a
more complex version of his feelings, particularly about poetry itself,
than those to more intimate correspondents who expected him to

share their prejudices. Thwaite went on to be Literary Editor of the *Listener* (1962–5) and of the left-wing *New Statesman* (1968–72) where he published many of Larkin's reviews and mature poems, including 'The Trees', 'Sad Steps', 'Vers de Société' and 'The Building'. Larkin later named Thwaite, together with the much younger Andrew Motion, as one of his literary executors.

In September 1958, in a bolt from the blue, it seemed that Larkin's secure position as Hull's Librarian might be about to end, and his life be ruined. Jean Hartley tells the story:

> in 1958 he received a letter on headed notepaper, putatively from the Vice Squad, saying that his name and address had been found on the mailing list of a pornographic publisher and that legal proceedings would be taken against the subscribers. Philip appeared on our doorstep trembling, white-faced and panic-stricken. He was certain that his mug-shot and crude headlines would be blazoned over the *News of the World* and the *Hull Daily Mail* and that he would lose his job, along with the respect of his colleagues. He might even be sent to prison. What should he do? Burn the contents of the cupboard? Tea and sympathy were offered and a waiting game advised.[47]

He visited his solicitor, Terry Wheldon, to explore his legal position. The danger evaporated, however, when Robert Conquest revealed that the letter was a practical joke. Astonishingly, once the alarm was over, Larkin ruefully appreciated the prank, and remained on cordial terms with Conquest.[48] He wrote to him on 9 September 1958, with a mixture of discomposure and relief, accusing his friend of inflicting 'a frightful scar on my sensibility'. In future 'nude pics will act as a detumescent [. . .] not that I shall ever have the courage to buy any. You've probably turned me homo, come to think of it. Perhaps you'll be the first to suffer the fearful consequences of this. What?'[49] He had no desire to put an end to his correspondence with so interesting and original a friend. A year later, in a letter to Monica, he described a visit to Conquest's chaotic flat in London. He had risen early on the Sunday and done 'all the accumulated washing up – I get great satisfaction from washing up, given hot water & Daz'. Conquest, he told her, 'prepared fairly eatable brecas, just what I have myself. "Will you have fruit juice and bacon? I should perhaps warn you there's — all else." He had his usual litter around him – *Astounding Science Fiction*, *The Polish Revolt*, *London Magazine*, *Frolics at St Freda's*. He *is* an odd chap. A real character [. . .]'[50]

George Hartley had decided to make audio recordings of key Marvell Press poets, and on 24 October 1958 Larkin and he travelled to the HMV studios in London.[51] By this time there was a constant tension between the two men over one thing or another. The record sleeve of *The Less Deceived*, for instance, featured carefully posed photographs of the poet in Spring Bank Cemetery. Larkin wrote to Judy Egerton: 'I had a row (too mild) with the Thing from Outer Hessle, who gave himself credit for the sleeve photos focussed & set with *my* camera loaded with *my* film on *my* tripod *by me*; he just pressed the cable release.'[52] When the record finally appeared in January 1959 he wrote that it was 'quite distractingly upset by bumps & various other polter-geistic activities in the background, nor do I think much of my readings. One or two are not too bad – unimportant ones for the most part – but I don't make much of the party pieces & a lot of the time it all goes dull and rather insignificant.'[53] For all his reservations his beautifully modu-lated, unforced readings have an authority beyond any which have followed them.

After the acerbic 'Self's the Man', Larkin returned, in 'Home is so Sad', to his new impersonal but generous lyric voice. Dated in the workbook to the last day of 1958, it focuses on a tragic archetypal living room seen through the eyes of an uncharacterized speaker. The original inspiration of the poem was intensely personal; indeed this is an anni-versary poem. Like the living room of his parental home in Warwick following his father's death a decade earlier in 1948, the room stays 'as it was left, / Shaped to the comfort of the last to go'. But the life for which it was decorated and furnished has ended. Like 'Love Songs in Age', this is a retrospective, ironic epithalamium. The room, unobtru-sively personified, is 'bereft / Of anyone to please', and the relics of the hopeful start of family life ('A joyous shot at how things ought to be') have become symbols of inevitable failure. In an arresting apostrophe the poet suddenly speaks as if he and the reader are standing together in the room: 'Look at the pictures and the cutlery. / The music in the piano stool. That vase.' 'That vase' is a completely unspecific signifier. It may be one of the loving couple's early purchases, or a prized or despised wedding present, or a casual insignificant holiday souvenir. Whichever of these it is, it has become over the years a familiar metonym of 'home'. Few readers will fail to recognize the equivalent of this vase in their own lives. With his instinct for contrast, Larkin followed this intimately emotional poem with the coolly impersonal meditation 'Far Out' (dated in the workbook 1 February 1959), contemplating the galaxies of deep space with their 'evasive dust' of stars, unmythologized and offering neither guidance nor delight to humankind. It remained unpublished until *Collected Poems* (1988).

In addition to running the Library day to day and overseeing the building programme, Larkin also had the Library Committee minutes to write, the Bookshop Committee to attend, and a yearly speech of introduction to the new first-year students to give, a task he found particularly stressful. It is not surprising that when in 1959 he was included for the first time in *Who's Who*, he gave his occupation as 'librarian', on the principle that 'a man is what he is paid for'.[54] But his life in the Library also had its lighter moments. He encouraged a decorous playfulness among his staff. In July 1959, just as the summer holidays began, in a benign echo of Conquest's practical joke of the previous year, Mary Wrench, Betty Mackereth and Maeve Brennan delivered mock letters of resignation, all in the same envelope, citing the impossible strains of the job. A few days later Mary, left solitary in the Library, wrote to Betty, telling her: 'we've had a brilliant creative reply from Sir', from the Kirkwall Hotel, Orkney, where he was on holiday with Monica. Mary copied out his letter:

25 July 1959

My dear Mary, Betty, Maeve,

It was delightful to get your letters yesterday [. . .] Your resignations are, individually and collectively, refused. I am sorry you find your working conditions intolerable, but that is implicit in the very phrase *working* conditions. How many times must I tell you that you don't come to work to be happy? [. . .] In any case, I am compelled to point out that you are by now hopelessly unfitted for work anywhere else. Does Betty think she could still take down a letter delivered at normal speed? Or Mary endure a post where G.M.T.[55] was still accepted? Or Maeve undertake duties that weren't one long languorous dalliance with romantic Scotchmen?[56]

It is no wonder his staff remember working in the Library with such pleasure. In the current jargon he was a natural and instinctive 'human resource manager'.

The Library staff had to take their holidays early so as to be on duty for the final move into the new building in August 1959. Larkin had a number of stout wooden boxes with handles specially made in the University workshop, three feet long, into each of which a shelf-full of books could be packed for the short drives to and fro across the campus in two vans hired from Hammonds, the Hull department store. Larkin was stationed at the receiving end, and carefully assigned each batch to the correct pink or blue colour-coded stacks. After the move they enjoyed a party, the only time Betty remembers seeing Philip really drunk. The Vice-Chancellor, Sir Brynmor Jones, gave them a day off and Betty, Maeve, Mary and Wendy Mann took the opportunity for a long weekend in the impressive hotel on the cliff-top at Ravenscar, which had an open-air swimming pool. Betty remembers 'there was a lot of giggling'.[57]

In the midst of all this activity, Larkin completed 'Afternoons', dated in the workbook '14.9.1959'. The albums 'lettered / *Our Wedding*' lie near the television as the mothers watch their children playing on the recreation ground. 'Something is pushing them / To the side of their own lives.' By September the Library move was finally over, and Larkin experienced a certain awe at the up-to-date facilities over which he now presided. He told Monica on 7 October: 'This building is like a tiger I have got on & can't get off.'[58] This might have seemed the ideal time for him to have followed the example of his friends Amis, Conquest and

Wain, and taken one of the proffered opportunities to make a short or long-term visit to America. Amis and Conquest both sang the praises of the USA and urged him to go. But perhaps Monica's earlier refusal of her chance made this difficult for him. Would she expect to accompany him? Perhaps he was too comfortable where he was. However this may be, it seems that, by this stage in his life, he was firmly decided against the USA. In April, he had turned down an offer from the University of Cincinnati to be 'their Something lecturer for six weeks in 1960 for 200 gns A WEEK and expenses. Sounded pure hell to me. Betjeman was it in 1957. Can't help feeling flattered, but am refusing, of course.'[59]

In late 1959, as the Library upheaval subsided, his relationship with Monica hit a crisis which changed its character for ever and put the seal on its permanence. His feelings for her were still in a lacklustre phase. On 11 August he expressed himself baffled by his contradictory emotions: 'As usual when you aren't here I should like to scramble to bed with you!!! How to reconcile this with my apathetic exhaustion in your presence is more than I can fathom.'[60] But now his feelings were intensely engaged. Her mother and father both fell seriously ill. He scarcely knew them, and was at an emotional loss. He wrote to Monica on 7 October: 'I don't like to think of you all alone with two such ill people, & parents at that, on your hands.'[61] Then, on 11 October, Monica sent him a dramatic telegram announcing her mother's death. He responded as best he could: 'Dearest, I was very upset to get your telegram & did feel for you strongly.' He expressed regret that he had met her mother only twice, and, in clumsy consolation, deferred to Monica's Tory views, welcoming reports of the election results: 'To die with Conservative gains coming in is not the worst of ways!'[62] He was clearly afraid of involvement. There is a distinct awkwardness in the wording of his letter of 13 October: 'I thought of you yesterday, and deeply hoped you were not being simultaneously ravaged & numbed by it all.'[63]

Then in December Monica's father also died, and she sank into depression. In a fascinating psychological twist, the crisis sent Larkin back to the draft of a poem he had begun in 1957, 'Letter to a Friend about Girls', which contrasts his attitudes towards Kingsley and Monica in terms of comic caricature. Larkin's correspondence with his friend still preserved, in a time warp, the masculine lewdness of their early relationship. During the Amises' visit to Princeton in 1958–9 Kingsley boasted in his letters about his sexual exploits, and on his return to England he and Conquest shared a life of promiscuity. Larkin wrote to Monica in August 1959 after a weekend visit to London to see them both: 'Everyone is having affairs with all the old people & lots of new ones.'[64] In 'Letter to a Friend' Larkin defers to Amis's self-image as a glamorous sexual success. The poet's friend enjoys erotic 'skirmishes / In train, tutorial and telephone booth' in a Platonically perfect world where 'beauty is accepted slang for yes'. The poet, however, finds himself in a separate 'league'. He has, somehow, always met 'a different gauge of girl from yours'. It is, he asserts in mock-heroic resignation, one of those things which, in Hamlet's words, lie beyond philosophy.

The caricatures, however, are deployed within a complex dialectic. From a feeble defence of his own wimpishness the poet slips into a sour but empathetic defence of the lives of the girls of his own 'gauge'. The 'My Darlings' or Margaret Peels with whom he is fated to spend his life do not inhabit a Platonic world of beauty and sex. Instead they 'work, and age'. Against a male caricature of rampant licentiousness the poem pits a female caricature of prissy homeliness. The women in the poet's league are confined within social proprieties. They 'put off men / By being unattractive, or too shy'. Some of them go 'quite rigid with disgust / At anything but marriage'. The poet concedes that the lives of such women may not amount to much, compared with that of his friend. But he humbly asks his friend at least to 'notice' them. The humour of the poem is uncomfortable, and Larkin made no attempt to publish it. His recourse to comic stereotype at precisely the moment of Monica's deepest grief no doubt shows his determination to distance himself from her. But, on a more profound level, the poem is a gloomy acknowledgement of their bond. They share the same gauge.

Andrew Motion interprets Philip's attitude towards Monica at this point as unfeeling and strategic: 'He was too self-absorbed to respond to her grief, and his obsession with his independence made him emotionally stingy. His defence of his actions could not disguise their cruelty.'[65] This seems wrong. Larkin failed to rally to Monica's side because he was in danger of being overwhelmed by her grief. Loyalty was his strongest instinct, and his inability to console Monica at this time distressed him deeply. Betty Mackereth recalls him saying to her with feeling, following the death of Monica's father, 'I am the only one in her life.'[66] In March 1960 he told his mother that Monica was 'very depressed & low. I sometimes wonder if she will ever get over all this: her work seems to weigh her down so much & she feels so alone in the world.'[67] Later, when Jean Hartley queried Philip's assertion that he really ought to marry Monica, he responded lugubriously: 'well at least she's an orphan'.[68]

Protective sympathy, and also perhaps sexual feelings aroused by Maeve Brennan, produced a marked change of tone in his letters to Monica during 1960. Complaints about holiday disasters and analyses of their sexual incompatibility give way to warm solicitousness, erotic tenderness and sentimental rabbit language. Motion writes: 'By turning to Maeve when he did, Larkin ensured that Monica could not become too dependent on him.'[69] The opposite seems to be the case. The fresh delight in life which he derived from Maeve gave him the emotional strength to offer continuing support to Monica. Without it he would have been dragged under by Monica's despair. Her bereavement had set the final seal on her dependence on him. After this trauma, for better or for worse, he would never be able to abandon her.

14

Here
1960–1

The University was expanding rapidly. By 1960 student numbers had risen to 1,660 and Larkin's Library staff had virtually doubled to twenty. With the new building and reorganization to his credit, it seemed logical to make another career move. He applied for the post of Librarian at Reading. On 7 March he visited the Egertons in London on his way to the interview. Something of his apprehension is perhaps audible in the poem he wrote that night. Before going up to bed the Egertons' ten-year-old daughter Bridget sketched a figure holding a lamp under the extravagant heading 'Good night World'. Larkin's accompanying words are rich in self-indulgent escapism: 'Goodnight World / Your toils I flee / Send no importunate / Messengers after me.'[1] On 9 March he fled his appointment with destiny. He was given a tour round the Library and looked round the town. But, instead of attending the interview, he caught the train back to Hull. On his return he wrote to Monica, saying that after a rest he felt 'more cheerful – I'm not going to Reading: didn't care for the looks of it: withdrew my application what. Just withdrew what [. . .] I have lots of good reasons for this, but I was certainly in a funk too, and I shouldn't wonder if it was just that.'[2] The idea of moving away from Hull put him in turmoil, but he was evasive about the reason. A relocation would have interrupted his involvement in the further development of Hull's Library. A 'Stage 2' building programme was provisionally approved only a week later with a target date of 1966–8 and a costing of £600,000.[3] However, a more private 'good reason' for staying must have been his growing attraction to the 'latest face' of Maeve Brennan. Indeed, it seems likely that the application to Reading was an attempt to escape this new threat to his relationship with Monica.

Despite, or because of, the complications of his personal and professional life, Larkin's poetry continued to broaden in scope and deepen in emotion. 'Faith Healing', completed on 10 May 1960, offers a variation on the theme of our 'almost-instinct'. The immediate impetus for the poem was the 'dramatized documentary' *The Savage Eye*, which won a BAFTA award in 1960, and featured a prayer meeting filmed in Los Angeles. As in the poem an evangelist with a 'deep American voice', silver hair, dark suit and white collar asks a stream of elderly women, many of them in a highly emotional state, 'What's the matter?' or 'What's the trouble?', before directing God to cure an eye or a knee.[4] At the end of his poem Larkin modulates from the brutal realism of 'Moustached women in flowered frocks' to an almost embarrassing empathy with their longing for a life lived 'according to love':

> To some it means the difference they could make
> By loving others, but across most it sweeps
> As all they might have done had they been loved.
> That nothing cures. An immense slackening ache,
> As when, thawing, the rigid landscape weeps,
> Spreads slowly through them.

The less deceived sentiment echoes that in Gray's 'Ode on a Distant Prospect of Eton College':

> all are Men,
> Condemned alike to groan;
> The tender for another's pain,
> Th' unfeeling for his own.[5]

An appeal to common humanity transcends cynicism.

A week later on 17 May Larkin completed 'MCMXIV',[6] one of the impersonal set-piece meditations characteristic of his middle period. He had recently read Leon Wolff's *In Flanders Fields: The 1917 Campaign* (1959) and been 'stunned at the awfulness of it all'.[7] The opening image of the poem, a line of young men queuing up to enlist 'as if it were all / An August Bank Holiday lark', recalls a sepia photograph or a jerky scrap of film from the sunny summer of 1914. The form of the date is that on the Cenotaph and monuments 'For the Fallen' on village greens and in town squares. But the poet has no ideological investment in a sentimentalized Georgian past. This England, with its 'differently-dressed' servants, living in 'tiny rooms in huge houses', where children were named after royalty and men queued like sheep to die for their country, is no nostalgic idyll. The details imply no ideology, being purely contingent: tin advertisements for 'cocoa and twist', bleached sunblinds over shopfronts, place-names 'all hazed over / With flowering grasses', and 'The dust behind limousines'. He is concerned with the tragedy of the war, not with sociology or politics. The conclusion develops into an ironic retrospective epithalamium. The men leave the gardens tidy, and their new marriages last 'a little while longer', but without substance, since the husbands are already as good as dead. Only an attitude remains, in the form of monuments with quaint Latin inscriptions. The insistent repetition of 'never' hints that this collective memory of innocence is only almost true, while the omission of the expected main verb ('As changed itself' rather than 'Has changed itself') makes the entire poem into a single complex noun phrase.[8] The poem does not record a real historical 'change'. It embodies a collective myth.

On 20 June 1960 the Queen Mother officially opened 'Stage 1' of the Library redevelopment. Both Eva and Monica came to Hull to celebrate this milestone in Philip's career. The ceremony saw Larkin at the apex of his public role, and he was proud of his achievement. The Vice-Chancellor introduced him to the royal visitor with the words, 'This is Mr Larkin our poet-librarian', and the Queen Mother replied, 'Oh, what a lovely thing to be.'[9] For some time afterwards he delighted in imitating Brynmor Jones's Welsh lilt and the Queen Mother's high-voiced reply. Four decades later Maeve Brennan remembered the occasion vividly: 'I wore an elegant chocolate and coffee-coloured dress of satinised cotton with cream hat and gloves.'[10] Maeve had already met Eva, who visited her son in Hull every year. The two women found they had much in common and liked each other. At the ceremony Eva introduced Maeve to Monica. Maeve recalled later that she was 'mildly interested to meet my boss's girl-friend!' She was not to speak to Monica for another twenty-five years.[11] In July Larkin spent a week in Minehead with his mother, before going on holiday with Monica to the island of Sark. This 'village surrounded by sea', as he called it, was to become one of their favourite holiday retreats.[12] His letters to Monica at this time, addressed to 'Dear bun' or 'Dearest bunny', show increasing affection. On 4 August he wrote: 'I miss the drink and the laziness of our holiday, & your company & readiness to trade chuckles and gull cries.'[13]

'Talking in Bed' was completed on 10 August 1960, the day after his thirty-eighth birthday and exactly ten years since he and Monica had first slept together.[14] Apart from the uncomfortable seduction by Patsy Strang in 1952–3 Larkin remained faithful to Monica, in strictly sexual terms at least, for a quarter of a century, from 1950 until 1975. This is Larkin's most intensely felt love poem, describing a committed relationship, for better or for worse. Its impact is muted and bleak but it is charged with restive verbal expressionism. It opens with a 'bad' pun: 'Lying together' carries a sexual and also a moral meaning. Like the earl and countess, the lovers form an 'emblem of two people being honest', which 'goes back so far': as far indeed as Adam and Eve, who lay together following the Fall and then lied to God about it. The first few lines maintain detachment, but there is a strain between the intimate subject and the dispassionate tone. Then in line eight a gesture of extravagant despair breaks the poem's composure: 'None of this cares for us.' The hissing monosyllable 'this' with its high short vowel seems arrogant; the lower vowel of 'us', unprotected by an opening consonant, is defenceless against it. A verbal perversity unique to this poem intensifies the emotional excess. The double negative phrase 'incomplete unrest' conveys a meaning more logically represented by 'complete unrest', but the grammatically correct 'complete' would imply restfulness. This wedding-wind is agitated and anxious. The final sentence presents the reader with a series of verbal tripwires. The phrase 'this unique distance from isolation' actually means unique closeness to isolation, but the poet disregards correct grammar in order to make sure that all three words in the phrase express alienation ('distance, 'from', 'isolation'). His meaning would be expressed correctly by 'distance *and* isolation'; but this would be limp in comparison. The concluding Hardyesque double negative, 'not untrue and not unkind', should logically resolve itself into 'true and kind'. Instead it conveys something more subtly intimate and tragic. The poem's tricksy verbal contortions do not detract from its gravity. Rather their far-fetched strangeness serves to give the poem an emotional power quite out of proportion to its length: twelve tetrameter lines.

Three days after this (13 August 1960) Larkin returned to complete a poem, 'Pets', first drafted in 1954, retitling it 'Take One Home for the Kiddies'. It is a terse reflection on children's passion for the novelty of 'living toys': 'fetch the shovel – / *Mam, we're playing funerals now.*' Seven days later he completed 'A Study of Reading Habits', on the surface a similar class-biased satire, this time on the facile conventions of popular literature. Beguiled by adventure stories in his youth, the speaker imagined himself a hero dealing out 'the old right hook / To dirty dogs twice my size'. Later, he graduated to gothic fantasies of vampirism. With his 'cloak and fangs' he broke women up, in a malicious rhyme, 'like meringues'. In the final stanza disillusion has set in: 'Don't read much now [. . .]' He has seen through the clichés, now those of the Western: 'the dude / Who lets the girl down', 'the chap / Who's yellow and keeps the store'. On the simplest level this is a didactic warning against subliterary escapism. But there is an oblique subtext of self-mockery. The poet is not so different as one might at first think from the poem's speaker. His responsible professional role has required him to outgrow his own literary dreams. Six years earlier the poet-librarian had feared his employer's reaction to 'Toads'. Now, his status safely established, he ensures that one of his most quotable lines will be: 'Books are a load of crap.'

Larkin had encouraged his staff to take the Library Association examination, offering to coach them in lunch-time tutorials. Half a dozen signed up, including Maeve Brennan. But, by the autumn of 1960, as Maeve recollected, 'all my colleagues had dropped out for one reason or another – they got married, or moved away, or became pregnant – and only I stayed the course'.[15] By the time she took the examination in December their relationship had intensified. On one level Maeve seemed to Larkin a *genius loci* of Hull: an ordinary, conventional Catholic girl with a sound but limited education and a charming innocence. She was the daughter of a dentist and at the age of thirty still lived with her parents. In her memoir she depicts herself as one of the crowd, attracted like the other library assistants by Philip's shyness and vulnerability: 'his stammer was [. . .] still pronounced and his diffidence of manner never completely left him. In fact his reserve was the key to his popularity with women – of all ages and status – making them feel protective towards him.'[16] But he also impressed them with his cosmopolitanism and sophistication. He would cook in his flat, serving 'fare we did not have at home, such as haggis and smoked kedgeree. He introduced me to avocado pears and asparagus which were then only just beginning to appear in the more upmarket shops in Hull.' He also had about him the glamour of a published novelist and poet. Culturally and intellectually the relationship between Philip and Maeve was an unequal one. She remarked in retrospect: 'how this unlikely friendship came about never ceases to surprise me'.[17] Her conclusion was that it was based on spiritual affinity. In 1960 she had 'a steady boy-friend', also called Philip; 'we were both Catholics and our outlook on life was therefore similar. But ironically, as I was soon to discover, Philip Larkin and I were on a much closer spiritual level than Philip C. and I had ever been.'[18]

The Hartleys were surprised by the freshness of Philip's affection. He was, Jean says, intensely 'in love': 'Maeve began to be mentioned and, quite soon, brought round to our house and introduced. This was not done in Philip's usual neutral manner when referring to his women friends. Whenever he spoke of Maeve or looked at her, it was with a sense of having won first prize.'[19] More intimately, Maeve later confided to Jean that Philip had told her that she kept him in 'a state of continuous excitation'.[20] Margaret Fowler, who was Maeve's assistant in the Periodicals and Binding Department of the Library, remembers that he started to 'wander in' to their small work room during the day, 'and, oblivious of my presence, was like a teenager in love for the first time; "besotted" was my word for it'.[21]

Two years earlier he had written to Monica that he was '*not* a highly-sexed person, or, if I am, it's not in a way that demands constant physical intercourse with other people'.[22] Maeve's Catholic propriety generated more erotic intensity than his physically fulfilled relationships. He became more sexually alert. In a letter to Judy Egerton of September 1960 he described visiting the cinema to see *The Nudist Story*, 'the sort of thing I do when alone. It confirmed my impression that bad films aren't so bad when the characters haven't any clothes on.'[23] Late in 1960 he mounted an exhibition in the Library to celebrate the success of the court case which opened the way to the publication of the unexpurgated *Lady Chatterley's Lover* by Penguin. The exhibits included his own signed copy.[24] Richard Bradford takes a different view of the relationship with Maeve, conjecturing that it resulted from 'mental imbalance', induced by envy of the 'recklessly licentious' Kingsley Amis. Bradford refers to Maeve's 'combative, well-defined features' that we 'readily associate with maleness', and argues that Larkin saw in her 'anxiety, insularity, shyness' his 'depressing mirror image'.[25]

It is difficult not to conclude that this new stimulus made him more sympathetic towards Monica's neediness. On 4 October 1960 he recalled her recent visit to Hull: 'I am thinking of you and wondering if you are in bed & rested. I do hope so. It was nice your bolting here: I hope you found it cheered you up. You are such a nice rabbit – really thoroughly nice. Much love'.[26] On 27 November he wrote:

I did love being with you last weekend. I treasure the memory of your lovely looks, really as I say lovelier than ever. Beautiful handsome girl! You're really horribly attractive, especially your legs, as you know. It must be all this milk you're drinking, don't you think? I wish you had put on the silk dress, but as you said it would probably have come to grief.[27]

But Monica remained sunk in mourning depression. He wrote to his mother: 'she is so low and unhappy and lonely [. . .] she really does seem so near giving up, or perhaps paralysis wd be a better word'.[28]

To celebrate the completion of Maeve's examinations in December 1960 Philip took her to dinner at the White House, the best restaurant in Hull. Afterwards she felt too inebriated to go directly home and they went first to his flat for coffee. She promised him that if she passed the examination she would take him out to dinner in return. But, despite his growing feelings for Maeve, Philip still felt bound in loyalty to Monica: 'I have built her in my own image and made her dependent on me, and now I can't abandon her.'[29] On New Year's Day he wrote to Monica with a mixture of sympathy and briskness: 'I'm terribly sorry you feel so miserable these days, though not surprised – it is a most trying position to be in, and I should hate it and feel utterly down and out, hopeless and scared to death, just as you do.'[30] A few days later, on 10 January 1961, he wrote to her again, more affectionately, following a visit they had made together to Lincoln:

I saw your white furred face turn to go back in the station, as if you were quick to get on with the next thing. In fact I then saw the best view of the cathedral I had had all day: straight up the High Street, floating as if in mid-air, its four red lights on. This is the view Paul Morel and his mother must have had, emerging from the station after coming from Nottingham [. . .] It's a pity we never turned round: did you see it?[31]

Monica would, he knew, understand what this Lawrentian epiphany meant to him. Their shared literary background bound them together in a way he would never be bound to Maeve.

Since the end of November he had been working on 'Ambulances', dating the final draft '14/1/61', and then making further changes before it was published in the *London Magazine* in April.[32] The poem is a set of variations on the grammatical device of the noun phrase, moving away from the literal through ever increasing levels of elaboration and elusiveness. The nouns are at first simple: a 'wild white face' is shut away behind 'fastened doors'. But the phrases become more abstract:

> For borne away in deadened air[33]
> May go the sudden shut of loss
> Round something nearly at an end,
> And what cohered in it across
> The years, the unique random blend
> Of families and fashions, there
>
> At last begin to loosen.

In one of Larkin's hallmark 'what . . .' constructions, the grammatical subject, 'what cohered in it', becomes a fading abstraction, and the verb is delayed by yet another, more intricate noun phrase ('the unique random blend'). Despite the hopefulness implied by the anacrusis 'there [. . .]', which restores the reader's grammatical balance, this is the beginning only of the end. When the long-delayed verb does come we realize that the grammar has broken down. The words 'what' and 'blend' are singular, so the verb should be 'begins'. However what cohered within this blend has now loosened, so the plural is sadly accurate.

In the first three stanzas the poet has viewed the scene from outside. In the last two stanzas poet and reader share the ambulance with the dying patient:

> Far
> From the exchange of love to lie
> Unreachable inside a room
> The traffic parts to let go by
> Brings closer what is left to come,
> And dulls to distance all we are.

The subject of the sentence is yet another elusive noun construction enclosing a series of subordinate phrases, and once again the verb ('Brings') is delayed, as though the poet is reluctant to face its implications. The parallel grammatical construction in the last two lines is subtly modulated. First the positive-sounding verb 'brings' focuses the meagre 'what is left to come', then the negative verb 'dulls' governs an existential summary of the whole of life: 'all we are'. The selfish less deceived 'what I am' which emerged in 'Best Society' becomes here the more generous and tragic (if equally less deceived) 'all we are'.

Maeve was successful in her exams, and in early February 1961 she fulfilled her promise to take Philip to the Beverley Arms for dinner. Afterwards they walked arm in arm to the taxi rank through the 'bright, frosty night',[34] and as she puts it 'from that evening our friendship entered a new and headier phase'. Shortly afterwards he called her into his office and, with a show of embarrassment which made a great impression on her, presented her with a gift of Elizabeth Arden *Mémoire Chérie* perfume: 'never before had I been given so romantic a gift in such touching circumstances – and my quest for romance had always been strong, though hitherto a vain one'.[35] For all the differences between Philip and Maeve they shared a simple impulse for romance. Philip's imagination was taken with the fact that she bore the name of an ancient Irish queen, and that her father, though a Hull dentist, had in his youth been a member of the Republican Irish Volunteers in Dublin and had walked the same streets as Yeats and Maud Gonne. He even compared Maeve to Yeats's muse, much to her father's derision: *'You* like Maud Gonne? Don't be ridiculous. *She* was very beautiful [. . .]!'[36]

As his literary reputation grew, Larkin became more confident in taking public initiatives. In January 1961 his friend Peter Coveney, the Warden of Needler Hall of Residence, introduced him to Donald Mitchell, a music critic who worked for the *Daily Telegraph*. Mitchell suggested Larkin as a jazz reviewer for the newspaper. He was taken on, and his first review appeared on 11 February 1961. He was to continue to write monthly reviews for the remainder of the decade and beyond.

On 16 January 1961, Larkin sent a letter to the novelist Barbara Pym

offering to write a 'general essay' on her work for the *Spectator* when her
next book appeared.[37] He was unaware that *No Fond Return of Love* was
just about to appear, and his offer was rather late. He asked to be sent
a proof copy of her next novel, so that he could write his essay when it
appeared.[38] He could not have suspected that this next work would not
be published for another sixteen years. His approach, however, initiated a correspondence, which lasted until Pym's death in 1980. It seems
likely that there was a strategic, sexual-political motive in Larkin's
public assertion of affinity with Pym. His sister Kitty, as well as both
Monica Jones and Maeve Brennan, were keen readers of Pym's novels.
She, like him, was a misogamist, preferring romantic dream over the
ties of marriage. By associating himself with this respectable woman
writer, Larkin made his stubborn misogamy seem less antisocial. His
was not, he deceptively implied, the lonely artistic dedication of the
poète maudit, but a normal, even perhaps a 'typically English' life choice.
He thus complicated the abrasive masculine 'Movement' context
imposed on him by critics. Pym cast herself as 'this old brown spinster';[39] Larkin increasingly cast himself as the bachelor hermit of Hull.

On 22 February 1961 Larkin put the final workbook touches to one of
his most radically ambiguous poems: 'Naturally the Foundation will
Bear Your Expenses'. He explained its inspiration later as 'a mixture of
finding that a number of my friends had gone to India and hearing, as I
usually do, the broadcast of the service at the Cenotaph'.[40] On one level
the poem is satirical: he wrote to Robert Conquest, 'I hope it annoys all
the continent-hopping craps.'[41] But Conquest himself, of course, was
both a 'friend' and a 'continent-hopping crap'. Conquest and Amis had
recently urged Larkin to follow their example. The mention of India
seems almost a diversionary tactic, the USA being his friends' usual destination. The poet's attitude towards the speaker on his expenses-paid
jaunt is not simple condemnation: 'Certainly it was a dig at the middle-
man who gives a lot of talks to America and then brushes them up and
does them on the Third and then brushes them up again and puts them
out as a book with Chatto'.[42] His wording is concessive: 'Certainly it was
a dig'; this dig is not the real point of the poem.

The poet's attitude towards the Armistice Day ceremony is also not as clear as most commentators have assumed. Though he allowed his emotions full rein in writing to Monica, declaring that hearing the Cenotaph service with the massed bands of the Guards playing Elgar's 'Nimrod' 'harrows me to my foundations',[43] nevertheless in a 1964 interview he defended his speaker against patriotic critics: 'Why he should be blamed for not sympathizing with the crowds on Armistice Day, I don't quite know.'[44] Indeed, in writing of the 'solemn-sinister / Wreath-rubbish' of the official ceremony, Larkin will certainly have had in mind Siegfried Sassoon's image in 'At the Cenotaph', of the Prince of Darkness attending the ceremony in the hope that it will foster nationalistic jingoism.

A further ambiguity is provided by the poem's intimate association with W. H. Auden. The speaker refers to himself, in a sophisticated poeticism, as dwindling 'down Auster', the South Wind:

> – But I outsoar the Thames,
> And dwindle off down Auster
> To greet Professor Lal
> (He once met Morgan Forster),
> My contact and my pal.

The Byronic double rhyme 'Auster / Forster' cannot help but bring Auden to mind. It seems not too fanciful to suggest that 'Auster' came to Larkin as a rough portmanteau of 'Wystan Auden'; Auden, like Forster, was a continent-hopping homosexual. The circuit of which the speaker is taking advantage was pioneered by writers like Auden and Dylan Thomas in the years following the Second World War. Larkin derided Auden for descending from the 'superb, magnetic, wide-angled poet' of the 1930s to 'the great American windbag' of his later years, crossing continents on reading tours.[45] Nevertheless the jaunty freeloader of Larkin's poem, published in *Twentieth Century* in July 1961, presented an attractive enough picture to prompt Auden's own genial self-satire, 'On the Circuit', published in *About the House* in 1966. Auden's speaker clearly owes something to Larkin's:

> Another morning comes: I see,
> Dwindling below me on the plane,
> The roofs of one more audience
> I shall not see again.
>
> God bless the lot of them, although
> I don't remember which was which [. . .][46]

Auden's persona, like Larkin's, relishes his sky-borne elevation above the audience that pays for his lifestyle. Larkin's attitude towards the literary 'circuit' is envious as well as disapproving. His poem is not morally didactic: 'I shouldn't call myself a satirist, or any other sort of -ist [. . .] To be a satirist, you have to think you know better than everyone else. I've never done that.'[47] Before it was published Larkin remarked to Monica that everybody seemed to be misreading the poem. Brian Cox, then in the Hull English Department, and editor of *Critical Quarterly*, thought it 'a bit hard on the Queen'.[48] His secretary, Betty Mackereth, joked that its animus against travelling would be attributed to his recent illness; 'not that I think she gets it any more than Cox did. How to read a page. Ogh ogh ogh [. . .] Well, it may not be a good poem, but it's a good title.'[49] He teasingly omits to explain how this particular page 'should' be read. Subsequent commentators continue to interpret the poem as angry moral satire. Motion calls it 'a piece of savagery'.[50]

On 6 March 1961, at a point when he was at the peak of his achievement in both professional and literary terms, Larkin suddenly collapsed during a Library Committee meeting and was rushed to Kingston General Hospital.[51] The doctors dismissed his immediate explanations: that his shirt collar was too tight or that his new spectacles had induced dizzy spells, though a recent analysis of Larkin's spectacles has suggested that a rogue prescription could indeed have been responsible for his disorientation.[52] However, in the case of a sensibility so radically psychosomatic as Larkin's it is tempting to seek personal causes for his mysterious breakdown. Over the previous months he had been overworked and under stress. He had managed the Library transfer and had endured the public exposure of the official opening. More relevantly, perhaps, he was aware that, though he could claim to be still faithful to Monica in physical terms, he was betraying her emotionally by his involvement with Maeve. Richard Bradford suggests a different reason for Larkin's collapse: intense jealousy of Kingsley Amis's success in being appointed Official Fellow and Tutor at Peterhouse College, Cambridge.[53] This is not an explanation which occurred to Larkin at the time, nor to anyone else since.

The next few weeks saw him subjected to extensive medical tests and deeply worried. He wrote compulsively from the ward to Monica. A letter dated 11 March runs to eighteen sides, written uncharacteristically in ballpoint and with an unwonted unsteadiness of hand. It begins with a PS at the top of the first page: 'I'm afraid this becomes rather a "frightened" letter, & isn't much fun to read [. . .]':

 It is Saturday & I've just had some lunch: it's 10 to one. There is nothing much to report. I haven't been x rayed yet, or brain-waved, as I believe they intend to do.

 I *feel* about the same – that is, there is something wrong with my vision, wch makes me have to focus specially sometimes, & I feel rather distant from my feet: this is all summed up by being *aware* of my right eye. In addition to this, I am out of sorts in a 'flu-y kind of way – no appetite, coated tongue, bowels sore, & ready to sweat easily. This last symptom seems to interest them.[54]

He is effusively grateful to her: 'I must thank you, dearest dearest love, for coming to see me so quickly, and for sending me cards & letters.' However, he refused to allow her to stay in his flat because 'I had left a few private papers & diaries lying around. Such things, which I suppose I keep partly for the record in the event of wanting to write an autobiography, & partly to relieve my feelings [. . .] will have to be burned unread in the event of my death [. . .]' He continues, 'I've been writing for an hour now, partly because I like talking to you, partly to see how my eyes & brain stand it. If this looks legible & makes sense I suppose I'm not too far gone yet [. . .] Oh darling I wish you were here!'[55] Pages of abjection follow, with little sign of his usual élan and wit: 'I can't bring myself to do anything but lie either whining to you or shudder-ing to myself.' 'I hardly know if I ought to send letters like this. You see, darling, I'm afraid I'm *seriously* ill, & really this is all that's in my mind, and nobody can give me any comfort. It would be comforting to have you here to talk to, if you could stay all the time, but it wdn't be any *ultimate* comfort, wd it?'[56] He wonders whether the problem may be with his liver: 'the liver *can* affect vision, can't it? You know what horrors are associated with livers for me, through my father.'[57]

The following day, Sunday 12 March 1961, he wrote to Maeve in a more reticent tone: 'I don't want to write very much at present. I don't feel in good enough spirits: I should only moan [. . .] but with all this time to spare, & without getting better, I have not been able to keep from worrying rather.'[58] On the same day he wrote a six-page letter to Monica which continued into Monday (beginning at 6.30 a.m.). He wrote again on the same day (eight sides), complaining about the television on the ward, and discussing their plans to attend the Test match at Lord's: 'Suppose there is something seriously wrong with my brain! Should I not say these things to you? Is it unfair of me?'[59] But his panic was subsiding. On 15 March he wrote only four sides to Monica, discussing the recent heavyweight boxing match involving Ingemar Johansson. On 16 March he wrote six sides, mentioning the radio soap opera *The Archers*, the marriage of Picasso and the death of Sir Thomas Beecham. Peter Coveney offered to let him move into Needler Hall when he was discharged. On 30 March Eva Larkin travelled up to Hull and looked after him there until 4 April. If his breakdown was a subconscious bid for sympathy and attention, it had certainly succeeded.

He was advised not to return to work immediately and paid for further tests in London by the eminent doctor, Sir Walter Russell Brain. Monica and Eva took rooms in different London hotels and he was visited by Kingsley and Hilly Amis,[60] Robert Conquest (who brought him pornography), Stephen Spender and John Betjeman. Brain found a 'deep-seated abnormality in the left cerebral hemi-sphere', and commented: 'He has epilepsy of late onset with no

George and Jean Hartley printed Larkin's poems 'Spring', 'Dry-Point' and 'Toads' in their magazine *Listen* (1954). In 1955 they founded the Marvell Press and published *The Less Deceived*.

Maeve Brennan was a Library Assistant when Larkin arrived in Hull in 1955. She recalled: 'On Monday mornings he would ask: "Well, any more engagements this weekend; or better still, any disengagements?"'

Larkin's first University of Hull library staff portrait, 1957, taken by delayed-action shutter release. *Front row:* Maeve Brennan, Arthur Wood (Arnold in 'Self's the Man'), Larkin, John Farrell, Mary Wrench. *Back row, second from left:* Larkin's newly appointed secretary, Betty Mackereth; *Middle row, second from left:* Wendy Mann.

Larkin met Judy Egerton in Belfast in 1951, and they corresponded regularly. She became Assistant Keeper of the British Collection at the Tate Gallery from 1974.

Anthony Powell, Hilly Amis, Kingsley Amis and Philip Larkin in London.

bring them sprouts, cabbages, pieces of bread, and cake. When there is none of this available they eat grass.

I hope you have a happy New Year. Do not tell Uncle Alec where your money box is, if he should ask.

With love from
Philip.

Extract and drawings from a letter to Judy Egerton's six-year old daughter, Bridget, 4 January 1956. Larkin has modified his handwriting to make it more legible.

Pearson Park, Hull: the lake, and the poet at the Venetian window of no. 32. Philip Larkin moved into his top-floor flat in October 1956, and this self-portrait is dated 1958, the year he completed his poem 'The Whitsun Weddings'.

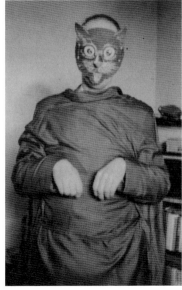

In 1957 Larkin shared a discreet intimacy with Library Assistant Mary Wrench (later Judd). She recalled his 'innocent natural sense of fun'; 'he called me and miaowed and when I turned round he had put on a cat mask'. Mary married in 1960 and Larkin and Betty Mackereth were godparents of her first child.

Maeve Brennan, *c.*1960. Jean Hartley commented: 'Whenever he spoke of Maeve or looked at her, it was with a sense of having won first prize.'

Monica Jones in tights given to her by Eva Larkin. Philip wrote to his mother in January 1960: 'Monica liked the striped tights, but they don't fit exactly – the feet are too big, and the ankles too large.'

The new University of Hull library under construction, October 1958. Larkin's shadow here shows his flair for photography.

'The Main Undergraduate Reading Room', from the booklet commemorating the opening of the library.

Larkin with the Queen Mother and the Vice-Chancellor, Sir Brynmor Jones, at the official opening of the new University of Hull library, 20 June 1960. This was the high point of Larkin's career as a librarian.

The view of the Humber estuary from the train inspired Larkin's lines 'Where sky and Lincolnshire and water meet' ('The Whitsun Weddings'), and 'the widening river's slow presence, / The piled gold clouds, the shining gull-marked mud' ('Here').

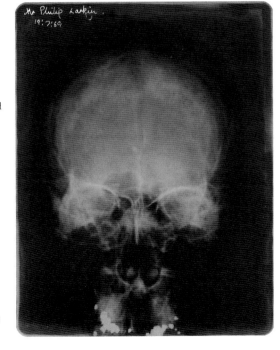

Inside the poet's head: X-ray, 19 July 1969. Larkin commissioned a number of X-rays during his various health scares.

Spurn Point, with remains of wartime defences: the
'beach / Of shapes and shingle' in 'Here'.

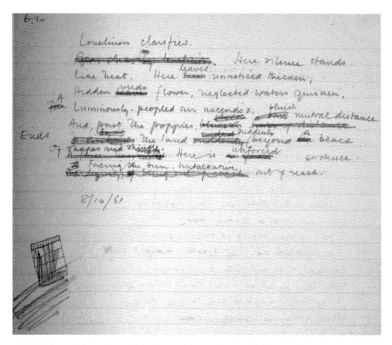

The final page of 'Here' in Workbook 6. On the tenth page of drafting Larkin wrote out a near
immaculate version of the first three stanzas. Continuing on to this eleventh page he was so sure
of his corrections that he did not make a fair copy of the final stanza, leaving the remainder
of the page blank. Before the poem was published he changed 'unforced' to 'unfenced'.

positive evidence of an organic cause.'[61] Later X-rays of his head, taken in July 1969, were among Larkin's papers after his death.[62] On 10 April 1961 he wrote to Maeve in a chastened tone, noting that in the hospital 'you can see so many people worse off than yourself [. . .] It was good of you to take it kindly & not tell me to pull myself together *etcetera*! Not that I should have taken such an exhortation particularly kindly, but it might have been justified.'[63] However, three days later he told her that he had contracted ear infections from the hospital tests, and was 'in a great mood of fury & irritation & wishing I'd never set foot in this lazar house.'[64] Later in life he blamed his increasing deafness on these infections. On the same day (13 April) he wrote to Betty, expressing pleasure that the Library Assistant Wendy Mann, who was also ill at this time, had avoided surgery, going on to praise his 'very charming' doctor, Miss Yen: 'At present they think my chest interesting. (I feel like Marilyn Monroe.)'[65] On 18 April he wrote to Maeve, in the characteristically sincere tone of their correspondence: 'It has meant a great deal to me to have your sympathetic letters. I don't connect them with flirtation or my taking advantage of you [. . .] just one person showing kindness to and concern for another. And this is a jolly rare thing in my experience. Thank you, dear, thank you with all my heart.'[66]

Maeve had been impressed by his consideration for others while he was in hospital. Philip would always ask after Wendy Mann, and after his return to Hull phoned her every week until she returned to the Library.[67] Maeve had come to believe that, though he did not share her religious faith, Philip shared her values: 'I discovered how deeply sensitive he was, and that his yearning for warmth, affection and idealism was as great as my own.'[68] Their relationship was a sensuous one. Philip told Jean Hartley that though she rejected 'sex before marriage', 'God knows we do everything but.'[69] However, as Maeve put it, 'I wasn't prepared to cut myself off from the sacraments.'[70] Eva was eager for her son to resolve the situation. But he could not abandon Monica. He joked in a letter to Maeve: 'Do you think this ailment I am undergoing is God's way of putting a stop to something He thought might be getting out of hand?'[71] In the event, however, things did not get 'out of hand' nor was he forced to make a decision. The situation remained unresolved for the better part of the next two decades. It was not until 1978 that, as Maeve recalled, 'he finally broke with me in favour of Monica'.[72]

Following his illness, he returned to work, and his correspondence with Monica resumed its equilibrium. On 11 June he wrote: 'How are you? I can remember of course that you were here, & what we did, but you slip so easily into my life, making no disturbance, it's almost like trying to pick out a rabbit among bracken. Not that rabbits have lovely legs like yours. Your legs are the only legs I ever see the point of, except for walking about on, of course.'[73] A week later he completed a sexually charged poem, 'The Large Cool Store', 'unsuspectingly inspired', Maeve explained, by herself. The poet is puzzled by the contrast between the two worlds implied by the clothes in the shop: on one hand shirts and trousers, 'Set out in simple sizes plainly', belonging to the weekday world of 'factory, yard and site'; on the other 'Modes For Night' in 'Lemon, sapphire, moss-green rose', belonging to an apparently unrelated ideal world. He concludes that this exotic nightwear shows:

> How separate and unearthly love is,
> Or women are, or what they do,
> Or in our young unreal wishes
> Seem to be: synthetic, new,
> And natureless in ecstasies.

The word 'natureless', which occurs nowhere else in Larkin's work, recalls Yeats's ascent 'out of nature' in 'Sailing to Byzantium'. On the 'Listen' recording of *The Whitsun Weddings*, made under the auspices of the Marvell Press, Larkin notes that this has been called a 'silly poem about nighties'.[74] It is in fact a moving evocation of the awesome impersonal power of sex.

Maeve's account of the occasion of the poem bowdlerizes its erotic content:

He was very taken with a smart summer handbag I had bought at Marks and Spencer's. He found it hard to believe that I had found anything quite so stylish there: in 1961 their merchandise was generally less well designed than in later years. The following Saturday Philip went along to 'the large cool store' which he saw through the eyes of working-class women whose humdrum existence was far removed from the tantalizing world represented by the store's 'Modes for Night'. Caressing the 'Bri-Nylon Baby-Dolls and Shorties', ethereal in colour, texture and design, the women imagine how possession of such a garment might transform their lives [. . .][75]

In her decorous misreading, male fantasies about sex become female fantasies about fashion. Paradoxically, however, this muse's reimagining of the poem is, in its very incomprehension, an illustration of its central insight. In 'our' unreal male wishes, women are rapt in a natureless, self-involved perfection. Maeve's response to the poem shows exactly this narcissism. Gautier would have interpreted her reaction in the familiar sexist terms of nineteenth-century Romanticism: 'It is true that women have no more understanding of poetry than has a cabbage or a rose, and this is quite natural and to be expected, since they themselves are poetry or at least the best instruments of poetry; a flute neither hears nor understands the air that is played upon it.'[76]

The balance, or imbalance, of Philip's relationship with Monica was restored. They took their 1961 summer holiday again in Sark. He told Conquest, 'Had a good time, except that I became shagged with late nights and drink.'[77] Shortly afterwards Monica took her cue from Philip's birthday to suggest that they both make wills ('I *don't* want my relations to inherit all that I have'). He was baffled by her anxiety about what would happen to the money she left him when he himself subsequently died: 'You seem to be wanting me to do something & I don't know what it is.' Unnerved, he told her, 'it isn't a topic I relish thinking about'. Then, still clearly not understanding her urgent reasonings, he attempted to placate her: 'I do see that it is a serious matter and ought to be settled. I also see that you are offering me a great kindness, and I'm properly grateful.'[78] A letter of several days later reveals a different, literary cause of friction. She had praised Sir Walter Scott, and he responded with crushing decisiveness: 'I don't think I recovered from being advised to read *The Heart of Midlothian* – was it? At different times I've tried that, and *The Antiquary*, and *Old Mortality*. All fell from my nerveless fingers. I *want* W.S. to be good – heavens, one wants anyone to be good [. . .] – but I don't know, there seemed nothing in his books, no imagination, humour, malice, style, perception, story even.'[79] In September a new, more stable pattern to their relationship was established when Monica bought a second home in Haydon Bridge, near Hexham, Northumberland, on the banks of the Tyne. Haydon Bridge was conveniently far away, but near enough to Hull for Philip easily to join her there for short breaks and longer holidays.

Larkin's life reached its apogee in late 1961. In 'Here', the fifth of his ten great contemplative elegies, completed on 8 October, there is a sense that he has attained the still midday of his life.[80] All the poet's skill is bent to distil a timeless, universal poem from an intensely local, personal inspiration. The poem takes as its title not the topographical 'Hull' but the existential adverb 'Here'. In an extraordinary grammatical manoeuvre the 'I' and 'we' of 'The Whitsun Weddings' and 'Ambulances' are ingeniously excluded, making the centre of consciousness the reader her or himself. There is momentous gravity in the poem's opening phrases. The subject of the first sentence is an elaborate noun phrase, whose repeated gerunds (present participles used as nouns), 'Swerving [. . .] swerving [. . .] swerving', create a slow-building climax. The main verb ('Gathers') is held back by this spacious grammar until the beginning of the second stanza. Then, in order to throw the emphasis on momentary experience rather than literal topography, this 'swerving' gathers not to a town, but to 'the surprise of a large town'. Though the first sentence could end here, the poet prefers the continuing impetus of a colon followed by 'Here [. . .]'. The first sentence does not end until the first line of the final stanza.

Though the unnamed city at the centre of the poem is indeed, in every detail, a 'literal' place with unique characteristics, ships up streets, a slave museum, consulates and tattoo shops, it is also a 'pastoral', if an unorthodox 'terminate and fishy-smelling' one. This 'urban, yet simple' world has the idyllic innocence of Theocritus' or Virgil's artificial visions of nymphs and shepherds. Its inhabitants, a 'cut-price crowd', are precisely observed as they push through plate-glass doors to their desires: 'Cheap suits, red kitchen-ware, sharp shoes, iced lollies'. But this vignette is also an archetype of the social existence of all readers, wherever our particular 'here' may be. It is surprising, to put it mildly, to find Larkin describing the poem to Conquest as 'plain description'.[81]

Larkin pulls out all the organ-stops of rhyme and assonance to create a sumptuous music of consonant clusters and shifting vowels, unlike anything else in his poetry: 'shadows / fields / meadows / shields / solitude / pheasants / presence / mud / [. . .] / stands, thicken / quicken / ascends / distance / beach / existence / reach'. Four octaves of commodious pentameters are orchestrated in alternating variation. Stanzas one and three both rhyme ababcddc, while stanzas two and four rhyme, with more formal closure, abbacdcd. He originally titled the poem 'Withdrawing Room', the archaic form of 'drawing room', imaging the ever-moving moment of being here as the most intimate of the rooms into which we withdraw. *Stanza* is the Italian for 'room' (usually in the plural, *stanze*: a suite of rooms). Here, in this spacious, patterned stanza-form, Larkin has found the comfortable withdrawing room of his own which he had been seeking since 'Dry-Point' and 'Best Society'.

No vehicles are mentioned, but 'here' moves implicitly from sitting in a swerving train approaching the city to walking around the streets, to pedalling a bicycle through suburbs and out across the flat landscape to the sea. The goal is ambiguous. On one reading the movement is a withdrawal inwards, from a larger public world of industry and 'traffic all night north' to crowded provincial cityscape, and then deeper and deeper into 'retired' self-possession. On another it is an opening outwards, from the enclosure of a railway carriage to the roads and shops of the town to a sublimely cleared attic of 'unfenced existence: / Facing the sun, untalkative, out of reach'. Both readings lose time in place. There are no events in the poem, only an undated present. For all its forward movement, largo – allegretto – andante, this is an anti-narrative, stopping the clock. Larkin was aware that his life had reached its point of balance. The photograph of Philip and herself outdoors which Maeve chose for the cover of her memoir is dated October 1961, and shows the poet radiating fulfilment. Larkin had always been uncannily sensitive to life's climacterics, and had long anticipated the moment when he would reach his 'prime'. If one were to put a date on this moment it would be October 1961. After 'Here' the way is downward.

To remind himself of cruel reality, Larkin followed this sublime poem with his coldest, most reductive work, headed in the workbook '18/10 *Life is slow motion dying*' and completed three pages later on 25 October. It was published as 'Nothing To Be Said' in the *London Magazine* on 11 February 1962. In an elliptical anthropological summary the poet reviews a spectrum from the rituals of primitive nomads and pig-hunters through 'cobble-close' working-class family life in mill towns to the civilized rituals of garden-parties and law cases. All of them amount to no more than a slow advance on death. The poem ends with a riddling play on words: 'saying so to some / Means nothing; others it leaves / Nothing to be said'. Some people are optimists, some are pessimists, and that is all there is to it. As the year approached its end Larkin followed this poem, on 3 November, with a mood-piece, 'And now the leaves suddenly lose strength'. Autumn is over, and seeing another year gone an assortment of people from different eras, 'Frockcoated gentleman, farmer at his gate, / Villein with mattock, soldiers on their shields' all silently watch 'the winter coming on'. He did not publish it.

But it was not winter yet for Larkin. Three days later, he completed, in two days of concentrated drafting (5–6 November), one of his warmest works, and the one with the most explicit biographical association with Maeve. On Sunday 5 November she attended a concert at Hull's City Hall which opened with the 'storms of chording' of Elgar's 'Introduction and Allegro for Strings'. The resulting poem, 'Broadcast', is the only work in which Larkin explicitly addressed his Hull muse. On the 'Listen' record he calls it 'about as near as I get in this collection to a love poem. It's not, I'm afraid, very near.'[82] His repeated stress on nearness ('about as near', 'not very near') seems almost a joke, since the relationship in the poem is so much a matter of carefully observed distance. Paradoxically what most excites the poet is his separation from his beloved: she in the concert hall hearing the music, he listening over the radio, a mile away, picturing her in his mind. The orchestra's chords overpower him not directly through their sound, but 'By being distant'. In a tenuous pun he hears her hands 'on air', electronically: 'tiny in all that air, applauding'. This is more rarefied than the 'real untidy air' of 'Bargains, suffering, and love'. The contrast with 'Talking in Bed' is stark. In that poem a uniquely intimate closeness made communication impossible. Here it is the very distance between the lovers which imparts the bloom to their relationship. The imagined details on which the poet focuses: her face, her unnoticed glove, her shoes, create an icon in his mind, and this artifice is underpinned by the echo of the medieval 'blazon', a poem of courtly love listing parts of the beloved's body.[83] Her face 'Beautiful and devout', true to the Petrarchan tradition, both inspires and forbids desire. For years afterwards Philip would send Maeve Christmas cards playing on this ambiguity. He would annotate each card according to the nature of the illustration: 'Devout but not beautiful'; 'Beautiful but not devout' or, more rarely, 'Beautiful *and* devout'.[84]

The phrase 'new, slightly outmoded shoes' was a private joke. Philip was particularly taken, Maeve revealed, by this pair of shoes which were 'an unusual colour of pearlized bronze, very smart, with stiletto heels and long, pointed toes, popularly known as winkle-pickers'.[85] Twenty years earlier Larkin would 'do the foot fetishist' for his undergraduate friends.[86] Now he acted out a version of this mime for Maeve's amusement, or bemusement.

> Philip raved about the shoes. He used to take them off my feet, hold them up, stroke them, put them down on the sofa and continue to admire them; not just once, but every time I wore them. He thought they were the last word in fashion, until one day, slightly exasperated, I teased: 'I don't know why you go on so about these shoes. They're almost out of fashion now. You know how I haven't the nerve to wear anything until it's been in vogue for six months.' He laughed and said: 'Well. I still adore them even if they are slightly outmoded!'[87]

One may doubt that Maeve was quite as innocent as she depicts herself in *The Philip Larkin I Knew*. But by this account the cross-purpose between their different shoe-fetishisms is total: eroticism on his part, narcissism on hers.[88] Larkin's inscription in Maeve's copy of the *Listener* in which 'Broadcast' first appeared on 25 January 1962 reads: 'To Maeve, who wd. sooner listen to music than listen to me.' The unfeeling muse ignores her poet's service.

Maeve was a more complex muse than Penelope Scott Stokes or Winifred Arnott. They were both soon lost to sight. Maeve broke the pattern by positively relishing their long-drawn-out delayed court-ship. Over the period of the relationship he was to write more than 200 letters to her, without any of the pungency or literary complexity of his letters to Monica or Judy Egerton. He soon found an appropriate animal language for their intimacy. At Christmas 1961 he gave her a gold chain with a pearl pendant, and shortly afterwards introduced her to the *Rescuers* series of novels for children by Margery Sharp, featuring the mouse Miss Bianca, who shared Maeve's initials and always wore such a chain. He became Miss Bianca's admirer, 'a rather commonplace-looking mouse named Bernard'.[89] His letters to her are sometimes adorned with drawings of 'Miss Mouse', in contemplative mood, or weighing herself on bathroom scales or choosing material in a shop.[90]

Maeve believed that Philip's tolerance of the delay in physical consummation was a result of his respect for her beliefs: 'he may at times have found my strict adherence to the Church's teaching on sexual ethics disconcerting. However, he understood and respected my principles with a facility which struck me as remarkable.'[91] Even when, after his death, she discovered more sides to his personality, her perception was unchanged: 'Knowing, as I do now, of Philip's darker side, it seems all the more remarkable that his view of love coincided so closely with mine.'[92] In fact his restraint owed less to respect for religion than to a Keatsian relish for trembling incipience. Maeve kept alive this frisson by remaining sexually unavailable. In late autumn 1961 she gave Philip a copy of Evelyn Waugh's *Unconditional Surrender* and, realizing the possible double entendre of the title, she forestalled him by saying: 'Now don't think for a moment that this gives you the green light to go ahead because that's the last thing I have in mind!'[93] Her limited moral code and unreflecting gender double standard allowed her to feel self-approval for forbidding her lover 'pre-marital sex', while at the same time overlooking his own 'pre-marital sex' with Monica. It never occurred to her that it was only Philip's regular sexual relations with Monica that enabled him to preserve the decorum of their prolonged, unreal courtship. On 18 January 1962, a week before he wrote the *Listener* dedication to Maeve, he had told Monica, 'I should like to stroke your little rabbit brow & large rabbit hindquarters,' and related to her how he had paid 4s 6d to sit 'among giggling Chinese' at the cinema watching *Nudes of the World*.[94]

Just as John Kemp had determined to keep the innocent Jill from Warner and his world, so Larkin kept the innocent Maeve from Amis and his world. Had his more cosmopolitan friends met Maeve, they would have seen only a grotesque mismatch, and would not have understood his feelings. Judy Egerton recalls a rare visit to Hull, when she stayed in the Pearson Park Hotel. On knocking at the door of Philip's flat she heard a furtive scramble, and when the door was opened Maeve was blushingly rearranging her dress. Egerton's impression was that the Library Assistant was 'absolutely thrilled – tickled pink' to be discovered in this liaison with her boss.[95] Most importantly, it was essential that Kingsley Amis should never meet Maeve. Even if he had only glimpsed her for a minute or two, Amis could have repeated the pattern of *Lucky Jim* and featured in his next novel an hilarious simpering, social-climbing 'Maud Brosnan' or 'Mavis Byrne', radiating comic vulgarity and smug prudishness.

Monica was deeply hurt when 'Broadcast' was published, and Philip was forced on to the defensive. He was, he wrote on 8 February 1962, 'ashamed of myself for causing you embarrassment *vis à vis* old Charity-Boots [. . .] I don't know that it's worth saying anything except that my delight in you isn't pretended: you blot out anyone else.' This was 'the first "love" poem I've written since *Maiden name* in about 1954, & I shd think both are pretty tenuous, pretty remote, as far as general approach goes. In fact I think this one just a shade ludicrous!'[96] This may seem at first sight an improvised excuse, cooked up simply to pacify Monica. But on reflection the word has real justification. There was indeed something 'ludicrous' about writing a love poem to someone with whom, in intellectual, cultural and social terms, his relationship was so insubstantial.

15

Sitting It Out
1961–4

Once again the poet felt compelled, as it were, to spill beer on the perfect photograph, answering 'Broadcast' (6 November 1961) with the sour misogamist poem 'Breadfruit' (19 November). This is one of his poems drafted during one day on a single page (though it was revised before publication in *Critical Quarterly*).[1] Larkin dismissed it in a letter to Conquest as a 'little squib': 'just about the worst poem I have ever let get set up'.[2] Its imagery calls on cartoons of the 1950s and 1960s showing puny weaklings with spectacles and tiny bumps for biceps gawping at curvaceous native girls in grass skirts. In the boys' dreams the girls bring them breadfruit as bribes to teach them sexual positions on the sand.[3] This fantasy impels the boys to play tennis, jive at the Mecca and use deodorants in order to lure ex-schoolgirls into marriage, with inevitable consequences: 'A mortgaged semi- with a silver birch; / Nippers; the widowed mum; having to scheme / With money; illness; age'. Though the mode is reductive stereotype, the vivid detail 'with a silver birch' gives an authentic poetic inflection, as does the relentless list, modulating into bleak elegy: 'illness; age'. After this cadenza, the poem ends with the boys, now old men, still dreaming of naked native girls bringing breadfruit, 'Whatever they are'.

The moment of serene stasis recorded in 'Here' had passed. As the year of his fortieth birthday, 1962, approached Larkin's thoughts turned to his physical condition:

I have simplified my own grub down to chopped cabbage, grated carrot, cheese, with egg (raw) and Worcester sauce on the side, with milk and wholemeal bread and butter. This is at the instigation of my secretary, who's certainly never ill and is full of energy. Unfortunately she says it'll be two years before the poison is worked out of my system.[4]

On 28 December he wrote to Judy Egerton that he had 'felt pretty depressed over Christmas, & spent some time labelling packages for my executors. I really have no sense of the future now, except as the approach of death'.[5] The new year, however, saw a hesitant return of vitality. The unpublished poem 'January' answers 'And now the leaves suddenly lose strength', celebrating what Eliot called 'midwinter spring', when life stirs beneath the debris of winter. In an urban wasteland a decrepit figure reminiscent of a Samuel Beckett character turns towards the faintest hint of spring:

> Some ajar face, corpse-stubbled, bends round
> To see the sky over the aerials –
> Sky, absent paleness across which the gulls
> Wing to the Corporation rubbish ground.
> A slight relax of air. All is not dead.

There is a touch of self-parody here: 'we are all on a one way trip to the grave, etc. etc. etc.' He wrote to Monica that he was taking 'two phenob.'s at night, & tranquillisers during the day' to calm his 'boiling' brain.[6] In April he told Judy Egerton with grim cheeriness: 'I am taking Yeast Tablets in the hope they will give me Fresh Force at Forty.'[7]

He was also plumbing murkier erotic depths. In the magazine *Encounter* John Sparrow riddled out the obscure passage in *Lady Chatterley's Lover* where Mellors and Constance indulge in anal sex as a way of burning out 'shame' and confronting the ultimate obscenity of physical being. In a letter to Monica of 23 January 1962 Philip reflects that, though it seems 'much too difficult technically, all things being equal it would please me to share it with *you*, as fit expression of a feeling you're well aware of [. . .] I can't imagine there is much in it for you, though.'[8]

His letters of the time bristled with edgy discontent. On 9 December he complained to Conquest that George Hartley, or 'the ponce' as he called him on account of his natty appearance, had allowed *The Less Deceived* to go out of print for six months: 'Jesus, he's got the best selling prospect since the ShrLad and he can't even keep the frigging thing in print.' At the same time Hartley was, he wrote, wasting money making a 'Listen' record of 'old Davie droning out his tosh'.[9] On 20 February he grumbled about Al Alvarez's Introduction to *The New Poetry*, which compared 'At Grass', quoted without permission, with 'something of the Mexborough Marvell's' (Ted Hughes's 'A Dream of Horses'). 'Says I'm badly dressed, too, which I take a bit hard.' He then skewered the humourless clergyman-poet R. S. Thomas in an unforgettable cameo: 'Our friend Arsewipe Thomas suddenly was led into my room one afternoon last week, and stood there without moving or speaking: he seems pretty hard going. Not noticeably Welsh, which is one comfort.'[10] On 27 March he wrote to Anthony Thwaite, then Literary Editor of the *Listener*, declining to review Robert Graves's *New Poems* in case it encouraged other editors to approach him, adding: 'if he says publicly just once more that he has a large family to support, I shall write to the papers asking whose fault he thinks that is'.[11]

In May 1962, in the midst of discussions about the Stage 2 Library building programme, he completed 'Wild Oats', putting the final full-stop against his relationship with Ruth Bowman:

> Parting, after about five
> Rehearsals, was an agreement
> That I was too selfish, withdrawn,
> And easily bored to love.
> Well, useful to get that learnt.

His sulky masculine shrug shows that he still felt bruised by this failure. His next poem was at an opposite extreme of philosophical detachment. 'Essential Beauty', substantially completed in June, and published

in the *Spectator* in October 1962, presents itself as a satire on the decep-
tiveness of advertisements which 'Screen graves with custard, cover
slums with praise / Of motor-oil and cuts of salmon'. However, these
naive images of perfection – the milk in the meadow, the stock cube
towards which all hands stretch – are presented with affectionate
humour. Larkin commented when the poem was broadcast that bill-
boards 'seem to me beautiful and in an odd way sad, like infinitely-debased
Platonic essences':[12]

> they rise
> Serenely to proclaim pure crust, pure foam,
> Pure coldness to our live imperfect eyes
> That stare beyond this world, where nothing's made
> As new or washed quite clean [. . .]

The poem's title is quite unironic. There may be anger in the portrayal of
the dying smoker's glimpse of the perfect girl of the advertisements,
'Smiling, and recognising, and going dark'. But it is not the fault of adver-
tisers that she is beyond reach; it is the fault of the human condition. The
indignation of a cheated consumer is lost in sorrow over mortality.

On 10 August, prompted no doubt by his birthday the previous day,
he returned to the drafts of what was to become 'Send No Money',
originally begun nearly two years earlier under the title 'What Goes
On'.[13] It is a howl of tragi-comic bitterness. As he had hoped, his dedication to his artistic vocation has given him a clear sight of the truth.
But this truth has been of no more use to him than a 'truss-advertise-
ment', proving 'Sod all'. He does not reproach himself for having made
the wrong decision. He had been well aware from the beginning that
the rough-tongued bell of art offered nothing in return for his service.
But in his youth the pleasures of creativity had amply outweighed this
bleak knowledge. Even now the poet still derives cathartic satisfaction
from writing a good poem about failure. But now that 'Half life is over'
he can no longer sustain his self-congratulation at having sat life out
rather than having 'a bash' at marriage and procreation. Two days later
he lamented to Monica that he had 'done nothing with that fat

fillet-steak part of life, 20 to 40'.[14] But, even if he had made different choices, his face would still be this 'bestial visor, bent in / By the blows of what happened to happen'. Among Larkin's effects, bought by the Philip Larkin Society after Monica Jones's death, was a circular swivel-mirror on a metal stand, one side of which is concave, reflecting a hugely magnified image of every pore and blemish.[15]

Compared with Monica's, however, his life was full of satisfaction and interest. She felt unfulfilled and longed for their lives to be united. But his visits to Haydon Bridge, and their regular holidays *à deux* can only have convinced him that living together would have been a challenge. It is to this period that Motion dates their defacing of Monica's hardback first edition of Iris Murdoch's 1956 novel *The Flight from the Enchanter*, though this might have been done earlier.[16] Few pages are unmarked and it is dismaying to contemplate the many hours of sterile boredom represented by their trivial, repetitive graffiti. It is not always possible to distinguish which of the two has made a change, but it is clear that Monica is as foul-mouthed as he. The title is altered, probably in her handwriting, to *The Shite from the Non-Enchanter*, and he changes the publisher's details to 'Shatto and Break-Windus Shit-shovellers to Greater London Council "You Write It – We'll Shift It"'. Most of the alterations are grossly lavatorial or sexual. 'Rosa sat up abruptly' becomes 'Rosa shat abruptly'; 'She swung her arms about a lot' becomes 'She swung her tits about a lot.'[17] 'Sit' and 'sat' are mechanically altered to 'shit' and 'shat'; 'uncurling their long legs' becomes 'uncurling their long pricks'; 'made as if to kiss Rosa's hand' becomes 'made as if to kiss Rosa's cunt'.[18] And so it goes on, page after page, a total of about 1,300 alterations. To return after a spell of this kind of thing to Maeve's innocent propriety must have been a great relief.

One or two of the marginalia show a nasty xenophobia. Murdoch's dedication to Elias Canetti, with whom she had had an affair, is elaborated in Philip's handwriting: 'To a Wop Tool – Peelias Canetti (Eytie for "little cunt") (he shagged me)'. The chapter heading 'Three' becomes 'Any Greek's Breath reeks'. The character Jan is described, in Monica's handwriting, as 'a dirty scrounging sex-mad foreigner'.[19] Her anti-Semitism, which was an undercurrent in *A New World Symphony*, is also in evidence. Once, when Philip and Monica were staying with the Thwaites in the 1960s or 1970s, she shocked everyone by declaring in the middle of a casual conversation: 'Well. What can you expect when they're *Jews*!'[20] Her insecurities drew Philip into a narrow, defensive intimacy. When she took the well-known photograph of him sitting on an 'ENGLAND' road-marker, after their holiday in Scotland in 1962, Monica was confirming what she saw as one of the sure foundations of their relationship.[21] Like Amis, she demanded that he reduce himself to her version of him.

It was a version he was determined should not become permanent. At the end of September 1962 Monica wrote an abject letter pleading for him to share his life with her. She was 'very conscious of what a short time we are here for, & how little of that time we have left, you & I; it isn't much, and for all we know it might be very short, & I wish I could spend what is left with you, or more of what is left than I do spend'. She continued: 'tears are behind my eyes, making eyes & head ache'.[22] In reply he rebukes her emotional blackmail: 'I don't say I want to bore you with my feelings, or be bored, so to speak, by yours, but I have a curious feeling that in some ways we are not in sympathy [. . .] you either know me too well or don't know me enough.' After criticizing his own anti-social tendency, he concluded: 'I do think you dislike people more than I do.'[23] Philip was committed to Monica but, except for short periods, a woman with her limitations could not but disappoint and bore him. On 1 October, she ruthlessly spelled out the truth at which he hinted, 'you don't like me enough to marry me', adding bitterly: 'it seems rather unkind for you to want to *tell* me so, & perhaps tell me all the things that are wrong with me'.[24] He responded characteristically by taking all the blame on himself: 'I do feel terrible about our being 40 & unmarried. I fear we are to turn slowly into living reproaches of the way I have dallied and lingered with you [. . .]'[25] She was socializing a good deal with one of her students, Bill Ruddick, and Philip experienced a certain jealousy: 'It gives me a queer disagreeable feeling to think of you with someone else.'[26] But he made no active intervention.

Later, on 10 October, in more cheerful mood, Larkin completed a genial riposte to 'Send No Money'. In 'Toads Revisited' the Librarian's voice replaces that of the *poète maudit*.[27] Instead of a lonely romantic artist dissociating himself from his contemporaries of middling sensuality, the speaker is now a bourgeois conformist, distancing himself from those too stupid or too weak to hold down a job. He expresses *faux naïf* puzzlement that his idle stroll in the park does not feel 'better than work'. The park's inhabitants, the palsied elderly, the jittery neurotics and tramps, have, after all, succeeded in dodging work, as he had longed to do in 'Toads'. But the price they have paid for their exemption is too high. At first he exclaims with distaste: 'Think of being them!' Then, having given the idea some thought, he repeats the phrase without the exclamation mark and in a more pensive tone. He is no heartless Norman Tebbit berating the workshy. Indeed their detachment from the flux of getting and spending gives their lives a hint of lyrical beauty:

> Watching the bread delivered,
> The sun by clouds covered,
> The children going home;
> Think of being them,
>
> Turning over their failures
> By some bed of lobelias [. . .]

But the comic misrhyme 'failures / lobelias' unsettles the brief epiphany. The poet is still thankful for his secure pensionable life. He even pieces together an alternative epiphany of his own out of the prosaic material of work itself: his in-tray, his loaf-haired secretary and the importunate telephone:

> What else can I answer,
>
> When the lights come on at four
> At the end of another year?
> Give me your arm, old toad;
> Help me down Cemetery Road.

A week or so later in 'Sunny Prestatyn' Larkin gave a new turn to the meditation on Platonic perfection of 'The Large Cool Store' and 'Essential Beauty'. The image on the holiday poster depicts what Larkin calls on the 'Listen' recording 'the universal symbol of happiness, a pretty girl'. Innocent though she is, however, she inevitably offers erotic invitation. Behind her a 'hunk' of coast and a hotel 'with palms / Seemed to expand from her thighs and / Spread breast-lifting arms'. The 'hunk' and 'palms' hint, through crude sexual puns, at the male viewer wanting to get his hands on her thighs and breasts. And the sexual message has indeed hit home, as is shown by the response of the vandals, who make the subtext brutally explicit by giving her 'Huge tits and a fissured crotch'. Larkin has been accused of misogynistic enjoyment of this degradation. On the 'Listen' record he acknowledges that 'some people think' the poem was intended to be 'funny', others that it is 'horrific'. He, the poet, thinks it was 'intended to be both'.[28]

The vandals' response is ambiguous. On one level they reinforce the satirical theme. They are not deceived by the advertiser's trick. Like the feminists who object to airbrushed photographs, they know that real girls in real places do not have perfect teeth and may squint. But more crudely they simply lust after her:

> the space
> Between her legs held scrawls
> That set her fairly astride
> A tuberous cock and balls [. . .]

However, there is more here than an impulse to rape. The cock and balls are 'Autographed *Titch Thomas*'. This diminutive vandal seems ironically aware of his own sexual inadequacy. More sombre, even sinister, is the ferocity with which another anonymous vandal has 'used a knife / Or something to stab right through / The moustached lips of her smile'. There is despair in this violence. The girl's image taunts the vandals not only with beauty but also with happiness ('her smile'). Their desecration may be seen as the thwarted expression of a yearning for perfection. It is a sad, self-hating impulse. Again, the poem is not satire or social analysis, but elegy. The perfect girl is 'too good for this life'.

The poem has complex genre associations. It is an 'ekphrastic' poem, a description of a work of visual art, albeit a stereotypical poster rather than an archetypal painting by Bruegel as in Auden's 'Musée des Beaux Arts' and Berryman's 'Winter Landscape'. It is also an Eros-Thanatos elegy, juxtaposing sex and death in the contrasting posters with which it begins and ends. Its theme is a version of the 'death and the maiden' motif of Western art, the girl's violated image recalling those medieval and Renaissance paintings in which amorous skeletons drag their buxom victims by the hair into yawning graves as they struggle to cover their modesty with a winding-sheet.[29] Larkin's version lacks the moralizing sexism of the traditional version. Instead, more simply and sadly, a vision of beauty is vicariously dismembered and subjected to the humiliation of disease. 'Very soon, a great transverse tear / Left only a hand and some blue. / Now *Fight Cancer* is there.' In the 'Listen' reading Larkin stammers momentarily at the word 'cancer'.

Larkin's moods always ran to extremes, and three days after he completed 'Sunny Prestatyn' he experienced an exalted epiphany during one of his solitary cycle rides in the country. He wrote to Monica on 23 October that he had stopped at the small village of Wawne, to the north of Hull, where he had 'poked about in the churchyard, turning up chestnuts in the grass, & noting George Beulah, who had outlived two wives before dying in 1909':

a woman called that if I was going into the church, wd I be careful to shut the door, as the heating was on. I hadn't really intended to, but thought I would, as the heating was on! I was glad I did, because it was all decorated for Harvest Home! Really *very* thrilling, & funny, the lines of cabbages and cauliflowers, piles of tomatoes in little stone niches, a box of dates (!) on the harmonium, celery up the aisle, chrysanthemums everywhere, a big sheaf of corn, then on the table a bunch of black grapes, a pot of honey (home-made), and a loaf, specially baked I should say. I don't think I have seen a church so decorated for years, and the shock of it was tremendous – of course I thought of you, although rabbits would be unlikely to take part in such a ceremony, or at least not in the way intended. You *would* have liked it. I left them a pound, and shut the door carefully – all *I* harvest is money, but they were welcome to some of that.[30]

This glowing prose poem reads as an alternative version of 'Church Going'. Omitting any reference to religion or belief, he responds emotionally to the 'thrilling, & funny' social ritual of Harvest Home. In contrast to the ironic Irish sixpence of 'Church Going', he gives a pound note, a very large sum in 1962: 'all *I* harvest is money, but they were welcome to some of that'.

The next poem Larkin completed, on 7 December 1962, has the bold title 'Love'.[31] Its epigrammatic tone and its structure owe much to Blake's 'The Clod and the Pebble'. With anti-intuitive logic the poet argues that the difficult part of love is 'being selfish enough' to upset an existence 'Just for your own sake'. On the other hand unselfish love seems to him equally unacceptable: 'Putting someone else first / So that you come off worst? / My life is for me.' Nevertheless he concedes, 'Love suits most of us.' The speaker, who excludes himself from both 'virtuous' unselfish love and 'vicious' selfish love, is a social outcast:

> Only the bleeder found
> Selfish this wrong way round
> Is ever wholly rebuffed,
> And he can get stuffed.

After this egotistical poem, he spent eight pages, as the year drew to an end, drafting a poem evoking the early life of his parents: 'Increasingly I think of them as young.' But he could not find his way beyond the second stanza. The next poem he completed, early in the New Year, was 'Long Last', a selfless meditation prompted by the death of one of his mother's friends. Effacing his own personality, he tells the poignant story of an eighty-year-old woman left unable to cope when her younger sister dies. She is taken away in a van, her feeble 'No' disregarded:

> This long last childhood
> Nothing provides for.
> What can it do each day
> But hunt that imminent door
> Through which all that understood
> Has hidden away?

This is the first glimpse in Larkin's poetry of the subject of senility which he was to make peculiarly his own in 'The Old Fools' ten years later.

His mother was now seventy-six. One of his Sunday letters to 'My very dear old creature', dated 16 December 1962, shows his consistent cheery, comforting tone: 'Hasn't it been windy! but what a relief to have it mild. I found my spirits soaring when I stepped out into the dark rushing rainy morning – it always cheers me up more than most people. When I went to London Tuesday–Wednesday it was beastly cold.' As he describes recording a reading for radio, he slips affectionately into the Midland idiom which he and she shared when he was a child: 'I didn't stammer hardly at all, but I got into a mess by reading a singular as a plural: had to start again.' He ceremoniously apologizes for having sent only one postcard during his two-day trip: 'I'm sorry I didn't after all send a card for Saturday – Friday was a tiresomely busy day & I had so much to do it just went out of my head. I hope you weren't disappointed.'[32]

Through February and March 1963 Larkin worked on 'Dockery and Son', the last-written poem to be included in *The Whitsun Weddings*, and the sixth of his ten great contemplative elegies. A year earlier, on 12 March 1962, he had attended the funeral in Oxford of Agnes Cuming, his predecessor as Librarian at Hull, and the following day had jotted the first two lines of the poem in his workbook. The occasion of his visit explains his punning description of himself as 'Death-suited, visitant'. He is dressed in mourning black; but he is also 'suited', in the more general sense, for death. He is making a brief 'visit'; but also he is a ghostly visitant, haunting his past life. The Dean casually mentions that the son of one of his college contemporaries is now in residence, and the poet recalls being disciplined as an undergraduate by a previous Dean. He tries 'the door of where I used to live: // Locked'. The preferred location for a Larkin speaker is secure in his room, gazing out through closed windows at a skyscape ('The piled gold clouds') or a framed glimpse of the lives of others ('someone running up to bowl'). Only in moments of greatest stress and self-dissatisfaction, in 'Dry-Point', 'Reasons for Attendance' and here in 'Dockery and Son', does he find himself outside, denied entry. Others, sons of Dockery and his like, are now living where he used to live. He cannot simply open the door and walk back into his youth. His response is irrational shock. As he emerges from the staircase 'The lawn spreads dazzlingly wide.' He feels exposed and vulnerable. 'A known bell chimes,' haunting him with recollections. It is only when he is safe in his railway carriage that his memories dwindle to a picturesque vista: 'I catch my train, ignored. / Canal and clouds and colleges subside / Slowly from view.' The brief trauma is over.

During his return journey he reflects on the young man who now lives in his place. To be already an undergraduate, Dockery's son must have been born in 1943. But he cannot even recall which of his dimly remembered contemporaries Dockery was. He dozes off, waking only at Sheffield, where 'I changed [. . .]', the omission of 'trains' giving the word a playfully ominous implication. Waiting for his connection he casually contemplates a suitable metaphor for these long perspectives:

> and walked along
> The platform to its end to see the ranged
> Joining and parting lines reflect a strong
>
> Unhindered moon.

He is awed by Dockery's confidence in starting a family so young. What Dockery saw as increase the poet sees as dilution. He philosophizes desultorily on the differences in their attitudes. After all, Dockery, he concludes, did not really know what he wanted and got it. Rather his and Dockery's lives, with their different 'Innate assumptions', have both been determined by what happened to happen. Dockery has had a bash and now has a grown-up son. In contrast, the poet has 'Nothing with all a son's harsh patronage'. Even without a child to patronize him he cannot escape the humiliation of age. The poem ends with one of Larkin's most splendidly lugubrious verdicts on life:

> Life is first boredom, then fear.
> Whether or not we use it, it goes,
> And leaves what something hidden from us chose,
> And age, and then the only end of age.

Larkin felt that this poem marked a watershed in his life. He commented to Monica later: 'I don't think I shall ever get past "Dockery and Son".'[33] After completing it he set about putting the poems for his next volume in order, and on 11 June he sent *The Whitsun Weddings* to Faber. His reputation was now established and he received an acceptance after only two days, with the offer of an advance 50 per cent larger than usual. Then, at the end of June, he began an ambitious poem, 'The Dance', initially with the idea that it could be inserted at the last minute into the forthcoming collection. Ten years earlier, in 'Reasons for Attendance', he had declined to attend the dance of social engagement, attending instead to his art. Now, in 1963, three years into his relationship with Maeve, he attempted to argue himself into the opposite decision. It was Maeve who had taught him, literally, how to dance 'in the privacy of his flat'.[34] Could he now join her in the public dance of society? Even as he was debating marriage to Monica in his letters, he was debating marriage to Maeve in this poem. Had he completed it, it would have been a self-epithalamium, celebrating his marriage to the muse of his latest volume. The couple had reached the stage of tentative discussions about domestic arrangements: 'You would have to give up work. It wouldn't do for the wife of the Librarian to work.'[35] He even acquired, without telling her, a copy of the Roman Catholic marriage service.[36]

Larkin was at the crossroads of his life. Was he to submit to the customs and establishments of society: even to a church sacrament? Or was he to remain an existential vagrant? On the crudest level he needed to sort out his sex life. He had asked ingenuously in 'Reasons for Attendance', 'what / Is sex?' And the question was a real one for him. In a letter written to Monica on 17 August 1963, he discussed his desire for 'unreal' erotic images of her, rather than the 'real' woman:

> When you talk about hair under the arms and bare breasts and nipples and the like it makes me think of *you* in these respects and I get *colossally* excited, almost unreally really – well, really unreally, I suppose [. . .] It's this mood that prompted the talk of Polaroid cameras – in one sense there's nothing I'd like more than photographs of you in your private clothes, or in no clothes at all, but I can't feel it's right when it seems more exciting than the reality.[37]

His 'live imperfect eyes' crave pure, 'essential' sex, rather than the woman herself. Years earlier he had explored with Amis and Hilly the possibility of pornographic photographs.[38] A Polaroid Land camera was found among Larkin's effects after Monica's death.[39] The photographs he took with it, however, have not survived.

Byron accused Keats of 'frigging his *Imagination*' in his poems,[40] and it is easy to detect a similar masturbatory impulse to that of 'The Eve of St Agnes' in such Larkin works as 'Lines on a Young Lady's Photograph Album' and 'The Large Cool Store'. Larkin has the intense erotic idealism found in both aestheticist art and soft-core pornography. In an early letter to Conquest, of 10 March 1956, he writes: 'So you're a Harrison Marks man too, are you?'[41] Marks specialized in photographs, sent under plain cover, of well-built 'nudes' in statuesque poses. He founded his magazine *Kamera* in 1957.[42] But the erotic fantasies which Larkin feared might vitiate his 'real' love life covered a wider spectrum than this, from the tastefully aesthetic to titillating stocking-and-suspender hijinks and 'real girls' of the 'readers' wives' genre. His fundamental instincts were, Conquest told Motion, 'really very unchallenging. Perhaps a bit of spanking, that's all, but nothing violent.'[43] Jean Hartley was 'neither stirred nor impressed' by the samples he showed her to satisfy her curiosity, though she reflects that he might have shown her a 'beginner's selection'.[44] In the 1960s Amis would avail himself of flats in London, hired by Conquest for the purpose of casual sexual liaisons. Larkin's tastes, however, were of a 'more introversive, voyeuristic' kind, and he never availed himself of this opportunity.[45] For him a relationship with an actual woman would inevitably entail respect and commitment.

In order to do the 'right thing' by marrying either Monica or Maeve, Philip would need to overcome not only the obstacle of his poetic vocation, but also its less culturally glamorous, if equally 'glamorous', shadow: the self-possession of bachelor auto-eroticism. Larkin's pornography collection is almost entirely lost. However, among his effects there survived a tattered manila envelope with the postmark 11 June 1959, sent to 32 Pearson Park from Harrison Marks's premises in Kingston upon Thames.[46] It contained thirty-one black and white photographs from nine different 'sets', possibly not all by Marks, nor of the same date. The nearest approach to 'hard-core' is a group of five images of a woman with huge breasts, her face turned anonymously away, perfunctorily 'bound' with tapes looped loosely around her curves. Ten of the images are from a set showing the model Sophia Dawn in striking poses.[47] Some feature further well-built Marks-style nudes and others a half-dressed woman sitting or lying coquettishly on a bed. Three are from a set in which an older 'headmistress', in flowered frock and high heels, canes an equally implausible 'schoolgirl' in her twenties, wearing a gymslip, stockings, suspenders and high heels. It seems that Larkin kept part of his pornography collection in the sturdy plastic-covered eggshell-blue ring-binders circulated annually around the University to update Regulations and Procedures. They were lettered boldly on the spine 'Staff Handbook', a designation equally appropriate to their new use.[48]

Larkin worked on 'The Dance', single-mindedly, for ten months, from 30 June 1963 until 12 May 1964. The last forty pages of Workbook 6 show him returning purposefully to the text, dating each new phase of drafting at the top left. In a contradiction of his usual practice he seems to have drafted no other poems during this period. By the time he abandoned it, 'The Dance' had become, at 140 lines, by far the longest poem he ever attempted. It took its origin from a University Staff Sports Club dance in May 1963, at which Philip's jealousy had

been inflamed by Maeve's flirtation with another man. It is a bold
attempt at a new genre for him: a serio-comic narrative poem, a 'Love
Song of P. Arthur Larkin', dramatizing the inability of a middle-aged
social misfit to ask the overwhelming question. In order to sharpen his
fictional narrative he makes two omissions from his own actual situation. Firstly the poem's protagonist claims no poetic vocation to excuse
his antisocial attitudes. Secondly, and crucially, his dilemma is not
complicated by other attachments. There is no equivalent of Monica in
the poem.

The speaker opens with a sulky monologue in which he prefers the
unadulterated pleasures of 'Drink, sex and jazz' to the 'muddled middle-
class pretence' which dilutes these things into a public 'dance'. He has
nothing but contempt for himself, dressed up in 'The shame of evening
trousers, evening-tie'. He departs for his ordeal, leaving behind his
private world with its brief epiphany of chestnut blooms and sunset:
'White candles stir within the chestnut trees. / The sun is low.' In
contrast as he arrives at the dance the parked cars, the strident music,
the brightly lit windows all signal to him *Alien territory . . .* The first
sight of his beloved comes as a shock, *Not you, not here*. He isolates her
by perverse syntax from her unworthy company: 'with some people at
some table, you'. Dancing with her takes on the aspect of a hostile
encounter: 'I face you on the floor.' The emotion intensifies as the
protagonist feels a challenge in the 'whole consenting language' of the
woman's body. He is hit by 'The impact, open, raw, / Of a tremendous
answer banging back // As if I'd asked a question'. In prosaic terms he
guesses that she expects a proposal. In an uncomfortably clumsy archa-
ism he finds himself 'descrying love':

> Something acutely local, me
> As I am now, and you as you are now,
> And now; something acutely transitory
> The slightest impulse could deflect to how
> · We act eternally.
> Why not snatch it? Your fingers tighten, tug.

Can he provide the question to her answer and achieve the transcendence, or at least the permanence, of marriage ('how / We act eternally')? Ominously there is more apprehension than epiphany in his words ('tighten, tug').

The narrative modulates into comedy as he is buttonholed by a shoptalking shit and his 'bearded wife'. Bemused he drinks coffee and listens to small talk while inwardly 'rent' by speculation on 'who has got you now'. As he escapes back to the bar, he catches sight of her, 'Loose to the music' with a 'weed from Plant Psychology'. She is apparently giving the same signals to this man as she had earlier given out to him ('So you looked at me, / As if about to whistle [. . .]').[49] The tone lurches from anguished sexual jealousy to the caricature comedy of a versified *Lucky Jim*. His 'tense elation' dissipates. Her shabby provincial world, he concludes, is not his. She dances in 'innocent-guilty-innocent' ignorance of his anguish, crudely teasing him by switching partners in her own 'sad set'. More embarrassingly, it is useless at his age to invite 'The sickened breathlessness of being young' back into his life. He decides to call a taxi and leave. But making for the bar to get pennies for the telephone, 'I see your lot are waving [. . .]' With an awful *déjà vu* 'The evening starts again' with 'omen-laden music'. By now the worse for drink he sits and beams about him, patiently listening to the 'Weed' explaining how to make wine from beetroot.

As the poem approaches its climax he finds himself again on the dance floor. The reader may doubt whether his anticipations of epiphany are the product of poetic insight or of gin-sodden inebriation. 'Something in me starts toppling.' Is he about to propose after all? Would this be a positive conclusion to the poem? Ten years earlier in 'Long roots moor summer to our side of earth' a vision of burgeoning nature had left the poet with no other reply than 'to be married'. Here in 'The Dance' he attempts to persuade himself not with images of leaves and sun-drenched fields, but with a vision of the blowsy rituals of a degraded 'Whitsun Weddings'. He sees behind his partner's half shut hazel eyes 'Endless receding Saturdays, their dense / And spotlight-fingered glut / Of never-resting hair-dos'.[50] Then, with an anticipatory anacrusis, he brings himself to the moment of truth, announcing that he has finally come to

understand[51]

> How the flash palaces fill up like caves
> With tidal hush of dresses, and the sharp
> And secretive excitement running through
> Their open ritual, that can alter to
> Anguish so easily against the carp
> Of too-explicit music [. . .]

In a *poesis interruptus*, the revelation falters into cloying descriptive detail ('spot-light-fingered glut', 'flash palaces'). Nevertheless, he remains determined to force an epiphany:

till
> I see for the first time as something whole
> What earlier seemed safely divisible[52]

At this point the draft breaks off, eight lines into an eleven-line stanza, without punctuation. The 'something whole', which the poet sees for the first time, remains unwritten. The final page in Workbook 6 shows a virtually immaculate draft of this final incomplete stanza, with the date at the top left: '12 May 1964'. 'The Dance' seems to belong to that unusual Romantic poetic form, the purposefully incomplete 'fragment'. Its irresolvable theme demanded that it remain unfinished. The final words seem contrived to leave the reader on a forever suspended cliffhanger. The poet could no more marry his muse than the poet of 'The Whitsun Weddings' could leave his train and join in the festivities.

Even as he wrestled with this epiphany of commitment, Philip was more headily embroiled with Monica than ever. In April 1964, tormented by the fear that he was about to abandon her for Maeve, she suffered a nervous collapse:

No tears, no reproaches could have shamed me more than your being sick. I feel quite awful, as if I had, well, kicked something to death – I'm not, I hope, being melodramatic: kicked something & seen it vomit as a result, perhaps. You know I feel I ought to take care of you – I have always felt this since your parents died, and it has caused enormous conflict & worry in me, that from time to time I've tried to explain, in that I did not ask you to marry me – I think I am mad & odd too: sometimes I am tempted to say how much I'm affected by sex fear & auto-erotic fantasies [. . .][53]

He apologized for having left the situation unresolved, but his language was cold and analytical: 'if I could have said last September "I'm in love with Maeve, goodbye", I wd: as it was, I couldn't – perhaps too fond of you, perhaps not fond enough of her, perhaps just too cowardly all round'.[54] But, despite the cruel home truths, he submitted to Monica's emotional blackmail, attempting to persuade her that his relationship with Maeve was all but over:

Sometimes I think Maeve is a kind of 40-ish aberration of mine, and her family & religion & desire for marriage and children & all that wd scare me out of the country if I were left alone with them. At others I think we have – that's you & I have – got into a sort of rut that will become increasingly ludicrous and painful as the years waste by. In a way you reflect what I am, she what I might have been – manager of a local insurance branch, I should guess. But you know how potent what one isn't can become![55]

His relationships with both women, he felt, suffered from his addiction to unreal dreams: erotic, but also social. He wrote to Monica the day after his birthday: 'I wonder if there *is* a "situation" – do I *really* want an RC wedding with Maeve and a "reception somewhere in Hull" etc. – I don't, of course, not really or even unreally.'[56] The implication is that the very 'unreality' of his dream makes it attractive to him.

To Maeve he painted a different picture, showing her drafts of the poem and telling her meaningfully on 27 December 1963, 'this is a great obstacle in my creative life: shan't write anything till it's out of the way'.[57] After its abandonment the poem still haunted him. In a letter of 29 July 1965 he told Maeve, 'I should really like to write a *winter* poem about you – not a Christmas one exactly [. . .] even with a bit of "The Dance" in it', and in January 1967 he copied out the initial encounter with the beloved and most of the final stanza in his seventh workbook.[58] In the early 1970s, when his relationship with Maeve was coming to a temporary halt, he gave her a typed copy, inscribed 'given to Maeve by Philip long afterwards with undimmed memories'.[59] Among his effects he left a tape recording of himself reciting the poem against a quiet background of dance music.

When *The Whitsun Weddings* was published, on 28 February 1964, it had at its centre not this personal poem, but the earlier collective epithalamium after which the volume is named. He could not dedicate the volume to Maeve without offending Monica, but he told Maeve that *The Whitsun Weddings* was 'her book', inscribing her copy: 'To Maeve, who can read between the lines'.[60] Within two months the volume had sold 4,000 copies; 3,000 more were sold over the next year. Days after its publication he could tell Monica with pride that '2 people asked me to autograph TWW's in the train – the Ringo Starr of contemporary verse.'[61] Two reprints were required before the end of the decade. The success of the volume lies, as Motion exactly puts it, in the way it transcends biography, diversifying the personal origins of poems, 'until they become exemplary'.[62] It is also impressively coherent in its impact, the poetic sequences being calculated to make the volume itself a larger poem. As Larkin said, with deceptive levity, its poems are arranged, 'like a music-hall bill: you know, contrast, difference in length, the comic, the Irish tenor, bring on the girls'.[63] Readers can remind themselves of its 'score', as it were, by running their eyes down the table of contents.[64]

These modulations, however, bear no relation to the time and circumstance in which each poem was written. The volume begins in October 1961 ('Here'), and ends in February 1956 ('An Arundel Tomb'). The earliest-written poems, 'Days' (August 1953), 'For Sidney Bechet' (January 1954) and 'Water' (April 1954), were composed before the *Less*

Deceived poems 'Church Going', 'Myxomatosis' and 'Maiden Name'. And they predate the last-written poems in *The Whitsun Weddings* by almost a decade. In the published sequence, 'The Importance of Elsewhere' is followed by 'Sunny Prestatyn', then 'First Sight', 'Dockery and Son' and 'Ignorance'. The reader is taken from meditative philosophizing through 'Georgian' pastoral to disillusioned dramatic monologue and pithy epigram. In terms of their composition, however, these poems move forward and backward in time from 1955 to 1962 to 1956 to 1963 to 1955.

To read the poems, instead, in the order in which they were written is to see the poet reaching fulfilment, then leaving his youth behind to embark on a troubled middle age. The anxieties of Larkin's return to England which lie behind 'Mr Bleaney' and 'The Importance of Elsewhere' thaw into the emotional well-being of 'The Whitsun Weddings', 'Here' and 'Broadcast'. Then bleak self-questioning sets in in 'Send No Money' and 'Dockery and Son'. The three journey poems in the collection tell an eloquent story. First, 'The Whitsun Weddings' (1958) celebrates a composed, open-hearted progress out into the world through a busy social landscape. 'Here' (1961) offers an intimate celebration of the poet's proper ground, culminating in serene stasis and a glimpse of transcendence. Finally 'Dockery and Son' (1963) traces a journey home in a mood of antisocial self-examination and disillusion. The spinning top had made its first stumble. Larkin's 'prime' had bloomed and faded within the period of the *Whitsun Weddings* poems.

16

Living for Others
1964–8

Following the acclaim which greeted *The Whitsun Weddings*, the television director Patrick Garland persuaded Larkin to appear in a BBC *Monitor* television feature with John Betjeman as his interviewer. Filming took place in Hull between 3 and 10 June 1964, and the resulting programme, *Down Cemetery Road*, gave visual form to his popular image.[1] Larkin manages his public persona with care. He is seen in his flat, a cigarette between long fingers, in faintly stilted conversation with Betjeman. They sit among the gravestones in Spring Bank Cemetery, reflecting on death in brilliant sunshine. Then, on the ferry in mid-Humber, the poet becomes a gauche tourist-guide with an enthusiasm for cloud formations. He cycles self-consciously up the path to a church, re-enacting the removal of his cycle clips 'in awkward reverence'. He wanders about the fish-docks, at a loss. He strides into the Library and up the stairs to leer with pantomimic sinisterness over a book in a dark corner. He had written to Monica: 'I shall be typed as just another Betjeman.'[2] But, in the event, there was no danger that he would be eclipsed by his media-savvy interviewer. However, the self-impersonation was a strain. On 8 June he wrote to Monica that it was 'nice' to have his favourite places filmed, but 'they seem less mine now. In fact *I* feel less mine now, if you follow me. I shall be glad when I see the whole caravan of sound, lights & cameras disappearing up the road towards London.'[3] Not owning a television, he drove with Maeve to the house of the Professor of History, John Kenyon, to watch the broadcast on 12 December 1964.

The bicycle had already fallen into the past. He had begun taking driving lessons in early 1964, and with sad symbolism bought his first car on the day *The Whitsun Weddings* was published, 28 February 1964. Until now he had avoided the accumulation of possessions and, apart from the houses which he bought for himself and his mother in 1948 and 1950, this was his first ever purchase of a major item of property. 'I feel I ought to go out and see that I have locked the boot & that no one can steal my jack, spare tyre, etc. Oh dear! Isn't it all *untypical*! I feel as if I had somehow slipped through into a different character.'[4] In the mid-1960s a large shift was taking place in Larkin's life. Public and professional activities came to the fore, and his poetry retreated into a more private space. In 1963 he had been instrumental in setting up an Arts Council Manuscripts Committee, to acquire the papers of living British poets for the National Collection, and in May 1964 he gave his weight to the programme by donating his first workbook to the British Library. He was to act as Committee Chairman from 1967 until 1979. In March 1964 he agreed to serve on the Board of the Poetry Book Society. In April he was elected a Fellow of the Royal Society of Literature.[5] In the autumn he made a 'Listen' LP of *The Whitsun Weddings*.[6] In 1965, he was awarded the Queen's Gold Medal for poetry. In 1966 he agreed to be on the Committee dispensing Gregory Awards for young poets.[7]

With its ever-growing staff the Library was losing its ingenuous, family atmosphere. But this was slow to fade. Larkin appeared in two of the three silent slapstick films made after working hours by the University photographer Alan Marshall and shown at staff parties in the early 1960s.[8] In the first, in black and white, Marshall scratched numerous crosses and ticks on the frames of the film to make the Librarian materialize in a shower of sparks. (He had the reputation of appearing out of nowhere just when members of staff thought they were safely out of view.) In the second film, in colour, Marshall directed Larkin to look out of his window, clapping his hand to his head in horror. He recalls that Larkin roared with laughter when the film was finally shown, and the splicing of shots made it appear that he was watching precious bound volumes of *The Times* falling past his office, dropped gleefully by a Library Assistant from the window of the Map Room above. (These volumes were so heavy that there was real concern over the strain on the joists above his desk.) In another sequence, engineered by means of a makeshift dummy and reversal of the film, Arthur Wood jumped off the Library roof and bounced before cheerfully walking away.[9] Brenda Moon, who joined the staff as chief cataloguer in 1962, entered into the fun. She was shown searching efficiently through the drawers of the card-catalogue. Horrified at a spoof index card reading *Mickey Mouse Times* she was soon dementedly tearing up card after card and tossing them about her head in a paper blizzard.

In letters to his proud mother casual references to Larkin's new status are mixed with the trivialities of his domestic life. On Thursday 28 January 1965, some days after her seventy-ninth birthday, he sent her a notecard relating how he had driven his car in for a service, taking the opportunity to 'collect my new dress suit, and to take back a pair of trousers for further alteration'. Then a photographer arrived from *Time* magazine '& I had to go through the usual mill'. He told her about his new cooker and carpet: 'much browner than I remember. The doors will just about open, but are very stiff [. . .] How lovely about the azalea – you will be pleased.' He inserted a drawing of a large-eyed seal in a frilled mob-cap bending solicitously over a pot-plant on a small table, and ended: 'I'll write again on Sunday – in the meantime, do please keep warm & dry. Tell Kitty I'm sorry about her cough.'[10]

His stamina for chat and affectionate concern was inexhaustible. In a four-page Sunday letter of 21 March 1965 he told Eva about a trip to Leeds to preside at a meeting of the Standing Committee of National and University Libraries (SCONUL): 'what Daddy wd call "The Branch"'. '[I]t rained, & near Leeds began to snow! and I couldn't find the hotel where we were lunching with the speaker.' He had also been to London to meet the Library architects and 'the Editress of Vogue', followed by drinks with 'the Features Editress ("a fat Belfast girl [. . .] far less glamorous than, for instance, Kitty . . .")'. The following day he had sat on a board 'for giving money to young poets to encourage them'. He tells Eva that he fears 'great West Indian & Pakistani germs hopping on me in the tubes [. . .]'. He devotes much space to her concerns: 'A pity I didn't get your letter on Thursday in view of the misunderstanding about Auntie Nellie's visit.' A brief touch of irritation, in his father's voice, interrupts the anodyne flow: 'You must stop putting the apostrophe in the wrong place in words like "isn't". It indicates that the "o" of "not" has been left out, & should go in its place. You are writing "is'nt".' Then he returns to the flow: 'How nice that your azalea is still flowering. There are a few green shoots in the garden here.' He mentions changes in the rules for the Old Age Pension, and reflects on how elderly 'boyish figures of the Thirties' such as Anthony Eden and the Duke of Windsor now look, and ends: 'Am thinking of you a lot – do take care – Much love. Philip'.[11]

In 1963, Barbara Pym, with whom he had been corresponding since 1961, had suffered a rejection at the hands of her publisher, Jonathan Cape. The publisher's readers, William Plomer and Daniel George, concluded that her seventh novel, *An Unsuitable Attachment*, would not sell enough copies to be commercially viable. Larkin praised the typescript and made some minor suggestions for improvement. She was as self-critical as he, and it was only after extensive rewriting that she sent it to Faber and Faber. Now, in August 1965, Larkin wrote twice to Charles Monteith at Faber, pressing him to accept it: 'This is in the tradition of Jane Austen & Trollope, and I refuse to believe that no one wants its successors today. Why shd I have to choose between spy rubbish, science fiction rubbish, Negro-homosexual rubbish, or dope taking nervous-breakdown rubbish?'[12] But his repeated 'rubbish' sounds strident. Larkin knew that the novels of Graham Greene, James Baldwin and Sylvia Plath were not rubbish. Indeed Pym herself was impressed by Baldwin's writing, despite its difference from her own. Moreover Larkin seems in danger of selling Pym short, ignoring her subversive wit and depicting her in moralistic terms as a writer of dogged respectable conservatism: 'I like to read about people who have done nothing spectacular, who aren't beautiful or lucky, who try to behave well in the limited field of activity they command [. . .]'[13] Unsurprisingly, Faber were not persuaded by his arguments. Pym's next novel did not see print for fourteen years, and *An Unsuitable Attachment* appeared only after her death.

Their friendship became warmer. From December 1963 onwards they addressed each other as 'Barbara' and 'Philip' rather than 'Miss Pym' and 'Mr Larkin'. He offered her crucial support during the years of rejection which followed. As Hazel Holt writes, she 'badly needed the sort of intelligent, perceptive and affectionate criticism and advice that he gave her. He also cheered her up by sending her lively, funny letters, which told her *just* the sort of ordinary, frivolous things she liked to know about people.'[14] His letters to Pym are full of domestic practicalities, with an occasional self-conscious conservative, 'English' touch:

> I had a few quite pleasant days in Shropshire & Herefordshire, looking at eccentric decaying churches, then to Salcombe for a week, which I didn't really care for [. . .] I was consoled slightly by passing Michael Cantuar[15] in a narrow lane one day. I finished with a visit to some friends who now have a 'country' house near Newbury: he is turning into a farmer, & most of the meals came out of a 'deep freeze' [. . .] The meat was fantastically tough, like some sort of well-tested plastic floor covering.

He entertains her with details of his University routines: 'On Tuesday I have to address the freshers on "Books" ("How to Kill, Skin & Stuff Them").'[16]

Larkin remained a champion of Pym's work, appreciating her 'gay, confident gift' for subtle verbal comedy and her 'ironic perception of life's absurdities', tempered by 'a keen awareness of its ability to bruise'.[17] But he was not an uncritical admirer. In 1966 he wrote to Monica of *Jane and Prudence*: 'there is a sort of woman's magazine quality there – a kind of cosyness – surely the best novels aren't cosy – reassuring, perhaps, but in BP all characters seem potbound, nobody's ever going to *do* anything, Harry isn't going to screw Wilmet, Prudence isn't *really* having an affair with Fabian, do you think, even, that Piers buggers Keith?'[18] Larkin puts his finger here on an element of Pym's writing that causes problems even for her greatest admirers. As her first love and lifelong friend Henry Harvey commented: 'She was without sensuality. Her passions, in so far as they were not kept back to being pretend play passions, stayed in her head and heart.'[19]

A larger opportunity for Larkin to make his mark on the culture of the age came in January 1966 when, following Louis MacNeice's sudden death, Oxford University Press invited him to take over as editor of the new *Oxford Book of Modern Verse*. Andrew Motion expresses surprise at his acceptance of this task, since it 'involved a great deal of work which he, an efficient but a lazy man, was bound to resent'.[20] This is a puzzling comment. Laziness was not one of Larkin's qualities. He saw his task of updating Yeats's 1936 volume as one of restoring balance to the canon, requesting a change in title to *The Oxford Book of Twentieth Century English Verse*, dissociating it from the 'modern poetry' of Yeats's volume. He wrote to Dan Davin of OUP: 'I am interested in the Georgians, and how far they represented an "English tradition" that was submerged by the double impact of the Great War and the Irish-American-continental properties of Yeats and Eliot.'[21] He intended, he said, to select good poems rather than deferring to the big names. His programme sounds persuasive, and not overly polemical or subjective. But he felt defensive and insecure, fearing that he would caricature himself as a philistine traditionalist.

Closer to home, Larkin found he needed to exert retrospective control over his own early oeuvre. In April 1965 R. A. Caton's Fortune Press capitalized on the success of *The Whitsun Weddings* by producing an unauthorized edition of *The North Ship*. The Society of Authors advised Larkin that, since there was no formal contract for the original publication, he could best reclaim his copyright by authorizing a new edition from Faber. Faber pressed him to include other early poems in a new larger collection. But he resisted a retrospective revision of his career, adding only the single key transitional poem 'Waiting for breakfast, while she brushed her hair'. His Introduction is self-deprecating. But reading between the lines it is clear that he had a higher regard for his first volume than he generally admitted. In late 1965, after rereading the poems, he wrote to his mother: 'I had a sneaking feeling that some of them weren't bad.'[22] The new edition was published on 15 September 1966, and Caton was forced to withdraw the Fortune Press copies from sale.

Meanwhile Larkin continued to perform the tasks of a full-time University librarian. Stage 2 of the Library rebuilding did not offer him the same satisfaction as Stage 1. A huge tower was built over the airy daylit undergraduate reading room which had been so attractive a feature of the original 'New Library'. Staff who had been involved in the move of 1959 insisted on terming the new Stage merely 'the extension'. The North Wing of Stage 2 was completed in March 1967, at which time the Library was renamed the Brynmor Jones Library after the Vice-Chancellor of the University from 1956 to 1972. Brynmor Jones and Larkin were pioneers in creating the first new post-war British university library, and their professional relationship was good. However, they had little in common. Larkin wrote jocularly in a letter to Monica: 'BJ's the man in charge, / He shouldn't be at large, / *I'm butter, he's marge.*'[23] After Larkin's death Sir Brynmor told Andrew Motion: 'people who have written about him have made too much of his poems and not enough of him as a librarian'.[24]

The tension between his relationships with Monica and Maeve continued throughout the decade and into the next. On 23 July 1964 Philip wrote to Maeve with arch suggestiveness: 'Writing in bed ought to be easiest . . . It's just midnight & I am scribbling a note to you because if I don't heaven knows when I shall [. . .] I go up to Hexham tomorrow as you know [. . .] I shall hope to be agreeable to Monica & not make the visit a disappointment, but one can never be sure how one will behave.'[25] He felt no qualm about casually referring to 'Talking in Bed', a poem intimately associated with Monica.[26] The compartments of his love life remained securely separate. He even jokingly suggested that Maeve should write an article for the *Times Literary Supplement*: '"Writing in Bed"! The life & letters of Maeve Brennan'. A few days later, on 5 August, he wrote to Monica in tones of relaxed, rather gross eroticism: 'I was terribly hot last night. I lay thinking how nice it would be to have you beside (or under!) me, &

not to be *drunk*, or *tired*, or *watching the clock*, just gathering your great smooth hips under me & shoving into you as I felt inclined. How rarely this has happened!'[27]

In a letter to Monica of 14 September 1964 he represented his affair with Maeve as in its last throes: 'We are quite friendly & have to see each other daily – the *real* breach & dismay is yet to come, I feel. And I suppose it will come.' But Monica did not believe him and felt deeply hurt. She wrote with passionate and probably inebriated sarcasm in the margin of this letter: 'Note the style, the irony of style, & no intention of doing anything like what is said – perhaps style indicates.' Running out of space she continued in a different margin: '& both of you had my sympathy – what a good giggle for both of you too, later. I was terribly upset for *both* of you while you were giggling together.' An asterisk directs the reader to the bottom of the page, where she added: 'I learned a good deal more later.'[28] Ten months later, on 20 July 1965, he was still making ineffectual apologies:

> I feel that as long as I was faithful, you could somehow accept the unsatisfactoriness of our relation – we might not be married legally, but we were different and perhaps superior – at least your sacrifice of yourself to me was superior to frogmarching me or anyone to the altar rails. But when I am unfaithful – not technically but spiritually – you can only feel duped and made light of, quite apart from the awful upsetting emotion [. . .][29]

He knew, however, that Monica gave the literary imperatives which governed his life a respect beyond Maeve's comprehension. Monica's humility was painful. 'Dear,' she told him apologetically, 'you have to put up with someone who will never distinguish herself.'[30]

Appropriately enough his abandonment of 'The Dance' had happened to coincide with the end of his sixth workbook. On 14 July 1964 he wrote glumly to Barbara Pym: 'poetry has deserted me'.[31] When it returned it took a new form, very different from the social commentary characteristic of his *Whitsun Weddings* period. He wrote in the centre of the first page of his seventh workbook: 'Never write anything because you think it's true, only because you think it's beautiful.'[32] He could not have said this to Monica Jones, nor to Amis.

He was returning to his aestheticist roots. The first work in the new book, 'Solar', completed six months after the abandonment of 'The Dance' on 4 November,[33] is the most austerely impersonal poem in his oeuvre. Larkin remarked in an interview: 'some of my favourite poems have not rhymed or had any metre', and 'Solar' is the most severely rhymeless of his works.[34] One might perhaps recall Milton's rejection of 'the jingling sound of like endings' as inappropriate in a serious religious poem. For, though the title implies godless scientific objectivity, 'Solar' is a pagan incantation: a hymn to the sun. Source of all life, the sun gives without limit, making no emotional demands, and taking no sentimental interest in human affairs. It pours 'unrecompensed'. These are the materialist perspectives of Lucretius, Housman and Hardy. Nevertheless the tone is one of exalted spirituality, and the poem's spare staccato imagism distils an intense metaphorical concentration. The twenty-one lines are packed with the metaphors through which humanity seeks to accommodate its understanding to this awesome force. The sun, in an 'unfurnished' sky, has a lion's face. It is a stalkless flower with a 'petalled head of flames'. Heat, in an extraordinary synaesthesia, is an 'echo' of its gold colour. It is 'coined' among horizontals. It uncloses 'like a hand'. Our needs, recalling Jacob's ladder in Genesis, ascend to it 'like angels'. The form, three stanzas each of seven lines, may perhaps hint at arcane numerology. Three and seven have since antiquity been regarded as numbers of mysterious significance. To be comprehensive Larkin's oeuvre needed to include a prayer, and this was the point in his life when the form was most appropriate to his situation. He was, however, disappointed that he could not make this key poem as large and monumental as its theme demanded. He told Monica: 'it's the sort of thing anyone could write, and indeed it ought to be much longer & deeper & altogether better'.[35]

Nineteen-sixty-four saw a definitive shift in Larkin's work. At this point the hitherto dominant theme of marriage disappears for ever, except in retrospect. Whatever the future contortions of his love life, the pros and cons of his own commitment to a woman cease to be a concern in his poetry. The themes of ageing and death come to the fore. His style begins slowly to harden, while at the same time it develops ever more surprising and ingenious rhetorical strategies. The gestures of comedy, bitterness and yearning of his earlier work are reprised in new mannered forms and abrupt mixtures. And an acute, unacknowledged contradiction develops between his public image and his poems. Acting up to the version of himself reflected by such correspondents as Monica Jones, Amis and Conquest, he appears in interviews and essays as a reductive, plain-spoken traditionalist. His poetry, however, becomes ever more self-ironic and elusive. The hard-won poems of the next five years are rich in literary allusion: elliptical, symbolist, sometimes even difficult.

In a characteristic swing of the pendulum his next completed poem after 'Solar', 'Ape Experiment Room', originally titled 'Laboratory Monkeys' (24 February 1965),[36] is a poem of anti-vivisectionist propaganda. (He was to leave half his estate, ultimately, to the RSPCA.) Forgetting his guiding principle of not making poetry 'do things', he writes with shallow ideological indignation, attacking the animal experimenter: 'a Ph.D. with a beard / And nympho wife who —'.[37] The caricature is loose, and mention of the beard shows nothing more than topical prejudice. As if aware of this the speaker stops before he gets into his stride. Larkin did not publish the poem, perhaps conscious that he had forced his inspiration. The real poet is however glimpsed in the chilling incongruity between the animal's 'eared / Head like a grave nut' on the one hand and the lights and sterilizers of the white rooms in which it is 'buried' on the other. Its apparently human gesture of 'the arms folded round' is no sentimental anthropomorphism. This enigmatic body language has a simian not a human meaning.

The first drafts of what was to become 'High Windows' followed, at the bottom of one page of which Larkin dashed off under the date '3.3.65' a quatrain titled first 'Time & Motion Study' then 'Staff Management', and finally 'Administration'. An office manager notes the strengths and weaknesses of his staff: 'Who deserves a smile, and who a frown'. Then with candid political incorrectness he observes that the girls you have to tell 'to pull their socks up / Are those whose pants you'd most like to pull down'. He did not publish the poem, and such feelings did not spill over into his actual behaviour. One member of staff who worked in the Library in the early 1970s commented: 'He never ogled the girls unlike some of the academic staff [. . .] He did like big busts, preferably with a pretty face above, but not in a creepy fashion.'[38]

He abandoned work on 'High Windows' for the time being and on 24 November 1965, more than a year later than 'Solar', completed 'How Distant'. Its theme is historical: the emigration of young men at the start of the century, keen to get away from 'married villages' and make a new life elsewhere. From on board they watch the 'fraying cliffs of water' and the 'differently-swung stars', or they glimpse a girl doing her laundry in the steerage:

> This is being young,
> Assumption of the startled century
>
> Like new store clothes,
> The huge decisions printed out by feet
> Inventing where they tread,
> The random windows conjuring a street.

At this point in their lives all is incipient opportunity; impressions have not yet hardened into habit. The poem evokes a detached distance between the present and the beginning of the century. But echoes of 'Single to Belfast' and 'Arrivals, Departures' suggest that Larkin is also thinking of a more personal distance. The poem is a fictionalized reminiscence of his own emigration to Belfast fifteen years earlier.

The sonnet 'Friday Night in the Royal Station Hotel', completed six months later on 20 May 1966, also has a personal subtext. Its evocation of life at the terminus revisits 'Here' five years on, in tones which point the way towards his 'late' style. The atmosphere of the Royal Hotel in Hull, a frequent venue for meetings with Maeve, is still today much as evoked in the poem.[39] But realist description is merely the starting point for an elaborate metaphor. In 'Here' the reader was transported across country to an epiphany of unfenced existence. In 'Friday Night' he or she is exiled in the stasis of a waiting room. The rhetoric is playfully surreal. 'Light spreads darkly downwards' like a thick liquid. The personified chairs 'face each other' in sinister confrontation. Reality is defamiliarized by a grammar which subordinates material things (chairs, doors, knives, glasses, carpet) to abstractions (light, loneliness, silence). The dining room elaborately 'declares / A larger loneliness of knives and glass', and the overextended 'octave' of nine lines (a 'nonave'?) ends on a note of orotund vacuity:

> And all the salesmen have gone back to Leeds,
> Leaving full ashtrays in the Conference Room.

The scene has the uncanny quality of a painting by René Magritte. As in 'Here' there is no explicit centre of consciousness. With camp lugubriousness a disembodied, unlocated voice describes the hotel's headed paper: 'made for writing home / (If home existed)'. Kafka's K. and Beckett's Krapp would recognize this room. The poem ends with an unexplained shift into italics, 'panning back' from the isolated fort-like hotel in an abrupt epiphany: '*Now / Night comes on. Waves fold behind villages.*' The euphoric sunny sea- and skyscape of 'Here' has turned to dusk and foreboding. This melancholic, 'funny' poem shows the richness of his *Whitsun Weddings* style hardening into the mannerism of *High Windows*.

In his letters he continued to declare his love for Monica and for Maeve with undiminished intensity. On 4 June 1966 he concluded a letter to Monica by squeezing 'Love, love, love, love, love, love, love, love, love' into the right margin. Two months later, however, he wrote playfully to Maeve from Haydon Bridge where he was staying with Monica: 'You know I'm never anything but happy to take you in my arms and enjoy that kind of kiss that seems to be your own speciality, or patent.'[40] Back in Hull on Sunday 30 October, while catching up on work in the University, he became so eager to see Monica that he leapt into his car and travelled as far as Bawtry before he realized he had too little money with him for the necessary petrol.[41] Shortly afterwards, in

November, an unexpected note was struck when Patsy Strang paid a sudden visit to Hull in an attempt to revive their love affair and, in the course of much drinking (port and gin), accused him of 'not being continental & so on'.[42] After her departure things fell back into their familar pattern. He wrote drily to Monica on 20 November: 'One thing about M., she's never idle. Hurt her feelings and she's soon making up to someone else, and letting you know about it.'[43]

Commentators generally agree with Larkin's own verdict on this love-triangle: 'There isn't any need to make my situation any better-sounding than it is: a self-centred person conducting an affair containing almost no responsibilities with one girl getting mixed up with another, heedless of the feelings of either. Well, not heedless, but not heedful enough to do anything about it, anyway.'[44] However, it is difficult to see how he could have broken the stalemate. Despite what he said, Monica's abject dependence imposed a crushing emotional responsibility upon him. Maeve was also, if to a lesser extent, dependent upon him, but gave his life a freshness and spontaneity lost in his relationship with Monica. He had to an extent created both women. As he had written earlier to his mother: 'I have built her [Monica] in my own image and made her dependent on me, and now I can't abandon her.'[45] In 1966 he wrote in not dissimilar terms to Monica about Maeve: 'You may wonder why I don't end it, in my own interests as well as yours. Partly coward-ice – I dread the scene. Partly kindness – if I've encouraged her to depend on me it seems cruel to turn her away. If she wanted to be free it wd be different.'[46] Neither woman wanted to be free of him. Both knew they would find no other partner so attentive and life-enhancing as he. Kindness did indeed require him to continue both relationships. And kindness required also that he take all the blame upon himself: 'it's my own unwillingness to give myself to anyone else that's at fault – like promising to stand on one leg for the rest of one's life. And yet I never think I am doing anything but ruin your life & mine. I suppose one shouldn't be writing letters like this at 44, one ought to have got it all sorted out twenty years ago.'[47]

It is possible to conclude that Monica and Maeve were taking advan-tage of Philip, rather than he taking advantage of them. He was the

victim of the breadth and generosity of his sensibility and the narrow-
ness of theirs. The rut of Monica's reductive pessimism on the one
hand, and the limitations of Maeve's complacent Catholicism on the
other, meant that to reduce himself to a one-legged relationship with
either of them would have brought pain to all three. It would also have
put an end to his poetry. Consequently they all, for their different
reasons, allowed the situation to continue from month to month, year
to year, sapping his emotional energies with guilt. As he wrote to Judy
Egerton on 5 March 1966: 'in pretty low spirits [. . .] largely because of
increasing dissatisfaction with me of Maeve & Monica'.[48] On the same
day he told Robert Conquest: 'Yes, life is pretty grey up in Hull. Maeve
wants to marry me, Monica wants to chuck me. I feel I want to become
something other than a man – a rosebush, or some ivy, or something.
Something noncontroversial.'[49]

The 'yearly frame' of his life was, for the time being, settled. Regular
short holidays with his mother in a spa hotel or seaside resort were
followed, or preceded, by longer holidays with Monica, often in
Scotland. He would spend Christmas in a state of frustration, with his
mother in Loughborough. Maeve he would meet within the decorous
context of the Library and social events in Hull, or in brief snatched
moments elsewhere. Without subterfuge they could socialize at meetings of SCONUL, in Bangor, Reading, Liverpool or Manchester,[50] and
for several years in the 1960s they visited Scarborough together on
Christmas shopping trips to Rowntree's department store, taking lunch
at the Pavilion Hotel.[51] He pursued his own interests on trips to London,
where he would visit Liberty's department store and the art dealer
Abbott and Holder with Judy Egerton,[52] and share pornographic bookshop expeditions in Soho with Robert Conquest.

He was working up to his limit, and living a full and, in his own
terms, fulfilled life. In addition to day-to-day responsibility for the
Library, he was serving on national committees, writing literary reviews,
composing a monthly jazz review for the *Daily Telegraph* and producing a steady stream of correspondence, personal, professional and
literary. In informal contexts he let off steam in ever more waspish
aphorisms. In a letter to Amis he commented on Ted Hughes: 'No, of

course Ted's no good at all. Not at all. Not a single solitary bit of good. I think his ex-wife, late wife, was *extraordinary*, though not necessarily likeable. Old Ted isn't even extraordinary.'[53] When Ray Brett of the Hull English Department remarked that the second volume of verse by an academic contemporary was 'at least up to the standard of the first', Larkin replied, 'You can't fall off the floor.'[54]

It was not until almost ten months after 'Friday Night in the Royal Station Hotel', on 12 February 1967, that Larkin returned to the March drafts of 'High Windows' and completed the poem on a single page. He was moving deeper into symbolism. Edna Longley observes: 'Although Larkin scorned the idea that *High Windows* might be called *Hautes Fenêtres* the English title reeks of the nineties as influenced by French symbolism.'[55] It is, however, a symbolism in tension with a less deceived demotic realism. The poem's caricature of permissive youth is the product of an embarrassingly raw envy. As University Librarian he himself had little direct contact with students, but his correspondence with Monica echoes her complaints about their loutishness and growing radicalism: 'The devils began their exams today (I think).'[56] In the poem, however, there is no trace of moral censure: 'When I see a couple of kids / And guess he's fucking her and she's / Taking pills or wearing a diaphragm, / I know this is paradise // Everyone old has dreamed of all their lives –'.

The speaker first seeks to reason with himself, putting his feelings into historical context by imagining the hypothetical resentment of an older generation for his own younger free-thinking self: '*That'll be the life; / No God any more* [. . .]' Then in a sudden, unanticipated shift of tone he leaps from this self-argumentative bluster to the purest poetic epiphany:

He
And his lot will all go down the long slide
Like free bloody birds. And immediately

Rather than words comes the thought of high windows:
The sun-comprehending glass,[57]
And beyond it, the deep blue air, that shows
Nothing, and is nowhere, and is endless.

The poem ends on a note of transcendence. But the poet himself remained dissatisfied. The climactic 'endless', which sounds like a triumphant assertion of permanence, is after all merely a trick of syntax. The normal word order, 'endless blue air' or 'endless nothing', would dispel the sublime effect. Larkin knew that his loss of youth could not be countered by a rhetorical sleight. At the end of the March drafts he wrote as an alternative to the final words: 'and fucking piss'.[58] This has now become an inextricable part of the poem; indeed it makes it a more profound work.

Increasingly Larkin was looking backwards, regretting his lost youth, and disliking the overworked, overweight, older man he was becoming. On 27 March 1967 he met Bruce Montgomery in All Souls, Oxford, and found himself picking up the relationship 'as if there hadn't been a ten year gap'.[59] But the meeting could only impress upon him the distance he had travelled since his Oxford days. Another long perspective opened when he re-encountered his first muse, Penelope Scott Stokes, who since their brief encounter twenty-five years earlier had followed his career and in 1965 had sent him a volume of her own poems. Penelope's vulnerable personality had made for a difficult life. In 1966–7 she spent some time in the Quaker psychiatric hospital, The Retreat, in York, and it was here that Larkin visited her on 8 May 1967, taking her out to Young's Restaurant for dinner. She found him charming and amusing; as she wrote to her young daughter:

> We had some very interesting conversation about John Betjeman and particularly about a poet called Elizabeth Jennings, whose work I very much like – apparently, she is about 39 & is always in and out of the Warneford (mental hospital near Oxford). At the end of the evening Philip said he seemed to have made a series of tactless remarks, but that just wasn't true [. . .] Actually he has a *huge* (quiet) sense of humour.[60]

Not surprisingly, in the account he gave to Monica he adopted a disparaging tone, calling Penelope's poems 'no good' and describing her as 'alert, dowdy & a bit toothy'.[61] However, he continued to correspond with her occasionally until his death.

Larkin was no longer the lanky young man who had left school at ten stone seven pounds. Over their meal Penelope noticed his concern with his weight, which 'has gradually crept up from 12 to 14 stone'. 'So he made a pretty half-hearted attempt at certain points during the goluptious dinner to have a *small* helping of something really rather fattening.'[62] He was aware of inexorable physical decline. However, his efforts at dieting were half-hearted. He wrote to Monica: 'Oh dear, I'm fat again! 3½ lbs up. Needle well clear of 14st. Isn't it grim! [. . .] I really must eat less, or something. My breakfast is juice, yoghurt, tea. Perhaps half an apple.'[63] To add to his sense of decline, his hearing was tested in 1967 and declared to be 'at the threshold of social adequacy'.[64] Over the following years increasing deafness contributed to his isolation. His casual assumption that he would die at the same age as his father was hardening into a fixed prediction. On 27 March 1967 he wrote to Monica from Loughborough, lamenting that he was still tied to his mother: 'I suppose I shall become free at sixty, three years before cancer starts. What a bloody sodding awful life.'[65] His prediction was only partly accurate: his cancer was indeed diagnosed when he was sixty-three but his mother had died eight years earlier, when he was fifty-five.

During 1967 Larkin encouraged Jean Hartley during her 'O' and 'A' level examinations, which she was taking as a mature student. She recalls that he 'had taken a close paternal interest in my progress since I first began my studies, even to the extent of calling round to go through each literature paper after I'd sat it and discuss the answers I'd given'.[66] On hearing that she had been awarded a B in 'A' level English he wrote to Monica: 'Not bad for someone who was in hospital and anyway had never taken an exam in her youth.'[67] When Jean began a degree course at Hull University the following year he opened a £25 account for her at Brown's Bookshop[68] (in 1968 Penguin paperbacks cost typically between four and six shillings).

Like 'High Windows', 'The Trees', begun on 9 April and dated in the workbook '2 June 1967',[69] contrives a fragile epiphany out of mere rhetoric. The first two stanzas prepare the ground. A beautiful description of buds relaxing and spreading into full leaf leads to a *faux naif* question, 'Is it that they are born again'? No, the poet answers, 'they die too'. The trees' apparent immortality is a 'trick' betrayed by their rings of grain. But then he side-steps logic, creating an upbeat ending through emotional sound-writing: 'Yet still the unresting castles thresh / In full-grown thickness every May [. . .] Begin afresh, afresh, afresh.' To a sentimental reader the final line will read as ecstatic affirmation. To a less deceived reader it will read as imperious command, reminding us that the time will come soon enough when we will be unable to respond. Larkin recognized that this would be one of his most popular poems, but he was unpersuaded by his own achievement. In a letter to Monica he called it 'very corny',[70] and in the workbook he added after the date: 'Birthday of T. Hardy 1840 / bloody awful tripe'.[71]

The next page of the workbook features a startling contrast of tone and manner. 'Annus Mirabilis' was begun on 16 June and completed, apart from typescript adjustments, after only one more page of drafting on 12 July.[72] It is a public poem, making out of the 'annus mirabilis' of 1963 a cultural myth to which readers of subsequent generations can easily relate:

> Sexual intercourse began
> In nineteen sixty-three [. . .]
> Between the end of the *Chatterley* ban
> And the Beatles' first LP.

Like 'MCMXIV' the poem has a Latin title, and refers to a specific date. Its theme is also an artificially reified social myth, though here in mock-heroic rather than tragic mode. Sex did not really begin in 1963 any more than innocence ended in 1914. Well-read readers will recognize the reference to Dryden's patriotic poem concerning the year 1666–7, describing the Fire of London, the plague and sea battles with the Dutch. The poet impudently asserts that 1963 is a date of similar national importance. There is no propaganda against the 'permissive society', as it was then called. The poet's self-mocking presence, '(Which was rather late for me)', merely adds piquancy, 'me' being a stereotype of old-fashioned inhibition. Indeed, the poem is delightfully politically incorrect (though the term did not come into use until the 1990s).

Larkin's forty-fifth-birthday poem, 'Sympathy in White Major', completed on 31 August 1967, shows his symbolist *High Windows* manner fully developed. Like his youthful 'Brunette' renderings of Villon and Baudelaire, the title makes an irreverent English reference to a French original: Théophile Gautier's 'Symphonie en Blanc Majeur'.[73] When asked in an interview in 1964 whether he read much foreign poetry Larkin responded in the voice of his crudely philistine persona: 'Foreign poetry. No!'[74] However, the title of this poem is incomprehensible without knowledge of Gautier. Whether or not he read foreign poetry, it still haunted his imagination. He had commented that the last line of 'Absences' sounded 'like a slightly unconvincing translation from a French symbolist'.[75] The title of 'Sympathy in White Major' is, precisely, an unconvincing translation from a French symbolist.

'Symphonie en Blanc Majeur' is a central document in the doctrine of 'L'art pour l'art', a sumptuous white-on-white description of a swan-maiden descending to humankind from a chill empyrean of dispassionate aesthetics. It concludes: 'Oh! Qui pourra mettre un ton rose / Dans cette implacable blancheur?' 'Who could infuse a rose tint into this implacable whiteness?' Who would dare sully such purity with the colour of blood and emotion? This is the Platonic perfection which Larkin had celebrated from the beginning: the angled features of the Polish airgirl, beyond all 'humanity of interest', the essential beauty of pure foam, pure coldness. He opens with his own cynical version of Gautier's white-on-white prescription:

> When I drop four cubes of ice
> Chimingly in a glass, and add
> Three goes of gin, a lemon slice,
> And let a ten-ounce tonic void
> In foaming gulps until it smothers
> Everything else up to the edge,
> I lift the lot in private pledge:
> *He devoted his life to others.*

In this clear ice, liquid and foam he will drown his sorrows. In the second stanza he insists that unlike his contemporaries, who wore other people 'like clothes' in their lives, he had set himself to bring 'the lost displays' to the select few 'Who thought I could'. A true aesthete, he has devoted himself to art for art's sake. His verdict now is as dismissive as it had been five years earlier in 'Send No Money': 'It didn't work for them or me.'

But the theme of the poem is peculiarly doubled: Anglo-Saxon as well as Gallic. In a typescript of the poem inserted at the end of Workbook 7, Larkin has written the title in capitals: 'SYMPHONY IN WHITE MAJOR'.[76] He has then crossed out the first word in pencil and replaced it with 'SYMPATHY' (the only appearance of this word in Larkin's mature oeuvre).[77] It was an inspired afterthought. By replacing Gautier's 'Symphonie' with 'Sympathy' the speaker imparts the rose tint, perverting the poem's focus from poetic vocation to moralized emotion.[78] In the light of experience his pursuit of beauty no longer appears as the simple antithesis to playing the socially responsible 'white man' which it had seemed to be in 'Reasons for Attendance' and 'Send No Money'.[79] He has attempted to follow both vocations, bohemian and respectable, and they have led to the same bitter outcome: the sacrifice of his life to others. The two voices blend and merge. In roman type he speaks as a lonely dedicated aesthete; in italics he speaks as a loyal pillar of the community shouldering the white man's burden: '*A decent chap, a real good sort, / Straight as a die, one of the best* [. . .]'. The bitter, histrionic irony builds up, phrase after phrase, into an excruciating self-epitaph: '*Here's to the whitest man I know* – Though white is not my favourite colour.' In a letter written shortly before the appearance of *High Windows* in 1974, Larkin revealed that the title he 'really wanted' for his final volume was *Living for Others*; 'only I could never write the title-poem'.[80] Had this poem been less elliptical and elusive it could have fulfilled that function.

Larkin's next two completed poems continue the process of stock-taking. 'Sad Steps' (dated 24 April 1968) offers a tragic point-by-point riposte to the tenuous transcendence of 'High Windows'. The earlier poem concluded with an empty daytime windowscape. 'Sad Steps' opens with a crowded night-time windowscape. The 'wedge-shadowed gardens' and 'wind-picked sky' are reminiscent of Laforgue, but this 'laughable' epiphany goes off half-cock, and the poet becomes, as in 'High Windows', entangled in words: not now words of envy and frustration, but of another bad translation from a French symbolist: 'Lozenge of love! Medallion of art! / O wolves of memory! Immensements!' In Laforgue's 'Complainte de cette bonne lune' the moon is 'le médaillon', and in 'Litanies des premiers quartiers de la lune' it is a 'blanc médaillon'.[81] But the less deceived English poet rejects his role as decadent *Pierrot lunaire* with a quiet monosyllabic 'No', and the poem ends where 'High Windows' began, with a vision of youth – not this time in the form of a shallow caricature generated by envy, but with tragic gravity, in the form of an intimate recollection of:

> the strength and pain
> Of being young; that it can't come again,
> But is for others undiminished somewhere.

'High Windows' ended in a suspect escape into an absolving 'nowhere' of clear blue air. 'Sad Steps', daring to impart the rose tint of human pathos, contemplates a 'somewhere' where youth still exists undiminished: but not for him. Larkin did not feel the need to add any disparaging comment to the draft of this more profound poem.

In 'Sympathy in White Major' Larkin had reviewed his achievement through a grotesque combination of French symbolism and British clubbability. In 'Posterity' (dated in the workbook '17.6.68') he delivered another scathing verdict on himself, this time in the trans-Atlantic tones of his own future biographer, Jake Balokowsky. The poem is a point-by-point variation on 'Naturally the Foundation will Bear Your Expenses', written more than seven years earlier. Both poems are monologues by professionals in the literary business: one a blithe British freeloader, the other a dissatisfied American on the academic treadmill. Both poems show a dynamic ambiguity in their attitude towards the speaker. Instead of teaching school in Tel Aviv as he would prefer, Jake has to bend to the demands of his wife's family and achieve tenure.

Consequently he is stuck with 'this old fart' (Larkin) for 'at least a year'. 'Just let me put this bastard on the skids, / I'll get a couple of semesters leave // To work on Protest Theater.' The poem is satire only on the surface. Jake may represent the cynicism of the academic racket but, more profoundly, he is a victim of the system. Like the poet whose work he is studying he is fouled up by the gulf between his dreams and hard reality. He also submits himself with a bad grace to living for others. Different though he appears from Larkin, Jake is the poet's intimate alter ego. His description of his subject conveys the poet's self-judgement: 'Not out of kicks or something happening – / One of those old-type *natural* fouled-up guys'. Jake's boring task is to write the biography of the author of 'Toads'. The toad with whom Jake is walking down Cemetery Road is Larkin.[82]

By 1968 the downward direction of Larkin's life was firmly established. His poetry had become a widely spaced series of ever more subtly successful poems about failure. As if to mark the loss of his past, in September the Hartleys, his first friends in Hull, split up, and Jean left Hull Road, Hessle, with her daughters.[83] He remained friends with Jean after George left Hull, but kept 'very much on the sidelines', unwilling to complicate his already difficult relations with his publisher.[84] His health was in steep decline. He told Brian Cox that, after a party for *Critical Quarterly* in October, he woke up feeling so terrible that he went 'on the wagon for a month'.[85] He was aware of being full of shallow anger, often out of proportion to any cause. In November he complained to Robert Conquest that the University was licking 'the blacking off the boots of all students in sight'.[86] Later in the month he broke into a heartfelt lament in a letter to Monica over the lost simplicity of his years in Belfast and the early time in Hull:

> Oh dear, it's such a nice day. I wish I could go out on my bike as in my youth, instead of taking the car to the Library, *for work*. As I said in an earlier letter, I spend my days in meetings, & then there's all the post stuff to be fitted in somewhere. I'd fit it into the lavatory pan & no error. And then the evening will be all bed changing & eating & bill paying & washing up. No time for anything.[87]

In addition, though he had done his best to live for others, he was beset by guilt over his failure to satisfy the demands of his mother, Monica and Maeve. In a letter to Monica written from his mother's house in Loughborough on Boxing Day and headed '<u>GLUM LETTER</u>', he exclaimed: 'God! It seems a waste of a life. I suppose someone someday will explain what went wrong. I can't believe I am so much more unpleasant than everyone else. How sick I am of it all.'[88]

17

Jazz, Race and Modernism
1961–71

Ever since February 1961 Larkin had been writing his monthly jazz review in the *Daily Telegraph*. In 1968 he collected the pieces into a volume and wrote an introduction. At first his intentions were modest. Indeed he had already given the text to a local Hull printer when he wrote to the book's intended dedicatee, Donald Mitchell, who had originally recommended him to the *Telegraph* and was now a commissioning editor at Faber: 'My idea is to print a small edition privately, just enough to send to the copyright libraries and distribute among friends, with perhaps some minor sales conducted personally.' Might Faber, he asked, help distribute the book? It was, he wrote, 'not over serious, but I think it might be of interest to people who like jazz and who have heard of me'.[1] Faber dismissed this naive idea and took over the project. But the book, particularly the Introduction, retains an uneasy private tone. There is perhaps even a hint of antagonism in the title. The heading of one of the reviews is the question 'All What Jazz?' Either this phrase, or the indicative answer, *All That Jazz*, would have been a natural title for the volume. Instead Larkin preserves 'what', but omits the question mark, stranding the phrase between interrogative and indicative.[2] Is this a subtle nuance or an attempt to catch the reader out? *All What Jazz: A Record Diary 1961–68* was published by Faber on 9 February 1970. Larkin continued to write his column, finally giving it up in December 1971, six months after the death of Louis Armstrong.

The reviews of 1969–71 were added to the second edition, which was published in 1985 as *All What Jazz: A Record Diary 1961–71*.

Jazz was essential to Larkin.[3] Misquoting mischievously he proclaimed 'the truth of Baudelaire's words: "Man can live a week without bread, but not a day without the righteous jazz."'[4] (Baudelaire actually wrote 'not a day without poetry'.) Though Larkin rarely expressed the same passion for other kinds of music, his musical tastes were wide. He was listening to records of Monteverdi in Belfast in the early 1950s at a time when this was very much a minority taste. His LP collection included the 1982 three-disc boxed set of early Mozart symphonies, Volume 1 in the series made by Christopher Hogwood with the Academy of Ancient Music playing on original instruments.[5] When he comments that ragtime, the early precursor of jazz, had 'a bizarre classicism, like plantation Scarlatti', the exactitude of the judgement relies as much on his knowledge of eighteenth-century styles as on his knowledge of ragtime.[6] And when he deplored the popularity of Jacques Loussier's 'Play Bach', he was as indignant at the travesty of Bach's baroque integrity as he was at Loussier's tepid 'jazz': 'tasteless expanses of real Bach themes distracted with aimless bits of syncopation [. . .] the acme of pallid vulgarity'.[7] Of the eight records he chose for the *Desert Island Discs* radio programme in 1976, three (his first, fourth and seventh choices) featured jazz musicians: Louis Armstrong ('Dallas Blues'), Bessie Smith ('I'm Down in the Dumps') and Billie Holiday ('These Foolish Things'). But his other five were a Newcastle street song from the 1790s, Thomas Tallis's motet 'Spem in Alium', the medieval 'Coventry Carol', Elgar's Symphony No. 1 and the closing chorus of Handel's oratorio *Solomon*.[8] His taste extended also to pop music. As Jean Hartley recollected: 'he had an affection for the more romantic Beatles numbers. He bought Maeve a copy of "Yesterday" and played it over and over.' Under the influence of 'Gin and the ambience' he declared Bob Dylan's 'Mr Tambourine Man' to be 'the best song ever written'.[9]

Jazz was not a taste he shared with the women in his life. Though she tolerated references to jazz in letters, Monica Jones preferred 'Classical. Mozart. Beethoven' and had no notion of the differences between jive, hotcha and boogie-woogie.[10] For Larkin jazz was a private passion, shared with a small number of male friends. He never tired, in particular, of the 'inexhaustible vitality of the blues', which in his view were 'fundamental to jazz'.[11] Mezz Mezzrow, he wrote, found in the blues 'the key to a relaxed vitality white America lacks'.[12] He himself, as a white British schoolboy at a further cultural remove from black America than Mezzrow, found in the blues a release from emotional inhibition and the boredom of his bourgeois boyhood. 'I suppose everyone has his own dream of America,' he wrote, and jazz music, particularly the blues, provided his earliest, most intimate and consoling version of this dream.[13] From the beginning he expresses his lyric appreciation of life in the vocabulary of jazz: 'Oh, yeah, man. The ultimate joy is to be alive in the flesh. Shake that thing.'[14] Bechet's held note evokes the 'appropriate falsehood' of his own private dream: 'Everyone making love and going shares –'. It conjures up '*My* Crescent City': 'On *me* your voice falls as they say love should, / Like an enormous yes.' Jazz allowed Larkin to indulge his longings without the censorship of reality. More specifically the jam session, in which 'hot' music was created by improvisation, offered him an ideal of spontaneity and freedom. He wrote in dispassionate retrospect, 'Nothing's arranged, we were told. Everyone just plays. Well, perhaps they did.'[15]

But jazz also taught him a more impersonal lesson in artistic rigour. The twelve-bar blues formula, that modern version of the ancient aubade ('Woke up this mornin' . . .'),[16] gave him the example of a strict but infinitely variable artistic discipline: 'for all its formal simplicity it is rarely monotonous. Somehow in this most characteristic music of the American Negro has been imprisoned an inexhaustible emotional energy. You can go on playing or listening to the blues all night.'[17] The jazz records over which he enthused with his schoolfriend James Sutton gave him a model for his own poetic practice of 'preserving' emotion. Larkin belonged to the first generation of listeners to experience their music largely through the private encounter with repeatable recordings, rather than, as in previous centuries, through their own playing or the fugitive public performances of the salon and concert-hall. The 'work' is now no longer an interpretable score but the particular recording. As Larkin wrote, 'it is not "Weary Blues" we want but Armstrong's 1927 "Weary Blues"'.[18] This new twentieth-century model of performance profoundly influenced Larkin's ideas about poetry. In his poetic theory the artist preserves the moment by creating a device in which the normal rhythms of speech are played off against the formal pattern of metre: 'When you write a poem, you put everything into it that's needed: the reader should "hear" it just as clearly as if you were in the room saying it to him.'[19] He could have learnt this from Shakespeare or Marvell, but the extreme meticulousness with which he organizes his devices imitates the exact nuances and subtleties of recordings. In a sense, it could be said, the reader 'plays' a Larkin lyric, just as one might 'play' a recording of Louis Armstrong or Bessie Smith. The poet aims at the identity and repeatability of impact of a record. In this context it is significant that the readings of his own poems which he recorded in 1980 for the Watershed Foundation show only very slight variations of inflexion and intonation from those made in 1958 and 1964 for the Listen label.

From the first, Larkin adopted in his reviews a pithy, opinionated voice capable of engaging even a reader who knows nothing about the subject. Larkin is a master of 'occasional' spontaneity. His critical voice commands respect largely because of the freshness and exactitude of each individual judgement: 'I have never heard a band whoop in the last ride-out as in this one [Count Basie's 'Jumpin' at the Woodside'], and how striking the accompaniments are – the menacing trombone figure behind Clayton, the harsh falling single note behind Young repeated like an accusation.'[20] He catches exactly the 'characteristic excitement' of the solos of the clarinettist Pee Wee Russell: 'their lurid snuffling, asthmatic voicelessness, notes leant on till they split, and sudden passionate intensities [. . .]'.[21] Russell's timing in 'D. A. Blues' 'is perfect, his phrasing oratorical without being melodramatic, his tonal distortions involuntary, and all is conceived in [a] vein of unique hard hitting lyricism'.[22] Elsewhere he lovingly evokes the qualities of the New Orleans trumpeter Henry 'Red' Allen: 'by the end of his life an Allen solo was a brooding, gobbling, stretched, telegraphic thing of half-notes and quarter-tones, while an Allen vocal sounded like a man

with a bad conscience talking in his sleep'.[23] Thelonious Monk's hesitant chords are, he writes, 'like suitcases just too full to shut properly',
and he characterizes Fats Waller's piano playing as 'a baroque trivial-
ity'.[24] He can also recognize when critical decorums become irrelevant:
'Listening to his "Moon River", a piece of slop if there ever was one, I
came to the conclusion that it is Armstrong's staggering and economical sincerity that makes this kind of number succeed.'[25] Larkin persuades
us that his ear is experienced and discriminating: to be trusted.

In the 1968 Introduction to *All What Jazz* Larkin describes his initial
intention as to adopt a posture of uncritical benignity. 'In literature, I
understood, there were several old whores who had grown old in the
reviewing game by praising everything, and I planned to be their jazz
equivalent [. . .] It didn't really matter, therefore, whether I liked things
at first or not, as I was going to call them all masterpieces.'[26] He was
after all no expert, and his taste, particularly in relation to recent developments, would need educating. Thus the fifth review, published in
June 1961, 'Bechet and Bird', judiciously juxtaposes the two reed-
players, Sidney Bechet of the older generation and Charlie Parker of
the new, as 'two players with nothing in common except that they
manifestly stood head and shoulders above their contemporaries'.[27] He
lovingly evokes the older performer's 'Blue Horizon': 'six choruses of
slow blues in which Bechet climbs without interruption or hurry from
lower to upper register, his clarinet tone at first thick and throbbing,
then soaring like Melba in an extraordinary blend of lyricism and power
that constituted the unique Bechet voice, commanding attention the
instant it sounded'.[28] He then goes on to summarize the shift from
'trad' to 'mod' in the mid-1940s, and ends with a paean to the original
genius of Parker:

> the new modern jazz that Parker and Gillespie founded was in part a
> reaction against the ossified platitudes of 1940 big-band jazz which they
> were both forced to play. Driven to desperation by the fag-end of the
> swing era, they and a few other young Negro musicians produced a
> music among themselves that was technically, melodically and rhythmi-
> cally beyond their elders and their audience alike. By doing so, they

recaptured for their race the jazz initiative, and, incidentally, split the world of this music into two camps. But on the evidence of these solos alone it would be absurd to call Parker's music a reaction. As well call leaping salmon a reaction.[29]

There is no affectionate evocation of particular felicities, and the analysis is objective and socio-historical. Nevertheless the eloquent final sentence strikes a note of sincere admiration.

But this show of even-handed balance was short lived. As the reviews proceeded Larkin showed himself as a partisan of traditional jazz, and Parker and Gillespie were increasingly denigrated. In January 1963 he wrote: 'Trad, everyone agrees, is dead, but it shows no more signs of lying down than modern does of sitting up.'[30] Elsewhere he notes that though Bop has been called development 'there are different kinds of development: a hot bath can develop into a cold one'.[31] His attitude accurately reflected the taste of most British jazz-lovers at the time, and many since: 'I am afraid that the modernist tradition in jazz – I am not for the moment thinking of gifted individuals such as Parker and Gillespie – strikes me, even in historical perspective, as no better than the modernist tradition in other arts – that is, as tending towards the silly, the disagreeable and the frigid.'[32] He notes that 'Even the magazines have a traditional reviewer and a modern reviewer,'[33] and devotes separate paragraphs to records which 'All modernists will want' and those of specifically 'traditional' interest.[34] Magnanimously rising above his prejudices, he finds 'the BBC's decision to ban modern jazz from its weekly "Jazz Club" on the grounds of public uninterest, a regrettable step in view of Britain's many fine modern musicians such as Tubby Hayes'.[35] Occasionally he will express enjoyment of a particular performance by Charlie Parker, Miles Davis or even John Coltrane. He seems genuinely prepared to be pleased by each new record, even against his expectations: 'I continue to listen gamely to Archie Shepp (who is wearing a beard now) in the hope that it will one day all cease to sound like "Flight of the Bumble Bee" scored for bagpipes and concrete mixer.'[36] He was wary of his own disputatiousness, and in the Introduction to *All What Jazz* expressed the hope that the reviews themselves 'are tolerably free from such polemics', conceding that his 'was not the only ear in the world'.[37]

Usually however, whenever the names of Parker, Davis, Coltrane, Monk, Ornette Coleman or Archie Shepp appear, the reader learns to anticipate an acid drop of delightful wit. Larkin's dislike varies in tone. His response to Davis shows a lively humour, as though he were marvelling that talent could be so wilfully perverted: 'his lifeless muted tone, at once hollow and unresonant, creeps along only just in tempo, the ends of notes hanging down like Dali watches';[38] 'the fact that he can spend seven or eight minutes playing "Autumn Leaves" without my recognizing or liking the tune confirms my view of him as a master of rebarbative boredom'.[39] 'I freely confess that there have been times recently when almost anything – the shape of a patch on the ceiling, a recipe for rhubarb jam read upside down in the paper – has seemed to me more interesting than the passionless creep of a Miles Davis trumpet solo.'[40] 'To my surprise, I found myself liking at least two tracks of "Miles in the Sky" (CBS), not of course as jazz, but as a kind of soundtrack to some bleak pastoral such as a film of the Paston Letters.'[41] Even a reader unsympathetic with Larkin's opinions will surely wince with delight at his deadpan judgement on an LP of Davis in concert: 'for me it was an experience in pure duration. Some of it must have been quite hard to do.'[42]

In writing of John Coltrane, however, Larkin's poise is less secure. On some level he seems deeply, personally offended by Coltrane: 'John Coltrane, that relentless experimenter, intersperses the vinegary drizzle of his tone with chords (yes, two notes at once) that hardly seem worth the effort';[43] 'in the main the effect is like watching twenty monkeys trying to type the plays of Shakespeare'.[44] This antagonism reached its extreme in the notorious 'Looking Back at Coltrane', written following Coltrane's death in 1967. There is something chilling and unpleasant about Larkin's refusal of any glimmer of generosity. He begins, in a most unLarkinesque way, by rebuking *The Times* and *Melody Maker* for not paying proper respect to his authority, in their praise for Coltrane. 'I do not remember ever suggesting that his music was anything but a pain between the ears [. . .] Was I wrong?'[45] It is the most rhetorical of questions, and he goes on to speak ill of the dead in a tone of deliberate malice, concluding: 'I regret Coltrane's death, as I regret the death of any man, but I can't conceal the fact that it leaves in jazz a vast, a blessed silence.'[46] Unsurprisingly the *Daily Telegraph* refused to publish this review. Surprisingly, however, Larkin was not chastened by the rejection. Though his next reference to Coltrane shows rare approval – 'On "Catwalk" in particular Coltrane is light and appealing'[47] – four months later he describes his solos as 'the scribbling of a subnormal child'.[48]

The reason for his ill will lies deep. Coltrane's playing exemplified for Larkin a fundamental artistic crime. For Larkin, art exists for its own sake; it does not 'do' anything. It has no ulterior designs on the audience. His obituary of Louis Armstrong stresses that the trumpeter humbly served his art and his audience: 'Armstrong was an artist of world stature, an American Negro slum child who spoke to the heart of Greenlander and Japanese alike. At the same time he was a humble, hard-working man who night after night set out to do no more than "please the people", to earn his fee, to pay back the audience for coming.'[49] He cited Armstrong's criticism of Parker for failing to please the audience: 'you got no melody to remember and no beat to dance to'.[50] Coltrane, in Larkin's view, takes this perversity a stage further than Parker:

> He did not want to entertain his audience; he wanted to lecture them, even to annoy them. His ten-minute solos, in which he lashes himself up to dervish-like heights of hysteria, are the musical equivalent of Mr. Stokely Carmichael. It is this side of his work that appeals to the Black-Power boys such as LeRoi Jones and Archie Shepp.[51]

Some see such views as racist. Ben Ratliff comments: 'for Larkin Coltrane's aesthetic problem [. . .] was that he was an American Negro'.[52] But this argument does not convince. Louis Armstrong and Bessie Smith were also American Negroes. It is not Coltrane's colour that rouses Larkin's hostility; it is Coltrane's attitude towards his colour and, crucially, the effect of this attitude on his art.

Larkin's earliest enthusiasm had been specifically for the exuberant rhythms of black musicians. As a schoolboy in 1939 he regretted that 'America is in the grip of the white bands [. . .] I'd back coloured against white most times.'[53] At this early stage his preference seems entirely aesthetic, with no ideology behind it. Awareness of the socio-political context followed later. The mature Larkin of the *Telegraph* reviews fully acknowledges the social and economic context of the blues and jazz. 'Behind the blues spreads the half-glimpsed, depressing vista of the life of the American Negro', he writes in a review of Paul Oliver's *The Story of the Blues*.[54] In a review of Nat Hentoff's book *The Jazz Life* he refers to 'the continual indignities endured by the Negro entertainer, who may well be refused admission at a club front door over which his name blazes in lights'.[55] Elsewhere he relates how the Ellington band was unable to find food during the interval of a concert in St Louis, since there was no segregated black restaurant close by, and a racist drugstore owner refused to make sandwiches for a white go-between.

Larkin draws an historical lesson in moral consequences, relating this episode to the insulting behaviour of Charlie Mingus towards his white audiences on a European tour in 1964.[56] Ellington had returned to the concert after his humiliation, still aiming to give pleasure; Charlie Mingus in contrast retaliated against his white audiences, refusing to be obedient to their pleasure. In a review headed 'The End of Jazz', Larkin quotes Mingus: 'Don't call me a jazz musician. To me the word jazz means discrimination, secondclass citizenship, the whole back-of-the-bus bit.'[57] As Larkin wrote in his weekend *Telegraph* essay 'Requiem for Jazz', 'Where there had been joy and relaxation, there was now tension and antagonism.'[58] This he registers as objective history: 'The Negro did not have the blues because he was naturally melancholy. He had them because he was cheated and bullied and starved. End this, and the blues may end too.'[59] Jazz, in the sense that he means the word, is destined to become 'an extinct form of music as the ballad is an extinct form of literature, because the society that produced it has gone'.

The American Negro is trying to take a step forward that can be compared only with the ending of slavery in the nineteenth century.

And despite the dogs, the hosepipes and the burnings, advances have already been made towards giving the Negro his civil rights under the Constitution that would have been inconceivable when Louis Armstrong was a young man. These advances will doubtless continue.[60]

As he puts it in the 1968 Introduction to *All What Jazz*: 'The tension between artist and audience in jazz slackened when the Negro stopped wanting to entertain the white man, and when the audience as a whole, with the end of the Japanese war and the beginning of television, didn't in any case particularly want to be entertained in that way any longer.'[61]

Modern black musicians show:

> a desire to wrest back the initiative in jazz from the white musician, to invent 'something they can't steal because they can't play it'. This motive is a bad basis for any art, and it isn't surprising that I found the results shallow and *voulu* [. . .] The constant pressure to be different and difficult demanded greater and greater technical virtuosity, and more and more exaggerated musical non-sequiturs.[62]

This was the source of the 'new inhumanity' which he heard in the playing of Miles Davis and John Coltrane. 'From using music to entertain the white man, the Negro had moved to hating him with it.'[63] It is a travesty to suggest that Larkin would have preferred blacks to remain oppressed and ill-educated so that his beloved pleasure-giving jazz might continue. His antagonism towards the modernizers might sometimes be mistaken for racist condescension: 'like most of his Negro contemporaries [Davis's] increasing preoccupation with musical theory is in direct ratio to his liability to make an ass of himself'.[64] But Larkin dislikes Davis's affectation of theoretical complexity not because he is black but because it leads him into unpleasant 'calculated perversity',[65] a perversity he shares with many white artists.

Indeed, Larkin's disappointment with modern jazz gains intensity from his respect for the contribution of traditional jazz to world culture. In his obituary of Louis Armstrong, he refers to 'the great ironical takeover of western popular music by the American Negro (and remember the saying "Let me write a nation's songs, and anyone you like may write its laws"), Armstrong stands with Ellington and Waller as one of the Trojan horses that brought it about.'[66] Shortly after Armstrong's death Charles Monteith of Faber suggested that Larkin might write Armstrong's biography. In his reply Larkin showed his appreciation of the historical gravity of the subject: 'It is already accepted – or if it isn't, it soon will be – that Louis Armstrong was an enormously important cultural figure in our century, more important than Picasso in my opinion, but certainly quite comparable.'[67] One approach to the biography might be 'cultural', 'taking Armstrong as a kind of Trojan horse of Negro values sent into white civilisation under the cover of entertainment'.[68] Any biographer, he stresses, must be fully aware of Armstrong's significance as 'a cultural phenomenon of the twentieth century, not overlooking the part he has played (with, of course, other artists such as Duke Ellington, Fats Waller and so on) in "Negroising" western culture. This may sound a tall order: it certainly isn't a description of me!'[69] He concludes that he is underqualified for the task.

In view of Larkin's enthusiasm for this 'Negroising' of Western culture, it seems strange that in his correspondence with Faber's Donald Mitchell concerning *All What Jazz* he should have commented: 'It's about time jazz had its Enoch Powell.'[70] Larkin's temperament constantly runs to contradictory extremes, but this surreal remark seems at first quite baffling. Powell's notorious 'rivers of blood' speech had been made a few months earlier on 20 April 1968, and following his subsequent dismissal from the government Powell had become the focus of widespread opposition to West Indian immigration into Britain. In terms of the politics of the day Larkin's comment should mean that he intends to take up Powellite cudgels against the 'Negroising' of British culture. Powell's own ideas were complex, but the ideological constituency to which he appealed was in the main crudely racist. Clearly Larkin does not intend his jazz criticism to be Powellite in this sense. It seems that, ignoring the immediate political implications, he is using Powell's name to signify simply a refreshing, bloody-minded candour on delicate issues. Larkin in jazz, like Powell in politics, will give voice to the inconvenient but deeply held feelings which others are too mealy-mouthed, or too intimidated by political correctness, to express.

But inevitably his mention of Powell will remind the reader of the handful of references to 'niggers' and 'pakis' in Larkin's correspondence of the later 1960s and 1970s. It is these which have led to the careless assumption by some critics that he is, in Lisa Jardine's words, 'a casual, habitual racist'.[71] Larkin does on occasions entertain some of his correspondents with expressions of pungent bigotry. However, these are performative riffs, always requiring inverted commas. They never come directly in his own voice or without subversion. He wrote to Monica on 19 November 1968, after he had completed his Introduction to *All What Jazz*:

> Dearest, For once I feel pretty cheerful – 11.20 pm on a Saturday night, on wch I *think* I have finished the preface, & eaten haggis, neeps & claret, reading the *Noctes*:[72] then a glass of Glenfiddich, & by God wasn't the toast 'Mr Enoch Powell'! Then jazz records *to my taste*, especially Armstrong, 'How Long Has This Been Going On', 'Let's Do It', & 'others about as good', as he himself once said.[73]

The smooth transition of approval from Powell to Armstrong makes a comic show of his own self-contradiction. Similarly in June 1970 he gave Robert Conquest his ultra-nationalist prescription for success at the ballot-box: 'Remember my song, How To Win The Next Election? "Prison for Strikers, Bring back the cat, Kick out the niggers, How about that?" How about it indeed. Yeah man.'[74] The slogans are held up provocatively for examination; they are not proposed as his sincere political creed. And the closing exclamation, 'Yeah man', evokes a 'Negro' jam session. He later inserted the quatrain in a letter to his old schoolfriend, Colin Gunner, adding 'Ooh, Larkin, I'm sorry to find you holding these views –'.[75] Gunner could read as much or as little irony into this comment as he liked. A less ironic manifestation of his nationalism came in his obituary of Louis Armstrong, when he expressed satisfaction that the trumpeter had in his final years been better appreciated in Britain than the USA: 'let us take pride in "The

Melody Maker Tribute to Louis Armstrong"' (a set of LPs from the seventieth-birthday concert held in the Queen Elizabeth Hall). 'I defy anyone to listen to the final "Sleepytime" track without being glad that this country made its feelings about Armstrong clear once more before his death.'[76] Nationalism was alien to Larkin's sensibility, and this is perhaps the most passionate assertion of nationalism in his writing.

Worried about his health, Larkin might sound off comically about 'fat Caribbean germs' chasing him in the Underground, or lament 'all manner of germs brought into the country by immigrants (Powell for Premier)'.[77] Or later, in a letter to Colin Gunner, he might deplore the behaviour of black spectators at Test matches: 'I don't mind England not beating the West Indies, but I wish they'd look as if they were *trying* to beat them [. . .] And as for those black scum kicking up a din on the boundary – a squad of South African police would have sorted them out to my satisfaction.'[78] But characteristically he begins with a reminder of the inferior skill of the English players. The verbal comprehensiveness at which Larkin aims in his writing meant that he would inevitably find a place for every conceivable kind of word. He could thus speak of 'the paki next door' in a letter to a friend without the slightest implication that he lacked respect for his neighbour, or would treat him differently from people of his own ethnic group. For all his verbal transgressiveness, it is impossible to imagine Larkin ever acting with racist motives.

Philip and Monica frequently dined with R. K. Biswas, an Indian colleague in the English Department at Leicester, and his wife.[79] In August 1971 Larkin travelled to All Souls for a farewell dinner given for Biswas, who had been a fellow there. Larkin approached publishers on behalf of the young poet and novelist Vikram Seth.[80] And in a letter to Anthony Thwaite he gave a glimpse of his contribution to a meeting of the Arts Council Literary Panel: 'You should have heard me pleading for ethnic culture.'[81] When the President of Senegal, Léopold Sédar Senghor, visited Hull, Larkin was disappointed not to meet the poet of *négritude* and the translator of T. S. Eliot into French. He wrote to Conquest: 'Didn't get introduced to His Nibs [. . .] I suppose I repre-sented Litherachoor. Apparently His Nibs is stuck on it.' But his casualness is affected. He had taken the trouble to read Senghor's poetry, and gave an incisive verdict on its combination of Gallic suavity and swooning *négritude* in terms of a cocktail recipe: 'I read his poems (in translation) and thought them Whitman-and-blackcurrant-juice-and-catpiss.'[82] This judgement may be felt to be too wickedly accurate, but it shows no racism.

In 1972 a student sit-in occurred in Hull when it was revealed in the press that Reckitt and Colman, a local company in which the University held a large investment, was paying black workers in its subsidiary factory in South Africa wages below the official UN poverty minimum. Larkin's comments on the merits of the issue were neutral. He told Barbara Pym on 22 March: 'I felt it was all rather halfhearted, and it failed to achieve its end anyway. The Admin Building stank for a week after the sitters-in ("activists") had departed.'[83] This issue was the source of ongoing tension in the University. I myself became involved as a young lecturer, securing the signatures of half the University staff on a petition to the University's Council requesting that the University sell their shares in Reckitts. Over lunch in the staff bar Larkin was asked about this petition, and replied: 'He's performing a valuable function. It will be handy to have a complete list of all the pricks in the University.' John Howarth, a Mathematics lecturer who was in the bar at the time, felt impelled to interject: 'There's one thing to be said about a prick. It usually has a pair of balls associated with it.' Larkin made an appreciative gesture of concession, as if to say *touché*.

It is unfair that Larkin has suffered so disproportionately for the flashes of performative racism in correspondence with his more prejudiced correspondents. D. H. Lawrence immersed himself in racist theories and fascism for a time in the early 1920s, and T. S. Eliot showed the nasty anti-Semitism of his class and generation in 'Gerontion' and essays of the 1930s. In contrast Larkin had no cultural investment in ideas of racial 'inferiority' or 'superiority'. It could never have crossed his mind, for instance, that Sidney Bechet must be an inferior musician to Pee Wee Russell because he was of an 'inferior' race.[84] He was not a racist, either 'casual' and 'habitual' or, for that matter, consistent and systematic. The speaker of 'Sympathy in White Major' declares, 'white is not my favourite colour', and throughout his work Larkin subjects the customs and establishments of his own culture to scathing ridicule. When *All What Jazz* was reissued in 1984 he reflected: 'It now reads very anti-black, insofar as most of the people I bollock are black [. . .] Coltrane, Coleman, Shepp. But then most of the people I praise are black too.' He added with a twinkle: 'Better play safe.'[85]

But the issue of Larkin's supposed racism only came to the fore after his death, with the publication of his letters. In the 1970s the controversy focused instead on his loud attack on 'modernism' in the Introduction. In his initial approach to Mitchell, Larkin had written diffidently: 'I thought it might amuse you to read the introduction, which is a *jeu d'esprit* not perhaps to be taken very seriously.'[86] There is something puzzling in his fatalistic anticipation of the trouble he was making for himself. He was determined to have his say, while at the same time he hoped not to be taken seriously. He repeats later to Charles Monteith that the Introduction was 'really only a *jeu d'esprit* in the manner of Mencken or someone like that', and anticipates that 'to pass it off seriously will earn me the biggest critical clobbering I have ever experienced'.[87] As publication approached he attempted to disarm criticism by suggesting that the book be promoted as a 'freak publication'. He wrote to Faber's Sales Director: 'I don't think it will earn me anything but execration [. . .] Treat it like a book by T. S. Eliot on all-in wrestling.'[88] To Anthony Thwaite he wrote: 'Try to imagine a book by Humphrey Lyttelton saying that modern poetry is no good, while at the same time charmingly admitting he's never read any since 1940, and you will get some idea of how mine will be handled.'[89]

But however hesitant he may have been it is clear that by prefixing the Introduction to the volume Larkin intended to cause controversy in literary circles and to secure a readership beyond the jazz world:

If it has any interest at all, I think it is the thesis of the introduction, namely, that post-Parker jazz is the jazz equivalent of modernist developments in other arts, such as are typified by Picasso and Pound in painting and poetry. I don't think this has actually been said before, and,

while it may not be wholly defensible, I think it sufficiently amusing to
say once.[90]

In the Introduction Larkin turns the story of his personal taste into an
engaging comic tale of hubris and punishment. Having, he explains,
lost touch with jazz in the later 1940s when he lived 'in a series of
provincial lodgings where jazz was not welcome', he had remained
largely unaware of the transition from 'trad' to 'mod'. When he was
reunited with his record collection in 1948, he was content for a time
'to renew acquaintance with it and to add only what amplified or
extended it along existing lines'. Consequently when he began to review
records for the *Telegraph* in 1961 he was 'patently unfitted to do so and
should have declined'.[91] Retribution for his hubris followed as the
records arrived month by month at his door:

> Had jazz been essentially a popular art, full of tunes you could whistle?
> Something fundamentally awful had taken place to ensure that there
> should be no more tunes. Had the wonderful thing about it been its
> happy, cake-walky syncopation that set feet tapping and shoulders jerk-
> ing? Any such feelings were now regularly dispelled by random
> explosions from the drummer ('dropping bombs'), and the use of non-
> jazz tempos, 3/4, 5/8, 11/4.

The accessible, happy Negro jazz of his youth had, he discovered, been
spoiled by experimental free forms and (warming to his theme in a riot
of alliteration) 'all the tawdry trappings of South America, the racket of
Middle East bazaars, the cobra-coaxing cacophonies of Calcutta'.[92]

Eventually, after months of puzzlement and dismay, it at last it dawned
on him that what had happened to jazz was only a version of what had
already alienated him in the other arts: 'this was *modern* jazz, and Parker
was a modern jazz player just as Picasso was a modern painter and Pound
a modern poet. I hadn't realized that jazz had gone from Lascaux to
Jackson Pollock in fifty years, but now I realized it relief came flooding in
upon me after nearly two years' despondency.' What had seemed merely
a private disappointment revealed itself as an aspect of a larger cultural

crisis with which he was already familiar. Parker, Davis and Coltrane were 'modernists', and 'the term "modern", when applied to art, has more than chronological meaning: it denotes a quality of irresponsibility peculiar to this century, known sometimes as modernism, and once I had classified modern jazz under this heading I knew where I was'.[93]

The Introduction to *All What Jazz* has served to perpetuate the image of Larkin as a pugnacious philistine. But it is not its basic argument which has made it notorious. Though, as he claimed, the jazz angle of his attack on modernism is original, his is otherwise, as he wrote, 'an ordinary tale, and perhaps hardly worth telling'.[94] Ever since the 1920s, when Eliot proclaimed that modern poetry must inevitably be 'difficult', voices have been raised to warn that modern art is losing its audience through obscurity and wilful experimentation. Larkin expresses a common and widespread concern which still persists: 'I dislike such things not because they are new, but because they are irresponsible exploitations of technique in contradiction of human life as we know it. This is my essential criticism of modernism, whether perpetrated by Parker, Pound or Picasso.'[95] What makes Larkin's treatment of the issue such a strenuously provocative read is the shamelessly point-scoring manner in which he puts his case. The final rhythmic phrase here, 'Parker, Pound or Picasso' has an alliterative bounce which disrupts the tone of serious debate. And there is histrionic bluster in his picturesque list of modernist 'irresponsibilities'. 'Piqued at being neglected', Larkin tells us, the modernist artist has:

> painted portraits with both eyes on the same side of the nose, or smothered a model with paint and rolled her over a blank canvas. He has designed a dwelling-house to be built underground. He has written poems resembling the kind of pictures typists make with their machines during the coffee break, or a novel in gibberish, or a play in which the characters sit in dustbins. He has made a six-hour film of someone asleep. He has carved human figures with large holes in them.[96]

Comic verve sweeps aside any sense of critical proportion.

He goes on to satirize the appropriation of art by the educational establishment, adopting the voice of a Further Education lecturer in a novel by Kingsley Amis:

> 'You've got to work at this: after all, you don't expect to understand anything as important as art straight off, do you? I mean, this is pretty complex stuff: if you want to know how complex, I'm giving a course of ninety-six lectures at the local college, starting next week, and you'd be more than welcome.'[97]

This is good fun. Moreover many readers will sympathize with Larkin's irritation at Yves Klein's publicity stunt in which models covered with paint rolled across canvases, and will share Larkin's irritation at 'concrete' poetry in typographical shapes. Many also will be left cold by Andy Warhol's 1964 'anti-film' of John Giorno asleep for five hours and twenty minutes. Other readers, however, will object that the idea of typographically shaped poetry goes back as far as George Herbert in the seventeenth century, while Picasso's *Guernica* ('both eyes on the same side of the nose'), Beckett's *Endgame* (characters in dustbins) and Henry Moore's statues ('with large holes in them') are certainly not 'in contradiction of human life as we know it', any more than is Le Corbusier's ecologically inventive architecture ('a dwelling-house [. . .] underground').[98] Nor had these highly successful artists much reason to feel pique at being neglected. That is mere wishful thinking on Larkin's part. His *jeu d'esprit* did indeed earn him, as he had forecast, 'the biggest critical clobbering I have ever experienced'.[99] And he deserved it.

Earlier in his career Larkin had been unwilling to pick public quarrels about art. He had been hesitant in 1956 about being too closely identified with Robert Conquest's claim that *New Lines* represented a new 'empirical' poetic 'Movement'. Now he cast discretion to the winds, and let rip, spoiling for a fight. There is little point in engaging with the details of his attack; nor does Larkin really intend the reader to do so. There may be some truth in what he says, but he says it with too much intemperate gusto. His moral indignation may be genuine, but it is also hectic. In Larkin's defence, however, it could be said that his Introduction suffers, to some extent, from the way the word 'modernism' has changed in usage over time. As happened also with 'Romanticism', what began as a polemical strand within a period has ultimately become the label for virtually every artist of the time. The term 'modernism', or 'Modernism', is now used in a much broader way than it was in 1968. Then it would have seemed highly provocative to call D. H. Lawrence a 'modernist'. Now it is normal. Earlier in his career Larkin had been sensitive to 'modernity' in the more inclusive sense. His earliest ideas on jazz have the heady tone of T. S. Eliot or Wyndham Lewis theorizing about the 'modern' spirit in art: 'The modern unconscious has chosen to symbolize its predicament of subjection through the mode of a subject people; its predicament of imprisonment through the unvarying monotony of the 4/4 rhythm; its panic at the predicament through the arresting texture of the jazz tone.'[100] At this point it seems he would have described his beloved blues as 'modern' or even 'modernist'. A quarter of a century later, Larkin specifies as his target something narrower than this, that quality 'known sometimes as modernism'. What he is attacking is not so much what we would now call 'modernism' as extreme avant-gardist experimentalism. And, though his examples are loosely and provocatively chosen, he has a point.

The Introduction to *All What Jazz* did the poet real damage by perpetuating in the minds of a readership deaf to the implied inverted commas in his writing the image of a reductive one-dimensional Larkin. The brilliance with which he 'pretends to be' himself in the Introduction has persuaded too many readers that this *is* actually Larkin. Thus one of the greatest poets of the twentieth century, a man with the widest and most exact appreciation of the various arts of his day, and with the most delicate and organic sense of literary history, ends up in the preposterous position of announcing: 'I don't like modernist art.'[101] Amusing though it is, there is something dismaying about his attempt to reduce himself to a philistine.

What ultimately raises the Introduction above this level is its personal, biographical narrative. He never quite accepts his own attempt to make a serious theory out of his unique individual experience, constantly questioning his own claim to authority, and conceding that, after all, the real problem may be simply that his tastes are old fashioned. At the beginning and end of the essay he takes a longer perspective, placing himself in an objective historical context: 'For the generations that came to adolescence between the wars jazz was that unique private excitement that youth seems to demand. In another age it might have been drink or drugs, religion or poetry.'[102] He presents the book very much as the work of a middle-aged man.[103] In the early pages of the Introduction he paints an intensely nostalgic picture of two schoolboys playing and replaying records in a room overlooking a tennis court, sharing their private jazz secret. In the thirties, he reminisces, jazz 'was a fugitive minority interest, a record heard by chance from a foreign station, a chorus between two vocals, one man in an otherwise dull band. No one you knew liked it.' He recalls battering away on the drum kit his father had bought him.[104] The Introduction to *All What Jazz* is ultimately as much elegy as polemic. As he wrote later: 'My objection to modern jazz is not that it is pretentious, but simply that it isn't anything like the jazz I loved and began collecting [. . .] What comes after may be technically brilliant and racially justified, but it leaves me cold.'[105] He was outraged less by irresponsible modernist art than by the realization that he was no longer young: 'Something, I felt, had snapped, and I was drifting deeper into the silent shadowland of middle age. Cold death had taken his first citadel.'[106] One factor in his dislike of more recent jazz, indeed, might have been his increasing deafness, which took the freshness off his experience of new sounds.

At the end of the essay he foreshortens this long perspective in a vision of the declining years of all the jazz-loving Dockerys of his generation, as they slip into the shades. These are the men for whom he wrote his reviews:

Sometimes I imagine them, sullen fleshy inarticulate men, stockbrokers, sellers of goods, living in 30-year-old detached houses among the golf courses of Outer London, husbands of ageing and bitter wives they first seduced to Artie Shaw's 'Begin the Beguine' or The Squadronaires' 'The Nearness of You'; fathers of cold-eyed lascivious daughters on the pill, to whom Ramsey Macdonald [*sic*] is coeval with Rameses II, and cannabis-smoking jeans-and-bearded Stuart-haired sons whose oriental contempt for 'bread' is equalled only by their insatiable demand for it [. . .] men whose first coronary is coming like Christmas; who drift, loaded helplessly with commitments and obligations and necessary observances, into the darkening avenues of age and incapacity, deserted by everything that once made life sweet.[107]

This gorgeous purple prose, funny and at the same time moving, is hugely cathartic.

18

Politics and Literary Politics
1968–73

Aware, as he wrote in an early letter to Sutton, that when it came to politics 'I don't know anything at all about anything, and it's no use pretending I do,'[1] Larkin's instinct was to avoid the subject. In November 1967, after presenting a rare jazz-record recital to undergraduate students, he wrote that, even when his deafness allowed him to hear what his audience had said, he did not know what to answer: 'Which side are we on – North or South Vietnam? Aawgh.'[2] Only once did the question of politics crop up in discussion with Jean Hartley. Jean recalls: 'An emotional scene ensued during which we each voiced our gut reaction to the other's views.' She told him:

> 'I have to be a socialist out of sheer self-preservation. A hundred years ago my counterpart would have been sent up chimneys or had to scrub someone else's floors from dawn to dusk as my mother did.' He shrugged disbelievingly and eased his jacket out of the iron-pronged chair which always managed to trap him. Socialism, for Philip, was on a par with modern jazz – a descent into chaos. Eventually we had a tacit agreement not to discuss politics.[3]

The argument had no effect on their personal friendship.

Larkin had anticipated the general election of 1964 with uneasy detachment, attempting to associate Monica with his own distaste:

'You'll hate it more than I shall, I expect, as you are more politically conscious.'[4] However, as the political temperature rose under the Labour government of Harold Wilson (1964–70), he increasingly began to take sides, expressing right-wing Cold War attitudes: hostility towards union militancy, contempt for leftist intellectuals and fear of the Soviet Union. The influence of Monica's unreflecting conservatism was reinforced by the wider perspectives of Robert Conquest. On 19 August 1968 Larkin wrote to Conquest that he was reading his friend's magisterial account of Stalin's purges of the 1930s, *The Great Terror*, 'as a change from writing my frigging annual report'.[5] Three days later, to the dismay of Western socialists, 2,000 Soviet tanks and 200,000 Warsaw Pact troops brutally suppressed Czechoslovakia's attempt to develop 'Socialism with a Human Face'.

Closer to home, the University was undergoing its own political upheavals. The 1960s saw an unprecedented democratization of the education system with the introduction of 'comprehensive' schools and a rapid expansion in University provision following the 1963 Robbins Report on Higher Education. A new generation of students arrived on campus with no recollection of the war or of post-war austerity, and with an idealistic social agenda. In May 1968 student protests led to a national strike in France and unrest on the streets of Paris. Hull saw its own provincial version of this revolt. In June 1968 the Student Union voted for an occupation of the Administration Building and Larkin found himself briefly imprisoned, along with others attending a meeting of Senate. A sign reading 'Under New Management' was posted on the door. He described the episode to Barbara Pym with exasperated resignation:

> Well, we have had our sit-in, our baptism of fire: I expect you saw it in the papers early last month. It was a disagreeable experience: I suppose revolutions always are. I wish I could describe it, or say something pene-trating about it [. . .] The universities must now be changed to fit the kind of people we took in: exams made easier, place made like a factory, with plenty of shop-floor agitation and a real live strike.[6]

The students' demands were voiced by a Joint Politics and Sociology undergraduate, Tom Fawthrop, who had walked out of his examinations, calling on others to do the same. (No other student had followed him.) Fawthrop became an instant national celebrity, writing a book, *Education or Examination*, and speaking in support of sit-ins in other universities:

> Exams are more a matter of luck than judgement [. . .] Actually doing a question in forty minutes – it's not an intellectual exercise. If you can do it in 40 minutes the essay isn't worth doing. In other words, can three years' work be adequately assessed by twelve or fifteen hours of exams? Critics of the system argue that it does not allow for the possibility of creativity and originality which a genuine educational process should seek to encourage.[7]

Larkin the bohemian poet might perhaps sympathize with Fawthrop's idealism, but the University Librarian was outraged at his irresponsibility. 'Did you see that poncing student of ours shooting off his mouth to the Press Association?' he wrote to Conquest. 'The guy who tore up his exam paper? What has actually happened is that he's been treated exactly the same as if he had *failed* the exam (since our regulations don't have any provision for people tearing up exam papers) –'.[8] In his poems at this time Larkin envies the freedom of the young; in his letters he resorts to the slogans of generational and class prejudice. In a letter to Monica he refers to students as a 'filthy pack of commie bastards'.[9] He wrote to Barbara Pym more wittily: 'It may sound snobbish, but I do think that now we are educating the children of the striking classes.'[10]

The influx of a new generation of academic colleagues added to his sense of embattlement and alienation. When I arrived in the Hull English Department in 1968, having picked my way through a sit-down protest on the way to the interview, there were so many newly appointed lecturers that a special welcoming dinner was held in a packed staff refectory. The same ritual was necessary the following year. I soon discovered that one of my colleagues in the English Department was a

charismatic apologist for Stalin's purges. Towards the end of the year
Larkin wrote to Monica:

> a nasty little maths lecturer called Jarvis who sells treasonable literature
> *in the street* has been *in hospital* after selling it in 'The Grapes' in Clough
> Road: a man [. . .] asked him (Jarvis) if he remembered him telling him
> to 'shove his *Newsletters* up his arse' last week? Jarvis said he didn't. The
> chap *waited outside* & beat him up. There's a man to admire! While we
> sit with our cigarettes & our attitudes, here's a sincere & conscientious
> man who puts aside comfort & pleasure & *does something about it* [. . .]
> Doesn't it warm your heart? Just what the medico commanded.[11]

Larkin's relish for this brutality is distinctly unpleasant. He enclosed a
cutting from the student magazine *Torchlight* in which Trevor Jarvis
described being kicked several times in the face: 'I was taken to the
Hospital where I had two stitches in my forehead and I couldn't open
my mouth and one eye for two days.'[12]

Larkin's relationships with his academic colleagues were formal and
professional. In the 1950s and early 1960s several distinguished scholars
had worked in the English Department. Richard Hoggart, Malcolm
Bradbury, Barbara Everett and Rosemary Woolf all taught in Hull
before moving on elsewhere. In 1959 Brian Cox, who had arrived
shortly before Larkin, founded the influential Leavisite literary magazine *Critical Quarterly*, together with his former student friend A. E.
Dyson, the pioneering campaigner for homosexual rights, who was at
Bangor. The magazine became central to the development of English
Studies, publishing the criticism of Raymond Williams, Frank Kermode
and David Lodge, and the poetry of Ted Hughes, Thom Gunn and
Sylvia Plath. During the 1960s Larkin gave Cox's magazine a number of
poems which focused on contemporary social mores: 'A Study of
Reading Habits' (1960), 'Breadfruit' (1961), 'Love' (1966) and 'High
Windows' (1968).[13]

Cox, who moved to a Chair at Manchester in 1966, saw the 1968
student unrest as the symptom of mistaken educational theory, and
conceived the idea of publishing 'Black Papers' on education attacking

the 'White Papers' in which government policy was published. Eventually five appeared, attacking the excesses of 'progressive educa- tion' and the introduction of 11–18 'comprehensive' education, which was replacing the socially divisive system of 'grammar' and 'secondary modern' schools. The Black Paper contributors deplored what they saw as a collapse of intellectual rigour resulting from the headlong expan- sion of the university sector. Kingsley Amis, a prominent contributor, was loud in disapproval of new university courses in Sociology and associated subjects, which he saw as cover for Marxist subversion. Uninhibited by the fact that he had failed his BLitt at Oxford, he deplored declining standards. His epigrammatic summary of the state of Higher Education, coined in 1961, was: 'more will mean worse'.[14]

Following the stir caused by the first Black Paper, *Fight for Education*, Larkin was persuaded to lend his celebrity to the second, *Crisis in Education*, published in March 1969. His contribution was a snappy trochaic quatrain, set out on the page in octameters instead of tetram- eters to form an uncouth, loping couplet:

When the Russian tanks roll westward, what defence for you and me?
Colonel Sloman's Essex Rifles? The Light Horse of L.S.E.?

Albert Sloman was Vice-Chancellor of Essex University, then a hotbed of radicalism, while students at the London School of Economics routinely disrupted meetings addressed by right-wing speakers. The implication of Larkin's lines is that the fellow-travelling radicals of the British education system will offer scant defence against the Red Army's advance across Europe.

But Larkin was not writing as one who had seriously considered education policy, any more than 'Breadfruit' or 'High Windows' embodied the Leavisite moral earnestness of *Critical Quarterly*. A more personal insecurity lies behind his public attitudes at this time. Students, for instance, unsettled him on a more primitive level than ideology. As he wrote to Cox in October 1968: 'Tomorrow I have to address the freshers [. . .] and feel as usual scared of it.'[15] This annual public expo- sure was an ordeal. And there is a tone of abject exhaustion in his comment to Pym a fortnight later: 'Wretched term has started again, & the place is full of replicas of Che Guevara & John Lennon, muttering away and plotting treason. How wearisome it all is! I wish I didn't have to work so hard: every day, all day . . . and about two evenings a week are snatched into the maw as well. How do you find time to write?' Characteristically, he had found time, despite everything, to read a draft of Pym's latest novel, *The Sweet Dove Died*, and in the same letter offered dispassionate and useful advice.[16]

But the dominant tone of his letters at this time is of a man overworked and at the end of his tether. He let loose in a letter to Monica of 27 November 1968:

Dearest bun,

> Morning, noon & bloody night,
> Seven sodding days a week,
> I slave at filthy *work*, that might
> Be done by any book-drunk freak.
> This goes on till I kick the bucket:
> FUCK IT FUCK IT FUCK IT FUCK IT

Nice to be a *pawet*, ya knaw, an express ya *feelins*. Eh? The last line should be *screamed* in a paroxysm of rage.[17]

His personal unhappiness increasingly displaced itself in shallow political rant. His verdict on the Wilson government in a letter to Amis was intemperate: 'Fuck the whole lot of them, I say, the decimal-loving, nigger-mad, army-cutting, abortion-promoting, murderer-pardoning, daylight-hating ponces, to hell with them, the worst government I can remember.'[18] It is difficult to believe that he was genuinely agitated about the decimalization of the currency or the adjustment of clocks to British Summer Time. In a letter to Monica of 3 March 1968 he broke off from such complaints to exclaim: 'But isn't it an *angry* time – how easily one gets cross, how when left to oneself irritation begins to ferment like some neglected juice! [. . .] Only drink releases me from this bondage.'[19]

Inwardly Larkin may have shared the desperation of Guy the Gorilla in London Zoo, two photographs of whom he kept on his desk at work, but he remained all the while a highly professional university librarian. Trevor Jarvis recalls that the local Association of University Teachers always found him constructive in negotiation and scrupulous in carrying out agreed policy, unlike some other members of Hull University's management.[20] Larkin's relations with John Saville, then Senior Lecturer in Economic History at Hull, whose promotion to professor was allegedly held back because of his radical views, show how complex Larkin's politics really were. As the University's Librarian, he gave Saville every assistance in what he jokingly called his 'seditious' projects, building up the Library's Archive of Labour History into an essential reference collection. In particular he supported Saville's acquisition of the early archive of the National Council for Civil Liberties (now Liberty) and the papers of the political cartoonist 'Vicky' (Victor Weisz). He was also instrumental in the acquisition of papers concerned with Jock Haston (1913–86), a Trotskyist merchant seaman who contested a seat in Parliament in the 1945 election as a member of the short-lived Revolutionary Communist Party.[21] Larkin would occasionally lunch with Saville and they would share their passion for jazz. After his death Saville commented that he was 'an efficient librarian who really knew what he was about [. . .] his very conservative politics did not confuse his role as a librarian [. . .] I mourn him still.'[22]

Nevertheless during the angry time of 1968–9 Larkin came closer than before to becoming the conservative caricature he frequently impersonated. He wrote to Monica on 7 February 1968:

Listening to *My Word* over supper[23] I heard them cite a bit of *Ver*'s song from *LLLost*, & this sent me tumbling to the bookcase for my New Temple – aren't the 2 songs lovely together! My eyes fill with tears [. . .] 'When turtles tread, and rooks, and daws, And maidens bleach their summer smocks' – oh darling! I can hardly write for tears, & only you can share it with me. Isn't it marvellous for there to be Shakespeare, & for him to be English! Or for *us* to be English!

It is dispiriting to see his spontaneous sense of the beauty of the poetry being reduced to a narrow defensive nationalism: 'only you can share it with me'. He congratulates Monica on not being 'a Czech, ceaselessly grumbling', and himself on not being 'a Yank, writing a thesis on water-imagery in Ezra Pound'.[24] But later in the same letter his reflection on literary nationality grows more complex. He describes being shown round the Oxford University Press Printers and seeing 'a queer thing called *Dictionary for Advanced Readers of English* – "What's that," I said. "Oh, that's a dictionary for 'emergent nations'," he said, giving the inverted commas.' The reprints, Larkin was told, were never fewer than a quarter of a million, most of which went to Africa. He was moved: 'I must confess I felt touched to think of them all winging their way there. Troops out, books in. I don't know.'[25] The diffident phrasing ('I must confess', 'I don't know') deflects any possible explosion to the right by Monica against this soft liberalism.

On 30 June 1968 he described 'Posterity' to her:

> It gets in Yanks, Yids, wives, kids, Coca Cola, Protest, & the Theatre – pretty good list of hates, eh? I long to write a political poem – the withdrawal of troops east of Suez started me, now I see someone boasting that in a few years' time we shall be spending 'more on Education than "Defence"' – this shocks me *to the core*, & I seriously feel that *within our lifetime* we shall see England under the heel of the conqueror – or what *used* to be England, but is now a bunch of bearded layabout traitors & National Assistant 'Black Englishmen' – if I had the courage I wd emigrate – terrible –[26]

Several months later, in January 1969, he completed his only substantial poem directly concerned with topical politics, 'Homage to a Government'. He was more than usually hesitant about this particular poem, though he did send it to the *Sunday Times*: 'if they print it I'll say why it fails. But they may send it back. Probably the kindest thing.'[27] It appeared on 19 January. His motive was fundamentally literary. Determined to explore every available form and genre at some point in his career, he intended this deliberately as 'a political poem'. The topic he chose, the withdrawal of British troops from the outpost of Aden on the Persian Gulf, was indeed a promising one for a right-wing polemicist. The Labour government stood accused of bungling the troop withdrawal because of its ideological commitment to pell-mell 'decolonization' at all costs.[28] It was also alleged that domestic finance played a greater role in the decision than foreign policy, a sore point in view of the current union agitation for higher pay.

Larkin made a poem out of this situation, not by forthright satire, as in the Black Paper epigram. Instead he aimed to rouse the reader's moral indignation through Swiftian indirection, adopting the *faux naïf* persona of an honest citizen attempting to justify to himself the corrupt motives of his government:

> Next year we are to bring the soldiers home
> For lack of money, and it is all right.
> Places they guarded, or kept orderly,
> Must guard themselves, and keep themselves orderly.
> We want the money for ourselves at home
> Instead of working. And this is all right.

The repetition 'it/this is all right' conveys the speaker's lack of conviction, while the rhyme scheme, abccab, listlessly repeats exactly the same words in each stanza ('home, right, orderly, orderly, home, right', etc.). As a dramatization of disillusion this is effective. But the tone is insecure. Is the persona meant to be genuinely naive, or is he speaking with heavy irony? Sarcasm certainly breaks the surface in the crude point-scoring phrase 'Instead of working', which seems interpolated from a more vigorously polemical poem.

The poem's attitude towards the specific military incident which had brought Aden into the news is also problematic. Opinion had been polarized by Lieutenant Colonel Colin Campbell Mitchell, 'Mad Mitch', who in 1967 led the Argyll and Sutherland Highlanders in reoccupying a district of Aden taken over by local nationalists in anticipation of the troop withdrawal. To many at the time the bloodshed of what was dubbed by the press 'the Last Battle of the British Empire' seemed gratuitous. The Labour MP Tam Dalyell asked in Parliament whether Mitchell had 'disobeyed operational and administrative orders of his senior officers',[29] and Mitchell's men were accused of brutality. Larkin's reference to this scandal in the poem is oddly oblique and mild. He concedes to his left-wing readers that 'from what we hear / The soldiers there only made trouble happen'. If the satire is to work effectively the phrase 'from what we hear' should strike the reader with heavy irony ('from what we hear from communist subversives'). But it does not. Indeed the tone seems to imply real doubt. Larkin's poetic integrity prevents him from simplifying the situation. He could not stop himself exploding (or at least fizzling momentarily) 'to the left'.

Crucially the poem fails to address the larger issue of imperialism itself, though this is central to its ideological context. Larkin's new-found interest in the British Empire fails to convince. He had shown not the slightest interest in the decolonization of Africa and the Middle East during the previous decades. Harold Macmillan's 'Wind of Change' had passed him by. 'You know I don't care at all for politics, intelligently.'[30] He quickly realized that this was not, after all, a 'political poem' in any true sense of the phrase. In a later interview, he clumsily denied that he had intended to take a political stand at all: 'Well, that's really history rather than politics [. . .] I don't mind troops being brought home if we'd decided this was the best thing all round, but to bring them home simply because we couldn't afford to keep them there seemed a dreadful humiliation.'[31] He does not mention the poem's allegation that the withdrawal served to line the pockets of workshy strikers. He was uneasily aware that decolonization was considered 'the best thing all round' by politicians of the right as well as the left. And as Blake Morrison comments: 'financial motives are as involved in the posting of troops to colonies as they are in the withdrawal of them'.[32] In everyday life, however, Larkin was less circumspect, acting out the stereotype of a Tory loyalist. When Mitchell later headed a national campaign against the dissolution of his regiment, Larkin's car sported a 'Save the Argylls' bumper sticker.[33]

His attempt to unite his University and poetic roles by involvement with the Compton Lectureship in poetry brought him disappointment of a more personal kind. In 1968 he was co-opted on to the Arts Council committee administering a bequest by the philanthropist Joseph Compton. He proposed that some of the money be used to set up a fellowship, installing a writer in a university for a year. He hoped that students and staff from across the disciplines would take advantage of this opportunity: 'both music and poetry tend to be thought of in terms of the departments that teach them [. . .] This seems to me quite wrong. Both are forms of art, and art is universal, not simply a subject to be taught.'³⁴ His proposal of Hull as a suitable place for the Fellowship was accepted. He had recently inaugurated a 'Poetry Room' in the Library, complete with records and audio-tapes. He approached Betjeman as a possible first Fellow, but he declined. His next choice, Cecil Day-Lewis, accepted, and gave his inaugural lecture on 17 January 1969. The arrangement was for Day-Lewis to be available for consultation in the University once a fortnight, and to deliver a lecture once a term. Larkin congratulated himself on his coup when Day-Lewis was appointed Poet Laureate late in 1968, shortly before taking up the Fellowship. However the literary politics of the time were not propitious. The generation gap was too wide and students were apathetic towards such official initiatives. Moreover, Day-Lewis was not a charismatic personality, and his poetic reputation was fading (Larkin himself called his poetry '*harshit*', horse-shit).³⁵ On the first day Day-Lewis and Larkin waited, but no one came. His subsequent visits to the University were only slightly more successful. The Fellowship was continued over the following four years. Richard Murphy, Peter Porter, Ian Hamilton and Douglas Dunn all served as Compton Fellows. But the initiative met with only modest success. The paper concerning the Fellowship which Larkin delivered later at a meeting of SCONUL was entitled, with litotes, 'A Faint Sense of Failure'.³⁶

Early in 1969, as if to confirm the loss of his youth, he heard that he was to be awarded an Honorary DLitt by Queen's University Belfast, which he had left fourteen years earlier. His supposed Orange sympathies did not extend to admiration for Loyalist politicians, and he hoped that the ceremony would not 'involve writing an ode to the

Reverend Ian Paisley'. He could not, however, resist penning a suitable quatrain:

> See the Pope of Ulster stand,
> Spiked shillelagh in each hand,
> Vowing to uphold the Border,
> Father, Son, and Orange Order.

He added: 'I had better make sure of getting my Doctorate first.'[37]

The established routines of his life continued. In August he snatched a week's holiday in Norwich with his mother in 'marvellous weather', followed by a touring holiday in Ireland with Monica in his new car, an 'enormous 4-litre Vanden Plas Princess, *with a Rolls Royce engine . . .* 2nd, or even 3rd, hand'. It was 'love at first sight', he told Barbara Pym.[38] He wrote to Maeve about the number of Brennans they had encountered, including one Maeve Brennan: 'I can't forget you, even if I had any inclination to, which I haven't. Accept a big kiss and some spectral maulings – are you wearing tights? Or stockings?'[39] Stage 2 of the new Library building had been opened in spring 1969, and he took pride in the imposing seven-storey tower which won awards from the Civic Trust and the Royal Institute of British Architects.[40] However, by the beginning of the academic year in autumn 1969, he already felt displaced within it: 'There are so many new members of staff that I feel like a stranger in my own building.' He was relying increasingly on Betty Mackereth, who had now been his secretary for twelve years. As he told his mother in October 1969: 'My mainstay is Betty: boundless energy, always cheerful & tolerant, and if she doesn't do half my work she sort of chews it up to make it easier for me to swallow. I'd be lost without her.'[41] Betty had learned to cope with his volatile moods. One morning she might receive a phone call shortly after nine in the accent of a Yorkshire pub landlord: 'We've got a geezer 'ere. Been under t'table all night, dead to t'world. And 'e says 'is name's Philip Larkin.' On another day he would sit at his desk staring at nothing, and she would flit silently in and out to collect the necessary papers.[42]

Increasingly deaf, overworked and alienated, Larkin was being pushed to the side of his own professional life. His response was to engineer an escape from Hull, if only a temporary one. Since early 1966 he had been giving occasional attention to his OUP *Twentieth-Century Verse* anthology. He could now reasonably request leave in Oxford, where he would have access to the Bodleian copyright Library and could finish work on the project. He wrote to Barbara Pym on 3 February 1970:

> I am hoping to go to All Souls for 6 months in the autumn – a 'Visiting Fellow'. I went there recently: it's rather like an academic nursing-home. 'We don't want you to have *any* worries while you're here.' My excuse is to finish off this wretched Oxford Book – or let it finish *me* off. I have dreams of reliving my youth – of doing all the things I never did – going to Bach choir concerts – the Playhouse – having coffee at Elliston's – walking to those places I've never seen, like *Bagley Wood* & all that Scholar-(Gipsy/Gypsy) jazz. Bet I don't.[43]

It was indeed, to a large extent, an 'excuse'. Looking at his final selection of poems, it is difficult to believe that the major poets would have been any differently represented had he not spent this time in the Bodleian, though it did provide him with a number of less well-known works. Most importantly the Fellowship took him away from the stresses of Hull and its Library.

He spent the winter and spring terms of 1970–1 in Oxford. The historian A. L. Rowse told Motion that, on his arrival, Larkin seemed to be 'Falling over backwards to be philistine' and was an alarmingly heavy drinker.[44] His expectation of an escapist idyll was more or less fulfilled: 'I did experience a remarkable return to youth – I bought a college scarf [. . .] and *nearly* bought a pipe, but reason remounted her throne in time. I tried to do all the things I said I would, like watch the OURFC,[45] and go to the theatre & the Bach choir, but this collapsed after a while: the theatre was just as boring as ever, and I never got as far as the Bach Choir.'[46] He lived at Beechwood House in the village of Iffley, south of Oxford, though he frequently spent weekends with his mother and Monica in Loughborough and Leicester. In the fine weather of the first months of his stay he would walk into Oxford along the Thames towpath and spend the morning on the fourth floor of the New Library. After lunch in the King's Arms he would move to the Upper Reading Room, where he would be provided with xeroxes of poems which had caught his attention earlier in the day. After tea in college he would return to Beechwood, often along the towpath again. He would then drive back into college for dinner. He continued his work through the winter. It was not until November that Maeve visited him for a weekend; he searched out a suitable Catholic church for her to worship at. After spending Christmas with his mother he returned to Oxford on 14 January 1971, and shortly afterwards he showed his selection to Anthony Thwaite, who had earlier drawn up a helpful list of 'musts, probables and possibles'. Larkin took little notice of his recommendations.[47] The anthology was submitted to the publisher in early spring, allowing time for negotiation and revisions.

In 1966 Larkin had reassured Dan Davin at Oxford University Press that 'it is none of the business of an Oxford book of this character to be eccentric'.[48] Both he and Davin were concerned to avoid the perversity of Yeats's notorious 1936 *Oxford Book of Modern Verse 1892–1935*, which began with an invented *vers libre* 'poem' by Walter Pater, omitted Wilfred Owen on the empty pretext that 'passive suffering is not a theme for poetry', and devoted many pages to Yeats's personal friends, Oliver St John Gogarty ('one of the great lyric poets of the age'), AE, Lady Gregory, Walter James Turner, Shri Purohit Swami and Yeats's lover at the time, Margot Ruddock.[49] A measure of Yeats's and Larkin's different editorial intentions is the contrast between their prefatory comments. Yeats's lengthy idiosyncratic Introduction surveys the literary scene and makes magisterial judgements. Larkin confines himself to a Preface of little over a page, in which he sets out his principles of selection in a businesslike tone. Whatever reservations there might be about Larkin's anthology it is at least free of Yeats's shameless egocentricity and partisanship.

In 1966, at the beginning of the project, Larkin had written to Monica, 'the book would be half Hardy if I had my way'.[50] It is intriguing therefore that, in an interview after publication, Anthony Thwaite could query the fact that Hardy and Auden had been given only twenty-four pages each, while Eliot had twenty-nine. Larkin was defensive, taking his interviewer half-heartedly to task for 'counting pages': 'I thought I had given the maximum representation to Hardy: he certainly got more poems than anyone else. You must remember that some people write longer poems than others.'[51] Larkin was right to point out that mere counting exercises are suspect; but they are inevitable if any analysis is to be done. Numbers of lines perhaps provide a more objective comparative measure than either Thwaite's number of pages or Larkin's number of poems. A count of lines yields some surprises. In what cannot but appear as a deliberate policy Larkin allocates almost equal proportions of lines to the 'traditional' Hardy (699 lines, twenty-seven poems), and the 'modern' Yeats (684 lines, nineteen poems). But their sections are dwarfed by that of Eliot, who has 1,047 lines (nine poems). This is by far the largest allocation of lines to any poet in the volume, and contradicts the idea that Larkin is pursuing an anti-modernist programme.[52] Larkin's Eliot selection is indeed slightly more 'modernist' than Yeats's, including 'Prufrock' and 'The Waste Land', which Yeats excluded. Larkin omits the other high modernists, Pound and Stevens, as American. But Wyndham Lewis is represented by the 104 lines of 'The Song of the Militant Romance' (no. 178), a raucous call for the revitalization of English poetry in baggy free verse. 'I am the master of all that is half-uttered and imperfectly heard. / Return with me where I am crying out with the gorilla and the bird!'

After Hardy, Yeats and Eliot, the next best-represented poet of the early generation, in terms of lines, is Monica's favourite, Kipling, with 652 (thirteen poems). Back in 1951 Larkin had disputed Monica's high valuation of Kipling, whom she had compared to Dryden as a public poet. Larkin retorted that while Dryden wrote for the discriminating ear of 'the ruling gang', Kipling wrote 'for the press, the penny (or half-penny) press at that'. Since the time of Dryden, 'A process of vulgarisation has set in & gone a long way.'[53] Now, two decades later, he is content to take Kipling at Monica's high estimation. No ideological motive is detectable, however. The Kipling selection includes fine poems with no imperialist associations. Similarly puzzling is the contrast between A. E. Housman, given only 126 lines in eight poems, and Robert Bridges, represented by 298 lines in five items, including a turgid 115-line extract in sham medieval spelling from 'The Testament of Beauty' (no. 34).

It is difficult to identify any consistent unifying programme. Larkin's allocations contradict his known preferences in haphazard ways. It is tempting to conclude that he simply lost his way during his Bodleian holiday. His initial aim of rediscovering an English 'Georgian' tradition, submerged by the Great War and the dominance of Yeats and Eliot, had soon been abandoned. He wrote to Judy Egerton on 19 April 1968: 'I'd always vaguely supposed that the by ways of 20th century English poetry were full of good stuff, hitherto suppressed by the modernist claque: now I find that *this isn't so.*' He was depressed to discover, for instance, that the 'Dymock' poet, Wilfrid Gibson, despite a career of regular publication, '*never wrote a good poem in his life.* Grim thought.'[54] In view of this comment it is puzzling that, in the event, he gave Gibson 222 lines in his selection, though only six poems. Perhaps his judgement changed between 1968 and 1971, or perhaps he felt he needed to keep faith with his original conception, even if half-heartedly. Rupert Brooke is given a handful more lines than Gibson at 240 (six poems); Walter de la Mare has 179 lines; Edward Thomas 160 lines, W. H. Davies 97 lines. These allocations do not seem eccentric. The poets of the Great War also receive even-handed treatment. Owen is represented by 251 lines (though neither 'Futility' nor 'Strange Meeting' is included). Sassoon is accorded 93 lines, but perversely only two of the seven chosen poems belong to the war-protest genre on which his permanent reputation rests.

The major voices of the 1930s and 1940s are given rough justice. Uncontroversially enough, W. H. Auden has 764 lines (sixteen poems), the next highest representation in the volume after Eliot. Betjeman is represented by an overgenerous 629 lines (twelve poems), more than twice as many as Louis MacNeice at 279 lines (eight poems). Perhaps traces of an 'English', middlebrow agenda can be glimpsed here. MacNeice had been the original intended editor of the anthology, and it is fascinat-ing to reflect how different his selection would have been from Larkin's. Stephen Spender, whose poetry had been the butt of Larkin's contempt since his schooldays, has a generous 134 lines: more than A. E. Housman. The Poet Laureate, Day-Lewis, who was to die in 1972 before the volume appeared, is accorded a respectful 185 lines, in six poems, including 'The Album', concerning a book of photographs. The hero of Larkin's student days, Dylan Thomas, is accorded 342 lines, 287 fewer than Betjeman, but 63 more than MacNeice. Stevie Smith has a respectable 170 lines. In 1953 Larkin had insisted to Monica that he could find no right-wing writer worthy of respect.[55] Now he gives the supporter of Franco, Roy Campbell, a substantial 187 lines. The works selected, however, justify inclusion on poetic grounds and show no hint of politics.

One problematic issue was nationality. Larkin's Preface begins:

> I have taken 'twentieth-century English verse' to mean verse written in English by writers born in these islands (or resident here for an appreciable time) [. . .] These terms of reference mean that I have not included poems by American or Commonwealth writers [. . .] No doubt in making up the collection I have unwittingly broken most of these self-imposed limitations at one time or another.[56]

In 1936 Yeats had included the Americans, Pound and Eliot, arguing that they seemed to English readers 'part of their own literature', by reason of 'subject, or by long residence in Europe'.[57] He had also included, quite arbitrarily, Sir Rabindranath Tagore and Shri Purohit Swami. But by the time of Larkin's anthology history had moved on, and editorial policy needed to be more clearly defined. Larkin had compounded his problem by insisting on the word 'English' in the title, with the vague implication of cultural consensus. Thus he includes the by now naturalized Eliot, but excludes Pound and Frost, both of whom were resident in England 'for an appreciable time' and made a significant impact on the English literary scene. One might suspect that it was convenient for him that his 'rules' excluded Pound's modernism. But, though Pound's very 'English' poem 'Hugh Selwyn Mauberley' is excluded, Larkin does, surprisingly, include Basil Bunting's 'Chomei at Toyama', a derivative Poundian monologue of 321 lines spoken by a medieval Japanese Buddhist. A similar arbitrariness prevails in his exclusion of Sylvia Plath, despite his high opinion of her work. Plath wrote all her mature poetry in London and Devon, and had an English husband. One cannot help but wonder if Larkin would have included Plath had Monica Jones not been so close to the selection process.

The question of Ireland was also vexed. Yeats could scarcely be excluded, despite having been a Senator in the Irish Free State. Fortunately most of his career fell before Irish independence. However the inclusion of a ninety-line extract from Patrick Kavanagh's 'The Great Hunger' is problematic, since Kavanagh was a native of County Monaghan and wrote all his works as a citizen of the Irish Free State. The Northern Irish Heaney could be omitted since his reputation was so recent, though Larkin included four English poets born later than Heaney, among them Douglas Dunn and Brian Patten.

Problems emerge also in relation to the Anglophone 'Commonwealth', which by the late 1960s included, as well as the old Dominions, a number of independent nations in Africa and the Caribbean.[58] This was a problem which any editor of the time would have found difficult, and one to which Larkin's political instincts were inadequate. Its intractability is indicated by the fact that there are now separate *Oxford Books* of American poetry, Caribbean verse, Canadian verse, Australasian verse and Irish verse. Larkin's solution was haphazard. He excluded major Canadian and Australian poets, but included 179 lines by Derek Walcott, a poet born in St Lucia and resident mainly in the Caribbean and USA.[59] Larkin's breaking of his own rules in this case cannot have been inadvertent. 'Letter from Brooklyn' is included, one suspects, because it so eloquently mourns the death of Walcott's father a quarter of a century earlier.

Larkin wrote in his Preface that in the case of the top 'two or three dozen names' he could 'let the century choose the poets while I chose the poems'. With hindsight it seems that, apart from the exclusion of Pound and Frost and a few questionable emphases, Larkin's representation of major poets does avoid eccentricity. His other choices, he wrote, were mainly 'poems judged by me to be worthy of inclusion without reference to their authors'.[60] Yeats's anthology featured 98 poets; Larkin's has 207, many of whom are represented by only two or three poems, and 88 by a single poem. On its publication most of the debate about the volume focused on particular individual poems, apparently chosen in accordance with a residual 'Georgian' agenda, or because they would appeal to his friends, or because they resembled or anticipated his own poems. On a few occasions he made a genuine discovery: May Wedderburn Cannan's war poem 'Rouen', for instance (no. 283),[61] Joan Barton's 'The Mistress' (no. 395), Jon Silkin's moving elegy on his son (no. 552), David Gascoyne's haunting evocation of the great surrealist's paintings 'Salvador Dali' (no. 462). Other inclusions are more intimately personal, Martin Bell's 'Winter Coming On: A caricature from Laforgue' (no. 470) for instance. Two poems reflect his fear of disease: J. B. S. Haldane's 'Cancer's a Funny Thing' (no. 252), and James Kirkup's 'A Correct Compassion', concerning a *mitral stenosis valvulotomy in the General Infirmary at Leeds*' (no. 509). These examples are intriguing and characterful. But there is also a large number of unimpressive poems which wear their crudely 'Larkinesque' credentials on their sleeves: the sour sing-song celebration of sterile spinsterhood, 'The Old Ladies', by Colin Ellis for instance (no. 270), the shamelessly middlebrow 'Good and Clever' (no. 29) by Elizabeth Wordsworth, C. H. Sisson's four-line assertion of atheism 'The Temple' (no. 451), and many more. One early attack on the volume, in the *Listener*, focused on the inclusion of Brian Patten's 'Portrait of a Young Girl Raped at a Suburban Party' (no. 583), which inevitably reminds the reader of 'Deceptions'.

In his Preface Larkin thanks 'Miss M. M. B. Jones for her constant encouragement and for many valuable suggestions for the book's improvement'.[62] The eighteenth-century Georgic pastiche by Victoria Sackville-West (no. 250) seems specifically intended for her. Judy Egerton felt that Monica played a key part in 'buttressing his resolve' or, as some might feel, his stubbornness.[63] Other inclusions are compliments to particular friends. The anti-Soviet propaganda of Sir Alan Herbert's poem (no. 246) would appeal to Robert Conquest, while Amis and Conquest would both appreciate Edgell Rickword's 'Augustan' satire on a fashionable literary avant-gardist (no. 302). Larkin's jazz friends would be amused by Robert Garioch's 'I Was Fair Beat' (no. 402), in which the speaker recalls in broad Scots dialect 'a nicht amang the cognoscenti', during which he heard 'modern jazz wi juicy / snell wud-wind chords [. . .] // Man, it was awfie.'

But the most idiosyncratic strand is the large number of poems concerning animals. Larkin wrote to Douglas Dunn on 16 January 1971: 'Most of it is about animals (you know I'm a life member of the RSPCA). Perhaps OUP could get a subsidy from them.'[64] And shortly before the volume appeared he joked to Judy Egerton that it would be better titled 'the Oxford Book of *Nineteen & a Half Century's Right-Wing Animal-Lovers Verse*'.[65] Some of the animal poems are genuine finds: Patricia Beer's 'The Lion Hunt' (no. 510) for instance, and Hal Summers's 'My Old Cat' (no. 415). Others have little more effect than to remind the reader that the anthologist is Philip Larkin. Dorothy Wellesley's 'Horses' (no. 240) can have been included only because of its anticipation of 'At Grass', while F. R. Higgins's more moving 'The Old Jockey' (no. 284) clearly earned its place for the same reason. Other anthologists would surely have overlooked Ralph Hodgson, but the author of 'At Grass' cannot resist including the lengthy evocation of animal retirement 'The Bull' (no. 114). Hodgson's 'Hymn to Moloch' (no. 116), attacking the trade in bird-feathers, is also a natural choice for the author of 'Take One Home for the Kiddies'. Startlingly, the allocation given to Hodgson, 272 lines, dwarfs that of Housman or Edward Thomas. But this number is exceeded by Sir John Squire's 'The Stockyard' (no. 180), dedicated to Robert Frost, with its harrowing description in almost 300 lines of the slaughterhouse at Chicago, 'the filthiest place in the world'.

As his time in Oxford ran its course Larkin became fatalistic and dispirited: 'as I feared, I'm drawing English poetry in my own image, & it isn't going to make a good book'.[66] Nevertheless his choices among his contemporaries and successors largely avoid contentiousness. He restricted his own representation to 191 lines. Though he included only 35 lines by Sidney Keyes, he rose above his personal antagonisms to include 137 lines by Ted Hughes, 151 lines by Donald Davie and 49 lines by Charles Tomlinson. Thom Gunn is given 123 lines. Kingsley Amis has an overgenerous 144 lines in comparison with Anthony Thwaite's 111 lines (including the Larkinesque 'Mr Cooper'). At the time, however, none of these allocations caused concern. Instead, with a certain arbitrariness, Dan Davin of OUP objected to the exclusion of the Scottish communist Hugh MacDiarmid and the visionary 'Apocalyptic' poet David Jones. Given the by now compromised nature of the whole exercise, Larkin could easily have given way. But he felt at bay. In a letter of 2 April 1971 he disputed Davin's suggestions in a bristling tone, concluding sulkily: 'I know this is a matter of opinion, and *tot homines quot disputandum est*[67] and all that, but this is no more than saying that I am the editor and not anyone else.' He continues: 'I am so averse from [MacDiarmid's] work that I can hardly bring my eyes to the page, but I agree a lot of people will expect to find him there [. . .] if you like I will make another effort to find some stretch of his verbiage that seems to me a trifle less arid, pretentious, morally repugnant and aesthetically null than the rest.'[68] In what looks very much like a rueful private joke, he eventually gave MacDiarmid 191 lines, exactly the same number as himself. Arbitrarily, however, he dug in his heels over David Jones. Davin did not have the heart for another quarrel, and Jones remained excluded.

The anthology was finally published on 29 March 1973. It immediately became apparent that the lack of coherence in the selection process extended also to the mechanics of its compilation. Monica Jones, having exerted her influence on his choices, might have been expected to have brought the discipline of her scholarly profession to the proof-reading of the volume. But she had not done so. Christopher Ricks wrote to Larkin to draw his attention to the fact that his carelessness with xeroxed pages had caused the omission of half of William Empson's 'Aubade'. The same fate had befallen the last two stanzas of Thom Gunn's 'The Byrnies'. Larkin was mortified. He wrote to Thwaite in April 1973: 'I can see myself joining Bowdler & Grainger: "*to larkinize*", v.t., to omit that part of a poem printed on verso and subsequent pages, from a notorious anthology published in the latter half of the twentieth century.'[69]

The expected clamour from the critics ensued, Donald Davie in the vanguard. 'Recoiling aghast from page after page', Davie accused Larkin of not taking poetry seriously, and of privileging 'amateur verse' over the poetry of David Jones, Elizabeth Daryush, I. A. Richards and Roy Fisher. 'This volume is a calamity,' he declared, adding gleefully: 'and it's very painful that it falls to me to say so.'[70] Larkin responded with disdain, reflecting, in a letter to Jon Stallworthy on 14 May 1973, that Davie 'must feel like a mill that has been given a lovely big lot of grist'.[71] He resorted to the defence that he was appealing over the heads of the academics and professional literati to the genuine audience of the common man and woman. 'I made twentieth century poetry sound nice.' 'My taste', he bravely proclaimed, 'is much more akin to that of the ordinary person than it is to that of the professional student or practitioner of literature.'[72] There is some truth in this. And in hindsight it does seem that much of what was confidently alleged against the volume was beside the point. Whoever is chosen to edit an official collection of this scope, the resulting volume will be bound to contain a large number of good poems. It will also, inevitably, bear the individual stamp of its editor. Moreover, the large anthology is so capacious a genre that any reductive summary or evaluation will be bound to be partial and arbitrary. Every reader encounters a quite different Larkin *Oxford Book*, depending on which combination of its 207 poets he or she happens upon. Over time the volume has performed its intended function of introducing readers to the variety of modern poetry as effectively as any conceivable alternative could have done.

19

Larkin's Late Style
1969–72

Larkin's public and professional commitments were driving his poetry deeper and deeper into a private space. It was not until nearly nine months after his 'political poem', 'Homage to a Government', that he completed his next poem. As one might expect it shows him at his most intimate and personal. He confided to Barbara Pym in a letter of 8 October 1969: 'I have just written a poem, which cheers me slightly, except when I read it; when it depresses me. It's about the seaside, & rather a self parody.'[1] In 'To the Sea' the speaker is pleased to find the rituals he remembers from his youth still 'going on'. Larkin wrote to Monica that the poem 'was aimed at being a Boudin, in its own way of course', referring to the French painter Eugène Boudin (1824–98).[2] As in a Boudin painting, exactly observed details depict 'The miniature gaiety of seasides': the low horizon, the white steamer 'stuck in the afternoon', the 'uncertain children [. . .] grasping at enormous air', and the rigid old in their wheelchairs feeling a 'final summer'. The poet reminisces about his childhood spent searching in the sand for cigarette packets with their cards of 'Famous Cricketers', and concludes, with the afternoon fading, the steamer gone and the sunlight 'milky':

> If the worst
> Of flawless weather is our falling short,
> It may be that through habit these do best,

> Coming to water clumsily undressed
> Yearly; teaching their children by a sort
> Of clowning; helping the old, too, as they ought.

There is indeed a self-parodic element in the studied hesitancy of tone ('If the worst'; 'It may be'), and the familiar Larkinesque assumption that flawless weather makes us feel inadequate. The halting last line is sincere and heartfelt, but the tone is weary and a touch pious. Larkin wrote to Anthony Thwaite on 13 January 1970: 'I am very pleased to know that you liked "To the Sea", though I am not too keen on it myself – it seems rather Wordsworthian, in the sense of being bloody dull.'[3]

'The Explosion' was completed three months later in January 1970. Like 'At Grass', written exactly twenty years earlier, it was suggested by a film. At Christmas Larkin had watched a television documentary on the mining industry with his mother, which had included the moving ballad 'The Trimdon Grange Disaster', by 'The pitman's Poet' Tommy Armstrong (1848–1919). Mindful of his public distrust of poems not based on direct experience, he told Monica: '*Don't tell a soul* where I got the idea from.'[4] Sixty-nine miners had been killed in an explosion at Trimdon, Durham on 16 February 1882 at 2.30 in the afternoon. In Larkin's poem, however, the explosion takes place, more symbolically, at noon, and for the sake of its central image of the eggs, the season is changed to early summer. The tone is highly mediated. The pitmen, in their beards and moleskins, recall early scenes from Lawrence's *Sons and Lovers*. This is one of Larkin's most riskily artificial poems. He claimed that he was at first unaware that it was falling into the trochaic metre of Longfellow's *Hiawatha*.[5] The effect is of archaic formality, though if the reader tunes into the metre too consciously it can sound over-insistent and mechanical. The image of the eggs, which one of the miners finds as he chases after rabbits, may also seem sentimental: 'Came back with a nest of lark's eggs; / Showed them; lodged them in the grasses'. After the explosion, these eggs reappear in the vision of the wives who:

saw men of the explosion

Larger than in life they managed –
Gold as on a coin, or walking
Somehow from the sun towards them,

One showing the eggs unbroken.

The reference to the men seeming 'Gold as on a coin' sounds forced, with its awkward period allusion to sovereigns; and 'Somehow' sounds loosely emotive. Moreover, the image will fail to deliver its full meaning of 'unbroken' life for some readers. The miner has already killed these eggs by pulling the nest up. Lodging it back 'in the grasses' will not help. He has ensured that, broken or unbroken, they can never hatch.[6]

A short meditation, 'How', followed, completed on a single work-book page on 10 April 1970. Like 'To the Sea' it has an element of the self-parodic with its repeated Larkinesque adverbial phrases: 'How high they build hospitals! [. . .] / How cold winter keeps [. . .] / How few people are.' He gave the poem to Ted Tarling, 'a local chap who I think deserves encouraging',[7] for publication in the autumn 1970 issue of his little magazine *Wave*, printed in Hull on Tarling's own hand-operated press. Tarling's imprint, the Sonus Press, also published Joan Barton's volume *The Mistress*, the title poem of which Larkin included in *The Oxford Book of Twentieth Century English Verse*. Tarling was an artist of some accomplishment, and later two of his gouaches hung in Larkin's house.[8]

Larkin's next completed poem is again the product of an indirect, secondary inspiration. Since 1965 his imagination had been haunted by the image of brutal, peasant contentment which he had encountered in the paintings of the seventeenth-century Flemish artist Adriaen Brouwer. On 15 May 1965, he had written to Monica that the Acquisitions Department of the Library was agitating for the return of a book of Brouwer's paintings which he had borrowed:

fine stuff: a comforting world of its own – you are a great fat oaf, three quarters drunk, sitting on a bench with a jug of beer in your hand, surrounded by cronies as ugly and disgusting as yourself. You are all smoking clay pipes: there's a good fire in the hearth. One man is flat out on the floor, having spewed (dogs are licking it up), another is pissing out of the back door. The candlelight shows patched clothes, broken cupboards: outside is wind, mud, winter. *But you are all right.*[9]

Over the months and years he had elaborated on this image. On 23 November 1967 he wrote to Monica: 'I think about Jan Hogspewer (flor. 1600) sometimes these days – I would write a poem about him if I believed poems about works of art were licit.'[10] The image sounds exclusively masculine; nevertheless he alludes to it in letters to Monica as a hard-core alternative to their cosy rabbit-burrow. On 10 December 1967 he writes: 'Darling: I do look forward to your being here. We shall be two Hogspewers together. Friday is it?'[11]

Finally, after this long gestation an imagined Brouwer painting became the basis for one of his most original late works, 'The Card-Players', completed in three days, from 6 to 8 May 1970 on two pages of Workbook 7. This is his fourth and final mature sonnet to be published, and like the others it has its own unique formal structure.[12] No division is indicated after line 8, eliding the traditional progression from expository octave to reflective sestet. The picturesque squalor of the 'lamplit cave' is built up without pause over thirteen lines, with a false conclusion, one line early, on the sordid couplet rhyme 'farts / hearts'. The final, typographically isolated fourteenth line then leaps out, unexpectedly, in an exclamation of brutal euphoria: 'Rain, wind and fire! The secret, bestial peace!' The feeble half-rhyme of 'peace' with 'trees' satisfies the scheme only nominally; the final line is effectively unrhymed, its denial of literary decorum matching the poem's denial of social decorum.[13] The sonnet becomes a symbolist ode, its final apostrophe recalling similar effects in Gautier, Baudelaire and Laforgue, and of course Larkin's own 'Absences', written twenty years earlier.

Like Brouwer's paintings, the poem transfigures its low-life subject in a sublime celebration. The storm outside and the scene inside the 'cave' both embody the four elements of nature: Earth (mud, clay, mussels, ham), Water (piss, rain, ale, gob), Air (belch, snore, gale, 'wind' in both senses), Fire (cinder, smoke, lamp, grate). The elements are in continuous flux between inner and outer worlds. The rain outside mingles with Hogspeuw's piss, and when Dirk pours himself 'some more' the grammar makes it sound as though it is rain as much as ale that he is pouring. The 'mud' of the cart-ruts outside is also the 'clay' of Dirk's pipe. Dirk's cinder and Prijck's fire relate to the element of fire in the outside world. The 'Rain, wind and fire' of the final line are the elements as much of the interior world as of the exterior.[14] Rather than looking upwards for transcendence, as do 'Absences' and 'High Windows', 'The Card-Players' finds profundity below. In this chthonic world the composed self-possession the poet usually guards so jealously is euphorically cast aside. All the barriers between outer and inner which preserve his self-possession are transgressed. Almost uniquely in his work this room is exposed to the elements, its door wide open on the dark.[15] Larkin has, like Brouwer, fused together a selfish, secular poetry of low life with a selfless spiritual poetry of ineffable epiphany.[16]

The most original element is the farcical 'double-Dutch' of the characters' names: Jan van Hogspeuw, Dirk Dogstoerd, Old Prijck. Though recognizable as 'Dutch', they bear only a superficial relationship to the language; 'speuw' is not far from the Dutch *spuwen*, but the extra 'e' makes hyper-Dutch nonsense of it, while the other elements are crude English projections of Dutchness. 'Hog' should be *barg*, 'Dog' *hond*, 'turd' *drol*; while *prijk* and *prijken* have no sexual connotation in Dutch.[17] Clearly the poet knows no Dutch; nor does he want to know any. His concern is not to blend the two languages, but to invent an idiom which evokes the context of a Dutch genre-painting by *sounding* like Dutch to an English-speaker. It is a complex effect, similar to the false-French of 'Immensements' in 'Sad Steps'. Paradoxically, however, the mistranslation shows the opposite of cultural provincialism. Rather it acknowledges the universal cultural currency of this image of peasant earthiness, familiar in the work of Flemish painters such as Bruegel, Teniers and Brouwer.[18] Larkin made clear that, unlike Auden's 'Musée des Beaux Arts' or Berryman's 'Winter Landscape', his poem makes no reference to an actual painting.[19] The scene described is, nevertheless, a perfectly visualized Brouwer composition.

'Dublinesque', completed on just over a page in the workbook between 1 and 6 June 1970,[20] though very different, is also heavily mediated, and set in a mythic past. This is no literal nostalgic recollection of his holiday in Ireland the previous year. He told Maeve Brennan that the poem's origin was 'a dream – I just woke up and described it'.[21] This is the 'Dublinesque' of a sensitive tourist who knows his Joyce and his Jack B. Yeats. The light is 'pewter', the afternoon mist brings on the early lights in the shops, above 'race-guides and rosaries'. As in a dream the poet feels euphoric gratitude at being spectator at the mourning ritual of the streetwalkers in their wide flowered hats, leg-of-mutton sleeves and ankle-length dresses. There is 'an air of great friendliness':

> And of great sadness also.
> As they wend away
> A voice is heard singing
> Of Kitty, or Katy,
> As if the name meant once
> All love, all beauty.

It is an exquisite, fragile poem, like 'The Explosion': just this side of sentimentality.

While in his poems he was conjuring these elusive epiphanies, his social image in Hull was hardening into that of an irascible hermit. A recently arrived lecturer in American Studies, who occupied the flat below his for a short time, remembers hearing him striding about his room alone reciting *Macbeth* with great feeling.[22] Another lecturer in American Studies, who occupied the same flat with his wife in 1970–2, invited him to tea and found him distantly amiable. He played with their cats and they discussed jazz. But then, when the lecturer left Larkin a note suggesting they might share the shed in which he kept his bicycle, the response was an official letter from the Estates Office indicating that the shed was for Larkin's sole use. Later he asked the poet to sign a copy of *The Oxford Book of Twentieth Century English Verse*, intended as a wedding present for some friends. Larkin rebuffed him, remarking that copies of his books were beginning to turn up in second-hand bookshops shortly after being signed. However, this refusal gave Larkin an uneasy conscience. Later the same day he phoned, asking if he might come across from the Library and sign the book after all, since he realized that recipients of a wedding present were unlikely to sell it on.[23]

Larkin's spell in Oxford working on his anthology disrupted his usual drafting processes. He completed no poems in his workbook for nearly a year between 'Dublinesque' on 6 June 1970 and 'Vers de Société' on 20 May 1971.[24] He did however complete two poems outside the workbook. 'Poem about Oxford' is inscribed on the flyleaf of an illustrated history of Oxford which he gave to Monica at Christmas in 1970. Movingly, he inserted the draft in the manuscript of his Brunette Coleman novella of three decades earlier, *Michaelmas Term at St Bride's*, which he must have reread at this time. As in 'To the Sea' Larkin was returning nostalgically to his earlier life. The poem is dedicated 'for Monica', and is possibly an anniversary poem, ten years on from 'Talking in Bed'. The form is the favoured metre for occasional verse in the eighteenth and nineteenth centuries, anapaests in alternate rhyme, with the added joke of carefully contrived 'slapdash' double rhymes ('touchstone / much tone; certain / Girton; notecase / Boat Race; cake-queues / break-throughs'). Larkin pitches his tone carefully to suit the poem's addressee. Its nostalgia is edgily anti-nostalgic, and there is 'Hogspewer' cynicism in the mockery of the 'arselicker'· who stays in Oxford. Since they had shared the city 'without knowing', emphasis inevitably falls on generic period detail, in a kind of 'Oxonesque'. Apart from 'more durable things' (their first-class degrees and literary educations), they shared 'Dull Bodley, draught beer, and dark blue, / And most often losing the Boat Race –'. And, in a beautiful zeugma, to these poignantly trivial memories 'You're added, as I am for you.'

On 14 April 1971 Larkin enclosed in a letter to Anthony Thwaite a typed version of 'This Be The Verse' with slightly different wording from that finally published.[25] Like the previous poems it is allusive and mediated. He joked: 'I've dashed off a little piece suitable for Ann's next Garden of Verses', alluding to the annual of new writing for children, *Allsorts*, which Ann Thwaite edited between 1968 and 1975.[26] The title refers to Robert Louis Stevenson's 'Requiem' ('This be the verse you grave for me'), published in *Underwoods*, 1887.[27] The reference is, however, highly ironic, and this is one of Larkin's most original works. He reasserts his own voice against the literary clutter of the previous months in the confident Armstrong-like trumpet line of this, his most pungently 'Larkinesque' comic poem. No doubt also, in a familiar dialectic of contraries, he felt the need to answer the filial piety of 'To the Sea' with something less 'bloody dull'. His elliptical late style is evident in the way the first line appropriates, and as it were copyrights, the most commonplace of phrases. The sentence 'your parents certainly fuck you up' or 'your mum and dad always seem to fuck you up', or even Larkin's precise formulation, 'They fuck you up, your mum and dad', must have been uttered millions of times in ordinary conversation. But simply by ordering the words into a neat tetrameter in a brisk abab stanza of facile rhymes, he makes it into an unforgettable aphorism:

> They fuck you up, your mum and dad.
> They may not mean to, but they do.
> They fill you with the faults they had
> And add some extra, just for you.

This sentiment will now always be a quotation from Larkin. The casual inflections are perfect for recitation, and the malicious relish of that final insinuating phrase 'some extra, just for you' has the verbal taste of vermouth in a martini. The poem takes the imperious form of a crude syllogism: thesis, antithesis, synthesis: i) Your parents fuck you up; ii) *but* they were fucked up too; iii) *because* we are all fucked up. To add to the fun the concluding synthesis modulates into ripe fatalistic orotundity ('Man hands on misery to man'), and portentous 'apocalyptic' imagery ('It deepens like a coastal shelf'). The poem's sentiment is sad, but the poem is full of *jouissance*. This must bid fair to be the funniest serious English poem of the twentieth century. It must also already rival Gray's 'Elegy' in the number of parodies and pastiches it has generated.

The following month Larkin completed 'Vers de Société' (20 May 1971), reworking the antisocial theme of 'The Card-Players', but replacing Hogspeuw's sordid cave with a civilized withdrawing room of aesthetic privacy. In a recasting of the unpublished 'Best Society' of exactly twenty years earlier, the ageing poet accepts defeat at the hands of society. Torn between an evening with a '*crowd of craps*' and the solitude of his breathing gas fire and darkly swayed trees outside, he decides to reject Warlock-Williams's invitation, unwilling to see more of his 'spare time' flow 'Straight into nothingness by being filled / With forks and faces'. The lamp, the wind, the moonlit windowscape offer implicitly to repay his time with poetic inspiration. But he no longer feels unquestioningly obedient to the call. 'The time is shorter now for company,' and solitude no longer seems unambiguously the best society. The contemptible room of social intercourse offers at least an escape from loneliness; 'sitting by a lamp more often brings / Not peace, but other things.' At the end he returns from the shifting rhyme-schemes of the middle stanzas to the direct aabbccdd couplet stanza with which he began, and begins to write – not a poem, but an acceptance of the invitation. 'Beyond the light stand failure and remorse / Whispering *Dear Warlock-Williams: Why of course –*'. There is perhaps a private, self-derisive joke in the use of the word 'remorse' which Bruce Montgomery had so ridiculed in Larkin's early Yeatsian poetry.

Two weeks later, on 2–3 June, Larkin completed the exquisite lyric 'Cut Grass', one of his poems drafted on a single workbook page. (He made a second column of text so as not to spill over on to the next page.)[28] Its economical but intensely charged poetic diction recalls Edward Thomas: 'young-leafed June', 'hedges snowlike strewn'; and 'that high-builded cloud / Moving at summer's pace'. In a letter to Monica Jones he criticized the poem's pure lyric beauty:

> Its trouble is that it's 'music', i.e. pointless crap. About line 6 I hear a kind of wonderful Elgar river-music take over, for wch the words are just an excuse [. . .] There's a point at wch the logical sense of the poem ceases to be added to, and it continues only as a succession of images. I like it all right, but for once I'm not a good judge.[29]

He had no reason to doubt his judgement. It is difficult to understand what he means by 'the *logical* sense of the poem' which allegedly prevails in the first five lines, or to hear how this is lost after that point. But his less deceived superego compels him to disown mere 'wonderful' music.

On 22 July 1971 Barbara Pym wrote to tell him that she was to undergo a mastectomy, and he attempted to boost her morale by congratulating her on having 'nobbled it quickly'.[30] His mother was now becoming frail. In the previous year, 1970, when he and his sister took their holidays at the same time, they had persuaded her to spend a fortnight in an Abbeyfield House residential care home in Loughborough. The same problem occurred in August 1971, and she again spent a fortnight in respite care.[31] A longing to be free of such domestic anxieties is perhaps one element in 'Forget What Did', which Larkin completed on 8 August 1971, the day before his forty-ninth birthday. It is another intertextual work. In Chapter 2 of Susan Coolidge's girls' classic *What Katy Did* the sisters read the diary of their 'pale, pudgy' six-year-old brother, Dorry, and find, alongside entries like 'played', or 'Had rost befe for diner, and cabage, and potato', several which read simply 'Forgit what did'.[32] Larkin kept a diary all his life, but, strong as was his impulse to self-examination, it was matched by the desire to escape the self. He had had the idea for a poem about giving up a diary as early as 1952, and the first drafts of this poem date to January 1967. By a symbolist leap Dorry's casual phrase licenses the poet's 'blank starting'. In future, he resolves, the pages of his diary shall be empty, or if they are ever filled, it shall be with records only of 'Celestial recurrences, / The day the flowers come, / And when the birds go'.

In September 1971, shortly after his return from his holiday with Monica in Islay, Jura and Mull, he received a letter from his old schoolfriend Colin Gunner, with whom he had had no contact since the 1940s. Gunner had led a varied life, serving in the army in North Africa and Italy, converting to Roman Catholicism and then moving through a series of short-term jobs. Though Larkin prudently did not meet his old friend, he read the 'almost-illegible typescript'[33] of Gunner's account of his service in the Irish Guards, *Adventures with the Irish Brigade*, and gave him advice. It had the faults of an 'amateur's book',[34] and he suggested that Gunner might boil it down to an article for *Blackwood's* magazine. He went to the trouble of approaching publishers. Eventually Gunner decided to have it printed privately and in a letter of 26 July 1973 Larkin agreed to write a short foreword.[35] Gunner's book finally appeared, with the foreword, in 1975 in an edition of twenty-four copies. Gunner's letters show him to have been the most uninhibitedly bigoted of the poet's later correspondents.

The poet's life was briefly shadowed at this point by an omen of the future. On 7 October the University's Medical Officer, Dr Raines, sent him to Hull Royal Infirmary for X-rays. He wrote gaily to Judy Egerton on 4 November 1971: 'My neck is *incurable* . . . because there is nothing wrong with it. Ha ha. [. . .] The X-ray languidly reported "Possibly some narrowing of the joints (what joints?) that might be indicative of a pre-arthritic state" or some such jazz.'[36] As Christmas approached, Eva's determination to observe the accustomed rituals in York Road, Loughborough, even proposing to cook a duck, prompted an outburst of exasperation rare in the letters to his mother: 'Let us have peace, and not all this blasted cooking and eating (and washing up!).'[37]

Nevertheless his poetic momentum was growing stronger. Early in October he had completed 'I have started to say', in which the speaker expresses horror at having become, as it were, 'historical', finding himself saying 'A quarter of a century' or 'thirty years back' about events in his own life. The poem remained unpublished, but the thought prompted an ambitious sequence of historically distanced dramatic monologues, 'Livings', written towards the year's end. 'Livings I', completed on 16 October 1971, has an archaic quality, reminding the reader of the world of Arnold Bennett or Somerset Maugham. A commercial traveller meditates on his routines:

> Afterwards, whisky in the Smoke Room: Clough,
> Margetts, the Captain, Dr. Watterson;
> Who makes ends meet, who's taking the knock [. . .]

The formal surnames and the slang have a dated feel. Though the speaker gives a close-up picture of his life, he occupies an 'historical present' deeper than mere grammatical tense. Then, in the third stanza, sociological detail and literary colour are left behind in an epiphany of pure living:

> Later, the square is empty: a big sky
> Drains down the estuary like the bed
> Of a gold river, and the Customs House
> Still has its office lit.

His dull world is briefly touched with beauty before he returns to the comic hunting pictures and 'ex-Army sheets' of his hotel, musing on whether he needs a change in his life. He wonders 'why / I think it's worth while coming. Father's dead: / He used to, but the business now is mine. / It's time for change, in nineteen twenty-nine.' The facile rhyme ('mine / nineteen twenty-nine') underlines the speaker's ignorance of the significance of the date. His desultory aimlessness is about to be overwhelmed by the Great Crash. But there is no heavy Sophoclean irony. The date simply intensifies the reader's sense that life is only ever a fragile livelong minute.

The initial intention was for 'I deal with farmers' to be the first of a sequence entitled 'Vocations'. The title Larkin finally settled on, 'Livings', is more existentially abstract, and lacks any hint of an artistic calling. Also 'living' is more purely lyrical, being a gerund in the present participial form, rather than a static noun like 'Vocations' or 'Lives'. In the event the sequence extended only to three works. Larkin wrote to Brian Cox on 23 February 1972 that he found them 'rather fun to do [. . .] Perhaps I shall do some more: they are miniature derivatives of Browning's dramatic lyrics, I suppose. As for LIVINGS: well, I don't know – the way people live, kinds of life, anything like that. I thought LIVINGS brought in the Crockford element, too.'[38] *Crockford's Clerical Directory*, first published in 1858, lists all the livings of the Anglican clergy.

The central poem in the triptych, completed on 23 November 1971, adopts a purer lyric register, stripped of literary mediation. A lighthouse-keeper celebrates his isolation in the grip of light, atop a seventy-foot tower. This is one of Larkin's most uncompromisingly symbolist poems. Ever since he first moved to Hull in 1955 he had been engaged in building his own tower. At the beginning of Stage 1 of the new Library the Viennese sculptor Willi Soukop had created bas-reliefs over the entrances. Larkin wrote to Judy Egerton in 1959 expressing doubt about his 'Genius of Light', 'an abstract figure bearing a torch that is already sprawled in rough over the front door'.[39] The image incorporates a pun on the name of the University's founder Thomas Ferens, whose name in Latin signifies bearing or carrying: hence the University's motto *Lampada Ferens*, 'bearing the lamp'. Larkin always appreciated a good, or bad, pun. For the whole of his mature life the poet-librarian entered his place of work, which eventually became the dazzling tower of light of Stage 2, through the doorway beneath this 'Genius of Light'.

Since 'Sympathy in White Major' the aesthete's ivory tower had offered the poet only a compromised romantic glamour. Rather than a man with a vocation, the keeper of the light in 'Livings II' is a kind of sublime Mr Bleaney. He keeps himself to himself, and passes the time in familiar routines. The poem's uncompromising unrhymed, 'modernist' trimeters express his edgy selfhood:

> By day, sky builds
> Grape-dark over the salt
> Unsown stirring fields.
> Radio rubs its legs,
> Telling me of elsewhere [. . .]

The sound of the radio, like that of a cricket which has strayed inside from the sterile salt 'fields' of the sea, keeps him company while making no social demands. He prefers the best society of his uncomfortable lighthouse to the warm sociability of cosy inns ashore, their sea-pictures 'kippering' humorously in the tobacco-smoke: 'Keep it all off!' In 'The Card-Players' the sociable lamplit cave of the drinkers was wide open to the flux of the elements outside. Here, the antisocial lamplit attic of the keeper is safely locked, and he plays cards only with himself. But paradoxically he is still at one with the surrounding elements of nature: 'Creatures, I cherish you!' This innocuous Lucifer, 'Guarded by brilliance', seems to have penetrated the padlocked cube of light of 'Dry-Point'. He has somehow succeeded in inhabiting the out-of-reach skyscape of 'Here', the cleared attics of 'Absences'. For all its self-doubt and irony this is an extravagantly romantic poem.

The final poem in the triptych was completed on 10 December 1971, shortly before Larkin departed to spend Christmas with his mother in York Road. He had heard the first sentence of the poem, 'Tonight we dine without the Master', with its archaic Oxbridge formality, in February, in casual conversation before dinner at Pembroke College, Oxford. Realizing that the words made a perfect tetrameter, he commented that this would make a good first line of a poem.[40] 'Livings III' evokes a more subdued version of 'The Card-Players', set not in a lamplit cave but amid the thin candleflames of a seventeenth- or eighteenth-century college common room. Outside are vapours and muddy fields; inside the jordan is set behind a screen making it unnecessary to brave the cold. These port-drinking dons are, like Brouwer's peasants, '*all right*' in their aimless learned gossip and college politics; 'assertions fly / On rheumy fevers, resurrection, / Regicide and rabbit pie'. And above them, with a touch of muted transcendence, 'Chaldean constellations / Sparkle over crowded roofs.'

About this time he was asked to write a poem to preface the report of a Government Working Party on 'The Human Habitat' chaired by Raine, Countess of Dartmouth. For the first time in his career, he agreed to write to a commission, and early in the new year completed 'Going, Going' (25 January 1972). Required to strike an attitude, he wrote as a public spokesman, lamenting the loss of 'England'. His introspection is uncharacteristically egocentric: 'I thought it would last my time –'; 'I knew there'd be false alarms'; 'what do I feel now?'; 'I feel somehow'; 'I just think it will happen'. With tragic portentousness he laments 'that will be England gone', 'England' being defined by five emotive epithets: 'The shadows, the meadows, the lanes, / The guildhalls, the carved choirs'. The word 'England' appears elsewhere in his mature poetry only in neutral or uncomfortably ironic contexts:

in 'I Remember, I Remember' ('Coming up England by a different line'), 'The Importance of Elsewhere' ('Living in England has no such excuse') and 'Naturally the Foundation will Bear You · Expenses' ('O when will England grow up?'). 'Going, Going' contains the only unambiguously positively charged use of the word in his poetry; and it strikes a false note.

The poem does, however, paint a moving picture in terms of Larkinesque social stereotypes. It seems, at first, that the degradation of the environment is to be blamed on the lower orders: 'The crowd / Is young in the M1 café; / Their kids are screaming for more – / More houses, more parking allowed, / More caravan sites, more pay.' But, Larkin at once corrects the balance:

> A score
>
> Of spectacled grins approve
> Some takeover bid that entails
> Five per cent profit (and ten
> Per cent more in the estuaries): move
> Your works to the unspoilt dales [. . .]

The suggestion that capitalist greed might be as environmentally destructive as better pay for the working class proved too much for the Countess and her Committee. Larkin wrote to Conquest in May 1972: 'Have you seen this commissioned poem I did for the Countess of Dartmouth's report on the human habitat? It makes my flesh creep. She made me cut out a verse attacking big business – don't tell anyone. It was a pretty crappy verse, anyway, not that she minded that.'[41] When the poem appeared in *High Windows* the offending lines were restored. He described the poem to Charles Monteith as 'thin ranting conventional gruel'.[42]

The drafts of this piece of 'required writing' had run across the end of the seventh workbook, and on to the first three pages of the eighth and – as he must have realized – last. Then, on the fourth page of the new book, on 13 January 1972, he began the confident draft of a new 'inspired', rather than 'required', poem. 'The Meeting House' was different from, and more ambitious than, anything he had attempted since 'Dockery and Son' and the ill-fated 'The Dance' almost a decade earlier. After four pages devoted to the new poem he forced himself to return to the commissioned piece on 24 January, but was uncomfortable at having to 'cut across' his new inspiration with 'thinking about the environment'.[43] The new extended elegy, soon renamed 'The Building', showed a return from the intertextuality and symbolism of his recent works to the more direct and universal lyric mode of his *Whitsun Weddings* style. It was to usher in the last great flowering of his genius.

20

Winter Coming
1972–4

On 24 January 1972, the day before Larkin completed 'Going, Going', his mother fell and cracked a bone in her leg. It was no longer possible for her to stay in her own home. On 30 January Larkin and his sister Kitty looked over Berrystead Nursing Home on the London Road between Leicester and Loughborough, and on 2 February Eva made her final move.[1] A week later, on 9 February, Larkin completed 'The Building'. It had been almost nine years since he had been confident enough to address a wider audience in one of the long Keatsian odes or reflective elegies which had formed the backbone of his early work ('At Grass', 'Church Going', 'An Arundel Tomb', 'The Whitsun Weddings', 'Here', 'Dockery and Son'). Now he resumed the sequence, and over the next six years would complete four more, all focused directly or indirectly on the theme of death: 'The Building', 'The Old Fools', 'Show Saturday' and finally 'Aubade'.

Since his forty-fifth-birthday poem, 'Sympathy in White Major', Larkin's poems had been distilled intertextually from earlier literature or art, or had evoked a reified historical past or an exotic location. Now he returned to the contemporary social scene of his middle-period work. But the modulations are more abrupt and the tone harder. In 'The Building' the poet struggles to assert an elevated poetic register against the drag of despondent prose; or his idiom fuses the flatly literal and romantically poetic together. This strange effect is seen in the footnote, isolated at the bottom of the second page of drafting: 'We must never die. No one must ever die.'[2] The businesslike imperative is contradicted by embarrassingly ingenuous emotion and naive repetition. The opening simile of the poem has a similarly mixed tone. It sounds rhetorically confident: 'Higher than the handsomest hotel'. But the aspirated 'h' alliteration gasps exhaustedly.[3] The phrase 'lucent [honey]comb' strikes a rich Keatsian note, but is also an exact photographic description of the yellow-lit Hull Royal Infirmary on the Anlaby Road.[4] A strained elevation is maintained in the description of the 'close-ribbed' streets: 'Like a great sigh out of the last century'. But towards the end of the stanza the poet's figurative nerve collapses: into flat description ('The porters are scruffy'), superstitious circumlocution ('not taxis') and the gallows humour of zeugma ('in the hall / As well as creepers hangs a frightening smell').

Prosy description follows: 'There are paperbacks, and tea at so much a cup.' Then the tone becomes more detached and impersonal with the stumble of a loosely appositional noun phrase: 'Humans, caught / On ground curiously neutral'. The chillingly abstract noun 'Humans', used here for the only time in a serious mature poem, strips the people of their families and fashions.[5] Faced with biological extinction, only the fundamentals remain. Two crushing noun phrases rub in the point with the same repeated grammar and rhythm: 'The end of choice, the last of hope', an effect so Larkinesque as to border on self-parody. Poetic metaphor flickers back into life with a variation on Larkin's familiar room imagery. The 'rooms' of 'The Building' are at the same time more literal than the attics, dens or towers of his recent symbolist poems, but also more awesome: 'rooms, and rooms past those, / And more rooms yet, each one further off // And harder to return from'. These oubliettes offer the same escape from the self which the poet longed for in the 'padlocked cube of light' in 'Dry-Point' and the attics of 'shoreless day' in 'Absences'. But in this context of reductive biology the surrender to extinction brings no euphoria.

In stanzas six and seven metaphor stands on its head as the 'real', dull ordinary world takes on the glowing inaccessibility of a Grecian urn or mythical Byzantium: 'Red brick, lagged pipes, and someone walking

[. . .] / Out to the car park, free'. Outside lies the gorgeous normality of traffic, terraced streets and, in an elegiac metonym of life as glamorous as anything in Keats or Yeats, 'girls with hair-dos' fetching their separates from the cleaners. This achingly poignant evocation of the loveliness of everyday things prompts an impassioned apostrophe which no other twentieth-century poet could have risked:

> O world,
> Your loves, your chances, are beyond the stretch
> Of any hand from here![6]

In the building the solid, accessible world of humdrum normality has become 'unreal', 'A touching dream' of togetherness, from which we all 'wake [. . .] separately'. Reality awaits us after we are 'borne across' into the metaphorical world of extinction. Towards the end of the poem the language descends again to prose: 'Each gets up and goes / At last. Some will be out by lunch [. . .]' In a wan parody of the elect ascending to heaven the others go to join the 'unseen congregations whose white rows / Lie set apart above'.

In the past we tried to keep our 'thought of dying' at bay through faith. Now, though secular medicine may outbuild cathedrals:

> nothing contravenes
> The coming dark, though crowds each evening try
>
> With wasteful, weak, propitiatory flowers.

Superstitious propitiation is useless, as are gestures of love and sympathy. The language combines the formal Latinate eloquence of 'contravenes' and 'propitiatory' with the homely Anglo-Saxon plainness of 'dark', 'weak' and 'wasteful'. The 'w' alliteration has a hint of exasperation and, after the emotional stammer of the cluttered polysyllable 'propitiatory' the voice falls, in a Mozartean diminuendo, to the open vowel of 'flowers'.

'The Building' adopts a roomy stanza of regular interwoven rhyme characteristic of Larkin's earlier reflective odes. But there is a hidden complication. The eight-line rhyme-scheme (abcbdcad) naturally suggests regular eight-line stanzas. Wilfully, however, the stanzas are only seven lines long. Thus the rhyme-scheme completes itself at line 1 of stanza two, at line two of stanza three, at line three of stanza four, and so on. It is not until the eighth stanza that the completion of the rhyme scheme coincides, for the first time, with the end of the stanza. But, instead of concluding here, Larkin adds a further, ninth stanza, necessitating a final single isolated line to complete the scheme. It is difficult to imagine any reader actually hearing this. Larkin is playing a private game, like the numerological patterns or acrostics of medieval poetry and music. But it is a game on which he has expended a great deal of imaginative energy. I have argued elsewhere that this device could be seen as leading the reader through a suite of similar rooms, each different from the last and with confusingly rearranged furniture.[7] Alternatively, the slippage between stanza and rhyme could be felt to throw the poem off balance, resulting in a game of catch-up as the initial 'a' rhyme of each abcbdcad rhyme-unit moves down the order in each succeeding stanza, hidden (like an undiagnosed cancer?) to take its final form as 'die' at the beginning of the ninth. It seems relevant here that the nine seven-line stanzas bring the poem to its sixty-third line. In his fiftieth year, Larkin was already certain that he would die at sixty-three, the same age as his father. The hopeful mathematics of this poem force the poem beyond that limit into a sixty-fourth line. However, like the wasteful and weak flowers themselves, this superstitious magic is pathetically ineffective.

Larkin followed this poem, just under a month later, with a more direct response to his mother's plight, 'Heads in the Women's Ward', drafted on a single page dated 6 March 1972. The poet describes the senile heads in crisp couplets: the staring eyes, the taut tendons, the bearded mouths talking silently. A sixty-year perspective returns them to their youth, when they smiled 'At lover, husband, first-born child'. But time and place are now different:

> Smiles are for youth. For old age come
> Death's terror and delirium.

The rhythm suggests a nursery rhyme suitable for recitation by those in their 'second childhood'. He published the poem immediately, placing it in the Rationalist Association's journal *New Humanist* (May 1972), which has been campaigning on behalf of scepticism since 1885.

Larkin was deeply affected by his mother's loss of independence. He wrote to Barbara Pym in March, reluctantly conceding that Eva would never now return to her own home: 'it's clear she can't go back to living, as she did, more or less on her own. Indeed I wonder if she will ever emerge from the Nursing Home [. . .] since Christmas I have been going back there on Saturday & returning Sunday, which leaves considerably less time than usual for letters.'[8] In May, to add to his gloom, Cecil Day-Lewis died. Larkin had visited him days before the end, and had shown him the Sonus Press publication of Joan Barton's *The Mistress*. Despite his condition Day-Lewis had gone to the trouble of reading the poems and dictating a complimentary letter to the author. Larkin was chastened at this generosity of spirit: 'Catch me doing that. I really think he was a nice man.'[9] In the same letter to Conquest he briefly reflected on Roy Fuller as a possible successor to Day-Lewis as Laureate. Had he himself been offered the post at this point, he would have accepted.[10] In the event Betjeman was appointed. In June 1972 Larkin allowed Anthony Thwaite to persuade him to make a rare 'personal appearance' during his visit to the University of East Anglia for a SCONUL conference. He commented apprehensively, 'The awful thing is that people may be expecting too much – a combination of Rupert Brooke, Walt Whitman and T. S. Eliot, instead of which they get bald deaf bicycle-clipped Larkin, the Laforgue of Pearson Park.'[11] He is echoing Dylan Thomas's description of himself as 'the Rimbaud of Cwmdonkin Drive'.

Unusually, 'The View', his fiftieth-birthday poem, was drafted almost entirely outside the workbook. Larkin dramatizes his feelings with the zestful gusto of a stand-up comedian. In a wildly inappropriate image he depicts himself as an 'overweight and shifty' mountain climber, ascending the peak of age. His weight was by this time fifteen stone. Experienced climbers assure him that the view is 'fine from fifty'. He should expect: 'fields and snowcaps / And flowered lanes that twist'.

But having reached this vantage point he is disappointed to find that, beyond his toecaps, the track 'drops away in mist'. A fifth line tacked on to each quatrain turns the knife with a third malicious recurrence of the rhyme. 'The view does not exist' gives the unmistakable cue for a pantomimic shrug.[12] Short-syllable throwaway rhymes ('twist / mist / exist') alternate with grotesque double rhymes ('fifty / shifty; snowcaps / toe-caps; lifetime / unwifed, I'm'). The flow runs clear only in the pensive open vowels of the final rhyme ('drear / clear / near'):

> Where has it gone, the lifetime?
> Search me. What's left is drear.
> Unchilded and unwifed, I'm
> Able to view that clear:
> So final. And so near.

With an elliptical virtuosity characteristic of Larkin's late style the poem modulates at the last minute into pensive self-elegy. Puzzlingly he did not publish it. Eight years later in 1980 he sent it to his friend Anthony Thwaite on his fiftieth birthday with the compliment 'But it would have been far worse without you.'[13] He wrote to Ann Thwaite, Anthony's wife: 'He's not to go publishing it.' In the event it did not appear until the publication of *Collected Poems* in 1988.

In August 1972 the BBC Third Programme broadcast a radio feature, *Larkin at Fifty*, prompting his Belfast muse, Winifred Arnott, now Bradshaw, long ago married, divorced and remarried, to write to him. They resumed an intermittent correspondence which lasted until the poet's death. This year Philip holidayed with Monica in Wester Ross. He wrote in their joint diary with disconcerting candour:

> My specs are splashed with lobster.
> My lobster's splashed with snot,
> No woman makes my knob stir –
> A bloody cold I've got.[14]

On top of his other reasons for depression his unhealthy lifestyle and heavy drinking were causing a loss of sexual vigour. In November Patsy Strang wrote to him from a nursing home for alcoholics. He replied regretting that they had lost touch with each other and sorry that she was in '"Clinholme" – word of fear'. Concerned as ever about his mother he told Patsy: 'I now go & see her every other weekend, which is a little wearing, but of course one does what one can, which isn't much.'[15] As another augury that he was becoming 'historical', he was approached by Barry Bloomfield, who had recently completed a bibliography of Auden, with a proposal to make him his next subject. He wrote that this would be 'wonderful', and speculated on whether he would be ethically justified in hiding from Bloomfield any 'terrible poem' tucked away in a magazine.[16]

At the beginning of December 1972 Larkin heard that Ansell and Judy Egerton were to separate. He had been writing to the Egertons, first as a couple, then regularly to Judy, since their first meeting in Belfast in 1954. He visited with the Egertons once or twice a year, and for many years he and Monica would take them out annually to dinner during the Lord's Test match. In 1974, together with Harold Pinter, Ansell Egerton sponsored Larkin for membership of the MCC. Judy Egerton was at this time developing her career as an art historian, and in 1974 was to become Assistant Keeper of the British Collection at the Tate Gallery. The news of the separation came as 'a great shock'. In a tactful letter of 5 December 1972, Philip expressed his sympathy ('I can guess the loneliness isn't easy [. . .] no, it's sad. I do feel that'). He went on to thank her for her advice on muesli for breakfast and congratulate her on the recent purchase of a watercolour, in a bidding competition against 'these grabbing Yanks'. He boasted that the Ferens Gallery in Hull had bought its Atkinson Grimshaw '*in 1950 for £10* ARRGHGH. It's lovely: so delicate', and went on to discuss the progress of the Egertons' younger daughter Fabia, then studying English at Cambridge.[17]

In January 1973 he wrote to Judy that he had 'finished a long dreary poem that had been dragging on since September'.[18] His great Ode to Senility, 'The Old Fools', completed on 12 January, again breaks new expressive ground. The meditative authority of his extended reflective elegies is here, uniquely, inflected into a series of blunt questions: 'What do they think has happened [. . .]?'; 'Do they somehow suppose [. . .]?'; 'do they fancy [. . .]?' One might see this as an example of Larkin's characteristic *faux naif* technique. The poet already knows the answers to his rhetorical questions. But the effect is actually less strategic than this. The questions sound genuine, and bitterly reproachful: 'Do they somehow suppose / It's more grown-up when your mouth hangs open and drools, / And you keep on pissing yourself [. . .]?' He shockingly refuses to displace this familiar anger into our usual patronizing sentimentalism towards 'the old dears'. He goes on to answer his questions by evoking their absent minds. They sit 'through days of thin continuous dreaming / Watching light move'. The last phrase cruelly parodies a typical Larkin epiphany: the wind tousling the clouds in 'Mr Bleaney', the luminously peopled air in 'Here'. In the curt two-stress line with which the stanza ends, the poet asks: 'Why aren't they screaming?' He seems genuinely puzzled. As he wrote to Brian Cox the following month: 'I felt I had to write it. It's rather an angry poem, but the anger is ambivalent – we are angry at the humiliation of age, but we are also angry at old people for reminding us of death, and I suppose for making us feel bad about doing nothing for them.'[19]

The second stanza shifts to composed philosophical meditation. In an atheist trope familiar from Hardy and Housman the poet contemplates our (or rather 'your') physical atoms 'speeding away' from each other in dissolution. He rationalizes that you are merely returning to the oblivion from which you emerged at birth. But there is no emotional consolation in this. After all, 'then it was going to end'. When our mothers gave us birth we became part of a 'unique endeavour / To bring to bloom the million-petalled flower / Of being here'. When oblivion resumes 'you can't pretend / There'll be anything else'. This thought unsettles the poet's philosophical composure and he reverts to awed jeering, mimicking the old fools' witlessness: 'Not knowing how, not hearing who, the power / Of choosing gone' ('Oh, ow, eeh, oo, ow, oo'). The final short line in this stanza returns with a mocking rhyme to the raucous disrespect of the opening: 'they're for it; / [. . .] How can they ignore it?' Georges Bataille wrote: 'Obscenity is our name for the uneasiness which upsets the physical state associated with self-possession, with the possession of a recognized and stable individuality.'[20] There is something radically obscene about 'The Old Fools'; and about old fools.

In the third stanza the familiar gibe 'the lights are on, but nobody's at home', generates one of the most poignantly beautiful effects in Larkin's work. The rooms they inhabit are no longer the literal rooms of homes or hospitals. They have retreated in their senile confusion into archetypal living rooms inside their heads:

> chairs and a fire burning,
> The blown bush at the window, or the sun's
> Faint friendliness on the wall some lonely
> Rain-ceased midsummer evening.

They achieve transcendence by living 'Not here and now, but where all happened once'. The effect is unbearably moving. As a materialist Larkin sees the fading rooms as 'Inside your head' rather than inside your mind, and so at the mercy of physical decline. They 'grow farther, leaving / Incompetent cold, the constant wear and tear / Of taken breath'. Riskily, Larkin changes metaphor at this point, shifting to the mountain climbing of 'The View'. The old fools are perhaps so near to the icy peak of 'Extinction's alp' that they can perceive only the 'rising ground' of day-by-day existence. Since the 1940s Larkin had been writing about the approach of death, but his internal verbal censor had stopped him from using the key word 'extinction' until the context arrived when it would exert its full 1,000-watt force. He uses the word only here in 'The Old Fools' and once again in 'Aubade' ('the sure extinction that we travel to'), in unforgettable phrases differentiated from each other in grammar and idiom. As the poem draws to a close the rhetorical questions return ('Can they never tell / What is dragging them back [. . .] Not at night?') to be 'answered' in the chilling final short line:

Well,
We shall find out.

For many readers this commonplace phrase has become a quotation from Larkin.

Three days after the completion of 'The Old Fools', and shortly before the publication of *The Oxford Book of Twentieth Century English Verse*, Charles Monteith wrote proposing that he and Auden nominate Larkin for the Oxford Professorship of Poetry. Larkin found the offer 'immensely flattering': 'the biggest compliment I have been paid for many years'. However, he declined: 'I have really very little interest in poetry in the abstract; I have never lectured about it, or even written about it to any extent, and I know that I could never produce anything worthy of such a distinguished office and audience.'[21] His instinct was sound. He could not have written the kind of sustained reflection on the poetic craft which Auden produced in his Oxford lectures, *The Dyer's Hand*. In the event he supported the candidacy of his friend John Wain. He wrote to Judy Egerton on 11 June 1973: 'I went to Oxford for the poetry election, & got very drunk.' Wain was elected.[22] In February 1973 the business of poetry had penetrated to Hull in a different form when Robert Lowell gave a poetry reading at the invitation of the Professor of American Studies, Geoffrey Moore. Though Larkin was uncomfortable with Lowell's 'confessional' mode, Lowell's admiration for his work, and capacity for hard drinking, created a short-lived friendship. They corresponded, and later, in 1974, Larkin visited Lowell at his home in Kent.[23]

The Oxford anthology appeared on 29 March 1973 in an edition of 29,300. A reprint of 13,550 copies followed in June. Whatever damage the volume might do to his reputation, it would certainly make him money. As he commented later, 'I was over fifty before I could have "lived by my writing" – and then only because I had edited a big anthology.'[24] He was by now already a man of substance, an uncomfortable thought for so purely lyric a poet. As Wordsworth wrote: 'Getting and spending, we lay waste our powers.'[25] His response was the late masterpiece 'Money' completed on 19 February 1973, a month or so before the

anthology was published. The poet reviews his quarterly accumulation
of dividends and interest payments and finds himself at a loss. It is
eloquent of the gulf between man and poet at this point that while in
the letters he complains about the bills he has to pay, in the poems it is
the accumulation of wealth that oppresses him. He is, it seems, making
a good living, but without living. With so much money why does he
not feel fulfilled? Money, a medium of exchange with no intrinsic use,
is Larkin's most thought-provoking metonym of life. It is the metaphorical abstraction of all our dreams of happiness and fulfilment; or,
as he reductively puts it, 'goods and sex'. It reproaches him: 'You could
get them still by writing a few cheques.' His friends and neighbours
have used their money, he slyly observes, to obtain 'a second house and
car and wife'. But a poet's life cannot be measured in houses, cars or
wives. For him the reflection that 'money has something to do with life'
is deeply puzzling. He reflects on its lyric elusiveness: it exists only in
being used. Like life, money is ours by leasehold. It will in the end buy
us only the final shave given to the corpse before it lies in the chapel of
rest.

So far the poem, with its briskly rhymed couplets (set out capri-
ciously with indentations appropriate to alternate rhyme) might seem
to be light and playful. But at this point Larkin springs a beautiful
surprise. If money is a metonym of life, it is equally a metonym of
poetry, as Wallace Stevens perceived: 'Money is a kind of poetry.'[26] In
the final stanza Larkin pulls out the symbolist throttle and gives
expression to this insight in one of the least anticipated epiphanies in
his work:

> I listen to money singing. It's like looking down
>   From long french windows at a provincial town,
>   The slums, the canal, the churches ornate and mad
>   In the evening sun. It is intensely sad.

This is a coup worthy of Verlaine or Rimbaud. Yet two years earlier he
had written to Douglas Dunn while at work on the Oxford anthology:
'my own mind is so shallow that I can only respond to lighter poems,

written in total explicit style. No obscurities!'[27] Significantly, however, he held back from contradicting Barbara Everett's appreciative analysis of his symbolist mode (1980),[28] and when Andrew Motion published his short monograph on Larkin's work in 1982,[29] he commented non-committally in a letter to Anthony Thwaite: 'his line on the poems is rather école d'Everett – Larkin as Mallarmé, and so on. Well, it makes a change.'[30]

Larkin was by now a national figure. In early April 1973 he and Monica were invited to a Garden Party at Buckingham Palace. He commented to Judy Egerton: 'Queen was pleasant enough, but I didn't have enough of her to lose my nervousness [. . .] I got on well enough with the Keeper of the Royal Stamps.'[31] In May, Faber published a paperback edition of *The North Ship*. However his professional life was becoming more stressful. With the oil crisis of 1973 the quinquennial grant, the government's funding mechanism for universities, was suddenly reduced. Nevertheless it remained national policy for higher education to expand. Student numbers at Hull grew inexorably while staffing was reduced. The elitist replica of Oxbridge which Larkin had entered in 1955 was under pressure to turn itself into an institution of mass education.[32] Between 1974 and 1977 there was a net loss of 13.5 full-time equivalent posts in the Library.[33] Despite this contraction the work was becoming more complex and technologically more complicated. A full-time archivist was appointed, and the first experiments in computerization were made. Larkin was never comfortable with the new technology, which he delegated to Brenda Moon, Deputy Librarian from 1962 until 1980. By the beginning of 1974 he listed among 'Crises at Hull': 'New Computer to be stuffed into vital Library area, because they've nowhere to put it, me going down fighting'.[34]

His mother was now eighty-seven and in the midst of all his activities he found time to keep her supplied with an unbroken flow of news and reassurance. In a one-page letter of Thursday 3 May 1973 he tells her, 'It's a grey day here, windy and rather chilly.' He describes an interview with the local radio station about the Oxford anthology. 'I had a nice letter from you this morning – thank you for taking the trouble to write. I don't expect you have got your *new* spectacles yet, but I know they have been ordered. It will be nicer when they come, you'll be able to read more easily.' He inserts a charming cartoon of a seal in a mob-cap reading a newspaper, and ends, 'Have you had any of Brenda's cake?' There is something deeply moving about this lifelong correspondence: intimate, polite and interminable.

In the late 1960s and early 1970s Larkin had succeeded in making for himself the private creative space for the poems which he was still able to write. But he was aware that his inspiration was failing. Now, in June 1973, having completed two new reflective elegies ('The Building' and 'The Old Fools'), and despairing of being able to produce a collection of the extent of *The Less Deceived* (twenty-nine poems) or *The Whitsun Weddings* (thirty-two), he assembled a volume of twenty-five poems (counting the 'Livings' sequence as three), including the uneasy 'Homage to a Government' and the commissioned 'Going, Going'.[35] He sent it to Faber with an apologetic letter: 'if I thought I were likely to write five more poems in the space of a few months I should hold back until I had done so. Unfortunately I don't feel this.'[36] He knew that this would be his final volume. At the age of fifty he had all but fulfilled his literary potential, and was burnt out.

His valedictory mood was intensified by the death, in September, of his boyhood idol W. H. Auden. He wrote to Anthony Thwaite: 'So Auden is no more. I felt terribly shocked when I saw the news. I imagined he would knock on another ten years, he seemed to have life taped.' He added dispassionately: 'At the same time I still don't think he'd written much worth reading since 1939, and in some respects ("Graffiti") he'd become a positive embarrassment.'[37] A memorial service was held at Christ Church Cathedral, Oxford, on 27 October 1973. After the ceremony Betjeman confided that he was considering resigning the Laureateship and asked Larkin if he might be prepared to take it on.[38] Larkin evaded the question. It was already too late.

His next poem, the poignantly lacklustre 'Show Saturday', reflects the valedictory gloom of this time. For many years Philip and Monica had made regular visits to the Autumn Fair in Bellingham,

Northumberland. Now as winter 1973 came on, he clung for stability to this fixed ritual. He dated a near-final draft in the workbook '3.12.73', and a week later wrote to Anthony Thwaite: 'I don't know whether to shove it into HIGH WINDOWS, of which I have now had the proofs and which they want back by January 4th. It would add bulk and roughage, I suppose – both much needed qualities.'[39] There is more here, perhaps, than his customary self-critical reflex. Though 'Show Saturday' has the form and extent of one of his major reflective odes, its impact is moody and subdued in comparison with 'The Building' and 'The Old Fools'.

It is by far the most crowdedly 'literal' of Larkin's works, reading at times like jotted directions to the director of a documentary film: 'Grey day for the Show, but cars jam the narrow lanes. / Inside, on the field, judging has started: dogs / (Set their legs back, hold out their tails) [. . .]' The visual details catch exactly the mix of business-deals and homespun holiday pleasure of such country fairs ('Bead-stalls, balloon-men, a Bank; a beer-marquee that / Half-screens a canvas Gents'). But there is little sense of charm or enjoyment. The poet seems listless and bemused, willing himself into enthusiasm for these quaint rituals: 'The jumping's on next [. . .] There's more than just animals [. . .]' However, a contrasting undercurrent of surrealist abstraction makes the proceedings seem weird and enigmatic:

> Folks sit about on bales,
> Like great straw dice. For each scene is linked by spaces
> Not given to anything much, where kids scrap, freed,
> While their owners stare different ways with incurious faces.

The kids have 'owners' rather than parents. This depersonalization continues in the slow-motion gymnopedic description of the wrestlers: 'One falls: they shake hands, / [. . .] They're not so much fights / As long immobile strainings that end in unbalance / With one on his back, unharmed, while the other stands / Smoothing his hair.' The Harrington Brothers were a fixture in the Bellingham programme and Larkin photographed them on more than one visit. But this description has no familiarity or affection about it. It is formal and abstracted: Seurat or Satie rather than Surtees.

The poet's attention turns to the 'tent of growing and making'. There is a hint of boredom in the listing of the categories to be judged:

> four brown eggs, four white eggs,
> Four plain scones, four dropped scones, pure excellences that enclose
> A recession of skills. And after them, lambing-sticks, rugs,
>
> Needlework, knitted caps, baskets, all worthy, all well done [. . .]

The bald prosiness is hardly redeemed by the makeshift poetic waffle of 'pure excellences that enclose / A recession of skills'. Is the speaker perhaps irritated at being required to feign an interest in these trivialities ('all worthy, all well done')? Can we read a subtext of refracted dialogue here, as the poet and his companion roam about the show, she holding the programme of events, directing his attention to the next attraction, while he, unable to snap out of his depression, pays listless attention? It seems painfully obvious that the poet has no real interest in knitted caps or lambing-sticks. Andrew Motion suggests that 'Show Saturday' is in some sense a love poem to Monica.[40] And this may account for the way it sometimes reads like a conversation with a shadowy companion who comes between poet and reader.

It is in the final three stanzas that the work realizes its poetic potential; but in a strangely indirect way. The car-park thins as the community breaks up into its constituent families, returning to private addresses 'In high stone one-street villages, empty at dusk'. There is a wan echo here of the affirmation of social community of 'The Whitsun Weddings'. Common humanity is embodied in stereotypes, though with less warmth than in the earlier work: 'dog-breeding wool-defined women, / Children all saddle-swank, mugfaced middleaged wives / Glaring at jellies [. . .]' The humour lacks élan. Moreover 'one-street villages, empty at dusk', make an ambiguous image of continuing life. The poet's valediction implies an ending more conclusive than seems justified by the subject. They all return: 'To winter coming, as the dismantled

The solitary bachelor hesitating on the brink of conformity and marriage, in 'The shame of evening trousers, evening tie' ('The Dance', 1963–4).

Larkin's pornography. *Left*: a characteristic 'nude study' of the model Sophia Dawn by the founder of *Kamera* magazine, Harrison Marks. *Right*: a naughty schoolgirl photograph.

Philip and Monica in the flat at 32 Pearson Park. Larkin used the imagery
of his later poem 'The Card-Players' in looking forward to a visit
from Monica in 1967: 'We shall be two Hogspewers together'.

The view from the Pearson Park flat
remained unaltered from October 1956,
when he moved in, until June 1974,
when he left for Newland Park.

'Veronica', Larkin's wicker rabbit,
sat beside his chair during his interview
with Betjeman in the BBC *Monitor*
television feature of 1964.

The cube of light which dominates 'Stage 2' of the Brynmor Jones Library, opened in 1969. Larkin wrote to his mother: 'There are so many new members of staff that I feel like a stranger in my own building.'

Librarian and Secretary: Betty and Philip in 1972. 'I'd be lost without her.'

he'd decided to stay the night. He had his wife with him. The place was just filling up for a dance, & the fat chap offered me another drink — I could see myself staying the night! So I fled. I drove very carefully, & only nearly had an accident in the lighted streets of Loughborough, staring at the legs of a booted miss Poet Dies. Hull Man Fatality.

I think I'll rewrite the cancels thing, & enclose the revision.

Love as ever

Philip

Extract from a letter to Betty Mackereth, 18 January 1969. He describes a stop-over in Bawtry on his drive down from Hull and encloses documents for Betty to type. At the end he stipples a Texas library stamp, anticipating the time when his papers might be acquired by the Harry Ransom Center.

Maeve Brennan, 1970. Maeve's caption for this photograph in her memoir *The Philip Larkin I Knew* is 'Shades of D. H. Lawrence'.

Monica Jones on Jura or Mull, 1971. Philip and Monica's holidays in the remoter parts of Scotland or on Sark became an annual routine.

I am getting well with my anthology — it's terrific having all one's time free to devote to a single interesting project. Really, I wonder if I shall ever grapple with 'work' again.

From a letter to Maeve Brennan, 19 October 1970, written from All Souls, Oxford, where Larkin was working on *The Oxford Book of Twentieth-Century English Verse*. Maeve is 'Miss Bianca Mouse'.

Anthony Thwaite in 1972. Larkin chose the poet and former Literary Editor of the *Listener*, *New Statesman* and *Encounter* as his literary executor. At Anthony's suggestion, he also recruited the young Andrew Motion.

How lovely about the azalea — you will be pleased!

I'll write again on Sunday — in the meantime, do please keep warm & dry. Tell Kitty I'm sorry about her cough. Much love Philip

CORN, BIRDWEED, POPPIES and SILVERWEED
with CLOUDED YELLOW BUTTERFLY.
◄ TERSTON ►

Eva Larkin in the garden of 21 York Road, Loughborough, 1970. Larkin returned regularly to mow this lawn until the house was finally sold after Eva's death in 1977.

Larkin wrote to his mother twice a week from the late 1940s to the 1970s. In this note of Thursday 28 January 1965 she appears as a seal in a mob-cap.

Eva (*left*, 1970; *right*, 1972) moved into Berrystead Nursing Home in February 1972 and died there five years later. 'Smiles are for youth. For old age come / Death's terror and delirium.' ('Heads in the Women's Ward').

During the 1960s and 1970s Monica and Philip frequently visited Bellingham Show, Northumberland. Larkin was intrigued by the wrestling of the Harrington Brothers: 'long immobile strainings that end in unbalance'. ('Show Saturday', 1974).

Self-portrait, 1974, the year in which Larkin moved to Newland Park, and began 'Aubade'. The first draft began: 'I work all day, and hit the jug at night'.

Hedgehog in the garden of 105 Newland Park, March 1979. On 11 June Larkin killed a hedgehog while mowing his lawn, prompting him to write 'The Mower'.

With Betty Mackereth, 1981. In 1975 Larkin 'seduced' his secretary of eighteen years. His poems 'Dear Jake' and 'We met at the end of the party' were inspired by her. During the following years they would escape to the North York Moors around Kirkbymoorside.

6.10.78

That spreads through other lives like a tree
And sways them on in a sort of sense
And say why it never worked for me.
There is ~~there would have need~~ a great difference ~~of~~
~~there would have been / have been~~
~~objectives, different rewards~~
~~Right at the start~~
A long way back; but the rewards
Can easily be imagined. Easily.

24·10·78

That spreads through other lives like a tree
And sways them on in a sort of sense
And say why it never worked for me.
There would need ~~need~~ to have been a great difference
A long way back, and ~~that~~ the rewards
~~It brought~~ Might not have meant much personally.

25·10·78

That spreads through other lives like a tree
And sways them on in a sort of sense
And say why it never worked for me.
Something to do with ~~violence~~ violence
~~A long way back~~, and wrong rewards,
And ~~wanting~~ arrogant ~~eternity~~...

20/9/79

The final page of 'Love Again' in Workbook 8. It is a sign of Larkin's faltering inspiration that he returned to the page after nearly a year to complete the poem.

Show / Itself dies back into the area of work'. With its private subtex-
tual reference to Laforgue's poem, this is more self-elegy than celebration
of communal solidarity. Like the architecture of the hospital in 'The
Building', the Show is an elaborate displacement activity, 'something
people do' to keep the thought of death at bay:

> Let it stay hidden there like strength, below
> Sale-bills and swindling; something people do,
> Not noticing how time's rolling smithy-smoke
> Shadows much greater gestures; something they share
> That breaks ancestrally each year into
> Regenerate union. Let it always be there.

The incantatory language, with its ceremonious conservative rhetoric
('ancestrally [. . .] Regenerate union') only underlines the feebleness of
the command: 'Let it always be there.'

It is difficult to detect in any of this the nationalistic celebration
which some critics have found in the poem. Motion calls it 'a huge
hymn to old England'. Neil Corcoran feels that the final lines 'witness
to a genuine religious feeling' attached to 'an enduring Englishness'. In
a characteristic misreading Seamus Heaney misquotes the final phrase
to give it more ideological fervour, 'Let it always be so,' and asserts that
the conclusion 'beautifully expresses a nostalgic patriotism which is
also an important part of this poet's make-up'.[41]

On 8 January 1974 Larkin wrote to Anthony Thwaite thanking him
for his positive verdict on 'Show Saturday'. His final collection was
complete and he took the opportunity to take stock of his achievement:

> you know I am a self-deprecating sort of character – I don't think I write
> well – just better than anyone else – No, seriously, this book does seem
> a ragbag, and I *do* think that the word will go forth 'Donnez la côtelette
> à Larquin!' ('Give Larkin the chop') – in a way it's a compliment (only
> big trees get the axe) but in another it's melancholy [. . .]
>
>   Talking about la côtelette, I had a *French* translation of 'Livings' sent
> me today. Bloody funny. The first line is

> Je fais des affaires avec les fermiers, dans le genre bains anti-parasites et
> aliments pour bestiaux

Quite Whitmanesque, isn't it? 'Our butler, Starveling' comes out as 'Notre maître d'hotel, Laffamé'.[42]

His comment that he doesn't write well, 'just better than anyone else', would be vanity from any other poet. But he does genuinely doubt the quality of even his best work. And he is right that, in comparison with the earlier mature volumes, *High Windows* is something of a 'ragbag'. The inspiration of many of the poems is heavily mediated and second-ary, and the style elusive and elliptical: the work of 'Larquin' rather than Larkin. In this final volume however we find the most unpredict-ably beautiful colours in his oeuvre. 'Strangeness' always made more sense to him than his own familiar 'establishments', and poems like 'The Card-Players', 'The Old Fools', 'Livings II' and 'Money' have the strangeness of unique originality.

Larkin's final collection was named after the high-windowed room in which he had lived for most of the last two decades. Now, shortly after Christmas, he learnt that this room was no longer to be his. The University intended to sell off some of its 'worst properties', including 32 Pearson Park. In a letter to Anthony Thwaite of 30 December he anticipated his rehousing with grim gusto:

> This was Mr Bleaney's bungalow,
> Standing in the concrete jungle, o-
> ver-looking an arterial road –
> Here I live with old Toad.[43]

Unable to contemplate buying the house in Pearson Park himself, and becoming a landlord, he set about finding a new home (if home existed). He was at last forced to own his own establishment and, to make things worse, he chose to live at ground level, overlooking neither a green park nor an arterial road. His class prejudice took him to the most expensive and exclusive residential area of Hull, Newland Park.

Despite its name, it is a cul-de-sac in the form of a figure of eight, the outer loop of which issues at two points on to the Cottingham Road, opposite the University. The houses, the earliest dating from the 1880s, but with many later infills, are detached and individually designed, with large gardens (hence 'Park'). Pressured by the need to vacate his beloved flat, and with no relish for house-hunting, Larkin took the first house to become available, number 105. Built in the 1950s, it lies down a slight slope, and in his day presented to the road a blank white garage door.[44] It is at virtually the midpoint of the inner loop, as far away from the main road as possible. However, apart from seclusion, it shared none of the characteristics of the compact rented flat in Pearson Park with its blue windowscape.

The end of an era, in a larger sense, was foreshadowed at the end of 1973 by a request from the Hull construction company, Fenner, for Larkin to write the words to a cantata to mark the completion of the Humber Bridge, work on which had begun the previous year. This new link with the south would end Hull's precious isolation which he so valued. The world which had formed him was slipping into the past. On 15 January 1974 he wrote a formal letter to Benjamin Britten asking whether he 'would be prepared in any circumstances to entertain a suggestion that has recently been made in Hull – namely, the completion of the Humber Bridge in (it is hoped) 1976 should be commemorated by the composition and performance of a choral work by yourself (with words by myself) [. . .] My own part in the project is simply due to the fact that I have lived in this neighbourhood for nearly twenty years, and have written one or two poems about it.'[45] However, this joint work by Britain's greatest poet and composer was not to be. Britten replied through his secretary that, having recently undergone a serious operation, he 'must very regretfully turn down your request for him to compose the music for a choral work to a text by yourself'.[46] Anthony Hedges, Reader in Composition at Hull, whose delightful Ayrshire Serenade had been written in 1969, was commissioned to write the music instead.

A month later, on 17 February, Larkin wrote to Judy Egerton on his familiar 32 Pearson Park notepaper, making as much lugubrious fun as he could of his situation:

my days in Pearson Park are coming to an end. I have blindly, deafly, & dumbly said I will buy an utterly undistinguished little modern house in *Newland* Park (plus ça change, plus c'est la même parc) [. . .] I can't say it's the kind of dwelling that is eloquent of the nobility of the human spirit. It has a huge garden – not a lovely wilderness (though it soon will be) – a long strip between wire fences – oh god oh god [. . .] So Larkin's Pearson Park Period ends, & his Newland Park Period commences.[47]

He attempted to raise his spirits by mentioning his recent election to membership of the MCC and hoping that his and Monica's annual 'Lords dinner' get-together with the Egertons, which had survived the couple's separation, would continue. He complimented her on the success of the Liberal Party in the polls, and looked forward to the collapse of the economy following the recent Middle Eastern oil crisis: 'Hull University will be shut down. I shall earn a few pence sweeping crossings [. . .] *You* can sell your pictures – at rock bottom prices. Gloomy old sod, aren't I?'[48]

A few weeks later, in the cruellest month, April, he began 'Aubade', the initial intensive drafts taking up nine workbook pages, dated between 11 April and 7 June. Unusually, he left the verso of the final page blank as if anticipating the poem's early completion.[49] He reached a near-final version up to the opening of the third stanza, though he was to change some phrases in the final version: 'I have the leisure to remark / That more than half of life has elapsed by now / (Two-thirds; three quarters'); 'Ancient interrogation'; 'The endless absent dark we travel to'. This, the tenth and last of his major contemplative elegies, is also the only one of his aubades to announce its genre in the title. Here there is no traditional parting of lovers. Dawn in 'Aubade' prompts the poet's farewell to life itself. The grip of light has become ominous and threatening.

The theme is the 'dread / Of dying and being dead'. The celebration of 'being here', always the *raison d'être* of Larkin's poetry, falters as the poet imagines the extinction of his imagination. Figurative language fails him, and a dispirited prosiness prevails: 'I work all day, and hit the jug at night' (in the final version: 'and get half-drunk at night'). In bitterly ironic self-quotation he falls back on familiar, richly romantic vocabulary recycled from his earlier work. In 'The Trees' (1967) the 'unresting castles' of leaf, renewing themselves each year, told the poet to 'Begin afresh'.[50] Now with the end of such renewals in sight, the adverb 'afresh' is attached not to rebirth but to the thought of death, which 'Flashes afresh to hold and horrify'. In the final draft three years later he cruelly transferred 'unresting' from the living foliage to death itself. It is an indication of the precision with which he imposes his linguistic authority that he confidently expects his readers to hear the verbal echoes of the earlier, already 'canonical' poem.

The stanzas preserve the richly interwoven form of the intricately rhymed Horatian or Keatsian ode, and there are poignant flickers of poeticism: 'that vast brocade, / Moth-eaten and musical' (in the final version 'That vast, moth-eaten musical brocade'). But this ornamental complexity is contradicted by bald indicative prose: 'nothing more terrible, nothing more true'. However, the poem's failure of élan is itself paradoxically eloquent, and the anti-rhetorical rhetoric is immediately accessible to the reader. The phrase 'the open emptiness for ever' (in the final version 'total emptiness') is instantaneously memorable, while 'Not to be here, / Not to be anywhere' has a naturalness which will make it sound to many readers like a quotation from themselves. This is the poetry of 'What oft was thought, but ne'er so well exprest'.[51] Few poets have succeeded in conveying so directly our familiar dismay at death. Mortality annihilates 'What I am'; it dissolves 'all we are'. Larkin's lyric naivety generates a candid dismay which other poets would repress in embarrassment. Any reader who has felt outraged at the sight of a loved one reduced to an inanimate mannikin in an empty room will respond to this.

Copies of *High Windows* arrived from Faber in May 1974, in the middle of his drafting of 'Aubade'. The grey cloth cover reminded Larkin of Auden's *Look, Stranger* which he felt to be 'a specially good omen'. It was, indeed, in terms of poetry publishing, a best-seller. The initial impression of 6,000 copies was sold by September; 7,500 more were printed, followed by another 6,000 in January 1975.[52] His poetic future, however, was bleak. He was aware of having all but completed his oeuvre, and his inspiration was guttering. It is thus perhaps not as surprising as it might at first seem that, having drafted half of one of his greatest poems, he abandoned it for the time being. No doubt the upheaval of his removal interrupted the flow. Perhaps, also, the manifest status of 'Aubade' as his 'last' poem inhibited him from putting the final touches on the tenth, blank page. He was not yet prepared to throw in the poetic towel. Larkin was to live for another twelve years following the end of his 'Pearson Park Period', and a brief poetic Indian summer lay ahead, in the poems he wrote to Betty Mackereth in the following year. But, with the final completion of 'Aubade' three years later in 1977, his literary life would be effectively over.

21

The End of the Party
1974–6

All his life Larkin had avoided 'furniture and loans from the bank'.[1]
When he moved house on 27 June 1974 he no longer needed loans.
But he did at last have to furnish his life in the expected manner. He
described the upheaval to Anthony Thwaite with gloomy wit: 'I've
been v. upset [. . .] in most senses: feel like a tortoise that has been
taken out of one shell and put in another.' He had had to cope with
a jammed door, lost key and ill-fitting carpet, and needed to 'buy
heap furniture fast'. Moreover, 'The garden is growing. Feel like
Hölderlin going bonk.' He concluded in the plaintive tones of an
exile: 'Drop me a line occasionally.'[2] Judy Egerton helped him choose
a stylish lampshade in London.[3] He bought a new washing machine
and no longer had the pleasure of wringing out his socks and under-
wear by hand, as he had done all his life. He mourned the loss of his
simple attic existence. He could not find a satisfactory place to work,
so he recreated his flat, sitting in an armchair by the fire downstairs,
his back to the garden, bookshelves within reach. He wrote to Barbara
Pym, 'Perhaps I shall produce a version of *About the House* (Auden's
sequence about his Austrian "pad"),' adding a grim self-quotation:
'"Well, we shall find out."'[4]

Andrew Motion's interpretation of Larkin's state of mind at this
point seems ungenerous. He sees the move to Newland Park as a
devious strategy, a 'form of creative suicide, one which left his

achievements untarnished, his put-upon identity intact, and his need for sympathy undiminished [. . .] he could both relish his success and seem not to enjoy it. He could freeze his talent to avoid the responsibility of having to live up to his reputation.'[5] The letters and poems of this period do not bear out this picture of manipulativeness and 'put-upon' self-pity. Larkin was not perversely freezing his talent. He was struggling to keep up his spirits and maintain his dying inspiration.

To all outward appearances his life had reached its zenith of success. *High Windows* was universally praised. He was awarded honorary degrees by St Andrews and Sussex Universities.[6] The eminent photographer Fay Godwin visited to take photographs which established a potent iconic image in the public imagination. He wrote to Godwin on 12 July 1974, saying that he liked some of her images 'very much indeed. I wish I always looked like that.' But he was apprehensive of the effect of others in reinforcing a negative stereotype. 'The photographs I "didn't like" [. . .] were simply the ones where I am peering out from among dark shelves with a somewhat furtive/whimsical appearance.'[7] Later, in 1982, he refused permission for one of these photographs to be used in Thwaite's *Larkin at Sixty* tribute volume. Later still, on 11 November 1983, he wrote to Godwin: 'I think it must have been to Fabers that I gave vehement instructions that the ones of me among the shelves on sheet 1892 should never be used. However, I take heart from your assurances that insofar as it lies within your control the Boston Strangler will not reappear.'[8] It is regrettable that Faber chose one of these images for the front dustwrapper of Martin Amis's selection of Larkin's poems in 2011, repeating it on the back, cropped to show a single sinister, bespectacled eye.[9]

His poetry was, for the time being, at a stand. After abandoning 'Aubade', he completed nothing until the day before his fifty-second birthday, eight months later. 'The Life with a Hole in It' (8 August 1974) was, he wrote, using Bruce Montgomery's *nom de plume*, 'what my old friend Edmund Crispin calls "demotic", I believe'.[10] Its jokey reference to the advertisement for Polos ('the mint with the hole') announces a richly self-parodic poem in 'Movement' vein. It is one of those works composed on a single page of the workbook, with only minor corrections. Never has an attack of the sulks been dramatized with such *jouissance*:

> When I throw back my head and howl
> People (women mostly) say
> *But you've always done what you want,*
> *You always get your own way* [. . .]

The women may be sympathetic and genuinely puzzled, but in his extravagantly self-pitying mood he hears only, as the italics suggest, a caricature feminine nagging. Then, determined to give offence (if he hasn't already), he turns the minimal civility of '(women mostly)' into the crude insult of 'the old ratbags'. All he can be justly accused of, he protests, is never having 'done what I don't'. He may have managed not to do what he doesn't want (marry and settle down). But this does not mean that he has done what he wanted. In this 'demotic' context what he wanted is imaged in terms not of symbolist transcendence, but of a novel-writing career in Ian Fleming mode. However, this turns out to be another dead end, since the life of 'the shit in the shuttered chateau' with its 'bathing and booze and birds', clearly repels him. Well, at least he has avoided the destiny the old ratbags would have preferred for him. He is not a 'spectacled schoolteaching sod' with six children, a pregnant wife and her parents coming to stay. The poem's real subject now emerges. This staged and artificial bellyaching is a displacement activity intended to distract him from 'larger gestures'. Choices of life are becoming irrelevant as age advances. In a grand didactic finale of emphatic noun phrases he declares that life is an 'immobile, locked' stasis, a struggle between 'Your wants', which remain unmet, 'the world's [wants] for you', which you strain to fulfil, and the ultimate winner, the 'unbeatable slow machine' which will bring 'what you'll get'. 'Days sift down it constantly. Years.'

At the time of his move from Pearson Park, Philip's relationship with Maeve was in abeyance. Her impatience with his indecision had resulted in frequent brief estrangements. 'I repeatedly dispatched him to sort himself out.'[11] The longest break in their affair had begun in

1973 and lasted sixteen months. Now it was briefly broken when he presented her with a copy of his new volume, inscribed 'For Maeve, with affectionate gratitude for so much – Philip'. She thanked him, a little puzzled, and, as she recalls, he responded: 'Oh Maeve! You have taught me so much about the breadth and depth of human emotions, and more about my own than anyone has ever done.'[12] Though they remained on distant terms for several more months, his words impressed her.

His routines repeated themselves. In September 1974 he and Monica spent the customary holiday in Scotland, and the same month he attended the SCONUL conference, which was held once again in East Anglia. In November he broke his usual rule and agreed to give a reading of his own poetry at his old college, St John's. In the haunts of his youth he relaxed, drank too much and ended the evening berating 'that shit Yeats, farting out his histrionic rubbish'.[13] Back in Hull his evening routine had now settled into a pattern: gin and tonic first, food accompanied by wine, then a nap followed by a menthol cigarette and another drink before bed.[14] His health steadily deteriorated. Occasionally he would host record-playing sessions with his jazz friends including the Professor of History, John Kenyon, Mike Bowen of the University's Audio-Visual Centre and John White from the American Studies Department. At the end of the year he edited the *Christmas Supplement* of the Poetry Book Society, and included 'The Life with a Hole in It'. The turn of the year brought his usual attack of despair. He wrote to Judy Egerton on 2 January 1975, 'What an absurd, empty life! And the grave yawns.'[15]

Nineteen-seventy-five however was to see an unexpected emotional and poetic flowering. Early in the year his estrangement from Maeve ended. Because the quarrel had lasted longer than usual, the reconciliation was particularly warm and, momentously, their relationship at last became fully physical. As she told Motion in 1992, she 'yielded to temptation, but only on *very* rare and isolated occasions, and at a cost of grave violation to my conscience, since I never, in principle, abandoned my stand on pre-marital sex'.[16] It is difficult, and perhaps unnecessary, to be sure exactly what occurred between them. Feeling that she had been too confiding to Motion in the early 1990s, she was very reticent when writing her memoir in 2000–2. However, more than one informed source attests that, overweight and undermined by drink, Larkin was by this time descending into impotence. Perhaps his own perception of inadequacy, unsuspected by her, gave Maeve's late access of passion a disorientating intensity for him. The statue of her beauty was walking, and he found himself wading in her wake. From Maeve's innocent viewpoint 'we embarked on the most serene phase of our relationship'.[17] Following this reconciliation, she wrote, 'our friendship continued on this heady course until 1978'.[18] Her language is characteristically decorous. Friendship is not usually described as running a 'heady course'. The tone of their relationship is illustrated by their innocent, chatty correspondence. Following his first encounter with Barbara Pym, whom he had finally arranged to meet on St George's Day 1975, in the Randolph Hotel, Oxford, he wrote to her:

> The day has turned into a really pleasant one as far as the sun is concerned – very warm & friendly. B. Pym was a bit like Joyce Grenfell, but very pleasant and accommodating.
>
> She is still under care after her mastectomy (is it?) and of course she did have a sort of stroke recently, but she seemed quite normal.
>
> How are you, dear? I hope the disagreeable impact of returning to work has worn off, and Brenda C. has come back. I dread the start of term [. . .][19]

There is a disingenuousness in his naive phrases: 'mastectomy (is it?)', 'a sort of stroke'.

He now occupied a secure place in the canon; Alan Brownjohn published a pamphlet on his work in the British Council 'Writers and their Work' series. On 16 June Harold Pinter, Charles Osborne and Ian Hamilton participated in a celebratory *Evening without Philip Larkin* at the Mermaid Theatre in London. His public image was on display at the end of May 1975 during a visit to Hull by Ted Hughes. Larkin wrote to Charles Monteith: 'He filled our hall and got a great reception. I was in the chair, providing a sophisticated, insincere, effete, and gold-watch-chained alternative to his primitive forthright virile leather-jacketed *persona*.'[20] A fortnight later he let rip more maliciously in a letter to Conquest: 'At Ilkley literature festival a woman shrieked and vomited during a Ted Hughes reading. I must say I've never felt like shrieking. We had the old crow over at Hull recently, looking like a Christmas present from Easter Island. He's all right when not reading!'[21] Larkin positioned a framed photograph taken on this occasion above the cistern of his downstairs toilet. It shows Hughes standing mid-stage, a sexually magnetic shaman, while Larkin, the poet-librarian, sits uncomfortably at a table to one side. Opposite this picture, high on the wall he hung an antique ceramic plate bearing the legend 'Prepare to Meet thy God' in ornate letters, a reminder perhaps that one should not be surprised to meet one's maker with one's trousers about one's ankles. He was making his domestic environment into a self-parody.

He now turned to his second commissioned poem, in celebration of the Humber Bridge. After initial drafts in the eighth workbook between January and 3 April 1975, Larkin bought a small dark-red 'Collins Ideal 468' hard-backed manuscript book, in which he continued drafting between the end of May and the end of July.[22] Was this perhaps because the poem was 'required' rather than 'inspired' writing? His heart was not in this celebration of community. Anthony Hedges recalls Larkin telling him that he 'felt more like writing a threnody for the things he loved about the region which the bridge would put an end to'.[23] Hedges estimated that 250 lines would be needed for a piece lasting forty minutes. In the event Larkin wrote forty lines, and when Hedges said he needed more, the poet regretted that there was nothing he could do. The composer recalls, 'I produced a long slow introduction and lots of repetition.' Larkin's ambiguous feelings about the project inhibited him from giving the work a title. Hedges headed the manuscript 'A Humberside Cantata'. But Sidney Hainsworth from Fenner, the company that had commissioned the work, insisted on the title 'Bridge for the Living'. Hedges recalled: 'Philip told me he thought it made it sound like a card game Instruction Manual for adults.'[24]

The words lend themselves well to a musical setting. The sections are clear and easily apprehended, beginning with an apostrophe to the 'Isolate city' by the sea, 'Half-turned to Europe', and continuing with contrasted word pictures of Holderness in summer and winter. The register is a pastiche of 'Here', diluted with dignified poetic diction ('Isolate', 'parley', 'manifest'). Arresting phrases catch the ear above the music:

> plain gulls stand,
> Sharp fox and brilliant pheasant walk, and wide
>
> Wind-muscled wheatfields wash round villages,
> Their churches half-submerged in leaf.

Larkin also gave Hedges the opportunity for fugato chiming effects in the lines 'Tall church-towers parley, airily audible, / Howden and Beverley, Hedon and Patrington'. The description of the suspended single span of the bridge, 'A swallow-fall and rise of one plain line', takes up, appropriately, one plain line. As the final four quatrains turn to the impact of the new bridge the first-person plural pronoun becomes prominent, asserting the new community created by the bridge: 'our solitude', 'our dear landscape', 'our lives', 'we may give', 'we are', 'we live'. Descending briefly to vacuous blarney, the poet reviews the 'Lost centuries of local lives', which fell short 'where they began', but which now 'reassemble and unclose', having been 'resurrected' by the new connections provided by the bridge. 'Here' culminated in a vision of unfenced existence, out of reach; 'Bridge for the Living', in contrast, ends with the bridge 'reaching' grandiosely 'for the world'. Nevertheless, it is a rhetorically effective work, with a memorable final line: 'Always it is by bridges that we live.'[25]

The new 'heady' relationship with Maeve, delightful and fresh though it was, was not as simply 'serene' for him as it seemed to her. Indeed the poem which it inspired is anguished and despairing. Her 'pre-marital sex' was for him touched with the anxious intensity of pre-mortality sex. When she departed for Ireland in 1975, leaving him to take his regular holiday in Scotland with Monica, he felt unaccountably bereft. He wrote to her on 7 August: 'I wish you hadn't gone away just when you did: I miss you. A fearful boiling night was diversified by two dreams about you, both "losing dreams" – you going off with someone else – wch was all very silly, for how can one lose what one does not possess?'[26] These dreams precipitated 'Love Again', on which he worked over the following months. Its title appears to be an ironic reference to the song made famous by Marlene Dietrich, 'Falling in Love Again'.[27] The poet's beloved has left a party with another man and he has returned home for an unsatisfactory wank at ten past three in the morning. In genre the poem is a blues anti-aubade of the small hours. In a bitter echo of 'Broadcast' the woman is inaccessible and the poet contemplates his imagined picture of her. But in 'Broadcast' the vision was fresh and beautiful; here it is wilfully coarsened by obscene language ('Someone else feeling her breasts and cunt'), the more shocking since Maeve was herself verbally innocent. When Motion showed her the poem after Philip's death she thought that 'wanking' was 'waking' mistyped.[28] These are the only appearances in Larkin's poetry of 'cunt' and 'wanking'. He seems to have been aware, at this last gasp of inspiration, that these key words, with the unique quality they would bring, remained to be used. Without them his oeuvre would be incomplete.

On the hard-core, impersonal level the poem depicts sex as a simple biological imperative, the time-honoured irritant of 'Dry-Point', again subjecting the poet to humiliating desire ('spilt like petrol' as he puts it in an early draft),[29] followed by the usual post-masturbatory pain, 'like dysentery'. Worse, the familiar dreary and compulsive situation opens up the long perspective of his failed bachelor life. In 'Round Another Point' in 1951 Larkin's persona, Miller, had painted a grim picture of Geraint's unmarried future: 'Well, I hope you enjoy yourself – that's about all you will enjoy [. . .] when you're sitting, a wanked-out seventy, in your third-floor bed-sitter in Bayswater staring at a hole in the carpet, waiting for the pubs to open [. . .]'[30] Now, at fifty-three, the poet finds himself already in something like this situation.

The bedroom hot as a bakery,
The drink gone dead, without showing how
To meet tomorrow [. . .]

It seems likely that the title also has a more personal, private significance. In a letter of 8 January 1946 the young Larkin had organized the first meeting between Kingsley Amis and Ruth Bowman. He ended the letter to Kingsley in his customary jokey style: 'love / philip foot-warmer'. Then, apprehensive about the coming confrontation between his abrasive masculine and gentle feminine sides, he added a long, anxious postscript detailing train times and connections. He eventually signed off for a second time: 'Love again (Don't look like that.)'[31] There seems little doubt that this casual phrase stayed with him, reminding him of this traumatic meeting, and the lifelong failure to 'sort himself out' which it symbolized.[32]

But the emotions of the poem did not affect the new 'serenity' of the relationship as it was perceived by Maeve. On 3 November, she wrote telling him not to be anxious about his forthcoming trip to London to receive the CBE: 'you are bound to carry off the occasion with grace and great dignity'. She went on to wonder at the continuing freshness of their affection:

It is very hard for me to believe that after all this time I have not grown stale for you. Needless to say, it is also the most wonderful thing that ever happened to me. It wouldn't be like that with any marriage partner after 14/15 years, so look what we have gained!

I shall look forward to hearing all about your visit to London, to see the Queen![33]

Clearly, whatever the exact nature of their renewed relationship it had brought her a deep satisfaction. Touchingly, she abandons her Catholic instincts, if only momentarily, and defers to his misogamist relish for uncommitted evanescence. A decade and a half after their relationship had begun he remained caught, with a new intensity, between his love for Maeve and his duty to Monica. When later in the month he travelled to Buckingham Palace for the CBE award ceremony, it was, of course, Monica who accompanied him.

At this point Larkin transformed his situation in the most dramatic and creative way. He brought a third woman into his life by initiating a love affair with his secretary of eighteen years, Betty Mackereth. Betty's description shows how deliberate the 'seduction' was on his part. Philip had driven Betty and Pauline Dennison, who was in charge of the Library issue desk, to a dinner at the Pipe and Glass Inn in the village of South Dalton with representatives of Castle Park Dean Hook, the architects of the new Library. Driving back at the end of the evening, Betty was puzzled that he contrived a circuitous route which involved dropping off Pauline first. When they arrived at Betty's house he surprised her by asking if she was going to invite him in for coffee. He later revealed to her that he had worked out the whole sequence beforehand. She told Andrew Motion later: 'Nothing much occurred that evening, though Philip did break a saucer! But once on the slippery slope, there seemed nothing I could do to stop (nor did I want to).'[34] The broken saucer seems oddly significant. Was it a sign of his guilt and nervousness, a symbol of transgression; or was it a careless assertion of masculine assurance?

On one level perhaps there was an impulse towards justice in this unexpected move. The new intensity of Maeve's love cannot but have sharpened his appreciation of Betty's opposite virtues, and of Betty's very different but equally devoted affection for him. Over a decade earlier, Mary Judd had detected a 'jealousy and antagonism' between the two women in relation to Philip: 'you could not have found two people more different'.[35] Betty had always felt that her own robust qualities were of more use to Philip than Maeve's naive narcissism.[36] He must frequently have felt himself, as on Lisburn Square in 1953, in the position of an early Christian between lions in the Roman arena. As his secretary, Betty would also be gratified by the absolute secrecy of the affair. After they became intimate, she immediately told him: 'Don't worry, Philip. I will never, ever say a word to anybody.'[37] Nor did she until more than a decade later, when Andrew Motion finally riddled out the clues. (She has never forgiven him.) From the point of view of his own emotions, an affair with Betty, who describes herself as 'quite unromantic',[38] would cut through the heady 'unreal' relationship with Maeve. Betty, as she says with precision, was not 'in love with' him, but over the years had grown to love him.[39] His affection for her had also become deep, and physical intimacy will have seemed a natural culmination of their long relationship. More crudely, they were both in their early fifties. It would soon be too late.

Betty recalls: 'The whole thing took me by surprise. As far as I was concerned we could have gone on as we were. We were good buddies. I worked with him. I was organized. I knew who to put straight through on the telephone: "Only Downing Street, my publisher and the VC". Of course I would also put the Chairman of the Library Committee through [. . .]'[40] She felt 'excited' by the new relationship, not having expected such a thing at her 'time of life'. Philip was finally acknowledging that their feelings went deeper than a professional relationship. One surprising element which drew them together was her misogamy. As she says: 'I knew all along, deep down, that I would never ever in this life get married.'[41] On the other hand her relationship with Philip had some aspects of a marriage: 'I knew everything a wife knows, more than some wives know, probably.'[42] She was enough of a woman of the world to be unconcerned by his taste for pornography, and in an echo of the swearing episode with his colleague in the Warwick Fuel Office in 1942, they had developed that most intimate of relationships for men and women of their generation: one in which obscenity was allowed. By the 1970s, when he irritated her at work she would explode, 'Well, *fuck you!*' and then reproach him for teaching her such bad habits.[43] Maeve, she knew, would be quite unable to understand any of this.

The affair was happy and long lasting. Over the remaining years, until Monica came to live in Newland Park, Betty would visit him occasionally in the evenings, leaving badminton in Hull at 9.00, and taking a shower before going to Newland Park. She would not go earlier because by this time, their written correspondence in decline, Philip rang Monica every night at 8 o'clock and they spoke for an hour. If, by chance, Betty did happen to be there earlier, he would have to leave her in bed and go downstairs for the phone call with Monica. She recalls:

'And if he didn't ring she would have to know why. Where had he been? What had he been doing?'[44] Philip and Betty would also take occasional day and weekend trips together to the Wolds or the North York Moors around Kirbymoorside. Their secret was not difficult to keep.

Another motive for this affair also irresistibly suggests itself. Larkin realized that it would give him a last precious access to poetic inspiration. The sexual intensification of his relationship with Maeve had revived the theme of love in his poetry, dormant since the abandonment of 'The Dance' over a decade earlier. But 'Love Again' was refusing to come right. Its tangled obscenity also suggests that, in descending to sex, the untouched muse of 'Broadcast' had become, on some level, spoiled. In a middle-aged version of the youthful lover on Keats's urn, the poet is racked, in his desolate attic, by the 'burning forehead' and 'parching tongue' of consummation. After having worked on the poem since August he abandoned it for the time being on 16 December. If he was ever to write love poetry, or muse poetry, again it would have to be in a new relationship. He turned instead, two days later, to his first poem addressed to Betty, completing 'When first we faced, and touching showed' on 20 December 1975.

'Face' (or 'faces') occurs, as noun or verb, forty-eight times in Larkin's poetry after 1945. The husband in 'To My Wife' regrets having exchanged 'all faces' for 'your face'. In 'Maiden Name' the five light syllables no longer 'mean your face'. In 'An Arundel Tomb' the earl's and countess's faces are movingly 'blurred' by the passage of the years. In 'The Dance' 'I face you on the floor', uncomfortably. In 'Broadcast' the poet pictures 'your face among all those faces'. 'Here' ends raptly, 'facing the sun', while in 'Solar' the sun's 'Suspended lion face' gives for ever. In 'Vers de Société' the phrase 'forks and faces' sums up the inane sterility of social life.[45] It is only in 'When first we faced' that Larkin uses the word as an intransitive verb, and with an unusually active connotation. There is a hidden intimacy here. Betty is much taller than Monica Jones or Maeve Brennan, closer to Larkin's height, so she 'faced' him more directly than they could.[46] The poem is a new version of 'Latest Face' written twenty-six years earlier, revised to fit lovers in their fifties. This face is not the object of aesthetic reverence that Winifred's had been in 1950. Behind the lover's 'inch-close eyes' lie the decades of a different life inaccessible to the poet, which 'Belonged to others'. Both poet and beloved are laden with depreciating luggage. Nevertheless this is his most tenderly affectionate love poem. Their middle-aged affair possesses the newness of first love:

> But when did love not try to change
> The world back to itself – no cost,
> No past, no people else at all –
> Only what meeting made us feel [. . .]

'I love you' is always a quotation, but everyone who says the words feels his or her situation to be unique. Even the last face is also a latest face. Larkin sent Betty a copy of the poem on 30 December. As if to under-line the complexity of his emotional life at this time, on the following day, the last of the year, he wrote to Maeve: 'I am very close to Monica and very fond of her . . . But it's you I *love*; you're the one I want.'[47] At the age of fifty-three he was involved in three intensely committed relationships.

At the end of 1975 and early in 1976 Larkin wrote four more substan-tial poems addressed to Betty. How largely did the promise of new poetic occasions feature in his decision to embark on the relationship? As an artist, Larkin certainly grasped every poetic opportunity Betty offered. The poems cover the widest spectrum of sharply differentiated styles. The initial warm love poem 'When first we faced' was followed less than a month later by a witty and subtle sonnet 'Dear Jake', which he sent to her on 23 January 1976. Well before their affair began, the appetite of 'Texas' for his manuscripts had become a joke between them. On 18 January 1969 he wrote to Betty from Loughborough about Library business, signing off 'Love as ever Philip', followed by a care-fully stippled imitation of a circular stamp reading 'TEXAS / MSS / 487'. On the card which accompanied 'When first we faced' he referred to the way British literary manuscripts were being bought up by the Harry Ransom Center in Austin. His typescript, he was aware, had a commercial value: 'Flog it to Texas if it seems embarrassing.'[48] In 'Dear

Jake' he elaborated this idea into a witty satire on Balokowsky, the academic biographer from 'Posterity'. In 'Posterity', Jake had 'this page microfilmed'. When I first wrote this paragraph in 2011, 'Dear Jake' had not yet been published, and I was reading it from my own digital photograph of Larkin's typescript. In 1976 Larkin was already wrong-footing any Jake or James who might eventually come on the scene.

The poem cites Balokowsky's account of 'the last singular comic episode' in his subject's love life, in which he accuses the poet of unloading 'love and pain and duty' on to one who was not fitted to cope with them, and assumes that she 'must have been thankful when it ceased'. The implied circumstances of Jake's account exactly match Larkin's biography. Four lives are threatened by the 'singular' affair, and its victim has been mentioned earlier 'on page thirty', when Betty's appointment in 1957 would have been recorded. But the biographer's language observes the decorum demanded by his University press, and the poet finds his mealy-mouthed pretence irritating: 'I know you really mean "Hey, Mac, / This old goat was so crazy for a fuck he –"'. This is the only appearance of 'a fuck' in Larkin's poetry; the verb has been used once in each of its idiomatic senses, as a participle ('fucking') in 'High Windows', and in the metaphorical phrase 'fuck up' in 'This Be The Verse'. Here, as a noun, its force has a unique brutality. The octave runs smoothly into the sestet, the temperature rising up to Jake's accusatory obscenity, which the poet then interrupts with weary resignation. After this, the final three lines have the quality of a combative retort:

> Well, it was singular; but, looking back,
> Only what men do get, if they are lucky.
> And when it came there was no thought of age.

From beneath the elaborate hijinks of the posthumous poet's address to his biographer emerges a delicate compliment addressed in the present to the lover herself. What to Jake is 'singular' in the sense of ridiculous is to the poet 'singular' in its precious uniqueness. As one might expect, the word 'singular' does not occur elsewhere in Larkin's poetry.[49]

The next poem presents yet another contrast. In February 1976 Larkin gave Betty a typed copy of 'Morning at last: there in the snow', his purest, most classically impersonal aubade.[50] In his Booker Prize Chairman's speech of the following year he reflected that whereas in novels 'the emotion has to be attached to a human being, and the human being has to be attached to a particular time and a particular place', the poem, in contrast, 'is a single emotional spear-point, a concentrated effect that is achieved by leaving everything out but the emotion itself'.[51] The lovers in this poem are ungendered, without indication of age or cultural baggage, and the relationship is reduced to a charged metonym: the 'small blunt footprints'. A lover has stepped in and out of the poet's life through that universal symbol of transience, snow. When the footprints have been washed out by the rain, the lovers will be left with 'What morning woke to'. The form is as simple as possible: three tetrameter triplets with a progression of plangent diphthong rhymes from a long back 'oh' ('snow / go / show'), through a high front 'i' ('wine / sign / mine') to a low front 'ai' ('rain / remain / pain'). The progression enacts a primitive emotional sequence, 'oh – eye – eh', like the formula of a sigh. The simplicity of this poem asserts the anti-ironic spirit which is so frequently the key to Larkin's emotional power.[52]

Larkin drafted 'When first we faced' and 'Morning at last' in the final, eighth workbook and made typed copies. The workbook also shows two pages of heavily corrected drafting for 'Dear Jake', dated '22.1.76'. However, the final drafting of 'Dear Jake' and the drafts of the remaining two works addressed to Betty, 'Be my Valentine this Monday' and 'We met at the end of the party', were written not in the workbook but instead at the end of the small manuscript book in which he had drafted 'Bridge for the Living' in the summer of 1975. Perhaps he was making a confused attempt at privacy. The workbook was less central to his writing process in the final stage of his career, when he knew he was no longer accumulating works for another volume. Nor could there be any possibility of publishing these particular poems during his lifetime, though the fact that he left typescripts of three of the four major poems surely indicates that he intended them to survive and become part of his oeuvre.

Years before, Philip had given Betty a comical soft toy crocodile to symbolize her role as the guardian of his privacy. On St Valentine's Day, Saturday 14 February 1976, knowing he was to be away at the beginning of the week, he left a card for Betty on her desk, depicting a grinning alligator with the caption 'See you later alligator!' and continuing inside, 'You tasty morsel!' The two stanzas written opposite the caption are light in tone, but have a hidden emotional complexity. He asks her to be his Valentine and to 'hyphen' with his heart (an appropriate image for someone who typed his letters, perhaps), even though they cannot be together on the day.

> You are fine as summer weather,
> May to August all in one,
> And the clocks, when we're together,
> Count no shadows. Only sun.

There is a hint of menace perhaps in this extraordinary image. Ever since he moved into the east-facing room in Wellington at the beginning of 1946, inescapable light had been for him an image of both euphoric epiphany and threatening exposure. Here, in a weird twist, the sundials stop the passage of time by 'casting sun' rather than shadow. Her sunny vitality leaves him no place to hide.

He sent the final poem, 'We met at the end of the party', to Betty from All Souls, Oxford, on 22 February 1976.[53] It offers another sharp contrast, being in a mixture of anapaests and iambs, a metre well suited to companionable chattiness. The imagery, however, is powerfully symbolic, and in a unique blend of genres it is both self-elegiac lyric and muse poem. By turning from Maeve to Betty, Larkin had replaced his spoiled muse of innocent beauty with an ageing muse of vitality, more relevant to his situation. Betty was 'certainly never ill' and was always 'full of energy'.[54] She was no physically untouchable conventional muse. She was tantalizing and out of reach in the vision of longevity which she embodied.

The poet and his lover encounter each other at the end of the party of life, when the drinks are dead and the glasses 'dirty'.[55] The sulky poet is bitterly convinced that his life is a spoiled remnant; she however, cheerful and optimistic, encourages him to make the best of what remains: '"Have this that's left," you said.' The second stanza follows the same syntactical sequence as the first but the imagery shifts to the seasons:

> We walked through the last of summer,
> When shadows reached long and blue
> Across days that were growing shorter:
> You said: 'There's autumn too.'

Autumn is too late for him. The precious moment of incipience has gone. This unromantic beloved is another of Larkin's muses of ordinary life: a real girl in a real place. What had made the young Larkin long to be the breathless girl in 'I see a girl dragged by the wrists' was not her beauty but her abandoned submission to life. This older muse also embraces willingly what life offers. She moves on, unafraid of the future: 'Always for you what's finished / Is nothing, and what survives / Cancels the failed, the famished.' There is a hint of nagging reproach in his words. He is intimidated by her ability to act as though they 'had fresh lives' from the moment of their meeting, as if:

> just living
> Could make me unaware
> Of June, and the guests arriving,
> And I not there.

The phrase 'just living' stumbles metrically and the final line disappoints the reader with only two stresses instead of three.

In 'Fourth Former Loquitur' three decades earlier, pathos was generated by a long perspective which transferred time into place. Having played out the cricket match to its close, the schoolgirls had gone to join the 'old girls' in the metaphorical pavilion of adulthood, leaving the fourth-former contemplating Jill's hat left behind, and the grass newly flattened by their girlish bodies. Now this long perspective is reversed. Where the fourth-former looked forward elegiacally from a vivid youthful present into a future of age and death, the poet in 'We met at the end of the party' looks back from an aged present to the vivid party of his young life, still about to begin. By the same elision of time with place he sees the guests arriving in June, while he, decades later in autumn, is unable to find his way back to greet them.

Betty recalls the debates between them which this poem distils: 'He said to me one day: "I can't understand why you, on waking in the morning, don't think of death." And I just looked at him and I said: "I cannot understand why you, on waking in the morning, *think* of death."' It is a poignant variation on the pattern of yearning poet and heartless muse. 'He said to me: "My father died when he was sixty-three" (I mean, he was *miserable*), "and I expect I shall die when I'm sixty-three." And I said: "Yes you will, because you are programming yourself to die at sixty-three."'[56] Though he criticized Sylvia Plath for living out a predetermined self-destructive myth in her work, in his own way Larkin followed Plath's example. He did die at the age of sixty-three, of the same disease as his father. As I write, in early 2011, Betty has, at the age of eighty-six, just set out in the snow for a Bridge Week at Scarborough. She only recently gave up her regular golf engagements, and braved the bitter cold to attend the unveiling of Larkin's statue on Paragon Station on his death day in 2010.

22

Death-Throes of a Talent
1976–9

In spring 1976 Larkin made his first excursion into Europe since his visit to Paris with Bruce Montgomery in 1952. He had been awarded the Shakespeare Prize of the Alfred Toepfer Stiftung F.V.S. Foundation, established in 1931 to promote European unification. It was a significant accolade; the prize had recently been awarded to Graham Greene, Harold Pinter and Peter Brook. Larkin, however, declared himself reluctant to have anything to do with 'those Nazis'.[1] He and Monica flew to Hamburg on 19 April, attended the ceremony on 20 April and flew back the next day. In a spirit of polite antagonism he made fun in his acceptance speech of the international 'circuit' of prizes and readings. In illustration of 'the miseries of the lecture tour' he quoted Auden's 'On the Circuit': 'very funny, but I think [. . .] rather dreadful too; the lecture circuit suddenly comes to resemble one of those other circuits described in Dante's *Inferno*'.[2] Nevertheless, writing afterwards to Winifred Bradshaw (formerly Arnott), he guiltily relished the hotel mini-bar which, since the Foundation was bearing their expenses, he and Monica had raided freely for half-bottles of champagne. He added more soberly: 'All these honours seem ironic; when I was really doing good stuff, no one knew or cared; now all these compliments are paid, and I can't write a line.' Taking stock of his life, he continued: 'To marry wd be an awfully big adventure, as Peter Pan nearly said, but I can't say my feelings on the subject have altered much. I suppose, if I

really have stopped writing, I might risk it.'³ The adventure to which
Peter Pan actually refers is, of course, death.

Also stressful was his appearance on BBC Radio's *Desert Island
Discs* programme. In a letter of 30 May 1976 he told his mother that
he was slowly recovering from the recording: 'I didn't think it went at
all well, principally because I was very nervous.'⁴ To contradict his
reputation for reactionary conservatism he chose Bernard Shaw's
Complete Plays as his book. He made a point of not listening to the
programme when it was broadcast on 17 July 1976. His correspondence with Conquest, Amis and Gunner was more peppered than ever
with splenetic outbursts:

> I want to see them starving,
>   The so-called working class,
> Their wages weekly halving,
>   Their women stewing grass [. . .]⁵

His holiday with Monica in 1976 was spent in the West Country,
where they visited the Hardy Museum in Dorchester. He wrote to
Barbara Pym: 'did you know he kept a calendar on his desk, set to
the day he met his first wife? Kept it all through his second
marriage till he died. What wives have to put up with!'⁶

In September he began the task of reading over and 'boiling down'
his diaries. He told Conquest: 'the idea is that I shall then burn them'.
It seems that he intended to preserve the 'boiled down' version,
though there is an odd (perhaps deliberate) ambiguity in his phrasing. But the project was doomed from the start. Though he whimsically
anticipated a time when he would be writing his diary one day,
'boiling it down' the next and burning it the next, he had so far
advanced only as far as 1940.⁷ Despite his sensitivity about his diaries
there is no evidence that they were as utterly disgusting as Andrew
Motion imagines: full of 'bile, resentment, envy and misanthropy',
functioning as:

a sexual log book full of masturbatory fantasies, and a repository for his rage against the world – his grimmest, sexiest, most angry thoughts [. . .] Even his most candid letters only hint at their intensity. To gauge the anger we might think of the sometimes seethingly bitter things he wrote to Sutton as a young man, then multiply them.[8]

The reference is puzzling since the Sutton letters are not notable for their seethingly bitter tone.

Over the years he had continued to encourage Barbara Pym in her attempts to write a novel which could be published. In 1968 he had commented on *The Sweet Dove Died*: 'there's more potential feeling in this book than in any you have written [. . .] I think it could be a strong, sad book, with fewer characters and slower movement.'[9] Lyric poetry had always meant a great deal to Pym and she was particularly impressed by 'Faith Healing', 'Ambulances' and 'Posterity'.[10] It was partly because of Larkin's influence that Pym left behind the cosiness of the earlier work. She includes a quotation from 'Ambulances' in her account of Marcia's pathetic last hours in *Quartet in Autumn*. In 1976 Larkin and Monica Jones visited Pym and her sister in their cottage in Finstock, where they stood together at T. S. Eliot's grave. On 27 September he wrote of the draft of what was to become *Quartet in Autumn*: 'It's so strange to find the level good-humoured tender irony of your style unchanged but dealing with the awful end of life: I admire you enormously for bringing it off so well.' He even offered to provide financial help: 'could you ask whether a *subsidy* wd make any differ-ence, &, if so, what it would have to be? Do please try. Or I will try if you like. Let me know.'[11] When in November she told him that she had received yet another rejection[12] he named her in the 'most underrated' author section of the 1976 *Times Literary Supplement* Christmas book feature. By chance Lord David Cecil made the same choice. Interest in Pym at once revived and Larkin responded by writing the essay he had planned years before. 'Something to Love: The World of Barbara Pym' was published in the *Times Literary Supplement* in January 1977.[13] After years of neglect Pym was approached by publishers and her earlier novels were reprinted.

At home in Hull, Larkin gave his support to a campaign to preserve the picturesque wilderness of Spring Bank Cemetery, near to Pearson Park. In February he travelled to his childhood home to receive the Coventry Award of Merit in the City's Guildhall. In the same month, he and Kingsley Amis attended a performance of *Larkinland*, an arrangement of poems and jazz made by Michael Kustow, the Associate Director of the National Theatre.[14] Larkin acted as Chair of the 1977 Booker Prize Panel, taking a pile of the long-listed novels with him to Scotland on his holiday with Monica in the summer. He favoured Pym's *Quartet in Autumn*, with its moving portrayal of loneliness and paranoia, but the award went to Paul Scott's *Staying On*.

On 1 September 1977 a sharp reminder of mortality came with the death of Patsy Strang. He wrote later to Amis: 'Did you know Patsy was dead? [. . .] Found literally dead drunk, it seems – empty Cointreau bottle, ½ empty Benedictine bottle. Fascinating mixture, what.'[15] Robert Lowell died a fortnight after Patsy, and Larkin tactfully declined an invitation from his widow to speak at the memorial service.[16] After the last poem addressed to Betty in February 1976 poetry had all but deserted him, the only significant new work in 1977 being a fragile love poem written in a copy of *Thorburn's Mammals* which he gave to Monica: 'The little lives of earth and form, / Of finding food, and keeping warm, / Are not like ours, and yet [. . .]' Rather than a sentimental poem it is a meditation on the sentimental fictions with which we fend off hard reality. Abstracting Beatrix Potter into symbolist metaphor, the poet evokes a close-up world as it might appear through rabbit eyes: 'I see [. . .] / The flattened grass, the swaying stalk, / And it is you I see.' From the outside, however, this well-worn relationship could look very different. Martin Amis remembers, 'In Monica's presence, Larkin behaved like the long-suffering nephew of an uncontrollably eccentric aunt.'[17]

During the summer of 1977 he worked on 'Aubade', abandoned in the middle of the third stanza in June 1974 during his final days in Pearson Park. Over the three months between 18 May and 18 August 1977, he completed the third stanza and reached a near-final version of the last two, filling nine pages with continuous, closely worked redrafts.

His revisions make the poem more incisive and authoritative. He introduces the spoiled lyricism of sing-song nursery rhyme: 'nothing to think with, / Nothing to love or link with'; 'Being brave / Lets no one off the grave'. And he reduces the faint transcendence of 'the open emptiness for ever' to the bleak prose of 'the total emptiness for ever'. In the third stanza he dismisses with crushing finality both theological and secular arguments against the fear of death. The brief nostalgia of the 'vast, moth-eaten musical brocade' of religion is rejected as wishful thinking which we have now outgrown. But equally ineffectual is the materialist rationalizing of death, derived ultimately from Epicurus:

> And specious stuff that says *No rational being*
> *Can fear a thing it will not feel*, not seeing
> That this is what we fear – no sight, no sound,
> No touch or taste or smell [. . .][18]

'The anaesthetic from which none come round' is not a figure of speech, but a literal definition of death, from the Greek *an-aesthesis*, the negation of the senses. Recently the philosopher Richard Rorty has attempted to reopen this debate, arguing that '"fear of extinction" is an unhelpful phrase. There is no such thing as fear of inexistence as such, but only fear of some concrete loss.'[19] This is a distinction without a difference. Inexistence consists precisely of the concrete loss of vision, hearing, touch, taste or smell, and Larkin fears this loss. Moreover it is quite possible to imagine the state of being without one's senses, and to fear being reduced for ever to that state. There is nothing forced or tenuous about what Larkin called his 'in-a-funk-about-death poem'.[20]

The final stanza dramatizes 'The death-throes of a talent'[21] with ruthless candour. Metaphor, threatened from the beginning of the poem, collapses completely. The light 'strengthens', and the poet is granted his epiphany: 'It stands plain as a wardrobe, what we know'. Larkin no doubt has in mind Auden's bedroom intimation of mortality: 'The glacier knocks in the cupboard, / The desert sighs in the bed, / And the crack in the tea-cup opens / A lane to the land of the dead.'[22] But where Auden's metaphors are extravagant and masterful, Larkin's prosy metonym sounds flat and unrhetorical. As an image of 'what we know' this wardrobe is the hollowest of metaphors. It is scarcely even figurative. As an upended wooden box it is almost a coffin already.[23] As in 'Going' we are presented with a transparent riddle, the answer to which is 'death'. This is metaphor *in extremis*. The inverted, Larkinesque construction, 'It stands [. . .] what we know,' throws the weight of meaning cruelly on to the stark 'what' noun phrase. The live emotional charge of 'what I am' in 'Best Society', or 'What will survive of us' in 'An Arundel Tomb', short-circuits to a resigned 'what we know'. A more relevant intertext than Auden is perhaps John Wilmot, whose blunt atheist assertion, 'Dead, wee become the Lumber of the World', has a similar anti-poetic poetry.[24] In 'The Building' the death-bound patients saw unattainable beauty in a prosaic glimpse of ordinary life. But here the 'girls in hairdos' coming from the cleaners are replaced by a less consoling symbol of everyday life: telephones crouching, 'getting ready to ring', in a world where 'Work has to be done', and postmen and doctors 'go from house to house' ministering to our needs with the contents of their bags.[25] But for all its threats and ambiguities this dawn world of offices, typewriters and letters, under a clay-white sky, is still infinitely preferable to 'sure extinction'.

On 17 November 1977 came the death that mattered most. His mother, already for many months in the twilight of the old fools, died at the age of ninety-one. His dearest old creature was no longer there to expect his next letter. The following day Larkin kept an appointment with Anthony Thwaite at All Souls College, and asked his Anglican friend to accompany him to college prayers in the morning: 'I think my mother would have liked that.'[26] He had left 'Aubade' all but complete just over three months earlier, on 18 August. A week or so after his mother's death he returned to it, and on a single page, with '28.11.1977' at the top and '29.11.1977' at the bottom, he redrafted the last stanza. The final touch seems to have been the insertion of the achingly moving phrases 'all the uncaring / Intricate rented world begins to rouse'. Only minor adjustments were made in the subsequent typescript. His 'final' poem was at last complete. 'Aubade' was published in the *Times Literary Supplement* on 23 December 1977. He grimly anticipated the number of Christmas dinners it would spoil.

With 'Aubade' he consciously signalled that his oeuvre was complete, and his creative life was over. He was to succeed in blowing the embers briefly into life on only five further occasions over the remaining eight years of his life.[27] By the end of 1977 he had made his contribution to each genre and form; he had explored every verbal possibility open to him. His art was his life, and his grasp on life depended on his poetry. If new inspiration did not come in answer to his waiting he could not force it. Writing a poem, as he said, was 'not an act of the will'. The death of his art in 1977 was as natural and inevitable a process as his biological death in 1985. A flower which has bloomed cannot remake itself as a bud.

However, life went on, and work had to be done. In his daily life his instinct for blithe wit remained undiminished. In January 1978, he received a letter from the Friends of Dove Cottage telling him that, following a recent donation, he had been made a life member. He replied: 'In fact I was similarly enrolled a few years ago, when I made a similar generous donation, as you so kindly put it, so I now have the distinction of being a life member twice over. I very much fear, however, that they will have to run concurrently.'[28] Larkin now found himself saddled with the task of writing a third commissioned work. Fortunately it was a relatively minor affair: a quatrain celebrating the Queen's Jubilee to be engraved in Queen's Square, Bloomsbury near Faber's office. Ted Hughes, Faber's next most prominent poet, was also to provide a quatrain. Larkin wrote to Monteith at Faber on 2 March:

I'm no good at this lapidary lark. All three nights' thought can produce is

> In times when nothing stood
> But worsened, or grew strange,
> There was one constant good:
> She did not change.[29]

You are welcome to first British chiselling rights in that, but please don't print it. I'm sure Ted will do better.

He could not resist adding his own imagined version of Hughes's poem, in the style of *Crow*:

> The sky split apart in malice
> Stars rattled like pans on a shelf
> Crow shat on Buckingham Palace
> God pissed Himself —[30]

It is an amusing comment on the fate of official, public verse that Larkin's pastiche of Hughes will be more familiar to readers than either poet's official quatrain.[31]

A fortnight later Larkin finally and momentously 'sorted himself out' in relation to Maeve. After her mother's death in May 1977, she had moved with her father into a smaller semi-detached house in St Margaret's Close, Cottingham, and Philip had helped with the move, changing all the plugs on their appliances.[32] But by early 1978 it seems that he had come to a final decision that this unequal, 'unreal' relationship could no longer be sustained. There is an appearance of deliberation, irritation even, about his actions. On 16 March 1978, following its successful run in London, *Larkinland* was performed in the Middleton Hall in the University. Philip attended with Maeve, and she naturally expected to accompany him to the reception in Staff House afterwards. However, as they left the Hall he insisted on going on alone. She was forced to find a friend to drive her home.

> With Philip as the guest of honour, and me as his escort, it should have been an enjoyable evening for both of us. Alas, it turned out to be disastrous and resulted in the abrupt termination of our long intimacy. I still find it distressing to recall the details, let alone write about them [. . .] When we met a few days later, Philip had finally determined to end the vacillation of eighteen years and henceforth pledge himself to Monica Jones. I reluctantly accepted his decision: what else could I do?[33]

Philip wrote to her: 'I realize that you are very hurt, and that this explains the angry home truths [. . .] I know most of these are justified (not quite all), but they leave their sting. Perhaps when we feel better we can meet again. I don't say this vindictively: I am extremely sad about it all.'³⁴ There is anger between the lines, and he stands his ground.

Bereft of poetic inspiration, Larkin was fully occupied with literary business. Though he avoided contact with the University's English Department, he took an interest in a new lecturer, Andrew Motion, later to become his biographer. In a letter to Anthony Thwaite of 29 January 1978 he gave a thumbnail sketch: 'Like a latterday Stephen Spender – very tall, sissy voice, gentlemanly, good-looking, all that. I quite like him.'³⁵ In spring 1978 Larkin wrote an essay on Hull's first major poet, Andrew Marvell, for the tercentenary of his death.³⁶ In May a well-written letter from the young Vikram Seth, then a student of Economics at Stanford, induced him to break his usual rule of polite refusal to give advice to aspiring poets. He responded that he had read Seth's work with 'great interest and a good deal of enjoyment', though he felt that the subjects he dealt with were 'not quite as advanced' as his technique. He undertook to show Seth's poems to an editor whom he was to meet later in the week. There may not have been much substance in this promise. In July he wrote that he had been disappointed that the editor had 'not been very impressed by your poems'.³⁷

In July the Royal Society of Literature made Larkin a Companion of Literature. He agreed also to become an adviser to the committee revising the New English Bible, but the task was not congenial and he soon resigned.³⁸ In September 1978 Bruce Montgomery died. Latterly Montgomery had become an alcoholic and both Larkin and Amis had been embarrassed by his requests for loans. But Larkin was grateful for the part the confident, cosmopolitan young Montgomery had played in his early career. He wrote to Kingsley Amis on 19 September: 'I wish I'd seen more of Bruce when he was still on top of things. Whatever one thought of his books, and his sense (sometimes) of what was funny or desirable, he was an original nobody else was the least like, don't you think?'³⁹

As the year drew to its end Larkin succeeded in drafting a wan but deeply affecting poem, 'The Winter Palace'. In ramshackle, sometimes double-rhymed couplets ('older / shoulder; century / university') starkly separated on the page, the poet gives a brutally reductive account of his life. His second quarter-century was spent losing what he had learnt at university, and he is now beginning to experience bouts of forgetfulness. He welcomes these 'senior moments' (as we would now call them), since they blank out awareness of the damage of age, providing a foretaste of oblivion: 'Then there will be nothing I know. / My mind will fold into itself, like fields, like snow.' The 'palace' of the title is another withdrawing room of the mind, 'cleared of me'. But this thought now prompts weary resignation rather than awe or euphoria. His poetic spirits were so low that he failed to finalize the poem. The third and fourth lines, as printed in the 1988 *Collected Poems*, have been crossed out in the typescript, and the alternative wording at the bottom of the page reaches no clear alternative.[40] Burnett consequently excludes the poem from *The Complete Poems*, as unfinished.

An eloquent epitaph on Philip's relationship with Maeve is provided by a Christmas card which he sent to her at the end of 1978. It falls into the 'devout *and* beautiful' category, showing a reproduction of a Botticelli Madonna. Following the conventional printed greeting he has written simply 'and love / from / Philip'. The small size of the card (four inches square) made it useful as a bookmark and it survived in a well-fingered state in one of Maeve's books.[41] She intensified its 'devout' aspect by copying out four lengthy inscriptions into the blank spaces, one of them relating to the Pope's visit to Ireland in 1979: 'By governing with fidelity those entrusted to his care may he, as successor to the Apostle Peter and vicar of Christ, build your church into a sacrament of unity, love and peace for all the world.' Facing Philip's inscription Maeve has written another prayer: 'Father, we pray that the healing Power of your Sacraments may give us peace [. . .]' There is something moving about the way the flowing strokes of Larkin's fountain-pen are hemmed about on all sides by the neat ballpoint of Maeve's piety. Underneath the second prayer she has copied out a couplet which appealed to her poetic taste: 'I heard a bird sing in the dark of December. / A magical thing and sweet to remember.'[42]

The fiftieth anniversary of the foundation of the University's Library fell on 8 March 1979. For the occasion Larkin wrote the delicate verse

'New eyes each year', and the Deputy Librarian Brenda Moon oversaw its printing in a limited edition on the Library's recently purchased 1833 Albion press. Philip also wrote two more private poems for the occasion. On the inside cover of Brenda's copy of 'New eyes', he addressed his deputy in 'The daily things we do'. But the poem he wrote in Betty Mackereth's copy, 'New Brooms', has a more intimate warmth:

> New brooms sweep clean,
> They say, and mean
> Change and decay,
> Things brushed away;
> But for old rooms
> Where life has been
> And love seen,
> Keep the old brooms.

The touching play on the familiar proverb gives this poem more feeling than the other two.

In March 1979 Larkin had seen a hedgehog several times in his Newland Park back garden, and had fed and taken photographs of it. Then on 10 June he wrote to Judy Egerton: 'This has been rather a depressing day: killed a hedgehog when mowing the lawn, by accident of course. It's upset me rather.'[43] With Betty the following morning he was less reticent. She recollects: 'I could always tell what sort of day it was going to be from his mood when he came in. But this day it was different from anything. He just stood at the window of his office, looking out, and said: "I mowed the lawn last night; and I killed the hedgehog." And the tears rolled down his face.'[44] The following day, 12 June 1979, he devoted a single page of workbook drafting to a poem, 'The Hedgehog', subsequently retitling it 'The Mower' and making one or two adjustments in the typescript.[45] The animal elegy goes back to Catullus' poem on Lesbia's sparrow, and there are familiar examples by William Cowper, Elizabeth Barrett Browning and Matthew Arnold. Larkin's contribution to the form is unique in its gravity. Rhyme is natural in this sentimental, relatively light genre, and the rhymelessness of Larkin's poem sounds like a denial of consolation. The poem is also rendered verbally distinctive by one of Larkin's unique 'un-' words: 'I had mauled its unobtrusive world / Unmendably.'

> The first day after a death, the new absence
> Is always the same; we should be careful
>
> Of each other, we should be kind
> While there is still time.

Though this is a mere animal, its passing is registered as 'a death', as if it were a human being. 'Next morning I got up and it did not': the homespun idiom asserts common human and animal life-rhythms. Some readers may feel uneasy at this. Hedgehogs are nocturnal animals and do not 'get up' in the morning. Is this hedgehog perhaps a little too close to Mrs Tiggy-Winkle?[46]

On 21–2 March, Larkin had attended the second meeting of the new Manuscripts Group of SCONUL in King's College London, and delivered a version of his influential essay 'A Neglected Responsibility', warning of the threat of contemporary British poetic manuscripts being acquired by American libraries.[47] In a letter of 20 March 1979 Ted Hughes wrote to him asking him to join Charles Causley, Seamus Heaney and himself on the Arvon Foundation poetry competition prize panel. Hughes took the opportunity to tell Larkin that he had written him a fan letter on reading 'Aubade', though he had not sent it: 'a really great poem – an event'.[48] Hughes's admiration did not prevent Larkin from making his usual jokes to his friends when Hughes revisited Hull in August 1979 for another reading. A 'Meet Ted Hughes' reception was advertised at a cost of £4.50. Larkin wrote to Winifred: 'Feel like walking up & down outside with a placard reading "Meet P.L. for £3.95".'[49]

What was to be Larkin's last-completed major poem, 'Love Again', had been left unfinished in December 1975, at which time the first stanza and first two lines of the second had reached their final version. Larkin had already formulated the crucial twist of the argument, in which the speaker turns impatiently away from his sterile sexual jealousy: 'But why put it into words?' But the remainder of the second stanza needed to be finalized. His 1975 draft concluded with a vision of failure and mortality, as 'fear-locked squalid pain' spreads in 'other lives' and, in a moving final rhyme: 'death comes easily as rain'.[50] But much slow and discontinuous drafting still lay ahead. In March 1976 and again, after nearly two years in December 1977, he had returned to the draft in the workbook, developing the image of the tree, which spreads harmoniously in other lives, in an echo of Yeats's 'Among School Children'.[51] Then on 15 August 1978, apparently prompted by the sight of Maeve at a party with her new partner, David Bassett, a lecturer in South East Asian Studies, Larkin began the final pages of drafting, copying out the poem again from the beginning each time. At the end of one draft he wrote: '21.9.78 RBM's funeral'. After two months, on 25 October 1978, he had reached the final version of all but the last three lines, which were to provide the explanation of 'why it never worked for me'. But here the poem faltered into inscrutably private references: 'There would need to have been a great difference / A long way back, and the rewards / Might not have meant much personally [. . .]'[52] He left space on the page for the conclusion, and turned his attention in the workbook to 'The Winter Palace', 'The Mower' and a poem entitled 'Letters to my mind'.

Then, as the inserted dates show, nearly a year later, on 20 September 1979, he turned back with inspired decisiveness to the final page of the 1978 draft and added the resonant conclusion:

> Something to do with violence
> A long way back, and wrong rewards,
> And arrogant eternity.

The pattern remains as first conceived, with a Larkinesque modulation from irritable self-analysis to universal elegy. It also has a unique form, consisting of ababcb stanzas, linked together by the same c-rhyme: 'afterwards / words / rewards'. But now it ends in a tone of eloquent magnanimity rather than elegiac resignation. The penultimate two

lines rephrase 'They fuck you up, your mum and dad' with tragic gravity. But the ultimate reason why it never worked for the poet lies beyond
the problems of his childhood, in his awareness of 'arrogant eternity'.
The earlier diminuendo ending, 'And death comes easily as rain', is
replaced by a rhetorical cymbal clash. This is in some ways an atypical
poem, written, as the halting drafting process shows, at a time when
Larkin was forced to tend his inspiration carefully.

His next serious poem to be completed would have been 'Letters to
my mind', which occupies five pages of the final workbook, ending on
a page dated at the top '20.11.79'. The poet asks his mind: 'Are you still
on my side?' He complains that it is not 'friendly' of his mind to be
constantly replaying the 'fool-film of me', scalding him with humiliating recollections. What, he asks his mind, does it really want? Is it to be
'folded cleanly', 'waiting emptily' in a state of senile dementia? The
draft falters into unpunctuated silence:

> So that I know no more
> Today – or even less –
> Than when we first

The remainder of the page is blank.[53]

Late in 1979, shortly after the publication of Barry Bloomfield's
bibliography, Larkin agreed to give two interviews intended to
consolidate his public image. The first, with Miriam Gross of the
Observer, appeared in November, and the second, with John
Haffenden, appeared in the April/May 1980 issue of the *London
Magazine*. Both are interviews in the loosest sense, since Larkin has
clearly polished every phrase. The *Observer* piece, particularly, is
packed with brittle and outrageous aphorisms as quotable as anything
in Oscar Wilde. He dislikes public readings, he says, because 'I don't
want to go around pretending to be me.' But this very 'interview' is
itself the most histrionic of self-impersonations. He proves his claim
to be 'quite funny' with provocative aphorisms: 'most people *are*
unhappy, don't you think?'; 'you can't write more than two hours a
day and after that what do you do? Probably get into trouble.' He

gives an Amisian caricature of his early novelistic ambition: 'I'd had visions of myself writing 500 words a day for six months, shoving the results off to a printer and going to live on the Côte d'Azur, uninterrupted except for the correction of proofs. It didn't happen like that – very frustrating.' He quotes his own line 'Books are a load of crap' as expressing one of those 'sentiments to which every bosom returns an echo', adding like an after-dinner speaker: 'as Dr Johnson said'. Writing a poem makes him feel as if he'd 'laid an egg'. In philistine mode, he tells his interviewer: 'I read everything except philosophy, theology, economics, sociology, science, or anything to do with the wonders of nature, anything to do with technology – have I said politics? I'm trying to think of all the Dewey decimal classes.' He would like to visit China, but only if he 'could come back the same day'.

The *Observer* interview is his most exhilarating exercise in high camp wit, though there is also something of the self-epitaph about it. He simplifies his life into a delightful self-parody, claiming to have 'completely forgotten' his childhood, and wanly characterizing his parents as 'not very good at being happy'. 'Oxford terrified me,' he remembers, and wistfully envies more recent students who have seen the influx of women into formerly all-male colleges: 'it would have been nice to have been part of the experiment'. He imagines the new regime as probably 'cheerful and non-academic, like an American college musical'. Sincerity and irony are blended in an inscrutable mix, and his diffidence is so articulate as to be indistinguishable from confidence. Librarianship was a good choice of profession for him, he claims, since 'it has just the right blend of academic interest and administration that seems to match my particular talents, such as they are'. For a moment he masquerades as a Tory ideologue, spoiling for a fight: 'I identify the Right with certain virtues and the Left with certain vices [. . .] thrift, hard work, reverence, desire to preserve – those are the virtues in case you wondered: and on the other hand idleness, greed and treason.' But then he dissolves into the softest man of feeling as he recollects nearly crashing his car while listening to the radio on the motorway: 'someone suddenly started reading the Immortality ode, and I couldn't see for tears'. He likes living in Hull because it is 'On the way to nowhere, as somebody put it. It's in the middle of this lonely country, and beyond the lonely country there's only the sea. I like that.' His final comment has persuasive gravity: 'I want readers to feel yes, I've never thought of it that way, but that's how it is.'54

23

Extinction
1980–5

The new decade opened with the death of Barbara Pym. On 11 January 1980 she succumbed to a return of the cancer first diagnosed ten years before. Shortly afterwards a long perspective was opened up when Ruth Bowman (now Siverns) wrote to Larkin, prompted by the appearance of the *Observer* interview. He told Amis tersely: 'now living in Romsey, nice and far away. Widow, son at Varsity'.[1] As in their youth he withheld the full story from his friend. Ruth had experienced a difficult life. She had married, only to be widowed before her son was born. Converting to Catholicism she never remarried and spent many years as a teacher and single parent in Wolverhampton. Resilient and creative, she was at this time about to publish a charming children's story, *Barlow Dale's Casebook*, focused on a Blue Persian cat detective.[2] Philip and Ruth continued to correspond until his death but they never met again in person.[3]

Early in 1980, Larkin agreed to read a retrospective selection of his work for the Watershed Foundation in the United States, and the University's engineer made the recording on 24 February 1980.[4] The edited tape included twenty-six poems from all phases of his development, ordered without regard to chronology.[5] Some poems were omitted at the last minute because of the limited time available, and too much should not be read into the selection. As he later explained: 'The tape was made with America in mind (that is, no four-letter words or peculiarly English subjects).'[6] But it is intriguing that he chose three poems from *The North Ship*, including the symbolist 'I put my mouth', and also 'So through that unripe day'. No sooner were the recordings made than complications arose. The Foundation had not budgeted for the required permissions fees, and crucially George Hartley refused permission for the use of poems from *The Less Deceived*, 'in any way'.[7] After protracted negotiations Larkin gave up hope of wider dissemination, and retrieved what he could from the debacle by selling a copy of the tape to Harvard University's Poetry Room for £50 plus postage. His own copy of the tape was deposited in the archive at Hull, available to any listener who discovered its existence.[8] The tape preserves readings of a small number of poems unrecorded elsewhere, but Larkin's manner of recitation is remarkably consistent, and there are no significant differences from earlier readings.

On 7 May Larkin travelled to Nottingham University to open an exhibition of books and manuscripts by D. H. Lawrence, and in a gesture of sartorial independence bought a T-shirt depicting the novelist, which he wore thereafter when mowing the lawn.[9] Andrew Motion, feeling ill-fitted for academic life, had secured an Arts Council Fellowship and moved to Oxford to write. Larkin had advised him against giving up his lecturing post, and asked Anthony Thwaite in a letter of 6 July 1980 to try to cheer Andrew up: 'He's a nice lad, I think, but I think not really tough enough – in his writing, that is. Probably tough enough otherwise.'[10] He had detected the determined ambition that was to take Motion to the Laureateship.

Larkin was finding his duties in the Library increasingly uncongenial. In the summer the new GEAC computer system, which the Deputy Librarian, Brenda Moon, had chosen during a trip to Canada, arrived. Unfortunately for Larkin, at this point Brenda left Hull to become Librarian at Edinburgh University. Burnt out by years of overwork, isolated by his deafness and alienated by the new technology, Larkin requested early retirement. However, the Vice-Chancellor, Sir Roy Marshall, refused, since his presence on the staff was deemed 'of material advantage to the university'. He wrote to Barry Bloomfield on 16 July: 'I am worked to death [. . .] Computerisation proceeds apace, resembling a kind of lunatic professional hari-kiri: I've never knowingly destroyed a library before. It's a curious sensation: half-exhilarating, half-frightening.'[11] In a sad contrast, just as his literary and professional lives were crumbling about him, he was gaining ever greater public acknowledgement. On 6 September Melvyn Bragg visited Hull to discuss a *South Bank Show* television feature. In the same month Larkin was elected an Honorary Fellow of the Library Association.[12]

He spent Christmas 1980 in Haydon Bridge with Monica. The year had passed without any attempt to write a poem. He was, however, having to read a large number of poems by others, as judge for the Arvon Foundation prize. He told Judy Egerton on 10 December: 'I deeply wish I'd never got mixed up with it. About half the entrants are Yanks, all worrying about Vietnam and being Jewish. UK entries are all about dying and dolmens on cold moors.'[13] Early in the New Year he wrote to Brian Cox: 'When I said, Where are all the poems about love? and nature? they said, Oh we chucked all those out on the first round. I bet I should have liked some of them.'[14] On 11 April 1981 'A Bridge for the Living' was finally performed at Hull's City Hall, celebrating the long-delayed opening of the Humber Bridge. Five days later came the *South Bank Show* interview. Larkin found the experience intrusive and uncomfortable. Melvyn Bragg recalled that he 'decided he didn't want to be seen, which I thought was a bit mean of him. We looked over his shoulder and shot him from a distance and all that rubbish. Either it was a tease or he didn't like the way he looked.'[15] Working to his limit, he was nevertheless still capable of dynamic initiatives. In May he was elected Chairman of the Poetry Book Society, and immediately suggested that its membership could be increased by transforming it into a club providing books at reduced prices. The scheme was put in place over his two-year tenure, and membership increased over the next five years from 871 to 2,000.[16]

At this time Larkin showed a brief interest in theology, partly stimulated by his relationship with the young writer A. N. Wilson, whom he had met in All Souls and who became the Literary Editor of the *Spectator* in 1981. In July Larkin bought an OUP Bible for £120 which he set up on a lectern in his bedroom, 'to remind me of matters spiritual'. The result was predictable. He told Andrew Motion: 'It's absolutely bloody amazing to think that anyone ever believed any of that. Really, it's absolute balls. Beautiful, of course. But balls.'[17] In the summer Monica had taken early retirement from Leicester at the age of fifty-nine, and Larkin once again raised the possibility of early retirement for himself, in vain. (The University did, however, confer an honorary professorship on him the following year.) Like 1980, 1981 passed without poetry, apart from a light-verse sixty-fifth-birthday greeting to Gavin Ewart, 'Good for you, Gavin'. Larkin praises Ewart for the 'riotous road-show' of his poetry 'like Glenlivet nightly, / A warming to us all.' It is a nicely judged compliment, but it has only a flicker of Larkin's former subtle felicity. The two undated pages of drafts of this poem comprise the last entries in his final, eighth workbook.

Now in his sixtieth year, he wrote to Amis on 3 January: 'So now we face 1982, sixteen stone six, gargantuanly paunched, helplessly addicted to alcohol, tired of livin' and scared of dyin'', world-famous unable-to-write poet, well you know the rest.'[18] Early in the year he resigned from the Arts Council Literature Advisory Panel, sounding off to Amis in terms his friend would applaud: 'No subsidies for Gay Sweatshirt or the Runcorn Socialist Workers Peoples Poetry Workshop. Or wogs like Salmagundi or whatever his name is.'[19] He agreed to an interview with the *Paris Review* conducted by Robert Phillips, stipulating that he be sent the questions by post. The result was another witty piece like the *Observer* interview of two years earlier. The aphorisms are as incisive as ever: 'of course most people do get married, and divorced too'.[20] There are also thoughtful reflections on his life and art. He asserts, 'I didn't choose poetry: poetry chose me,' and to the question of what he is aiming to 'preserve' in his poetry he replies with simple eloquence: 'the experience. The beauty.'[21] In contrast there is philistine coarseness in his response to a question about poets who have also been librarians: 'Who's Jorge Luis Borges?', though he follows this up with an acute account of Archibald MacLeish's creative impact as Librarian of Congress in the USA.[22] His response to a question about foreign poetry is utterly misleading: 'deep down I think foreign languages irrelevant

[. . .] *Hautes Fenêtres*, my God!' Here and there a tone of weary defeat is detectable: 'Anything I say about writing poems is bound to be retrospective.'[23]

In his later years Larkin was approached by an increasing number of admirers, students, secretaries of societies and young poets in search of advice. Betty Mackereth still has her book of draft 'Refusal Letters', dated 1982, by which he evaded these requests. It is divided under the headings: 'Autographs', 'Being photographed', 'Biographical information', 'Criticism of poetry', 'Interviews', 'Judging poetry competitions'. Each category has a number of standard responses graded by level of politeness. In the case of 'Autographs', for instance, they range from the courteous – (a) 'grateful though he is for your interest in his work, he prefers not to autograph copies of his books for people not personally known to him' – to the blunt: (d) 'indiscriminate signing seems to devalue copies inscribed to friends, and [. . .] it has not been unknown for such copies to turn up in book-sellers' catalogues in a remarkably short space of time.'

His practice was inconsistent, however, particularly in the case of personal approaches. In 1981 a young PhD student in the English Department sent him a copy of *High Windows* explaining that her newly bereaved mother, reading her own copy on a recent visit, had been much moved by it. Could he perhaps sign this copy to be given to her as a present? A few days later the student was surprised when Larkin visited her in her postgraduate study in the University to explain that he did not sign books for people he did not know. He noticed that her thesis was on Thomas Hardy and they were soon involved in a lively discussion over a cup of Nescafé and powdered milk. Roy Morrell's 1966 study of Hardy, he told her, had missed Hardy's 'sensual cruelty'. An hour after his departure a University porter delivered a package containing the copy of *High Windows* signed for her mother, and also, for herself, a copy of *A Girl in Winter*, also signed: 'with all good wishes'.[24]

On 12 May 1982 Larkin attended a reception in Downing Street and met the Prime Minister, Mrs Thatcher. She misquoted a line from 'Deceptions' – 'Her mind was full of knives' – which persuaded him that she really had read his work: 'I took *that* as a great compliment – I thought if it weren't spontaneous, she'd have got it right. But I am a child in these things.'[25] The poetry scene in Hull was highly active at this time, and Douglas Dunn, who after graduating from Hull in 1969 had been for two years an Assistant Librarian under Larkin, assembled an anthology for publication by Bloodaxe Books under the title *A Rumoured City: New Poets from Hull*. Larkin agreed to write a short foreword, and in mellow, retrospective mood produced a glowing prose poem celebrating the city in which he had now spent the best part of three decades. He evoked the 'sudden elegancies' of Hull's city centre, and ended with a recasting of the conclusion of 'Here':

> People are slow to leave it, quick to return. And there are others who come, as they think, for a year or two, and stay a lifetime, sensing that they have found a city that is in the world, yet sufficiently on the edge of it to have a different resonance. Behind Hull is the plain of Holderness, lonelier and lonelier, and after that the birds and lights of Spurn Head, and then the sea. One can go ten years without seeing these things, yet they are always there, giving Hull the air of having its face half-turned towards distance and silence, and what lies beyond them.[26]

His private comments on the poets in the volume were not, however, favourable. Only the local poet Frank Redpath, whose well-crafted works are heavily influenced by his own, gained his approval.[27] He was reading little of the poetry of others by this time, and was even reluctant, initially, to write a review for the *Observer* of Andrew Motion and Blake Morrison's *Penguin Book of Contemporary British Poetry*.[28]

As his birthday approached, Anthony Thwaite sent him the pieces to be included in the Festschrift *Larkin at Sixty* which he was editing for Faber and Faber. Larkin was offended by the essay by his schoolfriend Noel Hughes which referred to the Larkin house in Manor Road as 'joyless' and claimed that Sydney Larkin had been a member of the Link group of Nazi sympathizers. Larkin accused Hughes of writing a piece that 'read like a posthumous article, to be published when I was no longer around to mind'.[29] Hughes made changes but Larkin retained his sense of injury: 'I and my sister continue to regard [him] as a reptile spitting venom hoarded for forty years.'[30] Early in June the *South Bank Show* feature was broadcast. The chemistry between Bragg and the poet had not been good, and his verdict, in a letter to Judy Egerton, was that the programme was 'inoffensive', but 'lacked subtlety and intelligence'; 'there was rather too much of four-letter Larkin for my liking'.[31]

In January 1982 Larkin had read an article on his work by the Canadian academic Terry Whalen, 'Philip Larkin's Imagist bias'.[32] On 24 July he completed his first true poem for three years, a concentrated imagist lyric in two- or three-stress couplet lines, evoking a hot summer day. It is a welcome breath of celebratory lyricism:

> Long lion days
> Start with white haze.
> By midday you meet
> A hammer of heat –
> Whatever was sown
> Now fully grown;
> Whatever conceived
> Now fully leaved,
> Abounding, ablaze –
> O long lion days!

The poet was not quite dead. As if to highlight its isolated, belated position in his output he titled it '1982'. Of less poetic interest are the thirty-seven lines of tetrameter couplets he contributed to *Poems for Charles Causley*:

> Dear CHARLES, My Muse, asleep or dead,
> Offers this doggerel instead
> To carry from the frozen North
> Warm greetings for the twenty-fourth
> Of lucky August [. . .]

It seems significant that of the poems he wrote in his final years, two were celebrations of sixty-fifth birthdays (Ewart's and Causley's). Was he, on some level, attempting to persuade himself that he might himself reach this improbable goal?

A month after his sixtieth birthday, on 10 September 1982, he responded to a letter from his Oxford contemporary Michael Hamburger:

> Many thanks for your kind wishes [. . .] Yes, it is a pity that the ability to write poems dies away as one goes down the vale, but I don't think there is much one can do about it. Silence is preferable to publishing rubbish, and better for one's reputation. However, it would indeed be lovely if we both had sudden Indian summers, and there is no harm in hoping; is there?[33]

Wordsworth and Auden also exhausted their inspiration well before their deaths. They fell into empty prolixity; Larkin fell into silence.

On 26 October Larkin was invited by Hugh Thomas, head of the Centre for Policy Studies, to a dinner at his home in Ladbroke Grove, arranged to allow Mrs Thatcher to meet Tory-sympathising artists and academics. His fellow guests were Stephen Spender, Anthony Quinton, Al Alvarez, Anthony Powell, Isaiah Berlin, J. H. Plumb, Dan Jacobson, V. S. Pritchett, V. S. Naipaul, Tom Stoppard, Nicholas Mosley and Mario Vargas Llosa. In a letter to the Thomases following the dinner, Mrs Thatcher wrote that she was 'a little worried that Philip Larkin was so silent'. Not hearing much because of his deafness, he had felt out of his depth among all the talk about foreign policy. Characteristically, his only significant contribution seems to have been a condemnation of the 'hypocrisy' of those who (like Mrs Thatcher) complained about the Berlin Wall while at the same time not wanting to see a united Germany.[34]

The remaining three years of Larkin's life were darkened by accident and illness. In October 1982 Monica fell and cut her head in Haydon Bridge. He wrote to her in hospital: 'Dear bun, I know how utterly alien hospitals are, but I hope this one is kind and friendly [. . .] Think if you would like to come here to convalesce when you "come out". I could fetch you away.' The following day, 14 October, he wrote again, distressed that his deafness had prevented him from hearing what the nurse had said over the phone: 'Feel worried and cross with myself. I shd *say* I am deaf. How wonderful it will be to talk to you again!'[35] Five months later, in March 1983, Monica developed shingles, and Philip drove her down from Haydon Bridge to Hull Royal Infirmary.[36] When she left hospital to convalesce in Newland Park he found himself for the first time since 1950 living day to day with another person. She was suffering from lethargy and double vision, but on 9 July was sufficiently recovered to allow him to make a quick visit to Coleraine to receive an Honorary DLitt from the New University of Ulster.[37] Then in August a spell of sneezing dispelled her double vision. The lease on Monica's Leicester flat had expired in July and the plan was that as soon as she was well enough she would move permanently to Haydon Bridge. Betty recollects calling at the Newland Park house at this time with a bottle of champagne for Philip's birthday. Monica asserted her precedence by raising the toast (in Betty's champagne) 'To Oxford Firsts!'[38]

When, in October 1983, Vikram Seth renewed their brief correspondence of five years earlier, asking for advice over his second collection, *The Humble Administrator's Garden*, Larkin was impressed enough to respond. He paid Seth the compliment of hard-hitting but helpful criticism, writing that though he liked Seth's 'clear, moving, funny' writing and the skilful way he handled metre and rhyme, he did not feel his poems were 'world-beaters'. 'Sometimes they were too long (for me), sometimes they had a kind of flaccidity.' He asked Seth to forgive his 'candour' and advised him to cut down the number of poems in the volume. After 'the initial cold shock', Seth took the advice to heart. Candour, Seth wrote, 'never harmed anyone'.[39]

In October 1983 Larkin contributed two couplets on Hull's Library, 'A lifted study-storehouse', to the celebrations for Sir Brynmor Jones's eightieth birthday. Urged on by Anthony Thwaite and Blake Morrison, he had made a selection of the best of his prose, and on 7 November Faber published *Required Writing*. The volume collected together various autobiographical pieces, the interviews with the *Observer* and *Paris Review*, a number of general essays and many of his reviews, including insightful pieces on Housman, Auden, Hardy, Owen, Betjeman, Pym and Plath. It concluded with the Introduction to *All*

What Jazz and a selection of his jazz writings. He dedicated it to his friend Anthony Thwaite, who had commissioned many of the reviews as Literary Editor of the *Listener*, the *New Statesman* and *Encounter*. In his Foreword Larkin claimed that the volume had 'little coherence', and in a letter to Colin Gunner he referred to it as 'a collection of hack journalism. I wanted to call it THE BOTTOM OF THE BARREL, but they wouldn't play.'[40] In fact it makes a unified and impressive impact, and it is not surprising that it won the W. H. Smith Award.[41] When I thanked him for his signature at the launch in Hull, he responded in character: '*I* should be doing the thanking,' he said, and mentioned the number of pence he received 'for every one of these they sell'.

When in January 1984 *Poetry Review* published a special issue on 'Poetry and Drink', Larkin was persuaded to provide a contribution, 'Party Politics'. The speaker depicts himself in the corner of a room of forks and faces, his glass never full:

> You may get drunk, or dry half-hours may pass.
> It seems to turn on where you are. Or who.

The political metaphor of the title fails to grow wings. There is little conviction in the poet's grumbling about the arbitrariness of social rewards, and he is all too literally intent on his next drink. In contrast, in a short interview with A. N. Wilson broadcast on Radio 4 on 29 March 1984 his funny side was to the fore: 'I haven't given poetry up, but I rather think poetry has given me up, which is a great sorrow to me. But not an enormous crushing sorrow. It's a bit like going bald.' Asked what he intended to do with the £4,000 tax-free W. H. Smith Award, he quipped, 'Well I think I shall buy a new suit. I need one and I gather they cost about that nowadays.'[42]

Early in 1984 Monica was prescribed antibiotics for another infection. Then in February Larkin himself was diagnosed with phlebitic thrombosis and took a week off from the Library. The following month Monica was well enough for him to drive her back to Haydon Bridge, though only for a fortnight to see whether she could cope. He wrote to her on 2 April as soon as he arrived back in Hull: 'I can't imagine you'll be any less *feeble* but I hope you find some satisfaction in being among your own things, and your own boss again. Be careful, dear, of *stairs* & *road crossings*, and be sensible about eating & drinking.'[43] But she was unable to fend for herself and later in April he brought her back to Newland Park, where she was to stay for the rest of her life. She cut a startling figure around the University in her flamboyant cape, elaborate spectacles and strange hats. One of the young Library staff at the time recalls: 'You couldn't miss her bright colours.'[44]

Betty retired on her sixtieth birthday, 27 June 1984, and Larkin officiated at her farewell ceremony. On the day she actually left, however, he was in Oxford with Monica, receiving an Honorary DLitt in the new specially purchased suit, 'like a walrus maternity garment'.[45] On 17 July he began a month of sittings with Humphrey Ocean, who had been commissioned by the National Portrait Gallery to paint his portrait. He wrote to Judy Egerton:

> It's inevitably rather tedious; in fact I tend to fall asleep, quite without malice, but wch holds things up. The trouble is, he doesn't want to talk – reasonably enough – and if I talk he doesn't just grunt, but feels obliged to lay down his brush and concentrate on what I am saying [. . .] What I can see looks very *brown* to me – a sort of sepia study.[46]

Larkin is respectful of the artist's procedures, but Ocean's insistence on not engaging with his subject infects the painting. With its muted contrast and dull colour it catches something of the somnolence Larkin describes. Judy Egerton, who liked the painting, conceded that it depicts Larkin the librarian rather than the great poet.[47] Larkin told Jean Hartley that 'at first he had been rather taken with it – it made him look like the young Mussolini – but after several hours more work it looked like Hitchcock at eighty'.[48]

The University had imposed a 20 per cent cut in Library expenditure for 1984, and Larkin now had the unpleasant experience of seeing several of his staff made redundant. He accorded each of them an individual, sympathetic interview.[49] He was briefly cheered by the purchase of a new car, a second-hand Audi (the name reminded him of Auden). Also in the summer he watched the Test match at Lords, and saw the George Stubbs exhibition mounted by Judy Egerton at the Tate Gallery. He did not share her enthusiasm for Stubbs's work, finding it '*voulu*'.[50] In September Larkin was photographed again by Fay Godwin. His letter of thanks shows his keen appreciation of her determination to do justice to her subject: 'The trouble, as always, is me [. . .] my sagging face, an egg sculpted in lard, with goggles on – depressing, depressing, depressing.'[51] As his life grows gloomier and more hopeless, his letters become ever more entertaining.

John Betjeman died on 19 May 1984 and in July Larkin attended the memorial service in Westminster Abbey. Despite Kingsley Amis's urgings, he had determined to turn down the Laureateship. As he wrote to Colin Gunner: 'I just couldn't face the fifty letters a day, TV show, representing-British-Poetry-in-the-"Poetry-Conference-at-Belgrade" side of it all.'[52] The offer came in December and he declined. Hughes would become the next Laureate. He wrote to Amis: 'the thought of being the cause of Ted's being buried in Westminster Abbey is hard to live with. "There is regret. Always, there is regret." Smoking can damage your bum.'[53] As if to fulfil Larkin's prognostication, Ted Hughes, born eight years later than Larkin, was accorded a memorial in Poets' Corner in 2010, barely thirteen years after his death.[54]

In March 1985 Larkin exchanged his last letters with Ruth Bowman. On 7 March she wrote to sympathize with him in his low spirits. Her limp, she told him, had now deteriorated to the point that she could walk only very short distances even with a stick. She apologized for sending him 'quite the gloomiest letter you could wish not to have'. On 27 March he wrote to her, offering to call on the £4,000 W. H. Smith Award to help pay for an operation. But the offer was ungraciously phrased, and he was clearly overwhelmed with his own problems. He mentioned Monica's lack of medical insurance:

> I have a nasty feeling that before the curtain falls she is going to need a lot of attention. I just don't know. But there may be a house to buy and alter so that she can live on one floor. There may be paid help. I don't

know. But I have a notion that I'm likely to *need* the rest of my money
[. . .] *I do want to help.* But I'm bound to consider the other factors I
have mentioned. I'm sure you understand. I hope this doesn't sound too
curtly brutal: it isn't meant to.

But Larkin's real worry was not money: 'For my own part, I fully expect
to be on the operating table before you – they are longing to get at my
oesophagus, which has misbehaved for years but isn't in any sense serious as I understand it. Drinking, well I haven't got it organized yet. But
I shall.'[55] Ruth took the hint; in any case she had already been offered
help from a different source.

Also in March Larkin had his first meeting with Hull's new Vice-
Chancellor, William Taylor, who, he told Gunner, seemed to be
'weighing me for the drop'.[56] But he was 'for it' in a more literal sense
than this. On 16 March Dr Richardson, the University's Medical
Officer, sent him to see Dr Clive Aber in the Nuffield Private Hospital
in 'the Avenues', opposite Pearson Park. Rather comically, Aber gave
the professional diagnosis that Larkin had 'acute depression and hypo-
chondria' and suffered from 'a cancer phobia and fear of dying'. He sent
him for a barium-meal X-ray which revealed a tumour in his oesophagus. An operation would be needed. Far too late Larkin cut down on
his drinking and put himself on a diet. To add to his problems, Monica
also fell ill. Before the operation he phoned several friends including
Betty and Maeve, to say goodbye, just in case. During his convales-
cence a rota of car-drivers, comprising Betty Mackereth, his jazz friend
Mike Bowen and the wife of the University's Professor of Russian,
Virginia Peace, was arranged to ferry Monica, who did not drive, to the
hospital. Maeve was touched that he 'stressed that after Monica, he
wanted me to be amongst his first visitors'.[57]

When the growth was removed, on 11 June, a further cancerous
tumour was found, too advanced for surgery. Monica decided that he
should not be told. While he was in the intensive care unit of the
Nuffield Hospital one of his visitors smuggled in a bottle of whisky.[58]
He drank most of it, nearly died and was rushed back to Hull Royal
Infirmary for emergency resuscitation. He was returned to the Nuffield

to recuperate. Kingsley Amis offered to come up to Hull, but Larkin put him off so as not to 'scare' him. Even in this extreme situation he carefully preserved the different textures of his intimacies. His visitors give widely varying accounts of his state of mind. Maeve was surprised by his high spirits: 'he poked his head round the screen and pulled such a comical face, accompanied by a cheery wave of the hand. He was obviously delighted to see me and appeared in positively buoyant mood.' She remembers that he told her: 'You look absolutely lovely.'[59] Betty Mackereth, in contrast, recalls finding Philip 'sitting up in bed with a faraway look on his face – about 5.00 in the afternoon. The t.v. was on, but he was looking past it. He was thinking about death.' He told her: 'Maeve came to see me. I didn't want to see Maeve. I wanted to see Monica to tell her I love her.'[60] Jean Hartley, who visited with Ted Tarling, recollects his remorse over earlier insensitivities: 'he said he had been a callous bastard over other people's illnesses. "Hadn't realized. Failure of imagination."'[61] To Jean and Ted he gave a more dispassionate verdict on Monica: 'There was always enough between us to prevent us drawing apart but never sufficient to bring us any closer together.'[62]

At one point Maeve was the only driver available to take Monica to the hospital. She recalled that the atmosphere 'bristled with emotional tension which could not have contributed to Philip's well-being'. When she withdrew to leave him and Monica alone, 'Philip reached out to me in a passionate embrace. Deeply embarrassed, I froze under the hostile glare of Monica.'[63] Still determined to win Philip for the Church, Maeve persuaded Anthony Storey, the Catholic chaplain of the University, with whom Philip had a friendly relationship, to visit him. Only too aware of the poet's atheism, Storey was reluctant, but he agreed in order to satisfy Maeve. He later recalled that Philip was dozing, so he leant over him and whispered: 'Hello, Philip, this is Anthony Storey.' Opening his eyes Philip saw the dog collar and, understanding Maeve's strategy, exclaimed: 'Oh, fuck!'[64] On 17 July his solicitor Terry Wheldon visited and Larkin revised his will, cancelling a previous bequest to Maeve, an action which distressed and puzzled her after his death.[65] He left his estate initially to Monica, and then, after her death, to be divided equally between the Society of Authors and the

RSPCA. He wrote to Judy Egerton on 16 July that he was 'very depressed – never be the same again, old age here, death round the corner etc, I dare say I needn't elaborate.'[66] On 19 July Michael Bowen drove him back to Newland Park.

He was largely housebound, and Monica wanted to stay with him, so their shopping was done by Mike Bowen and Virginia Peace. He abandoned his intention of returning to half-time work at the beginning of the autumn term. His energy was failing, and he was unable to write a review of Dylan Thomas's *Collected Letters*.[67] He also cancelled a meeting with the new Vice-Chancellor to discuss a proposal that a number of rooms in the Library be redesignated for teaching. At this time the students were campaigning to 'save Larkin's Library'.[68] He was unable to attend Maeve's retirement party on 21 November, and Professor Eddie Dawes of the Library Committee read a speech on his behalf.[69]

On 21 November 1985 Ted Hughes had occasion to write to Larkin concerning the Queen's Medal Committee on which they both served. He took the opportunity, with much hesitation, to suggest a miracle cure: 'I simply wanted to let you know somehow of the existence of a very strange and remarkable fellow down here, quite widely known for what seem to be miraculous healing powers.' This man, Hughes assured Larkin, had cured twelve cancers, six of them terminal: 'He explains his "power" as some sort of energy that flows from him and galvanizes the patient's own auto-immune system [. . .] It isn't absolutely necessary to meet him. All he seems to need is name, details of place – but best of all contact over the phone.'[70] Hughes gave the healer's telephone number, but Larkin did not call it.

Larkin was due to be made a Companion of Honour on 25 November but there was no question of him travelling to London for the ceremony. He told Monica that he was 'spiralling down towards extinction'.[71] Poetry may have deserted him, but he continued to make phrases as dissolution approached. On Friday 29 November he fell down twice, the second time, late in the evening, in the downstairs toilet. His legs were wedged against the door and his face was pressing against one of the central heating pipes. Monica could hear him whispering 'Hot! Hot!' But he was unable to hear her because he had not put in his hearing aid. She called an ambulance and he was taken to the Nuffield Hospital, begging her on the way to destroy his diaries. On Saturday 30 November Betty drove Monica to see him, but he was sedated and asleep. On Sunday the visit was repeated with the same failure of communication. He died on Monday 2 December at 1.24 a.m., four months beyond his sixty-third birthday. It may be, as the nurse in attendance reported, that his last whispered words were: 'I am going to the inevitable.'[72]

Postscript: Petals and Graves

Monica was too distraught to attend Philip's funeral on 9 December 1985 in St Mary's Church, Cottingham. Kingsley Amis came and gave an address, seeing Larkin's home ground of thirty years for the first time. He limited his visit to Cottingham, not penetrating as far as Hull or the University. His son, Martin, remembers him, on his return from the funeral, reflecting 'defeatedly': 'I sometimes wonder if I ever really knew him.'[1] A formal memorial service took place later in Westminster Abbey, not inappropriately, on St Valentine's Day 1986. Some weeks after Larkin's death Monica gave Betty the diaries to be destroyed in accordance with his wish. He had always seen the diaries as comprising a special, suspect category among his writings. As early as 1954, following Patsy Strang's intrusion upon them he had told Monica: 'Journals – diaries – are two-edged weapons! I really must arrange for mine to be destroyed when I die.'[2] At the other end of his life, in his interview with John Haffenden of 1981 he said: 'I kept a diary for a long time, more as a kind of great grumble-book than anything else. It's stopped now.'[3] In fact, since his abortive attempt to 'distil' them in 1976 he had continued to fill their pages and there were now thirteen thick notebooks covering 1949 to 1980. Betty took them into the Librarian's office, tore the pages from their bindings, shredded them and sent the contents to the incinerator. Her task took all afternoon.[4] Tantalizing cuttings, photographs and quotations survive, pasted on the inside covers.

Betty has no qualms about her action: 'He was very sure that that's what he wanted to happen. He told Monica and he told me.'⁵ However, she still feels uncomfortable about a second, unauthorized interference with Larkin's property. Before the destruction of the diaries, Larkin's solicitor Terry Wheldon visited the Newland Park house with her and removed the pornography in two large cardboard boxes. 'In later years I would have stopped that,' she says. 'But I just went along with it. He said to me: "I always do this, because leaving things like this upsets the bereaved."' But, Betty says, 'It wouldn't have upset Monica in the least. She would have loved it. Wouldn't she? She probably knew anyway.' Later Betty wrote to the University Archivist, Brian Dyson, questioning this interference with Larkin's estate.⁶

Fortunately, Larkin's will was self-contradictory. It had been altered during his first spell in Nuffield Hospital in 1985, at a time when his judgement may well have been damaged by his collapse following the episode of the smuggled whisky. One clause required his executors to destroy his unpublished work 'unread'. Another clause gave them full permission to publish what they wished from his papers. His executors, Anthony Thwaite and Andrew Motion, took advice from a Queen's Counsel and the will was declared to be 'repugnant', allowing them a free hand to do what they felt best. They earned the gratitude of succeeding generations by destroying nothing.⁷ Given Larkin's own instinct to preserve and archive every twist and turn of his life and writing, including his gift of the first workbook to the British Library, and given also his fascination with the posthumous papers of Thomas Hardy and Wilfred Owen, this seems right. Anthony Thwaite records that Larkin 'often referred [. . .] to work which would have to be left for "the posthumous volume" of his poems'.⁸

Larkin had failed to become a novelist in the 1940s. However, as if his creativity could not be contained by his death, its aftermath shows a vivid abundance of novelistic character and event. During his researches for his official biography Andrew Motion concluded that the unpublished 'When first we faced, and touching showed' must be the product of a secret relationship of which neither Monica nor Maeve was aware. Though Philip had never shown her the poem Maeve felt at first that it must be addressed to her. Otherwise she was baffled as to who the 'third woman' could be. At one point she visited Betty for coffee and asked if she could help with the mystery. Had Philip, perhaps, Maeve inquired, had an affair with Joanna Motion, Andrew's first wife? Later, on learning the truth, and discovering much else about Philip she had not suspected, such as his habitual use of four-letter words, Maeve became disillusioned. She 'regretted his selfishness', telling Motion that he had taken 'the best years' of her life and 'given little in return'. She quoted Byron, an odd choice in the circumstances: 'Were I to meet him again, that's how I should greet him, "with silence and tears".'[9] Her moral judgement was characteristically decisive: 'He had feet of clay, didn't he? Huge feet of clay.'[10] Later, however, her attitude mellowed and she enjoyed the celebrity of a famous poet's muse. She became Vice-Chairman of the Philip Larkin Society, and put together, with my help, an affectionate memoir, *The Philip Larkin I Knew* (2002).[11] At the time of her death in 2003 she was organizing a Society excursion to Scarborough to explore the site of her shopping trips with the poet in the 1960s. The excursion took place after her death.[12]

Monica retired into seclusion, leaving most of the house she had briefly shared with Philip exactly as it had been when he died. So it stayed for the remaining fifteen years of her life. Uniquely among his loves and muses she understood poetry, and took it as seriously as he did. Unlike the others also, she had a capacity for tragedy. She had never been deceived about the complexity of Philip's life: 'I didn't think he was straightforward.'[13] Whatever Philip's faults, she could not bear to be without him. 'He lied to me, the bugger, but I loved him.'[14] Money from the Larkin Estate maintained and redecorated the rooms where she slept and in which she spent her days reading the *Daily Telegraph*, tracing her lover's growing reputation in literary magazines, and watching boxing and cricket on television. Elsewhere his clothes and shoes remained in their cupboards, his books and records on their shelves. Unfortunately, however, no one was at hand to prevent her falling prey to a cold-caller and commissioning the construction of an expensive plastic and glass conservatory, which she left bare and empty.

I met Monica briefly in 1999 two years before she died, barging in with academic questions at the end of an event. She was bedridden but as firm and opinionated as ever. At one point, her carer came in for a chat, no doubt concerned that my questions were overtaxing her frail charge. She had, she said, taken Monica into the front bedroom recently 'for a change of scene'. 'We found Philip's old scarf and some of the dresses you used to wear when you went out together. It's happy memories isn't it?' Monica drove her fists into the bed on each side of her and strained forward from the pillow: 'I found it *terribly boring* actually.' The nurse laughed ruefully: 'I don't give up, Mr Booth.' Later she told me how she had to fight Monica in order to wash her hair: 'she was so stiffened against it. It's very long, and it's really beautiful when it's washed.'[15] At Monica's funeral two years later, a very Anglican affair with much mumbling and a brightly encouraging organ, the officiating priest commented that he was wearing the same robes as at Larkin's funeral. He remembered because they had been noticed on television, and he'd received admiring letters about them.

After Monica's papers had gone to the Bodleian, according to her wish, and Larkin's remaining books, records and letters had been taken to the Brynmor Jones Library, the Larkin Society bought the residual contents of the house: pictures, ornaments, furniture, cameras, blank workbooks. At first we thought there might be manuscripts hidden under the upstairs carpets, but the promising unevennesses were only accumulated piles of dust. Again, life imitated fiction, when, despite the most rigorous search, we failed to locate the manuscript book in which Larkin had drafted 'Morning at last, there in the snow', 'Be my Valentine this Monday' and 'We met at the end of the party'. This had fallen down the back of a small bedside cabinet and only came to light when the house-clearer whom we paid to take away the last debris heard it rattling on the way to the tip.[16] More movingly, in one drawer we found a small translucent envelope containing petals of a pressed dog rose, now brown, together with a lock of pubic hair.[17] Though the moment of passion it preserves is lost to memory, this poignant metonym of the spring of life preserves its emotional charge. Like the rose and hair, Larkin's poems have, also, with accumulating deaths, outlived their occasions.

Larkin's grave is in the cemetery in Eppleworth Road, Cottingham. The small plain white headstone bears the simple wording decided upon by Monica:

Philip Larkin
1922–1985
Writer

The stonemason initially placed inappropriate full-stops at the ends of the lines, and these had to be clumsily filled in: a homely touch which Larkin would have appreciated. The grave stands mid-row, and attracts tributes of flowers. For a time a weatherbeaten copy of the *Collected Poems* was placed there, and someone planted a small *Laurus nobilis*, or bay, close to one side. But the roots would have unsettled the surrounding stones and the Council removed it. However, the grave is picturesque, and looks much as the final resting place of a well-loved poet should look. By the time of Monica's death in 2001 mortality had completed Philip's row and filled three more. So, looking over Larkin's grave a little to the right one can see Monica's grave about twenty yards away. A stone of exactly the same form as Philip's was eventually erected over her, giving simply her full name:

Margaret Monica Beale Jones
7th May 1922 – 15th February 2001

It is quite untended.

Maeve Brennan's relationship with David Bassett lasted until his death. They did not marry, though they were effectively a couple. He died four years after Larkin in 1989 and, since he had no surviving close relatives, it fell to Maeve to wind up his affairs and make arrangements for his burial. His gravestone of purple marble, larger and more ornamental than Philip's, in accordance with Maeve's Catholic taste, is located at the very end of the same row as Larkin's. In due course, in 2003, when Maeve herself died, she was interred in the same plot. Thus, the visitor today encounters a densely worded gravestone giving David

Bassett's details and ending: 'A very dear friend'. Below, without explanation, is engraved: 'also Maeve Brennan, devoted sister of Dermot and Moira'. The inscription concludes with Maeve's favourite words of poetry: 'What will survive of us is love.' She had always been earnest that 'Philip really did mean' what he had written, insisting that there was no irony in the line. One can hear the ghostly less deceived snort across the grass from Monica's grave: 'Love isn't stronger than death just because two statues hold hands for six hundred years.'[18] What the ghost of David Bassett makes of the situation is a question perhaps for Larkin's favourite celebrator of life's little ironies, Thomas Hardy. At Maeve's funeral Betty commented wickedly: 'Now nobody can contradict me.' And during the third Hull International Conference on the Work of Philip Larkin, held in the nearby Lawns Centre in summer 2007, she stood beside Larkin's grave in the drizzle and recited 'An Arundel Tomb' to the assembled delegates.

One distinctive aspect of Larkin's poems concerning death is the absence of any reference to those who will remain to grieve his passing. He would never have written a poem like Hardy's 'Afterwards' in which the poet imagines his own afterlife in the memories of others ('He was a man who noticed such things'). Nor does Larkin imagine his body decaying physically after death. There is nothing in his work similar to Betjeman's elegy on his father: 'In Highgate now his finger-bones / Stick through his finger-ends.'[19] For Larkin beyond death there is simply nothing. In the words of Auden's elegy on Yeats, he has become his admirers. What will survive of him is poetry. But the thought of his literary afterlife was never of any consolation to him.[20] 'We must never die. No one must ever die.'[21]

Notes

Abbreviations

AGW	Philip Larkin, *A Girl in Winter* (London: Faber & Faber, 1975 edn).
AL	*About Larkin* (Journal of the Philip Larkin Society) (April 1996–April 2012); nos. 1–6 ed. Jean Hartley; nos. 7–14 ed James Booth; no. 15 ed. Jean Hartley and Maeve Brennan; no. 16 ed. Jean Hartley; nos. 17–21 ed. Belinda Hakes; no. 22 ed. Janet Brennan; nos. 23–37 ed. James Booth and Janet Brennan.
AWJ	Philip Larkin, *All What Jazz: A Record Diary* (London: Faber & Faber, 2nd edn, 1985).
BD1	'Biographical Details: OXFORD', *AL* 23 (April 2007), pp. 5–13.
BD2	'Biographical Details: OXFORD – Part 2', *AL* 24 (October 2007), pp. 4–19.
Bibliography	B. C. Bloomfield, *Philip Larkin: A Bibliography 1933–1994* (London: British Library and Oak Knoll Press, revised and enlarged edn, 2002).
Brennan	Maeve Brennan, *The Philip Larkin I Knew* (Manchester: Manchester University Press, Larkin Society Monograph 3, 2002).
Collected Poems	*Philip Larkin: Collected Poems*, ed. Anthony Thwaite (London: The Marvell Press/Faber & Faber, 1988, revised 1990).
Complete Poems	*The Complete Poems of Philip Larkin*, ed. with an introduction and commentary by Archie Burnett (London: Faber & Faber, 2012).
FR	Philip Larkin, *Further Requirements: Interviews, Broadcasts, Statements and Book Reviews 1952–1985*, ed. Anthony Thwaite (London: Faber & Faber, pbk edn with two additional chapters, 2002).
Hartley	Jean Hartley, *Philip Larkin, the Marvell Press and Me* (1989; London: Sumach Press, 1993).
Jill	Philip Larkin, *Jill* (London: Faber & Faber, 1975 edn).
LKA	*The Letters of Kingsley Amis*, ed. Zachary Leader (London: HarperCollins, 2000).
LM	Philip Larkin, *Letters to Monica*, ed. Anthony Thwaite (London: Faber & Faber/Bodleian Library, 2010).
Motion	Andrew Motion, *Philip Larkin: A Writer's Life* (London: Faber & Faber, 1993).

OBTCEV	Philip Larkin (ed.), *The Oxford Book of Twentieth Century English Verse* (London: Oxford University Press, 1973).
RW	Philip Larkin, *Required Writing: Miscellaneous Pieces 1955–1982* (London: Faber & Faber, 1983).
SL	Philip Larkin, *Selected Letters*, ed. Anthony Thwaite (London: Faber & Faber, 1992).
TWG	Philip Larkin, *Trouble at Willow Gables and Other Fictions*, ed. James Booth (London: Faber & Faber, 2002).

Archival Sources in the Hull University Collection, The History Centre, Hull

U DLN	Larkin family papers.
U DLN/6	Letters to Eva Larkin. These are cited in the text by date only.
UDP, DPL	Various papers related to Larkin deposited in the University of Hull Collection.
U DP/174/2	Letters to James Sutton. These are cited in the text by date only.
U DPL/1/2–8	Larkin's poetic workbooks 2–8 (1950–81).
U DX/329	Pictures, ornaments, etc. from 105 Newland Park in 2001–2, belonging to the Philip Larkin Society, inventoried by James Booth in 2003. Key items are deposited in the History Centre, Hull; others are on loan to the East Yorkshire Museums Service.

The U prefix is omitted in the notes.

Other Archival Sources

British Library Add. MS. 52619: Larkin's poetic workbook 1 (1944–50).

Unpublished letters not included in *Selected Letters*, *Letters to Monica* or *The Letters of Kingsley Amis* are cited by recipient and date only. The correspondences are held in the following institutions:

Kingsley Amis: The Huntington Library, California, AMS 353–428.

Monica Jones: The Bodleian Library, Oxford, Ms. Eng. c.7403–c.7445.

Introduction

1. Jonathan Raban, 'Philip Larkin', in *Driving Home: An American Scrapbook* (London: Picador, 2010), p. 88.
2. http://www.philly.com/philly/entertainment/literature/20120422_Collected_Philip_Larkin__A_sobering_triumph_of_exquisitely_finished_poems.html?viewAll=y&c=y#ixzz1snyCEM65.
3. 'Poets' poll crowns Larkin king of verse', *Guardian*, 15 October 2003, p. 8.
4. To Judy Egerton, 6 June 1982. *SL, p.* 674.
5. *Complete Poems*, p. xxvi.

6. 20 September 1945. *SL*, p. 110.

7. Oliver Marshall, 'Stories from the Doldrums', *Irish Times*, 18 May 2002, p. 8.

8. *Complete Poems*, p. xiii.

9. Dennis O'Driscoll, 'Scraping the bottom of the waste paper basket', *Irish Times*, 11 February 2012.

10. Paul Muldoon, *New York Times Sunday Book Review*, 19 April 2012.

11. To Patsy Strang, 12 July 1953. *SL*, p. 202.

12. W. N. Herbert and Matthew Hollis (eds), *Strong Words: Modern Poets on Modern Poetry* (Tarset: Bloodaxe Books, 2000), p. 150.

13. 'Statement', *RW*, p. 79.

14. 'The Pleasure Principle', *RW*, p. 89.

15. 'A Conversation with Ian Hamilton', *FR*, p. 24.

16. See R. J. C. Watt, *A Concordance to the Poetry of Philip Larkin* (Hildesheim: Olms-Weidmann, 1995).

17. Martin Amis, Introduction to *Philip Larkin: Poems* (London: Faber & Faber, 2011), p. x.

18. Motion, p. 313.

19. Interview with Mark Lawson, *Independent*, Sunday 7 March 1993.

20. Tom Paulin, letter to the *Times Literary Supplement*, 6 November 1992, p. 15.

21. David Mason, 'What Will Survive of Us', *Wall St Journal*, 14 April 2012.

22. Morten Hoi Jenssen, 'Larkin's Way', *Paris Review*, 3 April 2012.

23. William Logan, review of *The Complete Poems*, *Poetry* (Chicago), September 2012. http://www.poetryfoundation.org/poetrymagazine/article/244462.

24. Martin Amis, review of *Letters to Monica*, *Guardian*, 23 October 2010.

25. Amis, Introduction to *Philip Larkin: Poems*, pp. xvii, xxii.

26. Hartley, p. 209.

27. Ibid.

28. Ibid., p. 215.

29. *Absalom and Achitophel*, ll. 545–6.

30. Professor Raymond Brett, personal communication, 1974.

31. Betty Mackereth, interview with the author, 9 February 2013.

32. Brian Dyson (ed.), *The Modern Academic Library: Essays in Memory of Philip Larkin* (London: Library Association, 1988).

33. See James Booth, 'The Turf-cutter and the Nine-to-Five Man: Heaney, Larkin, and "the Spiritual Intellect's Great Work"', *Twentieth-Century Literature* 43.4 (Winter 1997), pp. 369–93.

34. Amis, Introduction to *Philip Larkin: Poems*, p. xvii.

35. Interview with the *Observer*, *RW*, 51; 'A Conversation with Ian Hamilton', *FR*, p. 23.

36. Raban, 'Philip Larkin', p. 89.

37. Interview with the *Observer*, *RW*, pp. 47, 53–4, 48, 47.

38. Tom Paulin, 'She Did Not Change: Philip Larkin', *Minotaur: Poetry and the Nation State* (London: Faber & Faber, 1992), p. 236.

39. Anthony Thwaite (ed.), *Larkin at Sixty* (London: Faber & Faber, 1982), illustration opposite p. 60.

40. 29 November 1952. *LM*, p. 94.

41. Interview with the *Observer*, *RW*, p. 52.
42. To Julian Barnes, 27 September 1985. *SL*, p. 751.
43. To Monica Jones, 16 November 1968. Not in *LM*.
44. Brennan, p. 24.
45. James Booth (ed.), 'Larkin's Second Dream Diary', *AL* 32 (October 2011), pp. 6–7.
46. Motion, p. 62.
47. Paul Bailey, *Independent*, 12 August 2005.
48. DX/329, inventory 600 pp. i–ix.
49. Nuala O'Faiolain, *Are You Somebody?* (New York: Henry Holt, 1996), p. 66.
50. Interview with the *Observer*, *RW*, p. 48.
51. To his parents, 2 February 1944.
52. To Eva Larkin, 10 December 1944.
53. Hartley, pp. 118, 81.
54. Bridget Mason (née Egerton), personal communication, 1 July 2011.
55. 'Letter to Bridget Egerton, aged Six', *AL* 32 (October 2011), p. 8.
56. Ann Thwaite, personal communication, 17 August 2011.
57. To Eva Larkin, 7 January 1951.
58. *Daily Telegraph*, 11 December 2010.
59. 'A Conversation with Ian Hamilton', *FR*, p. 23.
60. To Eva Larkin, 4 April 1954.
61. 6 August 1955. *LM*, pp. 174–5.
62. 'An Interview with John Haffenden', *FR*, 57.
63. Motion, p. 460.
64. Interview with *Paris Review*, *RW*, p. 66.
65. Angela Leighton, personal communication, 1984.

1: Dear Fambly (1922–40)

1. *LM*,p. 106.
2. Interview with the *Observer*, *RW*, p. 48.
3. To Sutton, 12–14 April 1943. Not in *SL*.
4. Autobiographical fragment at the beginning of Workbook 5. The first poetic draft in the workbook is dated 11 November 1953, and this fragment was presumably written immediately prior to this. DPL/1/5/1. Cited in Motion, p. 14.
5. Ibid.
6. Interview with the *Observer*, *RW*, p. 48.
7. Motion, p. 8.
8. 'These I have loved', *Journal of the Association of Local Government Financial Officers* 10.5 (January 1948), pp. 129–31. DLN/1/38.
9. Interview with the *Observer*, *RW*, p. 49.
10. Sydney Larkin obituary cutting. DLN/1/40.
11. DLN/2/2.
12. Noel Hughes told Andrew Motion that Sydney entered into correspondence with Schacht, though I have been unable to find any confirmation of this. Motion, p. 12.

13. DLN/1/34.

14. 21 and 22 August 1927. DLN/1/1.

15. 30 August 1929. DLN/1/1.

16. 19 August 1930. DLN/1/1.

17. 29 August 1931. DLN/1/1.

18. 13 August 1932. DLN/1/1.

19. James Booth, '"Snooker at the Seaside": The Birthday Walk in Scarborough', *AL* 16 (October 2003), pp. 29–31.

20. DPL/2/3/63/11. See Sheila Woolf, 'A Hearty Laugh? Philip Larkin at King Henry VIII School, Coventry', *AL* 28 (October 2009), pp. 15–16, at p. 16.

21. W. H. Rider, 'Colin Gunner Recollected', *AL* 13 (April 2002), p. 32.

22. Introduction to Colin Gunner, *Adventures with the Irish Brigade*, *FR*, pp. 120–1.

23. 'These I have loved'. DLN/1/38.

24. 1 August 1934. DLN/1/3.

25. 17 August 1936. DLN/1/5.

26. 'An Interview with John Haffenden', *FR*, p. 54.

27. Ibid.

28. Motion, p. 26.

29. Interview with the *Observer*, *RW*, p. 47. He may be alluding to King George VI's celebrated comment: 'Abroad is bloody.'

30. DLN/1/7 and DLN/1/8.

31. DLN/1/8.

32. Autobiographical fragment in Workbook 5. DPL/1/5/1.

33. Interview with the *Observer*, *RW*, p. 47.

34. 'Not the Place's Fault', *FR*, p. 7.

35. 'The young Mr Larkin', in Anthony Thwaite (ed.), *Larkin at Sixty* (London: Faber & Faber, 1982), p. 21.

36. 'Not the Place's Fault', *FR*, p. 9.

37. *SL*, p. 416.

38. To Sutton, 9 August 1939. Not in *SL*.

39. 'Not the Place's Fault', *FR*, p. 9.

40. *AWJ*, p. 16.

41. To Sutton, 'Friday night' (1939 or 1940). Not in *SL*.

42. *AWJ*, p. 16.

43. DLN/1/10–29. Sydney Larkin's wartime diaries are closed to researchers until 2015.

44. Motion, p. 12.

45. Richard Bradford, *First Boredom, Then Fear: The Life of Philip Larkin* (London: Peter Owen, 2005), p. 25; *The Odd Couple: The Curious Friendship between Kingsley Amis and Philip Larkin* (London: Robson Press, 2012), p. 7.

46. James Booth, 'Sydney Larkin's Little Hitler', *AL* 29 (April 2010), p. 27.

47. Motion, pp. 492–3.

48. Fred Holland, personal communication, 2011.

49. Autobiographical fragment. DPL/1/5/1.

50. To Sutton, 6 September 1939. Reproduced as the front endpaper of *SL*.

51. To Sutton, 1 April 1942. Not in *SL*.

52. To Sutton, 2 January 1943. *SL*, p. 53.

53. To Sutton, 'Friday night' (1939 or 1940). Not in *SL*.

54. To his family, 7 March 1943.

55. 'Not the Place's Fault', *FR*, pp. 10–11.

56. One minor difference is that Sydney almost always spells 'and' in full, whereas Philip generally uses a plus sign.

57. 'Not the Place's Fault', *FR*, p. 10.

58. Burnett gives the full official version. *Complete Poems*, p. 510.

59. Philip Larkin, *Incidents from Phippy's Schooldays*, ed. Brenda Allen and James Acheson, with illustrations by Rodney Fitzgerald (Edmonton, Canada: Juvenilia Press, 2002).

60. James Booth, 'Larkin's Schoolboy Writings', *AL* 13 (April 2002), pp. 21–8.

61. 'Stanley en Musique', 'À un ami qui aime', 'Stanley et la Glace'.

62. *Jill*, p. 78.

63. Booth, 'Larkin's Schoolboy Writings', pp. 21–8.

64. 15 October 1940. James Booth, '"Dear Pop and Mop": The Larkin Family Letters Arrive in Hull', *AL* 25 (April 2008), pp. 16–17, at p. 16.

65. Ibid.

66. *Jill*, p. 12.

67. 26 October 1940. Booth, '"Dear Pop and Mop": The Larkin Family Letters Arrive in Hull', p. 16.

68. 17 November 1940. DLN/1/32.

69. *Jill*, p. 214.

70. Letter beginning 'Dear fambly', 18 November 1940.

71. BD1, p. 10.

72. For the Lichfield context see David Gerard, 'Family Matters', *AL* 12 (October 2001), p. 31.

73. Motion, p. 41.

74. BD1, p. 6.

75. Kingsley Amis, 'Oxford and After', in Thwaite (ed.), *Larkin at Sixty*, p. 25.

76. See Janice Rossen, 'Larkin at Oxford: Chaucer, Langland and Bruce Montgomery', *Journal of Modern Literature* 21.2 (Winter 1997), pp. 295–311.

77. 'Writing Poems' (1964), *RW*, p. 84.

78. Ibid.

79. S. T. Coleridge, *Biographia Literaria* (London: J. M. Dent, 1956), p. 167.

80. T. S. Eliot, 'Tradition and the Individual Talent', *Selected Essays 1917–1932* (London: Faber & Faber, 1932), p. 15.

81. 'A Conversation with Ian Hamilton', *FR*, pp. 19–20.

82. Interview with *Paris Review*, *RW*, p. 74.

2: Exemption (1941–3)

1. Kingsley Amis, *Memoirs* (London: Hutchinson, 1991), p. 55.

2. Though Kitty's name was Catherine, he addresses the envelope in florid

copperplate 'Miss Katherine Larkin', mentioning the 'elaborate envelope' in which her own previous letter had arrived.

3. DLN/3/2.

4. To Sutton, 16 June 1941. Not in *SL*.

5. 'The Art of Jazz' (1940), in *Larkin's Jazz: Essays and Reviews 1940–84*, ed. Richard Palmer and John White (London and New York: Continuum, 2001), pp. 169–70.

6. BD1, p. 5.

7. To Sutton, 26 March 1941. Not in *SL*.

8. *Jill*, Introduction, pp. 14–15.

9. Motion, p. 54.

10. Ibid., p. 55.

11. Richard Bradford, *The Odd Couple: The Curious Friendship between Kingsley Amis and Philip Larkin* (London: Robson Press, 2012), p. 65.

12. See ibid., pp. 71-2.

13. Amis, *Memoirs*, p. 54.

14. Motion, p. 59.

15. *Jill*, p. 17.

16. BD1, p. 9.

17. Ibid., p. 8.

18. 'Our Group', *London Magazine*, December/January 1999/2000, pp. 26–7.

19. 'Story 1', *AL* 10 (October 2000), pp. 4–20, at p. 19.

20. 'Peter', *AL* 11 (April 2001), pp. 13–23, at p. 21. Two similar typed stories, as yet unpublished, are 'The Eagles Are Gone' and 'Maurice' (DPL/2/1/1/4 and DPL/2/1/1/6).

21. Trevor Tolley and John White (eds), *Larkin's Jazz*, Properbox 155 (four-CD set), disc 2 'Oxford', track 6.

22. 'Peter', p. 14.

23. Ibid., pp. 14–16.

24. Ibid., p. 19

25. Ibid., p. 22.

26. To Sutton, 9 July 1941. Not in *SL*.

27. BD1, p. 7.

28. Ibid.

29. Ibid.

30. DLN/3/2/2.

31. BD2, p. 5.

32. Ibid.

33. Ibid., p. 6.

34. 20 November 1941. *SL*, p. 28.

35. BD2, p. 6.

36. Ibid.

37. To Sutton, 20 November 1941. *SL*, p. 28. Passage not in *SL*. See Don Lee, 'Larkin attends a jam session at Abbey Road Studios (1941)', *AL* 27 (April 2009), p. 14.

38. Tolley and White (eds), *Larkin's Jazz*, disc 2 'Oxford', track 24.

39. 20 November 1941. *SL*, p. 27.

40. BD1, p. 9.
41. Ibid.
42. See David Gerard, 'Oxford Roundabout: Or Currents Turned Awry' (The Fourth Larkin Society Birthday Walk), *AL* 10 (October 2000), pp. 34–6, at p. 34.
43. Motion, p. 65.
44. Ibid., p. 74.
45. BD1, p. 9.
46. Ibid.
47. 'Larkin at Twenty: Warwick, August 1942', ed. Don Lee and James Booth, *AL* 14 (October 2002), pp. 5–10, at p. 6.
48. Presumably a reference to Alan Ross, author, publisher and editor, a contemporary of Larkin and Amis at Oxford. See LKA, p. 93.
49. Ibid.
50. Ibid., p. 7.
51. Ibid. Larkin refers to D. H. Lawrence's novel.
52. Ibid.
53. Ibid., p. 8.
54. Ibid., p. 9. Parts of this letter appear in *SL*, pp. 42–4.
55. Passage not in *SL*.
56. Ibid.
57. In *SL* (p. 43) Thwaite mistranscribed 'scoffing' as 'slobbering'.
58. Prince George, Duke of Kent, the fourth son of George V, was killed in a plane crash in 1942.
59. 'Larkin at Twenty', pp. 9–10.
60. Ibid., pp. 5–6.
61. Bradford, *The Odd Couple*, p. 48.
62. See ibid., pp. 51–2.
63. Motion, p. 61.
64. Nuala O'Faiolain, *Are You Somebody?* (New York: Henry Holt, 1996), p. 66.
65. Motion, p. 78.
66. In BD2, p. 5, I mistranscribed 'gently' as 'greatly'. Penelope's name was Scott Stokes, without the hyphen which Larkin has mistakenly inserted.
67. Susannah Tarbush, 'From *Willow Gables* to "Aubade": Penelope Scott Stokes and Philip Larkin: Part 1', *AL* 25 (April 2008), pp. 5–11, at p. 8.
68. Ibid., p. 5.
69. *SL*, p. 105.
70. *AGW*, p. 173.
71. DPL/2/2/39.
72. DPL(2)/1/4/4. Tarbush, Part 1, pp. 10–11.
73. Geoff Weston, 'Sidney Keyes and Larkin: A Postscript', *AL* 30 (October 2010), p. 15. See also David Wheatley, 'Larkin and Sidney Keyes, or, The Case of the Mechanical Turd', *AL* 28 (October 2009), pp. 17–19.
74. Burnett (*Complete Poems*, pp. xix–xx) is mistaken in asserting that the lines following the asterisk are 'not a continuation of the parody'. He also states incorrectly that

the first two lines are in a 'different metre' from the rest. In fact a rough pentameter metre is maintained in all eleven lines. Burnett's notion that the second and third sections are 'disparate pieces of text' is also misguided. They both refer to his parents, are woven together by rhymes and pararhymes and are clearly sequential.

75. BD1, p. 10.
76. BD2, p. 6.
77. 'Larkin's Dream Diary 1942–3, Part 1', ed. Don Lee, *AL* 27 (April 2009), pp. 5–13, and 'Part 2', *AL* 28 (October 2009), pp. 5–13.
78. 'Larkin's Dream Diary, Part 2', p. 6. Margaret Flannery appears in *Trouble at Willow Gables*, her name being subsequently altered to Margaret Tattenham.
79. 'Larkin's Dream Diary, Part 1' and 'Part 2'.
80. To Sutton, 7 January 1943. Not in *SL*.
81. 'Introduction to *The North Ship*', *RW*, p. 29.
82. 'Vernon Watkins, an Encounter and a Re-encounter', *RW*, p. 42.
83. *RW*, pp. 43–4.

3: Brunette Coleman (1943)

1. To his parents, 20 June 1943.
2. BD2, p. 8.
3. Ibid., p. 6.
4. *Jill*, Introduction, p. 19.
5. David Gerard, 'Oxford Roundabout: Or Currents Turned Awry', *AL* 10 (October 2000), pp. 34–6. Diana Gollancz married Prince Leopold of Löwenstein-Wertheim-Freudenberg (1903–74), who published a memoir following her untimely death in 1967, *A Time to Live – A Time to Die* (New York: Doubleday, 1971).
6. BD2, p. 8.
7. 6 July 1943. *SL*, p. 59.
8. To Sutton, 28 July 1943. Not in *SL*.
9. 'An Incident in the English Camp', *AL* 12 (October 2001), pp. 5–10.
10. Ibid., p. 6.
11. Letter beginning 'Dear fambly', 18 November 1940.
12. 'An Incident in the English Camp', p. 6. The reading is confirmed by the original deleted version: 'peanut shaped head'.
13. 'An Incident in the English Camp', pp. 7–9.
14. Ibid., p. 10.
15. Ibid.
16. BD2, p. 8.
17. To Sutton, 14 May 1943. Not in *SL*.
18. To his parents, 15 May 1943.
19. During the war Blanche Coleman's group performed at the Royal Opera House, Covent Garden, which had been converted into a dance hall for service personnel. She died in 2008. *The Times*, 6 May 2008.
20. To Amis, 11 January 1947. Passage not in *SL*.

21. *Jill*, p. 19.
22. To his parents, 27 June 1943.
23. *SL*, p. 60.
24. Motion, p. 106. A fragmentary *jeu d'esprit*, 'Ante Meridian: The Autobiography of Brunette Coleman' interrupts the manuscript of *Michaelmas Term at St. Bride's* for nine pages, but its broad farce and lack of girls'-school references set it apart from the main Brunette canon.
25. To Amis, 24 October 1943. Not in *SL*. Motion wrote parts of his biography by dictation, which causes some mistakes. Vicary becomes 'Vickery', Breary becomes 'Breany', Burch becomes 'Birch', and Melibee becomes 'Mellaby' (Motion, pp. 100, 93, 184). 'What Are We Writing For?' becomes, inadvertently, 'What We Are Writing For' (pp. 100–1).
26. Sue Sims, review of *Trouble at Willow Gables and Other Fictions* by Philip Larkin, *AL* 14 (October 2002), pp. 37–9, at p. 38.
27. *TWG*, p. 12.
28. Ibid., 49–50.
29. Théophile Gautier, *Mademoiselle de Maupin*, trans. R. and E. Powys Mathers (London: Folio Society, 1948), p. 17.
30. Ibid., p. 266.
31. *TWG*, p. 84.
32. Ibid., p. 89.
33. Vicary, *Niece of the Headmistress*, p. 119.
34. *TWG*, p. 105.
35. Ibid., p. 128.
36. Motion, p. 62.
37. 12 October 1943. *SL*, p. 75.
38. To Amis, 24 October 1943. Not in *SL*.
39. To Amis, 7 September 1943. Not in *SL*.
40. Julian Hall, *The Senior Commoner* (London: Martin Secker, 1934). See *TWG*, p. xiv. At one point in Hall's novel a visitor to the school recalls a particularly attractive pupil: 'A brunette, isn't he?' (p. 373).
41. 'The Lesbianism of Philip Larkin', *The Movement Reconsidered*, ed. Zachary Leader (Oxford: OUP, 2009), p. 96.
42. http://www.bodley.ox.ac.uk/dept/scwmss/wmss/online/modern/montgomery/montgomery.html.
43. 12 October 1943. *SL*, p. 75.
44. See 'A Catalogue of the Papers of Victor Gollancz', University of Warwick, MSS.157/3/P/DOM/3/1–67.
45. Bodleian, MS Eng. C.3894, fol. 132.
46. Trevor Tolley and John White (eds), *Larkin's Jazz*, Properbox 155 (four-CD set), disc 2 'Oxford', track 8.
47. *LKA*, p. 17.
48. *The Complete Works of George Orwell*, vol. 12: *1940–1*, ed. Peter Davison (London: Secker & Warburg, 1998), pp. 57–79.

49. *The Complete Works of George Orwell*, vol. 14: *1941–2*, ed. Peter Davison (London: Secker & Warburg, 1998), p. 65.

50. Rosemary Auchmuty, *The World of Girls* (London: The Women's Press, 1992), p. 205.

51. *TWG*, p. 256.

52. Ibid., p. 269.

53. Larkin kept one of the four copies of *Sugar and Spice* himself (now in the University of Hull Collection, The History Centre, Hull, DPL(2)/1/11), gave one to Bruce Montgomery (now in the Bodleian), one to Kingsley Amis (now in the Huntington Library, California) and one to Miriam Plaut, a possible model for Katherine in *A Girl in Winter* (see *SL*, pp. 77–8).

54. Fairlie Bruce's poem forms the epigraph to *Dimsie Moves Up Again*, p. 6. See *TWG*, p. 266.

55. 'The hills in their recumbent postures', *Complete Poems*, pp. 179, 542.

56. BD2, p. 8.

57. *SL*, p. 658.

58. *TWG*, p. 243.

59. *SL*, p. 66.

60. *TWG*, pp. 247–8. In l.2 Burnett has, incorrectly, 'whom I once knew' (*Complete Poems*, p. 227)

61. Charles Baudelaire, *Les Épaves* (1866).

62. See Graham Chesters, 'Larkin and Baudelaire's Damned Women', in James Dolamore (ed.), *Making Connections: Essays in French Culture and Society in Honour of Philip Thody* (Bern: Peter Lang, 1999), pp. 81–92.

63. The original names of the characters remain unaltered in the second novella.

64. *TWG*, pp. 168–75.

65. BD2, p. 8.

66. *TWG*, p. 181.

67. Ibid., p. 184.

68. Ibid.

69. Ibid., p. 188.

70. Ibid., p. 223.

71. Ibid., pp. 229–30.

72. To Amis, 7 September 1943. Not in *SL*.

73. Interview with the *Observer*, *RW*, p. 51.

4: Nothing So Glad (1943–5)

1. Ruth Siverns, 'Philip Larkin at Wellington 1943–1946', *AL* 1 (April 1996), pp. 4–5, at p. 4.

2. David Gerard, 'Wellington Walkabout', *AL* 8 (October 1999), pp. 27–30, at p. 30. 'Glentworth' still stands.

3. *SL*, p. 85.

4. To Sutton, 22 March 1944. Not in *SL*.

5. *RW*, pp. 31–5.

6. Ibid., p. 33.

7. To Sutton, 22 March 1944.

8. Maeve Brennan, 'Philip Larkin: a biographical sketch', in Brian Dyson (ed.), *The Modern Academic Library: Essays in Memory of Philip Larkin* (London: Library Association, 1988), pp. 1–19, at pp. 5–6.

9. 'Single-handed and Untrained', *RW*, p. 34.

10. Siverns, 'Philip Larkin at Wellington', p. 4.

11. Ibid.

12. Motion, p. 120.

13. Gerard, 'Wellington Walkabout', p. 29.

14. Motion, p. 122.

15. Gerard, 'Wellington Walkabout', p. 29.

16. To Sutton, 26 February 1944. *SL*, p. 87.

17. For Caton (1897–1971) see Timothy D'Arch Smith, *R. A. Caton and the Fortune Press: A Memoir and a Hand-List* (revised edn, North Pomfret, Vermont: Asphodel Editions, 2004).

18. *The North Ship* (London: Fortune Press, 1945; first Faber & Faber edn, 1966), Introduction, p. 9. The reprint in *RW* (p. 29) corrects the quotation to 'cast out remorse'.

19. Ibid., p. 7.

20. This is the reading in William Bell (ed.), *Poetry from Oxford in Wartime* (London: Fortune Press, 1944), p. 77, and also in the 1945 Fortune Press edition of *The North Ship* (not noted by Burnett). The 1966 reissue of *The North Ship* has the more correct but less tremulous plural 'seraphim'.

21. Letter from Bruce Montgomery to Larkin, 20 October 1944. Bodleian MS Eng. C.2762.

22. *The North Ship*, p. 8.

23. Ibid.

24. Ibid., p. 9.

25. R. J. C. Watt, '"Scragged by embryo-Leavises": Larkin reading his poems', *Critical Survey* 1.2 (1989), pp. 172–5, at p. 175.

26. 'Ephemera', l. 12: W. B. Yeats, *Selected Poetry*, ed. A. Norman Jeffares (London: Macmillan, 1962), p. 4.

27. Ibid., p. 10.

28. See Don Lee, 'Coventry Godiva Festival Weekend: 4–6 May 1999', *AL* 8 (October 1999), p. 19.

29. Postcard to his parents, 29 October 1946.

30. To Alan Pringle, 23 August 1946. *SL*, p. 123.

5: The Novels (1943–5)

1. John Banville, review of *Complete Poems*, *Guardian*, 25 January 2012.

2. Interview with *Paris Review*, *RW*, p. 63.

3. To Sutton, 10 August 1943. *SL*, pp. 61–2.

4. *RW*, p. 63.

5. *Jill*, Introduction, p. 13.

6. To Sutton, 28 December 1940. Not in *SL*.
7. *Jill*, p. 97.
8. To Sutton, 30 September 1943. Not in *SL*.
9. To Sutton, 16 August 1943. Not in *SL*.
10. To Sutton, 29 December 1943. Not in *SL*.
11. *Jill*, pp. 131–2.
12. Théophile Gautier, *Mademoiselle de Maupin*, trans. R. and E. Powys Mathers (London: Folio Society, 1948), p. 87.
13. *Jill*, p. 149.
14. Ibid., p. 152.
15. Ibid., p. 186.
16. Ibid., p. 188.
17. Ibid., p. 211.
18. Ibid.
19. Ibid., p. 212.
20. Ibid., p. 215.
21. Ibid., p. 218.
22. Ibid.
23. Ibid., p. 219.
24. Ibid., p. 124.
25. Ibid., p. 230.
26. Larkin must have in mind Earlsdon Library in Coventry, rather than the small, one-man library in Wellington.
27. DPL/4/4, 1.
28. To Sutton, 10 December 1944. Not in *SL*.
29. To Sutton, 14 September 1944. Not in *SL*.
30. To Sutton, 10 December 1944.
31. *AGW*, p. 27.
32. Ibid., p. 44.
33. Ibid., p. 48.
34. Ibid., p. 69.
35. Ibid., p. 142.
36. DPL/4/4, inside cover opposite p. 1; DPL/4/4, p. 4.
37. DPL/4/4, inside cover opposite p. 1.
38. To Amis, 30 June 1981. See *LKA*, p. 925n.
39. See Birte Wiemann, 'Larkin's Englishness: A German Perspective', *AL* 29 (April 2010), pp. 25–6.
40. *AGW*, pp. 87–8.
41. Ibid., p. 113.
42. Ibid., p. 130.
43. Ibid., p. 69; Carol Rumens, '"I don't understand cream cakes, but I eat them": Distance and difference in *A Girl in Winter*', *AL* 29 (April 2010), pp. 7–12, at pp. 8–9.
44. *AGW*, pp. 158–9, 166–9.

45. To Amis, 13 September 1945. Not in *SL*.

46. *TWG*, p. 474.

47. Thomas Hardy, '*In Tenebris* II', l. 14.

48. Motion suggests that the name is based on Astley-Jones, Chief Clerk of Wellington UDC, who had misspelled Larkin's name ('Larking') in the letter offering him the Wellington post. Motion, p. 159.

49. *AGW, p.* 210.

50. Ibid., p. 243.

51. Ibid., p. 248.

52. To Barbara Pym, 18 November 1961. *SL*, p. 334.

6: The Grip of Light (1945–8)

1. *SL*, p. 104.

2. Ibid., pp. 104–5.

3. From Ruth Bowman to Larkin, 12 April 1947. Motion, p. 170.

4. To Sutton, 9 March 1945. Not in *SL*.

5. From Ruth Bowman to Larkin, 27 October 1945. Motion, p. 135.

6. Ruth Siverns (née Bowman), personal communication, 2 April 1999. Philip preserved Ruth's letters to him, and directed that they be returned to her after his death.

7. Motion, p. 122.

8. The first completed draft in the new workbook was of 'If grief could burn out', dated 5 October 1944. DPL/1/1/3.

9. All except pp. 2–10 (which seem to be lost) are preserved in the University of Hull collection in the History Centre, Hull, DPL/2/1/14 and DPL/1/2/50. See Trevor Tolley, 'Lost Pages', *AL* 11 (April 2001), pp. 24–7.

10. The title is from a typescript in the Bodleian. In the workbook it was titled 'For my Father'. See *Complete Poems*, p. 577. The workbook page on which it is written was one of those later torn out.

11. 'Plymouth' and 'Portrait' were published in *Mandrake*, May 1946. In the typescript of *In the Grip of Light*, 'Portrait' was retitled 'The quiet one'. *Complete Poems*, p. 486.

12. Jean Hartley recalled Larkin's disconcerting lack of inhibition about farting in company. At the age of nineteen he had written to Sutton: 'I have just farted with the sound of an iron ruler twanging in a desk-lid and the smell of a west wind over a decaying patch of red cabbages.' 31 December 1941, *SL*, p. 30.

13. The house has been demolished. See David Gerard, 'Wellington Walkabout', *AL* 8 (October 1999), p. 30.

14. 'The Poetry of Hardy', *RW*, p. 175.

15. Ibid.

16. Ibid.

17. Philip Larkin, *Early Poems and Juvenilia*, ed. A. T. Tolley (London: Faber & Faber, 2005).

18. Counting 'Two Guitar Pieces' and 'Two Portraits of Sex' as two poems each, and 'Livings' as three.

19. Completed by 23 February 1946. The date given in the 1988 *Collected Poems* is incorrect. *Complete Poems*, p. 587.

20. 1 April 1946. *LKA*, p. 54.

21. 7 April 1946. *SL*, p. 116.

22. 24 June and 15 July 1946. *LKA*, pp. 76 and 79.

23. To Sutton, 28 July 1946. Not in *SL*.

24. To Sutton, 26 June 1946. Not in *SL*.

25. Postcard to his parents, 7 February 1945.

26. Letter to his parents, 31 March 1946.

27. To his parents, 24 June 1945.

28. To his parents, 30 June 1946.

29. To his parents, 7 July 1946.

30. While awaiting Jill's visit, John Kemp imagines that he knows 'for one curious transient second [. . .] how a bride feels on the morning of her wedding'. *Jill*, p. 185.

31. Burnett (*Complete Poems*, p. 358) claims that it is almost certainly this poem to which Larkin was referring in his 1973 comment that he had written his first 'good poem' when he was twenty-six. However, the poet had only just turned twenty-four in September 1946. Larkin may perhaps have meant 'An April Sunday brings the snow', written a few months before his twenty-sixth birthday, or 'At Grass', written when he was twenty-seven.

32. Motion, p. 153.

33. *The Poems of Andrew Marvell* (London: Routledge & Kegan Paul, 1956), p. 53.

34. DPL/2/3/63.

35. 'The Poetry of Hardy', *RW*, p. 176.

36. 'Larkin's Dream Diary 1942–3, Part 2', ed. Don Lee, *AL* 28 (October 2009), p. 12.

37. Only a single detached page of this second dream diary survives, loosely inserted into the second workbook (DPL/1/2/51). It is misdated 1942 in the catalogue on the assumption that it is part of the earlier dream diary. But the reference to Gillian Evans dates it to 1946. See James Booth, 'Larkin's Second Dream Diary', *AL* 32 (October 2011), pp. 6–7.

38. DPL/1/2/51.

39. 26 February 1947. *SL*, p. 135.

40. DPL/1/2/51.

41. 2 December 1946. *LKA*, p. 103.

42. 26 March 1947. *LKA*, p. 124.

43. From Kingsley Amis, 5 May 1947. Passage not in *LKA*.

44. 26 February 1947. *SL*, p. 136.

45. Anthony Thwaite, personal communication, 7 June 2013. Not in *Complete Poems*.

46. Motion, p. 119.

47. 15 March 1947. *LKA*, p. 117.

48. 21 December 1946. *LM*, p. 3.

49. Motion, p. 170.

50. Postcard to Sydney Larkin, addressed to 'Ward 2, Warwick Hospital', 24 February 1948. 'Nottingham have taken up my references.'

51. 14 January 1948. *SL*, p. 143.

52. 28 January 1948. *SL*, p. 144.

53. 'Going', 'Deep Analysis', 'Come then to prayers', 'And the wave sings because it is moving', 'Two Guitar Pieces', 'The Dedicated', 'Wedding-Wind', 'Träumerei', 'To a Very Slow Air', 'At the chiming of light upon sleep', 'Many famous feet have trod', 'Thaw'.

7: Just Too Hard for Me (1945–50)

1. A Conversation with Neil Powell, *FR*, p. 32.

2. Ibid.

3. Interview with the *Observer*, *RW*, p. 49.

4. 20 September 1945. *SL*, pp. 109–10.

5. To Sutton, 5 March 1942. Not in *SL*.

6. W. H. Auden, *The English Auden*, ed. Edward Mandelson (London: Faber & Faber, 1977), p. 238.

7. A Conversation with Ian Hamilton, *FR*, p. 24.

8. Ibid.

9. 12 October 1943. *SL*, p. 75.

10. Richard Bradford, *The Odd Couple: The Curious Friendship between Kingsley Amis and Philip Larkin* (London: Robson Press, 2012), pp. 91–2.

11. *TWG*, pp. 279–80.

12. See ibid., pp. xxxiii–xxxv.

13. Ibid., p. 313.

14. Bradford, *The Odd Couple*, pp. 91–2.

15. *TWG*, p. 324n.

16. Ibid., p. 324.

17. Personal communication, Ruth Siverns (née Bowman), 2 April 1999.

18. *TWG*, p. 356.

19. Interview with the *Observer*, *RW*, p. 49.

20. A Conversation with Ian Hamilton, *FR*, p. 24.

21. Pamela Hanley, personal communication, 18 October 2000. For reminiscences of Monica in Leicester see *AL* 12 (October 2001), pp. 14–20. For a sample of Monica's essay-marking style see James Booth, *Philip Larkin: Writer* (Hemel Hempstead: Harvester Wheatsheaf, 1992), pp. 26–7.

22. *TWG*, p. 371.

23. None of Larkin's contemporaries at Leicester is able to identify a model for Mrs Klein. There was a refugee from Germany at the University College, but she was nothing like Larkin's character. Monica Jones commented: 'There may have been someone Philip knew, but I didn't.' James Booth, 'Glimpses' (interview with Monica Jones), *AL* 12 (October 2001), p. 22.

24. *TWG*, pp. 371–2.

25. Ibid., p. 370.

26. Ibid., p. 463.

27. Ibid., pp. 450, 463.

28. 8 September 1948. *LKA*, p. 186.

29. LKA, p. 209.

30. The name is, appropriately, that of the minor society poet Winthrop Mackworth Praed (1802–39).

31. *TWG*, pp. 422–42.

32. Monica Jones, personal communication, 26 January 1999.

33. 'An Interview with John Haffenden', *FR*, p. 49.

8: Crisis and Escape (1947–50)

1. 6 December 1947. *LKA*, p. 145.

2. Motion (p. 180) misdates the marriage in August.

3. Letter to his parents, 27 May 1947.

4. *SL*, p. 143.

5. Ibid., p. 144.

6. Ibid., pp. 144–5.

7. *LM*, p. 5.

8. The last of these plum trees succumbed in 2012. See also David Gerard and Graham Landon, 'Plum, in the Middle: The Sixth Annual Birthday Walk', *AL* 14 (October 2002), pp. 20–4.

9. *Radio Times*, 16 August 1973, p. 11. Burnett (*Complete Poems*, p. 358) believes this poem was 'Wedding-Wind', but Larkin was only twenty-four when he wrote that poem.

10. DPL/1/1/72.

11. DPL/2/1/1/14. A.T. Tolley, 'Lost Pages', *AL* 11 (April 2001), p. 26. Burnett includes the lines in *Complete Poems* 'on the chance that they may constitute a complete poem' (p. 592).

12. 18 May 1948. *SL*, p. 147.

13. 11 August 1948. *SL*, p. 148.

14. When Trevor Tolley asked him about the torn-out pages in the early 1980s Larkin replied with evasive casualness: 'Some missing pages contained material I did not wish to make public, and probably still have somewhere; others were torn out simply when I wanted a sheet of blank paper, for any reason.' Tolley, 'Lost Pages', p. 26.

15. He even kept one half-page which is quite blank. Ibid.

16. Burnett corrects 'blocks' in Thwaite's *Collected Poems* of 1988.

17. Burnett (*Complete Poems*, p. 593) does not mention the original title. See Tolley, 'Lost Pages', p. 24.

18. Burnett mentions only the typescript and follows the 1988 *Collected Poems* in dating the poem '?1950'.

19. Burnett restores the parentheses omitted by Thwaite in the *Collected Poems*.

20. Interview with *Paris Review*, *RW*, p. 74.

21. *SL*, p. 152.

22. *LKA*, pp. 204–5.

23. 13 July 1949. *SL*, p. 153.

24. To Sutton, 3 October 1949. Not in *SL*.

25. *SL*, p. 156.

26. To Sutton, 26 January 1950. *SL*, p. 158.

27. To Sutton, 4 May 1950. *SL*, p. 161.

28. The workbook shows that in the final version Larkin excluded some explicit moralizing over the exploitation of the horses in the interests of human greed: 'They lived in terms of men, hedged in / By bet and bid'; 'money rode them, led them in'. DPL/1/1/82. See also Philip Larkin, 'Worksheets of "At Grass"', *Phoenix* 11/12 (1973/4), pp. 93–8.

29. He made further adjustments to the second stanza in November 1950 (DPL/1/2/24) and before its publication in *XX Poems*. *Complete Poems*, p. 381.

30. Hartley, p. 76.

31. Henry Mayhew, *London Labour and the London Poor IV* (1862; London: Frank Cass, 1967), p. 240.

32. Janice Rossen, *Philip Larkin: His Life's Work* (Hemel Hempstead: Harvester Wheatsheaf, 1989), p. 89; Joseph Bristow, 'The Obscenity of Philip Larkin', *Critical Inquiry* 21 (Autumn 1994), pp. 176–7. See also James Booth, *Philip Larkin: Writer* (Hemel Hempstead: Harvester Wheatsheaf, 1992), pp. 108–12.

33. Richard Bradford, *The Odd Couple: The Curious Friendship between Kingsley Amis and Philip Larkin* (London: Robson Press, 2012), p. 87.

34. DPL/3/1/3.

35. DPL/1/2/1.

36. DPL/1/2/6.

37. See for instance the photograph in *AL* 12 (October 2001), p. 17.

38. A deleted draft passage is even more metaphorically tangled:

> And the vertiginous wedge, would, would stick in her throat
> Like a half-chewed bandage, till she fell on her knees,
> An endless recession of motives patterning the light [. . .] (DPL/1/2/9)

39. Larkin considered 'unprintable', but took Amis's advice that this 'would just mean cunt, whereas unpriceable *probably* meant cunt but could mean all sorts of other things too'. 'An Interview with John Haffenden', *FR*, p. 55.

40. James Booth, 'Glimpses' (interview with Monica Jones), *AL* 12 (October 2001), p. 22.

41. *SL*, p. 165.

42. To Sutton, 18 June 1950. Not in *SL*.

43. To Sutton, 3 July 1950. Not in *SL*. My impression of Larkin's correspondence differs from Motion's: 'Larkin seldom hesitated to complain about whatever was bothering him to anyone who would listen.' Motion, p. 182.

44. To Sutton, 26 July 1950. Not in *SL*.

45. *SL*, p. 166.

46. To Sutton, 26 January 1950. *SL*, p. 157.

47. *LKA*, pp. 228–9.

48. *TWG*, p. 473.
49. Ibid., p. 476.
50. Ibid., p. 479.
51. Ibid., p. 482.
52. DPL/1/2/20. It is omitted as incomplete from the *Collected Poems* and the *Complete Poems*. Motion gives an edited version (pp. 196–7). Motion (p. 195) gives the date of Larkin's departure, incorrectly, as 16 September.

9: The Best Writing Conditions (1950–2)

1. Michael Innes was the pen-name of John Innes Mackintosh Stewart (1906–94), Scottish academic and author of crime fiction.
2. *LM*, pp. 9–10.
3. Ibid., p. 10.
4. Misdated 25 November in *LM*. Larkin writes on the first page 'Tuesday 28th Nov.' In 1950 25 November fell on Saturday.
5. *LM*, p. 23. The cartoon and dialogue are omitted in *LM*.
6. Not in *LM*.
7. *LM*, p. 42.
8. 23 May 1951. *LM*, p. 38.
9. 15 September 1951. *LM*, p. 58.
10. James Booth, 'Glimpses' (interview with Monica Jones), *AL* 12 (October 2001), pp. 21–6, at p. 21.
11. 21 November 1950. *LM*, p. 21n.
12. *LM*, pp. 45–6 and n.
13. Winifred Dawson (née Arnott), personal communication, 21 November 2011.
14. Motion, p. 202. Motion relates this comment to Larkin's reading of H. E. Berthon's *Nine French Poets 1820–1880* (London: Macmillan, 1930, with later reprints). But Laforgue (whose first volume was published in 1885) is not included in the volume.
15. Interview with *Paris Review*, *RW*, p. 58.
16. *LM*, p. 35. *LM* omits 'or the implied-conceit kind (*Moments of Vision*)'.
17. Ibid.
18. To Monica Jones, 14 February 1951. Not in *LM*.
19. Larkin to Barry Bloomfield, 1977. Motion, p. 215.
20. 'Going', 'Wedding-Wind', 'At Grass', 'Deceptions', 'Coming', 'Dry-Point', 'Spring', 'If, My Darling', 'Wants', 'No Road', 'Wires', 'Next, Please', 'Latest Face'.
21. Unpublished interview, *South Bank Show*, 16 April 1981. Motion, p. 216.
22. *LM*, p. 55.
23. Unpublished interview, *South Bank Show*. Motion, p. 215.
24. 26 November 1951. *LM*, p. 25.
25. Ibid.
26. DPL/1/2/28.
27. DPL/1/2/29. Not in *Complete Poems*.

28. 'Tes mollets farauds, / Ton buste tentant, / – Gai, comme impudent, / Ton cul ferme et gros, // Nous boutent au sang / Un feu bête et doux / Qui nous rend tout fous, / Croupe, rein et flanc.'

29. He did not recognize Verlaine's demotic form 'gas' for 'gars' ('lads'). It is excluded as incomplete from the *Collected Poems* and the *Complete Poems*. For a facsimile of the workbook page and a transcription of the poem see *AL* 36 (October 2013), pp. 4–5.

30. DPL/1/2/30.

31. DPL/1/2/34.

32. 'Poet's Choice', *FR*, p. 17.

33. Graham Chesters, 'Tireless Play: Speculations on Larkin's "Absences"', in Richard Bales (ed.), *Challenges of Translation in French Literature: Studies and Poems in Honour of Peter Broome* (Bern: Peter Lang, 2005), pp. 47–60.

34. 'Poet's Choice', *FR*, p. 17.

35. The word occurs a third time in 'Unfinished Poem' (October 1953), in which the poet hides away from Death in a squalid 'emaciate attic'. It seems likely that Larkin held back this poem from publication to avoid diluting the effect of the word. The odd form 'attic'd' appears as a self-parodic joke in the late light-verse exercise, 'Good for you, Gavin', written in 1981.

36. 13 January 1951. Passage not in *LM*.

37. 6 October 1951. *LM*, p. 63.

38. One draft has the title 'Tenth Days'. The final title was added in *The Less Deceived. Complete Poems*, p. 362.

39. Winifred Dawson (née Arnott), interview with the author, 21 October 2003.

40. Motion, p. 209.

41. Ibid., p. 212.

42. Ibid., p. 213.

43. Winifred Dawson (née Arnott), personal communication, 14 February 2011.

44. To Monica Jones, 13 July 1951. Not in *SL*.

45. The march took place on Sunday 20 May 1951 (*LM*, 41), and Larkin all but completed the poem by 25 May or shortly afterwards. *Complete Poems*, p. 602.

46. Burnett uses as copy-text a typescript enclosed with a letter to Monica Jones of 15 October 1951. In the 1988 *Collected Poems* Thwaite reproduced an earlier typescript with different wording.

47. Tom Paulin, 'She Did Not Change: Philip Larkin', *Minotaur: Poetry and the Nation State* (London: Faber & Faber, 1992), p. 236.

48. Motion, p. 210.

49. *LM*, pp. 48–9.

50. To Eva Larkin, 15 July 1951.

51. *TWG*, pp. 485–6.

52. Ibid., p. 487.

53. Ibid., p. 493.

54. Ibid., p. 495.

55. Ibid., pp. 496–7.

56. *LM*, p. 58.

57. Ibid.
58. To Winifred Arnott, 22 October 1951. Motion, p. 218.
59. To Eva Larkin ('My dear Mop-Moust-Haugh'), 29 April 1951.
60. DPL/1/2/49. James Sutton became a pharmacist, married and had two children. He died in 1997. See Maeve Brennan, 'James Ballard Sutton 1921–1997', *AL* 5 (April 1998), pp. 24–7.
61. 14 October 1951. Not in *SL*.
62. *SL*, pp. 179–80.

10: Single in Belfast (1952–3)

1. Motion, p. 217.
2. Ibid., p. 211.
3. *LM*, pp. 69–70.
4. Winifred Dawson (née Arnott), interview with the author, 21 October 2003.
5. Motion, p. 221.
6. George Gilpin, 'Patricia Avis and Philip Larkin', in James Booth (ed.), *New Larkins for Old* (Basingstoke: Macmillan, 2000), pp. 66–78, at p. 68.
7. *SL*, p. 183.
8. Motion, p. 222.
9. Winifred Dawson (née Arnott), interview with the author, 21 October 2003.
10. Gilpin, 'Patricia Avis and Philip Larkin', p. 70; *SL*, p. 184.
11. Gilpin, 'Patricia Avis and Philip Larkin', pp. 70–1. Not in *SL*.
12. Ibid., p. 71.
13. *LM*, p. 86.
14. Ibid., pp. 86–7.
15. Ibid., p. 90.
16. 12 November 1951. *LM*, p. 70.
17. *LM*, p. 94.
18. Winifred Dawson, 'The Day I Met Monica', *AL* 31 (April 2011), p. 6.
19. Winifred Dawson (née Arnott), personal communication, 10 June 2011. In return she lent him the very feminine *Ordinary Families* by E. Arnot Robertson.
20. To Eva Larkin ('My dear old creature'), 18 January 1953.
21. Winifred Dawson (née Arnott), interview with the author, 21 October 2003. Motion (p. 223) misdates the engagement to July 1952.
22. Gilpin, 'Patricia Avis and Philip Larkin', p. 72.
23. Motion, p. 220.
24. For example 1 November 1951. *LM*, p. 68.
25. Gilpin, 'Patricia Avis and Philip Larkin', p. 72. Patsy refers to the recasting of Dante's *Inferno* by James Thomson, published in 1874.
26. Gilpin, 'Patricia Avis and Philip Larkin', p. 74.
27. *TWG*, p. 492.
28. Winifred Dawson (née Arnott), personal communication, 14 February 2011.
29. Gilpin, 'Patricia Avis and Philip Larkin', p. 75.

30. Winifred Dawson (née Arnott), personal communication, 6 February 2011.

31. Gilpin, 'Patricia Avis and Philip Larkin', p. 75.

32. Ibid., p. 74.

33. Motion, p. 230.

34. Colin and Patsy divorced shortly afterwards.

35. *SL*, p. 208.

36. *LM*, p. 105.

37. Ibid., pp. 104 and 105n.

38. 7 August 1953. The passage and drawing are not in *LM*.

39. *RW*, p. 52.

40. Burnett notes this, but includes the work in *Complete Poems* without further explanation.

41. To Eva Larkin, 23 August 1953.

42. 25 October 1953.

43. Havelock Ellis, British doctor, and author of early academic works on sexuality.

44. Dawson, 'The Day I Met Monica', pp. 6–7.

45. It appeared in *The Fantasy Poets 21* in 1954, and subsequently in *The Less Deceived*. In 1993 Motion (p. 235) related the poem to the relationship with Winifred Arnott.

46. *SL*, p. 216.

47. Ibid., pp. 215–17.

48. The poem is mistakenly dated '1951?' in the 1988 *Collected Poems*. See *Complete Poems*, p. 607.

49. Published, posthumously, under her maiden name, Patricia Avis (London: Virago, 1996).

50. *SL*, p. 232.

51. *LM*, pp. 60–1.

52. *LKA*, p. 273.

53. 11 August 1951. *LM*, p. 51.

54. Janice Rossen, 'Philip Larkin and *Lucky Jim*', *Journal of Modern Literature* 22.1 (Fall 1998), pp. 147–64.

55. 24 July 1952. *LKA*, p. 288.

56. 8 September 1952. *LKA*, p. 292.

57. 11 September 1952. *LM*, p. 84.

58. Zachary Leader, 'Making *Lucky Jim*', in *The Life of Kingsley Amis* (New York: Pantheon, 2006). See also Ross Gresham, 'Larkin on the *Lucky Jim* Manuscript', *AL* 26 (October 2008), pp. 11–13.

59. Gresham, 'Larkin on the *Lucky Jim* Manuscript', p. 12.

60. Ibid.

61. Ibid.

62. Ibid., p. 13.

63. *LKA*, p. 292.

64. Richard Bradford, *The Odd Couple: The Curious Friendship between Kingsley Amis and Philip Larkin* (London: Robson Press, 2012), pp. 106–7.

65. Motion, p. 169.

66. Bradford., p. 107.

67. *LM*, 110.

68. 3 April 1953. *SL*, p. 195.

69. *SL*, pp. 201–2.

70. DPL/4/4; Motion, p. 240.

71. *SL*, pp. 221–2.

11: Various Poems (1953–6)

1. Hartley, p. 64.

2. 3 February 1954. *SL*, p. 222.

3. A Conversation with Neil Powell, *FR*, p. 31. Larkin was pleased that Auden noticed this complication.

4. Interview with *Paris Review*, *RW*, p. 70.

5. Robert Conquest, '*New Lines*, Movements, and Modernisms', in Zachary Leader (ed.), *The Movement Reconsidered: Essays on Larkin, Amis, Gunn, Davie, and their Contemporaries* (Oxford: Oxford University Press, 2009), p. 310.

6. 'Born Yesterday' was a late inclusion in *The Less Deceived*. 'Philip felt that although it was slight, Kingsley might be annoyed if he left it out, especially as he intended to dedicate his book not to Kingsley but to Monica Jones. He thought Kingsley might have been expecting him to make a reciprocal gesture as he had dedicated *Lucky Jim* to Philip, thereby taking his name into a million households.' Hartley, p. 85.

7. DPL/4/1/4.

8. *LM*, p. 416.

9. SL, p. 225.

10. See, for instance, N. F. Lowe, 'Bruce Montgomery and Philip Larkin: Evidence of a ruptured relationship', *AL* 6 (October 1998), pp. 11–12.

11. *SL*, p. 225.

12. Winifred Dawson, 'Photograph Albums Revisited', *AL* 13 (April 2002), p. 4.

13. Raphaël Ingelbien, 'The Uses of Symbolism: Larkin and Eliot', in James Booth (ed.), *New Larkins for Old* (Basingstoke: Macmillan, 2000), p. 134.

14. *LM*, p. 210.

15. '*Would you call yourself an Anglican?* Half way there. *God?* Well, half way.' James Booth, 'Glimpses' (interview with Monica Jones), *AL* 12 (October 2001), p. 23.

16. 3 August 1954. *LM*, p. 112.

17. Ibid.

18. J. R. Watson, 'The Other Larkin', *Critical Quarterly* 17.4 (Winter 1975), p. 358. See also R. N. Parkinson, 'To keep our metaphysics warm: A study of "Church Going" by Philip Larkin', *Critical Survey* 5 (Winter 1971), pp. 224–33.

19. Richard Perceval Graves, *A. E. Housman: The Scholar-Poet* (London: Routledge & Kegan Paul, 1979), p. 187.

20. Brenda Moon, 'Working with Philip Larkin', *AL* 8 (October 1999), p. 11.

21. 'A Conversation with Ian Hamilton', *FR*, p. 22.

22. See *SL*, p. 289 (21 October 1958).
23. Ibid., pp. 229–30.
24. To Patsy Strang, 28 October 1954. *SL*, p. 231.
25. 18 October 1954. *LM*, p. 120.
26. *LM*, pp. 130–1.
27. To Eva Larkin, 28 November 1954.
28. *LM*, p. 133.
29. 23 September 1954. *LM*, p. 116.
30. *LM*, p. 128.
31. Ibid.
32. See James Booth, 'Competing Pulses: Secular and Sacred in Hughes, Larkin and Plath', *Critical Survey* 12.3 (2000), pp. 4–27; and 'Larkin as Animal Poet', *AL* 22 (October 2006), pp. 5–9.
33. *LM*, p. 119.
34. Ibid., pp. 119–20.
35. Motion, p. 224.
36. Hartley, p. 64.
37. 20 December 1954. *LM*, p. 134.
38. *LM*, p. 137.
39. 15 February 1955. *LM*, p. 147.
40. 8 and 16 January 1955. *LM*, pp. 138–9.
41. *LM*, pp. 143–4n.
42. 29 January 1955. *LM*, p. 142.
43. *LM*, p. 145.
44. Motion, p. 262.
45. 'The Dedicated', 'Waiting for breakfast', 'Modesties', 'Oils', 'Who called Love conquering', 'Since the majority of me' and 'Arrival'. The Hartleys persuaded him to include 'Spring' and 'No Road', which he had initially excluded. *LM*, p. 143.
46. 8 April 1955. *LM*, p. 150. In a letter of 22 July 1955 Larkin told Monica that Jean Hartley had reported to him that 'Judy Egerton has opted out of the printed list – the only one to do so' (*LM*, p. 170). This was not the case. Judy Egerton's name appears in the list of subscribers, and in a letter of 10 February 1956 Larkin refers to the Egertons' copies as '*true bibliographical firsts*' (*SL*, p. 257).
47. 26 October 1955. *LM*, p. 188.
48. 12 May 1956. *LM*, p. 203.
49. *LM*, p. 192.
50. Blake Morrison, *The Movement: English Poetry and Fiction of the 1950s* (London: Methuen, 1980), p. 2.
51. Letter to the *Spectator* (8 October 1954). Anthony Thwaite, 'How It Seemed Then: An Autobiographical, Anecdotal Essay', in Leader (ed.), *The Movement Reconsidered*, pp. 247–54.
52. 'Statement', *RW*, p. 79.
53. Walter Pater, *The Renaissance: Studies in Art and Poetry* (1873), ed. Adam Phillips (Oxford: Oxford University Press, 1986), p. 152.

54. 'Statement', *RW*, p. 79.
55. Motion, p. 265.
56. 'Maiden Name', 'Church Going', 'I Remember, I Remember', 'Skin', 'Born Yesterday', 'Triple Time', 'Toads' and 'Lines on a Young Lady's Photograph Album'.
57. Introduction to Robert Conquest (ed.), *New Lines: An Anthology* (London: Macmillan, 1962), p. xv.
58. Letter to Conquest. Motion, p. 269.
59. Charles Tomlinson, 'The Middlebrow Muse', *Essays in Criticism*, 7.2 (April 1957), pp. 208–17.
60. Al Alvarez (ed.), *The New Poetry* (Harmondsworth: Penguin, 1962), pp. 20–1.
61. Interview with the *Observer*, *RW*, pp. 53–4.
62. Amis was unable to place this set of parodies in *Encounter* or the *London Magazine* (see Leader (ed.), *The Movement Reconsidered*, pp 5–6). Zachary Leader published them in *LKA*, pp. 1141–4.
63. The poem is misdated '1951' in the 1988 *Collected Poems*.
64. 27 September 1956. *LM*, p. 207.
65. David Lodge, 'Philip Larkin: The Metonymic Muse', in Stephen Regan (ed.), *Philip Larkin: Contemporary Critical Essays* (Basingstoke: Macmillan, 1997), p. 72.
66. Morrison, *The Movement: English Poetry and Fiction of the 1950s*.
67. Blake Morrison, '"Still Going On, All of It": The Movement in the 1950s and the Movement Today', in Leader (ed.), *The Movement Reconsidered*, p. 33.
68. Conquest, '*New Lines*, Movements, and Modernisms', p. 307.
69. Letter to William Van O'Connor, 2 April 1958. Motion, p. 243.
70. 'A Conversation with Ian Hamilton', *FR*, p. 20.

12: Hull (1955–7)

1. 27 April 1955. *LM*, p. 155.
2. Originally titled 'Lodgers', and focused on 'Mr Gridley'. W. I. Bleaney was one of the successful School Certificate candidates listed in the King Henry VIII school magazine, the *Coventrian*, in 1936.
3. Larkin is thinking not of Hull, but of Coventry or Oxford, with their vehicle-assembly plants.
4. In a sign of his working-class taste Bleaney prefers sauce from a bottle to properly prepared gravy. His 'plugging at the four aways' is an allusion to the 'pools', which, for a penny or halfpenny stake, gave punters the chance of winning hundreds of thousands of pounds by guessing the draws or away wins in Football League matches.
5. Published in the *Grapevine* (University of Durham Institute of Education), 4 February 1957.
6. 'The Circus Animals' Desertion', W. B. Yeats, *Selected Poetry*, ed. A. Norman Jeffares (London: Macmillan, 1962), p. 202.
7. Hartley, p. 59.
8. Ibid., p. 74.

9. Ibid.

10. 16 April 1955. *LM*, p. 152.

11. 1 May 1955. *LM*, p. 157.

12. *LM,* p. 167.

13. Alison Hartley, personal communication, 2012.

14. *LM*, p. 167. The hare is in fact wearing the garb of a medieval pilgrim, but characteristically Larkin does not 'bother' with such antiquarianism.

15. *SL*, p. 246.

16. Judy Egerton, interview with the author, 17 December 2010.

17. Ansell later became City Editor of *The Times*, 1962–7.

18. Hartley, p. 177.

19. *LM*, p. 171.

20. R. J. C. Watt, *A Concordance to the Poetry of Philip Larkin* (Hildesheim: Olms-Weidmann, 1995), p. 521.

21. To Eva Larkin, 25 January 1956.

22. Martin Amis, Introduction to *Philip Larkin: Poems* (London: Faber & Faber, 2011), p. x.

23. To Eva Larkin, 25 January 1956.

24. To Ansell and Judy Egerton, 31 May 1955. *SL*, p. 243.

25. Hartley, p. 67.

26. To Conquest, 24 July 1955. *SL*, p. 245.

27. *LM*, pp. 182–3.

28. Ibid., p. 178n.

29. Ibid., p. 192n.

30. 11 March 1956. *LM*, 201.

31. Letters and cards to Eva Larkin, 4, 11, 14, 16 and 20 December 1955.

32. To Eva Larkin, 9 September 1956.

33. To Eva Larkin, 8 January 1956.

34. To Eva Larkin, 14 February 1956.

35. He made minor adjustments to the text before publication. *Complete Poems*, pp. 435–6.

36. There may be a buried echo of Book 9 of Milton's *Paradise Lost*, ll. 385–6: 'Thus saying, from her Husband's hand her hand / Soft she withdrew.'

37. Simon Blackburn makes this point in his survey of the clasped-hands motif in medieval monuments and brasses, 'English Tombs and Larkin', *AL* 36 (October 2013), pp. 7–11.

38. Larkin was wryly amused when it was suggested that the clasped hands might be a Victorian restorer's addition. Trevor Brighton, 'An Arundel Tomb: The Monument', in Paul Foster, Trevor Brighton and Patrick Garland, *An Arundel Tomb*, Otter Memorial Paper 1 (Chichester: Chichester Institute, 1987), pp. 14–22. It is now thought that this feature was indeed original.

39. 6 October 1951. *LM*, p. 63.

40. DPL/1/4/24.

41. 21 February 1956. *LM*, p. 196.

42. Motion, p. 275. He had asked her, in crossword-mode, for 'something meaning a sign, two syllables'.

43. 4 December 1956. *LM*, p. 210.

44. To Monica Jones, 31 March 1956. Not in *LM*.

45. This public lavatory has received awards, and is to this day something of a tourist attraction.

46. Tranby Croft is a Grade II-listed country house at Anlaby, just outside Hull.

47. To Monica Jones, 22–23 April 1956. Not in *LM*.

48. John Malcom Brinnin, *Dylan Thomas in America: An Intimate Journal* (Boston: Little, Brown, 1955).

49. To Monica Jones, 22–23 April 1956.

50. To Eva Larkin, 23 September 1956.

51. Ibid.

52. Moira Phillips, 'Larkin Recollected', *AL* 33 (April 2012), p. 11.

53. To Monica Jones, 27 October 1956. Not in *LM*.

54. To Monica Jones, 18 November 1956. Not in *LM*.

55. *SL*, p. 276.

56. At a Larkin Society dinner held in 2010 to raise money for the statue by Martin Jennings now at Paragon Station, Maureen Lipman, standing beside a fibre-glass toad in the form of Philip Larkin, declared, in her best Hull accent, that this was the first time she had shared the stage with a 'turd'. Jackie Sewell, 'An Evening with Maureen Lipman CBE', *AL* 30 (October 2010), p .26.

57. Interview with the *Observer*, *RW*, pp. 54–5.

58. 7 January 1956. *LM*, p. 193.

59. 26 August 1956. *LM*, p. 204.

60. Motion, p. 259.

13: Poet-Librarian (1956–60)

1. To Eva Larkin, 26 May 1957.

2. Betty Mackereth, interview with the author, 4 August 2003.

3. Brennan, p. 23.

4. Ibid.

5. Ibid., p. 24. In 1967 the novel was made into a film starring Sidney Poitier.

6. Betty Mackereth, interview with the author, 9 February 2013.

7. Brennan, p. 28.

8. *LM*, pp. 173, 223, 256.

9. Brennan, pp. 25–6.

10. To Eva Larkin, 19 May 1957.

11. Mary Judd (née Wrench), interview with the author, 28 June 2011.

12. Brennan, pp. 29–30.

13. Ibid., p. 23.

14. Mary Judd (née Wrench), interview with the author, 28 June 2011.

15. Verso of p. 286 of diary no. 12, 1954–7 (DPL4/1/4). He gave the names of the

writers on a separate inserted list: Miss Cuming (Agnes Cuming, his predecessor as Librarian at Hull), J. B. Sutton, Jill McIver, Joan Loughlin, John Wain, Ruth Bowman, Robert Conquest, E. E. Larkin (his mother), Molly Terry, Judy Egerton, Patricia Murphy, Miriam Plaut, Hilly Amis, Margaret Sutton, Jane Exall, Vernon Watkins, Charles Madge, Bruce Montgomery, Philip Brown, Karl Lehmann, Peter Rose, Colin Gunner, Madeleine Boyall, Winifred Arnott, Kingsley Amis, John Betjeman, Philip Oakes, Harry Hoff, Pamela Hansford Johnson, C. P. Snow, Edward Du Cann, Eric Ashby, Janet Murphy, Elizabeth Jennings, Linda Murphy.

16. Letter to Monica Jones, 28 July 1956. Not in *LM*.

17. See Joan Redford, Jean Watson, Jean Humphries, Ann Connolly, John Yates and Margaret Austin, 'Monica at Leicester', *AL* 12 (October 2001), pp. 17–18; and Yvonne Rowland, 'Remembering Monica Jones in Leicester', *AL* 30 (October 2010), pp. 18–19.

18. 16 October 1957. *LM*, p. 229.

19. *LM*, p. 245. See Peter Keating, 'Monica', in *Autobiographical Tales* (Edinburgh: Priskus, 2013), for an account of Monica in Leicester.

20. 4 May 1957. *LM*, p. 221.

21. 8 December 1956. *LM*, p. 212.

22. *LM*, pp. 225–6.

23. To Monica Jones, 7 and 8 August 1957. Not in *LM*.

24. Letter from Mary Judd (née Wrench) to Maeve Brennan and Betty Mackereth, 15 April 1986.

25. Ibid. Mary married in 1960 and Philip and Betty Mackereth acted as godparents to her daughter. She left Hull in 1964.

26. 16 October 1957. *LM*, p. 229.

27. 29 January 1958. *LM*, p. 235.

28. To Eva Larkin, 6 May 1956.

29. *LM*, pp. 209–10.

30. Larkin dated the last complete draft in the workbook '1 Jan 57'; only minor adjustments followed. *Complete Poems*, pp. 397–8.

31. *LM*, p. 170.

32. Unpublished interview, *South Bank Show*, 16 April 1981. Motion, pp. 287–8.

33. 'An Interview with John Haffenden', *FR*, p. 53.

34. Ibid., p. 57.

35. To Thwaite, 17 March 1959. *SL*, p. 301.

36. *The Complete Poems of Thomas Hardy*, ed. James Gibson (London: Macmillan, 1976), p. 135.

37. Larkin perhaps recalls the biblical phrase 'all flesh is grass'. He may also have had in mind Auden's 'The crowds upon the pavement / Were fields of harvest wheat' in 'As I walked out one evening'. W. H. Auden, *Another Time* (London: Faber & Faber, 1996), p. 43.

38. Hartley, p. 125.

39. David Lodge, 'Philip Larkin: The Metonymic Muse', in Stephen Regan (ed.),

Philip Larkin: Contemporary Critical Essays (Basingstoke: Macmillan, 1997), pp. 71–82, at p. 77.

40. Ibid., p. 78.
41. In Christopher Ricks, 'The Pursuit of Metaphor', *Allusion to the Poets* (Oxford: Oxford University Press, 2002), p. 248.
42. Lodge, 'Philip Larkin: The Metonymic Muse', p. 76.
43. Motion, p. 280. Judy Egerton always received Larkin's letters with great pleasure. Interview, 17 December 2010.
44. 3 November 1958. *LM*, p. 245.
45. Motion, p. 284.
46. Anthony Thwaite, personal communication, 14 August 2011.
47. Jean Hartley, 'Larkin, Love and Sex', *AL* 30 (October 2010), p. 6.
48. Larkin, indeed, had played the same prank on his sister Catherine during the war, sending her a typewritten letter in an envelope with an official 'On His Majesty's Service' cover, informing her that she had been 'drafted to the Colliery at Pwllycracrach. Mon., for light duties at the shafthead'. Unlike Conquest, however, he revealed the joke in the PS: 'Well, I hope [. . .] that this didn't give you too much of a turn.' 8 September 1943. DLN/3/2/11.
49. Motion, p. 267.
50. *LM*, p. 256.
51. Hartley, p. 100.
52. 17 December 1958. *SL*, p. 297.
53. To Judy Egerton, 19 January 1959. *SL*, p. 298.
54. Motion, p. 294.
55. Greenwich Mean Time. He is alluding to Mary's poor time-keeping. Betty recalls Larkin standing at the issue desk, watch in hand in pantomimic censure, as Mary arrived late yet again.
56. Betty still has Mary's letter.
57. Betty Mackereth, interview with the author, 20 June 2011.
58. Passage not in *LM*.
59. 14 April 1959. *LM*, p. 248.
60. *LM*, p. 254.
61. To Monica Jones, 9 October 1959. Not in *LM*.
62. *LM*, pp. 259–60.
63. *LM*, p. 261.
64. 25 August 1959. *LM*, p. 256.
65. Motion, pp. 296–7.
66. Betty Mackereth, interview with the author, 20 June 2011.
67. To Eva Larkin, 20 March 1960.
68. Jean Hartley, 'Larkin, Love and Sex', *AL* 30 (October 2010), p. 8.
69. Motion, p. 297.

14: Here (1960–1)

1. The drawing and poem are reproduced in facsimile as the back endpaper of *SL*. Motion records that he stayed with Bruce Montgomery before the interview. Motion, p. 302.
2. *LM*, p. 265.
3. 16 March 1960. *LM*, p. 266.
4. Archie Burnett, 'Biography and Poetry: Philip Larkin' *AL* 36 (October 2013), pp. 7–14, at p.13. Jean Hartley recalled seeing the film with Larkin. John Osborne, 'Larkin and the Visual Arts', *AL* 36 (October 2013), pp. 15–17, at p. 15.
5. Thomas Gray, *Poems, Letters and Essays* (London: Dent, 1963), p. 6.
6. He had begun drafting it in late 1956, and had returned to it several times. *Complete Poems*, p. 417.
7. 4 July 1959. *LM*, p. 252.
8. Larkin commented to Barbara Pym some time later: 'it's a "trick" poem, all one sentence & no main verb!' *SL*, p. 367.
9. Hartley, p. 119.
10. Brennan, p. 36.
11. Ibid., p. 26. Betty Mackereth recalls that during the royal visit the Librarian's office served as the Queen Mother's 'retiring room', and was fitted with a set of net curtains. These were still incongruously in place when I arrived in Hull in 1968, and survived for many years afterwards.
12. 15 August 1960. *LM*, p. 270.
13. 4 August 1960. *LM*, p. 268.
14. He had been drafting it intermittently since the summer of 1959. *Complete Poems*, p. 419.
15. Brennan, p. 37.
16. Ibid., p. 28.
17. Ibid., pp. 33–4.
18. Ibid., p. 38.
19. Jean Hartley, 'Larkin, Love and Sex', *AL* 30 (October 2010), pp. 6–8, at p. 7.
20. Jean Hartley, personal communication, 4 March 2011.
21. Margaret Fowler, 'Larkin's Library Recollected', *AL* 32 (October 2011), p. 11.
22. 9 August 1959. *LM*, p. 239.
23. *SL*, p. 319.
24. 10 November 1960, *LM*, p. 275.
25. Richard Bradford, *The Odd Couple: The Curious Friendship between Kingsley Amis and Philip Larkin* (London: Robson Press, 2012), pp. 222–4.
26. *LM*, p. 273.
27. Ibid., p. 275.
28. To Eva Larkin, 6 November 1960.
29. Motion cites this comment from a letter to Eva Larkin of 1 January 1961 (Motion, p. 310 n. 12). However these words are not present in the letter of that date. The correspondence is not yet fully catalogued and it may be that the letter containing

this sentence has been misplaced, perhaps before the correspondence came to Hull. Richard Bradford (*The Odd Couple*, p. 223) repeats the quotation (presumably from Motion), but mistakenly applies it to Maeve rather than Monica.

30. To Monica Jones, 1 January 1961. Not in *LM*.

31. *LM*, p. 276.

32. *Complete Poems*, p. 423.

33. Larkin cannot resist the bad pun 'born / dead'.

34. She adds an arch parenthesis: '(why he didn't call [a taxi] from the hotel, I cannot think)'.

35. Brennan, p. 38–9.

36. Ibid., pp. 8–10.

37. *SL*, p. 323.

38. 5 March 1961. *SL*, p. 325.

39. Hazel Holt, *A Lot to Ask: A Life of Barbara Pym* (London: Macmillan, 1990), p. 89.

40. *Philip Larkin Reads and Comments on The Whitsun Weddings*, Listen Records, LPV 6 (Hull: Marvell Press, 1965).

41. 11 July 1961. *SL*, p. 330.

42. 'A Conversation with Ian Hamilton', *FR*, p. 25.

43. To Monica Jones, 13 November 1960. Not in *LM*.

44. *FR*, p. 25.

45. 'W. H. Auden', *FR*, p. 40; 'The Life under the Laurels', *FR*, p. 296.

46. 'On the Circuit', in W. H. Auden, *About the House* (London: Faber & Faber, 1966), p. 63.

47. Interview with *Paris Review*, *RW*, p. 73.

48. 11 February 1961. *LM*, p. 276.

49. 11 June 1961. *LM*, p. 283.

50. Motion, p. 311.

51. Motion (p. 311) and *LM* (p. 283n) give the date as 5 March, which was a Sunday. The letters to Eva show that it was Monday 6 March.

52. Colin Vize, 'Larkin's Refraction', *AL* 35 (April 2013), p. 23. Vize concluded that 'less than 1% of the population exhibit short-sightedness of the magnitude experienced by Larkin'.

53. Bradford, p. 224.

54. 11 March 1961. *LM*, p. 278.

55. *LM*, p. 279.

56. Ibid., p. 280.

57. Ibid., p. 281.

58. Brennan, p. 41.

59. To Monica Jones, 13 March 1961. Not in *LM*.

60. Larkin was hurt when Amis failed to follow up this hospital visit. On 11 July, following his recovery, he remarked to Conquest that he had received no letter from Kingsley: 'His joy at learning I was discharged without any discoverable defect must have rendered his right hand useless: give him my sympathy. It must be hell not being able to toss off' (*SL*, p. 331).

61. Motion, p. 313.
62. Larkin Society. DNX, box 1.
63. *SL*, p. 327.
64. Brennan, p. 42.
65. To Betty Mackereth, 13 April 1961 (unpublished).
66. Brennan, p. 42.
67. Ibid., p. 29.
68. Ibid., p. 39.
69. Hartley, 'Larkin, Love and Sex', p. 7.
70. Motion, p. 305. Maeve was offended by Alan Bennett's review of Motion's biography which depicted her as a northern 'lass' deceived by a sophisticated seducer. All Larkin 'really wants', Bennett concluded, 'is just to get his end away on a regular basis and without obligation'. Alan Bennett, 'Alas! Deceived', in Stephen Regan (ed.), *Philip Larkin: Contemporary Critical Essays* (Basingstoke: Macmillan, 1997), p. 243.
71. 10 April 1961. Brennan, p. 75.
72. Brennan, p. 43.
73. *LM*, p. 283.
74. *Philip Larkin Reads and Comments on The Whitsun Weddings*, Listen Records.
75. Brennan, pp. 56–7.
76. *Mademoiselle de Maupin*, trans. R. and E. Powys Mathers (London: Folio Society, 1948), p. 133.
77. 5 August 1961. *SL*, p. 331.
78. 9 August 1961. *LM*, p. 284 and n.
79. 17 August 1961. *LM*, p. 285.
80. It was published at once in the *New Statesman*, on 24 October 1961.
81. 21 September 1962. *SL*, p. 346.
82. *Philip Larkin Reads and Comments on The Whitsun Weddings*, Listen Records.
83. Shakespeare's anti-Petrarchan sonnet, no. 130 ('My mistress' eyes are nothing like the sun'), is an ironic example of the genre, and its conventions feature in Marvell's 'To his Coy Mistress': 'An hundred years should go to praise / Thine eyes and on thy forehead gaze [. . .]'.
84. Brennan, pp. 57–8.
85. Ibid., p. 57.
86. Motion, p. 46.
87. Brennan, p. 57.
88. Among the books which Maeve left at her death was Linda O'Keeffe's lavishly illustrated *Shoes: A Celebration of Pumps, Sandals, Slippers and More* (New York: Workman Publishing; special edition for Past Times, Oxford, 1996).
89. Brennan, p. 50.
90. Ibid., pp. 174, 184, 209.
91. Ibid., p. 73.
92. Ibid., p. 43.
93. Ibid.

94. *LM*, p. 289.

95. Judy Egerton, interview with the author, 17 December 2010.

96. *SL*, pp. 339–40.

15: Sitting It Out (1961–4)

1. *Critical Quarterly* 3.4 (Winter 1961), p. 309.

2. 9 December 1961. *SL*, p. 335.

3. *Critical Quarterly* misprinted 'bribes' in line 2 as 'brides', a mistake carried forward into the 1988 *Collected Poems*. The correct reading was restored in a reprint of *Collected Poems* later in 1988.

4. To Conquest, 9 December 1961. *SL*, p. 335.

5. *SL*, p. 336.

6. 23 January 1962. *LM*, p. 292.

7. 30 April 1962. *SL*, p. 342.

8. *LM*, p. 292.

9. *SL*, p. 335.

10. To Conquest. *SL*, p. 341.

11. *SL*, p. 342.

12. 'The Living Poet', *FR*, p. 81.

13. He finished the poem on 21 August and it was published in the *Observer* on 18 November 1962.

14. *LM*, p. 302.

15. DX/329, inventory p. 119.

16. Motion, p. 319. Iris Murdoch, *The Flight from the Enchanter* (London: Chatto & Windus, 1956). Copy in the University Collection, History Centre, Hull: MJ/B1/491, inscribed 'M. M. B. Jones' in Monica's hand, with '& Dr Larkin' beneath in his.

17. Hull copy of Murdoch, *The Flight from the Enchanter*, pp. 3, 78, 81.

18. Ibid., pp. 79, 308.

19. Ibid., pp. 5, 23, 79.

20. Anthony Thwaite, personal communication, 14 August 2011.

21. Anthony Thwaite (ed.), *Larkin at Sixty* (London: Faber & Faber, 1982), opposite p. 60.

22. *LM*, p. 304n.

23. Ibid., pp. 303–4.

24. Ibid., p. 306n.

25. 4 October 1962. *LM*, p. 305.

26. Ibid., p. 304.

27. Published in the *Spectator*, 23 November 1962.

28. *Philip Larkin Reads and Comments on The Whitsun Weddings*, Listen Records, LPV 6 (Hull: Marvell Press, 1965).

29. See for example paintings by Hans Baldung Grien (1484/5–1545) in the Kunstmuseum, Basel, Switzerland.

30. *LM*, pp. 306–7.
31. Published in *Critical Quarterly* 8.2 (Summer 1966), p. 173.
32. To Eva Larkin, 16 December 1962.
33. To Monica Jones, 7 August 1966. Not in *LM*.
34. Brennan, p. 43.
35. Ibid., p. 23.
36. DPL/10/3.
37. To Monica Jones, 17 August 1963. Motion, p. 339.
38. *LKA*, pp. 204–5.
39. DX/329, inventory 68. These cameras took self-developing film, avoiding the involvement of a chemist or photographic laboratory.
40. *Lord Byron: Selected Prose*, ed. Peter Gunn (Harmondsworth: Penguin, 1972), p. 357.
41. *SL*, p. 257.
42. See http://www.harrison-marks.com/hub.htm (accessed 27 April 2011).
43. Motion, p. 266.
44. Jean Hartley, 'Larkin, Love and Sex', *AL* 30 (October 2010), p. 6.
45. Richard Bradford, *The Odd Couple: The Curious Friendship between Kingsley Amis and Philip Larkin* (London: Robson Press, 2012), pp. 209, 237.
46. DX/329, inventory 600 i–ix. There were also 'Super 8' cine-reels such as were used for Marks's films: inventory 72a–d.
47. Sophia Dawn appeared in *Kamera*, issue 56 (1963). She was the principal model in Harrison Marks's Byronically titled hardback *She Walks in Beauty*, and appeared in two 8mm home movies, *The Bare Truth* and *Nature's Intended*. See http://www.harrison-marks.com/models_1.htm (accessed 27 April 2011).
48. DX/329, inventory 73 a–j. Ten ring-binders were found in the box room of 105 Newland Park. They were empty, but one showed the torn remnants of two black-and-white glamour photographs pasted to the inner front and back covers. Seven were Staff Handbooks. James Booth, 'Glimpses' (interview with Monica Jones), *AL* 12 (October 2001), pp. 25–6.
49. Presumably a jokey reference to the famous 'You know how to whistle?' scene from the film *To Have and Have Not* (1944), starring Lauren Bacall and Humphrey Bogart.
50. Thwaite inadvertently omitted the final stanza in the workbook draft from the 1988 *Collected Poems*.
51. Burnett omits the stanza break after 'understand'. *Complete Poems*, p. 309.
52. Burnett's rigorous editorial principles led him to print Larkin's shorter typescript version of the poem, adding subsequent lines from the 1967 fragment in Workbook 7 (see below). This fragment breaks off two lines earlier than the 1964 text, at 'Of an explicit music; then'. Burnett confusingly relegates the uncancelled final two lines of the substantive 1964 workbook version to his notes, as 'Additional lines'. *Complete Poems*, p. 637.
53. 25 April 1964. *LM*, p. 330.
54. *LM*, p. 331.
55. 29 April 1964. *LM*, p. 333.

56. To Monica Jones, 10 August 1964. Not in *LM*.
57. Brennan, p. 58.
58. DPL/1/7/16.
59. Brennan, p. 59; Motion, p. 423.
60. Brennan, p. 7.
61. 3 March 1964. *LM*, p. 326.
62. Motion, p. 343.
63. 'An Interview with John Haffenden', *FR*, p. 55.
64. In his selection of Larkin's poems, Martin Amis preserves the order of poems within the volumes, despite the fact that his omissions dispel Larkin's original sequence. Thus 'Here', completed in October 1961, and 'Dockery and Son', completed in March 1963, both come before the much earlier 'An Arundel Tomb', completed in February 1956. This is puzzling since Amis argues that Larkin's 'volumes of verse [. . .] get stronger and stronger by a factor of ten', a contentious point which would surely be better illustrated by arranging the individual poems in chronological order. Introduction to *Philip Larkin: Poems* (London: Faber & Faber, 2011), pp. xxii–xxiii.

16: Living for Others (1964–8)

1. *Bibliography*, G14.
2. 22 May 1964. *LM*, p. 335.
3. 8 June 1964. *LM*, p. 337.
4. 3 March 1964. *LM*, p. 326.
5. Motion, pp. 340, 345.
6. Ibid., p. 350.
7. Ibid., p. 362.
8. Brennan, p. 30.
9. A Law student working in the Library at the time rushed down to the entrance, fearing that someone had really committed suicide. Alan Marshall, interview with the author, 16 April 2013.
10. Card to Eva Larkin, 28 January 1965.
11. To Eva Larkin, 21 March 1965.
12. 15 August 1965. *SL*, pp. 375–6.
13. *SL*, p. 376.
14. Hazel Holt, *A Lot to Ask: A Life of Barbara Pym* (London: Macmillan, 1990), p. 202.
15. Michael Ramsey, Archbishop of Canterbury.
16. 3 October 1967. *SL*, p. 397.
17. 'The World of Barbara Pym', *RW*, pp. 240–1.
18. 26 November 1966. *LM*, p. 371.
19. Holt, *A Lot to Ask*, p. 49.
20. Motion, p. 362.
21. 20 January 1966. *SL*, p. 380.
22. To Eva Larkin, 24 October 1965.

23. 12 October 1961. *Complete Poems*, p. 301.

24. Motion, p. 302.

25. Brennan, pp. 170–1.

26. Ibid., p. 178.

27. *LM*, p. 339.

28. Ibid., p. 340 and n.

29. Ibid., p. 350.

30. Ibid., p. 352n.

31. *SL*, p. 369.

32. DPL/1/7/1.

33. Larkin made slight changes of wording before it was published in *Queen*, 25 May 1966.

34. 'A Conversation with Ian Hamilton', *FR*, p. 21.

35. 13 October 1964. *LM*, p. 342.

36. In the 1988 *Collected Poems* Thwaite adopted Larkin's second title, added in pencil to the typescript (DPL/1/7/76). Breaking his editorial principles Burnett prefers the first title (*Complete Poems*, p. 634).

37. For the possible background to this poem, see Gary Kriewald, 'Wasteful, weak, propitiatory poems: Larkin apologizes to the animals', *AL* 28 (October 2009), pp. 29–33.

38. Margaret Hersom, unpublished recollection. Burnett prints a version of 'Administration' sent in a letter to Gavin Ewart in 1977 (*Complete Poems*, p. 655).

39. Now the Mercure Hull Royal Hotel. It was burnt out in 1990, but was deliberately restored in the same traditional style in order to recall the poem, with high clustered lights and differently coloured chairs.

40. To Maeve Brennan, 6 August 1966. Motion, p. 365.

41. *SL*, p. 387.

42. *LM*, p. 369.

43. Not in *LM*.

44. To Monica Jones, 8 October 1966. *LM*, p. 364.

45. Motion, p. 310.

46. 8 October 1966. *LM*, p. 364.

47. *LM*, p. 365.

48. *SL*, p. 381.

49. Ibid., p. 382.

50. Brennan, p. 49.

51. James Booth, '"Snooker" at the Seaside: The Birthday Walk in Scarborough', *AL* 16 (October 2003), p. 29.

52. He would never take her advice, being 'very determined about what he liked and what he didn't'. Judy Egerton, interview with the author, 17 December 2010.

53. 3 June 1967. *SL*, p. 396.

54. Professor Raymond Brett, personal communication, 1969.

55. Edna Longley, 'Poète Maudit Manqué', in George Hartley (ed.), *Philip Larkin – A Tribute: 1922–1985* (London: Marvell Press, 1988), p. 230.

56. 23 May 1968. Not in *LM*.

57. This line was changed in the typescript from the workbook's 'The sunlight pouring through glass'.
58. DPL/1/7/18.
59. Motion, p. 371.
60. In Susannah Tarbush, 'From Willow Gables to "Aubade": Penelope Scott Stokes and Philip Larkin: Part 2', *AL* 26 (October 2008), pp. 5–10, at p. 7.
61. 10 May 1967. *LM*, p. 375. A selection of Penelope's verse and drawings, 'Poems by Pen Evans', is to be found in *AL* 27 (April 2009), pp. 15–21.
62. Tarbush, 'From Willow Gables to "Aubade"', p. 7.
63. 24 April 1968. Passage not in *LM*.
64. Motion, p. 374.
65. 27 March 1967. Motion, p. 369.
66. Jean Hartley and James Booth, 'Jean Hartley DLitt', *AL* 31 (April 2011), p. 10.
67. 23 August 1967. *LM*, p. 377.
68. Hartley, p. 134.
69. Published in the *New Statesman* on 18 May 1968.
70. 24 April 1968. Passage not in *LM*.
71. Workbook 7, 1/7/20.
72. The date in the 1988 *Collected Poems*, '16 June', is inaccurate. This was the date the poem was begun.
73. *Émaux et Camées* (1852).
74. 'A Conversation with Ian Hamilton', *FR*, p. 25.
75. 'Poet's Choice', *FR*, p. 17.
76. DPL/1/7/78.
77. The word appears elsewhere in his work only in the juvenile 'Last Will and Testament' (1940).
78. It is difficult also not to hear a horrible gauche pun here. 'White Major' evokes a Kiplingesque officer in the British army, the kind of person who would use the phrase 'a white man' to indicate decent, upright values. In a letter to an inquirer, however, Larkin denied that he intended this pun: 'you don't mention that "Sympathy in White Major" is an echo of "Symphonie en Blanc Majeure" (Gautier). Nothing about white majors!' *Complete Poems*, p. 444.
79. When Kemp in *Jill* allowed his room-mate to plagiarize his tutorial essay, Warner declared: 'That's awfully white of you, old man.' *Jill*, p. 119.
80. Oliver Marshall, 'A Letter from Loughborough', *AL* 15 (April 2003), pp. 18–19. Larkin had written a four-line squib with this title in Workbook 5 in 1959. *Complete Poems*, p. 298.
81. *Les Complaintes* (1885) and *L'Imitation de Notre-Dame la Lune* (1886).
82. Robert Giroux of Farrar, Straus and Giroux, the American publisher of *High Windows*, objected to this poem on the grounds of anti-Semitism. Without engaging in any argument Larkin directed that the poem either be included, or omitted with a note indicating that the omission had been made. Motion, p. 436.
83. To Monica Jones, 12 September 1968. *LM*, p. 391. Hartley, pp. 133–5.
84. Hartley, p. 194.

85. 4 October 1968. *SL*, p. 405.
86. 2 November 1968. *SL*, p. 407.
87. 24 November 1968. Not in *LM*.
88. 26 December 1968. Not in *LM*.

17: Jazz, Race and Modernism (1961–71)

1. 20 November 1968. *SL*, p. 408.
2. This may have been at the suggestion of John Kenyon, Hull Professor of History. John White, personal communication, 24 October 2010.
3. An anthology of Larkin's own favourite jazz recordings is available. Trevor Tolley and John White (eds), *Larkin's Jazz*, Properbox 155 (four-CD set), in association with the Philip Larkin Society. www.propermusic.com.
4. *AWJ*, p. 45.
5. Larkin's LP collection is held in the University Collection at the Hull History Centre.
6. *AWJ*, p. 106.
7. Ibid., p. 116.
8. *FR*, pp. 112–16.
9. Hartley, p. 139.
10. James Booth, 'Glimpses' (interview with Monica Jones), *AL* 12 (October 2001), p. 23.
11. *AWJ*, pp. 47, 36.
12. Ibid., p. 65.
13. Interview with *Paris Review*, *RW*, p. 70.
14. To Sutton, 23 June 1941. *SL*, p. 18.
15. *AWJ*, p. 35.
16. B. J. Leggett notes the parallel in relation to 'Aubade'. *Larkin's Blues: Jazz, Popular Music and Poetry* (Baton Rouge: Louisiana State University Press, 1999), p. 14.
17. *AWJ*, p. 36.
18. Ibid., p. 60.
19. Interview with *Paris Review*, *RW*, p. 61.
20. *AWJ*, p. 167.
21. Ibid., p. 47.
22. Ibid., p. 156.
23. Ibid., p. 243.
24. Ibid., pp. 86, 85.
25. Ibid., p. 119.
26. Ibid., p. 19.
27. Ibid., p. 40.
28. Ibid., p. 41.
29. Ibid., pp. 41–2.
30. Ibid., p. 78.
31. 'Requiem for Jazz', *Weekend Telegraph*, 23 April 1965; in *Larkin's Jazz: Essays and*

Reviews 1940–1984, ed. Richard Palmer and John White (London and New York: Continuum, 2001), p. 140.

32. *AWJ*, p. 112.

33. Ibid., p. 44.

34. Ibid., pp. 39, 43.

35. Ibid., p. 63.

36. Ibid., p. 211.

37. Ibid., 28. Trevor Tolley gives an account of Larkin's jazz tastes in the chapter on *All What Jazz* in *My Proper Ground: A Study of the Work of Philip Larkin and its Development* (Edinburgh: Edinburgh University Press, 1991).

38. *AWJ*, pp. 96–7.

39. Ibid., p. 126.

40. Ibid., p. 150.

41. Ibid., pp. 218–19. The Paston Letters were written by members of the Paston family between the years 1422 and 1509.

42. Ibid., p. 161.

43. Ibid., p. 46.

44. Ibid., p. 188.

45. Ibid., p. 187. The text has 'remembering' in error for 'remember'.

46. Ibid., p. 188.

47. Ibid., p. 201.

48. Ibid., p. 209.

49. Ibid., p. 282.

50. Ibid., p. 62.

51. Ibid., p. 187. Stokely Carmichael (1941–98) was a Trinidadian-American activist associated with the Black Power and Black Panther movements.

52. Ben Ratliff, *Coltrane: The Story of a Sound* (New York: Farrar, Straus & Giroux, 2007); cited in 'Ugly on Purpose', review of Richard Palmer, *Such Deliberate Disguises: The Art of Philip Larkin* (London and New York: Continuum, 2008). http://www.openlettersmonthly.com/january-2009-larkin-coltrane/ (accessed 14 November 2011).

53. To Sutton, 'Friday Night', 1939? Not in *SL*.

54. *AWJ*, p. 234.

55. Ibid., p. 68.

56. Ibid., pp. 117–18.

57. Ibid., p. 87.

58. 'Requiem for Jazz', in *Larkin's Jazz*, ed. Palmer and White, p. 141.

59. *AWJ*, p. 87.

60. Ibid. John Osborne refers to 'the radicalism and cosmopolitanism' of Larkin's racial ideology in his jazz writings. *Larkin, Ideology and Critical Violence: A Case of Wrongful Conviction* (Basingstoke: Palgrave Macmillan, 2008), p. 45.

61. *AWJ*, p. 24.

62. Ibid., p. 20,

63. Ibid., pp. 21, 24.

64. Ibid., p. 97.

65. Ibid., p. 55.

66. Ibid., p. 283.

67. 3 August 1971. *SL*, p. 443.

68. *SL*, p. 444.

69. Ibid., p. 445.

70. To Donald Mitchell, 9 December 1968. Motion, p. 386.

71. Lisa Jardine, 'Saxon Violence', *Guardian*, 8 December 1992, Section 2, p. 4. For good measure Jardine adds: 'and an easy misogynist'.

72. The *Noctes Ambrosianae*, a series of seventy-one witty and humorous discussions set in Ambrose's Tavern, Edinburgh, appeared in *Blackwood's Magazine* between 1822 and 1835.

73. To Monica Jones, 16 November 1968. Not in *LM*.

74. 19 June 1970. *SL*, p. 432.

75. 19 November 1973. *SL*, p. 493.

76. 21 August 1971. *AWJ*, p. 284.

77. To Judy Egerton, 15 November 1969. *SL*, p. 421.

78. 15 September 1984. *SL*, p. 719.

79. *SL*, p. 445.

80. DPL(2)/2/15/44.

81. 14 October 1980. *SL*, p. 629.

82. To Conquest, 12 November 1973. *SL*, pp. 492–3.

83. *SL*, p. 456.

84. See also John Osborne, 'Diasporic identities', in *Larkin, Ideology and Critical Violence*, pp. 229–45. Osborne sees Larkin's enthusiasm for jazz as an aspect of his modernity.

85. To John White, cited in Tolley and White (eds), *Larkin's Jazz*, CD liner notes, p. 13.

86. 20 November 1968. *SL*, p. 408.

87. 27 November 1968. Motion, p. 386.

88. To Peter Crawley, 19 June 1969. *SL*, p. 416.

89. 13 January 1970. *SL*, p. 425.

90. To Peter Crawley. *SL*, p. 417.

91. *AWJ*, pp. 17–18.

92. Ibid., p. 19.

93. Ibid., pp. 22–3.

94. Ibid., p. 25.

95. Ibid., p. 27.

96. Ibid., p. 23.

97. Ibid.

98. The 'novel in gibberish' is not immediately identifiable. Probably Larkin had in mind James Joyce's *Finnegans Wake*, which still remains problematic for most readers.

99. Motion, p. 386. Richard Palmer devotes a chapter to 'Larkin's Most Expensive

Mistake', analysing the 'determined perversity' of the Introduction to *All What Jazz. Such Deliberate Disguises*, pp. 13–33.

100. 'The Art of Jazz' (1940), in *Larkin's Jazz*, ed. Palmer and White, p. 169.

101. *AWJ*, p. 27.

102. Ibid., p. 15.

103. Palmer, *Such Deliberate Disguises*, p. 57.

104. *AWJ*, pp. 15–16.

105. *Larkin's Jazz*, ed. Palmer and White, pp. 6–7.

106. *AWJ*, p. 22.

107. Ibid., pp. 28–9.

18: Politics and Literary Politics (1968–73)

1. 10 March 1946. *SL*, p. 115

2. *LM*, p. 381.

3. Hartley, p. 159.

4. To Monica Jones, 14 September 1964. Passage not in *LM*.

5. *SL*, p. 403.

6. Ibid., p. 402.

7. http://senatehouseoccupation.wordpress.com/1968/07/02/are-examinations-really-necessary/ (accessed 10 December 2010).

8. 19 August 1968. *SL*, pp. 403–4.

9. 16 November 1968. Not in *LM*.

10. 24 March 1973. *SL*, p. 473.

11. 16 November 1968. Not in *LM*.

12. Ibid. (insertion).

13. *Critical Quarterly* 2.4 (Winter 1960), p. 351; 3.4 (Winter 1961), p. 309; 8.2 (Summer 1966), p. 173; 10.1–2 (Spring–Summer 1968), p. 55. Larkin also published in *Critical Quarterly* a review, 'Mrs Hardy's memories', 4.1 (Spring 1962), pp. 75–9, and his essay, 'Wanted: Good Hardy Critic', 8.2 (Summer 1966), pp. 174–9.

14. http://pubs.socialistreviewindex.org.uk/isj70/amis.htm.

15. 4 October 1968. *SL*, pp. 404–5.

16. 17 October 1968. *SL*, p. 406.

17. *LM*, p. 394.

18. To Kingsley Amis, 8 April 1969. Not in *SL*.

19. *LM*, p. 385.

20. Trevor Jarvis, personal communication, 2010.

21. University of Hull Collection, The History Centre, Hull: U DJH.

22. John Saville, *Memoirs from the Left* (London: Merlin Press, 2003), pp. 138, 139, 145.

23. A BBC radio quiz, based on literary quotations, starring Frank Muir and Denis Norden. It ran from 1956 until 1990.

24. In *LM* (384) the phrases 'aren't the 2 songs lovely together! My eyes fill with tears' are inadvertently omitted.

25. Ibid.

26. Ibid., p. 387.

27. To Monica Jones, 15 January 1969. *Complete Poems*, p. 461.

28. See http://www.britannica.com/bps/additionalcontent/18/23072911/The-Decline-of-the-AngloAmerican-Middle-East-19611969 (accessed 12 April 2011).

29. Mitchell left the army later in the year and unlike officers of similar rank was not awarded an OBE. The final evacuation of troops from Aden took place on 8 November 1967. Mitchell capitalized on the glamour of this exploit in a populist campaign to become a Conservative MP.

30. To Monica Jones. 5 August 1953. *LM*, p. 104.

31. Interview with the *Observer*, *RW*, p. 52.

32. Blake Morrison, *The Movement: English Poetry and Fiction of the 1950s* (London: Methuen, 1980), p. 256.

33. Trevor Jarvis, personal communication, 2010.

34. Motion, p. 381.

35. To Conquest, 7 April 1969. *SL*, p. 413.

36. Motion, p. 380.

37. To the Revd A. H. Quinn, 3 February 1969. *Complete Poems*, p. 641.

38. 8 October 1969. *SL*, p. 420.

39. To Maeve Brennan, 4 September 1969. Motion, p. 393.

40. Motion, p. 390. The official opening by the University Chancellor, Lord Cohen of Birkenhead, took place on 12 December 1970.

41. To Eva Larkin, 5 October 1969.

42. Betty Mackereth, personal communication, 7 January 2014.

43. *SL*, p. 427.

44. Motion, p. 404.

45. Oxford University Rugby Football Club.

46. To Barbara Pym, 29 May 1971. *SL*, pp. 438–9.

47. Anthony Thwaite, personal communication, 2010.

48. 20 January 1966. *SL*, p. 380.

49. W. B. Yeats (ed.), *The Oxford Book of Modern Verse 1892–1935* (Oxford: Oxford University Press, 1936), pp. xxxiv, xv.

50. 4 June 1966. *LM*, p. 361.

51. '"A great parade of single poems" – Philip Larkin, poet, librarian and anthologist, discusses his *Oxford Book of Twentieth-Century English Verse* with Anthony Thwaite', *Listener*, 12 April 1973, p. 472.

52. Motion (p. 431) reaches different conclusions by counting numbers of poems rather than numbers of lines.

53. 22 November 1951. *LM*, pp. 71–2.

54. *SL*, p. 401.

55. 5 August 1953. *LM*, p. 104.

56. *OBTCEV*, p. v.

57. Yeats (ed.), *The Oxford Book of Modern Verse*, p. xlii.

58. The Republic of Ireland was also a member of the Commonwealth until 1949.

59. Walcott's inclusion was presumably justified on the technical grounds that at the

time of publication, 1973, St Lucia had not yet gained its independence from Britain. Had the volume been published six years later Walcott would presumably have been excluded as a 'Commonwealth writer'.

60. *OBTCEV*, p. v.

61. *OBTCEV*, no. 283. Larkin's response to Cannan's work was critically scrupulous. He wrote to Monica that one of her poems was 'good by accident, wonderfully evocative of the first war [. . .] They probably aren't any good really.' *LM*, p. 413.

62. *OBTCEV*, p. v.

63. Judy Egerton, interview with the author, 17 December 2010.

64. *SL*, p. 435.

65. 18 January 1973. *SL*, p. 472.

66. To Judy Egerton, 16 January 1971. *SL*, p. 434.

67. Larkin's Latin is faulty. The quotation should be 'quot homines tot disputandum est'. The usual, more economical form is 'quot homines tot sententiae', from Horace.

68. *SL*, p. 436.

69. Ibid., p. 477.

70. 'Larkin's Choice', *Listener*, 29 March 1973, pp. 420–1.

71. *SL*, p. 481.

72. Motion, pp. 432–3.

19: Larkin's Late Style (1969–72)

1. *SL*, p. 420.

2. 30 October 1969. *Complete Poems*, p. 442.

3. *SL*, p. 425.

4. 6 January 1970. *LM*, p. 405.

5. Motion, p. 394.

6. See James Booth, 'Larkin as Animal Poet', *AL* 22 (October 2001), p. 6.

7. To Thwaite, 25 April 1972. *SL*, p. 457.

8. *Bowlby's Row*, signed 'E. Tarling 1978', and *Entrance to Albert Dock*. Larkin Society, DX/329, inventory 6 and 12.

9. *LM*, p. 348.

10. Ibid., p. 381.

11. Not in *LM*.

12. The others are 'Spring' (ababcdcd effgeg), 'Whatever Happened?' (aba, bcb, cdc, ded, ff) and 'Friday Night in the Royal Station Hotel' (ababcdcde fgefg).

13. Burnett (*Complete Poems*, p. 456) cites Roger Day, who indicates no rhyme in the last line.

14. The fourth element, 'earth', has to be omitted for the sake of the metre.

15. See V. Penelope Pelizzon, 'Native Carnival: Philip Larkin's Puppet-Theatre of Ritual', in James Booth (ed.), *New Larkins for Old* (Basingstoke: Macmillan, 2000), pp. 213–23, at p. 218.

16. See James Booth, 'The Card-Players', in Michael Hanke (ed.), *Fourteen English Sonnets: Critical Essays*, Studien zur anglistischen Literatur- und Sprachwissenschaft (28) (Trier: Wissenschaftlicher Verlag, 2007), 169–77.

17. I am grateful to Raphaël Ingelbien for his help with this poem.

18. Pieter Bruegel the Elder (1525–69), David Teniers the Younger (1610–90), Adriaen Brouwer (c. 1605–38).

19. Larkin wrote to Arthur J. Hobson on 15 December 1978: 'I had no particular picture in mind. I should not go quite as far as to say that Brouwer was my favourite painter, but he is the only artist of whose work I have bothered to buy a book of reproductions, and in general I like Dutch low-life painting very much indeed.' DPL/2/2/15/9.

20. Adjustments were made before its publication in *Encounter* 35.4 (October 1970), p. 41.

21. Motion, p. 395.

22. John Osborne, personal communication, 1996.

23. John Mowat, 'Larkin' About in Hull', in Cliff Forshaw (ed.), *Under Travelling Skies: Departures from Larkin* (Hull: Kingston Press, 2012), pp. 73–4.

24. In *Collected Poems* (1988) the final date of drafting of 'Vers de Société' is given as '19.5.71'. This is the date at the top left of the page. But Larkin has written '20/5/71' at the end of the draft. DPL/1/7/41, p. 159.

25. In *New Humanist*, 86.8 (August 1971), p. 253.

26. *SL*, p. 437.

27. *Complete Poems*, p. 463. Motion writes (p. 373) that Larkin began the poem on 'the same evening that he wrote Annus Mirabilis' (16 June 1967). But there is no sign of this in the workbook. DPL/1/7/21. Burnett (p. 38) prints the poem without indents.

28. DPL/1/7/42.

29. 1 August 1971. *LM*, p. 423.

30. 26 June 1971. *SL*, p. 440.

31. This was a short-term arrangement, while Philip and Kitty were both on holiday, not as Motion implies, a semi-permanent move (p. 414).

32. See Marion Lomax, 'Larkin with Women', in Michael Baron (ed.), *Larkin with Poetry: English Association Conference Papers* (Leicester: English Association, 1997), pp. 39–40.

33. Introduction to *Adventures with the Irish Brigade*, *FR*, p. 119.

34. To Colin Gunner, 26 October 1971. *SL*, p. 449.

35. *SL*, p. 487.

36. Ibid., p. 450.

37. 14 November, 1971.

38. *SL*, p. 453.

39. 13 July 1959. *SL*, p. 305.

40. Burnett (*Complete Poems*, p. 448) points out Motion's mistake in connecting this incident with the first line of 'Livings I' rather than 'Livings III'. Motion, p. 415.

41. 31 May 1972. *SL*, p. 459.

42. *SL*, p. 452.
43. Letter to Robert Jackson. DPL/2/2/10. Motion, p. 418.

20: Winter Coming (1972–4)

1. Motion, p. 419.
2. DPL/1/8/2.
3. Compare 'his hand, holding her hand' in 'An Arundel Tomb'.
4. Burnett (*Complete Poems*, p. 458), citing R. J. C. Watt, misidentifies the hospital as Kingston General, a Victorian building, now demolished, which bore no resemblance to a clean-sliced cliff.
5. The singular noun 'human' never occurs in Larkin's poetry. The plural occurs again only in the light verse 'Dear CHARLES, My Muse, asleep or dead'. 'Human' occurs as an adjective only in the juvenile 'After Dinner Remarks', and then, substantively, in 'Sympathy in White Major'. 'Humanity' occurs only once, in relation to the Polish airgirl in 'Like the train's beat'. R. J. C. Watt (ed.), *A Concordance to the Poetry of Philip Larkin* (Hildesheim: Olms-Weidmann, 1995), pp. 223–4.
6. There is an echo of Shelley's 'O world! O life! O time!' in 'A Lament'. *The Poems of Shelley* (Oxford: Oxford University Press, 1960), p. 643.
7. James Booth, *Philip Larkin: The Poet's Plight* (Basingstoke: Palgrave Macmillan, 2005), p. 169.
8. 22 March 1972. *SL*, p. 454.
9. To Conquest, 31 May 1972. *SL*, p. 458.
10. Brennan, pp. 86–7.
11. 13 June 1972. *SL*, pp. 459–60.
12. There may be a wry echo of 'That lone lane does not exist' in Hardy's 'Beyond the Last Lamp'.
13. Anthony Thwaite, personal communication, 22 April 2011. He also sent a hand-written copy to Anthony's wife Ann, for inclusion in a book of manuscript poems she was assembling at the time, offering to rewrite it if he had gone too close to the left-hand edge of the paper.
14. Motion, p. 424. Not in *Complete Poems*.
15. 25 November 1972. *SL*, pp. 465–6.
16. 29 November 1972. *SL*, p. 466. Bloomfield's *Philip Larkin: A Bibliography 1933–1976* was published by Faber in 1979.
17. *SL*, p. 467.
18. 18 January 1973. *SL*, p. 471.
19. 10 February. *SL*, p. 473.
20. Georges Bataille, *Death and Sexuality: A Study of Eroticism and the Taboo* (New York: Ballantine Books, 1969), p. 12.
21. 15 January 1973. *SL*, p. 470.
22. *SL*, p. 483.
23. Motion, p. 430.
24. Interview with *Paris Review*, *RW*, p. 62.

25. *The Poetical Works of Wordsworth* (London: Oxford University Press, 1950), p. 206.

26. 'Adagia', in Wallace Stevens, *Opus Posthumous*, ed. Samuel French Morse (London: Faber & Faber, 1959), p. 165. Larkin follows Stevens rather than Robert Graves, who expresses the more conventional view: 'If there's no money in poetry neither is there poetry in money.' Robert Graves, *Mammon and the Black Goddess* (London: Cassell, 1965), p. 3.

27. 16 January 1971. *SL*, p. 435.

28. Barbara Everett, 'After Symbolism', first published in *Essays in Criticism* in 1980; reprinted in Barbara Everett, *Poets in their Time* (Oxford: Oxford University Press, 1986), pp. 230–44.

29. Andrew Motion, *Philip Larkin* (London: Methuen, 1982).

30. 17 October 1981. *SL*, p. 658.

31. *SL*, pp. 476–7.

32. The first two tutorial groups I taught on my arrival in the English Department in 1968 consisted of a single student and three students. By the mid-seventies tutorial sizes were up to seven and later increased to sixteen.

33. Motion, p. 391.

34. To Judy Egerton, 11 January 1974. *SL*, p. 498.

35. The tally was to rise to twenty-six with the addition of 'Show Saturday'.

36. Motion, p. 435.

37. 4 October 1973. *SL*, p. 489.

38. Motion, p. 438.

39. *SL*, pp. 494–5.

40. Motion, pp. 437–8.

41. Motion, p. 437; Neil Corcoran, *English Poetry Since 1940* (Harlow: Longman, 1993), p. 93; Seamus Heaney, *The Government of the Tongue* (London: Faber, 1988), pp. 19–20.

42. *SL*, p. 497.

43. Ibid., p. 496.

44. The present owner, Miriam Porter, has transformed and improved the house out of all recognition, and installed a blue plaque recording Larkin's ownership. See 'Newland Park Garden Party', *AL* 20 (October 2005), pp. 54–7.

45. DPL/2/3/39.

46. Britten lived nearly three years longer and resumed composition. When he died at the end of 1976 he was composing a work for voices and orchestra, 'Praise We Great Men', to words by Edith Sitwell.

47. *SL*, p. 502.

48. Ibid., p. 503.

49. DPL/1/8/18, pp. 55–64. Motion (p. 442) writes that he started 'Aubade' 'on 11 March'. But there is no evidence for this. See *Complete Poems*, pp. 494–5.

50. In the then unpublished 'Long roots moor summer to this side of earth' (1954), 'unresting' had appeared in the gorgeous phrase 'River-castles of unresting leaf'. Otherwise both words appear in Larkin's poetry only in 'The Trees' and 'Aubade'. R.J.C. Watt, Concordance, pp. 6–7, p. 521. Some readers may hear an echo of 'the wind's incomplete unrest' in 'Talking in Bed'.

51. Alexander Pope, *An Essay on Criticism*, l. p. 298.
52. Motion, pp. 443–5.

21: The End of the Party (1974–6)

1. Letter to Sutton, 26 July 1950. Not in *SL*.
2. To Thwaite, 11 July 1974. *SL*, pp. 511–12.
3. Judy Egerton, interview with the author, 17 December 2010.
4. 5 June 1974. *SL*, p. 509.
5. Motion, p. 448.
6. Motion, p. 443.
7. *SL*, p. 512.
8. Ibid., p. 704.
9. See Terry Kelly, 'The Black Album: Review of *Philip Larkin: Poems*', *AL* 32 (October 2011), pp. 33–4.
10. To Barry Bloomfield, 4 December 1974. *SL*, p. 515.
11. Brennan, p. 89.
12. Ibid., p. 141.
13. R. J. C. Watt, '"Scragged by embryo Leavises": Larkin reading his poems', *Critical Survey* 1.2 (1989), pp. 172–5.
14. Motion, p. 449.
15. Ibid., p. 446.
16. Ibid., p. 447.
17. Ibid.
18. Brennan, p. 51.
19. Ibid., p. 219.
20. 2 June 1975. *SL*, p. 525.
21. 15 June 1975. *SL*, p. 526.
22. See James Booth, *Philip Larkin: The Poet's Plight* (Basingstoke: Palgrave Macmillan, 2005), Appendix, pp. 202–3. This book is now in Emory University Library, Atlanta, Georgia.
23. Motion, p. 487.
24. Ibid.
25. Burnett hears an echo of Kingsley Amis's poem 'Masters', from *A Case of Samples* (1946), pp. 22–3: 'For it is by surrender that we live, / And we are taken if we wish to give.' *Complete Poems*, p. 506.
26. Brennan, pp. 67–8.
27. Written originally to German lyrics by Friedrich Hollaender and sung by Dietrich in the film *The Blue Angel* (1930). The English lyrics were by Sammy Lerner: 'Falling in love again. / Never wanted to. / What am I to do? / Can't help it.'
28. Motion, p. 319.
29. 25 November 1975. DPL/1/8/22, at p. 73.
30. *TWG*, p. 497.
31. Ibid., p. xixn.

32. Larkin's verbal memory was hypersensitive. In a letter to Monteith of 16 April 1974 he asked for the word 'with' to be reinstated in the paperback reprint of *A Girl in Winter*, in a sentence ending 'you would have to deal with.' The word was, he writes, 'cut out by your super-efficient editors in 1946'. He had however intended it as 'a deliberate grammatical mistake [. . .] to show the muddle-headedness of the speaker'; 'it has irked me for over a quarter of a century'. *SL*, pp. 503–4.

33. Brennan, p. 221.

34. Motion, p. 451.

35. Mary Judd (née Wrench), interview with the author, 28 June 2011.

36. Betty Mackereth, interview with the author, 20 June 2011.

37. Ibid.

38. Ibid., 4 August 2003.

39. *Philip Larkin: The Third Woman*, BBC4 television feature, 7 December 2010.

40. Betty Mackereth, interview with the author, 20 June 2011.

41. Ibid.

42. Motion, p. 282.

43. Betty Mackereth, interview with the author, 4 August 2003.

44. Betty Mackereth, interview with the author, 20 June 2011.

45. See R. J. C. Watt, *A Concordance to the Poetry of Philip Larkin* (Hildesheim: Olms-Weidmann, 1995).

46. I am grateful to Suzanne Uniacke for this observation.

47. Motion, p. 453.

48. Kate Greenaway Valentine's Day card, dated 30 December 1975.

49. The noun 'singularity' occurs in 'Marriages' (1951).

50. A typescript inserted into Workbook 8 is dated '1/2/76'. *Complete Poems*, p. 651.

51. 'The Booker Prize 1977', *RW*, p. 95.

52. Larkin may have recalled the ending of Hardy's 'Beyond the Last Lamp': 'they seem brooding on their pain, / And will, while such a lane remain'. Thomas Hardy, *Complete Poems* (London: Macmillan 1976), p. 315.

53. The surviving drafts, dated between 7 and 21 February, are in the Collins manuscript book, now at Emory University, and the text as he sent it to Betty is in holograph. It is possible that Larkin never made a typescript.

54. To Conquest, 9 December 1961. *SL*, p. 335.

55. Larkin uses the word 'dirty' three times in his mature poems, each time with a different idiomatic nuance. In 'Success Story' (1954) the speaker celebrates having dodged the metaphorical 'dirty feeding' of domestic compromise. In 'A Study of Reading Habits' (1960) the word appears in a demotic cliché, as the speaker fights 'dirty dogs'. In contrast, in 'We met at the end of the party' the word has a simple physical application.

56. Betty Mackereth, interview with the author, 4 August 2003.

22: Death-Throes of a Talent (1976–9)

1. Motion, p. 457. Toepfer had indeed had Nazi connections, but the Foundation denied them.
2. 'Subsidising Poetry', *RW*, p. 90.
3. 26 April 1976. *SL*, p. 539.
4. To Eva Larkin, 30 May 1976.
5. To Conquest, 26 May 1976. *SL*, p. 541.
6. *SL*, p. 546.
7. 21 September 1976. *SL*, pp. 546–7.
8. Motion, pp. 460 and 221.
9. 17 October 1968. *SL*, p. 406.
10. Hazel Holt, *A Lot to Ask: A Life of Barbara Pym* (London: Macmillan, 1990), p. 247.
11. *SL*, pp. 547–8.
12. 28 November 1976. *SL*, p. 552.
13. *Times Literary Supplement*, 21 January 1977, p. 66.
14. Motion, p. 464.
15. 24 October 1977. *SL*, p. 571.
16. Motion, p. 466.
17. Martin Amis, Introduction to *Philip Larkin: Poems* (London: Faber & Faber, 2011), p. xxi.
18. 'So death . . . is nothing to us, since so long as we exist, death is not with us; but when death comes, then we do not exist. It does not then concern either the living or the dead.' Epicurus, *The Extant Remains*, trans. Cyril Bailey (Oxford: Oxford University Press, 1926), p. 85.
19. Richard Rorty, *Contingency, Irony, and Solidarity* (Cambridge: Cambridge University Press, 1989), p. 23.
20. Letter to Barbara Pym, 14 December 1977. *SL*, p. 574.
21. Ibid.
22. Auden, 'As I walked out one evening', in *The English Auden*, ed. Edward Mendelson (London: Faber & Faber, 1977), p. 228.
23. We may also recall that 'clothes make the man'. Mark Twain, *More Maxims of Mark*, ed. Merle Johnson (privately printed, 1927).
24. 'Senecas Troas Act 2d Chor', in *The Poems of John Wilmot Earl of Rochester*, ed. Keith Walker (Oxford: Blackwell, 1988), p. 51.
25. He commented to one correspondent: 'I can see the justice of your objection to the last line, and yet I do not know how else to say what I mean, namely that postmen, by going from house to house and bringing welcome distraction in the shape of letters, cure those awful waking thoughts as if they were a kind of doctor.' To B. Z. Paulshock, 16 August 1978. DPL(2)/2/15/51.
26. Motion, p. 466.
27. In 'The Winter Palace' (1978), 'The Mower' (1979), the concluding lines of 'Love Again' (1979, begun in 1975), '1982' (1982) and 'Party Politics' (1984).
28. DPL(2)/2/15/85.

29. *SL*, pp. 580–1.

30. Ibid., p. 581.

31. Hughes's lines assert a right-wing organicist concept of nationhood:

> A Nation's a Soul;
> A Soul is a Wheel
> With a Crown for a Hub
> To keep it whole.

Ted Hughes, *Collected Poems* (London: Faber & Faber, 2003), p. 381. For a discussion of the poems see Neil Roberts, 'Hughes, the Laureateship and National Identity', *Q/W/E/R/T/Y* 9 (October 1999), pp. 203–9.

32. Motion, p. 471.

33. Brennan, pp. 88–9.

34. Motion, p. 472.

35. *SL*, p. 577.

36. 'The Changing Face of Andrew Marvell', *RW*, pp. 245–53.

37. DPL(2)/2/14/44.

38. Motion, p. 469.

39. *SL*, p. 589.

40. DPL/1/8/50. See Burnett, *Complete Poems*, p. xix. For a facsimile of the typescript see *AL* 33 (April 2012), cover.

41. Between pp. 96 and 97 of M. V. Hughes, *A London Girl of the 1880s* (Oxford: Oxford University Press, 1982).

42. The card is reproduced in *AL* 30 (October 2010), p. 4.

43. *SL*, p. 601.

44. Betty Mackereth, interview with the author, 20 June 2011.

45. DPL/1/8/32 and DPL/1/8/47.

46. In 'Larkin as Animal Poet' (*AL* 22, October 2006, pp. 5–9) I suggested that the hedgehog might have been diseased or already dead, since it was out on the lawn in the daytime. However, Larkin says that he mowed the lawn 'last night', and hedgehogs are active in the dusk. I am grateful to Peter James for pointing out my mistake.

47. http://www.amarc.org.uk/Newsletter02.pdf (accessed 14 December 2010).

48. Ted Hughes, *Letters of Ted Hughes*, ed. Christopher Reid (London: Faber & Faber, 2007), p. 404.

49. 23 August 1979. *SL*, p. 603.

50. DPL/1/8/22.

51. DPL/1/8/26 and 1/8/28.

52. DPL/1/8/30.

53. For a facsimile and transcription see *AL* 34 (October 2012), pp. 5–9.

54. Interview with the *Observer*, *RW*, pp. 47–56.

23: Extinction (1980–5)

1. To Amis, 26 April 1980. *SL*, p. 619.
2. Ruth Siverns, *Barlow Dale's Casebook* (London: Macmillan, 1981).
3. In her last years Ruth Siverns became friends with Winifred Dawson (née Arnott), who happened to live in nearby Winchester. She died on 31 December 2012. Obituaries appeared, by myself (www.guardian.co.uk/books) and by Win Dawson, *AL* 35 (April 2013), pp. 5–6.
4. DPL/2/3/91.
5. 'Lines on a Young Lady's Photograph Album', 'MCMXIV', 'Toads', 'The Explosion', 'A Study of Reading Habits', 'Home is so Sad', 'Within the dream you said', 'Afternoons', 'The Old Fools', 'For Sidney Bechet', 'So through that unripe day you bore your head', 'Next, Please', 'The Trees', 'Church Going', 'The Whitsun Weddings', 'Days', 'Wires', 'An Arundel Tomb', 'Cut Grass', 'Vers de Société', 'I put my mouth', 'At Grass', 'Mr Bleaney', 'Coming', 'Toads Revisited', 'The Building'.
6. James Orwin, 'Serious Earth: Philip Larkin's American Tapes', *AL* 25 (April 2008), pp. 20–4, at p. 22.
7. Ibid.
8. The recording was omitted from Bloomfield's *Bibliography*. The readings were released commercially by Faber in 2009 under the title *The Sunday Sessions: Philip Larkin Reading his Poetry*. Orwin, 'Serious Earth: Philip Larkin's American Tapes', p. 23.
9. Motion, p. 483.
10. *SL*, p. 624.
11. Motion, p. 482.
12. Ibid., p. 484.
13. *SL*, p. 632.
14. 13 January 1981. *SL*, p. 637.
15. http://entertainment.timesonline.co.uk/tol/arts_and_entertainment/tv_and_radio/article4718715.ece (accessed 14 December 2010). Bragg gives a highly coloured account of a meeting at a restaurant at which Larkin became drunk, refused to leave and, according to Bragg, 'had to be forcibly ejected by policemen with dogs'.
16. Motion, p. 489.
17. Ibid., p. 486.
18. *SL*, p. 662.
19. 23 February 1982. *SL*, p. 665. The reference is to Salman Rushdie.
20. Interview with *Paris Review*, *RW*, p. 65.
21. *RW*, pp. 62, 68.
22. Ibid., p. 60.
23. Ibid., pp. 69, 58.
24. Jane Thomas, Philip Larkin Society website: 'Poem of the Month', June 2011 ('Love'): http://www.philiplarkin.com/histpom/proposer/thomas_j.htm (accessed 1 September 2012).

25. Motion, p. 497.
26. Douglas Dunn (ed.), *A Rumoured City: New Poets from Hull* (Newcastle upon Tyne: Bloodaxe Books, 1982), p. 9.
27. Hartley, p. 202.
28. Motion, p. 496.
29. Ibid., p. 492.
30. To Thwaite, 17 May 1982. *SL*, p. 671.
31. 6 June 1982. SL, p. 674.
32. To Virginia Peace. *SL*, p. 663. Whalen later wrote *Philip Larkin and English Poetry* (Basingstoke: Macmillan, 1990).
33. Michael Hamburger, *Philip Larkin* (London: Enitharmon Press, 2002), pp. 35–6.
34. Motion, p. 497. Janet Brennan, 'Philip Larkin and Margaret Thatcher'. *AL* 35 (April 2013), p. 11..
35. *LM*, pp. 442–3.
36. Motion, p. 498.
37. Ibid., p. 499.
38. Betty Mackereth, interview with the author, 20 June 2011.
39. DPL(2)/2/15.
40. *RW*, p. 11; to Colin Gunner, 2 August 1983, *SL*, p. 700.
41. In a letter to Daniel Weissbort of 25 November 1983, Ted Hughes paid rueful tribute to the way the 'spermicide' of Larkin's authority, and the 'subtle efficiency' of his 'sort of social one-upmanship', made other kinds of poetry seem 'a genetic mistake, unfit for [. . .] decent society'. 'Some of the pieces are awfully good & persuasive [. . .] He's a sour old cuss & the whole book's outrageous propaganda for his own tastes & limitations & prejudices, but perfectly timed – philistinism has been browbeaten too long!' Ted Hughes, *Letters of Ted Hughes*, ed. Christopher Reid (London: Faber & Faber, 2007), pp. 476–7.
42. 'Meeting Philip Larkin', *FR*, pp. 112 and 116.
43. 2 April 1984. *LM*, p. 444.
44. Jane Bottomley, personal communication, 27 July 2011.
45. Motion, pp. 508, 507.
46. *SL*, p. 713.
47. Judy Egerton, interview with the author, 17 December 2010.
48. Hartley, p. 178.
49. Jane Bottomley, personal communication, 27 July 2011.
50. Judy Egerton, interview with the author, 17 December 2010.
51. 16 September 1984. *SL*, p. 720.
52. Motion, p. 510.
53. 27 December 1984. Motion, p. 511.
54. In 1999 the then Dean of Westminster, Wesley Carr, responded to the Larkin Society's representations with reservations about Larkin's religious views, and the opinion that a poet should not be considered until at least twenty years after his or her death. The current Dean, John Hall, clearly adopted a different policy in relation to Hughes.

55. DPL/X4/5/5.
56. Motion, p. 513.
57. Brennan, p. 91.
58. Jean Hartley believed that it was Monica. Personal communication, 2011.
59. Brennan, p. 91.
60. Betty Mackereth, interview with the author, 20 June 2011.
61. Hartley, p. 207.
62. Jean Hartley, 'Larkin, Love and Sex', *AL* 30 (October 2010), pp. 6–8, at p. 8.
63. Brennan, p. 91.
64. Thomas McAlindon, personal communication, 23 October 2011.
65. Betty Mackereth, interview with the author, 20 June 2011.
66. *SL*, p. 743.
67. Motion, p. 519.
68. Personal recollection of the author.
69. Professor Dawes is now Chairman of the Philip Larkin Society.
70. Hughes, *Letters of Ted Hughes*, pp. 502–3.
71. Motion, p. 520.
72. Ibid., p. 521.

Postscript: Petals and Graves

1. Martin Amis, Introduction to *Philip Larkin: Poems* (London: Faber & Faber, 2011), p. xix.
2. 13 September 1954. *LM*, p. 116.
3. *FR*, p. 60.
4. DPL/4/1/1–DPL/4/1/13.
5. Betty Mackereth, interview with the author, 4 August 2003.
6. Ibid.
7. Motion, p. xvi.
8. *Collected Poems*, p. xxii.
9. Motion, pp. 519–20.
10. Ibid., p. 307.
11. Maeve wrote: 'James Booth undertook the task of editing my text and skilfully welded its different elements into a harmonious whole' (p. xii). My contribution was to encourage her to write at greater length and more candidly than she had originally intended. I helped her to distribute the material into chapters, provided the chapter headings and suggested the title. I also encouraged her to add the chapter 'Religion'. Otherwise I scrupulously avoided any attempt to influence the content or tone of her book.
12. James Booth, '"Snooker" at the Seaside: The Birthday Walk in Scarborough', *AL* 16 (October 2003), pp. 29–30.
13. James Booth, 'Glimpses' (interview with Monica Jones), *AL* 12 (October 2001), p. 22.
14. Motion, pp. 310–11.

15. Booth, 'Glimpses', pp. 23–4.
16. James Booth, *Philip Larkin: The Poet's Plight* (Basingstoke: Palgrave Macmillan, 2005), Appendix, pp. 202–3.
17. DX/329, inventory p. 584.
18. DPL/1/4/24.
19. John Betjeman, 'On a Portrait of a Deaf Man', *Collected Poems* (London: John Murray, enlarged edn, 1973), p. 96.
20. 'The current of his feeling failed: he became his admirers.' W. H. Auden, 'In Memory of W. B. Yeats', in *The English Auden*, ed. Edward Mendelson (London: Faber & Faber, 1986), p. 241.
21. Note in an early draft of 'The Building'. DPL/1/8/2.

Bibliography

1. Unpublished or partly published material

Larkin family papers, Hull University Collection, The History Centre, Hull, U DLN/1–6. (Letters to Eva Larkin, U DLN/6).

Larkin, various papers, Hull University Collection, The History Centre, Hull, U DP, U DPL.

Letters to Kingsley Amis, The Huntington Library, California, AMS 353–428.

Letters to Monica Jones, The Bodleian Library, Oxford, MS. Eng. c.7403–c.7445.

Letters to James Sutton, Hull University Collection, The History Centre, Hull, U DP/174/2.

Pictures, photographs, ornaments, etc. from 105 Newland Park, Hull University Collection, The History Centre, Hull (Philip Larkin Society deposit), U DX/329.

Workbook 1 (1944–50), British Library, Add. MS. 52619.

Workbooks 2–8: Hull University Collection, The History Centre, Hull, U DPL/1/2–8.

Workbook containing drafts of poems from 1975–6, Emory University, Atlanta, Manuscripts, Archives and Rare Books Library (MARBL).

2. Publications of Larkin's work

All What Jazz: A Record Diary (London: Faber & Faber, 2nd edn, 1985).

'Biographical Details: OXFORD', parts 1 and 2, *About Larkin* 23 (April 2007), pp. 5–13, and *About Larkin* 24 (October 2007), pp. 4–19.

The Complete Poems of Philip Larkin, ed. with an introduction and commentary by Archie Burnett (London: Faber & Faber, 2012).

'Country Beauty' ('Verlaine'), *About Larkin* 36 (October 2013), pp. 4–5.

Early Poems and Juvenilia, ed. A. T. Tolley (London: Faber & Faber, 2005).

Further Requirements: Interviews, Broadcasts, Statements and Book Reviews 1952–1985, ed.

Anthony Thwaite (London: Faber & Faber, pbk edn with two additional chapters, 2002).

A Girl in Winter (London: Faber & Faber, 1975 edn).

High Windows (London: Faber & Faber, 1974).

'An Incident in the English Camp', *About Larkin* 12 (October 2001), pp. 5–10.

Incidents from Phippy's Schooldays, ed. Brenda Allen and James Acheson (Edmonton, Canada: Juvenilia Press, 2002).

Jill (London: Faber & Faber, 1975 edn).

'Larkin's Dream Diary 1942–3, Part 1' and 'Part 2', ed. Don Lee, *About Larkin* 27 (April 2009), pp. 5–13, and *About Larkin* 28 (October 2009), pp. 5–13.

Larkin's Jazz: Essays and Reviews 1940–84, ed. Richard Palmer and John White (London and New York: Continuum, 2001).

'Larkin's Second Dream Diary', ed. James Booth, *About Larkin* 32 (October 2011), pp. 6–7.

The Less Deceived (Hull: Marvell Press, 1955).

Letters to Monica, ed. Anthony Thwaite (London: Faber & Faber/Bodleian Library, 2010).

'Letters to my Mind', *About Larkin* 34 (October 2012), pp. 5–9.

The North Ship (London: Fortune Press, 1945; first Faber & Faber edn 1966).

The Oxford Book of Twentieth-Century English Verse (London: Oxford University Press, 1973).

'Peter', *About Larkin* 11 (April 2001), pp. 13–23.

Philip Larkin: Collected Poems, ed. Anthony Thwaite (London: Marvell Press/Faber & Faber, 1988, revised 1990).

Philip Larkin: Collected Poems, ed. Anthony Thwaite (London: Marvell Press/Faber & Faber, 2003); excludes poems first published in 1988.

Philip Larkin: Poems, selected by Martin Amis (London: Faber & Faber, 2011).

Philip Larkin Reads and Comments on The Whitsun Weddings, Listen Records, 'The Poet's Voice', ed. George Hartley (Hull: Marvell Press, 1965).

Philip Larkin Reads The Less Deceived, Listen Records, 'The Poet's Voice', ed. George Hartley (Hull: Marvell Press, 1958).

'Poem for Penelope abt. the Mechanical Turd', in Susannah Tarbush, 'From *Willow Gables* to "Aubade": Penelope Scott Stokes and Philip Larkin: Part 1', *About Larkin* 25 (April 2008), pp. 5–11, at p. 11.

Required Writing: Miscellaneous Pieces 1955–1982 (London: Faber & Faber, 1983).

Selected Letters, ed. Anthony Thwaite (London: Faber & Faber, 1992).

'Single to Belfast', in Andrew Motion, *Philip Larkin: A Writer's Life* (London: Faber & Faber, 1993), pp. 196–7.

'Story 1', *About Larkin* 10 (October 2000), pp. 4–20.

Trouble at Willow Gables and Other Fictions, ed. James Booth (London: Faber & Faber, 2002).

The Whitsun Weddings (London: Faber & Faber, 1964).

'The Winter Palace', *About Larkin* 33 (April 2012), front cover.

'Worksheets of "At Grass"', *Phoenix* 11/12 (1973/4), pp. 91–103.
XX Poems, privately printed, Belfast, 1951.

3. Bibliography and Concordance

Bloomfield, B. C., *Philip Larkin: A Bibliography 1933–1994* (London: British Library and Oak Knoll Press, revised and enlarged edn, 2002).

Watt, R. J. C., *A Concordance to the Poetry of Philip Larkin* (Hildesheim: Olms-Weidmann, 1995).

4. Memoirs and Recollections

Amis, Kingsley, *Memoirs* (London: Hutchinson, 1991).

——, 'Oxford and After', in Anthony Thwaite (ed.), *Larkin at Sixty* (London: Faber & Faber, 1982), pp. 23–30.

Booth, James, 'Glimpses' (interview with Monica Jones), *About Larkin* 12 (October 2001), pp. 21–6.

Brennan, Maeve, 'Philip Larkin: a biographical sketch', in Brian Dyson (ed.), *The Modern Academic Library: Essays in Memory of Philip Larkin* (London: Library Association, 1988), pp. 1–19.

——, *The Philip Larkin I Knew* (Manchester: Manchester University Press, Larkin Society Monograph 3, 2002).

Dawson (Arnott), Winifred, 'The Day I Met Monica', *About Larkin* 31 (April 2011), pp. 5–7.

Dyson, Brian (ed.), *The Modern Academic Library: Essays in Memory of Philip Larkin* (London: Library Association, 1988).

Fowler, Margaret, 'Larkin's Library Recollected', *About Larkin* 32 (October 2011), p. 11.

Hamburger, Michael, *Philip Larkin* (London: Enitharmon Press, 2002).

Hartley, George (ed.), *Philip Larkin – A Tribute: 1922–1985* (London: Marvell Press, 1988).

Hartley, Jean, 'Larkin, Love and Sex', *About Larkin* 30 (October 2010), pp. 6–8.

——, *Philip Larkin, the Marvell Press and Me* (1989; London: Sumach Press, 1993).

Hughes, Noel, 'The Young Mr Larkin', in Anthony Thwaite (ed.), *Larkin at Sixty* (London: Faber & Faber, 1982), pp. 17–22.

Iles, Norman, 'Our Group', *London Magazine*, December/January 1999/2000, pp. 26–7.

Keating, Peter, 'Monica', in *Autobiography Tales* (Edinburgh: Priskus, 2013, pp. 77–155).

Moon, Brenda, 'Working with Philip Larkin', *About Larkin* 8 (October 1999), pp. 5–11.

Phillips, Moira, 'Larkin Recollected', *About Larkin* 33 (April 2012), p. 11.

Raban, Jonathan, *Coasting* (London, Collins Harvill, 1986).

——, 'Philip Larkin', in *Driving Home: An American Scrapbook* (London: Picador, 2010).

Rowland, Yvonne, 'Remembering Monica Jones in Leicester', *About Larkin* 30 (October 2010), pp. 18–19.

Saville, John, *Memoirs from the Left* (London: Merlin Press, 2003).

Sharpe, Norman, and A. K. B. Evans (eds), 'Monica at Leicester', *About Larkin* 12 (October 2001), pp. 17–19.

Siverns (Bowman), Ruth, 'Philip Larkin at Wellington 1943–1946', *About Larkin* 1 (April 1996), pp. 4–5.

Thwaite, Anthony (ed.), *Larkin at Sixty* (London: Faber & Faber, 1982).

Watt, R. J. C., '"Scragged by embryo-Leavises": Larkin reading his poems', *Critical Survey* 1.2 (1989), pp. 172–5.

5. Biographies

Bradford, Richard, *First Boredom, Then Fear: The Life of Philip Larkin* (London: Peter Owen, 2005).

——, *The Odd Couple: The Curious Friendship between Kingsley Amis and Philip Larkin* (London: Robson Press, 2012).

Motion, Andrew, *Philip Larkin: A Writer's Life* (London: Faber & Faber, 1993).

6. Select Secondary Sources

About Larkin (Journal of the Philip Larkin Society) (April 1996–April 2014); nos. 1–6 ed. Jean Hartley; nos. 7–14 ed. James Booth; no. 15 ed. Jean Hartley and Maeve Brennan; no. 16 ed. Jean Hartley; nos. 17–21 ed. Belinda Hakes; no. 22 ed. Janet Brennan; nos. 23–37 ed. James Booth and Janet Brennan.

Alvarez, A., 'The New Poetry, or Beyond the Gentility Principle', Introduction to *The New Poetry* (Harmondsworth: Penguin, 1962), pp. 17–28.

Amis, Martin, 'Philip Larkin, His Work and Life', introduction to *Philip Larkin: Poems* (London: Faber & Faber, 2011), pp. ix–xxiii.

Avis (Strang), Patricia, *Playing the Harlot or Mostly Coffee* (London: Virago, 1996).

Baron, Michael (ed.), *Larkin with Poetry: English Association Conference Papers* (Leicester: English Association, 1997).

Bennett, Alan, 'Alas! Deceived', in Stephen Regan (ed.), *Philip Larkin: Contemporary Critical Essays* (Basingstoke: Macmillan, 1997), pp. 226–49.

Blackburn, Simon, 'English Tombs and Larkin', *About Larkin* 36 (October 2013), pp. 7–11.

Booth, James, 'The Card-Players', in Michael Hanke (ed.), *Fourteen English Sonnets: Critical Essays*, Studien zur anglistischen Literatur- und Sprachwissenschaft (28) (Trier: Wissenschaftlicher Verlag, 2007), pp. 169–77.

——, 'Competing Pulses: Secular and Sacred in Hughes, Larkin and Plath', *Critical Survey* 12.3 (2000), pp. 4–27.

——, 'Larkin as Animal Poet', *About Larkin* 22 (October 2006), pp. 5–9.

—— (ed.), *New Larkins for Old* (Basingstoke: Macmillan, 2000).

——, *Philip Larkin: The Poet's Plight* (Basingstoke: Palgrave Macmillan, 2005).

——, *Philip Larkin: Writer* (Hemel Hempstead: Harvester Wheatsheaf, 1992).

——, '"Snooker" at the Seaside: The Birthday Walk in Scarborough', *About Larkin* 16 (October 2003), pp. 29–31.

——, 'Sydney Larkin's Little Hitler', *About Larkin* 29 (April 2010), p. 27.

——, 'The Turf-cutter and the Nine-to-Five Man: Heaney, Larkin, and "the Spiritual Intellect's Great Work"', *Twentieth-Century Literature* 43.4 (Winter 1997), pp. 369–93.

Brennan, Maeve, 'James Ballard Sutton 1921–1997', *About Larkin* 5 (April 1988), pp. 24–7.

Bristow, Joseph, 'The Obscenity of Philip Larkin', *Critical Inquiry* 21 (Autumn 1994), pp. 176–7.

Burnett, Archie, 'Biography and Poetry: Philip Larkin', *About Larkin* 36 (October 2013), pp. 7–18.

Carey, John, 'The Two Philip Larkins', in James Booth (ed.), *New Larkins for Old* (Basingstoke: Macmillan, 2000), pp. 51–65.

Castle, Terry, 'The Lesbianism of Philip Larkin', in Zachary Leader (ed.), *The Movement Reconsidered: Essays on Larkin, Amis, Gunn, Davie, and their Contemporaries* (Oxford: Oxford University Press, 2009), pp. 79–105.

Chesters, Graham, 'Larkin and Baudelaire's Damned Women', in James Dolamore (ed.), *Making Connections: Essays in French Culture and Society in Honour of Philip Thody* (Bern: Peter Lang, 1999), pp. 81–92.

——, 'Tireless Play, Speculations on Larkin's "Absences"', Richard Bales (ed.), *Challenges of Translation in French Literature: Studies and Poems in Honour of Peter Broome* (Bern: Peter Lang, 2005), pp. 47–60.

Conquest, Robert, Introduction to *New Lines: An Anthology*, ed. Robert Conquest (London: Macmillan, 1962), pp. v–xviii.

——, '*New Lines*, Movements, and Modernisms', in Zachary Leader (ed.), *The Movement Reconsidered: Essays on Larkin, Amis, Gunn, Davie, and their Contemporaries* (Oxford: Oxford University Press, 2009), pp. 307–16.

D'Arch Smith, Timothy, *R. A. Caton and the Fortune Press: A Memoir and a Hand-List* (revised edn, North Pomfret, Vermont: Asphodel Editions, 2004).

Dawson (Arnott), Winifred, 'Photograph Albums Revisited', *About Larkin* 13 (April 2002), p. 4.

Dyson, Brian (ed.), *The Modern Academic Library: Essays in Memory of Philip Larkin* (London: Library Association, 1988).

Everett, Barbara, 'After Symbolism', *Essays in Criticism*, 1980; reprinted in *Poets in their Time* (Oxford: Oxford University Press, 1986), pp. 230–44.

Foster, Paul, Trevor Brighton and Patrick Garland, *An Arundel Tomb*, Otter Memorial Paper 1 (Chichester: Chichester Institute, 1987).

Gilpin, George, 'Patricia Avis and Philip Larkin', in James Booth (ed.), *New Larkins for Old* (Basingstoke: Macmillan, 2000), pp. 66–78.

Gresham, Ross, 'Larkin on the *Lucky Jim* Manuscript', *About Larkin* 26 (October 2008), pp. 11–13.

Holt, Hazel, *A Lot to Ask: A Life of Barbara Pym* (London: Macmillan, 1990).

Hughes, Ted, *Letters of Ted Hughes*, ed. Christopher Reid (London: Faber & Faber, 2007).

Ingelbien, Raphaël, 'The Uses of Symbolism: Larkin and Eliot', in James Booth (ed.), *New Larkins for Old* (Basingstoke: Macmillan, 2000), pp. 130–43.

Kelly, Terry, 'The Black Album', review of Martin Amis's *Philip Larkin: Poems*, *About Larkin* 32 (October 2011), pp. 33–4.

Kriewald, Gary, 'Wasteful, weak, propitiatory poems: Larkin apologizes to the animals', *About Larkin* 28 (October 2009), pp. 29–33.

Leader, Zachary (ed.), *The Letters of Kingsley Amis* (London: HarperCollins, 2000).

——, *The Life of Kingsley Amis* (London: Jonathan Cape, 2006)

—— (ed.), *The Movement Reconsidered: Essays on Larkin, Amis, Gunn, Davie, and their Contemporaries* (Oxford: Oxford University Press, 2009).

Leggett, B. J., *Larkin's Blues: Jazz, Popular Music and Poetry* (Baton Rouge: Louisiana State University Press, 1999).

Lodge, David, 'Philip Larkin: The Metonymic Muse', in Stephen Regan (ed.), *Philip Larkin: Contemporary Critical Essays* (Basingstoke: Macmillan, 1997), pp. 71–82.

Lomax, Marion, 'Larkin with Women', in Michael Baron (ed.), *Larkin with Poetry: English Association Conference Papers* (Leicester: English Association, 1997), pp. 31–46.

Longley, Edna, 'Poète Maudit Manqué', in George Hartley (ed.), *Philip Larkin – A Tribute: 1922–1985* (London: Marvell Press, 1988), pp. 220–31.

Lowe, N. F., 'Bruce Montgomery and Philip Larkin: Evidence of a ruptured relationship', *About Larkin* 6 (October 1998), pp. 11–12.

Marshall, Oliver, 'A Letter from Loughborough', *About Larkin* 15 (April 2003), pp. 18–19.

Morrison, Blake, *The Movement: English Poetry and Fiction of the 1950s* (London: Methuen, 1980).

——, '"Still Going On, All of It": The Movement in the 1950s and the Movement Today', in Zachary Leader (ed.), *The Movement Reconsidered: Essays on Larkin, Amis, Gunn, Davie, and their Contemporaries* (Oxford: Oxford University Press, 2009), pp. 16–33.

Orwin, James, 'Serious Earth: Philip Larkin's American Tapes', *About Larkin* 25 (April 2008), pp. 20–4.

Osborne, John, 'Larkin and the Visual Arts', *About Larkin* 36 (October 2013), pp. 19–21.

——, *Larkin, Ideology and Critical Violence: A Case of Wrongful Conviction* (Basingstoke: Palgrave Macmillan, 2008).

Palmer, Richard, *Such Deliberate Disguises: The Art of Philip Larkin* (London and New York: Continuum, 2008).

Parkinson, R. N., 'To keep our metaphysics warm: A study of "Church Going" by Philip Larkin', *Critical Survey* 5 (Winter 1971), pp. 224–33.

Paulin, Tom, 'She Did Not Change: Philip Larkin', *Minotaur: Poetry and the Nation State* (London: Faber & Faber, 1992), pp. 233–51.

Pelizzon, V. Penelope, 'Native Carnival: Philip Larkin's Puppet-Theatre of Ritual', in James Booth (ed.), *New Larkins for Old* (Basingstoke: Macmillan, 2000), pp. 213–23.

Regan, Stephen (ed.), *Philip Larkin: Contemporary Critical Essays* (Basingstoke: Macmillan, 1997).

Roberts, Neil, 'Hughes, the Laureateship and National Identity', *Q/W/E/R/T/Y* 9 (October 1999), pp. 203–9.

Rossen, Janice, 'Larkin at Oxford: Chaucer, Langland and Bruce Montgomery', *Journal of Modern Literature* 21.2 (Winter 1997), pp. 295–311.

——, 'Philip Larkin and *Lucky Jim*', *Journal of Modern Literature* 22.1 (Fall 1998), pp. 147–64.

——, *Philip Larkin: His Life's Work* (Hemel Hempstead: Harvester Wheatsheaf, 1989).

Rowe, M. W.: 'The Transcendental Larkin', *English* 38.161 (Summer 1989), 143–152.

——, 'Unreal Girls: Lesbian Fantasy in Early Larkin', in James Booth (ed), *New Larkins for Old* (Basingstoke: Macmillan, 2000), 79–96.

——, *Philip Larkin: Art and Self: Five Studies* (Basingstoke: Palgrave Macmillan, 2011).

——, 'Unreal Cities: Gautier's Influence on "'For Sidney Bechet"', *About Larkin* 38 (October 2014), 17–19.

Rumens, Carol, '"I don't understand cream cakes, but I eat them": Distance and difference in *A Girl in Winter*', *About Larkin* 29 (April 2010), pp. 7–12.

Thwaite, Anthony, 'How It Seemed Then: An Autobiographical, Anecdotal Essay', in Zachary Leader (ed.), *The Movement Reconsidered: Essays on Larkin, Amis, Gunn, Davie, and their Contemporaries* (Oxford: Oxford University Press, 2009), pp. 247–54.

Tolley, Trevor, *Larkin at Work: A Study of Larkin's Mode of Composition as seen in his Workbooks* (Hull: Hull University Press, 1997).

——, 'Lost Pages', *About Larkin* 11 (April 2001), pp. 24–7.

——, *My Proper Ground: A Study of the Work of Philip Larkin and its Development* (Edinburgh: Edinburgh University Press, 1991).

—— and John White (eds), *Larkin's Jazz*, Properbox 155 (four-CD set), in association with the Philip Larkin Society. www.propermusic.com.

Tomlinson, Charles, 'The Middlebrow Muse', *Essays in Criticism* 7.2 (April 1957), pp. 208–17.

Vize, Colin, 'Larkin's Refraction', *About Larkin* 36 (April 2013), p. 23.

Watson, J. R., 'The Other Larkin', *Critical Quarterly* 17.4 (Winter 1975), pp. 347–60.

Wiemann, Birte, 'Larkin's Englishness: A German Perspective', *About Larkin* 29 (April 2010), pp. 25–6.

Woolf, Sheila, 'A Hearty Laugh? Philip Larkin at King Henry VIII School, Coventry', *About Larkin* 28 (October 2009), pp. 15–16.

Acknowledgements

My thanks are due to Larkin's literary executors, Sir Andrew Motion and Anthony Thwaite, for their ready cooperation and help. I am also grateful to Jeremy Crow at the Society of Authors, administrator of Larkin's estate, for his unfailing assistance.

Any biography of Larkin must acknowledge a huge debt to Andrew Motion's *Philip Larkin: A Writer's Life* (1993). Many times I have found myself strategizing how best to deploy some primary material, only to find that Motion has already anticipated what I was intending to say. There has, however, been an accumulation of documentation in the two decades since the publication of his biography. Also I have, where possible, returned to original sources, both human and written. My interpretation of Larkin's character differs from Motion's in some crucial respects.

Though I was for seventeen years a colleague of Larkin in the University of Hull, our encounters were limited to formal contexts. He avoided the English Department, and never gave readings. However, since his death I have come to know several of those who were closest to him personally or professionally, and have interviewed others. I owe particular debts to Anthony and Ann Thwaite, the late Ruth Siverns (Bowman), the late Monica Jones, the late Judy Egerton, Winifred Dawson (Arnott), Mary Judd (Wrench), Professor Eddie Dawes, the late Jean Hartley, the late Maeve Brennan, the late Father Anthony

Storey, Betty Mackereth, John White, Alan Marshall, Bridget Mason (Egerton) and Angela Leighton, all of whom have shared with me their insights into the Larkin they knew. Anthony and Ann Thwaite gave invaluable advice throughout, and Ruth Siverns, Judy Egerton, Winifred Dawson, Jean Hartley, Betty Mackereth, Rosemary Parry and John White read and commented on particular chapters.

A great deal of the new material in this book has been gathered as a result of the activities of the Philip Larkin Society, founded in Hull in 1995. I am grateful for the scholarly work of all those who have attended the three Hull international conferences which took place under the Society's aegis in 1997, 2002 and 2007, and others who have given lectures and talks to the Society, in particular Barbara Everett, John Carey, Archie Burnett, Janice Rossen, Judith Priestman, Edna Longley, Raphaël Ingelbien, István Rácz, Graham Chesters, John Osborne and Jim Orwin. The help of Ivor Maw and Philip Pullen, who are currently cataloguing the Larkin family letters in the University of Hull archive, has been invaluable.

For twelve of the seventeen years since the Society's foundation I have been editor or co-editor (with Janet Brennan) of the Society's journal, *About Larkin*, which has published much new documentary information and contextual research. I owe an immense debt to the officers and members of the Society. Significant new biographical perspectives have been opened up by Susannah Tarbush, Geoff Weston and particularly Don Lee, who with his partner Gloria Gaffney has been indefatigable in tracking the geography and associations of Larkin's early life. When, after the death of Monica Jones in 2001, the Society bought the non-literary effects left in 105 Newland Park, a team consisting of Eddie Dawes, the Society's Chairman, Maeve Brennan, Carole Collinson and David Pattison helped to catalogue Larkin's pictures, ornaments, cameras, spectacles, hearing aids, ties, etc., all still in place sixteen years after his death.

Archie Burnett generously allowed me pre-publication access to the 'Commentary' in his edition of *The Complete Poems* (2012). I am also grateful to the many friends and colleagues who have read all or part of my draft and made suggestions for improvement. Anthony Thwaite,

Ann Thwaite and Don Lee have read the entire text, while Graham Chesters, Christopher Reid, Angela Leighton, Trevor Tolley, Richard Palmer, Geoff Weston, Terry Kelly, Janet Brennan, Tom McAlindon, Jim Orwin, Trevor Jarvis, Elena Miraglia, Birte Wiemann, Carol Rumens, Suzanne Uniacke, Martin Goodman, Sheila Jones, Bruce Woodcock and Philip Weaver have made suggestions in relation to particular chapters. Remaining mistakes of fact or wrong interpretations are my own.

My thanks are due also to Judy Burg (Hull University Archivist) and the staff of the Brynmor Jones Library, Hull, and the History Centre, Hull, which now houses the University's Larkin archive, and also most of the Larkin Society collection.

I must also thank my wife, Jennifer, and daughters, Anne and Eleanor, for their understanding and forbearance during the writing of this book.

Index